People and Politics
An Introduction to Political Science

People
and
Politics
An Introduction
to Political Science
SECOND EDITION

Herbert R. Winter
Rhode Island College
Thomas J. Bellows
University of Arkansas

in collaboration with

Conrad Waligorski
University of Arkansas
and
Stanley Erikson
Augustana College

John Wiley & Sons
New York ☐ Chichester ☐ Brisbane ☐ Toronto

The capitol buildings that appear on the cover are as follows: (clockwise from upper right) Capitol Building, Washington, D.C., U.S.A.; Casa Gobiernoe, Managua, Nicaragua; Parliament Building, London, Great Britain; Kremlin, Moscow, U.S.S.R.; Reichstag, Berlin, Germany; National Assembly Building, Nanking, China; Colonial Parliament Building, St. John's, Newfoundland, Canada.

Photo Research by Mary Lang

Library of Congress Cataloging in Publication Data:

Winter, Herbert R   1928–
    People and politics.

    Includes bibliographical references and index.
    1. Political science.   2. Political sociology.
3. Comparative government.   I. Bellows, Thomas J.,
1935–   joint author.   II. Title.
JA71.W47   1981   320   80-20518
ISBN 0-471-08153-1

Printed in the United States of America

10 9 8 7 6 5 4 3 2

To Our Children:

John-Martin and Nadia Winter
Roderick, Adrienne, Jeannine,
Derek, Scott, Marshall, and
Justin Bellows

Preface

People and Politics: An Introduction to Political Science is a book for beginning students of political science—for those who will be majoring in the field as well as for those who are majoring in other areas but wish to understand the subject matter of political science. The book surveys the major areas and aspects of the political process, relating the parts of the political system to each other. The topics follow in logical order, progressing from the basics of political analysis through analysis of the political processes to international politics.

This second edition is an **extensive revision** of the earlier publication. Major structural changes include separate chapters for interest groups and political parties and the addition of a chapter on public policy. We have included a sizable glossary, which contains definitions and/or explanations of more or less specialized political science terms. These terms appear in bold print when mentioned first in the text. This approach should serve students as a handy reference in the course of their reading.

Part One of the second edition describes the foundation of political science: the scope of the discipline, its approaches and concepts, as well as major political theories and ideologies. Part Two examines the input activities, those forces that form the major popular participatory part of the political process. Included in this section are the formation of political attitudes, political participation as reflected in elections and representation, and the roles of interest groups and political parties. Part Three is devoted to an examination of the output agencies, which make, administer, and enforce policy. This includes the legislative system, the executive branch and the bureaucracy, as well as the judiciary.

Part Four deals with political change and international politics. Our discussion of political change emphasizes the process of political development and its variations. This is followed by an examination of politics among countries, of international law and organization, as well as regional integration.

Our framework of analysis, especially Chapters 4 through 11, is based on the systems approach, explained in detail in Chapter 2. By a systems approach we mean that politics can be viewed as an assembly or combination of mutually interacting units that affect each other and form a complex whole, such as the nation-state. By emphasizing how the different parts of the political system interact and affect each other, we can make some sense out of the seeming confusion of modern politics. The systems approach stresses that the political systems of the 160-odd nation-states of our time share certain similar characteristics.

All countries are influenced by their particular political heritages, which range from the lengthy evolution of democracy in Britain to the authoritarian tradition of Russian society. Political societies adhere to an ideology of one kind or another, be it liberal democracy, democratic socialism, Third World socialism, communism, or fascism. All countries contain processes for the socialization of the young and old—though again these processes differ from society to society and range from a ninth-grade civics class to totalitarian brainwashing.

The Western democracies have viable input agencies for articulation and aggregation, in the form of interest groups and political parties. They serve as instruments for popular participation, for expression of public opinion, and for the selection of candidates for public office. The input process is different in Communist countries; they have basically one-party systems, and interest groups follow the course set by the reigning party. The developing countries still have little in terms of established interest groups or viable political parties. As the economic systems of these countries become more developed, however, we anticipate that these societies will become more pluralistic, which usually induces the formation of interest groups and political parties.

All countries have means for selecting their legislative, executive, and judicial officials. In the Western democracies this selection procedure is constitutionalized: officials are elected or appointed according to established law. In contrast, in many other countries change still occurs by violence, and gross nepotism is execised in the appointment of government officials.

All countries have institutions for rule making, rule application, and rule adjudication in the forms of a legislature, an executive, and a judiciary. These agencies are more viable in certain countries than in others. For example, the United States has a fairly viable tripartite national government. In contrast, the executive branch dominates the governmental process in most of the developing countries. In these, legislatures and judiciaries have not yet developed to a state of equality with the executive. In the Communist countries the politburo of the Communist Party is the basic rule-making body, and the legislature, the executive, and the judiciary play second-ary roles.

All political systems are subject to change. Political change can take one of two forms: it can be evolutionary and relatively peaceful through such means as using the ballot, or change can be brought about by revolutionary means, using the gun to alter the political system. The latter is usually more drastic and far-reaching (for example, the Russian Revolution of 1917) than evolutionary change.

The systems approach permits us to use political features common to all socie-ties as convenient *starting points* for our analysis and discussion. It provides an or-derly framework for the comparative examination of political phenomena and is, perhaps, the most logical way to scrutinize a variety of political systems.

The examples used for illustrative purposes are drawn from many countries. However, we have made it a point to include in almost all of the chapters represent-ative examples from Western democracies, Communist countries, and non-Com-munist developing societies.

Some of our examples are drawn from the realm of micropolitics and others from macropolitics. Micropolitics focuses on the individual rather than political groups or institutions. Macropolitics focuses on groups and institutions. Micropolitics and macropolitics complement each other. The behavior of any group or institution manifests, in part, the attitudes and beliefs of the individuals involved. This book dis-cusses the various ways in which people organize to make political decisions or to influence the decision makers. Thus we examine political organizations as well as individual attitudes and behavior.

We believe our approach contains a healthy mix of traditionalism and behavioral-ism. No introductory text can include detailed discussion of all aspects of a discipline. We emphasize those subjects we consider important in teaching.

We hope that this book will give a better understanding of politics and the institu-tions and processes it entails. We also hope that it kindles in the reader a deeper in-terest in politics and political analysis and provides a helpful basis for more special-ized studies in political science. Our principal objective is to make it possible for the reader to participate more effectively in the political process.

Many people have been helpful to us in producing this second edition. We are grateful to those of our students who gave us their ideas for improving the book. We appreciate the constructive criticism which we received from many faculty mem-bers throughout the country who used the first edition. In particular, we thank Payge Dampier of Palm Beach Junior College, Darwin Gamble of Arkansas State Universi-ty, and Kenneth Town of Emory University for their most helpful reviews of the sec-ond edition manuscript. Our colleagues Eugene Perry, Carey Rickabaugh, and Robert Waste of Rhode Island College provided considerable help by offering con-structive suggestions on particular chapters.

We owe much to the entire Wiley staff for their help and attention in producing this second edition. In particular, we thank Wayne Anderson, who as usual, has been a terrific editor to work with; Connie Rende, who has been always available when advice was needed; Stella Kupferberg, who has been most skillful in finding the needed cartoons and pictures; and Cathy Starnella, who has been most helpful as production supervisor.

Herbert R. Winter
Thomas J. Bellows

Contents

Part One

Foundation and Fundamentals

Chapter One

The Nature and Scope of Political Science

Inflation, unemployment, human rights, corruption, and conflicts in Asia, the Middle East, and Africa are a few of the many issues confronting today's citizen. These are problems in the public realm, problems we expect to deal with through political action. The public realm includes the activities and effects of all input and output agencies. Input agencies include political parties, interest groups, public opinion, and even violence. Outputs include the activities, decisions, and regulations of governmental agencies at the local, state, national, and international levels. These interact in a system of politics to produce the complex and often interdependent problems that scream for our attention from the daily headlines. We are challenged to understand and deal with the world. Failure to do so may spell disaster for our country and ourselves.

Past generations also have had their share of crises and problems, but people often tend to feel that present-day public problems are more severe than those of the past. Modern politics is on a larger scale, involving more people and more questions than ever before. Governmental activities have expanded considerably in most countries.[1] This expansion has brought the government closer to the people while making it more complex and difficult to understand. More public services are available, but, concurrently, governments encroach increasingly on the day-to-day affairs of their citizens.

Contemporary people are better informed politically and more attentive than their forefathers; however, one may ask whether the increase in available information and the growth of governmental activities have made the citizen a more active political participant. One standard indicator used to examine political participation is

[1]For information on the growth of the public sector, see Charles L. Taylor and Michael C. Hudson, *World Handbook of Political and Social Indicators* 2d ed.(New Haven: Yale University Press, 1972).

1960

1970

1974

1980

The effect of inflation!

that of voter turn-out on election day. By and large, voter turn-out has remained fairly constant in the developed countries or has even declined slightly during the last two decades. It is still too early to ascertain trends of this type in the developing countries.

Rather than a general increase in the standard types of political participation, the two past decades have shown a pattern of "flash" activities and movements centering around specific issues. The many domestic demonstrations against U.S. military involvement in Southeast Asia illustrate this. Currently, we are witnessing a rising concern about pollution, natural resource depletion, and conservation. The composite picture of political behavior in the 1960s and 1970s seems to show an additional

"The Small Society" by Brickman © Washington Star Syndicate, permission granted by King Features Syndicate, 1973.

phenomenon. Rising interest in the public issues of the day has been accompanied by a specific concern about priorities set by governments and the corresponding allocation of resources.

Many of the demonstrations staged by students, members of minority groups, and others in this country have had to do with governmental priorities because these priorities are associated with individual and group welfare. Governmental decisions made in Washington may have a bearing on whether an American will have to fight in Asia or some other part of the world, whether his taxes will be increased, and whether a larger amount of his tax money will be used for furthering the arms race—or for improving medical services, public transportation, and conservation efforts.

Demonstrations protesting governmental policies are common outside the industrialized countries of the West. In many of the developing countries demonstrations are a common occurrence, as people who do not have a voice in public office attempt to make their wants known. The same applies to demonstrations in Communist countries. Thousands of workers and students rioted in Poland's port cities in December 1970 and widespread strikes occurred in the summer of 1980. Dissent in the Soviet Union has been expressed in the form of small demonstrations or clandestine publications, as when some Soviet citizens demonstrated in public in 1968 against the Warsaw Pact intervention in Czechoslovakia. One of those protesting was the renowned nuclear physicist Andrei Sakharov, who first became known in the West for his essay *Progress, Coexistence and Intellectual Freedom*.[2]

These criticisms indicate a growing civic awareness in segments of the population here and abroad. During the 1960s, rising civil and social consciousness among students in North America and Western Europe led to a burgeoning enroll-

[2]Andrei D. Sakharov, *Progress, Coexistence and Intellectual Freedom* (New York: W. W. Norton, 1968).

ment in social science courses, subjects that focus on the economic, political, and social behavior of man.

This book addresses itself to these interests and concerns by placing them into an analytic framework, that of political science.

WHAT IS POLITICAL SCIENCE?

Political science is a discipline within the social sciences. It deals with politics; the political behavior of individuals, groups, and societies; and the factors and conditions affecting politicians, political events, and institutions. It is akin to the other social science disciplines (anthropology, economics, geography, history, sociology, and social psychology) in that all of them examine related aspects of human behavior and of society. All social behavior occurs through the interaction of individuals and groups of people; therefore, all social science study is concerned with the nature of human interaction, group behavior, decision making, leadership, and so forth. An examination of human political behavior lends itself readily to the application of anthropological, economic, psychological, and sociological analyses. For example, Almond and Verba, in their famous comparative analysis, *The Civic Culture*, applied a broad range of modern social science research techniques to study the political aspirations, beliefs, emotions, and participation of people in Italy, Mexico, the United Kingdom, the United States, and West Germany.[3]

In the past, political scientists relied more on history and jurisprudence, but today they look to economics, sociology, social psychology, and statistics for research methods, tools, and analysis.[4]

Political science deals with a vast number of phenomena. This is indicated by the many subareas into which the field can be divided. Some major subareas are political theory, American politics, comparative politics, international relations, public administration, state and local politics, and public law.[5]

THE FOCUS OF POLITICAL SCIENCE

Political science, we have said, deals with human political behavior. In short, it deals with politics. Thus, there is no need to define political science further; rather, we should define and discuss politics. What is politics? What are its features and ingredients? The word "politics" stems from **polis**, the Greek word for city-state. Athens

[3]Gabriel A. Almond and Sidney Verba, *The Civic Culture* (Boston: Little Brown, 1965). See also, the follow-up anthology by the same authors, *The Civic Culture Revisited* (Boston: Little Brown, 1980).

[4]For a perceptive discussion of the relationship between political science and the other social sciences, see Seymour Lipset, ed., *Politics and the Social Sciences* (New York: Oxford University Press, 1969).

[5]For a more detailed discussion of the subareas see Marion D. Irish, ed., *Political Science: Advance of the Discipline* (Englewood Cliffs, N.J.: Prentice-Hall, 1968); Michael Haas and Henry S. Kariel, eds., *Approaches to the Study of Political Science* (Scranton, Pa.: Chandler, 1970); and Ronald J. Stupak et al., *Understanding Political Science: The Arena of Power* (Port Washington, N.Y.: Alfred, 1977).

was a *polis* at the time of Plato and Aristotle. Aristotle, in his discussion of human associations, stated that the "most sovereign and inclusive association is the *polis*, as it is called, or the political association."[6] The complexity of the term "politics" is illustrated by the variety of the following responses, which were given by students in an introductory political science class in an urban college in New England when they were asked to register their associations to the word:

authority	decision making	mudslinging
bargaining	democracy	patronage
bribery	dishonesty	political parties
campaign	elections	politicians
candidates	elite	power
coercion	equal opportunity	president
committee	favoritism	promises
competition	government	public interest
complexity	inflation	public office
compromise	graft	secrecy
conflicts	interest groups	struggle
Congress	law	summit meetings
corruption	leadership	taxes
debate	manipulation	voting
deception	money	Watergate

A search through political science textbooks confounds the student with a number of definitions, stating that politics is the process of making governmental policies, the making of decisions by public means, the authoritative allocation of values, the quest for power, and so forth. The ethical scope of political activities has been expressed candidly by Peter Merkl in the following words: "At its best, politics is a noble quest for a good order and justice; at its worst, a selfish grab for power, glory and riches."[7]

To most political scientists the word "politics" denotes all the activites and processes that take place in the public realm, some overt and others of a more covert nature. Our discussion in the following chapters will be limited to the public scope of politics.

The following are some of the more pertinent attempts to define politics. Quincy Wright, in his classic study of international relations, defines international politics as "the art of influencing, manipulating, or controlling major groups in the world so as to advance the purposes of some against the opposition of others."[8] This definition could be applied readily to domestic as well as international politics.

[6]Ernest Barker, ed. and trans., *The Politics of Aristotle* (New York: Oxford University Press, 1962), p. 1.
[7]Peter H. Merkl, *Political Continuity and Change* (New York: Harper and Row, 1967), p. 13.
[8]Quincy Wright, *The Study of International Relations* (New York: Appleton-Century-Croft, 1955), p. 130.

According to Vernon Van Dyke, politics can be defined as a struggle among actors pursuing conflicting desires on public issues.[9] A sizable number of American political scientists adhere to a definition attributed to David Easton: Politics is the authoritative allocation of values.[10] While Van Dyke's definition lacks reference to the outcome of the struggle between the actors and limits politics to the public realm, the definition attributed to Easton lacks reference to the competition and struggle that occur before an allocation of values can set in. But the two definitions complement each other. We suggest a comprehensive definition that contains elements of the thoughts of Van Dyke and Easton, namely that **politics can be defined as a struggle between actors pursuing conflicting desires on issues that may result in an authoritative allocation of values**. Political science involves the systematic analysis and study of politics in the public realm.

THE RANGE OF POLITICS

Political activities may be considered legitimate or nonlegitimate. Legitimate activities are sanctioned by law and custom. Examples of legitimate political functions would be the act of voting on election day, the passage of a statute by a legislative body, or a demonstration permitted by the authorities. But politics goes beyond the legitimate area: a demonstration held despite the authorities' refusal to grant permission is a political act though this type of politics might lead to turmoil and fighting in the streets. A coup d'etat is a political act, though it might involve military force. A revolution clearly has political overtones. The Prussian General Karl von Clausewitz went even further by saying that:

> War is not merely a political act, but also a political instrument, a continuation of political relations, a carrying out of the same by other means.[11]

While political scientists deal primarily with politics within the public realm, politics is **not** limited to the public realm. As stated by Robert Dahl, the political arena tran-

[9]Van Dyke's complete definition reads as follows: "Politics can be defined as (1) activity occurring within and among groups, (2) which operate on the basis of desires that are to some extent shared, (3) an essential feature of the activity being a struggle among actors, (4) to achieve their desires, (5) on questions of group policy, group organization, group leadership, or the regulation of intergroup relationships, (6) against the opposition of others with conflicting desires." See Vernon Van Dyke, *Political Science: A Philosophical Analysis* (Stanford, Cal.: Stanford University Press, 1960), p. 134.

A closely related definition comes from Meyerson and Banfield, who speak of politics as "the activity by which an issue is agitated and settled." See Martin Meyerson and Edward C. Banfield, *Politics, Planning, and the Public Interest* (Glencoe, Ill.: Free Press, 1955), p. 304.

[10]This definition is a loose paraphrase of statements made by David Easton. At no place does he give the above definition verbatim. See David Easton, "An Approach to the Analysis of Political Systems," *World Politics*, 9, 1957, pp. 383–400; *A Framework for Political Analysis* (Englewood Cliffs, N.J.: Prentice-Hall, 1965), p. 47 ff.; and *The Political System: An Inquiry into the State of Political Science*, 2nd ed. (New York: Alfred A. Knopf, 1971), p. 129 ff.

[11]Quoted in Frederick A. Hartmann, *The Relations of Nations*, 3rd. ed. (New York: The Macmillan Company, 1967), p. 171.

scends the public realm. In his words, "A political system is any persistent pattern of human relationships that involves, to a significant extent, power, rule, or authority."[12] His definition implies that politics is not limited to the public realm, but includes conflict-of-interest situations and struggles for power, as well as policy-making activities in business firms, civic groups, religious organizations, crime syndicates, college organizations, families, and other groups.

College students demonstrating against an undesirable policy set by their institution's administration are engaged in politics. Members of a minority group rioting in order to protest their miserable living conditions pursue politics. The phenomenon of politics can be found in the armed forces, be it in cases of promotion to high-level rank or the interservice rivalries having to do with areas of jurisdiction or budget allocations. Politics is found in business, where promotion to a high-ranking executive position may involve a great deal of maneuvering behind the scenes. Those who have been active in an established church probably are aware that the hiring or resignation of a minister involves, at times, a fair amount of politics. The world of academe involves, at some institutions, considerable politics.

There is also an enormous amount of politics in organized crime; politics that has to do with the maintenance of hierarchical order, promotions within the syndicate, discussions about the ends to be pursued and the methods to be employed, and debate about the division of territory among the families. There is also politics in the sense that in some communities the activities of crime syndicates are tightly interlocked with those of the established authorities.

The smallest group subject to politics is the family. The pursuit of desires and issues in the family often will have political overtones in that father and mother will pursue differing, or at times contradictory, aims and will compete for the children's support for their stand. The playing of favorites will serve as an enticement or as a payoff. Children, at times, will try to play the parents against each other. These examples, we hope, will serve to illustrate that the phenomenon labelled "politics" is an unavoidable fact of human life and that everybody is involved in it in one fashion or another.

THE IMPORTANCE OF POLITICS

Politics surrounds everyone. A modern citizen is unlikely to play, either by choice or by fate, the isolated role of Robinson Crusoe. People are, by necessity, either actors or subjects in the web of politics. Their roles will be of a given type in the societal authority structure; for example, one might be a leader, an active participant, a passive subject, or play a role somewhere in between. What importance does a certain role or position have? Politics, if used wisely, can enhance human freedom and well-being. While we cannot achieve all our desires, we can, through political pur-

[12]Robert A. Dahl, *Modern Political Analysis*, 2nd ed. (Englewood Cliffs, N.J.: Prentice-Hall, 1970), p. 6.

suit, exercise more choice and achieve some of our aspirations, to render our lives more secure and master a greater degree of our own fates.

The political role that an individual can play in a society depends upon the authority structure of a given society. A person living in a strongly regimented (totalitarian) society enjoys less freedom than a person in an authoritarian society, who in turn has less leeway than the person in a Western-type democracy. Freedom of action, in the above context, involves such matters as freedom of speech, assembly, press, religion, travel (both within and beyond one's country), and social and economic advancement and opportunity. All these freedoms are relative in the sense that there is no country where there prevails complete freedom and none where there exists no degree of freedom at all. A society's authority structure, however, has a considerable bearing on the degree of freedom that prevails.

Politics affects people's lives in many ways. One important example would be the allocation of scarce resources by government. This presumes that the resources people regard as important are never sufficient, whether we are talking about clean air, clean water, or money. This does not mean that government determines or influences all aspects of our lives. If it did, we would be living in a completely totalitarian state, as depicted in George Orwell's *1984*. But where government is involved, it usually is making a decision (a choice between alternatives) about how a resource shall be allocated. One situation that occurs regularly concerns appropriations for education. We may have to raise taxes or spend less on defense, highways, welfare measures, and so forth, if we are going to allocate more for schools.

Once man has gone beyond an idyllic **state of nature**—where populations are small, people are assumed always to be rational, and there are few, if any, conflicts—people are either forcibly organized or organize themselves into a society with rules and obligations. At this point some members of the society believe that certain objectives (for example, defense, security, or a transportation network) or values (such as respect for human life) can be achieved only by rules or laws that bind everyone. If many people are allowed legally to participate in deciding procedures, objectives, policies, and values, we have some form of what is commonly called democracy. If few have the right to participate, we have some type of authoritarian or totalitarian system. The institution that promulgates and enforces such laws is government, and government in one aspect or another is a subject in which all political scientists are interested. Disagreements, competing points of views, or conflicts that are appealed to government for response are called political conflicts. The age we live in is much more **politicized** than those of previous generations because many more conflicts involve government and therefore are political. There are several reasons for this:

1. Today there are more than 160 sovereign countries in the world. When the United States declared its independence in 1776, there were approximately 40 sovereign countries; there were 70 sovereign countries in 1945. Thus, the number of independent countries has more than doubled during the last 30 years. The main reason for this increase in sovereign nation-states is the dissolution of the colonial empires. Most of the people who have achieved independence from colonial rule since 1945 live in Africa, Asia, and the Middle East. These people are no longer the generally docile colonial subjects of an imperial foreign power. With independence they have progressively come to acquire a sense of common political identity and recognize they are now governed by individuals from their own country, although not necessarily from the same tribe or region. The effort to achieve independence, sometimes involving armed struggle, made the majority of the world's population more politically aware. The world is more politicized because more people are self-consciously organized into sovereign countries.

  2.   Related to the first point is the fact that on occasion more people are participating in the political system. Now, after several years of independence, many of the developing world's peoples have become involved in influencing government policy or political leaders. Over the last several years one can point to such countries as Ghana, India, Indonesia, Jordan, Nigeria, and Syria, where substantial elements of the population have been active in the political process since independence. In much of the developing world and even in most Communist countries, there are more or less regularly scheduled elections; however, in a majority of these political systems few if any opposition candidates are permitted. One purpose of single-party elections in these countries is to manipulate political awareness and create support for the government. In contrast, the United States serves as an example where enfranchising segments of the population has led to a meaningful increase in political participation due to the passage of the Nineteenth, Twenty-Third, and Twenty-Sixth Amendments to the United States Constitution. The Nineteenth Amendment, ratified in 1920, granted suffrage to women. The Twenty-Third Amendment, ratified in 1961, gave voters in the District of Columbia the right to vote for President and Vice-President of the United States. The Twenty-Sixth Amendment, ratified in 1971, gave citizens 18 years and older the vote in federal, state, and local elections. More people are participating in the political process in the contemporary world, whether mobilized by authoritarian governments or voluntarily, as in the United States.

  3.   We also have become more politicized in the last 100 years as citizens have turned increasingly to government to solve problems previously considered outside the jurisdiction of government. Formerly, most governments throughout the world were responsible principally for defense, internal security, and maintaining some form of transportation-communication network. Today governments often are held responsible not only for inflation and deflation, but also for the price of gasoline and sugar, for encouraging industrialization to provide jobs, for establishing minimum wages and working conditions, and for implementing retirement systems such as social security. The list could go on for several pages. The notion of what are government responsibilities has expanded several-fold within the last 100 years. As groups support certain issues, such as gun registration or increasing the minimum wage, other groups oppose them. It is inevitable that political competition and disagreement expand as more issues are being pursued by various groups or individuals. The cumulative impact leads to increased politicization.

The more complex, specialized, and interdependent the economic and social systems become within a country, and the more economic, political, and national security policies are influenced by international forces outside the country, the more governments must respond on behalf of the political community. Governments are expected to deal with multiplying problems, national and international. The balancing and accommodating of numerous demands and pressures and the choice among alternatives often are decisions only governments can make and enforce. Even in this age of specialization and division of labor, governments should not be expected "to do everything" and solve all problems; however, the role of political institutions is critical. The linchpin status of government today results in increased politicization.

4. Another reason for increased politicization is that we have experienced a communications revolution in this century. Radio increased political participation and awareness in the United States and abroad. Television has brought a new dimension to observing events and has replaced radio as the prime source of political information in the more advanced countries, though participation did not itself increase. Television is the principal source of news for approximately 70 percent of the population in the United States. Greater in-depth understanding does not necessarily occur, but awareness of the politically newsworthy and dramatic events of the moment is increased. Riots, wars, and the impeachment proceedings are filmed live or shown within hours of the event. This often takes the form of a dramatization of politics and may actually draw attention away from a reasoned and studied understanding of major political problems. This superficial politicization is a phenomenon that occurs in many countries that have developed mass communications systems (newspapers, radio, television).

In sum, the world of today is more politicized than ever before, and politics is an important element of our life.

THE LANGUAGE OF POLITICS

One other item merits discussion before we turn to the discipline of political science per se. The metallurgist speaking on iron or lead, the ornithologist speaking on bluebirds or goldfinches, the artist discussing the techniques of Rubens or Van Dyck can speak more objectively about his subject than the political scientist discussing democracy or communism. This is because these two labels refer to something of an amorphous quality, in contrast to the known entities of iron, lead, bluebirds, goldfinches, or the paintings of Rubens and Van Dyck. Many of the terms used to describe political phenomena have, at best, ambiguous meanings. This language complexity obviously is not unique to political science vocabulary, but presents a problem in other social science disciplines too.

While social scientists attempt to define their terminology with some precision, society at large often uses political labels very loosely. What do we mean by **democracy**, by **communism**, by **fascism**, by **socialism**? What is a **liberal**, what are the characteristics of a **conservative**? Which societies are democratic, which **authoritarian**, and which **totalitarian**? During the past three decades it has been in vogue in this country to speak of "the free countries," leaving the assumption that all countries not included in the above category are the opposite—enslaved countries. In discussions on matters of international politics, basic terms such as "state" and "nation" have been used quite loosely too.

We shall discuss the ideological terms in some detail in our chapter on political theory and ideology. For our present purposes we would like to point out that even within a society such as the United States, people's concepts as to what constitutes democracy, socialism, communism, or fascism differ considerably. While the social scientist may attach basic models to each of these "isms," only to find that these models have little applicability to contemporary societies, the layperson will use these terms in a still less thoughtful way. One's own political perspective will have a bearing on how one applies the labels. The language used during the demonstrations in the United States in the late 1960s serves as an interesting illustration. People strongly opposed to the demonstrations were quite likely to label the demonstrators "communists," while in turn some of the demonstrators who were taken into custody by the police would accuse the police (and other officials) of being "fascists" or "fascist pigs." Obviously, the labels, in their true meanings, do not apply to either of the groups.

Still more confusion arises about the proper use of such terms as "liberal" and "conservative." People sharing the political philosophy of Senators Goldwater or Tower (two leaders who generally are considered to be conservative) will view those who are less conservative as being "liberal." In turn, many supporters of such "liberals" as Senators Cranston or Metzenbaum will look upon those who are less liberal than they are as being "conservative." The point is that the terms "liberal" and "conservative" are used not so much in reference to ideologies, but in a relative way, describing a person's political philosophy relative to one's own.

In a related way, this thesis could be applied partially to the use of such terms as democracy, socialism, fascism, and communism. There has been a tendency among some Americans, including high-ranking government officials, to label as "Communists" those at home and abroad who have opposed one or several of our foreign policies, while some of the domestic and foreign adversaries to U.S. foreign policies have accused the government of this country of being "Fascist."

At the Yalta Conference in 1945, Churchill, Roosevelt, and Stalin agreed that a "democratic" government would be established in Poland after World War II. It is obvious that Stalin's concept of what this government was to be like differed considerably from that of his Western conference partners. The point is that the use of political words is often purely verbal, based on linguistic habits and conventions and telling us little or nothing about the matter of fact.[13]

Political vocabulary has more meaning if the user clarifies the use of a term and what is meant by it. One important service political scientists render is to help to define political vocabulary more clearly.

THE DISCIPLINE OF POLITICAL SCIENCE

After having examined the scope of political science, we would like to discuss the discipline per se. Political science is a relatively young academic field in the United States. The first political science courses were taught at Columbia University in the 1850s and 1860s. During the following decades the political science program at Columbia served as a model for similar programs being established at a number of American universities.[14] The discipline has grown rather speedily, and today political science departments exist independently at many colleges and universities in this country. In other colleges, political science is still part of a conglomerate social science department or forms a department jointly with history or economics. Among the approximately 2000 colleges and universities in the United States, 796 had independent political science departments in 1979; 118 of these offered a Ph.D. program in the field.[15]

The United States has more trained political scientists than all the rest of the world. According to Gabriel Almond, "Nine out of every ten political scientists in the world today are American, and probably two out of every three political scientists who ever lived are alive and practicing today."[16]

What do political scientists do? How successful are they in pursuing their aims? Most political scientists are teaching about politics at colleges and universities. Their teaching and research have largely to do with politics in the public realm. Very

[13]For a more detailed discussion of the complexities of political labels, see T. D. Weldon, *The Vocabulary of Politics* (London: Penguin Books, 1953), pp. 9 ff.

[14]The following are informative sources on the growth of political science in the United States: Albert Somit and Joseph Tannenhaus, *The Development of American Political Science: From Burgess to Behavioralism* (Boston: Allyn and Bacon, 1967); Bernard Crick, *The American Science of Politics: Its Origins and Conditions* (Berkeley: University of California Press, 1964); Francis J. Sorauf, *Political Science: An Informal Overview* (Columbus, Ohio: Charles E. Merrill Books, 1965); and Harold D. Laswell, *The Future of Political Science* (New York: Atherton Press, 1963), ch. 2.

[15]From data compiled by the American Political Science Association.

[16]Gabriel A. Almond, "Political Theory and Political Science," in Ithiel Pool, ed., *Contemporary Political Science: Toward Empirical Theory* (New York: McGraw-Hill, 1967), p. 3.

little has yet been written by political scientists about politics in the world of business, social organizations, religious organizations, or organized crime.[17] The importance of one of these categories to political scientists was stated some time ago by Hans Morgenthau:

> The curriculum of political science must take theoretical notice of the actual development of private governments in the form of giant corporations and labor unions. These organizations exercise power within their organizational limits, in their relations to each other, and in their relations to the state. The state in turn exercises power in regard to them. These power relations constitute a new field for theoretical understanding.[18]

A similar reasoning could be applied to the political importance of the other categories too. The fact is, however, that most political scientists have assumed, and perhaps still assume, that political science should deal with legitimate politics in the public realm. Only in recent years have such areas of inquiry as domestic turmoil and revolutionary change become panel topics at political science conventions and have scholarly publications bearing such titles as *Political Violence, The Dynamics of Aggression*, and *Revolutionary Change* begun to appear.

What are the legitimate tasks of those who teach political science? What are the values of studying political science? Most of us, presumably, would agree with Dwight Waldo, who speaks of teaching citizenship as the first pursuit of the political science teacher.[19] We are talking about teaching citizenship in the sense of providing data, facts, and methods of analysis pertaining to political processes and systems in the hope that students will become interested in politics and become more intelligent observers of, and participants in, the political arena. While political scientists do not have ready-made answers to all political issues and problems, they can—and should—educate students in citizenship.

A second task of those who teach political science is to provide preprofessional and professional training, such as preparing young people for public service. Each year thousands of college graduates take jobs with the federal, state, and local governments. Many of these are political science majors whose academic training has given them a suitable academic and preprofessional background for their future careers.

A third task, according to Waldo, is to train students for political science research. The last function is more applicable to graduate instruction than to undergraduate.

---

[17]Perhaps the most informative book on organized crime in the United States has been written by a former police officer and a journalist. See Ralph Salerno and John S. Tompkins, *The Crime Confederation* (Garden City: Doubleday, 1969).

[18]Hans J. Morgenthau, "Power as a Political Concept," in Roland Young, ed., *Approaches to the Study of Politics* (Evanston, Ill.: Northwestern University Press, 1958), p. 77.

[19]Dwight Waldo, "Values in the Political Science Curriculum," in Roland Young, ed., *Approaches to the Study of Politics* (Evanston, Ill.: Northwestern University Press, 1958), p. 110.

THE SCIENTIFIC CONTENT OF POLITICAL INQUIRY

How scientific a **science** can political science be? No single school or mood in political science provides the exclusive answer to the question. For, as Gaetano Salvemini has stated so succinctly:

> *Scientific research is a series of successive approaches to the truth, comparable to an exploration in an unknown land. Each explorer checks and adds to the findings of his predecessors, and facilitates for his successors the attainment of the goal they all have in common. This is why history and the social sciences, more than any of the physical sciences, need an atmosphere of free competition between different schools of thought, in which all hypotheses and all proconceptions [sic] can be pitted one against the other. If liberty is suppressed in favor of a single school, it is the death warrant of our studies. . . . If they do not demand free competition not only for themselves but for their rivals as well, the historian and the social scientist, more than any scholars, accept both moral and intellectual degradation.*[20]

"How're you doing, Professor?"

Allen Johnson, *Providence Journal.*

[20]Gaetano Salvemini, *Historians and Scientists* (Cambridge, Mass.: Harvard University Press, 1939), pp. 112–113.

Political science, as a social science, is not a science in the sense of the so-called hard sciences, such as biology, chemistry, or physics. These hard sciences deal with phenomena that can be examined in controlled experiments in a laboratory setting, while, in political science inquiry, it is just not possible to examine a voter, a political candidate, or an office holder in the same fashion.

In this context, the following anecdote may be of interest. The great physicist Albert Einstein was asked once by a colleague why mankind, on one hand, has been able to unlock the secrets of the atom but, on the other hand, has been unable to devise the political means necessary to keep the atom from destroying civilization. Einstein replied, "This is simple, politics is more difficult than physics."

The researcher of political phenomena has a certain amount of personal psychological involvement in the subject of his inquiry, be it an urban problem, an aspect of national government policy, or a particular issue of U.S. involvement abroad. A political scientist's findings are by nature more subjective than those of the natural scientist. The complexity of political phenomena and the influence of values make it impossible for the political scientist to be as objective as a colleague in the natural sciences. This does not mean, however, that political science inquiry is not scientific. Science starts with empiricism, the observation and verification of facts, and the formulation of generalizations and propositions. Scientific inquiry calls for adding new knowledge to what is known already. The perennial debate over the scientific nature of any or all of the social sciences has been influenced all too often by the commonly held notion that the term "science" should be reserved for those disciplines that show constant progress in obvious ways and use standard research techniques to achieve this progress.

We should take note, however, of Abraham Kaplan:

Each science—and indeed, each inquiry—finds some techniques appropriate and others inappropriate and even impossible. The microscope is of very limited use to astronomy (for the present, at least), while the biologist cannot learn much about terrestrial life with the telescope. But to note this difference is not to say that these two sciences have different methods.[21]

In his famous essay, *The Structure of Scientific Revolutions*, Thomas S. Kuhn defines science as "research firmly based upon one or more past scientific achievements that some particular scientific community acknowledges for a time as supplying the foundation for its further practice."[22] According to Kuhn, science has not been quite the logical process that many scientists have claimed it to be. Rather, he found that the history of science consists of a number of drastic changes, or revolutions, by which the theories of a given time, called paradigms by Kuhn, are rendered

[21]Abraham Kaplan; *The Conduct of Inquiry: Methodology for Behavioral Science* (San Francisco: Chandler Publishing, 1964), p. 31.
[22]Thomas S. Kuhn, *The Structure of Scientific Revolutions* (Chicago: The University of Chicago Press, 1962), p. 10.

obsolete by new discoveries. These lead to the shaping of new paradigms which, again, will become obsolete at some later date. According to Kuhn, the history of science is a continuous process, consisting of a chain of paradigms.[23]

Political science is self-conscious about the need to be as "scientific" as possible. It strives to be scientific in its methods, in the ways facts are collected, examined, and organized. The rigorous survey research that occurs in the United States is an example and outgrowth of this scientific research. Nationwide surveys by the Gallup and Harris polls or the Michigan Survey Research Center interview 1200 to 1600 adults. These surveys describe American political opinion or vote intention of more than 100 million adults within a maximum of 2 or 3 percent margin of error.[24]

As the student will see in the following chapters, political science is making progress in identifying and explaining political relationships. Moreover, new theories have been developed and older ones have been reexamined in new settings. New horizons have been opened for research. Political science has grown to become a more exact and more scientific discipline of scholarly pursuit. One other sign of its growth importance can be seen in the fact that in the past two decades the presidents of this country, as well as state executives, have increasingly sought the advice of selected political scientists.

Having examined the nature and scope of political science, we now turn our attention to the approaches or methods used by political scientists to study political phenomena and the key concepts involved.

SELECTED READINGS

An excellent collection of essays on the relationship between political science and the other social sciences is *Politics and the Social Sciences** (New York: Oxford University Press, 1969), edited by Seymour Martin Lipset. For a treatment of the relationship between political science and mathematics, see Hayword R. Alker, *Mathematics and Politics** (New York: Macmillan, 1965).

Among the more useful of the numerous studies that focus on the scope and methods of political science are Charles E. Hyneman, *The Study of Politics: The Present State of American Political Science** (Urbana, Ill.: University of Illinois Press, 1959); Vernon Van Dyke, *Political Science: A Philosophical Analysis** (Stan-

[23]*Ibid*, pp. 1–90.

[24]For further discussion of the scientific nature of political science, see Andrew Hacker, *The Study of Politics: The Western Tradition and American Origins* (New York: McGraw-Hill, 1963), pp. 5–8; Charles S. Hyneman, *The Study of Politics* (Urbana, Ill.: University of Illinois Press, 1959), pp. 75–80; Alan C. Isaak, *Scope and Methods of Political Science: An Introduction to the Methodology of Political Inquiry* (Homewood, Ill.: The Dorsey Press, 1969), pp. 22–30 and 45–57; Austin Ranney, ed., *Political Science and Public Policy* (Chicago: Markham Publishing Company, 1968); and Vernon Van Dyke, *Political Science: A Philosophical Analysis* (Stanford, Cal.: Stanford University Press, 1960), pp. 191–205.

*Available in paperback.

ford, Cal.: Stanford University Press, 1960) and, by the same author, "The Optimum Scope of Political Science," in James C. Charlesworth, ed., *A Design for Political Science: Scope, Objectives, and Methods** (Philadelphia: The American Academy of Political and Social Sciences, 1966); Harold D. Laswell, *The Future of Political Science** (New York: Atherton, 1963); David Easton, *A Framework for Political Analysis* (Englewood Cliffs, N.J.: Prentice-Hall, 1965) and, by the same author, *The Political System: An Inquiry into the State of Political Science,** 2nd ed. (New York: Alfred A. Knopf, 1971); William A. Welsh, *Studying Politics** (New York: Praeger, 1973); and Alan C. Isaak, *Scope and Methods of Political Science: An Introduction to the Methodology of Political Inquiry,* rev. ed. (Homewood, Ill.: The Dorsey Press, 1975). A good collection of essays on political science and the functions of political scientists is George J. Graham, Jr. and George W. Carey, eds., *The Post-Behavioral Era: Perspectives on Political Science** (New York: David McKay, 1972).

A superb analysis of the political environment of society is Robert A. Dahl, *Modern Political Analysis,** 3rd ed. (Englewood Cliffs, N.J: Prentice-Hall, 1976). Two other studies that focus on the same general topic are Harold D. Laswell, *Politics: Who Gets What, When, How** (Cleveland: The World Publishing Company, 1958), and David R. Segal, *Society and Politics: Uniformity and Diversity in Modern Democracy** (Glenview, Ill.: Scott, Foresman, 1974).

Very little has been written on "the language of politics." The best treatment is Chapter 3 in T. D. Weldon, *The Vocabulary of Politics** (London: Penguin Books, 1953). A useful and more recent study of the subject is Eugene F. Miller, Metaphor and Political Knowledge. *The American Political Science Review*, 73:1, (1979), 155–170.

Two informative books on the development of political science in the United States are Bernard Crick, *The American Science of Politics: Its Origins and Conditions* (Berkeley: University of California Press, 1964) and Albert Somit and Joseph Tannenhaus, *The Development of Political Science: From Burgess to Behavioralism* (Boston: Allyn and Bacon, 1967). For a discussion of its more recent status, see Heinz Eulau and James G. March, eds., *Political Science** (Englewood Cliffs, N.J.: Prentice-Hall, 1969). A thought-provoking study with emphasis on futurism is Albert Somit, *Political Science and the Study of the Future** (Hinsdale, Ill.: Dryden, 1974).

Good treatments of the subfields in political science are Marian D. Irish, ed., *Political Science: Advance of the Discipline** (Englewood Cliffs, N.J.: Prentice-Hall, 1968); Michael Haas and Henry S. Kariel, eds., *Approaches to the Study of Political Science* (Scranton, Pa.: Chandler, 1970); and Ronald J. Stupak, et al., *Understanding Political Science: The Arena of Power** (Port Washington, N.Y.: Alfred, 1977).

*Available in paperback.

Chapter Two

Political Science: Approaches and Concepts

APPROACHES TO THE STUDY OF POLITICS

Political scientists use various methods to conduct their inquiries. Modern political science has been shaped by different methodological approaches and considerable debate over the appropriateness of each. The period during the late nineteenth century was heavily legalistic, as illustrated by the title of one of the major works of that era, John Burgess' *Political Science and Comparative Constitutional Law* (1890). Many American political scientists of that time had received at least some of their graduate training at European universities and were influenced by the legalistic training in these schools, but during the late nineteenth century some political scientists in this country already had begun to shift away from constitutionalism and legal inquiry, moving toward a structural study of governmental institutions and organizations. This can be seen, for example, in Woodrow Wilson's *Congressional Government: A Study in American Politics* (1885).

A new mood or spirit entered political science in the 1920s, when some political scientists began to supplement their library research with interview and survey fieldwork, thereby adding a new vista to the historical, legalistic, and constitutional approaches employed by the traditionalists. The new movement, soon to become known as **behavioralism**, aimed at making political science a more scientific discipline, one which analyzed politics as it operated in the contemporary, real world.

Behavioralism initially focused on the beliefs and activities of individuals. The emphasis on individual and group behavior led the behavioralist to study the leadership role of a president, the performances of members of congress and judges, and how they carry out their responsibilities, instead of focusing on institutions such as the Constitution, the executive, the Congress, or the judiciary. In other words, while the traditionalist's concern was largely with formal institutions, the behavioralist stressed individuals rather than large political units.

The behavioralists have acquired some of the research tools used in anthropology, economics, mathematics, psychology, and sociology. They have advocated a more rigorous empiricism, extensive use of statistical methods for quantifying the data, and the recording of these on charts, graphs, scales, and tables.

The behavioral approach seeks to achieve a greater accuracy in identifying, explaining, and verifying "laws" of politics that apply to a variety of political systems. Science in the term political science is stressed. Some early behavioralists even believed that we could begin to predict or foretell political events, on the assumption that politics was an orderly system governed by universal, discoverable laws. Most political scientists now believe that after careful analysis we can perceive trends and probabilities but cannot predict. As one political scientist concluded, the behavioralist can "explain how under carefully given and controlled circumstances and conditions [a previous event] men have in fact acted."[1] We cannot forecast with precision, however, because we cannot identify and examine every condition or circumstance that will influence future political events.

The most successful areas of inquiry for the behavioralist have been studies of voting behavior and investigations of beliefs and attitudes held by individuals. This certainly has helped us better understand the political arena and direct us to information we did not use 50 years ago.

Table 2.1 is based on a study of some 4,000 people in 3 countries. All 3 countries were surveyed in 1959 and in the case of Germany, a second survey was conducted in 1978. In this latter case, German pride in governmental institutions increased significantly over the nineteen year period. The individuals surveyed were asked, "Generally speaking, what are the things about this country that you are most proud of?" This table indicates that Americans and the British took great pride in their political system in 1959. The Germans showed little pride in their political system in 1959, but such pride increased noticeably by 1978. Democracy, whatever its many faults, can better withstand challenges if there is substantial pride or satisfaction in the political institutions and their policies. Widespread alienation, distrust, or disinterest in the political process may prove a weakness if the political system is subjected to severe economic, social, or international stress. It is only through such political surveys of the behavioralists that we have become aware of popular attitudes in different countries and have been able to study the implications of these attitudes.

During the past decade behavioralism has become an integral part of the political science discipline, and many members of the profession now rely on a combination of methods of inquiry derived from the traditional and behavioral schools. In a very real sense almost all political scientists are behavioralists if we summarize the behavioral movement as an effort to make political science more scientific. This new synthesis is not concerned exclusively with individuals; it also is concerned

---

[1]Mulford Q. Sibley, The Limits of Behavioralism, in James C. Charlesworth, ed., *Contemporary Political Analysis* (New York: The Free Press, 1967), p. 61.

Table 2-1 Aspects of Country in which Respondents Report Pride, by Country (in percent)

	1959			1978
	U.S. %	U.K. %	Germany %	Germany %
Respondent is most proud of:				
Governmental, political institutions	85	46	7	31
Social legislation	13	18	6	18
Position in international affairs	5	11	5	9
Economic system	23	10	33	40
Characteristics of people	7	18	36	25
Spiritual virtues and religion	3	1	3	6
Contributions to arts and sciences	4	13	23	23
Physical attributes of country	5	10	17	14
Nothing, don't know	13	21	18	10
Total[a]	158	148	148	176
N	(970)	(963)	(955)	(2,030)

Source: David P. Conradt, "Changing German Political Culture," in Gabriel A. Almond and Sidney Verba (eds.), *The Civic Culture Revisited* (Boston: Little, Brown and Company, 1980), p. 230.

[a] Percentages exceed one hundred because of multiple responses.

with the functioning and impact of political institutions and the influence of relevant geographic, economic, historical, legal, and cultural factors. This combining of various approaches has been influenced increasingly by the political and social crises of our time and the awareness that so many factors influence political events. One important credo of postbehavioralism is relevance; that is, the effort to make political science teaching and research as relevant as possible to current domestic and international problems and, if possible, to contribute to solving these problems. A major subfield that has emerged in the last few years is called public policy, committed to improvement of government policy.

This text is designed to use the most appropriate approaches for the beginning student in his or her study of politics. We believe that a basic familiarity with political science principles will enable the student to better understand contemporary political issues and to analyze and contribute toward the making of government decisions by voting, working in a political campaign, or even becoming a government official. A democracy such as ours requires informed and interested citizens who are able to take part in the political process.

We believe that the most appropriate approach to political science for the beginning student is a combination of political systems analysis and functionalism. Both of these orientations are concerned with the interaction, cooperation, and conflict of diverse parts. The underlying organization of this book presumes that such a focus provides a useful means for beginning students to understand the political world.

THE POLITICAL SYSTEM

We do not consider here all the complexities and debates surrounding systems theory. We will use the concept of the **political system** as an approach to recognizing and understanding patterns or regularities when confronted with what is often a large, unorganized mass of political information. As one distinguished political scientist explained:

> *Anyone who attempts to study politics scientifically must at least implicitly think of politics as though it were functioning as some sort of system. That is, he must assume that more or less regular relationships can be discerned among various aspects of politics and between phenomena he describes as political and certain other phenomena not so described.*[2]

We have used the term "political system" several times. At this point a definition and more thorough explanation are in order. Most political scientists agree that we study political systems and not just government. Government is the focal point or center of the political system, but many other parts are involved. The political systems approach does two things: it enables us to perceive selectively and to organize what is significant politically when we look at the whole political process. It also alerts us to the interrelationships between obviously political phenomena—for example, political parties, the chief executive, civil service commission—and other phenomena in society that are sometimes politically important—such as the family, educational, or economic systems.

Any system, whether we are discussing the political system, the heating system in a house, or the individual's physiological system, has five characteristics:

1. The system is made up of many parts.
2. Some parts are more important than others.
3. The parts interact.
4. To varying degrees the parts are interdependent.
5. The system has boundaries.

A major difference between an example such as the heating system of a house and the political system is that in the former the boundaries are tangible and readily observable. The components of the heating system (thermostat, furnace, wiring, ducts) are apparent to the eye, and it is obvious where the physical boundaries are. This is not true with the political system; its boundaries are abstract and must be identified and explained by the political scientist. You are not participating in the po-

[2]Herbert J. Spiro, "An Evaluation of Systems Theory," in James C. Charlesworth, ed., *Contemporary Political Analysis* (New York: The Free Press, 1967), p. 164.

litical system if you have a date or go to a football game. You are in the political system if you attend a political rally, write a letter to a government official, vote, or study and discuss politics.

In any system some parts are more important than others, and some parts interact more than others. Changes in one part may or may not affect other parts or processes in the system. If you have your appendix removed, there is little apparent change in your physiological system. If you lose a kidney the consequences are serious, and without a heart the body will not function. There are similar variations in the political system. Political parties and elections are very important in the American political system. The military and/or bureaucracy may be the most important institutions to study in some other political system. In fact, the latter situation is true for many political systems in Africa, Asia, Latin America, and the Middle East, where there are many military governments. An understanding of what we mean by political system will assist you in studying political science and particular countries or processes (for example, elections, revolutions, rule making, political socialization), but the concept of political system will not itself explain particular events. The first step, however, is to organize data information within a general framework, in this case, the political system. Figure 2–1 (on the following page) will help you visualize what we are discussing.

GOVERNMENT DEFINED

Government is the focal point or center of any political system. Government is that institution in society that successfully upholds a claim to the exclusive regulation of the legal use of physical force in making and enforcing its rules within a given territorial (geopolitical) area. It is the most inclusive institution in society. No other organization (fraternity, sorority, trade union, church) in society includes everyone within its jurisdiction or membership.

Government sometimes allows other groups to use physical force, but only in a restricted manner. A parent may discipline a child physically, but this must be limited. Too much physical force becomes child abuse and child abuse is against the law. Generally, when physical force is used by other than government officials it is done illegally. Much violence that actually occurs in society is outside the law, or what is generally described as crime. If crime and violence become too widespread, government effectiveness rapidly diminishes. The existence of a particular government actually may be threatened. When individuals organize and declare a government illegal, initiate political violence in an effort to establish a different government or change drastically the existing political system, then there is an insurgency or a revolution.

The use of force is the ultimate government sanction. Generally, the less physical force required, the more effective government is and the more it is accepted by the population. The arbitrary and unpredictable use of force characterizes totalitarian governments, which seek to terrorize and thus more easily control their subjects. A

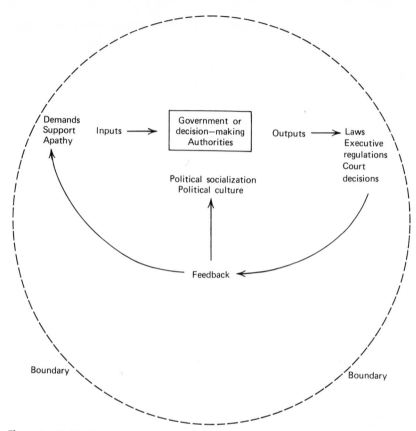

Figure 1. Political system.

government such as the American national government uses physical force relatively infrequently, but it is used. So that a government does not have to allocate extensive resources to internal security, 90 to 95 percent of the population should—out of commitment, understanding, self-interest, or habit—obey the law. If a police officer had to be on duty 24 hours a day to enforce stoplights, an unacceptable share of government resources (taxes, appropriations, personnel) would have to be committed to this area of government responsibility. Fortunately, most drivers obey traffic signals.

One example of the role of government and the uncommon but ultimate use of physical coercion by democratic governments is **eminent domain**. In the United States, eminent domain, or the acquiring of private property for public use after the payment of fair compensation, is usually accomplished without a court trial or resort to force. There are exceptions, such as the hypothetical individual who is required to sell his property for an interstate highway interchange. The person may believe the price the government offers for the property is too low; therefore, a jury trial becomes necessary to determine the price. On a few tragic occasions, government force is used. The following example also involves the question of whether or not "justice" was actually served.

> Consider the 1964 case of a Los Angeles resident named Steven Anthony who refused to vacate his home which had been condemned by Los Angeles County under the laws of eminent domain. The land was to be turned over to a private group for the construction of the Hollywood Motion Picture and Television Museum. For ten weeks Anthony barricaded himself in his home, holding off with a shotgun the deputies who sought to evict him. Finally, two plainclothes policemen gained access by posing as sympathizers. Anthony was arrested and jailed. The next day the house was demolished by court order. The judge labeled this previously unknown man "an anarchist, a rabble rouser, and a publicity seeker" and sentenced him to a year in jail for battery and resisting arrest. . . .
>
> All plans for building the museum have been abandoned due to dissension among the ranks of the Hollywood promoters. The property is currently being used as a parking lot.[3]

INPUTS

Government, because of its unique characteristics, is at the center of the political system, but many other activities and institutions are included as part of the system.

The **input** side of Figure 2–1 includes claims or **demands**, supports, and apathy. *Demands* refer to actions people want government to undertake or reject. The method by which to involve peacefully the largest number of people is that of competitive elections where most of the adult population is eligible to vote. Voters make few specific policy choices, but they do select candidates who have committed themselves on specific issues. Demonstrations, petitions, and individual letters to newspapers or government officials are also means of making input.

Interest groups and political parties, discussed in more detail in Chapters Five and Six, are also means of making claims. For example, the National Rifle Association actively and successfully opposes gun-control legislation. In a democratic political system, the opportunities are greater for groups to organize without the supervision or control of government. A variety of competing claims are made in this type of political system. Ultimately, some part of government makes a decision (or refuses to take action); whether it be a law, a court decision, or an executive order limiting the amount of oil that can be imported. Individuals also can make claims or present demands by writing letters, meeting a government official, running for office, and, of course, through the electoral ballot.

Supports are given to the political system as a whole and to that part of the system referred to as the regime. **Regime** refers to the overall constitutional process

[3]Susan Love Brown et al., *The Incredible Bread Machine* (San Diego: World Research, 1974), pp. 2–3. The original story appeared in the *Los Angeles Times*, April 4, 1965.

Poster encouraging young people to register and vote.

or political rules of the game, to "those arrangements that regulate the way in which the demands put into the system are settled and the way in which decisions are put into effect."[4] Supports generally evolve over decades or even centuries and are basically loyal to the system and regime, without necessarily being in agreement with the individuals or political party in office. You may have voted against the president or the member of congress representing you, but still be loyal to the existing political arrangement, which in the case of the United States is a constitutional representative government.

An increasingly common phenomenon, however, is **support-inputs** given to a particular government by a "supportive" foreign power. Inputs and supports are not only domestic in origin. In many countries in Africa, Asia, Latin America, and the Middle East, international inputs and supports are critical if a particular group of po-

[4]David Easton, An approach to the analysis of political systems, *World Politics*, 9: 1, p. 392.

litical leaders is to continue ruling. One example is the overthrow of the government of the Central African Empire and Emperor Bokassa in 1979. This is a small, land-locked country, formerly a French colony, in central Africa. It is dismally poor with a population of under 4 million. For over a decade the French provided 60 percent of the national budget. Bokassa was a cruel tyrant, who a few months prior to his over-throw had ordered 200 school children murdered for demonstrating against him. Shortly before his ouster, Bokassa had converted to Islam and was seeking to re-place French support with even larger amounts of financial and military aid from Libya and Russia. France first cut off its aid program and then its contributions to the Central African Empire's budget. Bokassa flew to Libya in an effort to replace French support-inputs with Libyan ones, but it was too late. While Bokassa was gone, a former president flew to the capital "at the head" of 500 French para-troopers, and the Central African Empire became the Central African Republic un-der a pro-French president. Many governments in smaller countries depend on foreign support-inputs to stay in power. When this is reduced or cut off, they must look for other foreign sources or very likely will be overthrown. This happened to Bokassa.

Within the political system, supports can be divided into two basic types: **tangible** and **symbolic**. Tangible supports are usually actions that show or promote loyalty and identity with the political system. Examples include voting as an act of citizenship or paying taxes because of a feeling of commitment and identity. Sym-bolic supports are states of mind, such as attitudes of loyalty, patriotism, and com-mitment. These attitudes sometimes become tangible supports; at other times they remain simply a psychological orientation that creates what may be described as indirect, emotional support.

Supports evolve because governments and regimes have responded over sever-al decades and generations (see "political integration" in Chapter Ten). Supports hold a political community together, even though there are sharp differences over particular policies or individuals in office. When the widely shared supports are few, the political system is threatened and radically different political arrangements may be imposed. During the closing days of Weimar Germany (1918–1933), shortly be-fore Adolf Hitler assumed full power in 1933, the Communists and Nazis together were winning 50 percent of the votes. (In the November, 1932, Reichstag elections, the Nazi Party won 33 percent of the vote and the Communists 17 percent.) This lack of support for constitutional democracy made it easier for the Nazis to achieve power and transform the German government from a representative to a totalitarian political system.

Apathy or indifference can be either a support or a potential reservoir from which revolutionaries can mobilize support. For example, in the United States ap-proximately 20 percent of the eligible electorate is apolitical or apathetic. Some peo-ple are apathetic because the electoral process involves so many people that they feel one vote makes no difference; others are uninterested because "things will not

get better," or they lack the mental ability to understand and organize political information. In some political systems fear and coercion encourage apathy. For others,
apathy reflects general satisfaction with the political system and the feeling that
there is no need to become concerned with political matters. People may be very intelligent and have many interests but simply not be interested in political issues. If
politics becomes so intense that it turns into a war of one side against the other, orderly procedures, such as secret ballot and the defeated candidate acknowledging
the winner's right to assume office, will soon be ineffective. Apathy, positively viewed,
reflects the genuine right of a person to be apolitical. This bloc of people, by their
presence, reduces the intensity of competition among the politically concerned.

Political apathy also can result from a sense of hopelessness and withdrawal
from the political system. Apathy in an authoritarian state is commonly a defense
mechanism. It does not directly challenge the regime, but it seeks to preserve in
one of the few ways possible a degree of individual privacy and autonomy. It prevents the complete politicization of the individual in the name of the state. Given the
proper circumstances, such apathy may be interrupted by spontaneous antiregime
demonstrations, as happened in East Germany in 1953, in Hungary in 1956, in
Czechoslovakia in 1968, and in Thailand in 1973. Apathy based on a sense of hopelessness or an underlying hostility is not a support, and it becomes a violent input
when triggered.

In the case of the Thai "student revolution," which occurred in Bangkok in October 1973, troops fired on students and at least 69 students died. High-ranking military officers then refused to order the troops against the students again. Three days
of demonstrations forced the most unpopular government–military leaders to flee
the country. The generally politically uninterested Bangkok population was mobilized by the students' actions. In Thailand, apathy had been a form of support for
many years. As this apathy moved from a form of support to quiet hostility, the student demonstration drew on and organized popular feelings. The result was input
that had crucial political implications. A civilian prime minister was appointed by the
king, and one year later a new, more liberal constitution was adopted.

Apathy, as we have seen, can provide support for the political system or it can be
a potential source for mass agitation against the system. If a government is struggling against an insurgency, the apathy of the population in their effort to stay alive
generally is a disadvantage for the government. A government under this type of
stress needs the positive support of its citizens and not their disinterest.

OUTPUTS
Outputs are government decisions. They may be laws, court decisions, executive-
administrative orders, or conscious refusals to make a decision. The work and even
intentions of the government are measured by its outputs. Public administration is
the subfield of political science that studies how decisions are implemented and if
implementation is efficient, often with more concern for procedures (such as budgeting and personnel policies) than substance of decisions. No-decisions, the re-

Thai students scatter to avoid fire from troops during clashes that led to the collapse of the military government, 1973.

fusal of government to intervene or take an action concerning a problem or dispute in society, is also a form of output. Examples include the refusal of Canada to develop nuclear weapons or allow nuclear weapons to be located on its territory and the refusal of the American Congress to approve gun-control legislation.

Laws as output are apparent: eighteen-year-olds are enfranchised by Constitutional amendment, social security benefits are raised, or the speed limit is set at 55 miles per hour by act of Congress. One of the most famous judicial outputs in the United States was the Supreme Court decision in *Brown* v. *Board of Education* (1954), in which racial segregation in public schools was declared unconstitutional. The implementation of that decision since 1954, though slow, has had a tremendous impact on society.

An example of an executive or administrative output was the action taken by President Ford in 1974 imposing a quota on the importation of Canadian beef and pork. President Nixon had suspended import quotas on foreign beef in 1972 to reduce inflationary pressures. President Ford's reimposition of quotas on Canada resulted from the American government's belief that Canada had established "unjustifiable import restrictions" on American products. A White House spokesman explained that the President's proclamation was intended "to bring an end to the Canadian quotas."[5]

Unfortunately, most political science writing is not concerned with the output side of the political system. Relatively little research is done on the impact that output decisions have or on the question of whether they actually accomplish their pur-

[5]*Washington Post*, November 17, 1974.

pose. Laws, rules, appropriations, and good administrative procedures do not guarantee that the result will be the one anticipated. Most political science literature focuses either on inputs or the government decision-making process and devotes little time to the effect of government policy.

CONVERSION AND POLITICAL CULTURE

Government in all of its parts (executive, legislative, and judicial branches) can be described as the decision-making authority that has **conversion** as a principal function:

> *The conversion processes, or functions, are the ways systems transform inputs into outputs. In the political system this involves the ways in which demands and support are transformed into authoritative decisions and are implemented.*[6]

The more people participate freely in making demands, the more effort required by government to balance, modify, approve, or reject some claims and convert the inputs into policy or outputs. Much of what political scientists study is concerned with government institutions: history, organization, and functioning. Government is crucial to political science because of its ultimate sanction—the legal use of physical force—and also because of its decision-making and conversion roles.

As government decisions are made and policies carried out, they pass through a feedback process that affects the political culture, as well as the more immediate input side. Political culture (discussed in detail in Chapter Four) is shaped in part by outputs, but it also affects the input process. Political culture refers to those aspects of our social heritage concerned with beliefs, attitudes, values, and behavior patterns affecting the way people perceive and behave in the political system. Political culture grew out of the concept of national character, which presumes the presence of modal national traits having political significance, for example, general acceptance of a ruling elite not subject to competitive elections. Modal behavior, or the mode, refers to the characteristic that occurs most often in the group. The characteristic is not present in everyone, and sometimes is not even present in a majority of the universe measured, but it is the most common trait or set of traits.

Political culture is important in the conversion process. It influences the thinking and actions of those actually making government decisions. It also influences the range of claims and the style (voting, letters, demonstrations, riots, or apathetic obedience) with which the conversion process must deal. For example, during the Tokugawa period (1603–1857) in Japan, the emperor was a figurehead and military lords, or *daimyo*, controlled the government. Rule often was arbitrary. The political culture enforced uniformity and self-conscious apolitical behavior. There were few, if any, popular demands and political claims were nil. An in-depth study of the period by an anthropologist shows how the samurai warriors enforced detailed government rules by instantly decapitating anyone whose actions were "other than expected." Those Japanese who survived in the Tokugawa political system "learned

[6]Gabriel Almond and G. Bingham Powell, Jr., *Comparative Politics: A Developmental Approach* (Boston: Little, Brown, 1966), p. 29.

in early childhood to keep their own counsel, trust no one, and conform fanatically to whatever might be ordered."[7]

FEEDBACK

Feedback is a result of the changing opinions and actions of citizens in response to government output. It may increase or decrease support for the system. It may affect the types of inputs or claims that are made (from lowering taxes to creating a totally new type of government), as well as how the claims are presented (from voting to revolution). Feedback in an authoritarian political system, as in the case of Tokugawa Japan, may be controlled by the government so as to compel obedience, with the result that popular input is nonexistent.

Relative satisfaction with output leads one to support the political system or even particular candidates and political parties. Often there is a direct and clear-cut feedback loop (see Figure 2–1). Political leaders may increase government benefits or programs shortly before an election in order to win votes. For example, in the fall of 1979, President Jimmy Carter ran against Senator Edward Kennedy in a popularity contest electing Democratic delegates to county caucuses in Florida. President Carter and his advisors believed he must defeat Ted Kennedy in "Carter country" or he had no chance to be renominated. Carter beat Kennedy two to one. One factor assisting President Carter was the rapid approval of numerous federal projects in the state shortly before the election. Clearly, many were announced to win support for the president. One member of Congress from Florida declared, "I've never seen anything like it. We're getting money for highways, for housing, for hospitals. One more grant and the state will sink under the weight of these projects."[8]

Another example of how feedback can affect general political orientation is the case of postwar Japan, which underwent one of the most successful land-reform programs in this century. The American occupation required the Japanese Diet (legislature) to enact far-reaching land-reform legislation in October 1946. The number of farmers owning all their land increased from 36 percent to 62 percent within 3 years, and the number of farmers owning less than half their land dropped from 17 to 7 percent. The new agrarian policy and the feedback related to these reforms were accomplished. The land-reform campaign was to change village relationships so that the mass of peasants were not dominated by a few landlords. Radical agrarian movements now found little support among the new peasant-owners. Political attitudes and input were greatly influenced by the government's agrarian policies. The peasants were interested mainly in conserving their new gains. The new peasant-owners "became the chief support of the conservative political parties."[9]

---

[7]Douglas G. Haring, "The Formation of National Character in Tokugawa and Meiji, Japan," reprinted in Thomas J. Bellows, Stanley Erikson, and Herbert R. Winter, eds., *Political Science: Introductory Essays and Readings* (Belmont, Cal.: Duxbury Press, 1971), p. 166.

[8]*New York Times*, October 7, 1979. p. 27.

[9]Franz H. Michael and George E. Taylor, *The Far East in the Modern World* (New York: Henry Holt, 1956), p. 546.

Communications and information are also part of the feedback loop. The presumption is that, with more information, governments are more effective. David Easton, the political scientist who has written the most extensively on political systems, believes that information is important for two principal reasons: public officials need as much information as possible about the political system so they can act to meet any possible loss of support; and public officials also should "be able to evaluate the consequences of whatever behavior they have already undertaken or are in the process of undertaking."[10] Feedback through elections, the party organization, newspapers, interest groups, and the like, provides information about the impact of outputs. Nevertheless, in this information-explosion era we live in, we often do not have sufficient information and are unable to utilize fully what we potentially have access to. Even in an open system with a wide range of competing inputs, the amount of information moving through the feedback loop often is inadequate or cannot be retrieved at the moment it is required. It almost appears at times that there is a dichotomy between the world of action and the world of thought. Former Secretary of State Henry Kissinger, who has achieved success in both worlds, as both a government decision maker and as an eminent political scientist at Harvard University, spoke on the difficulties confronting political leaders as they must make often-difficult and rapid choices and judgments. Dr. Kissinger says that under these pressures, which are common for political leaders, there is little time for reflection. Officials are so hard pressed that most of them "leave office with the perceptions and insight with which they entered."[11]

We are suggesting that even when all parts of the political system appear to be functioning very adequately, the system always will be less than "perfect." Even in a democratic political environment with considerable subsystem (interest group, parties, individual freedom) autonomy—resulting in a broad flow of claims and information feedback—policies and choices are subject to the "human factor." Anthony Downs has pointed this out in his analysis of the civil servant as a decision maker. Downs discusses several inevitable limitations to decision making.

1. Each decision maker can devote only a limited amount of time to decision making.
2. Each decision maker can mentally weigh and consider only a limited amount of information at one time.
3. The functions of most officials require them to become involved in more activities than they can consider simultaneously; hence, they must normally focus their attention on only part of their major concerns.
4. The amount of information initially available to every decision maker about each problem is only a small fraction of all the information potentially available on the subject.

[10]David Easton, *A Systems Analysis of Political Life* (New York: John Wiley, 1965), pp. 364–65.
[11]Review of Henry Kissinger's *White House Years* by Daniel Southerland, in *The Christian Science Monitor*, November 2, 1979, p. 15.

5. Additional information bearing on any particular problem can usually be procured, but the costs of procurement and utilization may rise rapidly as the amount of data increases.
6. Important aspects of many problems involve information that cannot be procured at all, especially concerning future events; hence, many decisions must be made in the face of some ineradicable uncertainty.[12]

The world we live in is imperfect. We can never achieve a mechanical functioning of the political system that will provide a perfectly harmonious, obviously understandable, and rational interaction. Nevertheless, we believe an understanding of the principal characteristics of the political system enables the student to understand better the vast amounts of often-unrelated political information available every day. It allows the student to organize much of the information into understandable categories (what events involve demands, supports, conversion). Systems analysis alerts us to the fact that while everything may relate to everything ultimately, during a given period time some things relate more than others. For example, we suddenly are aware that we live in an age of scarce natural resources. Economic contraction rather than growth may characterize the United States, Western Europe, and in fact most of the world for several years if not decades. This scarcity has led suddenly to important political inputs. Individuals and groups are demanding lower gasoline and fuel oil prices. Groups and rallies are organized to oppose nuclear power plants as a substitute for oil, in favor of solar or water power. Others argue that lifting price controls on petroleum in the United States will eliminate worldwide scarcity because more oil will be produced.

A declining natural resource—oil—has led to all varieties of claims on governments to deal with this new problem. Various governments have adopted different policies. A knowledge of what we mean by political system should help us in identifying important issues and the most important groups or individuals involved in the political system or arena during a given period of time. Beyond this, there are limitations.

CRITICISMS OF THE SYSTEMS APPROACH

A. It is difficult to test the whole systems model. It is easier to study parts or subsystems that are performing important functions, such as political parties, interest groups, or the bureaucracy. The components of a political system are distinct and different from one another. All of the parts do not depend on one another. Some parts are vital, some are intermediary, some are incidental. In one political system autonomous interest groups are important in maintaining competition and freedom of expression, while in a totalitarian system interest groups are just another instrument of control and provide no input. We must study a spe-

---

[12]Anthony Downs, *Inside Bureaucracy* (Boston: Little, Brown, 1967), p. 75.

cific political system in detail to determine which parts are essential and how they influence and are influenced by other parts. Change or destruction of one part will not necessarily have much impact on the system.

B.   Adjustments between parts and/or processes may be delayed. It often is difficult to predict response or determine with any degree of accuracy what a change in one part of the system (literacy, greater freedom of speech, lowered voting age) may have on another (increased political support, weakened extremist parties, the creation of revolutionary parties). Moreover, government responses to a problem often fail to achieve what is intended, as illustrated in the following cases.

1.   In 1977–1978, the Shah of Iran attempted to create more political stability and build support by permitting greater freedom of expression (rallies, releasing political prisoners, promising elections, and so forth) and choosing a member of the opposition to head a new civilian government. The result was the opposite of what was intended. Groups now allowed to participate openly in the political process were no longer interested in reform but in deposing the Shah. After months of riots and demonstrations, the Shah was forced to leave Iran in early 1979.

2.   The 1960s "war on poverty" in the United States was intended to involve the poor in planning and carrying out the program in their neighborhoods. Elections were held in poor neighborhoods to choose representatives to local Community Action Programs. Turnout was dismal, ranging from between one and five percent of those eligible. Individuals elected often helped only their friends and their handful of political supporters. Within a few years there were numerous indictments of antipoverty workers for forgery, kickbacks, and embezzlement.[13] Many of the antipoverty programs were hastily conceived, poorly administered, failed noticeably to improve the condition of the poor, and attracted little participation by the poor in developing and reviewing programs.

C.   Finally, we might note the frequent criticism that systems analysis is biased toward the status quo and is sympathetic toward only limited change. Although regularly denied, this is sometimes true. There is more than a suspicion in systems theory that the continuous interaction and interdependence of parts implies self-regulation and adjustment because the first goal is survival of the system. We cannot assume all parts are working for survival (for example, a revolutionary party), nor have any measures been constructed to determine when a system is being adequately maintained or being exposed to too much stress. What is the threshold, determined by measuring such crucial variables as caloric intake, literacy, employment, education, riots, or political assassinations, that, when taken as an interrelated group, will reveal to us that a political system is about to disintegrate or, having faced challenges, is stronger than before?

---

[13]George E. Berkley, *The Craft of Public Administration* (Boston: Allyn and Bacon, 1975), p. 305.

SUMMARY

Despite its limitations, systems analysis provides the political scientist with a useful framework for analysis. It is the beginning point for a study of one or more individual political systems or for a study of international politics. It provides a general orientation and reminds us that there are certain basic processes, such as inputs, decision making, conversion, outputs, and feedback, that are performed in all systems. Which parts are important, how they interact, and what functions each performs can be determined only by analyzing specific cases.

FUNCTIONALISM

Closely associated with systems analysis is **functionalism**, often called structural functionalism. Again, it is an approach to understanding politics rather than a theory explaining politics. Because many of the terms are used so widely in the discipline today, we will discuss briefly its major features.

The dedicated functionalist hopes to develop a general theory of politics. These individuals believe that every society must perform certain functions if it is to continue (goal attainment, reproduction, child rearing, rule making, and so on). These are called **requisite** functions. One difficulty is that there is no agreement among structural functionalists on the precise definition and number of requisite functions. Some writers identify as few as four broad functions; others list as many as twenty. Although this book does not use functionalism as a theory, a greater awareness of political functions will increase our understanding of politics. Institutions and functions cannot be separated, if for no other reason than the fact that institutions are important principally because of their functions.

This text places considerable emphasis on institutions (discussed later in this chapter) or structures. We believe, however, that institutions (parliament, political parties) are important in the first place because they perform significant functions. If one knows the contributions or functions of an institution in a political system, one can understand better why and how the institution adapts and survives. In terms of the political system, what consequences does the institution/function have in the polity? At least some individuals or groups must think the function is important or it would not continue. We consider here the functions of the individual (e.g. the president, the prime minister), of groups (e.g. political parties, interest groups), and of ideas (e.g. Communist ideology). This book does not limit itself, however, just to functions. Political analysis also should be concerned with the structure, history, and leadership characteristics of the political phenomena being analyzed.

Over the years, the political scientist who has written most widely and clearly on functionalism in political science is Gabriel Almond. He does not list a set of requisite functions; rather, he identifies functions that seem to occur in all political systems, whether it be a simple village society or an authoritarian, industrialized society such as the Soviet Union. The following are seven of Almond's functions that we believe the student will find useful.

1.   Recruitment involves filling new roles or jobs, replacing individuals, and promoting individuals to new positions. Whether a political system can maintain itself and adapt to new challenges depends in great measure on who occupies important roles or positions (presidents, members of congress, diplomats, military officers, financial experts) and how they reached (were recruited) to these positions or offices.

2.   Socialization is the shaping of attitudes and beliefs. As circumstances change, political attitudes may be shaped appropriately, maintained, or changed. Socialization occurs among the general population as well as among those who occupy the elite political positions.

3.   Interest articulation occurs when individuals or groups request/demand that government change, continue a specific policy, or take no action (do not introduce gas rationing). These demands often are associated with promise of political support (vote, financial contribution, work for an individual or political party). In a democracy, this function is performed by a large number of independent groups or individuals. In a more authoritarian system, interest articulation may be limited to elite groups of landowners, industrialists, military officers, and the leaders of the ruling political party.

4.   Interest aggregation occurs when demands are combined or aggregated into a smaller number of policy alternatives. This activity often is associated with political parties who try to absorb, adjust, or compromise numerous demands in order to build a broad coalition of electoral support.

5.   Policy making is the rule-making process in the political system. This is the authoritative setting of official objectives. Every political system has a set of rules that determines what institutions decide policy. In Great Britain it is principally the elected prime minister and the cabinet; in the Soviet Union it is a few people on the Politburo; in a tribal society it may be a council of elders.

6.   Policy implementation is the carrying out of policy. Often these policies are carried out through civil bureaucracies or the military. As we have already seen, policy implementation may not be successful. Declaring a policy does not mean it will be implemented. For example, over 50 political systems have established comprehensive land-reform programs since the end of World War II. Only a handful of these programs (in Taiwan, Japan, South Korea) have actually distributed land to the peasant and raised the rural standard of living. The remainder, for one reason or another, did not succeed.[14]

7.   Political communication refers to the flow of information dealing with politics including face-to-face contacts within nonpolitical groups such as the family, within political parties, interest groups, legislatures, political executives, the civil service and the mass media. It is not a separate function but precedes and is present in all of the above functions.[14]

Before enumerating the benefits of functionalism we might note a major criticism. Namely, that too much stress on functionalism tends to take us away from looking first at institutions (discussed on pp. 43–44) such as political parties, legislatures, and bureaucracies. It is often easier to begin our analysis with institutions and then look at functions. In fact, institutions are politically important only because of the functions they perform. It is easier to look first at institutions and then at their functions rather than look at functions first and then try to determine which institutions perform these functions.

The following list gives three ways in which functionalism will help the student to become a more effective political observer.

1.   Institutions perform more than one function. We should look closely at the several functions that are performed and what purposes they serve. In the nineteenth century, as legislatures grew in power in democratic political systems, their principal functions were to pass laws and appropriate money. Throughout its more than 50-year history, the Supreme Soviet has had no actual power in either of these areas, but it serves as a forum for the announcement and explanation of communist policy to the Russian masses. It also makes the political system seem more legitimate (legitimizing function) because, at least formally, laws are approved by the Supreme Soviet. A principal function of Singapore's parliament for the past decade has been to serve as a recruiting and testing ground. Since one party controls all 69 parliamentary seats, policy is decided by a few ministers in the cabinet. Legislators who are capable debaters and evaluators of government policies, as demonstrated in parliamentary debates, may be invited to become ministers. Ineffective members of parliament are not renominated by the ruling party in the next election. Legislatures in the USSR and Singapore perform different functions from the American Congress, and even a preliminary effort at political analysis should include an awareness that institutions perform several functions and these functions differ among political systems.

2.   Various institutions may perform some of the same functions in different political systems. In Imperial China, scholar-bureaucrats constituted the civil service, which held the empire together. These Chinese Mandarin elite were selected in highly competitive examinations. Learning and intelligence, rather than social status, generally determined success. Education and examinations are also recruitment institutions important in contemporary France. The National School of Administration recruits the most capable college graduates for a three-year course. Students who are able to complete the rigorous curriculum become the top civil servants. Even in ''classless communist'' societies there is an emphasis on knowledge and training when the party recruits. In the Soviet Union, the Central Committee of the Commu-

[14]See Gabriel A. Almond and G. Bingham Powell, Jr., *Comparative Politics: System, Process and Policy* 2nd ed.; (Boston: Little, Brown and Company, 1978), *passim,* for further discussion of these other functions.

nist Party is composed of highly educated persons who have performed well and are recruited from the military and the bureaucracy as well as the party itself. In the United States, recruitment for a government or political office can be through self-selection. It is not uncommon for an ambitious and skilled individual to organize a group of supporters and campaign successfully for political office. A final example is **ascriptive recruitment**, where individuals achieve government office because of their lineage and social status (the institutions of blood descent). A group of individuals form the pool of candidates, such as in Saudi Arabia where all important positions are held by members of the very large Saudi royal family.

    3.   The difference between **manifest** and **latent functions** is quite important in political analysis. The latent functions often are discovered only after careful study, and they sometimes may be the most important functions performed by the institution. Those functions that were intended when the institution or organization was created we call **manifest**. Those functions that were not intended originally or are not principally intended are called **latent**. Robert Merton's discussion of political machines (p. 42) identifies the importance of latent functions. Another example is India's caste associations. Caste membership is ascriptive. A person born into a caste has no way to change his/her membership. Caste prescribes occupations which can be pursued, religious rituals, marriage within caste, social position within society, and often place of residence. Habit and custom have determined caste activities and organizaton for centuries. It was the core feature of a rigid, traditional society, ruled by a few noble families. Membership in caste ruling bodies usually was hereditary, passed on to the senior members of certain families in the caste. Slowly and almost imperceptibly, caste associations began to participate in India's electoral politics after independence in 1948. Now there is active involvement, including attendance at caste meetings, paying membership dues, and voting for candidates supported by the caste association. Caste functions no longer are limited to organizing society along rigid, traditional lines. The new and slowly growing function of the caste is to act as a political interest group, making demands and delivering votes. This new function is the most important one for political scientists to study. It is bringing much of traditional, rural India into meaningful electoral participation. This latent function was not recognized until two political scientists studied the activities of Indian castes in the late 1950s.[15]

    Functionalism alerts us to the fact that institutions always and principally involve behavior or activities. Functionalism suggests we study what the behavior is and why it is important in the political system. We believe, however, that it is easier to identify and understand functions by identifying and studying them as part of the activities of specific institutions, such as elections, legislatures, the executive offices, universities, the military, and the bureaucracy.

[15]For an elaboration of the political functions of caste, see Lloyd T. Rudolph and Susanne Hoeber Rudolph, The political role of India's caste association, *Pacific Affairs*, 33:1, 1960, pp. 5–22.

DEFINING CERTAIN TERMINOLOGY

Having reviewed two of the basic organizing approaches of the book—systems theory and functionalism—we logically turn to the definition of certain terms that are useful to the understanding of politics in today's world. Political scientists may disagree on the effectiveness of particular approaches or specific methodologies. Most, though, agree on the range of phenomena we study. In the remainder of this chapter we consider certain terms with which the student should be familiar. The terms we discuss are **political analysis, institution, role, power and influence, authority and legitimacy, postindustrial society,** and **conflict and adjustment**.

POLITICAL ANALYSIS

The business of political scientists is **political analysis**. Most adults are aware of and discuss some political happenings. The political scientist, however, brings systematic training to bear on the study of politics. At its simplest, analysis is work undertaken by a trained person that requires studying a problem, issue, decision, policy, or situation by organizing the data into categories or elements and then relating these to one another. Basic to the analytical process is selective perception—choosing the elements or variables that are of primary significance as opposed to those of secondary importance or even irrelevant to the study. Analysis should lead to generalization, explanation, and the offering of hypotheses for further study. Scientific analysis seeks to relate two or more political phenomena (type of political leadership, for example, and effectiveness of government decisions) with one another.

Negating a generalization is also part of analysis. For example, for many years after World War II it was argued that democracy is unstable if religion is politicized and religious parties are active, as in Lebanon, Northern Ireland, and the French Fourth Republic (1946–1958). As this generalization has been tested in other political systems, such as postwar Germany, Austria, and the Netherlands, it was found that the relationships between religious political parties and instability did not always hold. Religious political parties do not inevitably lead to instability. Other factors or variables, still being determined, must be present.

Analysis requires training and a basic knowledge of the subject matter. The determination of crucial variables and identification of nonobvious patterns, such as channels of recruitment to political leadership, the policy role of the bureaucracy, and cultural fragmentation, are analyzed most effectively by individuals who have spent a good deal of time studying these problems. Certain assumptions about which institutions and processes are the key ones serve to determine the appropriate focus of the investigation and guide the selection and ordering of one's observations. Expectations and insights based on prior study and research are fundamental to sophisticated political analysis. One objective of this book is to help the student acquire basic political science principles and data for effective political analysis.

Robert Merton has described and analyzed American political machines in the late nineteenth and early twentieth centuries in a study widely quoted as an excellent example of political analysis. Merton pointed out the "human" side of the political machine, which saw its roots in the local neighborhood, where residents were principally concerned with personal problems and needs. The machine won its elections in the precincts through elaborate networks of personal ties and obligations.

> The precinct captain is forever a friend in need. In our prevailingly impersonal society, the machine, through its local agents, fulfills the important social function of humanizing and personalizing all manner of assistance to those in need. Foodbaskets and jobs, legal and extra-legal advice, setting to rights minor scrapes with the law, helping the bright poor boy to a political scholarship in a local college, looking after the bereaved—the whole range of crises when a feller needs a friend, and above all, a friend who knows the score and who can do something about it—all of these find the ever-helpful precinct captain available in the pinch.[16]

Political machines were corrupt. They often used public moneys to benefit the leader and their friends. But they also helped new migrants to the big cities to adjust to the problems of urbanization and industrialization. The machines helped these immigrants, some of whom could not speak English, to survive in an alien environment. Professor Merton's analysis shows how political machines helped to integrate people into society through welfare services and similar programs aimed at individual adjustment. These were latent functions, or functions not originally intended by political machines, which were created to win elections. The extended analysis goes on to suggest that in our study of organizations we should be alert to the importance of latent functions in a social or political system. Merton's analysis explained, generalized, and hypothesized.

The organization of components, their interrelationships, and how they function vary in many ways among the 160 plus sovereign countries in today's world. Analysis and understanding of political system A will not necessarily enable you to use the same approach or methods of analysis and arrive at a quick understanding of political system B. An expert on Ford automobiles will have little difficulty in working on a Plymouth motor. The same does not hold true for political systems. The importance of certain parts or institutions in one system does not mean they are important in another political system. If the relative importance of parts varies, the pattern of interaction obviously varies even more. For example, knowledge of the organization and functioning of American political parties will not lead to an immediate understanding of French parties. It will, though, make you better able to analyze the French party system. One reason for a large number of diverse examples in the text is to enable you to understand better when studying new material and new situations.

[16]Robert Merton, Social Theory and Social Structure, 3rd ed. (Glencoe, Ill.: The Free Press, 1968), pp. 127–29, passim.

INSTITUTION

Institutions are more than buildings made out of steel and brick, although many people think first of the physical structures when discussing institutions. Institutions are patterns of human relationships. They are regular and observable patterns of interaction, usually evolving over time, which then are formalized by custom or written form through rules of procedure or laws. Your college or university is an institution, the family is an institution. Institutions may develop rather quickly if rules are promulgated and behavior must conform to such rules. For example, one of the inheritances common to former British colonies is the Public Service Commission (PSC). The PSCs were introduced in the British colonies to handle recruitment, promotion, and often job assignments in the colonial civil services. Most such PSCs are less than 50 years old, yet these personnel procedures and the PSCs through which they are implemented have rapidly become important institutions in many of the now-independent developing countries formerly under British rule. In some developing countries the PSC may be one of the most important institutions in the political system because of its control over the bureaucracy. Institutions are the core of a functioning political system.

Political parties are also institutions. No mention is made of them in the American Constitution. Their crucial role today tells us much about the evolution of the American political system. American political parties and the party conventions that nominate the presidential and vice-presidential candidates have become important politi-

Republican presidential nominee Ronald Reagan and running mate George Bush are joined by former President Gerald Ford at the finale of the 1980 Republican Convention.

cal institutions in our nation. As parties and conventions evolved, states passed laws dealing with such matters as nondiscriminatory practices in primary elections and regulations affecting the choice or voting commitments of convention delegates (for example, a delegate must support, on the first convention ballot the individual who won the party's presidential primary in the state). Over the course of the nineteenth century, we can observe the institutionalization of party and convention processes.

The "action" in stable political systems occurs in the principal institutions. (By political stability we mean change without noticeable violence.) Institutionalization should not mean rigidity or ossification. To remain effective, institutions must be flexible in organization and adaptable in terms of performing new and discarding old functions. Institutions should allow for, respond to, and guide change, but not prevent it. Russian civil administration under the Czar prior to World War I represents an institution that collapsed when it could not adapt to fundamental challenges—World War I and the fight against the Austro-Hungarian and German Empires, along with the desperate domestic economic crises resulting from the war.

When we study institutions, an important aspect is the individual and the role he occupies and how he is limited by or expands the role.

ROLE
It is essential to appreciate the significance of **role** if one is to study institutions. Role refers to the relationship between individual and institution. In all societies people develop standard expectations about how they and others should behave in specific situations or within particular institutional contexts. When many people share generally similar expectations, we refer to this as a role.[17]

A role guides behavior in a socially defined position. It establishes the boundaries but not every detail. Students have rather clear ideas about the role of the student and the teacher in a college or university. Within the general role expectations, however, there is wide latitude for individual behavior.

Each American president must fulfill certain role obligations while he or she is in office. Examples include nominating members to the cabinet, making recommendations in the annual State of the Union speech, conducting foreign policy so as to protect American national security, recommending a national budget to Congress. Individuals are expected to perform certain actions and to function in certain ways. The individual in the role, considered to be the actor, also has the opportunity to modify or expand the role. Role suggests incremental but not radical change. Radical change would so alter the characteristics of the role that the new role would resemble only in name the previous role. The presidential role in the United States has undergone substantial incremental changes, but generally within restrictive yet adaptive guidelines. In an excellent analysis of the role of the American chief execu-

---

[17]This discussion of role draws heavily from Robert A. Dahl, *Modern Political Analysis*, 3rd ed. (Englewood Clifffs, N.J.: Prentice-Hall, 1976), p. 11.

tive, Louis W. Koenig has pointed out that it is individual presidents responding to great crises who have had the major impact on shaping the presidency:

Crisis is a crucible in which a President and his administration are tested as nowhere else. No other condition tries so vigorously the capacity of the President for decision, perceptiveness, physical endurance, self-confidence and prudence.[18]

An example of role adaptation is the regular holding and use of press conferences, which have become an important part of the presidential role. This was first mastered and developed by Franklin Delano Roosevelt (1933–1945) as part of his response to the Depression crisis:

Roosevelt's approach to the crisis was a massive venture in public relations. Like Hoover, interestingly, Roosevelt considered the root cause of the depression to be psychological. . . . "The only thing we have to fear is fear itself," he said memorably in his inaugural. He perfected two techniques to bathe the country regularly in the ointments of hope and optimism—the press conference and the fireside chat. He transformed the press conference . . . into a vehicle of lively and informative interchange between the President and the press.[19]

While reading the rest of this book, the student should be developing the ability to pick out the key institutions and roles in whatever political system is being studied. An understanding of role, institutions, and power is essential to analyzing politics.

POWER AND INFLUENCE

We can say that **power** is the ubiquitous phenomenon of politics. Robert Dahl has defined politics or a political relationship as involving to a significant extent "power, rule, or authority."[20] We are more restrictive because we limit our focus to power that is part of the political system in the public realm. We are not so much concerned with power, rule, and authority as they may affect family relationships, the election of a union representative, a business reorganization, or the selection of a college president, except if some of the activities of the preceding influence the public political system. We restrict politics in this text to the political system. We do not use it in the more popular sense, which refers to any situation (such as the election of a student body or club president or a new chairman of the board in Corporation X) that involves **influence**, power, authority, rules or regulations, and the person(s) exercising these.

Power is basic to the study of politics, because in many ways this is what politics is all about. Harold Laswell's often-quoted analysis of politics is entitled *Politics— Who Gets What, When, How*.[21] The "who" in the title refers to who has power or who has access to those holding power. Those with power are most able to control the allocation in society of scarce resources for which there is competition.

[18]Louis W. Koenig, *The Chief Executive*, 3rd ed. (New York: Harcourt, Brace, & World, 1975, p. 362.
[19]*Ibid*, p. 373.
[20]Robert A. Dahl, *Modern Political Analysis*, 2nd ed. (Englewood Cliffs, N.J.: Prentice-Hall, 1970), pp. 4–6.
[21]Harold Lasswell, *Politics—Who Gets What, When, How* (New York: McGraw-Hill, 1936).

We define power in the following way: one person or group exercises power over another when it is intentional and done in such a way as to affect in a predictable way the action(s) of another or others. Three aspects are involved: relationship, intention, and predictability. Power usually involves penalties or rewards, but the instruments of power also can be rational persuasion or appeals to the emotions.

The difference between influence and power is predictability. Power suggests that the intended outcome will more likely occur. Thus, the penalties and rewards are considerably more severe or greater in the hands of the person or group exercising power. A teacher can influence a student to study. Frequently, the penalty or reward, as the case may be, is the grade. For some students the grade is an important influence; for a few it is relatively insignificant because it is regarded as having only short-run consequences. In terms of grading, teachers generally have influence, not power.

The **power base** is composed of a few or many assets. The power base requires some but not all of the following: wealth, social status, control of force (military/police), office skills (legal, managerial, technical), personal magnetism, and friendships and other forms of extended personal relationships (family, ethnic group, religion). A person exercising power has one and usually more of the preceding. A public official not only has the office (legislator, judge, mayor) but also several other assets that enable him to achieve office. In the case of most democracies, a typically successful candidate will possess wealth, social status, education (legal training, for example), as well as some measure of personal magnetism. The following description of President Franklin Roosevelt indicates the importance of personality.

> *His flashing smile, his cigarette holder set at a jaunty angle, his ready humor and booming laugh were the trademarks of his self-possession against the pressures of crisis. A brief exposure to Roosevelt was enough to repair the panicky, quiet the agitated, and inspirit the downhearted.*[22]

Power is relational and reciprocal. It is affected both by the exerciser and the recipient. A country with adequate energy reserves is not nearly as dependent on the goodwill of the petroleum-producing countries as a nation that must import 90 percent of the energy resources it consumes. A poor person may be more responsive to the demands of a rich person than a rich person to another rich one. A person may be willing to endure severe penalties for a cause to which he or she is committed. Joan of Arc was not swayed by violence, even when she was under sentence of death and eventually executed.

The concept of **power motivated change** (PMC) is associated closely with the "relational" aspect of power. PMC refers to the effort or amount of change that the exerciser must expend if power is to be exercised. PMC is the adoption of a decision or policy needed to exert power or influence. When President Lyndon Johnson

[22]Koenig, *op. cit.*, p. 373.

sent several hundred troops to the Dominican Republic in 1965 to prevent what was believed to be a possible communist takeover, relatively little effort had to be expended by the United States. Compare the Dominican case with American involvement in Vietnam. The American objective was to prevent insurgents, supported by North Vietnam, from winning control of South Vietnam. Beyond that, one can only debate the extent to which the United States desired to influence the policies and choice of political leaders of the Republic of Vietnam. American offers to exercise power or influence in Vietnam extend back to President Truman's second administration (1948–1952).

Many power motivated changes occurred as the United States sought to influence developments in Vietnam. The PMCs that occurred would not have taken place if we were not attempting to exercise power or influence in this ravaged Southeast Asian nation. Examples of PMCs in the Vietnam case are higher taxes, an expanded military draft, larger defense budgets, increased military and civilian aid to the Republic of Vietnam, and troop dispositions—at one point more than 500,000 American military personnel were assigned to Vietnam. Eventually, these efforts became so burdensome and unpopular that the American government reduced its efforts to exercise power or influence and agreed to a truce agreement in Vietnam in January 1973. The ultimate result was a communist takeover in South Vietnam during the spring of 1975.

American involvement in Vietnam will be debated for many years, but it does illustrate a situation where the allocation of resources necessary to exercise power and influence became unacceptable and policy was modified accordingly. Frequently, the objective desired is not considered as important as the scarce resources that must be allocated to achieve the objective. Another example is a recent analysis that explores the growth of opposition political parties in the West. This book identifies several reasons for their emergence. Many of these have their origin in the unique historical circumstances of the political systems studied.[23] The common denominator is the fact that governments, which probably had the power to restrain opposition, ultimately decided that the efforts necessary to exercise this restraining power did not justify the objective:

> Opposition is likely to be permitted in a political system if (1) the government believes than an attempt to coerce the opposition is likely to fail, or (2) even if the attempt were to succeed, the costs of coercion would exceed the gains.[24]

Power motivated change is a key, but often overlooked, factor in analyzing power. Another facet of power and influence is authority, which in turn is related to legitimacy.

---

[23]In his preface to this study, the editor, Robert Dahl, observes that in 1964 there were "only about 30 . . . political systems in which full legal opposition among organized political parties had existed throughout the preceding decade." *Political Oppositions in Western Democracies* (New Haven: Yale University Press, 1966), p. *xiii*.

[24]*Ibid.*, p. *xiv*.

AUTHORITY AND LEGITIMACY

Authority is one type of power. Authority is power that is regarded by citizens as generally rightful or legitimate. This does not mean that one agrees in each instance with the decision by the person in authority. There is, though, a general belief in the rightfulness or appropriateness of the authority. There also should be an inverse relationship between authority and force. The greater the authority of the person or group exercising power, the less need there will be to use force.

Legitimacy is the principle upon which authority rests in a political system. Legitimacy has three dimensions:

1. Procedural norms should be used in acquiring power. In the Western democracies such procedures most commonly are competitive elections in which all adult persons may vote. Legitimacy is a relative term. What is legitimate in one political system may not be regarded as legitimate in another. In some societies rule by a council of elders (gerontocracy) has been considered appropriate. Age, experience, and wisdom are considered interdependent traits, and age is the criteria for membership on the council. For many centuries blood descent (as in a king or emperor) was regarded as the procedure for qualifying for office and power. Political systems with a monarch as the head of state actually exercising power (as opposed to a constitutional monarchy seen today, in which the king or queen is a figurehead) were based not on election or age but on the fortuitous circumstances of birth. Age or blood descent obviously are not regarded as legitimate in democratic political systems, but they were legitimate in many other political systems.

2. Procedural norms (generally accepted procedures) generally should be followed in exercising power. In constitutional systems, where a constitution and laws restrain government officials, even those at the highest level of power and discretion must follow the legal procedures expected of the office. This is contrary to some political systems where there are relatively few limitations on a ruler who has acquired office. For most of recorded history, it was regarded as an act of treason to remove even the most rapacious and incompetent ruler. Few people made an effort to justify rebellion. One famous political philosopher who did mention procedural standards in exercising power was Thomas Aquinas (1225–1274). Saint Thomas distinguished between a person who usurps power—a tyrant or *titulo*—and a ruler, who is the legitimate sovereign but who abuses his power.

> He [Saint Thomas] argues that a tyrant a titulo can legitimize his power if he governs with justice; that is, in the interest of his subjects. He admits that in extreme cases when tyranny becomes unbearable and inflicts sinful actions on his subjects, rebellion is justified.[25]

Only during the last few centuries have we made progress toward a commitment to limited or constitutional government. This means that in some political systems

---

[25]Gaetano Mosca, *A Short History of Political Philosophy* (New York: Thomas Y. Crowell, 1972), p. 60. Translated by Sondra Z. Koff. Originally published in 1937.

the rulers and other government officials will lose legitimacy, as happened to President Nixon as a result of Watergate, if they flagrantly violate the basic procedural norms in exercising their political office. In some cases this may only involve replacing (sometimes violently) one ruler or group of rulers for another, but not changing the fundamental rules of the game in the system. In other situations the political system itself may be altered drastically.

China represents both cases. During its 4000-year history, Imperial China experienced numerous rebellions and civil wars, often because the emperor was cruel and abused the population. Sometimes the rebel leader was victorious and a new dynasty was established. The imperial political system as such, with an emperor as head of state, was not changed. The Chinese revolution of 1911 was a sharp break with the past. Not only did new rulers seize office, but the political system was fundamentally changed. A republic replaced the empire, which had been based on blood descent. The Republic of China, led by Chiang Kai-shek, eventually was replaced by a communist state after fighting that lasted intermittently from 1927 to 1949.

3. Legitimacy also involves the notion that government and the political system should function in such a way that government generally performs the tasks citizens expect of it. Popular expectations of the functions, if not obligations, of government have changed measurably during the last 200 years. During the nineteenth century the most common political system was the "night watchman state." Governments were expected to maintain domestic security; protect the borders; and construct, maintain, and protect communication and transportation networks. For example, immediately after the American colonies won their independence, two of the most important cabinet departments were the State Department and the Post Office Department. Expectations about government responsibilities have evolved worldwide in the last 100 years. People now turn to government to solve inflation, unemployment, land reform, energy shortages, retirement benefits, protection of the environment, zoning, water and sewers, free public education, and so on. The obligations of government, or expected government outputs, vary among political systems; thus, political systems in the developing world, where governments have fewer monetary and technical resources, are not expected to provide extensive retirement programs or unemployment benefits.

We might only note that where governments do not provide the minimal outputs the prevailing values deem necessary, the government and the rules of the game may be completely changed. One of the most difficult situations any system confronts is an insurgency, often aided by outside powers. In such circumstances the preponderant allocation of resources goes to combat the insurgents. This almost inevitably erodes legitimacy because governments are unable to deliver other outputs (more jobs, village water systems, land reform) believed necessary in the contemporary world. The "revolution of rising expectations" refers in part to the services citizens expect from their governments; these cannot be provided effectively during an insurgency.

Legitimacy in all of its aspects is relative rather than absolute and varies among countries. It is a long and evolving process and is an objective for all political systems. In our discussion of the developing world, Chapter Twelve, we shall see that it is a difficult goal to reach in the short run.

POSTINDUSTRIAL SOCIETY

In Chapter Twelve we discuss the developing world, whose economy is dominated by agriculture or extracting and exporting of natural resources (petroleum, tin, copper). Once a country passes the point where under 50 percent of its labor force is in agriculture, it generally is moving toward an industrial society where an increasing percentage of the workforce is engaged in the manufacturing sector. Since World War II most countries of the industrial world (United States, Canada, Western Europe, and Japan) have been moving into what is called **postindustrial society**. These societies also constitute nearly all of the 30 to 35 democratic political systems in the world today. Postindustrial societies are the wealthiest, most productive, and most democratic political systems of the world. Because there are political implications for the world's 30 to 35 democracies, most of whom are in the postindustrial era, we will note the major features of postindustrial society, a term increasingly used in the mass media.

Certain elements appear to stand out. The service sector (including transportation, communication, trade, education, public administration) increasingly dominates in contrast to agriculture and industry. In 1970, service occupations in the United States, for example, employed 62 percent of the labor force.[26] White-collar rather than blue-collar workers predominated. Again, using the American case, the white-collar proportion rose from 31 percent in 1940 to an estimated 51 percent in 1970, while blue-collar employees dropped from 40 to 33 percent in the same period.[27]

Professional, technical, and managerial workers play an increasingly widespread and critical role in the economy. More and more people attend college or technical schools after high school. Some predict that by the year 2000 over half the adult population will be educated beyond high school level. Increased leisure time will be available as the work week average drops to below 40 hours.

When industrial society replaced agricultural society in what are now democratic political systems between 1830 and 1930, market demand and consumer goods were core elements of economic growth. To meet demands for cheap, available goods, large and complex industrial organizations emerged. Competition among numerous small companies in the open market was replaced by control through a small number of industrial corporations. The hidden hand of the free market was

[26]Samuel P. Hunington, Postindustrial politics: How benign will it be? *Comparative Politics*, 6:2, 1974, 171. Much of the material for this section is drawn from Huntington's article and Zbigniew Brzezinski, *Between Two Ages: America's Role in the Technetronic Era* (New York: Penguin Books, 1970), pp. 10–14.
[27]Huntington, *op. cit.*

replaced by managerial planning. There emerged a complex interdependence between the government (such as military procurement), scientific/educational institutions (often in terms of grants for research and development), and industrial organizations. The interaction of these various institutions, often highly technical and complex, meant that in many instances, power, influence, and decision making became even less visible and understandable to the average citizen. Until recently, however, most individuals in the Western democracies appeared to approve of the products resulting from the managerial/corporate economy, if not always approving the practices of the corporate giants.

Politically, postindustrial society suggests certain emerging trends, not all of them clear, and some contradictory. We will list a few examples.

1. Political alienation could become more common. Public participation in highly complex decisions far removed from the average citizen is difficult to ensure. Because experts with years of training have difficulty resolving problems, the conflicts and various proposed solutions seem far beyond the average citizen, who does not have the time or knowledge to understand the causes of the problem (such as **petroflation**) so as to vote or write a letter in order to record a choice based on substantial knowledge and understanding of the alternatives.

2. The influence of political parties and even mass-participation interest groups may decline as individuals are less involved in these organizations. Those that do exert influence may be dominated increasingly by the leaders and career bureaucrats in the organization. The latest, all-pervasive communication techniques can be utilized by magnetic personalities with heavy financial backing appealing directly to individuals. A growing reliance on television with emphasis on imagery can lead to an impressionistic and superficial political involvement and further erosion of factual knowledge and the significance of choices presented.

3. Frustration, if not confusion, also may be encouraged by the communications media (radio, newspapers, television). As one political journalist concluded, "The national media have put themselves into the role of permanent critical opposition to any government which does not instantly clean up the unfinished business of our time." Consequently, "no government will satisfy them."[28] It is in the nature of the mass media to have an interest in exposing, criticizing, and highlighting disagreement and inaction in government. This is further confirmed by an editor of the *Washington Post* who observed that "we of the media like conflict, tension, the suspense of contest. We like these things because they make good copy. Our banner might well carry the motto 'Let's You and Him Fight.' "[29]

4. As economic well-being spreads in the transition from industrial to postindustrial society, quality of life issues have growing political appeal. Government often responds by regulating business practices, but there is a real question as to whether this expanding government involvement achieves what it has promised. A

[28]Quoting Theodore H. White in Huntington, *op. cit.*, p. 185.
[29]*Time*, November 19, 1979, p. 116.

recent analysis concluded many government regulators are ineffective. Officials in the Consumer Product Safety Commission in Washington, D.C. have admitted that the 135 full-time investigators cannot begin to survey enough stores to make sure banned products are no longer sold. One official said, "Most of the time we don't know how well our orders are being carried out. We can only rely on good faith."[30] The appearance of a new government policy and agency has not led to a solution.

    5. The postindustrial systems suddenly are facing a basic issue that was not originally associated with this era. It commonly was assumed this would be a society of economic affluence, with only a few isolated pockets of poverty. The economic pie would continue to expand so all groups would receive benefits. Deep social and political cleavages would be eliminated because continued growth insured greater benefits for everyone concerned. Scarcity, belt-tightening, limited growth, and now a suggested lower standard of living confront a society that was to be characterized by technologically managed unlimited growth. A recently discovered scarcity of resources and limited or zero expansion are becoming the central political issues in a society that supposedly was based on unlimited growth. The superior ability of technology, combined with a faith in an infinite supply of natural wealth that can be extracted from the earth, are no longer believable. Issues not even conceived possible five years ago are beginning to challenge the postindustrial democracies. These societies now must deal not with improving life through growing economic abundance but a coming age of scarcity which will last for several decades. For example, the Worldwatch Institute reported that by 1984 it will cost $50 to fill the tank of a standard American car. Even then fuel may not always be available because cars will have to compete with more essential claimants for scarce petroleum. Such essentials include powering factories, heating homes, and running trucks and buses.[31]

    An anticipated epoch of political tranquility may be replaced by sharp political conflicts as political systems experience critical shortages in nonrenewable (petroleum, gold) and even renewable (grain, timber, clean air) resources. Social scientist Herman Kahn, founder of the Hudson Institute, which specializes in long-term trends and policies, has described the next decade for the postindustrial world as "the sobering 80s, an epoch of malaise" where we are neither sick nor well. Political systems will be less able to respond: "Our reaction time is longer when a crisis arises, and our policymakers tend to flounder. The confused and disorganized response to the energy situation is the classic example."[32]

CONFLICT AND ADJUSTMENT

In concluding this chapter, we note that in the first two chapters of this text we have provided the student with a basic overview of the underlying concerns of politics

---

[30]Caroline E Mayer, "Analysis: Too Much Regulation? Not As Regulators Tell It," *U.S. News and World Report*, October 8, 1979, p. 74.

[31]UPI reported in the *Arkansas Gazette*, September 30, 1979.

[32]Interview of Herman Kahn, in *U.S. News and World Report*, August 20, 1979, pp. 52–53.

and the academic discipline that studies it—political science. We also have discussed certain basic approaches, such as systems analysis and functionalism, which are the underlying approaches in the following chapters. These concepts are necessarily selective of many available in the political science literature. They represent what we believe are the more feasible ways of organizing a great bulk of material for students being introduced to political science. Although we focus on systems analysis and functionalism, we do not believe there is one approach or a single key to understanding politics. There are many writers who adopt an exclusive theme. One example is Hans Morgenthau, a distinguished author in the international politics field since the 1950s. Morgenthau believes all people share drives to live, reproduce, and dominate. He expands this assertion by declaring that all political life is a struggle for power.

> *Both domestic and international politics are a struggle for power, modified only by different conditions under which this struggle takes place in the domestic and international spheres.*[33]

We do not believe there is a single, underlying principle, such as a struggle for power, that is the basis for understanding politics. We believe that a broader approach will enable a student to understand better the ever-changing political world.

Our final point is implicit in much of what you have read so far. Change, transition, and competition are basic to what we are studying. The history of politics is development, adjustment, or regression. Seldom, if ever, is there a period that can be described as a time of status quo and no change.

Change, power, and competition are the ever-present phenomena of modern politics. When we study the political we inevitably deal with objectives and efforts in a constant state of flux. Many changes are consistent with the existing political and social institutions: one president is elected and another leaves office; one party replaces another as the majority party in parliament; the social security deduction or the income tax is raised or lowered. Institutions and the political process are not fundamentally altered by these changes.

A second type of change is more substantial and may fundamentally affect the functioning and organization of the political system: a presidential type of government replaces a parliament-dominated political system, as occurred in 1958 when the French Fifth Republic replaced the Fourth Republic. A hereditary monarch has his powers removed and in his place a junta of young, reform-minded, military officers makes government decisions, as happened in Ethiopia in 1974. Change may be peaceful or violent, but it always is pervasive. A never-ending task of political science is to attempt to explain the nature and types of change that are occurring.

Our analysis of change means that political systems that appear stable are actually in a condition of homeostatic equilibrium. By this we mean a relatively stable functioning of the political system with regard to ongoing competition among con-

---

[33]Hans J. Morgenthau, *Politics Among Nations,* 5th ed. (New York: Alfred A. Knopf, 1973), pp. 34–35.

tending individuals, groups, and ideas. Homeostatic equilibrium is present when institutions and procedures have evolved for peaceful rather than violent competition and encourage the peaceful adjustment of conflict.

Throughout the remainder of this text students should analyze carefully what they perceive to be those institutions that encourage the peaceful adjustment of disagreement in the most reasonable and fair manner. By fair we mean equity, responding as much as possible to the various viewpoints in resolving a conflict. We offer no solutions, except to note that political conflict probably will always exist, even with the best of intentions. John Stuart Mill stated it ably:

> As soon as any part of a person's conduct affects prejudicially the interests of others, society has jurisdiction over it, and the question whether the general welfare will or will not be promoted by interfering with it, becomes open to discussion. [It begins to be politically debated.] [34]

We believe political science should make it possible for the student to understand better the political process. The student is being trained to perceive selectively and to focus on the key factors in the political system; to organize data; to retrieve previously learned and relevant information as he or she interprets contemporary political systems or components of a system (for example, a city or state, the United States, one or more foreign governments, the international system, or specific institutions and processes such as political parties, legislatures, and political socialization, all discussed subsequently). Perception, organization, retrieval, and explanation as they relate to the political process are the capabilities students will begin to acquire as they read this book.

SELECTED READINGS

There are several brief introductions to the major questions in the discipline. These are read to better advantage by students who have had one or two basic courses. Three of the more useful works are Robert A. Dahl, *Modern Political Analysis*, 3rd ed.* (Englewood Cliffs, N.J.: Prentice-Hall, 1976); Francis J. Sorauf, *Political Science: An Informal Overview** (Columbus, Ohio: Charles E. Merrill, 1965); and Victor Wiseman, *Politics: The Master Science** (New York: Pegasus, 1969).

A more comprehensive review of most of the fields in political science, with an extensive bibliography, more appropriate for seniors or beginning graduate students, is Stephen L. Wasby, *Political Science: The Discipline and Its Dimensions* (New York: Charles Scribner's Sons, 1970). Also useful is Heinz Eulau and James G. March, eds., *Political Science** (Englewood Cliffs, N.J.: Prentice-Hall 1969). Albert

---

[34]John Stuart Mill, *On Liberty,* from Marshall Cohen, ed., *The Philosophy of John Stuart Mill* (New York: The Modern Library, 1961), p. 272.
    *Available in paperback.

Somit and Joseph Tanenhaus have traced major trends in the discipline from the "prehistory" (before 1880) period through the mid-1960s in *The Development of American Political Science* (Boston: Allyn and Bacon, 1967).

Two works that provide useful evaluations of the various approaches and methodologies in the discipline are James A. Bill and Robert L. Hardgrave, Jr., *Comparative Politics: The Quest for Theory** (Columbus, Ohio: Charles E. Merrill, 1973) and James C. Charlesworth, ed., *Contemporary Political Analysis** (New York: The Free Press, 1967). A basic overview and evaluation of the behavioral movement in political science is Robert Dahl's "The Behavioral Approach in Political Science: Epitaph for a Monument to a Successful Protest," *The American Political Science Review*, 60:4, 1961, pp. 763–72. A readable critique by a statistician of some of the quantitative methods used by political scientists is Edward R. Tufte, "Improving Data Analysis in Political Science," *World Politics*, 21:4, 1961, pp. 641–54.

The initiator and leading exponent of the systems approach in political science is David Easton. The most efficient introduction to his writings is "An Approach to the Analysis of Political Systems," *World Politics*, 9:3, 1957, pp. 383–400. A more recent and expanded interpretation of his theories is his *A Systems Analysis of Political Life* (New York: John Wiley, 1965). Evaluations and criticisms of the systems approach are found in the Bill and Hardgrave and Charlesworth works cited above. A difficult but a "must" evaluation of recent political research, including a section on the systems approach, is Joseph LaPalombara, "Macrotheories and Microapplication in Comparative Politics: A Widening Chasm," *Comparative Politics*, 1:1, 1968, pp. 52–78.

As emphasis has increased on the output side of political science, public policy has become a major subfield and we increasingly see comparative studies. An excellent one is Richard Rose, ed., *The Dynamics of Public Policy: A Comparative Perspective** (Beverly Hills: Sage Publications, 1976). Two relatively new journals representative of this output trend are *Policy Sciences* and *Public Policy*. The perspectives of almost 30 social scientists from several disciplines are found in Stuart S. Nagel, ed., *Policy Studies and the Social Sciences* (Lexington, Mass.: Lexington Books, 1975).

The most helpful introduction to power and its relationship to influence and authority is Chapter 3 in Robert Dahl, *Modern Political Analysis,** cited previously. Nelson Polsby, *Community Power and Political Theory** (New Haven: Yale University Press, 1963) is a well-written effort to organize the theoretical implications of local power studies. The volume edited by John R. Champlin, *Power** (New York: Atherton Press, 1971) includes various viewpoints on the definitions and applications of power.

*Available in paperback.

Part I of *Administrative Behavior*, 4th ed.* (New York: The Free Press, 1976) by Herbert Simon is especially useful in discussing the limits of power in administrative settings. An article that is quite thought-provoking on power in general, as well as in the international setting, is David A. Baldwin, "Power Analysis and World Politics," *World Politics*, 30, 1979, pp. 161–94.

Robert E. Lane, *Political Life** (Glencoe, Ill.: The Free Press, 1959); and Seymour Martin Lipset, *Political Man** (Garden City, N.Y.: Doubleday, 1960) discuss some of the major generalizations about how humans behave politically. Students will find these two books provide valuable background as they follow and participate in political events after leaving college.

Academic analyses of the role of corruption in a political system are in short supply. A work that argues that the United States has the worst rate of corruption of any modern democracy is George C.S. Benson, Steven A. Maaranen, and Alan Heslop, *Political Corruption in America* (Lexington, Mass.: Lexington Books, 1978). A series of essays discussing postindustrial society, focusing on the United States, is Seymour Martin Lipset, ed., *The Third Century: America as a Post-Industrial Society* (Stanford: Hoover Institution Press, 1979).

Finally, we might note that essays and bibliographies on most of the terms and concepts used in this chapter are available in the *International Encyclopedia of the Social Sciences* (New York: Macmillan and Free Press, 1968); and Fred I. Greenstein and Nelson W. Polsby, eds., *Handbook of Political Science*, 8 vols. (Addison-Wesley, 1975).

A dated but still useful work because the statistics can be updated is Charles L. Taylor and Michael C. Hudson, *World Handbook of Political and Social Indicators* 2d ed.; (New Haven: Yale University Press, 1972).

*Available in paperback.

Chapter Three

Political Theories and Ideologies

INTRODUCTION

The study of political theory and ideology are integral parts of political science. Both are analytic methods, or ways of looking at political phenomena, which are an important part of politics. As noted in Chapter One, values and value arguments are part of politics and are among the most important things studied by political theorists. Moreover, in reviewing the development of political theory, we are looking at the origin of both political science and many of our basic institutions and values. For this reason, we now turn to political theory and ideology, to help provide the foundation for understanding the political value conflicts that make up the heart of subsequent chapters.

Political theory generally deals with people and government. From early times people have speculated about their relationship to the political system, the various kinds of government, and the best way to attain a just society. The Western political tradition is still the source of much wisdom, and many basic concepts of modern political life had their origin in the Greco-Roman world and the Middle Ages.

In developing their theories, many great political thinkers have attempted to find an answer to some political problem or crisis of their day. An example is Karl Marx, who made the evils of the industrial revolution in the middle of the nineteenth century the basis of his philosophy. In this sense, philosophers are dated, but all the great thinkers, in developing answers, have raised issues and answers that transcend the problems of their day. It is this feature that gives their works a timeless quality.

That political thought influences actual political institutions is unquestionable. The relationship between Karl Marx and the political and economic developments in the Soviet Union is obvious. This is not to suggest that present-day Russia is a blueprint of Marx's ideas, for it obviously is not. There are many developments that Marx did not anticipate, and many of his ideas have perhaps worked out differently from what he expected; yet it would be hard to think of the Russian Revolution without Karl Marx.

There is also a close relationship between the ideals of John Locke, the English philosopher of the late seventeenth century, and American political principles and practices. Not only is the American Declaration of Independence a restatement of Locke's philosophy, but such concepts and practices as limited government, a written constitution, and a bill of rights are derived from Locke as well as similar theorists.

In this brief survey of leading Western political philosophers, the student should not ask which one is "right," for none has provided a complete answer to the perennial problems of politics, although some developed a metaphysical system they believed was final. Rather, the question should be what insights these people offer in helping to understand the great issues of politics.

In answering the above question, it does not necessarily follow that a recent philosopher in time, say John Dewey, is necessarily more relevant than John Locke. Although John Dewey still has his followers, many believe his rather facile optimism is superficial because it reflects an exaggerated and unjustified confidence in the ability of the scientific method to solve our political problems. Furthermore, those whose philosophical systems we may reject as erroneous may still offer many insights. We may reject the "dialectical materialism" of Marx, but few can deny the truth of his analysis of the evils of mid-nineteenth-century capitalism.

ANCIENT AND MEDIEVAL BACKGROUND

Plato and Aristotle are the leading, seminal political theorists of all time. Plato (427–347 B.C.) was an Athenian aristocrat. He was influenced greatly by his friend and teacher, Socrates, whose death, decreed by the Athenian state, led Plato to distrust Athenian democracy, which was at its height in the fourth century B.C. In Athens citizens were entitled to participate directly in the government of the city by voting in the assembly of all citizens or serving on a jury. Selection for office was very democratic. The procedures employed were lot and rotation in office. Although the Athenians prized their democracy and citizenship highly, there was also a dark side to their political system. Only a minority of the inhabitants of Athens were citizens, and slavery was accepted as natural. Demagogues as well as statesmen were elected to office.

Plato's greatest political work is *The Republic*, in which he describes the ideal state. *The Republic* was not a utopia in the modern sense, for Plato regarded the ideal state to be the most real state and the standard by which actual states were to be judged. Plato believed that behind the world of appearances there was an inner reality. To him, objects perceived through the senses were particular manifestations of universal ideas. To understand these universal categories was the task of philosophy. For Plato, the idea of the triangle was more real than a particular tri-

Plato.

angle. To understand the ideal state was more important than studying actual historical states. These principles were the exact opposite of the school of philosophers known as Sophists, who argued that there is no truth or absolute moral principle, only opinion and social convention. To Plato, the Sophists' philosophy was not only erroneous but dangerous.

Justice was the cornerstone on which *The Republic* was to be based. By this term Plato meant a society in which each person performed a function in society for which he was best suited. The structure of society was aristocratic, with an artisan class of workers, farmers, and merchants at the bottom who performed economic functions. Above them were the auxiliaries, consisting of men and women whose role was that of defense. At the top was the ruling class of philosopher, or a "philosopher-king" if one was available. The philosopher class was to undergo a long period of training and education as preparation for the task of governing, which Plato regarded as an exacting science.

More important than the details of *The Republic* are the political ideals it reflects. Plato's concept of the philosopher-king as the ideal ruler is a magnificent idea and consistent with his basically aristocratic philosophy: that those of superior wisdom and virtue should rule. Plato firmly believed that humans by nature are moral beings and that good people are also good citizens. Despite his distrust of Greek democracy as exemplified in Athens, Plato was not a believer in arbitrary government. To him, tyranny was the worst form of government.

Like Plato, Aristotle (384–322 B.C.), a student of Plato, believed that humans are rational, moral beings who could attain the good life only through the state, which Aristotle considered the highest form of organization. Aristotle believed that by nature humans are "political animals" and that the state is the result of their social instinct. He believed the state grew out of the household and was the ultimate human organization.

Unlike Plato, Aristotle was less concerned with the ideal state and more concerned with the best practical state, which he called "polity" or a mixture of aristocracy and democracy. Aristotle laid great stress on economic conditions as the basis of a good state. Extremes of wealth and poverty worked for political instability. Polity would be possible in a political society with a strong middle class. The idea of a government under law was important in Aristotle's philosophy. Plato, in his ideal state ruled by philosophers, dispensed with the need for law. But *The Statesman*, a product of Plato's old age when he realized the ideal state was unattainable, stressed the need for law as a "second best," to compensate for the inability to find all-wise philosophers.

There are obvious shortcomings in Greek political thought. Both Plato and Aristotle were unable to go beyond the Greek city-state, which was already becoming obsolete. Aristotle, for example, served as tutor to Alexander, son of Philip, king of Macedonia. Within a short time Macedonia was to conquer the Greek city-states and, under Alexander the Great, establish an empire for the Hellenistic world. Yet Aristotle's experience at the Macedonian Court as tutor to the young Alexander apparently made no impression on his political thought. Both Plato and Aristotle had a conception of citizenship limited to a leisure class that would be free of economic concerns. Aristotle in particular defended slavery and assumed the natural superiority of Greeks to the "barbarians."

Yet both Plato and Aristotle laid the basis for a science of politics. Both men accepted the civic ideal of a state based on reason and aimed at the good life. Aristotle in particular established a logical method of political inquiry. And Plato accepted the complete equality of the sexes.

Following the death of Aristotle in 322 B.C., and with the advent of world empires in the Western world—for a brief time Alexander's empire and subsequently the Roman Empire—political thought showed a marked change as the independent city-state became politically obsolete. The dominant school of thought was that of Greek and Roman Stoics. Stoicism was a school of thought rather than a philosophy identified with a particular individual. The Stoics equated God with universal reason, which they believed to be immanent in nature and in humanity. Politically, the Stoics emphasized the basic equality of all people, regardless of differences in wealth or social position. Gone was any distinction between Greeks and barbarians. Even a slave was a "laborer hired for life." The individual was a citizen not only of the secular state into which he was born but of the community of all humanity as well.

The Stoics also introduced the concept of natural law, which was to dominate Western political thought through the eighteenth century. Just as God was regarded as the reason governing the universe, so the souls of human beings were part of that reason, which is the same everywhere and binding on all humanity. **Natural law**, in the words of the Roman philosopher and politician Cicero, a great popularizer of **Stoicism**, was "right reason in agreement with nature; it is of universal application, unchanging and everlasting; it summons to duty by its commands, and averts from wrongdoing by its prohibitions."[1] This law was considered the foundation of the state as it existed from eternity, and the state or commonwealth existed to promote ethical purposes or it was nothing.

Although no attempt was made to implement Stoicism in a political sense, it is unlikely that political democracy in the modern sense could develop unless the idea of the basic equality of all people won general acceptance. The Stoic idea of the role of natural law probably has contributed to the later concept of natural rights and the present-day practice of judicial review.

Christianity as a body of thought was consistent with Stoicism in stressing the basic equality of all people. It also believed government to be of divine origin and stressed the duty of obedience, but it introduced a dualism unknown to the ancient world. A person is not only a citizen of an earthly kingdom but also, potentially at least, a member of the kingdom of God. Thus, there is a potential divided loyalty as illustrated in the Gospels—a loyalty to Caesar and to God. Perhaps, as George Sabine has suggested, civil liberties would not have played the role they have in the modern world were it not for the concept of divided loyalty.[2]

The idea of divided loyalty or rights against the state was unknown to the Greeks. To Plato and Aristotle the state served a moral purpose and people could achieve their complete development only through the state. But the state was considered prior to the individual and the idea of the individual asserting rights against the state was unknown to them.

Following the decline and eventual disintegration of the Roman Empire in the West, beginning in the late fourth century A.D., Europe entered into a period of turmoil and political disorder out of which the Middle Ages emerged in about 800 A.D. The Middle Ages were as rich in political philosophy as the ancient world.

The greatest contribution of the Middle Ages was its emphasis on law and kingship. A just king ruled according to law. Thomas Aquinas (1225–1274), the great Medieval philosopher, developed the concept of natural law, which he took from the

[1]Michael B. Foster, ed., *Plato to Machiavelli. Masters of Political Thought, vol. 1.* Cambridge: The Riverside Press, 1964, p. 188.

[2]George H. Sabine and Thomas Landon Thorson, *A History of Political Theory,* 4th ed. (Hinsdale, Ill.: Dryden Press, 1973), pp. 180–181.

Stoics. The philosophy of natural law in modified form was transmitted to the modern world by John Locke, as will be seen later in this chapter.

With the passing of the Middle Ages between 1400 and 1500 A.D., Europe entered the modern age. One of its many important characteristics was the rise of individualism, which now will be taken up.

THE RISE OF INDIVIDUALISM

One of the characteristics of the modern age, which began about 1500 A.D., is the rise of **individualism**, which was manifested in all walks of life. In religion, individualism is identified with the Protestant Reformation, which stressed individual salvation made possible by God's grace without the intervention of the Catholic Church. The modern age was associated with the rise of capitalism, which emphasized individual endeavor and financial rewards for those who were successful. Another influence was the Renaissance, which was characterized by a revival of interest in the Greek and Roman classics. The result was a new humanism centering on humanity as the "measure of all things." Fundamentally, the new individualism was a rebellion against the existing restraints of the traditional social order and a movement toward personal autonomy.

MACHIAVELLI

Machiavelli (1469–1527), a Florentine, was one of the most important figures of the Renaissance.[3] He introduced a new type of political writing. Before Machiavelli, all political philosophy dealt with the state as a means to the good life. Machiavelli ignored theories about the state as such. He was an individualist in his admiration of the successful ruler who makes power an end in itself, divorced from all considerations of morality, religion, and ethics.

The Prince, Machiavelli's chief work, is an accurate description of politics in the Italian city-states of the fifteenth century, a period characterized by low political morality and factional strife among the able but cruel Italian despots.

The able ruler made the safety and success of the state superior to all considerations of morality or religion. The latter he accepted as facts of life to be used if they advanced the interests of the state but to be disregarded if they did not serve the interests of the ruler. In general, Machiavelli believed it better for a prince to be feared rather than loved. To Machiavelli, the success of a ruler's policy was determined by his ability to control *fortuna* and *virtu*. By *fortuna* he meant the uncertainty of history. *Virtu* referred to the ability to show mastery amid the uncertainty of events.

Machiavelli saw himself as an Italian patriot and scientific historian with a realistic philosophy who sought the unification of Italy. Although he had a romantic and

---

[3]For an excellent discussion of diverse evaluations of Machiavelli, see *Machiavelli: Cynic, Patriot, or Political Scientist*, edited by De Lamar Jensen in *Problems in European Civilization* (Boston: D. C. Heath and Co., 1960).

idealized vision of the Roman Republic, he believed that the Italians of his era were too corrupt to make a republic practical. More importantly, Machiavelli assumed the corrupt politics of his time to be the norm. He identified power politics with the whole of political reality, thus dismissing the moral imponderables, such as humanity's desire for freedom.

THOMAS HOBBES

In political philosophy, the new individualism gave rise to the social contract theory of government, which, unlike previous political philosophy, began with the autonomous individual rather than the state. The individual, according to the new approach, created the state through the social contract. The leading advocates of the new school were Thomas Hobbes (1588–1679) and John Locke (1632–1704), both English. Although the social contract philosophy frequently stresses limited government and the right of revolution, this type of thinking is not always present. Certainly in the thought of Hobbes it was absent. Instead, Hobbes' philosophy led to emphasis on the dangers of anarchy and the need for a strong government to make life tolerable. Hobbes' philosophy reflected the social and political turmoil of his age characterized by the struggle between Charles I and the Puritan majority in Parliament, the subsequent civil war between the king and his supporters and the Puritans, the execution of Charles I, the rule of Oliver Cromwell, and the royalist restoration.

Yet Hobbes was an individualist in the sense that the starting point of his philosophy was the state of nature, a presocial state, characterized as a condition in which life was "solitary, poor, nasty, brutish, and short." To make life tolerable, people created an "artifical" community, the state, to which they turned over all power. As the state was the beneficiary of the contract and not a party to it, there was no possibility of asserting rights against the state.

Hobbes was also a materialist who ridiculed the traditional, natural-law philosophy and revealed religion. To him the only law was that made by the sovereign of a state. It was the sovereign who would determine the religion of the state. In every state, according to Hobbes, there was a sovereign in which ultimate power rested. In a democracy this might be a parliament; in a monarchy, the king. Whoever the sovereign might be, he was all powerful except for the rather ineffective right of the individual to resist the infliction of death or injury on himself. What liberty there might be in a state existed only at the sufferance of the sovereign, whether the latter was a king or a democratic parliament. The only difference between the all-powerful state and a democracy was the way in which sovereign power was exercised.

To Hobbes, monarchy was the best government. Despite his preference for a strong monarchy, Hobbes should not be considered an advocate of modern dictatorship as exemplified in twentieth-century Fascist or Communist countries. Hobbes' monarch would preserve order and suppress any movements leading to possible anarchy, but he did not expect the monarch to engage in thought control and purges as contemporary dictators do. The ideal monarch would provide security and presumably a limited area of intellectual freedom for enlightened men like Hobbes.

Hobbes' overemphasis on the dangers of anarchy is in part a product of the age in which he lived. Without doubt Hobbes was overly pessimistic about the possibilities of limited government, and he overstressed the role of force in maintaining order; yet, today we may find some insights in Hobbes in a period characterized by revolutions, riots, and social unrest. Even in a democratic state, force is the ultimate weapon in maintaining order when the community is threatened by disorders.

JOHN LOCKE

Of greater significance for Americans was John Locke (1632–1704), the defender of the "glorious revolution" of 1688, which deposed James II, the last of the Stuart kings and the last English monarch claiming to rule by divine right. In his place the English Parliament, representing the nation, called William and Mary, rulers of the Netherlands, to the throne.

In his *Second Treatise on Government*, Locke, like Hobbes, assumed that humanity originally lived in a state of nature; however, Locke's primitive state was prepolitical rather than presocial like Hobbes'. Locke accepted the traditional philosophy of natural law. To this he added **natural rights**, the rights to liberty and property that people enjoyed in the state of nature. To better secure these rights, people entered into a social contract, thus creating a political society.

John Locke.

The next step is the formation of a government by majority decision, as contrasted with the unanimity necessary for the social contract. To Locke, the government was trustee of society's rights. A government that failed to protect the individual's rights to liberty and property violated the trust and could no longer claim the obedience of its citizens. For a flagrant abuse of power, the people could resort to revolution.

Locke's philosophy not only justified the English Revolution of 1688, but the American Revolution as well. In the Declaration of Independence, Thomas Jefferson restated the essentials of Locke:

That, to secure these Rights, Governments are instituted among Men, deriving their just Powers from the Consent of the Governed; that, whenever any Form of Government becomes destructive of these Ends, it is the right of the People to alter or abolish it, and institute new Government, laying its Foundation on such Principles, and organizing its Powers in such Forms, as to them shall seem most likely to effect their Safety and Happiness.

The American Constitution, with its emphasis on the powers of government being limited to those delegated and implied, reflects Locke's influence, and the Bill of Rights is a practical application of the idea of natural rights.

Today the philosophy of natural law and natural rights is not as strongly held as formerly. Few if any now believe in the social contract as a historical fact; nevertheless, Locke's philosophy is still of great significance. It is a way of explaining the importance of the individual and his priority to the state and the state as a constitutional relationship based on consent.

THE POLITICAL COMMUNITY

Political thought in the eighteenth century was influenced greatly by the French Enlightenment. The political philosophy of the Enlightenment undermined the intellectual foundations of the absolute monarchy in France. The basic assumptions of the Enlightenment were:

1. Confidence in the ability of human reason and science to cure the social ills of humanity.
2. The belief that social evils are the result of bad institutions but that human nature is essentially good.
3. Belief in the idea of progress.
4. Opposition to revealed religion.
5. Glorification of nature and worship of the God of nature.

Jean-Jacques Rousseau (1712–1778), one of the great political philosophers of the eighteenth century, shared many of the tenets of the Enlightenment, but he was atypical in stressing the primacy of feelings and emotion over reason. Rousseau was a romanticist who disliked the abstract, deductive reasoning characteristic of the Enlightenment.

"Man was born free and everywhere he is in chains," states Rousseau in his famous book, **The Social Contract**. But paradoxically the freedom of the state of nature can be regained through the establishment of a legitimate civil society to which citizens give up their natural freedom, in return for which they participate in the **general will** of the community. As each individual agrees to be ruled as well as to rule, all are made free. This is the social contract.

One of Rousseau's basic contributions is popular sovereignty. The political community created by the social contract alone possesses supreme power or sovereignty. All legitimate governments, according to Rousseau, are basically democratic. In a democracy the people rule directly. Even a monarch rules only as long as the sovereign people permit. Rousseau did not approve of representative institutions, for they violated his idea of direct rule by the people. He also believed the only state that could be based on his philosophy was a small one comparable to the Greek city-state.

The concept of the general will is another important contribution of Rousseau. The general will is an expression of what the common good requires. Although the general will is central to Rousseau's political philosophy, it is a mystical and somewhat illogical conception of what the common good requires. It is more than an expression of the majority viewpoint, which is merely the sum of private interests. But, in Rousseau's opinion, as mankind is naturally good, the general will is uncorrupted. Thus, the general will represents the common interests of humanity.

The weakness in the idea of the general will is that Rousseau failed to safeguard minority rights. Only in the creation of the political community is unanimity required. Otherwise, the will of the majority prevails. The people are never wrong according to Rousseau, but he acknowledged that they might be misled. In all democracies there will always be dissent, but Rousseau believed that dissenters, if they are not in agreement with the general will, must acknowledge their error. They may be "forced to be free" if necessary—that is, coerced. This is clearly not democratic and suggests the confusion inherent in the concept of the general will.

Although Rousseau was a democrat, his philosophy, with slight modification, can lead to totalitarianism. The general will need not be the will of the majority. It is conceivable that a small group or even one person might speak for the community. Hitler claimed to express the will of the German nation and Stalin spoke not only for the Russian Communist Party but for the entire nation.

Rousseau's influence has been tremendous. The Declaration of the Rights of Man of the French Revolution stresses popular sovereignty. American democratic thought in the nineteenth century also reflects Rousseau's philosophy that all power is derived from the people.

Yet Rousseau presents a utopian conception of democracy. Today it is hard for many to believe that the people are never wrong and are naturally good. Instead, it has been argued that it is the weakness of human nature that makes democracy a necessity, not humanity's innate goodness. And, as has been stated, Rousseau's rather mystical idea of the general will also can support totalitarianism.

EDMUND BURKE AND CONSERVATISM

Edmund Burke (1729–1797) was, without question, the outstanding critic of the philosophy of the Enlightenment, especially the philosophy of Rousseau. Burke did not write any systematic work on political science. Instead, his ideas are scattered through speeches, letters, pamphlets, and books. Burke was a member of the House of Commons from 1765 to 1794, a period covering both the American and French revolutions.

Burke was particularly critical of metaphysical and abstract political theory. It was such theorizing, rather than practical reason, that he attacked. To him morality is not comparable to mathematics. The most important qualification for a statesman was practical wisdom rather than the abstract, deductive reasoning of the leaders of the French Revolution, who believed it possible to create a new civilization by drawing up a new constitution based on theoretical "rights of man."

According to Burke, man is a complex animal of both reason and passion. Reason is influenced by passions, loves, fears, and habit. Although Burke accepted the idea of natural law, he regarded the social contract theory of government as an oversimplified fiction. A political society was not a human invention but a living organism, with roots deep in the past, that evolved slowly over the years and reflected the political experience of a particular nation. He considered the British settlement of 1688, with its limited monarchy and division of power between the king and Parliament, to be the best possible reconciliation of liberty and authority. No wonder Burke often has been called the philosopher of "common sense."

Burke defended the American Revolution while bitterly criticizing the French. The Americans in his opinion were fighting to retain the ancient liberties of Englishmen, which were threatened by the policies of the king and Parliament. The French Revolution, on the other hand, was seeking to overturn the entire political order and create a new order based on abstract rights without concern for history or tradition.

Burke was not opposed to all change or reform, as his attitude toward the American Revolution indicates. No doubt he idealized the British House of Commons and overlooked its unrepresentative character. Also, in criticizing the excesses of the French Revolution, he minimized the evils of the old regime in France. Nevertheless, Burke performed a great service in showing the weaknesses of a philosophy that assumed the perfectibility of human nature and the belief that all social evils result from a bad environment and can be eradicated overnight by a revolution based on abstract theories.

Burke's *Reflections On the Revolution in France* (1790) usually is considered the beginning of **conservatism** as a philosophical movement. There have been far fewer conservative than liberal writings, and conservatism has been far more influential in Europe than in the United States. Although European conservatism began as a reaction against the French Revolution and its philosophy, it is not inherently a reactionary movement opposed to all social change. Conservatism originated among the aristocracy of Europe, but it was accepted by considerable sections of the working class. Conservatism is characterized by basic attitudes rather than specific beliefs.[4] Support of established churches, whether Protestant or Catholic, and a belief that traditional institutions such as the family are important, are part of the conservative creed. Traditionally, conservatives supported monarchy and generally still do where constitutional monarchies continue to exist. Conservatives also believe in an organic conception of society similar to Burke and accept the traditional class structure of society.

Although conservatives support private property as necessary for political and economic stability, they have not been committed to a belief in economic laissez-faire, as were many liberals in the early nineteenth century. Nineteenth-century English conservatives such as Benjamin Disraeli favored not only enfranchisement of the working class but paternalistic legislation to protect them against the evils of industrialism.[5]

LIBERALISM

Liberalism, as George Sabine and Thomas Thorson have suggested, is used in two different senses. In a narrower sense it designates a position that is midway between conservatism and socialism. It is thus favorable to reform but opposed to radicalism. In a broader sense it is belief in a democracy in a popular sense, as opposed to dictatorship, whether Fascist or Communist. In this sense liberalism is identified with the defense of democratic suffrage, representative and responsible government, and constitutionalism.[6]

Earlier liberalism often is identified with individualism and the philosophy of John Locke, who, as has been explained, put the individual prior to the state in his social contract theory of government. Early English liberalism was a middle-class movement, which advocated traditional civil liberties, representative government, and constitutional monarchy. In economics early liberals advocated laissez-faire, the doctrine that the state should as a matter of principle not regulate the economy. The latter policy would abolish traditional mercantilist restrictions on trade and industry. As the rising middle class was identified with trade and industry, removal of these restrictions served middle class interests. Its political policy served to check the power of monarchy and the landed aristocracy. Although the liberal movement was primarily middle class, its program transcended purely middle class interests. Its philosophical roots, as set forth by Locke with emphasis on natural law, were definitely Christian.

In the nineteenth century, as a result of the industrial revolution, the liberal movement faced a crisis. A liberal movement that opposed state intervention in the economy as a matter of principle meant that the working class would find no relief from

---

[4]Compare the section on liberalism.
[5]See F. J. C. Henshaw, *Conservatism in England* (London: MacMillan, 1933), pp. 22–23.
[6]George H. Sabine and Thomas Landon Thorson, *op. cit.,* pp. 668–669.

sweat shops, subsistence wages, child labor, and a host of other such evils of early capitalism.

Some liberals, such as the English sociologist Herbert Spencer (1820–1903), who was a follower of Darwin, developed a philosophy of rugged individualism that assumed that society was based on a ruthless struggle for existence. To him it was futile for the state to try to interfere through welfare legislation, since it was natural that some should be poor and others rich as a result of the struggle for existence. Spencer's concept of the role of the state was distinctly negative and limited to preserving order.

In the closing decades of the nineteenth century and early part of the present century, Spencer's extreme individualism was perhaps the dominant political philosophy of the United States. Even the United States Supreme Court read Spencer's doctrine, "freedom of contract," into the Constitution. The Court ruled that many labor laws setting maximum hours, and all minimum wage laws, violated "freedom of contract," which in the Court's opinion were part of the concept of "due process of law" included in the Fourteenth Amendment.[7]

Today some American "conservatives," like Senator Barry Goldwater of Arizona, are really adherents of the older liberal tradition of Spencer in their strong opposition to state intervention in the economy. But in the late nineteenth century, the main body of the liberal movement broke with laissez-faire philosophically.

The English philosopher who rejected laissez-faire and laid the foundations for the welfare state was Thomas Hill Green (1836–1882). To Green, victims of poverty in modern industrial society had no share in the civilization of England. Genuine freedom must be an actual as well as a legal possibility. The state may pass legislation to remove obstacles to the achievement of the good life, such as gross inequalities in bargaining power between employer and employee. Green favored laws abolishing child labor and setting maximum hours of work when necessary.

Green also believed that there is a social impulse in human nature and that there should be a mutual relationship between the individual and the community. A liberal society, according to Green, recognizes the social impulse and should create conditions that will make its realization possible.

The new liberalism in England, which Green helped to fashion, gave rise to the liberal legislation of the period 1906 to 1914, when the Liberal government of that country laid the basis for the present welfare state by enacting laws that removed barriers against trade unions and provided for unemployment insurance, old-age pensions, and other welfare legislation.

In the United States the flowering of liberalism was in the Progressive movement of the early part of the century and the New Deal legislation of the 1930s. The former stressed making democracy more effective by such reforms as the direct

[7]See the opinion of Justice Peckham in *Lochner versus New York* (1905) and Justice Holmes' dissent in the same case, for a criticism of the majority for reading Herbert Spencer's social philosophy into the Constitution.

primary, the strengthening and better enforcement of antitrust laws, effective regulation of monopolies such as the railroads, and reform of the banking system. The New Deal was a response to the Depression and led to a modified capitalism in which the role of government regulation of the economy was vastly extended and extensive welfare legislation was passed to protect the disadvantaged in society.

The philosophical basis of American liberalism grew out of Dewey's pragmatism more than Green's idealism. John Dewey (1859–1952) regarded the search for truth as a process of inquiry. In solving governmental problems, Dewey favored a process of trial and error under the guidance of the scientific method, which had been so successful in our natural sciences. Dewey had a great dislike of traditional metaphysics and was totally uninterested in such issues as the state, sovereignty, natural rights, and similar "abstractions" that had intrigued earlier philosophers. Despite his dislike of metaphysics, Dewey assumed certain axioms. Among these were confidence in human nature and our ability to disinterestedly apply the scientific method to social problems if freed from certain mistakes of the past, including belief in ideas such as first causes and ultimate goals. This approach disavowed Marxism, with its belief in the class struggle and the inevitability of revolution, as well as traditional liberalism and conservatism. There is an affinity between Dewey's thinking and the experimental nature of Roosevelt's New Deal. Dewey also reflected the traditional American optimism in his belief that all problems are capable of solution. His thinking also has much in common with certain types of democratic socialism, especially Fabian socialism.[8]

SOCIALISM

Today when the term "socialism" is used, the doctrines of Karl Marx are often thought of. In fact, some individuals would tend to identify socialism primarily with Marx or with the interpretations of Marx by such Soviet and Chinese revolutionary leaders as Lenin and Mao Zedong. Marx is perhaps the leading and most influential socialist philosopher, but there are many variations of socialism, and it is not at all necessary that one be a Marxist to be a socialist.

Socialism is a response to the industrial revolution and to the conditions it created. The early socialists of the first part of the nineteenth century were known as utopian socialists. Their socialism was based on a humanitarian outlook and belief in the perfectibility of human nature. They hoped to bring about an ideal socialist society as a result of the soundness of their arguments and were opposed to force and revolution.

An early French socialist was Count Henri de Saint-Simon (1780–1825), who proposed a new social order based on the leadership of the producing class. Society

---

[8]See section on "revisionist or democratic socialism," later in this chapter.

would be a productive association similar to an ideal factory. More important was Robert Owen (1771–1858), an English factory owner, who sought to create utopian communities organized along socialist lines. He set up such communities for brief periods in New Lanark in Scotland and New Harmony, Indiana.

Socialists believe that human progress and justice are hindered by private ownership of the means of production. The problem, as they see it, is to limit or abolish private property. The answer for the socialist is the common ownership, to varying degrees, of the means of production and exchange. In this way the inevitable unequal distribution of wealth under capitalism will be corrected. The difference between communism and socialism is in the means used to transform capitalism into socialism. Socialists believe the transformation can and should be attained through peaceful and democratic means. Communists, on the other hand, believe that the change must be accomplished by revolutionary means and that dictatorial government is necessary at least for a transitional period. The term "Communist" is usually applied to the revolutionary regimes of the Soviet Union and the People's Republic of China.

MARXIAN SOCIALISM

Karl Marx (1818–1883) was born in the Rhineland, Germany, but spent most of his life as an exile in England because his radical views brought him into conflict with the Prussian authorities. In his political activity and writing, he worked closely with his lifelong associate, Friedrich Engels.

As a young man Marx had studied the **dialectical philosophy** of George Wilhelm Friedrich Hegel at German universities. Marx took Hegel's philosophy and transformed it. According to Hegel, the dialectic is the way the human mind learns the truth about anything. A doctrine is advanced about some subject, but such a doctrine is necessarily partial and one-sided because of human fallibility and is limited by the historical perspective of the period. Critics develop an opposite doctrine to correct the errors in the initial thesis. As this second doctrine, or antithesis, also will be one-sided and only partial in its truth, it will lead to a third doctrine, or synthesis, of the true elements in the original thesis and its opposite antithesis; however, the synthesis is not the complete truth and the dialectical process will start again with another antithesis. To Hegel this dialectical process was more than a way of acquiring knowledge; it was the essence of reality itself and its unfolding was the will of God or the Absolute.

Marx took Hegel's dialectic and transformed it into **dialectical materialism**, which assumed that the ultimate reality is matter in motion. Reality is in a constant state of change and truth is no more than what the general laws of motion bring about. The Marxian dialectic works itself out in history. For example, the practical methods of industrial production, such as tools and machines, and the physical and cultural conditions of production, such as topography and climate, create various

Karl Marx.

Cover of Manifesto of the Communist Party, first edition.

relationships, such as landlord and tenant or factory owner and laborer. These economic forces and relationships determine the character of the state and its institutions and the cultural and religious ideas of any given period. What is produced in society and how it is distributed are the ultimate causes of social change. The human mind and ideas about truth and justice reflect changes in the methods of production and exchange.

Marx regarded religion as the opium of the masses and an illusion, since it is not God who creates humanity but humanity who creates God. To him religious ideas merely reflected alterations of economic relations.

Marx believed that the history of all human societies is a record of class struggles. Capitalism grew out of feudalism. With the discovery of America and the opening of new markets throughout the world as the result of progress in navigation, commerce, and industry, the old feudal order disintegrated. The development of capitalism led to the industrial revolution, which brought about the modern industrial working class, or proletariat. Under capitalism, labor becomes a commodity to be bought or sold and the wage earner becomes a wage slave as the average wage tends to become a subsistence wage.

Capitalism tends to destroy itself. The accumulation and centralization of capital leads to overproduction of both capital and commodities as the purchasing power of the masses or workers is inadequate to purchase the output of industry. Economic depressions become more frequent and severe. The middle class is destroyed and sinks into the proletariat. Eventually, there will be a final collapse of capitalism, as there remain only the factory owners and proletariat whose economic lot becomes one of increasing misery. As the working class increases in size, its poverty becomes more pronounced. As its members become more class conscious, a Communist movement develops among the proletariat. To Marx, the Communist movement is an instrument of history and a mechanism for the creation of a new social order.

Marx's mistake was in assuming that his diagnosis of capitalism was of universal application and unchanging. He did not foresee that the lot of the working class would generally improve rather than grow worse as he predicted. Also, many of his specific economic doctrines have not stood the test of time.

To Marx, the state or the government was always the tool of the dominant class. As the state was essentially an instrument of suppression under capitalism, the ruling bourgeoisie would use force against the proletariat if the latter sought to better itself. The idea of the state as an entity based on law, which sought to treat all groups and classes equally, was rejected by Marx.

Marx was not always consistent in his views as to how the transition to a socialist society would take place. In general he believed a violent revolution to be necessary; however, late in life he suggested that in England, America, and perhaps Holland, there was hope of a peaceful change.[9]

The revolution, according to Marx, will be followed by the "dictatorship of the proletariat," by which he apparently meant the rule of the working class. But he was not clear as to the meaning of this phrase except that the proletariat would use political power against the bourgeoisie. Just how the proletariat was to be represented in the governing group was never explained.

The dictatorship of the proletariat would continue during the transition from capitalism to communism. There would still be differences in pay as labor would be compensated on the basis of skill. There would be no exploitation, however, because the means of production would be owned by the state.

At some point, according to Marx, the dictatorship of the proletariat will destroy the last vestiges of capitalism. When this occurs there will be a classless society and no further correction will be necessary. Under the dictatorship of the proletariat, the political power of the state is used to destroy the remnants of the bourgeoisie. With the advent of the classless society, the state as an administrative machinery for managing the instruments of production remains, even though it no longer employs force.

[9]J. H. Hallowell, *Main Currents in Modern Political Thought* (New York: Henry Holt and Company, 1950) p. 428.

With the new society, religion, the family, and marriage will all disappear, according to Marx. Marriage, in the traditional sense, will be replaced by alliances between the sexes based on mutual affection. With the abolition of private property, the family will be superfluous.

REVISIONIST OR DEMOCRATIC SOCIALISM

Following the death of Karl Marx, many of his followers became **revisionists**. They realized that Marx was not an infallible guide and criticized him in a number of respects. Many revisionists believed individuals and nations develop an increasing freedom in shaping their progress, contrary to Marx and the materialist interpretation of history. The revisionists also contended that the lot of the proletariat was improving and that a violent revolution was not necessary in democratic states.

The revisionists, like Edward Bernstein (1850–1932) in Germany, accepted Marx as a great thinker who proved that capitalism does exploit the great majority of workers and does tend to undermine itself. But to Bernstein and others, Marx's philosophy would have to be revised in the light of experience, as he had been proven wrong on a number of points. The growing socialist parties in France and Germany tended to accept parliamentary democracy in practice, even though in theory they might remain orthodox Marxist parties.

In England, Marx had relatively little influence. The Fabians, a group of intellectuals including such distinguished men of letters as H. G. Wells and George Bernard Shaw, took their name from the Roman general, Fabius, who through delaying tactics ultimately defeated the Carthaginians even though he lost many battles. The "Fabian Essays" presented the case for a democratic and evolutionary socialism in plain language that everybody could understand. Sidney and Beatrice Webb (1859–1947) and (1858–1943) were the leading theorists of the society.

Fabian socialists regarded socialism as a logical next step in the progress of society. To them socialism was a scheme under which the means of production and exchange would be under the administration of the civil service. They had no doubt that trained civil servants would administer the economic system fairly. The injustices of the industrial system that Marx denounced were, in the eyes of the Fabians, the result of inept social arrangements. They also assumed that their version of socialism was completely compatible with political democracy.

Fabian doctrine had great influence upon the British Labour Party, which was organized in 1906 and is now one of the two leading British parties. Fabian leaders, such as Sidney Webb, also served in Labour cabinets when that party was in power.

In the United States, democratic socialism has not been a factor of great significance in recent years, because it does not have much working class support. During the first quarter of this century, however, it did have some labor support and was a third party of some importance. In 1912 it received about 5% of the total presidential vote. However, in no election did a Socialist win the electoral vote of any state.

The main importance of the Socialist party has been to propagate reform proposals later adopted by the two major parties, especially the Democratic. Much of the New Deal program originated with the Socialists.

Socialism, however, has been a powerful force in Europe. In Britain and the Scandinavian countries in particular, Social Democratic parties have been in power for considerable periods of time. Socialism also promises to be of importance in the new nations of Africa and Asia. We will now take up developments in African socialist thought.

AFRICAN SOCIALISM

African socialism is a product of a particular environment, especially one with the absence of distinct classes and a pre-capitalistic economy. President Nyerere of Tanzania has said that socialism, like democracy, is an attitude of mind rather than a set of doctrines. To Nyerere and others, the beginning of socialism is found in the traditional African way of permitting a person to occupy a piece of land only if he uses it. In Africa, there would be no need for an agrarian revolution to create the "landed" and "landless" classes, or an industrial revolution to create the modern capitalist and proletariat. Instead, African socialism would develop out of tribal socialism, under which members of a tribe would prosper if the tribe prospered.

Thus, African socialism emphasizes the group or community and opposes the concept of the "class struggle"; yet, at the same time, some African socialists call themselves Marxists. Clearly, African socialism is still in a process of definition and development.

Nyerere has compared governments in developing countries to governments at war. In developing countries the immediate goal is freedom from fear of starvation. Because economic planning and strong government are essential in wartime, such luxuries as opposition parties cannot be permitted. Democracy, according to Nyerere, is consistent with the one-party system as long as freedom of discussion is preserved and government by force avoided.[10]

Tanzania is the African country in which both the theory and practice of socialism has been most extensively developed. The charter of Tanzanian socialism is the Arusha Declaration of 1967, providing for the nationalization of all major industries. The most radical measure was the resettlement of millions of peasants into villages intended to become replicas of the model village of Luthanga, which has a village-owned dispensary, clinic, furniture shop, a women's cooperative that sells milk and soft drinks, and a private plot of land for each family.

It is the hope of President Nyerere that village socialism can modernize and raise the standard of living of his country, which ranks among the 25 poorest countries of the world. Progressive taxes have produced an extremely egalitarian society. The

[10]See Julius K. Nyerere, *Freedom and Unity* (London: Oxford University Press, 1966), pp. 162–171.

ratio between the earnings of the highest and lowest paid citizen is now 9 to 1 instead of 100 to 1 as it was at the time of independence in 1967.

In other respects, the results are far from successful. The economy is approaching bankruptcy. There has been a shortage of consumer goods, widespread smuggling and corruption, except among higher officials, and a lack of concern and enthusiasm in all aspects of life. Tanzanian officials describe their difficulties as temporary due to failure to develop a vision of a better life. In practice, foreign aid has kept the economy afloat.[11]

COMMUNISM

The various types of socialism that we have discussed thus far are essentially democratic, except for some aspects of African Socialism. An outgrowth of Marx's thought that has led frequently to totalitarianism is Communism.

SOVIET COMMUNISM

As a result of the Russian Revolution of November, 1917, there was for the first time in history a government established on the principles of Marxian socialism. The man who headed the new regime, Vladimir Lenin (1870–1924), was an unusual combination of active revolutionary and political and economic theorist. Lenin's philosophy was based on Marx, but a Marxism modified in the light of developments in Russia. Lenin differed from Marx in a number of respects. First, since Russia was not a well-developed capitalist country, it was not a likely candidate for the type of revolution Marx predicted. Lenin explained the Communist victory in Russia as a result of the country having experienced capitalism "vicariously," through contact with the more advanced capitalist countries of the West. Second, he believed that capitalism had entered the imperialist phase because the European powers were engaged in a worldwide imperialistic war in a struggle for world markets. Consequently, revolutionary activity was possible anywhere and Russia, as a result of World War I, had an unusually unstable government.

Lenin also differed from Marx in his interpretation of the role of the proletariat in bringing about revolutionary activity. Unlike Marx, Lenin believed the working class by itself was not capable of developing a revolutionary consciousness. A revolution according to Lenin could come about only through a vanguard of dedicated revolutionaries who would supplant the old regime as rulers. Thus the dictatorship of the proletariat became the dictatorship of the Communist Party in Russia. The party ruled in the name of the proletariat.

Lenin was more explicit than Marx about the period of transition following the revolution. He believed that an extended period of time was necessary before the attainment of communism was possible. Following the revolution, there would be a

---

[11]"Socialism: Trials and Error," *Time*, 111, March 13, 1978, p. 40.

period of revolutionary transformation during which time suppression of the minority of exploiters still remaining would be necessary. The state would continue but would rule in the name of the proletariat. During the period of transition, inequalities of wealth would still exist but exploitation of the many no longer would be possible, for the means of production would cease to be in private hands. Only when society is capable of attaining the formula of "from each according to his ability—to each according to his needs" will the state disappear. At what time this stage would occur was not clear.

On the question of revolution, Lenin believed that a violent overthrow of the old regime was necessary. He also had only contempt for the institutions of parliamentary democracy that were common in Western Europe.

Lenin's emphasis on the need for a revolutionary vanguard to instigate the revolution and to rule in the interim period before the state withers away prepared the way for the Soviet dictatorship, which began under Lenin and has continued to the present. While Lenin lived, dictatorial power was vested in the Communist Party leadership. Under his successor, Joseph Stalin (1879–1953), power gravitated into the hands of Stalin alone, who acquired nearly absolute power through purges of party members. Since Stalin's death in 1953, the dictatorship has been relaxed in some respects. The Soviet Union, however, is still far from the democratic republic it is supposed to be according to its constitution, which on paper provides for a bicameral legislature with a cabinet responsible to the legislative branch. Actual power still does and always has been lodged in the party Central Committee and Politburo. There is no sign of the withering away of the state.

In economic terms the Soviet Union has achieved a high degree of socialization and is now a leading industrial power, but this accomplishment has been at a very high cost in human terms. Industrialization was achieved through a series of five-year plans, which imposed the cost of industrial progress on the masses through the maintenance of a low standard of living. Thus, drastic limitations on the production of consumer goods was the necessary price for rapid industrialization, and collectivization of agriculture led to liquidation of millions of peasants who resisted the abolition of private property in agriculture. Some were executed and others perished in forced labor camps.

CHINESE COMMUNISM
Chinese communism is of importance for several reasons. First, it marks the second major try to accept the creed of Marx. Second, the Chinese interpretation of Marxism has some ideological characteristics of its own that differ from the Soviet version. Lastly, the People's Republic of China, instead of strengthening the worldwide Communist movement by becoming a partner of the Soviet Union, as first seemed likely, has accentuated divisions in the Communist world by following policies of its own and attacking the Soviets as bitterly as any capitalist power. The prin-

cipal charge against the Soviets was that of deviating from the principles of Marxist Leninism.

The Chinese Communists, through their leader Mao Zedong (1893–1976), have emphasized the revolutionary doctrines of Marx rather than the philosophical and economic aspects of his philosophy. Since China is a developing country, Mao based his revolutionary techniques on the peasants rather than the proletariat, which was virtually nonexistent in China. Since 1949, great efforts have been made to develop a proletariat through industrialization.

Probably the most important contribution of Mao to Communist ideology is the theory of guerrilla warfare as both a military and political principle. The military principle emphasizes attacking isolated enemy forces, winning rural areas and small cities first and big cities later, mobile warfare, and making use of the periods between campaigns to consolidate the revolutionary forces. To retain the revolutionary army, a strong territorial base is necessary. This requires control of an area where there is a revolutionary peasant government that has redistributed land. By following the above tactics, the Chinese Communists were able to defeat the forces of the Chinese Nationalist Government headed by Chiang Kai-shek between the end of World War II in 1945 and 1949.

The tactics of the Chinese Communists following their victory in the mainland in 1949 were to apply the principles of Mao's pamphlet *On the People's Democratic Dictatorship.* A coalition government was formed, which originally included non-Communist elements. Agrarian reforms were introduced. To carry out these changes landlords, as well as other "counterrevolutionary" individuals, were publicly executed. In 1953 the first five-year plan to nationalize most of the economic structure was introduced. By 1956 most Chinese farmers were organized into cooperative farms.

In 1966 China launched the Great Proletarian Cultural Revolution. Young students, organized into Red Guards, were used to bring about an extensive cultural revolution and political purge of party members guilty of "bourgeois" thinking. For a while the revolutionary movement got out of control and Chinese society approached a condition of anarchy until the army restored order. According to Thomas L. Thorson, the apparent purpose of the Cultural Revolution was to preserve Chinese society from the threat of destruction by industrialization and excessive bureaucratization of life.[12]

Since the death of Mao in 1976, his successors have brought the changes he inaugurated to an abrupt halt. The new leaders of China have not only introduced a more conservative policy but downgraded Mao as a leader as well. Emphasis has been placed on economic development, and less regard for party ideology has been shown.

[12]George H. Sabine and Thomas Landon Thorson, *op. cit.,* p. 788.

EUROCOMMUNISM

In theory at least, **Eurocommunism** is a demand by the Communist parties of Eastern and Western Europe for independence from the Soviet Union. Such independence would give each Communist party the right to determine its own road to socialism. The problems faced by the Communist parties in Eastern and Western Europe are not identical.

In Western Europe the Communist parties exist primarily in democratic countries with a pluralistic society. The Soviet government traditionally has exercised considerable control over local Communist parties in Western Europe. The problem confronting Communist parties in the West is not only their relationship to Moscow but to non-Communist parties as well. The problem is particularly important in France and Italy, where the Communist parties are fairly large and at times play an important role by holding the balance of power in parliament.[13]

In Eastern Europe the Communist parties have existed in one-party dictatorships, with varying degrees of Soviet control, ever since these governments were established after World War II. The first signs of revisionism in Eastern Europe occurred in 1948 with the break between Stalin and the Yugoslav Communists. Although Marshal Tito, the Yugoslav ruler (1892–1980), alleged that ideological differences with the Soviet regime were the cause of the break, the controlling factor seems to have been opposition to Stalin's policy of treating Yugoslavia as a satellite state. Tito created his own revolution, and, unlike the other Communist countries in Eastern Europe, Yugoslavia was never occupied by the Soviet army. Following the break with Stalin, doctrinal differences developed. The Yugoslavs have alleged that the Soviet Union had become a state capitalist country rather than a socialist country; because the party and the bureaucracy had become independent of popular control.[14]

As Yugoslavia is a confederation of six republics, the Communist party is organized on a similar basis. The party does not control the government to the same degree as in the Soviet Union, and some degree of internal democracy exists within the party. The Yugoslav experiment is a less extreme type of dictatorship.

Following the breach between Stalin and Tito, a cold war developed between the two countries. This has been followed by frequent thaws since Stalin's death.

After the passing of Stalin, some liberalization took place in Poland, Hungary, and Czechoslovakia. The pace of change has varied from country to country; in some, progress has been followed by setbacks. In Poland, liberalization was the result of the transfer of power from one wing of the local Communist party to another, and progress has been limited. In Hungary, a revolution in 1956 was put down by the So-

---

[13]See Jean-Francois Revel, The myths of Eurocommunism, *Foreign Affairs*, 56:2, 1978, pp. 295–305, for a discussion of the political aspects of Eurocommunism.

[14]See Max Mark, *Modern Ideologies* (New York: St. Martin's Press, 1973), pp. 190–200, for a discussion of Eurocommunism in Eastern Europe.

viet army, yet there has been progress toward liberalization in that country since 1956. In Czechoslovakia on the other hand, the triumph in 1968 of the liberal Communist, Alexander Dubcek, was followed by suppression by the Soviet army and the installation of a Soviet-controlled regime.

A problem for intellectuals in East European Communist countries was how to restore faith in Marxism after its long identification with Stalin's policies. The answer was found in Marx's concept of alienation.[15]

The discovery of Marx's early writings has had an impact on Marxist thought in the past 10 years, particularly in Eastern Europe. The early Marx stressed humanity's **alienation** from society, which he attributed to the division of labor and private property. He believed that the worker creates capital for the capitalist; thus, a worker's labor becomes an object with an independent existence, outside of the worker, and alien to him or her. People become nothing more than an extension of the machine.

In Eastern Europe this idea of alienation has been used to criticize Stalinism. It has been argued that the worker under Stalinism was as alienated as under capitalism because he had no part in the decision-making process and was subject to the power of the bureaucracy. Some of the Eastern European writers such as Milovan Djilas, Georg Lukacs, and Roy Medvedev, among others, contend that Marxism must reject many of its own doctrines and return to the humanism of the early Marx. They are hoping to develop a new version of communism that will give more importance to the individual.

The issues in the West concern not only obedience to policies made by Moscow but also the right to criticize Soviet policy and to form electoral alliances, particularly with non-Communist parties on the Left. In France, as far back as the 1930s, the Communists formed an electoral alliance with other parties of the Left for a brief time. Recently an electoral alliance with the socialists was formed but broke up shortly thereafter. Italian Communists have even developed a tenuous cooperation with the ruling Christian Democrats by voting to support the government on some occasions, though this cooperation has eroded recently.

It has been suggested that some of the West European Communist Parties are guided by an independent principle or tendency that often is labeled "Eurocommunism." This, if true, may be the result of two developments in the past twenty years: (1) a growing awareness in Western Europe of the failure of Soviet Communism and (2) an effort on the part of Communist parties to adjust their brand of communism to the needs of advanced industrial societies.[16] In this way they hope for growing popular support, which would increase their chances for participating in governments.

Is it possible to believe that the Communist parties of Western Europe are now on the road to independence from Moscow and to democratization? It should be noted

[15]Mark, *op. cit.,* pp. 202–207.
[16]Revel, *op. cit.,* pp. 304–305.

that only in Yugoslavia and Albania have the local parties broken with the Soviet Union. Tension between the Soviet Union and the local parties in Eastern Europe is common, but a complete break is unusual. Furthermore, a complete break would not of itself transform local parties into democratic parties. As Jean-Francois Revel has said, "Nothing . . . makes it possible to believe that communists do not have as their goal, today as yesterday, the monopoly of power."[17]

THE NEW LEFT

Eurocommunism is not the only important political trend to develop since World War II. One of the more important ideological developments in recent years has been the rise of the **New Left** in Western Europe and the United States. According to one prominent American political scientist:

> The term New Left is used to describe the general movement of agitation, protest and revolt organized and led in great part by young people and university students in the 1960s. The system under attack was, and continues to be, that of the modern industrialized societies—democratic or not.[18]

This trend is "new" in the sense that it represents a new type of radicalism that does not fit into the mold of any existing type of Marxism. In the United States it is the outgrowth of such traumatic events as the Vietnam War and the violent opposition it aroused. It also has ties with the Civil Rights Movement and the Women's Liberation Movement.

The dominant philosopher of the New Left is the late Herbert Marcuse (1898–1979), whose utopian philosophy is based on certain ideas of Freud and Marx. Marcuse agreed with Freud that repression is a cause of human unhappiness. Unlike Freud, who believed repression was a necessary result of culture, Marcuse regarded it as a result of a culture based on work.

Although modern industrial civilization makes individual freedom possible, Marcuse believed the economic structure of both the Soviet Union and the West inhibits this development. The revolution in the Soviet Union was betrayed, in his opinion, by a repressive bureaucratic regime. Western capitalism maintains itself on the constant increase of artificial wants, warfare, and the exploitation of developing countries.

Marcuse accepted the fact that a majority in the West approved of capitalism, but he believed somewhat illogically, that this was due to the fact that radical points of view do not get a fair hearing, even though there is broad toleration of diverse

---

[17]*Ibid.*, p. 305.
[18]Roy C. Macridis, *Contemporary Political Ideologies: Movements and Regimes* (Cambridge, Mass.: Winthrop Publishers, 1980), p. 241.

points of view. As a result, the public's confidence in the political system is strengthened due to its policy of toleration. The crux of Marcuse's position is that there cannot be equal toleration of truth and falsehood. According to Marcuse:

> In the last analysis, the question of what are true and false needs must be answered by the individuals themselves, but only in the last analysis; that is, if and when they are free to give their own answer.[19]

The only solution, according to Marcuse, is a revolution that goes beyond socialism. As for traditional socialism, nationalization of the means of production is condemned as only a quantitative change. Only a total reconstruction of society will make possible the real freedom of humanity from compulsive work, a freedom that modern technology makes possible. His hope rests on the Third World of developing countries.

The New Left is very critical of the basic values of Western society. A special target of criticism is the university, not only in the United States but throughout the world. The gist of its criticism is that the university is a tool of the status quo and that many courses are irrelevant to the needs of the student.

Three basic values of the movement are (1) the importance of action, (2) the concept of "participatory democracy," and (3) the need for revolution. The stress on action reveals the anti-intellectualism of the New Left, which assumes that change will not result by speech or the pen but only by action. Great emphasis is placed on "participatory democracy," a vague phrase that implies that traditional law-making bodies should be replaced by a number of smaller bodies that presumably would be closer to the people. Another basic tenet is that it will take a revolution to destroy the present corrupt society in order to prepare the way for a new order; however, there has been no agreement on the kind of revolution needed. Many in the movement stress the need for a violent revolution, and emphasis has been placed on the idea of a "permanent revolution."

As might be expected, the New Left has been subjected to strong criticism. Critics have denounced its intolerance of groups opposing its ideas and programs. The utopianism that assumes the perfectibility of human nature has been challenged for assuming that all social ills are due to faulty environment. Other criticism has been directed at its conspiracy theory of political power, which assumes all important political decisions are made by a small elite motivated by sinister purposes. The strongest criticism has been directed at the violence associated with the movement. A notorious example of violence is the 1978 kidnapping and murder by the Red Brigade of Aldo Moro, the Christian Democratic leader in Italy. This murder was reminiscent of the assasinations committed by the Nihilists in Czarist Russia.

---

[19]Herbert Marcuse, *One-Dimensional Man: Studies in the Ideology of Advanced Industrial Society* (Boston: Beacon Press, 1964), p. 6.

Another shocking action was the bombing of the University of Wisconsin's Mathematics Research Center in 1970, which resulted in the death of a graduate student. There is also the kidnapping of Patty Hearst by the bizarre group known as the Symbionese Liberation Army. For many Americans, the New Left was best known for the violent antics of the "Weathermen" faction of the now defunct "Students for a Democratic Society."

It is impossible to predict with certainty whether the New Left will continue as a mood or to guess what its long-run consequences will be. Perhaps it already has created a climate for a greater tolerance of the politics of protest and political violence.

FASCISM AND NATIONAL SOCIALISM

The New Left and the various types of Marxist thought that we have discussed are doctrines of the Left. There remains one important political theory of the twentieth century to discuss: Fascism, a philosophy of the Right.

Even though the two leading Fascist powers—Germany and Italy—were defeated in World War II and their regimes overthrown, it would be a mistake to assume that the conditions that led to the creation of these regimes could not recur in some country. There were considerable differences between the two Fascist countries, but the similarities were greater. It is therefore appropriate to call both regimes Fascist, even though the German system was called National Socialism. Primary consideration will be given to Hitler's dictatorship, as it was the most powerful militarily and was the more extreme in its ideology.

Fascist writers do not contribute a great deal to an explanation of the ideology of the movement. Mussolini stressed the "will to power" and the supremacy of the state over the individual. German writers like Alfred Rosenberg stressed the myth of Aryan racial superiority. The basic elements of Fascist ideology, however, would seem to be the glorification of the irrational, a social Darwinism employed to justify national and racial superiority, a totalitarian one-party state, and the leadership principle.

The Nazis stressed Aryan supremacy and justified the extermination of "inferior" races, such as the Jews, whom the Nazis blamed for the ills of Germany. The nationalism of both the Italian and German versions of fascism glorified war as the climax of human achievement.

Perhaps most important, though, was the leadership principle. Hitler as *Führer* presumably embodied within himself the ability to speak for the entire German nation. Only Hitler could express the will of the German people. This might be considered a perversion of Rousseau's concept of the general will. Hitler as leader provided religious as well as political values to the regime. Hermann Göring, a Nazi leader, claimed Hitler was infallible.

There is no agreement among scholars as to the exact nature of fascism, except that Fascist systems are dictatorships. There are, however, a number of important theories that have been advanced.[20]

One interpretation, the Marxist, holds that fascism is the final stage of capitalism, in which capitalists conspire to save themselves by establishing a dictatorship. In support of this view, it is pointed out that a number of German capitalists subsidized Hitler financially since he promised to save the country from communism. Although many of these financial angels regarded Hitler as a demagogue, they believed that he could be managed so that their economic interests would be protected. Hitler was strongly anti-Communist and appealed to the fear of communism not only among the industrialists but the middle class as well. Supporters of this view point out that Germany was in a state of severe economic crisis when Hitler came to power and that a probable alternative regime was a Communist one.

This interpretation has elements of truth but ignores the fact that Hitler's dictatorship encroached upon property rights to such an extent that many industrialists were reduced to the status of paid managers of their own enterprises. Some businesspeople had their property seized by the Nazi government. The Marxist interpretation also ignored the strong popular support for Hitler among the masses and the broad appeal of the Nazi movement as a new form of socialism.

Fascism also has been described as essentially a personal dictatorship comparable to the rule of Napolean. This view ignores the mass support of the Nazis and obscures the totalitarian character of the dictatorship, which goes beyond the realm of the political and includes all aspects of individual life.

Another interpretation stresses the fact that Hitler's movement grew out of the strong military tradition that had roots deep in Germany history. According to this theory, the Nazi dictatorship was basically a new and extreme version of German militarism. This explanation overlooks the fact that Hitler differed in kind as well as degree from such older militarists as the German Emperor William II of World War I or Bismarck or Frederick the Great. These men were militaristic and authoritarian but they did not repudiate the basic values of Western civilization as Hitler did. They did not believe in the Nazi racial theories or seek military domination to the same extent as the Nazis.

A fourth view of fascism interprets it as a political manifestation of a crisis of Western civilization that occurred in Germany and Italy because of special circumstances in those countries. But these conditions could develop anywhere. The basis of fascism, according to this view, is despair caused by the loss of faith on the part of the German and Italian people in the ability of their political and economic institutions to solve their social problems. As a result, they accepted a tyranny that promised to restore some degree of order and provide a meaning to life; however, the

---

[20]This discussion follows to a considerable degree the analysis of John H. Hallowell, *op. cit.,* pp. 591–617. Hallowell considers the fourth interpretation to be the most satisfactory.

new order was the embodiment of naked power, and it repudiated reason and all Western values. The last court of appeal in a Fascist system is the will of the leader, who is not influenced by reason or justice.

The preceding explanation contains elements of truth the other three ignore, but this approach is perhaps too philiosophical and intellectual. Having surveyed the main currents of political theory, we now will discuss ideology, which takes us beyond pure theory.

AN AGE OF IDEOLOGY?

Ideology may be defined as an extension of political theory, simplified in form so as to arouse the masses in order to win popular support. It refers to emotionally charged beliefs concerning the ideal political and economic system. Every ideology asserts the primary importance of some value system. It may be equality or justice. In communism it is belief in revolution as the road to a new society. Fascists believe that the state represents the spirit of the people of the nation. There is also a utopian element present, such as the eventual "withering away of the state," in Marxism. A characteristic common to both is emphasis on seizing power rather than ruling. In general, ideologies consist of a political plan, and frequently an economic plan as well, together with a body of doctrines, myths, and symbols for curing some political or social evil. They also are excessively moralistic.[21]

Ideology has been affected to a considerable degree by the Industrial Revolution, which gave credence to the belief that human life is capable of being changed and improved by human knowledge and effort. In earlier times there were political philosophies, but it was generally believed people would go on living in much the same way as their ancestors had for centuries. Thus, it is not surprising that the beginning of ideology often is associated with the French and American Revolutions, each of which occurred in the early stages of the Industrial Revolution.

Clearly, the role of ideology reached its climax in the twentieth century and now has spread from the Communist world and the United States and Western Europe to the Third World. The main ideologies of the twentieth century are the two totalitarian ideologies, communism and fascism, and the two moderate ideologies, democratic socialism and liberal democracy.

Totalitarian regimes like Soviet or Chinese communism and German fascism are complete ideological systems, with belief systems that cover almost all aspects of life. No other competing belief systems are tolerated. Of course, totalitarian regimes differ in the degree to which complete orthodoxy is enforced. It has been seen that the Tito government in Yugoslavia has been more tolerant than the Soviet

---

[21]For an excellent historical discussion of ideology, see Frederick M. Watkins, *The Age of Ideology: Political Thought, 1750 to the Present.* In Robert A. Dahl, ed., *Foundations of Modern Political Science Series.* Englewood Cliffs, N.J.: Prentice Hall, 1964.

Union's. Even within the same regime, as in the Soviet Union, the dictatorship may be relaxed slightly under some leaders. For example, the dictatorship was more complete under Stalin than it is today.

Being pluralistic, democracies, whether capitalistic or socialistic, have less complete belief systems. They permit competing ideas to exist, and allow freedom of speech and the press.

Many modern ideologies have characteristics of religion. This is particulary true of communism and fascism. In fact, they have been referred to often as secular religions that provide meaning to life. Marx is as important for his ideology as his economic doctrines and his realistic analysis of the evils of capitalism in mid-nineteenth-century England. His doctrines became the basis of a secular religion. Perhaps, as Christopher Dawson and others have suggested, Marx was of the "seed of prophets" and offered a secularized version of the ancient doctrine of the Jewish prophets concerning the coming of the Messianic kingdom.[22] Despite Marx's antireligious point of view, the Marxian dialectic possessed religious values, for it was to serve as an instrument of universal salvation that would usher in a new and pure social order on earth. The God of tradition was rejected but was returned in a modified form in the dialectic that provided a new source of meaning to life. For Marx, private property is the source of evil that eventually will be purged from life.

These "spiritual" promises of Marxism, rather than the basic economic doctrines that frequently were obscure and sometimes mistaken, were the basis of the appeal of the new creed to the working classes of Europe. This appeal compensated for the inadequacies of his purely economic doctrines and led to the formation of socialist parties throughout much of Western Europe.

Although there is no doubt of the importance of ideology in the earlier part of this century, in the last 20 years a debate has taken place on the question of whether the role of ideology is declining. In 1960, Daniel Bell wrote that ideologies had exhausted themselves in the West. He and other members of the "end of ideology school" argued that ideologies were too simplistic and harmful for complex Western societies.[23]

What Bell is referring to are the old ideologies that developed in the nineteenth century, especially the various types of Marxism. Bell goes on to say that the rising countries of Asia and Africa are creating new ideologies with a different appeal: "the ideologies of industrialization, modernization, Pan-Arabism, color, and nationalism." The goals of the new ideologies are economic development and national power, whereas the goal of the old faith was social equality. The models for the new faith are Russia and China. Even though communism is not accepted as such, there

---

[22]J. H. Hollowell, *op. cit.,* p. 436.

[23]See Daniel Bell, *The End of Ideology*, 2nd ed. (New York: The Free Press, 1962), for a well-stated argument about the decline of ideology in today's world. Bell is a distinguished professor of sociology at Harvard University.

is debate over whether democratic procedures will be used to attain these goals or whether totalitarian means will be accepted to transform their countries.

Although the picture is a mixed one, there is considerable evidence to support Bell. There is no doubt that the appeal of Soviet communism has been declining in the past 40 years. What weakened the movement ultimately was, first, the Nazi–Soviet nonaggression treaty of 1939, which gave Hitler the green light to start World War II. This traumatic event made it increasingly difficult to believe in the anti-fascism of the Soviets. Second, the tyranny of Stalin was a fact even "true be-lievers" found hard to ignore. Lastly, the development of the Cold War and the Korean War dealt a fatal blow to Communist sympathizers in the United States. To-day, relatively few look at the Soviet Union through rose-colored glasses. Although there are some intellectuals who find evidence for idealizing the Chinese commu-nists, there is no group comparable in numbers or influence to the Soviet sympa-thizers of the 1930s and 1940s.[24]

In Western Europe the Communist party has yet to come to nationwide power in a free election in any country with the exception of small San Marino. The Commu-nists failed to make the expected gains in elections in France in 1978 and Italy in 1979, despite a growing independence of the French and Italian parties from the dictates of Moscow. Neither in Spain nor in Portugal have the Communists been successful, despite the revolutionary situation in those two countries.

The preceding discussion indicates that the influence of Soviet Communism, the orthodox ideology of the 1930s and 1940s, is declining, but other varieties of Com-munism still exist and have their followers. The main enemy of Communism—Fas-cism—is, of course, dead for the present. Revisionist or democratic socialism, as exemplified in Social Democratic parties in Western Europe, is not in very robust health. In the United States, democratic socialism as a political force has shown no progress. Democratic Socialist parties still continue and are in office in West Ger-many and some of the Scandinavian countries, but the Labour Party went down to defeat in Britain in 1979 and is hardly the "way of life" it once was.

Furthermore, Socialism in office often has been the program of the "middle way" of reformed capitalism, with emphasis on the welfare state rather than nationaliza-tion of industry. Today many socialist leaders themselves disavow nationalization. In Britain it is primarily "sick" industries—the railroads, coal mines, and electric util-ities, which were experiencing economic difficulties under capitalism—that were taken over by the government. In short, democratic socialism today has eroded doctrinally, so that it is in some respects hard to distinguish from liberal democracy.

"The end of ideology" debate is by no means over. Advocates of Bell's ideas ar-gue that many people in the United States reject the concept of ideology because they realize the intractable nature of many social problems, such as inflation and

---

[24]Sheila K. Johnson, To China with love, *Commentary*, 4:6, 1973, pp. 37–45.

poverty, and because they have lost confidence in the ability of government to find solutions.

But to others, the rise of the New Left, which is clearly an ideological movement, is a refutation of Bell's position.[25] This may be so only to a limited degree. Although the New Left is ideological, it is essentially a protest movement that lacks a positive political theory comparable to that of Marxism. All that can be said is that while the old faiths are losing their ideological appeal, the new faith has yet to develop a more complete philosophy. It also must prove that it is more than a passing phenomenon.[26]

CONCLUSION

In looking back on the various schools of political thought that have developed since the birth of democracy at Athens, several diverse trends are apparent. The basic approach of Plato and Aristotle was to look upon the state as an agency for moral improvement and to see the individual as part of the state. This approach was revived by Rousseau in the eighteenth century, with his emphasis on the importance of the community. T. H. Green, in justifying state intervention in the economic life of the community as a way of removing obstacles to the full development of the individual, stood in this tradition. The great insight of this approach is the recognition of humans as social beings. The great weakness is that too often the rights of the individual are not protected adequately, as in Rousseau.

Stoicism, the second great school of thought discussed here, differed from Plato and Aristotle in developing the concepts of natural law and the basic equality of all people.

Individualism for the first time starts with the individual, for whose benefit the state is created, in the social contract philosophy of Locke. It is important to remember that present-day liberalism had its origins in Locke's social contract, with his emphasis on limited government and natural rights, which were reinforced by his doctrine of natural law. The weakness of Locke is his concept of the state as a "passive policeman," which if unmodified in an industrial age can lead to the extreme and unrealistic ideas of Herbert Spencer. Perhaps one of Locke's great insights was his idea of the political community and its values, which were brought into existence from the social contract. Today Americans can appreciate the buffeting the political community has received as a result of the stresses and strains induced by the Vietnam War, the Watergate scandals, and the Civil Rights movement.

Another important philosophy is socialism. That Marxian doctrine has led to totalitarianism in the Soviet Union and the People's Republic of China is perhaps as much the result of the absence of a strong democratic tradition in those countries as it is of Marx's ideas. It would not have surprised Edmund Burke to learn that the

[25]See Mark, *op. cit.*, pp. 230–234, for a criticism of Bell.
[26]Chaim I. Waxman, ed., *The End of Ideology Debate* (New York: Simon and Schuster, 1968), p. 5.

new order in these countries includes much of the undemocratic past. Socialism, where it has been democratic, as in Western Europe, has served liberal values. But socialism in terms of pure economic policy can be as unliberal or inhumane as the worst capitalistic state, as evidenced by the Soviet Union. On the other hand, democratic socialism seems to differ from modern liberalism in degree rather than in kind. The dominant philosophical trend in the Western democracies is either liberalism or democratic socialism.

The development of Marxism led to the age of ideology, which only in recent years has shown some signs of having passed its peak due to the decline of socialism and Soviet communism as fighting faiths. The New Left is a more recent trend but it is not clear whether it is more than a transient movement.

Lastly, more recent liberal political philosophy, which is dominant in the United States, has been "realistic" and pragmatic in the tradition of Dewey. Whether modern liberalism can continue to promote traditional liberal values when divorced from its philosophical roots, which assumed a world of transcendental values as set forth by Locke and Green, remains to be seen. Nevertheless, the current trend of liberal thought is away from such abstractions as the nature of the state, natural law, and natural rights and toward emphasis on political theory that is useful and factual.

The survey of political theory in this chapter points the way to our major focus— discussion and analysis of major political institutions and processes. We will begin to use and apply the insights developed in the first three chapters. As you progress in your reading, keep in mind the ideas previously developed: that politics is part of a wider system of interactions and processes and that we are studying these interactions.

SELECTED READINGS

George H. Sabine and Thomas L. Thorson, *History of Political Theory*, 4th ed. (Hinsdale, Ill.: Dryden Press, 1973) is an excellent survey of Western political theory from the Greeks to the twentieth century. Thorson updates this classic work of the late George Sabine. For an interpretation of political thought from Locke to the twentieth century from a Christian and natural law point of view, see John H. Hallowell, *Main Currents in Modern Political Thought* (New York: Henry Holt, 1950).

A recent challenging study of political thought is John Rawls, *A Theory of Justice** (Cambridge, Mass.: Belknap Press of Harvard University Press, 1971). Rawls presents a theory of justice that rejects utilitarianism and reinterprets the traditional theory of the social contract, as represented by Locke and his successors, as its philosophical justification. For a work that surveys in detail the scientific foundation of twentieth-century political thought, see Arnold Brecht, *Political Theory* (Princeton: Princeton University Press, 1959).

*Available in paperback.

Hannah Arendt is the author of two excellent studies on certain aspects of political thought. *The Origins of Totalitarianism,* * 2nd ed. (Cleveland and New York: A Meridian Book, World Publishing, 1967) analyzes the historical roots of totalitarianism. *Between Past and Future* (New York: The Viking Press, 1968) consists of eight essays in political thought. Chapter 3, "What is Authority?" is particularly outstanding.

For a modern study of the state as an instrument for satisfying human needs under changing conditions, see R. M. MacIver, *The Modern State,* rev. ed. (London: Oxford University Press, 1964). Another book about the state is Sir Ernest Barker's *Principles of Social and Political Theory** (London: Oxford University Press, 1961). Barker discusses the state and society historically and the development of justice and law.

Of the many books on the political philosophy of Plato and Aristotle, mention will be made of only one. Sir Ernest Barker, *The Political Thought of Plato and Aristotle** (New York: Dover Publications, 1959) analyzes the philosophy of these classic Greek thinkers within the framework of T. H. Green's political thinking.

There are several good studies of ideologies. Kenneth M. and Patricia Dolbeare in *American Ideologies** 2nd ed., (Chicago: Markham Publishing, 1973) present an introduction to current competing American political beliefs, such as various schools of liberalism, conservatism, capitalism, Black Liberation, the New Left, and American Marxism. C. Wright Mills, *The Marxists* (New York: Dell Publishing, 1962) is a primer on Marx and various schools of thought developed by his followers. More recent discussions of ideologies are Lyman T. Sargent, *Contemporary Political Ideologies*, 4th ed. (Homewood, Ill.: The Dorsey Press, 1978); and Roy C. Macridis, *Contemporary Political Ideologies: Movements and Regimes* (Cambridge, Mass.: Winthrop Publishers, 1980).

There are a number of philosophical books dealing with democratic theory. *Plato: Totalitarian or Democrat?* edited by Thomas L. Thorson (Englewood Cliffs, N.J.: Prentice-Hall, 1963) is a collection of essays on the question of whether Plato's philosophy was totalitarian or democratic in its implications. R. H. S. Crossman and Karl Popper view Plato as the ancestor of totalitarianism, while John Wild and John H. Hallowell see him as the ancestor of democracy. Henry B. Mayo, *An Introduction to Democratic Theory** (New York: Oxford University Press, 1960) develops a few basic principles necessary to the operation of a political system. They are popular control, elections, the franchise, political freedoms, and majority rule and its limits.

An unconventional vindication of democracy and criticism, of its traditional defense is made in Reinhold Niebuhr, *The Children of Light and the Children of Darkness* (New York: Charles Scribner's Sons, 1944). The "children of light" are those

*Available in paperback.

who believe that self-interest should be brought under the control of a higher law, whereas the "children of darkness" are the moral cynics who recognize no law above their self-interest. A dilemma known to professional students of politics is that of choosing between justifying political systems or being scientific. Thomas L. Thorson, *The Logic of Democracy** (New York: Holt, Rinehart and Winston, 1962) explores this problem and proposes a solution. Walter Lippmann, *The Public Philosophy* (Boston: Little, Brown, 1955) is an eloquent plea for a restoration of belief in the "public philosophy," an objective order based on natural law.

For a classic study of the optimism of the eighteenth century Enlightenment, which had great influence on political theory, see Carl L. Becker, *The Heavenly City of the Eighteenth Century Philosophers* (New Haven: Yale University Press, 1932). Louis Hartz, *The Liberal Tradition in America* (New York: Harcourt, Brace and World, 1955) is an excellent interpretation of American political thought since the Revolution, with emphasis on the liberal tradition.

*Available in paperback.

Part Two

The Input Agencies

Chapter Four

Formation of
Political Attitudes

Political life involves a constant interaction among institutions, individuals, values, ideology, and group activities. It includes attitudes, attitude formation, and many aspects of a country's culture. These help shape how institutions and processes operate. In this, the opening chapter to our discussion of input processes, we will look at the formation of political understanding and attitudes. Attitude formation is an important input in terms of helping to regulate how people view their political system and what they will be willing to do for it. Attitude formation is also an important output of the political process because it helps to determine what people will demand and expect from their political system. This fact encourages people everywhere to attempt to regulate and control the content and direction of political learning.

Each of us probably has asked where a particular person acquired his or her political ideas. Quite often we ask where they may have gotten their ''crazy'' ideas. In this chapter we will look at one answer to this question. Political culture—the political-social-economic-cultural-value milieu within which individuals and institutions operate—and political socialization—the process by which individuals learn to participate in or oppose their society—help explain the origin of many political values and behaviors. They illustrate the mechanism through which common values and orientations necessary to maintaining political-social cohesion operate, as well as offer clues as to why people in other nations or in previous eras have acted in ways we may consider incomprehensible or self-destructive. Fundamentally, we are what we consciously and unconsciously learn to be. Transferring a newborn infant from one cultural-political environment to another means he or she will learn a different language, religion, set of values, and expectations about politics. In asking ''why,'' we will examine factors influencing formation of political attitudes, values, and norms.

WHAT IS POLITICAL CULTURE?[1]

Culture refers to the widely shared rules, values, norms, cognitions, and ways of life of the members of a particular social group. This includes cognitive orientations, "basic premises and sets of assumptions."[2] Political culture is a specialized part or aspect of a whole culture, referring to the dominant or typical attitudes, values, and beliefs that are relevant to politics in any society. They include empirical beliefs about what actually is happening in a society, generalized beliefs about the goals and values of that society, and beliefs and values that may be relevant to politics, even though they are not specifically political. Common attitudes, values, and orientations include such things as what citizens typically expect from politics and the political economy; political and economic ideologies; how people habitually act politically, whether passively or as active participants; whether deferential or assertive behavior is common; and many other common behaviors and expectations. Thus people in each country tend to develop unique approaches to the inputs and outputs of their system; common feelings evolve, of trust or mistrust toward government and of support or hostility for political, social, and economic systems. Whether implicit or explicit, these widely shared styles, approaches, traditions, and stereotypes tend to be expressed in individual and group political thinking and behavior, helping to distinguish one system from another.[3]

This attitudinal environment, in which every political system operates, affects and sets limits to that system as much as actual political institutions. As noted by Sidney Verba, political culture affects and helps to determine people's interaction with other people: who talks to whom; what roles and attitudes of superiority or deference they may have; the nature of political processes; how formal institutions operate; how ideologies are interpreted in daily activities; and what the orientation of members of a political system is to the functioning and structure of that particular system.[4] Political culture provides clues to proper collective and individual behavior, as well as defining the content of specific roles and the relationship between roles. It can be a dynamic and changing concept if we emphasize mutual interaction and interdependence of values, factual knowledge, and everyday experience.

In a traditional political system, dominant values may indicate that the majority of people are unable or incompetent to participate in politics. Government may be

---

[1]This discussion of political culture draws heavily from Gabriel A. Almond and Sidney Verba, *The Civic Culture* (Princeton: Princeton University Press, 1963); George M. Foster, *Traditional Cultures and the Impact of Technological Change* (New York: Harper and Row, 1962); Lucian W. Pye and Sidney Verba, eds., *Political Culture and Political Development* (Princeton: Princeton University Press, 1965); James C. Scott, *Political Ideology in Malaysia: Reality and the Beliefs of an Elite* (New Haven: Yale University Press, 1968); and Donald J. Devine, *The Political Culture of the United States* (Boston: Little, Brown, 1972), pp. 1–32.

[2]Foster, *op. cit.*, p. 11; George M. Foster, "Peasant Society and the Image of Limited Good," in Jack M. Potter, May N. Diaz, and George M. Foster, eds., *Peasant Society: A Reader* (Boston: Little, Brown, 1967), pp. 300–323.

[3]Walter A. Rosenbaum, *Political Culture* (New York: Praeger, 1975) pp. 4–9.

[4]Pye and Verba, *op. cit.*, pp. 517–518.

treated as a mystery, understandable only by the high-born, the highly educated, or by initiates into an arcane philosophy or ideology. Society may be pyramidically or hierarchically organized—the major injunction is obey the law and be loyal; do not question, do not participate.

In a democratic system, dominant values may emphasize participation—the idea that common people are rational and intelligent enough to participate, that we can trust other citizens, that interest groups are legitimate, and that governors gain their privilege of governing and decision making only from the consent of the governed. Whether or not these values actually operate, they set limits to government and spell out relations between the governed and the governors that could not exist in traditional political cultures.

Obviously, attitudes affect politics. Where they are supported by political and economic institutions they can be conducive to stability. Where they clash with new or changing institutions, or where older values, such as the primacy of self-help, clash with new realities, such as an urbanized, industrialized, highly interdependent economy, psychic dislocation and civil strife will result.

People socialized to an older political culture, one that emphasized authority, obedience, and deference, as in pre-World War II Germany, or to local ties, limited opportunities, and stability of expectations, as in many developing countries, may find it difficult or impossible to cope with their new situation. Their familiar political culture may be gone or disappearing, and the new world confusing and alien. Orientation becomes difficult because the old behavior clues no longer refer to reality.

Since it refers to a set of understandings, values, and assumptions, political culture is not uniform between or within political systems. Diversity and even inconsistency are common. Political culture is the result or "product" of the history of any system, as well as the individual socialization of its members. While we may speak of a common political culture in any society, its interpretation and meaning will vary greatly, depending on the roles, socialization, and experiences of different groups. Subcultures and countercultures may develop. These are groups who have or develop substantially different social and political values from those that are dominant within their country. Differences of opinion and orientation are very common. Different political cultures distinguish the United States from Germany, and, to a more limited extent, eastern, white, elite values from southern, black, agricultural values.

Political culture and political socialization are related to each other. Political culture provides the environment within which socialization occurs. Political culture may be viewed as the "macro" level, the sum total of values, attitudes, and orientations that affect politics and political behavior. Political socialization may be viewed as the "micro," or individual, level "as the acquisition by an individual of the political culture which surrounds him."[5] Political culture and political socialization interact, with dominant political values largely determining the content of political socializa-

[5]Edward S. Greenberg, *Political Socialization* (New York: Atherton, 1970), p. 7.

tion, while the process of successful socialization helps maintain and transmit the political culture. When culture and socialization are similar, political stability usually results. Where they diverge and disagree, the likely result will be political instability unless there is widespread agreement on the desirability of changing dominant values.

WHAT IS POLITICAL SOCIALIZATION?

In the same way that political culture is a specialized part of culture, **political socialization** is a specialized part of socialization. Socialization refers to the total process of learning how to interact with other people and of developing our individual personalities. There is fairly widespread agreement on the components of a definition of political socialization, even though political scientists disagree about whether we should emphasize child learning, the content of what is learned, and/or adult learning about politics.

"Political socialization is the gradual learning of the norms, attitudes, and behavior accepted and practiced by the ongoing political system." Its goal "is to so train or develop individuals that they become well-functioning members of the political society," that is, a person "who accepts (internalizes) society's political norms and who will then transmit them to future generations."[6]

Or, "socialization refers to the process by which persons acquire the knowledge, skills, and dispositions that make them more or less able members of their society."[7]

Political socialization is a process of learning about politics. People are taught to participate or not to participate. They are taught what is proper behavior, how to interact with other people and with government. In modern developing systems people may be taught to focus their energies on national development. In democratic countries people may be taught they have a right, perhaps even a duty, to participate. In most political systems people are taught to disapprove of dissent. The essence of political socialization, therefore, involves learning, teaching, acceptance, and transmission of group values and norms.

As a working definition, we may consider political socialization as the continuing process by which people acquire motivations, information, norms, attitudes, and values about their society, economy, political system, and their role or place in these. People become members of their political system through political socialization. They learn what is expected of them and how to live and interact with society and the political system. The content of this learning is different from system to system, and even within the same political system, because of different experiences

---

[6]Roberta Sigel, Assumptions about the learning of political values. *Annals of the American Academy of Political and Social Science*, 361 (September, 1965), pp. 1–9.

[7]Orville G. Brim and Stanton Wheeler, *Socialization After Childhood* (New York: John Wiley, 1966), p. 3.

and milieus. Regardless of the content, however, political socialization refers to political learning, and that is where its importance lies. Throughout the rest of this chapter we will be concerned largely with the process of political socialization, which shows less variations within and across systems than does the content of political socialization.[8]

THE IMPORTANCE OF POLITICAL SOCIALIZATION

Today, as in the past, people fervently hold an almost infinite variety of political-social-economic beliefs. People have supported every system from emperor worship to anarchism, from total state control to complete laissez-faire, from systems based on slavery to those promising equality. These illustrate the way in which human beings may be shaped and molded, particularly when we emphasize fairly general characteristics and societal averages rather than individual attributes. This does not mean that an individual's personality can be shaped in any direction. It does mean that the institutional-value milieu within which people develop has an important input into their political-social-economic behavior and largely determines the nature of the values that are passed from generation to generation or, as the case often is, are modified in the process of transmission.

Political socialization is important because it permits us to carry on an organized social-political life. Without political socialization there could be no continuation of political life. The very concepts of government, the state, and society would cease to exist. Clearly this is inconceivable and impossible. Some political learning always will go on, simply because political learning is necessary to maintain any political system, no matter how simple or complex. By creating common values, assumptions, and loyalties, it enables us to develop stable expectations about the behavior of others and integrates us into whatever common enterprises society is engaged in by supplying us with understanding of our position and roles. The choice is simple. Either people agree on some common values and ways of running their political system, or the system will be based on force and coercion. Yet even force and coercion are ultimately based on agreement to use them, that is, on some value agreement.

Therefore, while we are not certain of the exact relation between learning and particular features and characteristics of political systems, it is clear that what people learn about politics ultimately affects community and regime characteristics. This fact has held out to many people the possibility that manipulation of the learning process may create a more desirable political system.

---

[8]For a discussion of some of the different ways political scientists view political socialization, see Fred Greenstein, A note on the ambiguity of 'political socialization:' Definitions, criticisms, and strategies of inquiry. *Journal of Politics*, 32 (November, 1970), pp. 969–978.

POLITICAL SOCIALIZATION IN POLITICAL THEORY

Political socialization is one of the oldest issues in political literature. The Greek philosopher Plato (427–347 B.C.), in his *Republic* and *Laws*, considered citizen training and education to be society's most important function. He proposed that everyone would have access to basic physical and mental training. This would be the first step in sorting people out to their different roles and activities. People who did not have the necessary intellectual equipment to master advanced education would be trained to accept unquestioningly the duties of citizenship. Internalization of citizen duties, loyalty, and acceptance of their social role as absolutely unchangeable and just, as well as physical remoteness from other sources of influence, guaranteed for Plato widespread acceptance of the values and ideas that produced a stable political system.

In addition to basic education, the most talented would be selected for further training and education. Their education, directed toward discovering and creating the guardians and **philosopher-king**, revolved around training the gifted few to understand and carry out what was necessary to achieve stability, justice, and congruence between society and what Plato considered to be the fundamental reality of the universe. Ultimately, good government depended upon this elite's understanding of the ideas or forms which Plato considered to be the basic reality behind the transitory nature of physical existence. This understanding, in the *Republic*, would give the philosopher an absolutely perfect claim to rule. Through the proper system of education, society literally could be made perfect. No other theorist has claimed more for either philosophy or education.

Other theorists emphasized education. Aristotle discussed the necessity of legislation that would insure that young men received the education necessary to fulfill their role as citizens, to be able to rule and be ruled in turn. The Italian Renaissance theorist Niccolo Machiavelli (1469–1527) argued that civic loyalty and civic virtue made Republican Rome great, and that a resurrection of civic loyalty, or devotion to the affairs of the state, could unite Italy, freeing it from foreign invaders. In *The Prince*, he indicated that the prince should attempt to create the kind of loyalty and sense of duty that would accomplish this. In his *Discourses* he presented models of civic devotion that he felt exemplified dedication to the state.

In the eighteenth century, Jean-Jacques Rousseau, in his *Consideration on the Government of Poland*, emphasized the need for training, which would make people willing to dedicate their lives to a strong united Poland. In his *Social Contract* the only possible way the "general will" could operate would be through citizens trained to accept and articulate the same values. Throughout the eighteenth, nineteenth, and twentieth centuries, theorists as diverse as Thomas Jefferson, Alexis de Tocqueville, Karl Marx, and John Dewey emphasized some form of education and civic training as prerequisites to citizen participation in their ideal political systems. Today, B. F. Skinner's *Walden Two* represents an extreme belief in socialization and the effects of psychological conditioning as means to produce a cooperative, well-adjusted person. Based more on faith than empirical analysis, Skinner's model culminates more than 2300 years of efforts to argue for an ideal political system through manipulation of the educational system or, in some cases, the entire learning process.

POLITICAL SOCIALIZATION AND POLITICAL LIFE

Control over political socialization is always a basic political issue. If philosophers have dreamed of manipulating education, power holders and social-political factions have attempted continuously to use education to achieve their ends or to perpetuate the values and institutions they upheld. Every political system that has existed anywhere, at any point in time, has been concerned with what kind of values and attitudes people were learning and, more importantly, how these affected behavior. In ancient Greece and Rome, although there was no formal educational system for the masses of people, the various governments were deeply concerned with controlling the population. Civic religions, games, and family training all contributed to maintaining political continuity. In the Middle Ages the Church helped teach peasants proper political deference through emphasis on religious sanctions. Thomas Jefferson proposed a system of universal primary education to insure a population sufficiently educated to participate in public affairs and create an American republic of liberty. Throughout the nineteenth century in Europe and North America political reformers and civic leaders emphasized the need for widespread popular education to improve the position of the newly created industrial working class, but fought bitterly over who would control the content of education.

Socialization is a political concern throughout the world, particularly during crisis periods or when old values and institutions appear to be weakened or in danger. Since World War II vocal and angry public debates have occurred in the United States, France, West Germany, Canada, the United Kingdom, and elsewhere over whether the educational system and mass media were inculcating values necessary for national survival. In the twentieth century, particularly in totalitarian states, or in response to their challenge, mass education has been consciously and systematically politicized. This is particularly true where the leadership attempts to control all social and cultural institutions, such as schools, clubs, and youth organizations. This enables the government to insure that children will receive the same message of dedication and loyalty to the regime, while countering the possibility that families will teach or inculcate antiregime values. Such education emphasizes the child's usefulness and duty to the country, rather than development of individual talents and potential as ends in themselves.

In the Soviet Union, Lenin and Stalin emphasized the absolute necessity of teachers' conforming to the regime's values. Starting with virtually no school facilities and a largely passive and illiterate population, Soviet leaders created an educational system designed both to train effective workers and develop loyal citizens. In

Disciplined North Korean schoolchildren march to President Kim Il Sung's birthplace in Pyongyang.

the process of creating an advanced educational system, they employed formal methods, such as teaching history and economics from their ideological perspective, and informal methods, such as emphasizing cooperation and the individual's duty to society, to instill loyalty and pride in the Soviet Union. In addition, Young Pioneer and Komsomal organizations provide out-of-school reinforcement.

Nazi Germany reveals a slightly different pattern.[9] When Hitler came to power in 1933 he did not need to create an efficient educational system; he only needed to take an advanced and sophisticated system and convert it into an active instrument of Nazi politics. The new Nazi government forbade Jews to teach and subjected teachers to vigorous indoctrination and observation to insure that they were politically reliable. Hitler demanded that German education be concerned with creating healthy, racially "pure" bodies; development of obedience to authority; and teaching of useful tasks. This was supplemented by strong doses of historical studies, which were to teach patriotism, love of country, and willingness to sacrifice for Germany. History was taught as a struggle, out of which a racially "pure" Germany was emerging.

[9]See George Frederick Kneller, *The Educational Philosophy of National Socialism* (New Haven: Yale University Press, 1941); William L. Shirer, *The Rise and Fall of the Third Reich* (New York: Simon and Schuster, 1960), pp. 248–256.

Based on prior socialization patterns, which emphasized obedience to authority, German education was centralized in the Ministry of Education, thereby ending state educational independence and a tradition of university autonomy. The entire educational curriculum was changed to reflect Nazi teaching. Exceptions were forbidden. Most teachers and students rapidly cooperated.

In the process, German education suffered a catastrophic decline. Between 1933 and 1939 the number of university students declined from 127,920 to 58,325.[10] The quality of education also suffered. Even before the war, scientists had begun to complain that new graduates were unfit for creative work. To Hitler, that did not matter, as long as they had the proper political attitudes.

Nonschool activities also were organized and centrally controlled. Organization of children started at age six in Hitler Youth. Modeled on traditional youth clubs and organizations, it was organized in 1925 to provide an auxiliary service to the Nazi

Young members of the Hitler Youth at a party rally in Nuremberg.

[10]Shirer, *op. cit.*, p. 252.

Party. After 1933, efforts were made to induce all youth to join, although it never achieved universal membership. At 18, young men went into the *Arbeitsdienst*, or Labor Service, for six months, where their political education was continued while they engaged in labor. All these organizations sought to socialize German youth to Nazi ideology and break down class barriers that could have prevented total dedication to Germany.

Following World War II the victorious Allies engaged in systematic "de-Nazification" programs, passing judgment on teacher certification, issuing new textbooks, and creating new youth groups, all aimed at resocializing German youth.

Without going to Nazi extremes, many leaders in developing countries emphasize education and new socialization patterns as keys to economic and social development. Given the strength of family, cultural, religious, ethnic, linguistic, and local groups in many developing countries common or nationwide patterns of loyalties, values, and expectations have not developed. This makes economic and social modernization difficult because people do not have the common images, trust, and patterns of interaction necessary to cooperate with each other. Instead, they often focus on the things that divide them. For the developing countries education has a doubly difficult task: it must provide the skills and motivations necessary to modernize economically and it must overcome the centrifugal forces of localism by providing value orientations that can produce national consciousness, common identity, and integration. In the absence of cohesion and widespread agreement on goals, leaders of developing countries seek control of socialization to achieve modernization.

POLITICAL SOCIALIZATION AND POLITICAL INDOCTRINATION

Students constantly challenge us to distinguish socialization from indoctrination. **Indoctrination** is a heavily value-laden word bound closely to our ideological expectations. It conjures up images of manipulation, control, and perhaps questionable purposes. Nevertheless, indoctrination occurs. Even though it is often difficult to distinguish socialization from indoctrination in specific cases, the distinction is important for the Western, liberal–democratic tradition.[11]

It is very easy to fall into the false belief that political socialization and civic education go on in systems we approve of, and indoctrination occurs in systems we disapprove of. Seriously, we may distinguish transmission of values, a neutral concept, from the content of values, which may have a heavy moral-normative content. Learning goes on in every system. In terms of Western, liberal-democratic values, political socialization involves more than learning common values. Ideally, it also

---

[11]This question cannot be answered in a completely value-free way. Some subjective elements must enter. Most, if not all, that people prefer doing is a result of past learning. No one ever has a completely free choice. There is always and perhaps inevitably some restraint on alternatives.

should emphasize individual development; flexibility; ability to respond to new and changing conditions; development of critical judgment, including analysis of accepted values and institutions; and the right to question values learned during socialization.

Conversely, indoctrination can be understood as teaching only what those in power want. It makes impossible the acquisition of alternative values and ideas. It forbids seeking of political-social-economic alternatives, emphasizes the absolute truth of one set of values to the exclusion of all others, demands uncritical acceptance of and dedication to a set of values prescribed by the group or government and includes injunctions that only one way of life is legitimate.

Given these criteria, no system is completely free of some elements of indoctrination. No matter how open the system, not all potential values are taught. As with so many other questions involving values or behavior, political socialization versus political indoctrination is not an either/or, yes/no question. Rather, it is a "more or less" question (see Figure 4-1). Societies may be ranked on a simple ordinal (ie., more or less) scale, depending on their relative openness and receptivity to criticism of accepted values. The difference between socialization and indoctrination is a matter of degree and purpose. We may argue that the more that conformity to a single standard is demanded, and as alternatives are forbidden, the more we are in a situation of indoctrination. The more critical awareness is emphasized and the tools and ideas necessary for critical analysis are developed, the more we are dealing with a situation of socialization. Still, some elements of indoctrination will be present in every system. Children do not have any choice as to what language they will speak, what religion they initially will follow, or what values their parents will support. No one can learn to think critically until she or he has learned to think, has developed analytic tools, and has some minimum facts. Even participation and aware-

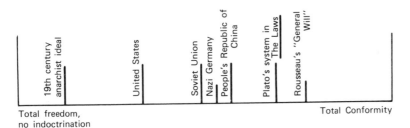

Total freedom,
no indoctrination

Total Conformity

Figure 1.　At the pole of total freedom there would be the danger that some values and information absolutely necessary to modern organized life would not be conveyed, such as, language, basic curbs on ego, ability to interact with other people, as well as simple conventions such as driving on the right side, rather than on the left side of the road, or stopping at a red traffic light rather than a green one. At the total conformity pole, children would be carbon copies of their parents, and there would be little or no intergenerational change. Neither pole is possible. (Note that distances are for illustrative purposes only and represent relative, not absolute, degrees of difference.)

ness are learned. In seeking our own answer to this perennial question, therefore, we must try to look at the purposes, tendencies, content, and orientation of the entire learning process.[12]

POLITICAL SOCIALIZATION: REFINING OUR DEFINITION

By now it is apparent that we favor a definition of political socialization that is wide enough to include all politically relevant learning. Political socialization has a number of facets or components. These refer to different aspects of the same process—learning about politics. First we may emphasize content and divide political socialization into "specifically political learning" and nonpolitical, but "politically relevant learning."[13] **Specifically political learning** refers to the acquisition of information, attitudes, and evaluations about politics. It includes learning about how the political system works, the structure of government and decision making, to whom the system responds, what roles individuals fill, what kinds of values are dominant, and so forth. Whether this learning is formal (as in schools) or informal (as from mass media) the important point is that this kind of learning is about politics.

Nonpolitical learning is also important, perhaps more important than specifically political learning. It refers to the political results or side effects, often unintended, of other learning. Through the political culture and formation of their personalities, people acquire attitudes and values which, while not specifically political in content, have an impact on how the political system functions and on their roles in the political system. In the family and at school, children learn attitudes and habitual responses to authority, order, and obedience which *may* have an impact on their political attitudes and the broader political system. In pre-World War II China and Japan children constantly were taught obedience to their parents and superiors, and this habit of obedience to authority figures may have transferred to military and political affairs. Adults who, as children, were encouraged to participate in family decisions tend to have a greater sense of personal worth and importance and tend to participate more in politics than adults from families that emphasized obedience to parental decisions and exclusion from family decision making. Attitudes toward sex, race, economics, and class, while not usually political in intent or content, condition people's involvement in politics. Attitudes that "politics is man's business" or attitudes of racial superiority are learned during childhood, usually informally, from parents and close associates, but they condition people's attitudes toward sex and race for the rest of their lives.

[12]For a discussion of indoctrination intended to develop unquestioning political loyalty, see Hoang Van Chi, "Political Indoctrination in North Vietnam," in Thomas J. Bellows, Stanley Erickson, and Herbert R. Winter, eds., *Political Science: Introductory Essays and Readings* (Belmont, Cal.: Duxbury Press, 1971), pp. 150–159.

[13]Fred J. Greenstein, *Children and Politics* (New Haven: Yale University Press, 1965), p. 12.

Identifying with a class or ethnic group and acquiring professional skills and social roles are not directly political but affect a person's understanding of and reaction to politics. If you add to this the high probability that personality—openness, adaptability, ability to cooperate, willingness to tolerate ambiguity, need for order, inflexibility, assumptions about progress, and so on—affects politics, and that basic personality patterns develop through our interaction with institutions and other people as we grow, it is easy to see the potential impact of nonpolitical learning on politics.

We also may distinguish **formal and informal political socialization**. They refer to the method by which people learn. Everyone is familiar with **formal** political socialization: deliberate efforts by schools, parents, groups, or government to teach information, values, and attitudes they feel may affect the political system. Content may be directly political, as when people are taught about political institutions and values; or it may be nonpolitical but politically relevant, as when people are taught obedience or cooperation. Typically, formal socialization takes place in a structured teacher–student situation. Reading patriotic literature and classroom history or civics instruction are the most common forms of formal political learning. In many states and countries, the law requires students to attend specific civics or history courses. While political scientists are uncertain of the exact impact of formal instruction, parents and governments constantly emphasize its importance to the continued existence of preferred values and institutions. If this formal learning is reinforced by other agents and experiences, it may have a profound impact on learning. Without agreement, formal learning may have a weak impact on personality and the political system.

Children and adults acquire a vast amount of political information and shape values and attitudes through **informal** learning situations. Much of our political and politically relevant learning occurs incidentally to other activities. Much of it is at the subconscious level, where information and attitudes are acquired in an unstructured forum. Children absorb attitudes and values from their parents without being aware of this. Casual remarks about other races or honesty in government; parental statements about honesty versus efforts to bribe a policeman instead of paying a fine; simple explanations about why a car cannot be parked in a particular area—all these help form a child's attitude toward government and his or her place in government. A black child does not need formal classroom instruction to discover discrimination. Women and racial minorities are taught the same formal values as dominant groups. Their lower rate of political participation and access to the professions is the result of informal socialization. Frequent demands for censorship, and the following discussion of television, illustrate a widespread appreciation of the impact of informal learning.

Thus, all of us are imbedded in an institutional-value milieu that constantly "teaches" us to accept or reject certain groups, ideas, or values. Even though political scientists have no precise way to measure this informal learning or its impact, it seems to have a profound impact on politics and attitudes toward political life.

A further distinction follows from what we have said—the differences among cognitive socialization, affective socialization, and evaluation judgments.[14] **Cognitive socialization** refers to "transmitting political knowledge and information."[15] This includes information about the formal structure of government, its officers and their roles and function, official values, the nature of political inputs and outputs, and information about accepted political behavior. Information may be acquired either formally or informally, but is specifically factual and political in content. Acquisition of information about the political system is of obvious importance because citizens could not know how to function without it. This knowledge, however, is often minimal. In the United States half of the 17-year-olds in a recent study did not know that presidential candidates are nominated at national party conventions, and 29 percent did not know the Supreme Court has the power to declare acts of Congress unconstitutional.[16]

Cognitive socialization alone is insufficient to explain political stability. While knowledge of how the system works is necessary, **affective socialization** helps explain feelings of loyalty, support, and affection for the system. Affective socialization refers to acceptance of commonly held values, feelings, and beliefs about the political system. People are taught to approve of and accept their political system. Patriotism, affection for the community, and respect for basic laws and institutions are taught in each country. Even before children acquire any understanding of their country's political system, they learn to have highly positive feelings toward it. In the United States:

> The child's early relationship to the country is highly positive although his conceptualization of it is vague. . . . This attachment develops despite a fragmentary and incomplete view of the nation and its government.[17]

This kind of development also appears in all other industrialized countries. Whether this teaching is formal or informal, it is more important to support for and the stability of the political system than cognitive socialization. Without feelings of support and affection, no system could survive for any extended period of time. This support and affection—or the lack of support—are taught in much the same way as factual information. As we will see below, families and schools are major agents teaching loyalty, affection, and support.

Evaluation judgments combine both factual information and values. They express judgments and opinions about the political system. Evaluation, or appraisal of

[14]Dean Jaros, *Socialization to Politics* (New York: Praeger, 1973), p. 9; Almond and Verba, *op. cit.,* p. 15. See also Lewis A. Froman, Jr., Learning political attitudes, *Western Political Quarterly,* 15 (1962), pp. 304–313.

[15]Jaros, *op. cit.,* p. 9.

[16]Review of a National Assessment of Educational Progress Report in *DEA News,* 2, Spring-Summer 1974, p. 6.

[17]Robert D. Hess and Judith V. Torney, *The Development of Political Attitudes in Children* (Chicago: Aldine, 1967), p. 26.

political phenomena based on moral criteria (good or bad) or empirical criteria (something is or is not working the way we agree it should work), is the essence of political judgment. Everyone constantly makes such judgments. Whether it is a question of personal conduct, such as extramarital sex, or political morality, such as calling a particular politician honest or crooked, we are expressing value judgments. These value judgments do not materialize out of thin air; rather, they are based on a set of acquired and developed assumptions about what is or is not proper conduct.

Regardless of the source of our value judgments, statements about proper political conduct condition people's responses to political events. They help to determine what people will consider legitimate or illegitimate. For a person who accepts the tenets of a free enterprise system, governmental control of major parts of the economy will be considered illegitimate. He or she probably would oppose a proposal that the federal government in the United States acquire control over steel mills. Differing value judgments and efforts to implement them provide much of the content of political conflict. They arise because people have been socialized to expect different conduct and actions from government. One of the purposes of indoctrination is to insure that people will make the same value judgments, and will approve uniformly of the conduct of their governments.

Finally, political socialization is not directed toward a simple, undifferentiated "thing," the political system. Political scientists distinguish among **community, regime**, and **government** or **authorities**.[18] Children first acquire affection for the country or larger political community. Such feelings change very slowly. Affection for and understanding of the regime—that is, the form and institutions of government—develops much later. Orientation to specific government authorities is the least stable. More importantly, a distinction among community, regime, and authority helps us to understand political stability in the midst of political disagreement. By being able to distinguish loyalty and affection toward the idea of maintaining a common community, values, and institutions from disagreements on specific issues or personalities, people are able to interact and disagree with each other without undermining the state or government. For example, during the Watergate crisis, politicians as different as Senator Barry Goldwater and Senator George McGovern could agree on the desirability of Richard Nixon's resignation (the individual) from the office of president (the regime) as a way of preserving that office and saving the nation (community) from a potentially divisive conflict. They were able to agree because of a common dedication to the regime and community, even though they disagree on most policy issues.

In short, socialization to community and/or regime provides the common stock of ideas and values that enable people in the same country to disagree over particular issues without resort to violence or civil war. Agreement on fundamental rules and institutions helps to account for the long-term stability of the United States and

[18]See especially, Jaros, *op. cit.*, pp. 33–50.

Great Britain. Where agreement is lacking, as in the question of the role of ethnic minorities, violence often results. In states where fundamental splits occur over whether there should be a single political community, as in Northern Ireland or Lebanon, socialization to different ethnic, religious, or national identities insures conflict and perpetuation of separate nationalisms. In the rare cases where several different groups and colonies joined together, as in the United States or Canada, it has been necessary to create a common community identification and to socialize people into accepting this identity.

POLITICAL SOCIALIZATION OF CHILDREN

By the time children enter high school they have acquired a vast amount of political and politically relevant information, ideas, and attitudes. Informal politically relevant learning may begin as early as age two or three, when children are forming their personalities and acquiring basic attitudes toward authority and rules. Ideas about law, justice, rules, government, and public roles develop long before children have any possibility of having an impact on politics. Childhood political learning is important because values, identification, loyalties, and attitudes acquired at a tender age may last through a person's life. They may condition a person's acceptance or rejection of institutions and values met in later life.

Logically there ought to be a link between childhood learning and adult attitudes and behavior; however, "the existing body of basic knowledge linking childhood experience and adult behavior is quite rudimentary."[19] We simply do not know the mechanism by which child socialization affects development of later policy orientations. At best we can say that child socialization has an as yet unspecified impact on later issue orientations, and probably has a basic, but not controlling, influence on adult attitudes and values. It appears that the earliest values we acquire, especially loyalty and attachment, are the most deeply rooted and long lasting. Children learn political and social values uncritically. They do not usually have the necessary experience to see alternatives. Much childhood politically relevant learning is unconscious, and people tend to take it for granted. Thus, we may not be completely aware of why we hold a belief. Many people dislike or fear people of other races, but when challenged to give reasons often find it difficult or impossible to articulate their feelings. Their race attitudes were learned, perhaps informally, uncritically, and unconsciously as children, and these early attitudes often have been reinforced, unquestioned, and unchallenged.

Moreover, early learning provides a framework for later learning. Early learning, or its lack, helps set foundations on which later learning may take place or build. Perhaps if we do not learn social cooperation as children, it would be difficult or impossible to learn it as adults. By a process called "psychologic," early learning also helps condition acceptance or rejection of later information and values. Most peo-

---

[19]Greenstein, *op. cit.*, p. 43. See also Donald D. Searing, et al., The structuring principle: Political socialization and belief systems, *American Political Science Review*, 67 (June 1973), pp. 415–432.

Mother and daughter at a Ku Klux Klan rally.

ple systematically, if unconsciously, screen the flow of information and stimuli to themselves. Already accepted attitudes and values help determine whether we will accept or reject new information. If new information agrees with what we already believe, we may pay attention to it. If it disagrees with what we believe, we tend either to ignore it or to make it conform to our beliefs. Thus, our earliest acquired values, images, and attitudes filter or reinterpret values, images, and attitudes that are incompatible with our basic core set of values and attitudes. As we will note later, people do not block out discordant messages forever but may change their beliefs and values when these no longer correspond with reality. Nevertheless, the values and attitudes each of us learned as children help set up a screening framework through which we view institutions, people, and values we meet in later life.

Childhood learning is important, but we must ask, what is its content? Specific content varies among political systems because political cultures vary. A child born in the People's Republic of China will be socialized to a set of duties and expectations about government different from those of a child in Canada or the United States.

Everywhere, childhood political socialization is a process of **mass socialization**; that is, it involves learning those common political attitudes, values, and behavior that are considered appropriate to the people of a particular political culture. This involves behavior that "may be performed by the overwhelming majority of people."[20] Appropriate behavior varies but always involves learning what will be expected from "typical" citizens. One country may emphasize a citizen's right, even duty, to participate in selecting leaders or influencing decisions, while another may emphasize the citizen's duty to labor ceaselessly to build a strong nation or reach an ideological goal. Socialization to special roles (such as political behavior appropriate to a certain profession) or to an incumbent role (a member of Congress or the school board) occurs later, usually during adulthood. Such socialization builds on, and often modifies, the mass socialization of childhood.

Political scientists have conducted more socialization studies in the United States than anywhere else. Although patterns of socialization are probably similar in most countries especially in moving from personification of government to acceptance of abstract concepts, we will speak mainly of the United States in the next few paragraphs.[21]

Initially, children probably conceive of their parents as all powerful. At about two years of age, they begin to become aware of a larger world outside their family and begin to realize this world impinges on their parents and themselves. By age four, children are becoming aware of authority, such as traffic lights and perhaps police officers. Children in the United States and Great Britain first become aware of larger political institutions by learning the names of a few prominent officials and initially identify government with these officials. Children idealize these officials, thinking they are benevolent and personally helpful. This idealistic assumption about the still-distant government encourages children to feel affection for the political system before they acquire information about it. Children also become aware of national symbols, such as the flag, Uncle Sam, or in Britain, the Queen, before they know what the country is. These symbols focus their affection on the country. Cynicism about politics and politicians does not develop until adolescence or adulthood.[22]

[20]Jaros, *op. cit.,* p. 27.

[21]This section on the United States is based on Greenstein, *op. cit.;* Jaros, *op. cit.;* and Hess and Torney, *op. cit.* See also Robert D. Hess and David Easton, The role of the elementary school in political socialization, *The School Review,* 70 (1962), pp. 257–265. See aslo Jack Dennis, Leon Lindberg, and Donald McCrone, Support for nation and government among English children, *British Journal of Political Science,* 1 (January 1971), pp. 25–48; and Barrie Stacey, *Political Socialization in Western Society* (New York: St. Martin's Press, 1977) pp. 10–23.

[22]For an argument that children's generally "highly positive views of politics may be a culturally bound phenomenon," see Dean Jaros et al., The malevolent leader: Political socialization in an American sub-culture, *American Poltical Science Review,* 62 (June 1968), pp. 564–575.

Pledging allegiance to the flag.

In the United States children are most familiar with the President, who serves to introduce them to the American political system. Up to grade four, they identify the national government almost exclusively with him. If aware of Congress at all, they tend to assume that members of Congress are the President's "helpers," and that it is wrong for them to oppose his policies. Though they do not understand who he is or what he does, they feel he is important, powerful, and personally interested in their welfare. They focus on his personal qualities, and only after age ten or so do they begin to distinguish the role of the President from the personal qualities of the man. Some political scientists speculate that the young child's high regard for the President is the result of feelings of vulnerability in a world over which children have no control. The President becomes a kind of distant protector. In the process they may transfer feelings about authority and helpfulness from the family to this distant political personage. The number of children who think the President makes the laws or runs the country decreases dramatically between the fourth and fifth grades. Children in the age group 9–13 make dramatic and rapid increases in knowledge about the political system's formal and institutional structure.

Similar development can be observed among English children as they mature (see Table 4–1). They also show a dramatic increase in understanding the role of the national legislature in making law as opposed to highly visible individuals such as the Queen or Prime Minister. In both countries this reflects a growing ability to

Table 4-1   The One Who Has Most to do with Making the Laws in Great Britain

	Age		
	8–10	11–13	14–17
Possible Chief Law-maker	(n = 140)	(n = 202)	(n = 190)
Parliament	14%	37%	59%
Prime Minister	18	16	8
Queen	44	11	3
Cabinet	5	19	21
Judges	12	4	2
Political parties	4	7	6
Don't know	4	5	2
Total	101	99	101

Source: Jack Dennis, Leon Lindberg, and Donald McCrone, Support for Nation and Government Among English Children. *British Journal of Political Science*, 1 (January 1971), 37.

think abstractly. Children develop the ability to understand government in terms of institutions instead of only individuals.

Acquisition of other attitudes and knowledge occurs at a later age. There may be an actual sequence. Initial development of political awareness is, as we have seen, first "attachment to the nation," followed by development of awareness of government officials and then attachment to them. This is followed by a child's awareness of the legal system, her or his relation to it, and a tendency to equate obeying the law with good citizenship. The child's awareness that citizens may have an impact on political decisions and that they, as individuals, may be in a position to influence public policy develops at a later age, generally after fifth or sixth grade.[23]

POLITICAL SOCIALIZATION OF ADULTS

Political socialization continues throughout our entire lives. The political information and values people learn as children, though important, are only part of an adult's necessary intellectual equipment. This is particularly true in modern, dynamic societies where institutions, values, and problems are changing constantly. In relatively stable societies, such as early medieval Europe or some isolated parts of the world today, childhood socialization may be sufficient training for many adult roles and attitudes. Since little in the environment changes, few changes become necessary in people's understanding of, and values about, the political system. Yet even here, the content of socialization changes at different stages of the life cycle. Adulthood may bring changes in status for which childhood socialization cannot prepare peo-

[23]Hess and Torney, *op. cit.*, p. 24ff.

ple. Even in simple societies, all of the skills necessary for handling adult roles cannot be learned during childhood.

Adult political learning is made necessary and is complicated by other important factors. Modern societies are typified by rapid and frequent socioeconomic change. The values and beliefs people learn in childhood may not refer to any existent reality 20 or 30 years later. In nineteenth-century Europe and North America, people born on farms often had to move into new and frightening urban industries because of changes brought about by the industrial revolution. Here they painfully had to learn new work habits, new patterns of interaction between employer and employee, new family and neighbor relations, and often new political behavior. **Future shock** refers to a phenomenon more than a century old but sums up the fact that information and values acquired during childhood may be inadequate to the new social, political, and economic realities of an altered world during adulthood.

Many other forces illustrate the need for continued adult socialization. Immigration from one country to another causes obvious environmental changes. Geographical mobility is a fact of life in most nations. Movement from one part of the country to another may place migrants in an entirely new social and political milieu. In the United States movement by a young professional from New York or Chicago to a small town in the Southeast or Midwest often involves movement from a socially permissive, politically liberal climate to one that tends toward political conservatism and conformity to dominant norms. Moreover, typical political participation may shift from interest-group activities to personalist politics, emphasizing who you know and manipulation of the political system from within. Simply because different behavior is expected, individuals may feel constrained to modify their behavior in order to function effectively in their new environment. Students entering college also meet a new environment and new stimuli. Typically, these operate to move them in the direction of political liberalism, social permissiveness, acquisition of new political information, and new ways of viewing the political processes.

Economic and social mobility, either upward or downward, may bring about similar changes in an individual's milieu. These changes also may require readjustment to new values, institutions, and ways of doing things. Quite often a process of "anticipatory socialization" occurs. In anticipatory socialization people consciously try to acquire and emulate the values and attitudes of people who are in the class or occupation into which they are moving. In the United States large increases in salary and movement into the suburbs often have foreshadowed a switch from the Democratic Party to either the Republican Party or an independent orientation.

ROLE SOCIALIZATION

So far we have discussed mass socialization. Acquisition of a specifically political role also entails new political learning. As noted in Chapter Two, role refers to a recognized and usually defined social position about which fairly specific performance expectations are made, regardless of who holds that role. Roles can be separated from the person holding a role, and one person may hold many roles. We expect a fire fighter to perform a primary role—putting out fires—regardless of who he or she is. Often, specific rules and a rigid organizational structure define a role, as in a bureaucracy. At other times general expectations, informal folkways, as well as some written rules, define a role, such as in a legislature. People may acquire a specifically political role when they become involved in politics beyond the activities expected of a "typical" or "average" citizen. Election to office, such as a school board, a local governing body, or Congress; lobbying and other direct involvement in interest group activities; and efforts to affect public policy through personal influence or public protest are all examples of role playing of one sort or another.

Every role, political or nonpolitical, has rules and expectations attached to it. Each role involves learning these basic rules and behavior patterns, which are different from behavior learned through mass socialization. A freshman member of Congress must learn informal Congressional procedures, approaches to other members, times to keep quiet, and how to function in a rather small group of proud individuals, if he or she is to have any chance of being effective. It is also possible that learning other nonpolitical adult roles—employer, employee, or parent—may affect political or politically relevant information and values. Such socialization occurs only when the individual is actually in a particular role. It is difficult to learn outside the role, and impossible that such role behavior could be learned during childhood.

AGENTS OF SOCIALIZATION

Numerous agents and events, as well as individual character, contribute to political socialization. There is no agreement about which agent is most important. The impact of different agents varies during an individual's life. Families are most important for young children, but peers become more influential during adolescence and adulthood. Importance also varies according to "the political and cultural milieu in which it operates."[24] In relatively simple, stable systems, the family may be the most important agent of socialization. In societies undergoing rapid change, where traditional or family values conflict with officially approved developmental values, schools may become the major socialization agents. In situations of extreme stress, a political party or religious group may become an important agent of resocialization. Mass media may become increasingly important in homogenizing socialization stimuli. These agents interact, producing a strong set of beliefs when they agree and confusion when they disagree.

[24]Kenneth P. Langton and David A. Karns, Political socialization and national development: Some hypotheses and data. *Western Political Quarterly*, 27 (June 1974), pp. 217–238.

Many people expect political socialization to cause political-social-economic- cultural change, as well as stability. This results in conscious efforts to modify socialization agents in a desired direction. Because so many agents are involved and the process of socialization is so complex, it may be difficult to change complicated phenomena such as race and sex attitudes by manipulating only one socialization agent. For example, introducing women's studies in universities will not eradicate sexism, since universities are neither dominant nor pervasive agents of socialization; removing violence from Saturday morning TV cartoons may have little influence in socializing children to nonviolence if they are exposed to it in other areas. Modification of all agents, particularly in a reasonably open, pluralistic society, is extremely difficult without either extensive voluntary compliance or force. Changing any one agent, therefore, may not produce desired results in the short run; moreover, an agent's influence is modified by different generational, class, sexual, or subcultural experiences.

THE FAMILY

For thousands of years students of politics considered the family the incubator of political man. They assumed that families provided the initial and longest lasting political-social education and that they therefore had to be concerned with family values as the first step toward their preferred political systems. Increasingly in the last two centuries other influences have competed with the family, introducing children to information, values, and ideas different from those inculcated within the family. In many instances this has created painful cross-pressures in which people are torn in different directions. A "generation gap" conflict over values may result from these cross-pressures. Nevertheless, the family is extremely important.

Our first political and politically relevant learning occurs within the family. Most of this learning is informal, unintentional, and often subconscious. Families initially provide everything necessary for a child to survive and grow—food, shelter, affection, and social interaction.[25] Because of this, families influence basic personality development and have great influence on acquisition of nonpolitical but politically relevant values. Children's basic personality orientation, such as capacity for trust and cooperation, receives its initial development within the family. Politically relevant ideas and values, such as proper conduct or orientation to authority, rules, and obedience, also develop within the family. Certain family characteristics, such as hierarchical, authoritarian family structure, may dispose people to obedience of authority figures and a tendency to tyrannize those they consider inferior.

Different family structures may encourage different kinds of expectations about the rest of the world; thus families that encourage child participation in family deci-

---

[25]James C. Davies, The family's role in political socialization. *Annals of the American Academy of Political and Social Science*, 361 (September 1965), pp. 10–19.

sions seem to encourage these children to participate in politics when they are adults. Children of politically active parents tend to be more active as adults. This is probably the result of children copying their parents, of transmission of some values to children, and of an enriched environment where awareness of political, social, and economic events is considered normal. Children whose parents deprecate political involvement or rarely discuss political, social, and economic events have few parental examples and less encouragement to participate themselves. Consequently, they tend as adults to be less involved in politics.

Families have a much smaller impact on specific issue positions.[26] A child's affection for the nation develops within the family. General attitudes toward other races also develop within the family. Adult political opinions on specific issues, however, have little measurable correlation with childhood experiences and learning. With the sole exception of party orientation or preference, parental attitudes have little or no direct influence on a child's later adult political opinions. In the United States, Great Britain, and probably in other countries with stable party systems, there is a high probability that if both parents prefer the same political party, the child will prefer the same party when he or she becomes an adult. Children in second and third grade "know" if they are Democrats or Republicans, Labourites or Conservatives, before they know what these labels refer to. Parents transfer their party preference for a number of reasons. In these countries parties tend to be stable over time and limited in number. As adult voters, children will face the same party choices as did their parents. Party identification is also simple. In most states it does not require any activity to be a party identifier; therefore, little conscious choice is involved. Schools do not teach preference for a particular party; in fact, they usually discourage it, so that the parents' preference is dominant during a child's formative years. Moreover, party preference, as with religious preference, becomes a part of a child's identity and milieu. As with so many things we accept uncritically, because learned informally or unconsciously, party preference is acquired before children develop the tools to distinguish different programs or purposes. Many other factors, such as adult experiences, affect party preference, but the family is the most important influence in this area.

None of these reasons operates for specific issue orientations. A child may not be aware of his or her parents' specific preferences on most public issues. In a dynamic society there are many rapidly changing issues, and parents and children may not be aware of them. Issues may be radically different from those experienced during childhood. One generation's experience with war and inflation may be different from an older generation's experiences with war and economic problems. Unlike the choice between two or three parties, there may be an almost infinite range of choices on policy issues. Moreover, many different forces—job, the mass media, friends—influence how we view issues and what information we receive

---

[26]See especially R. W. Connell, Political socialization in the American family: The evidence re-examined. *Public Opinion Quarterly*, 36 (Fall, 1972), pp. 323–333.

about issues. Therefore, while the family is extremely important in personality development, creation of politically relevant attitudes, and, in some countries, party identification, it has much less impact on development of particular issue preferences.

SCHOOLS

Though a great deal of informal and unconscious learning occurs in school, the school political socialization process is much more formal, conscious, and intentional than in the family. Schools are conscious societal instruments for transmission of desired values, information, and norms. In terms of helping people acquire necessary political-social tools, insuring intergenerational continuity, and providing a forum for value change, schools are among the most important socialization agents. They reinforce other agents while directly contributing to socialization. In adult life, level of education is highly correlated with political participation. In terms of transmitting political information and values and in developing politically relevant skills, schools have a greater impact than the family. They may serve to overcome some student differences that result from family differences by socializing children to a common citizenship behavior norm. By the time they reach high school, most children in Europe and North America have a fairly clear idea of the formal institutional structure of their political systems and of what citizen roles will be expected of them as adults.

The content of school political socialization is important. Cognitive socialization, toward understanding the formal structures of society, is very common. This includes how the system operates and who the major figures are. Schools emphasize voting as the main form of participation and civic duty. Young children tend to develop an image of a conflict-free political world. Given children's initial expectations about benevolent government, it is often difficult to make them understand political processes or the need for participation. Schools tend to ignore both the conflict attendant upon political decision making and alternative ways through which people make their influence felt, such as political parties, interest groups, and use of personal influence based on wealth or position. Potentially more forceful means of influence, such as organized dissent or resistance, usually are not considered. This tends to be true of schools in most countries. They emphasize social interaction, learning, and complying with rules and authority, and do not introduce critical and participatory norms until the upper grades, if at all.

Affective socialization is also an extremely important part of school. "The schools reinforce the early attachment of the child to the nation."[27] Particularly in the first five or six grades, they do this through patriotic rituals and songs, recitation of pledges of allegiance, emphasis on historical figures, and concentration on historically important buildings, as well as by placing children in an environment that emphasizes their relation to, dependence upon, and duty toward society and the political system. Schools do a much better job of transmitting such generalized atti-

[27]Hess and Torney, *op. cit.,* p. 105.

tudes as patriotism and mass citizen duties, for which there is general social support, than of transmitting attitudes about specific issues.

Given their importance, schools always have been major concerns of political systems. Though most western societies are dedicated to depoliticizing their schools, this occurs only when there is widespread agreement over the content of the political values schools are expected to teach. When that agreement breaks down, schools everywhere have become involved in political controversy. Schools were a major target for governmental control in Nazi Germany and, after World War II, for efforts to erase Nazism.

In the United States schools have again and again become centers of controversy over whether they were teaching proper American values. In the 1950s schools and teachers were subjected to harassment to "insure" that "communism" and "communists" were not influencing American children. In the 1950s and 1960s many white parents tried to form separate schools, to insure that their ideas about race and racial relations would be passed on to their children. The schools remained a battleground in the 1970s. Issues such as the busing of children to achieve racial balance illustrate the use to which schools may be put to achieve such social and political goals as equality. Demands for decentralization and for local control over school decision making reveal widespread appreciation of the impact of schools on value transmission. In 1974 and 1975, in Kanawha County, West Virginia, violence broke out over school textbooks. Many parents felt that approved books contained anti-Christian, anti-American, and obscene material. Concerned with maintaining their value system, many were willing to keep their children out of school rather than subject them to what they considered undesirable influences.

In many parts of the world schools have become battlegrounds, as linguistic, cultural, and religious groups seek to control and use them to maintain their special values or separate identities. Everywhere schools transmit information and values. Either to reinforce or change these values, parents and political leaders are concerned with the content of what schools teach, because that content will be an important factor in determining how the next generation will think, feel, and act.

PEER GROUPS

Peer groups refer to clusters of people with similar status and often similar interests. They are made up of people with close ties, persons who know and admire each other, such as close friends, colleagues, neighbors, small clubs, and informal associates. On an informal basis children and adults learn a great deal from their peers. Through frequent interaction they learn other people's values and ideas. Peer groups help people develop a sense of worth and are important in defining our personalities. Friends exchange ideas and information with each other, helping to shape their views of the outside world. Because people want to be liked, and if contact with a group is stable, people often modify their values and behavior to fit those of the people with whom they interact. This is especially true during adolescence, when contact with people of the same age probably shapes behavior more than any other factor.[28] If a person interacts with many different groups, he or she may not receive consistent reinforcement and therefore may not conform to the standards of one group. Peer-group contact is very important when there are generational conflicts or very different experiences between groups or generations. Peer groups then present the first and, in most cases, the most influential challenge to the values and attitudes taught in the family. Politically, peer-group contact is important if peer groups (Boy Scouts, Girl Scouts, and the like) reinforce dominant political-social values. It also becomes important when peer groups take on aspects of a subculture; members, especially the young, may develop alternative values or even life-styles. Much of the college-level opposition to American involvement in Southeast Asia in the 1960s and early 1970s grew out of extensive peer-group contact in an essentially age-group-isolated environment.

MASS MEDIA

Ever since the invention of printing opened the possibility of communicating a message to large numbers of people, the **mass media** have had an increasingly important impact on politics and political socialization. In the eighteenth and early nineteenth centuries the spread of cheap periodicals opened increasingly literate middle and working classes to influences from outside their immediate environments and helped make mass participation, as well as manipulation of the masses, possible. About the turn of this century movies made it possible to present complex visual images, and by the early 1920s radio made it possible to convey simultaneously the same message to millions. Today television makes it possible to present complex messages to tens of millions. In the United States children start to view television at about age two. In the primary grades children watch an average of 15 to 25 hours of television a week, with the number of hours tapering off in high school. By age 18 the average American child will have spent more hours watching television than in the classroom.[29] The important question is, what impact does this have?

We do not yet understand clearly television's impact on political socialization, and there is a great deal of controversy over this question. If television were completely controlled by government and presented a single-minded partisan message, measurement of television's impact would be relatively easy, but in most reasonably democratic states this is not the case. In Western countries television seems to have an impact largely in terms of informal learning, often subconscious, of politically relevant attitudes, rather than on acquisition of political information and values. This is true despite television's unequalled potential for influencing people through new information or through a presentation of different value systems. Nevertheless, television can have a direct impact on mass political socialization if it

[28]Richard E. Dawson et al., *Political Socialization* (Boston: Little, Brown, 1977), pp. 182–185.
[29]Robert M. Liebert et al., *The Early Window: Effects of Television on Children and Youth* (New York: Pergamon Press, 1973), pp. *x, xv,* 9.

presents a consistent message, particularly one that is at variance with messages from other agents. Increased cynicism and disillusionment among Americans may be attributable directly to the impact of seeing and hearing the Vietnam war and the Watergate scandals on television. Vietnam and Watergate helped to cause a significant decrease in support for the United States because of their revelation of practices so at odds with much of the value system implied in the American socialization process.

Much of television's impact is informal and indirect. This is illustrated by the ongoing argument over the effects of television violence on children. Children learn a great deal by observing adult behavior. Young children may not be able to distinguish fantasy from reality. Also, they are continually bombarded with examples of violence, pain, and injury. It becomes an important part of entertainment, raising the unanswered question of whether constant viewing of violence affects our emotions. More importantly, a constant diet of violence, particularly where it seems to teach that the "good guys" may use violence, deceit, torture, and clandestine activities to obtain their ends, may be breaking down the barriers to social and political violence. If television shows imply that it is legitimate to break laws, intervene in other states, and commit other crimes in order to maintain or get desired results, then they may be teaching a new generation that "might makes right."

Current research indicates that this, indeed, is happening. Television "does more than entertain us and our children; it communicates information about ourselves, others, and the world at large."[30] Information and images about social roles are very important, especially if these foster values inimical to political participation. In its early years television tended to perpetuate racial stereotypes by emphasizing white, middle-class professionals, though this is changing slowly as a result of pressure from civil rights groups who are concerned with white people's views of racial minorities and also with the self-image among members of minorities. Until quite recently television also perpetuated stereotypes of women and women's roles in society. Under pressure from such groups as NOW (National Organization for Women), stereotypes that portray women as passive and uninvolved are slowly disappearing. Nevertheless, many commercials continue to portray women as happy, but usually simple, even dumb, housewives. Women also are conspicuously absent from roles involving real intelligence. One also might ask if television ads perpetuate acquisitive values. Though not directly political, such values may have an impact on cooperation and willingness to be taxed for common social programs.

Television can have a positive and rewarding impact. It can teach cooperation as well as violence. It can open new worlds of information, experiences, and emotion. By bringing inflation, starvation, and war into our homes, it can make us aware of our finite world and increasing interdependence. All of these effects are potential. As with schools, much of the present controversy over television is over whose val-

---

[30]*Ibid.*, pp. 18–19 ff.

ues it will present. Whose picture of reality will be dominant? As with schools, that question involves more than temporary partisan advantage. It involves rival images of our future world because it contains disagreement over the values and information we want children to learn.

On a purely political level television's impact is hard to measure. The average voter has more information than at any time in history, but television has not encouraged a larger number of people to vote. Television has, however, changed our image of politics, and by changing our image may be changing what people learn to expect from politics. Television image building and the need to present complex issues quickly encourage simple alternatives. Television usually does not put a premium on careful analysis and explanation of long-standing problems. It also may change what we expect politicians to look like and do. The first Kennedy–Nixon televised debate in 1960 helped Kennedy, because many people concluded that he looked better and fresher.

Television also focuses on the more spectacular aspects of politics, such as national conventions, wars, and summit conferences, and obscures the day-to-day activities of regulatory agencies, local politics, interest groups, and compromise and consensus building that make government possible. This focus may encourage feelings of being a spectator only, while at the same time "teaching" some groups that the way to instant recognition is through an action that will get them national news coverage. Moreover, television may help to create new political demands by illustrating alternatives; portraying some kinds of political-social behavior while ignoring others; and by focusing on a few highly visible people, such as presidents and prime ministers, to the exclusion of the majority of people involved in government. Television's exact impact is unknown. It is changing our image of the world, however, and that makes it important to students of political socialization.

TRAUMA AND CHANGE[31]

Trauma and political-social-economic changes many disrupt people's lives, producing a gap between values and the institutions that embody and support them. Old values no longer seem to fit altered situations. New institutions or new practices seem to undermine or discredit long-established values. War, depression, revolution, immigration, and major changes in government have an impact on the world and people's image of it. Each of these may force a change in values and institutions. They affect political socialization by forcing changes in established attitudes or by introducing new content into the political socialization process. Other types of change are less obvious. Despite the most elaborate socialization processes, intergenerational change is common in active, vital societies. Each generation (which may be as short as five years in rapidly changing societies) experiences new events that condition its perception of the validity of older values and institutions or of

[31]See Jaros, *op. cit.*, p. 64 ff. See also Arthur H. Miller, Political issues and trust in government. *American Political Science Review*, 68 (September 1974), pp. 951–972.

whether institutions should be changed to conform to dominant values. Experience with economic hardship, especially at a fairly young age, may shift permanently people's loyalty to the party they perceive as eliminating that hardship. Such experience also may lead to emphasis on security from want, perhaps materialism, which a later generation, not knowing hunger, will decry. Experience in war may confirm one generation's belief in its political values, as in World War II. It may shake another generation's beliefs, as in Vietnam, because of the lack of congruence between "defense" of those values and war aims.

In the United States today many people seem to feel that the American system has somehow failed. Government lying about foreign policy; massive resistance to government over civil rights, by both civil rights' supporters and opponents; assassination; and discovery of domestic poverty disillusioned many people in the 1960s. Economic crises in the 1970s and early 1980s are undermining faith in every government and are providing new lessons about limitations and mutual interdependence. There repeated crises produce fear, disillusionment, and cynicism in people experiencing them. If these feelings or events are intense enough, as in revolution, they may cause a permanent change in political values and institutions and our socialization to these.

THE NONUNIFORMITY OF POLITICAL SOCIALIZATION

In distinguishing types of political socialization—mass socialization from role socialization, child socialization from adult socialization—and the different socialization agents, we have indicated that socialization is not a uniform process, even within the same political system. Even if the agents of socialization could operate uniformly on people, individual and environmental variations would produce different results. Despite many shared values, there are significant sources of variation in every political culture.

INDIVIDUAL DIFFERENCES

Individual characteristics help determine people's absorption of and response to the socialization process. People are not passive receivers; rather, they select, reject, and modify external stimuli. Personality is one such individual difference. We do not understand fully the complex relation between personality and behavior; nevertheless, people react differently to the same stimuli, and it becomes necessary to explain why, in terms of personality. Despite the fact that personality is formed through socialization, once developed, personality has an independent effect on political values, attitudes, and behavior. Different personalities lead people to perceive and respond to the world differently. A confident, open, and cooperative person may view politics as an opportunity and be able to participate easily. A more fearful, closed personality, seeking hierarchy, rigidity, and specific guidelines and rules for interpersonal activities, may feel threatened by an open political process. People who have been taught that they are significant are more likely to participate than are those who have been continually taught they are inferior or should only obey. Different personal needs also may determine people's responses, leading some to demand government protection, others to downgrade it.

Intelligence appears to be a very significant individual difference. Among American children, intelligence, in all social classes, accelerates acquisition of political information and attitudes. More intelligent children find it easier to conceive of politics as a system or set of institutions, rather than as people. This may be the result of a greater facility to abstract. Children with high intelligence appear to have a greater feeling of political efficacy and appear more willing to participate.[32] Greater intelligence may allow a person to see more opportunities for manipulation of politics, or lead to despair at the complexity of politics. It can encourage people to see their roles clearly, or can encourage antisocial feelings of superiority. Despite our inability to adequately define intelligence, it seems to be a significant variable in determining how people view the world and how they respond to it.

SEX, RACE AND CLASS

Sex[33]

Intelligence seems to be mainly an individual attribute affecting socialization. Sex and race, while individual, are socially defined. Attitudes toward sex and race are examples of generalized cultural values which, while not usually specifically political in content, affect the content of political socialization and the nature and direction of political participation. Everywhere, women participate less in politics than do men, even though this gap is closing in some Western countries under pressure from organized women's groups. Despite similar **formal** education and despite similar **formal** political values, women are subject to a variety of informal and often unconscious pressures that push them into politically nonactive roles. These pressures include widespread attitudes that assume women should be passive, have occupational roles that are not politically oriented, and beliefs that politics is a male prerogative. This, in turn, has tended to exclude women from politics by blocking their access to political roles.

Thus, the lower rate of participation by women can be explained only in terms of political culture. Men and women are socialized to expect lower participation from women and act to fulfill these expectations. Changes in attitudes held by men and women, as well as institutional changes to encourage greater participation, can reduce these differences.

---

[32]Hess and Torney, *op. cit.,* p. 128 ff.

[33]See Susan C. Bourque and Jean Grossholtz, Politics an unnatural practice: Political science looks at female participation. *Politics and Society,* 4 (Winter 1974), pp. 225–266.

Race

All of the available evidence indicates that different racial and ethnic groups in the same country develop dissimilar political attitudes and rates of participation due to their varied socialization experiences. Race affects politics and political socialization because attitudes among dominant racial and ethnic groups toward minorities affect socialization. Racial and ethnic identification develop early. In most countries racial and ethnic minorities often develop, or have imposed upon them, distinct views of the world and their place in it. Attitudes and values differ, because the real-life opportunities of racial and ethnic groups differ. Even if the formal socialization process is the same, children of different races in the same political system may learn different values and expectations because of informal learning and attitudes expressed outside the formal socialization process. This informal learning may be caused by dissimilar experiences with police and government, different treatment by dominant groups, different images of acceptable behavior and real opportunities from the mass media and peers, and even differences in the quality of schools.

As an example of differences caused by racial experience, take the fact that in the United States black children "tend to have lower feelings of political effectiveness than white children." They also "tend to have lower feelings of trust toward political leaders."[34] Similar variations are apparent among black and white adults.[35] Even when they are at the same economic level, black citizens participate less than do white citizens, particularly in terms of office holding. Studies of minorities in other countries would probably illustrate a similar situation. Such attitudes are due to differences in the political-social-economic environment in which minorities and majorities live.

CLASS AND OTHER GROUPS

Class membership varies in impact among different political cultures, though class differences everywhere affect the rate and direction of political participation, and different family patterns affect acquisition of politically relevant values. Socioeconomic class modifies and structures people's experience with law, police, and the political system; therefore, it affects their political learning. The same is true of membership in different subcultures. Many groups develop peculiar cultural patterns that distinguish them from the dominant political culture, even though they still share many values with it. Racial, class, cultural, linguistic, religious, regional and economic groups all may be subcultures. The thing they share in common, as distinct from the rest of society, affects their view of the larger society and how the larger society views them. This in turn may affect the nature and rate of value, information, and attitude formation/acquisition.

[34]Paul R. Abramson, *The Political Socialization of Black Americans* (New York: The Free Press, 1977), p. 3.
[35]*Ibid*, pp. 80–84.

SUMMARY

Political socialization is part of the ongoing political struggle and political processes in every society. Throughout history, governments and important groups have considered it too important to leave to chance. Political culture and political socialization help provide a common value system, common assumptions, and common attitudes about proper political behavior within specific political systems. In providing a common framework within which people of a particular political system can function, they make organized political life possible. Nevertheless, political culture and political socialization are not uniform within the political system. While they provide the common framework for political activity, important differences exist. Intergenerational changes, different agents, and different cultural patterns all work to make political socialization an uneven process. Even though political socialization tends toward maintenance of the status quo, enough variation occurs to insure political-social change. Whether this change is conscious or not, in our contemporary world political culture and political socialization are not static; rather, they are in a state of constant flux, affecting our perceptions of politics and the operations of every political system.

SELECTED READINGS

The opening chapter of Donald J. Devine, *The Political Culture of the United States: The Influence of Member Values on Regime Maintenance* (Boston: Little, Brown, 1972) is a superb introduction to the study of political culture. For a thorough discussion of political culture, see Chapter One of Gabriel A. Almond and Sidney Verba, *The Civic Culture* (Princeton: Princeton University Press, 1963). This book analyzes the interrelation between political culture and participation in the United States, Great Britain, Germany, Italy, and Mexico. Lucian W. Pye and Sidney Verba, eds., *Political Culture and Political Development* (Princeton: Princeton University Press, 1965) is both a summary of the concept of political culture and studies of the interrelation of political culture, development of national consciousness, and political development in 11 countries. Walter A. Rosenbaum, *Political Culture* (New York: Praeger, 1975) is a very readable and useful cross-cultural summary of political culture.

Dean Jaros, *Socialization to Politics* (New York: Praeger, 1973) is a basic introduction to political socialization, covering most of the topics in this chapter. Fred I. Greenstein, *Children and Politics* (New Haven: Yale University Press, 1965) is a basic study of the sources and content of childhood socialization in the United States. Pay particular attention to Chapter Four, which discusses the development of political information and attitudes. Richard E. Dawson, Kenneth Prewitt, and Karen S. Dawson, *Political Socialization** (Boston: Little, Brown, 1977) is an analysis

*Available in paperback.

of most of the topics discussed in this chapter, including political culture. This book is a good starting point for further reading. Roberta S. Sigel, *Learning About Politics: A Reader in Political Socialization* (New York: Random House, 1970) is a collection of articles and excerpts dealing with political socialization from a comparative perspective. Charles F. Andrain, *Children and Civic Awareness* (Columbus, Ohio: Charles E. Merrill, 1971) is an empirical study of fifth- through eighth-grade children's political values and information, set within a framework of how children learn about politics. Herbert H. Hyman, *Political Socialization** (New York, Free Press, 1959) is the first modern, full-scale treatment of political learning as a part of political science, summarizing research from other disciplines and concerns as relevant to political analysis. Edward S. Greenberg, ed., *Political Socialization* (New York: Atherton, 1970) is a collection of eight major readings, analyzing socialization in both dominant and subcultural settings in the United States. Greenberg's introduction critically discusses political socialization studies. "Political Socialization: Its Role in the Political Process" is the topic of the *Annals of the American Academy of Political and Social Science*, 361 (September 1965). This important issue includes discussions of the family, education, children's images of government, impact of socialization on personality, and black socialization. One of the most thorough studies into the sources, process, and content of childhood political socialization in the United States is Robert D. Hess and Judith V. Torney, *The Development of Political Attitudes in Children* (Chicago: Aldine, 1967). Based on a study of 12,000 grade-school children, this book examines both the development and content of basic political attitudes among American children.

Political socialization is part of the political process and is analyzed as such by David Easton and Jack Dennis, *Children in the Political System: Origins of Political Legitimacy* (New York: McGraw-Hill, 1969). Jack Dennis, ed., *Socialization to Politics: A Reader* (New York: John Wiley, 1973) is a collection of articles and excerpts covering most of the questions dealt with in this chapter. Kenneth P. Langton, *Political Socialization* (New York: Oxford University Press, 1969) is a cross-cultural analysis of the agents of political socialization. Richard W. Wilson, *Learning to Be Chinese: The Political Socialization of Children in Taiwan* (Cambridge, Mass.: MIT Press, 1970) analyzes childhood political socialization in Taiwan.

For a brief but insightful discussion of the criticisms and shortcomings of current political socialization research, see Fred I. Greenstein, "A Note on the Ambiguity of 'Political Socialization': Definitions, Criticisms, and Strategies of Inquiry," *Journal of Politics,* 32 (November 1970), pp. 969–978. Susan C. Bourque and Jean Grossholtz, "Politics an Unnatural Practice: Political Science Looks at Female Participation," *Politics and Society,* 4 (Winter 1974), pp. 225–266, is a critical analysis of the biases against women that the authors find in political socialization literature. Finding few differences in political attitudes between men and women, the authors call for a re-

*Available in paperback.

assessment and rejection of assumptions that explain differences in male–female political participation in terms of attitudes.

One of the most controversial political issues in socialization is the impact of television on children. For an excellent summary of research and findings on television's probable effects on American children, see Robert M. Liebert, John M. Neale, and Emily S. Davidson, *The Early Window: Effects of Television on Children and Youths* (New York: Pergamon Press, 1973). For a brief discussion, with specific policy recommendations, see "Violence in Television Entertainment Programs," Chapter 8 in National Commission on the Causes and Prevention of Violence, *To Establish Justice, To Insure Domestic Tranquility, Final Report* (Washington: U.S. Government Printing Office, 1969). *Television and Social Behavior*, 5 vols. of *A Technical Report to the Surgeon General's Scientific Advisory Committee on Television and Social Behavior* (Rockville, Md.: National Institute of Mental Health, 1972) extends beyond our discussion of political socialization but is a fundamental resource for studying television's impact.

The impact of socialization agents changes under different socioeconomic conditions. See Kenneth P. Langton and David A Karns, "Political Socialization and National Development: Some Hypotheses and Data," *Western Political Quarterly*, 27 (June 1974), pp. 217–238. Orville G. Brim, Jr., and Stanton Wheeler, *Socialization after Childhood: Two Essays* (New York: John Wiley, 1966), particularly in Part 1, emphasize that socialization continues throughout a person's life. This is especially true of role socialization in dynamic societies. The following two articles illustrate the need to distinguish between general attitudes and specific political beliefs in discussing socialization. R. W. Connell, "Political Socialization in the American Family: the Evidence Re-Examined," *Public Opinion Quarterly*, 36 (Fall, 1972), pp. 323–333, disputes the belief that the family is the most important socialization agent, claiming that the family, with the exception of political party preference, is "largely irrelevant to the formation of specific opinions" about politics. Donald D. Searing, Joel J. Schwartz, and Alden E. Lind, "The Structuring Principle: Political Socialization and Belief Systems," *American Political Science Review*, 67 (1973), pp. 415–432, claim that childhood orientations may not be associated with beliefs on specific political issues. Paul R. Abramson, *The Political Socialization of Black Americans* (New York: Free Press, 1977), critically reviews all of the available socialization research that examines feelings of political efficacy and political trust among black and white Americans.

*Available in paperback.

Chapter Five

Interest Groups

PLURALISM
In order to understand **interest groups** and their environment, we must review the concept of **pluralism**. We believe some form of pluralism is necessary if a political system is to facilitate the optimum level of human progress and freedom.

CHARACTERISTICS OF PLURALISM
Pluralism is defined as extensive participation in the political process through competing and autonomous groups and hence competing viewpoints. Citizens, though, continue to participate as individuals, as will be discussed. Pluralism recognizes that many, though not all, important political decisions are influenced most effectively by organized groups (interest groups) concerned with the political question at hand. Pluralism requires that there be various competing groups that are not government sponsored or manipulated. Most of all, the right to organize means freedom to oppose both individuals and policies and to support individuals seeking to replace incumbent office holders. The greatest proliferation of groups and the greatest freedom they possess are found in pluralistic societies.

In addition to a multiplicity of associations, there should be some multiple affiliations: "Individuals belong to several groups, no one group is inclusive of its members' lives."[1] In a pluralist system, often called a democracy, many groups have members with a variety of social characteristics (class, education, age, religion, ethnic, or racial identifications) and a majority of individuals will belong to more than one organization. The various organizations will serve different needs and will be independent of each other. No group will dominate a person's thinking. Multiple mem-

[1]William Kornhauser, *The Politics of Mass Society* (New York: The Free Press, 1959), p. 80.

berships will give the individual a variety of perspectives and sometimes even conflicting signals. It is hoped that the impact of various memberships will not be cumulative in a monolithic, doctrinaire way that gives the individual a rigid and closed view of the political world as, for example, the Communist who belongs to the Communist trade union, reads a Communist newspaper, and belongs to a social group whose members are all Communists.

One of the pioneer studies of pluralism and the importance of groups to a community was undertaken in the late 1930s in Newburyport, Massachusetts. One-third of the 357 associations studied in this city had members from 3 of the 6 social classes the authors had identified previously. Another third of the groups had members from 4 classes. Approximately 13,000 members were surveyed in conjunction with the study of the 357 associations. Almost two-thirds of these individuals belonged to associations in which 4 or more of the 6 classes were represented. More than 50 percent belonged to associations in which 2 or more of the 4 major religious faiths were represented. Pluralism, as in Newburyport, is based on a large number of organized groups.[2] This type of pluralism moderates political conflict. Associations composed of people with different religious, ethnic, and class characteristics prevent one line of social cleavage from becoming dominant in the organization. The actions of the group usually are moderated because the organization must respect the various identities of its members, lest it alienate any segment of its membership. This mixing of memberships and identifications is characteristic of a society where individuals have cross-cutting and often competing identifications.

Referring to Figure 5–1, note that we have used cross-cutting here in the sense of a grid. Vertical divisions in society, represented here by a vertical line, are principally inherited genetically or socially and include male–female, young–old, religion, language, and race. Vertical divisions generally do not involve a quantity, nor may the characteristics vary in the degree to which they are present. One is either Catholic or Methodist, a native Malay speaker or a native Chinese speaker. Horizontal divisions, represented here by horizontal lines, generally measure the degree of presence or absence of something, such as income (high or low) or education (grade school or university). An example of a person with cross-cutting identifications

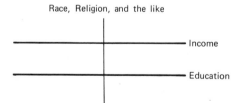

Figure 5–1.   Schematic of cross-cutting identifications.

[2]See W. Lloyd Warner and P. Lunt, *The Social Life of a Modern Community* (New Haven: Yale University Press, 1941), pp. 341, 346, and 349.

would be a high-school educated, wealthy businessman who follows a particular religion.

A cumulative or reinforcing set of traits not cross-cutting might typify a society where all members of a particular tribe or ethnic group are Muslims; almost all have a grade-school education or less and are living at the poverty level or below. Here each characteristic reinforces the other in such a way as to set apart the group from the rest of society. No identifications are shared with other groups. Interaction and tolerance among groups frequently break down. Barriers are erected that prevent accommodation of different needs and concerns of individuals and groups.

Pluralism presumes that the largest possible number of people will participate in the political input process through universal adult suffrage and interest-group activity. It also assumes that the widest range of alternative proposals will compete. Competition is subject to restriction only for those who call for deliberate violence, propose to drastically reduce participation, or substantially restrict the types of alternatives that can be proposed legally. One such example was the Nazi Party of Germany. The Nazis participated extensively and effectively in the competitive electoral system of Weimar Germany before forming the government in 1933. Yet the Nazis were dedicated to eliminating all political freedoms and all opposition parties and interest groups once they seized power. There is no absolute answer, but a realistic approach suggests that a pluralistic system must by some means restrict those who would participate in order to destroy the system.

Pluralism encourages individual action, such as voting, and collective action through group membership. These two types of participation are not necessarily contradictory or mutually exclusive. **Classical democratic theory** of the eighteenth and nineteenth centuries stressed individual responsibility and individual choice based on rational evaluation of all factors involved. This type of individual participation is still common in a pluralist system, as manifested in the private act of voting, writing a letter to a government department or a public official, or meeting with an elected official. The individual also may participate collectively through membership in and support of one or more interest groups. Commonly, this act of association with a group is a matter of individual choice; nevertheless, in a pluralist system, groups with an organized membership, monetary resources, administrative skills and contacts, and offices in the state, provincial, or national capitals are often the most successful in influencing policy. We live in a specialized, complex, and interdependent world. The most effective means by which an individual gains access to and influences decisions in the political system is frequently through the groups with which he is affiliated.

A recent and insightful study that addressed the concept of pluralism occurred in New Haven, Connecticut, in the late 1950s. This study was undertaken by political scientists at Yale University.[3] One of the conclusions of the study was that no single

---

[3]The first of several books to appear based on this study was Robert A. Dahl, *Who Governs? Democracy and Power in an American City* (New Haven: Yale University Press, 1961).

group dominates politics. Pluralism as it existed in New Haven, and was hypothesized as existing in the United States, identifies power with issues. Issues generally are transitory or semipermanent. Each issue provokes coalitions among different individuals and groups. Pluralism means limited participation in many situations because of specialized interest or limited time. When issues affecting a large number of people are involved, or when wide publicity is given the issue, wider participation is required. Nelson Polsby, who participated in the study, concluded that political decision makers were relatively free to deal with issues that were routine or minor. "Other kinds of decision-making—of a nonroutine, unbureaucratized, or innovative variety seem to require special consent by citizens who fall outside the small decision-making group."[4]

Pluralism sometimes means restricted participation, depending on the nature of the issue and the possibility of its becoming controversial. At times a broad popular mandate is required, as occurs at general elections or when questions such as city income tax or an amendment to the state constitution are decided as a referendum item on the ballot. Different groups and various numbers of people participate according to the issue, and no single group dominates most decisions. On critical issues, a broad consensus usually is sought from the general public. Specialization and limited participation in input are controlled by the need to maintain popular support.

Pluralists also usually support a division of power and a series of checks and balances so that no group, not even a popular majority, can exercise unrestrained power. Robert Dahl has summarized the basic principle of political pluralism as follows:

> Since even legal and constitutional arrangements will be subverted if some citizens or groups of citizens gain disproportionate opportunities for power in comparison with other citizens, the potential power of one citizen or group must be balanced by the potential power of other citizens.[5]

At the national level in the United States, for example, this balance and division of power was achieved by the Constitution: certain powers are denied to Congress (Article I); Congress is bicameral and legislation must be approved by both houses (Article I); the president can veto laws passed by Congress (Article II); the federal judiciary is largely independent of the president and Congress (Article III); and the national government is prohibited from undertaking certain acts, and rights are guaranteed to the citizens (Amendments 1 through 9).

Pluralism regards concentrations of power as dangerous, whether in government, large corporations, powerful trade unions, or landed estates. Pluralism sees

[4]Nelson W. Polsby, *Community Power and Political Theory* (New Haven: Yale University Press, 1963), p. 128.

[5]Robert A. Dahl, *Pluralist Democracy in the United States: Conflict and Consent* (Chicago: Rand McNally, 1967), p. 40.

countervailing centers of power as allowing broad inputs and checking the consolidation of private or public power. Competition and regulated conflict are accepted as inevitable. An important function of government is the maintenance of the rules of the game, in order to prevent undue accumulation of power in the private sector and to maintain individual freedoms. Interest groups not only should organize and express opinion and thus continually bear witness to the right of freedom of association, providing information to the public and government officials, but also act as a check on excessive amassing of power in the hands of government officials or in other interest groups.

Pluralism means negotiaticn and compromise. Decisions are reached more slowly and may not always be as logically consistent because of the need to accommodate diverse inputs. Multiple centers of power mean various groups may have the power to dilute, delay, or veto. Pluralistic politics is often consensual politics. Ideally, no affected group should be ignored in the solution, even if no group entirely realizes its objectives. Coalition building around specific issues and bargaining, negotiating, and accommodating diverse viewpoints are key aspects of pluralism. This process has been described at the national level of American politics as follows:

> The most conspicuous problem that American political parties face is to achieve a record of advocacy and accomplishment in public policy while harmonizing the interest of Presidential and Congressional wings. Legislative policy is approved or rejected by building a majority coalition through a process of bargaining and the proposal of objectives appealing to a wide variety of interests. With no central authority to dictate decisions, administrative politics requires the formation of coalitions among the many dispersed centers of power.[6]

The need to coalition build, whether between branches of government or within a multiparty legislature as in much of Western Europe, characterizes most pluralistic political systems.

CRITICISMS OF PLURALISM

Pluralism, as it has evolved in postindustrial political systems, has its critics, and objections have been raised to this type of political system. We now will discuss the six bases for these objections.

1.   Classical democratic theory emphasized the rational, informed, and thoughtful political participation of the individual. Pluralism, with its emphasis on political competition among groups, policy alternatives as advanced by various coalitions of group interests, and the resulting competition among leadership elites, implicitly rejects classical individual participation. It is charged that pluralists more generally consider the typical voter uninformed and only occasionally interested. Some con-

---

[6]Nelson W. Polsby and Aaron B. Wildavsky, *Presidential Elections*, 3rd ed. (New York: Charles Scribners Sons, 1971), p. 294.

tend that pluralists are overly concerned about "the role of demagogic leadership, mass psychology, group coercion, and the influence of those who control concentrated economic power;"[7] as a result, the individual's participatory capability is neglected. Meaningful political competition–participation is among elites. The masses exercise some power because of the right to vote among alternatives at regularly held elections. However, individual input at the mass level is limited.

   2.   Moreover, pluralism assumes that individuals identify with and belong to associations that advance individual as well as group interests. It anticipates that many individuals will belong to more than one interest group. Multiple memberships expose a person to various opinions and thus increase political information and political tolerance, but it is said that in actual practice group memberships may not be as extensive as often assumed.

   A cross-national survey by a Canadian sociologist asked the following question: "Are you a member of any organization now—trade or labor union, business organization, social group, professional or farm organization, cooperative, fraternal or veteran's group, athletic club, political, charitable, civic, or religious organization, or any other organized group?"[8] In the case of the United States, 57 percent belong to an organization and 32 percent belong to more than one association. Excluding union membership, 50 percent belong to one organization and 29 percent have multiple memberships. The figures for Canada were almost as high.

   Critics of pluralism point to the fact that more than 40 percent of the adult population in the United States and Canada has no organizational membership. Furthermore, those who do voluntarily belong are the better educated, the wealthier, and predominantly from the middle and upper classes. Group membership is even lower in most other democratic political systems. A significant strata of the population is thus on the periphery of a functioning pluralism.

   We might observe that if there is such a thing as a "perfect" pluralist political system, it comes closest to being realized in the United States and Canada. The sociologist who directed the cross-national membership survey described the United States and Canada as "nations of joiners."[9] Where memberships are voluntary in a political system, one cannot expect anything approximating 100 percent of the population belonging to one or more organizations.

   One point of comparison might be the level of group membership and voter participation in American presidential elections. Statistics for 1976 reveal that only 54 percent of the eligible adult population voted in the presidential race. Turnout among younger voters always has been low. Only about one-third of all citizens under 21 voted in 1976. We should, however, note that in many European countries, voter turnout is between 75 and 90 percent, despite the fact fewer Europeans be-

   [7]Jack L. Walker, A critique of the elitist theory of democracy, *The American Political Science Review*, 60:2, 1966, p. 285.
   [8]The results of the survey are analyzed in James Curtis, Voluntary association joining: A cross-national comparative note. *American Sociological Review*, 36, October 1971, pp. 872–880.
   [9]*Ibid.*, p. 875.

long to interest groups. One of the keystones of pluralism and also classical democratic theory is voluntary participation, which includes voting as well as interest-group membership. A political system that does not require participation must expect a measure of political uninterest or even apathy. Whether participation in groups and voting is high or low, and if this is caused by political pluralism, is a question still being studied. A person can, of course, still vote, write letters, go to see an elected official, or march in a demonstration, even if he or she does not hold any group membership.

3. Critics of pluralism also argue that interest-group competition dominates the political system and thereby restricts the input of individual citizens. Moreover, since many groups are dominated by the leaders, the average association member has little influence on the organization's policies. Robert Michels was the first modern scholar to conclude that the **iron law of oligarchy** was an inherent trait of organizations. Although Michels' analysis was of the German Social Democratic Party during the period before 1915, what he said subsequently has been used even more to criticize interest groups, alleging that whoever "says organization says oligarchy." Michels claimed that monopoly of organizations by the full-time professional staff was inevitable. Consequently, leaders' perspectives are no longer those of the members. A distinguished political scientist has summarized Michels' position concerning organization leadership as follows:

a. Superior knowledge, for example, they are privy to much information that can be used to secure assent for their program.
b. Control over the formal means of communication with the membership, for example, they dominate the organization press; as full-time salaried officials, they may travel from place to place presenting their case at the organization's expense; and their position enables them to command an audience.
c. Skill in the art of politics, for example, they are far more adept than nonprofessionals in making speeches, writing articles, and organizing group activities.
d. Those who become full-time officials of unions, political parties, or who serve as parliamentary representatives, "whilst belonging by social position to the class of the ruled, have in fact come to form part of the ruling oligarchy." That is to say, the leaders of the masses are themselves part of the "power elite," and develop perspectives and interests derived from their position among the more privileged elements.[10]

After summarizing Michels, the above political scientist then pointed out that the pessimistic, oligarchical, and unrepresentative structures described by Michels frequently have not come into being. More recent research reveals that many political parties and interest groups in the United States and Western Europe vary signifi-

[10]Seymour Martin Lipset, Introduction, in Robert Michels, *Political Parties*, Edan and Cedar Paul, trans. (New York: The Free Press, 1962), pp. 16–18.

cantly from the organizational structure described by Michels. Michel's forecast was "overdeterministic" and "the iron law of oligarchy" is not a universal phenomenon.[11]

A case study by Samuel Eldersveld of party organization in Wayne County, Michigan, discussed in the following chapter, reveals a fluid structure, where the leadership is heavily dependent on support from the membership. This is summarized as a **reciprocal deference system**, quite the opposite of the "iron law of oligarchy." Undoubtedly, some organizations are oligarchical; others are not. Additional data must be collected and analyzed before we can conclude that organizations have an inherent oligarchical nature that fundamentally undermines pluralism.

4.   Pluralism assumes checks and balances resulting from group conflict, with no group or coalition emerging permanently victorious. Critics claim that too often there is inequality of bargaining power among groups. Many times, well-led groups representing narrow interests have acquired much political expertise in achieving their goals. Their goals, such as higher oil prices, may be achieved at the expense of most other segments of the population. Related to this is the observation that producer groups, especially those producing essential products, even when the number of individuals involved is not large, achieve inordinate success under a pluralistic system. Consumer groups tend to be more amorphous, poorly organized, and less successful in the political system. The evidence is mixed, as will be described. The student who investigates this topic further will discover carefully analyzed examples on the several sides of the question.

5.   The issues to which interest groups address most of their efforts are often so technical as to discourage any popular participation or opposition by other interest groups, thus destroying the competition between groups so critical to pluralism. Benefits to be achieved are important to the group concerned but may imply no specific penalty on any particular group, except possibly the "public interest." One such example is the activities of the American Bus Association with reference to President Carter's energy program. The association has labored long and hard to provide aggregate tax credits of $1 billion between 1978 and 1983 for intercity buses in order to encourage energy saving. Opposition came principally from diverse groups opposed to losing tax revenue. Sometimes, even when simplified, the issue is unclear to the intelligent reader, as in the following case: "Dow Chemical Co., which generates some of its own electricity, circulated a proposal to give cogeneration equipment the same tax treatment that utilities would receive under the Administration's user plan, rather than the harsher treatment that industrial boilers would get."[12]

6.   The final argument advanced is more logical and deductive than replete with specific examples. It was advanced more than two decades ago, and occasionally

[11]*Ibid.*, pp. 27–33. See also Samuel Eldersveld, Chapter 1, in *Political Parties* (Chicago: Rand McNally, 1967).

[12]Richard Corrigan, "Lobbyists are Putting the Blitz on Carter's Energy Plan," *National Journal*, November 26, 1977, p. 1837.

has appeared in writing since that time. Simply stated, it is the "no government leadership" hypothesis, which maintains that the public interest, representing the essential concerns and needs of the whole political society, is neither articulated nor promoted in a pluralist system. Government does not advance specific **national interest** policies; rather, it plays an umpire role. As groups compete, government maintains the rules of the game in the political arena. The bargaining, negotiation, and compromises that ensue produce some benefits for the groups involved, but no group completely achieves its objectives. Equilibrium is a principal objective and government plays a key role in maintaining the dialogue, monitoring the competition, and finally, through laws and regulations, implementing the eventual compromises. Government is a responsive institution, which plays a regulative–balancing role. Government does not initiate policy or promote policies that will respond to a broad public interest beyond the narrower concerns of competing group interests.

PLURALISM: AN OVERVIEW

We have summarized the major criticisms of pluralism. They do not include all of the criticisms, nor does each critic include every major argument in an analysis of pluralism. We recognize that no series of political arrangements is beyond improvement. Pluralism is a form of democracy that has evolved; it was not constructed or deliberately planned. In no small measure it has emerged in the last two centuries as social and economic life became more specialized, complex, and interdependent. Undoubtedly, pluralism will continue to change. These changes may or may not be improvements. In the imperfect world we live in, however, we believe pluralism is a political form that makes possible organizational and individual freedom in the political system. It can be improved, but it has many virtues as it actually functions. It seems to be one means by which authoritarian politics can move toward more personal freedom and citizen input. A distinguished political scientist and proponent of pluralism, Robert A. Dahl, has observed how we must deal with the empirical political world we live in, not an ideal model that can never be realized.

Dahl first concludes that there are no students of modern politics who deny the proposition "that leaders do, as a matter of fact, have great weight in large, modern representative systems." Dahl goes on to state:

At the empirical level, experience with and systematic study of political life in cities and countries with democratic governments has turned up evidence that, if valid, raises interesting and important empirical questions. . . . This evidence seems to demonstrate rather conclusively, I think, that rates of participation vary widely, that a rather large fraction of adults participate in political life barely at all, and that a small proportion of adults participate a very great deal. Confronted by this evidence, political scientists have had either to reject it as factually false, which it is increasingly difficult to do, or to accept it provisionally as correct.[13]

[13]Robert A. Dahl, Further reflections on "The Elitist Theory of Democracy," *The American Political Science Review*, 60:2, June 1966, pp. 298–99.

Pluralism is not a utopian blueprint. It has evolved as societies became more specialized and interdependent. It exists today in fewer than 35 political systems. Pluralistic systems are concentrated in North America and Western Europe and scattered haphazardly in the rest of the world, for example, in Japan, Costa Rica, Sri Lanka, Singapore, Malaysia, Venezuela, and a few others. Part of the evolution of pluralism also has been in response to the rates of political participation described in the previous quote. Pluralism is an input process that potentially includes large numbers of people, despite the fact that many people in a democracy are only marginally interested in politics. In terms of interest-group politics, for better or worse, pluralism is the environment in which interest groups, free of government domination, function most effectively. Finally, like it or not, it is characteristic of most modern political systems commonly labeled "democratic."

INTEREST GROUPS

Most people are gregarious, at least in some of their activities. As society grows and people interact and depend on those beyond their immediate families, they tend to form groups to promote or protect their interests, and, as we discussed in the chapter on political theory, a principal reason democratic theorists believed organized government came into being was to protect and facilitate private interests. Much of politics, at least pluralistic politics, is about conflict, negotiation, and government decisions, which often represent a compromise. Many people get involved in politics for reasons of self-interest, or join groups they believe will watch out for their interests. A great deal of political participation is through membership in an organized group.

Robert Dahl of Yale University lists 20 institutional guarantees that are required if a democratic political system is to exist. The first "requirement" listed is the "freedom to form and join organizations."[14] In a major work published 15 years earlier, the same author noted that through groups (and other means) a democracy, which Dahl calls a polyarchy, extends "the number, size, and diversity of minorities whose preferences will influence the outcome of governmental decisions."[15]

A distinguished British political party specialist, R.T. McKenzie, observes that, in a pluralist system, interest groups, not political parties, **represent** the people by expressing their demands. Political parties "are teams of potential decision makers who offer themselves as prospective governors of the country between whom the voters have an opportunity to choose at a general election." Groups are the ever-present representing institutions. Once in office, elected officials must "contend with the *real* on-going expressions of group demands through the organized interests in the socieity."[16]

[14]Robert A. Dahl, *Polyarchy: Participation and Opposition* (New Haven: Yale University Press, 1971), p. 3.

[15]Robert A. Dahl, *A Preface to Democratic Theory* (Chicago: The University of Chicago Press, 1956), p. 133.

[16]R.T. McKenzie, "Political Parties Revisited," *Government and Opposition*, Vol. 12, No. 4 (Autumn, 1978), p. 528.

DEFINITION OF INTEREST GROUPS

An interest group is in most cases an advantage group; it is to an individual's advantage to join. It is an organized body that is supposed to look after the interests of its members. Interest groups are made up of people who share common traits, attitudes, beliefs, and/or objectives, and who organize to promote and protect these interests. Organized groups have by-laws, formal membership requirements, annual meetings, and elected officers; they provide information and other services to members and maintain a communication flow through such things as newsletters that include explanations of the organization's objectives and the efforts to achieve these objectives.

Although the terms interest groups and **pressure groups** often are used interchangeably, some political scientists do distinguish between the two. A pressure group is one that deliberately seeks to influence the public authorities. Some groups are organized specifically for this purpose, such as the Vietnam Veterans against the War or Concerned Citizens for Initiated Act X or for a state constitutional amendment (for example, a state-wide referendum on a state income tax). Others may be interest groups looking after the welfare of their members and only occasionally attempting to influence a public issue. One example would be the Automobile Association, which provides insurance, tour information, towing, repair services, and bail bonds; but may engage infrequently in political activity, such as opposing an increased gasoline tax or initiating legal action against a well-known and persistent speed-trap operation. We use the term interest group in this book because almost all such groups, at one time or another attempt to influence the public authorities on some issue. Interest groups attempt to influence government decisions and even support political candidates, they do not nominate candidates for public office. Moreover, most interest groups usually have narrower concerns, such as minimum wages, textile tariffs, gun control, milk supports, and the like, while political parties are concerned with all aspects of public policy, both domestic and international.

EVOLUTION OF INTEREST GROUPS

The twentieth century has witnessed a rapid increase in the number of interest groups. Two reasons are (1) functional specialization leading to the evolution of more specialized groups (such as the General Confederation of Beet-Growers in France and the Milk Producers Association in the United States), and (2) the fact that governments throughout the world are taking on more and more activities and responsibilities.

As the number of people allowed to participate legally (usually through enfranchisement) in politics increased and the scope of government activities expanded throughout society, it was natural that organizations would be created to respond to the new conditions. Interest groups developed as one instrument of mass political behavior in "urbanizing-industrializing-democratizing" societies. They also are found in many developing countries. Regardless of the stage of industrialization-urbanization, the emergence of masses of people in different types of politically relevant behavior has brought forth corresponding organizations. Organized interest groups also are called **secondary associations**, to distinguish them from primary, face-to-face associations, such as family, schoolmates, or fraternity or sorority.

Private groups now have much more to gain or lose as a result of government policies. In an effort to influence government decisions, a group is increasingly likely to encounter other organized interests with conflicting objectives, and this leads to greater activity. Government is more pervasive and is more likely to affect the private lives of persons than it was 30 or 50 years ago. In a superior study of the British Medical Association, Harry Eckstein found the growth of government an important reason for political activity by the BMA:

> The state of Britain today [1950s and 1960s] disposes directly of 40 percent of the national income; and that fact speaks for itself. We may regard political and actual groups ... drawn into politics chiefly through the impact of public policies, either policies actually adopted or policies which are "threatened" [by government].[17]

As a society becomes more economically differentiated, groups emerge to organize and represent these specialized producer interests. When one interest group begins to make claims on government, new groups are organized, or existing groups take on new tasks to counter these claims and increase their bargaining power and protect their clientele.

For example, with the energy crunch has come increased use of coal. A slurry pipeline has been proposed to move coal more quickly and cheaply from southern Illinois and Indiana to several southern states. Some estimates say such a pipeline would save utility customers in Georgia and Florida $15 billion in 20 years. The railroads, who now move 80 percent of the coal, vigorously oppose slurry pipelines and will not allow them to cross railroad right of ways. Slurry pipeline companies do not have the right to condemn land through eminent domain proceedings, as do railroads and utilities, for their transportation lines. The Slurry Transport Association is locked in battle with the Association of American Railroads before Congress and several state legislatures to secure eminent domain rights. Only Florida has approved eminent domain, but under railroad pressure, it adopted an amendment permitting the bill to take effect only after all other states along the proposed route pass similar legislation.[18]

Moreover, interest groups also cross national boundaries and are active in areas where there was no activity before. One astute observer of the respective attempts of Morocco and Algeria to secure American backing in the violent struggle of each to control a contested portion of the Maghreb desert notes: "The lobbyist firm hired to improve the Moroccan image in Washington has trouble competing with the skill-

---

[17]Harry Eckstein, *Pressure Group Politics: The Case of the British Medical Association* (Stanford: Stanford University Press, 1960), p. 27.

[18]For discussion of this clash between interest groups, see Peter N. Spotts, "Pumping Coal: New Energy Muscle for America," *Christian Science Monitor*, November 20, 1979.

ful maneuverings of Washington lawyer Clark Clifford (a former Secretary of Defense), the high-powered advocate of Algeria."[19]

Self-interest obviously leads to the formation of interest groups. Self-interest as first cause has been described in a general, summarized "exchange theory of interest groups," as developed by Robert Salisbury. All groups originally are based on a distinction between the **entrepreneur**, or organizer, and the individual member, or customer. People belong because they receive some benefits. The important fact about this explanation is that it provides specific examples of why formal associations are created by the entrepreneur organizer.[20]

The first broadly successful American farm organization was the Grange, followed by such associations as the Farm Bureau and the Farmers Union. The Grange was originally a lodge, with a secret ritual for both the farmer and his wife. One of its chief objectives was to foster scientific farming at lectures and discussion sessions. Within three years of its founding in 1867, the Grange was spearheading the fight to get state legislatures to regulate railroads, especially setting the maximum shipping rates railroads could charge. The Grange movement also was active in establishing cooperative stores, elevators, creameries, and so on.

Salisbury emphasized the creative and innovative role of the entrepreneur organizer, who offers future customers (potential members) benefits if they join the organization. When customers "buy" by joining, the group is in business. Organizations are created by leaders who develop a package of advantages that benefit both the leader and the member, and the organization takes shape and grows. This theory emphasizes the roles of specific individuals (entrepreneurs), whose efforts bring about the first visable signs of a new interest group. The student should not, of course, overlook the particular environment that allows certain types of organized responses, such as the poor conditions of the farms in nineteenth-century America, nor should the Constitutional freedom to organize be overlooked.

> The Grange was launched by Oliver Hudson Kelly who, by dint of considerable personal sacrifice and some generous friends, managed to survive until his organizational dream had begun to take hold. Similarly, Newton Gresham, having failed as a newspaper publisher, fed his family on credit and neighbors' largesse for more than a year until his Farmers Union began to attract enough dues-paying members to sustain him.[21]

Organizations then generally survive if members have the funds to invest. Members are compensated when benefits received exceed costs. There emerges a "cyclical pattern of group membership," which is dependent on a member's willingness to commit time, interest, and especially money. In prosperous times organiza-

[19]Davis Humphrey, "Myopia on Morocco," *Christian Science Monitor*, October 23, 1979.

[20]The material on the exchange theory is drawn from Robert Salisbury, who explains the origin and continuation of interest groups in terms of benefits and costs. Most of his examples are drawn from the history of farm organizations. See his An exchange theory of interest groups, *Midwest Journal of Political Science*, 13:1, 1969, pp. 1–32.

[21]*Ibid.*, pp. 12–13.

tions grow because members and potential members have dues money to invest. In hard times, despite the fact that the organization may represent fundamental needs under adverse circumstances, membership declines because there is so little money available for dues. During the Depression of the 1930s farm membership dropped, but during the prosperous decade, between 1940 and 1950, "The three main general farm organizations, the Grange, the Farmers Union and the Farm Bureau went from a combined total of 866,224 family memberships to 2,108,849."[22]

Interest groups emerge and grow for a variety of reasons. These are usually a combination of factors including social, economic, and political conditions interacting with the motivations and abilities of individuals who initiate the organizations.

TYPES OF INTEREST GROUPS

We will discuss three interest-group typologies so that students can be aware of some of the different ways interest groups are classified and analyzed.

Classification by Type and Scope

One method of classifying groups is according to the type and scope of interests they speak for. The most common is the **restrictive interest group**, which speaks principally for the specific interests of its members: The National Rifle Association, Real Estate Brokers Association, and the State Cattlemen's Association are examples of this. However, numerous interest groups, among them the AFL-CIO and the National Association of Manufacturers, have come to take public positions on matters of general concern, such as foreign aid, the United Nations, and civil rights. These groups can be classified as permanent, **multi-issue interest groups** that promote the specific self-interests of members as well as broader interests they believe will benefit not only their members but most of society. Another fairly common phenomenon on the political scene is the **single-issue group** that emerges in response to a controversial public question. Often, ad hoc groups will organize to support or oppose specific bond issues or urban renewal projects. Others are of a more permanent nature. They have had their greatest growth in the United States but are expanding rapidly in most postindustrial societies. These single-cause groups are devoted uncompromisingly to supporting or opposing such causes as abortion, women's rights, tax reduction, and nuclear power plants, and are currently a growing force on the American political scene.

Many interest groups, however, are not organized to represent the specific functional or material interests of the membership. These are **promotional** or principle **groups**. In fact, a sizable number of these groups—such as the American Civil Liberties Union, Common Cause, the League of Women Voters, or the British Royal Society for the Prevention of Cruelty to Children—are supporting continuously posi-

[22]*Ibid.*, p. 9.

tions they believe will improve society in general or in a specific area. These groups are not organized primarily to promote the special positions of their members.

Almond's Fourfold Classification

Gabriel Almond's fourfold classification of interest groups is based on the style or method of interest articulation, "the process by which individuals and groups make demands upon the political decision makers."[23] Almond lists four types of interest groups.

1. **Anomic** interest groups are spontaneous, immediate-action oriented. Riots, demonstrations, strikes, and the early stages of a revolution are characteristic of their tactics. They often are alienated, and spontaneously respond to a precipitant, whether it is a speaker or the arrest of an individual. Many of the 1978 Iranian demonstrations against the Shah were anomic, at least in the initial stages.

2. **Nonassociational** interest groups are categoric groups, people who share one or more characteristics in common but are not formally organized as such. Examples of these include ethnic or racial, kinship, geographic location, social class (landowners), religion, sex, and age groups. These groups are represented informally and intermittently through village or family heads, individual representatives, or cliques. An unofficial spokesperson for a group of manufacturers in a developing country who export a large percentage of their products may complain to the ministry of foreign trade that the government is not providing enough assistance in finding new markets or is not underwriting the travel expenses required to attend trade fairs. A group of local religious leaders may ask a town official to help build or maintain a mosque, church, or religious school.

3. **Institutional interest groups** originally came into being to perform functions other than interest articulation. Presumably these groups were the agents of the policy makers and it was not intended that they spend part of their energy advancing their own interests. Examples include the army, bureaucracy, schools, and church. These groups have certain advantages, among them a professionally staffed organization with a longer history than most other groups in society. Because of the important functions these groups perform (national security, administration, education), many of them traditionally have been close to the centers of power. These groups commonly are assumed to dominate interest articulation in the developing world. Frequently it is believed that the interests skillfully articulated by institutional interest groups are narrowly self-serving and serve primarily to enhance the position of one segment of an already too-powerful oligarchy.

Two qualifications should be made: (a) there are innumerable institutional interest groups in developed political systems; the American state university that lobbies for

[23]For the most elaborate discussion of interest articulation, see Gabriel A. Almond and G. Bingham Powell, Jr., *Comparative Politics: System, Process, and Policy*, 2nd. ed. (Boston: Little, Brown, 1978), Chapter VII.

increased appropriations from the state legislature is one example and (b) institutional interest groups also may speak for other groups in society. In developing political systems they may be the only ones with the expertise and access to make claims effectively. Elements of the church, bureaucracy, or the military may speak for social and economic development of certain regions of the country or for land reform.

In recent years, segments of the Catholic Church in the Philippines and several Latin American countries have spoken out forcefully for economic justice and the end of political oppression. The military in Brazil, an institutional interest group that has become the government, represents different points of view. (Both the church and the military are characterized by diverse viewpoints within each group.) Since 1964, the military has dominated the Brazilian political system. Within the military there are three basic groups striving to direct policy: (a) On one side is the hard-line group, mostly young colonels, who believe that the civilian leadership is hopelessly corrupt and lacks direction. They desire a disciplined effort to industrialize, which brings them into conflict with the big landowners of the rural, frontier northeast. (b) At the other end of the continuum is the soft-line group, which seeks to clean up the system and have the military progressively return to the barracks. They oppose the harsh policies of the hard-liners. (c) In the middle are officers associated with the War College, who believe not all problems can be solved by the military. They turn to the highly educated technocrats to deal with such social and economic problems as inflation and industrialization. The result is a "two-Brazils" approach. The frontier, the resource-rich northeast now being developed, is run by the military in a tough, arbitrary manner; it is a garrison state where opposition is not tolerated. In the southern, urbanized, industrialized, developed Brazil, the military has moved more cautiously, and there is some effort to work with various groups who do not openly oppose army rule.[24]

4. Associational interest groups are specialized organizations who have interest articulation as a principal function. They are characteristic of political systems in which some degree of autonomous input is permitted. These groups are well-organized, with a full-time professional staff who have regular procedures for influencing public policy. Examples include trade unions, farm organizations, business associations, professional groups such as the American Medical Association, and promotional groups discussed previously, like Common Cause.

Classification According to Benefits
A third interest group typology categorizes groups according to three principal benefits members perceive themselves receiving from the organization.[25] The first is

---

[24]For background see Jordon M. Young, "Brazil," in Ben G. Burnett and Kenneth F. Johnson, eds., *Political Forces in Latin America*, 2nd ed. (Belmont Ca.: Wadsworth Publishing, 1970).

[25]This approach to interest groups is rather common and is summarized in Salisbury, *op. cit.,* pp. 16–22.

material benefits, which are tangible—personal rewards such as higher wages, an industrial park that will increase the general business volume in the community, or higher prices for the farmer. The second is **solidarity values**, in which psychological, nonmaterial needs are realized. These would include such needs as affiliation, social interaction, sense of group identification and belonging, status, fun, and congeniality. The third is **purposive benefits**, which are usually suprapersonal and are not confined to the persons promoting these objectives. Examples would be to save the environment, oppose the spread of nuclear power plants, promote freedom of expression or civil rights, oppose increased defense spending, and encourage patriotism and national loyalty. The expression and support of these values is often personally satisfying. Benefits that result accrue to large numbers of people who have not joined the organization or may not even be aware a group exists promoting an objective.

Individuals may belong to an organization and in the process receive more than one type of benefit, or one person may perceive one type of benefit while another person perceives a different benefit. The benefits to members also may change over the years. Veterans' organizations are one example of such variations in benefits. The late V. O. Key concluded that "every war has been followed by the establishment of a society of veterans to bring pressure for the creation of conduits from the Federal Treasury to the pockets of the veterans."[26] One of the most successful veterans' organizations in the United States, founded at the end of World War I, is the American Legion, which has nearly 3 million members. The Legion and other veterans' groups have been highly successful in securing such material benefits as bonuses, medical care, educational allowances, and the veterans' 10-point test preference when applying for federal jobs. As these benefits have been secured, solidarity values have become more relevant. For many veterans and their families the American Legion building is a center of social and recreational activities. Purposive benefits are also an aspect of veterans' organizations. Various patriotic contests are held and awards made to high-school students and others. In 1921 the Legion was a founding sponsor, with the National Education Association, of American Education Week (now also cosponsored by the Department of Education and the National Congress of Parents and Teachers). During American Education week, programs are undertaken that alert communities to the achievements and needs of the local schools. A strong America and loyalty to it are important objectives of most veterans' groups. The material benefits were emphasized initially, after major wars when millions of new veterans returned home. The other benefits became more important as material objectives were achieved. Although no survey has been taken, we may assume that veterans belong for different reasons. Some may be most interested in the social benefits, while others may believe membership is the most ef-

[26]V. O. Key, Jr., *Politics, Parties, and Pressure Groups*, 5th ed. (New York: Thomas Y. Crowell, 1974), p. 106.

fective way to identify with and support educational and patriotic goals. The delivery of benefits may change over the years as well as the fact that different benefits are seen as important by different individuals at a given moment in time.

FUNCTIONS OF INTEREST GROUPS

The first, if not always obvious political function of an interest group is to influence public policy in an effort to provide benefits to its members. In so doing, it helps to communicate popular feelings and demands to the government. Where a competitive party system exists, part of an interest group's political effort is devoted to influencing one or more of the political parties. A political party in turn attempts to reconcile as many conflicting interests as the party judges ideologically acceptable or practical in order to win electoral support. Interest groups lobby or seek to persuade public officials, including bureaucrats, and they often contribute time, money, and people to support political candidates (electioneering). Many interest groups also function as a source of information to bureaucrats and lawmakers. This information generally must be "straight" and not obviously and systematically manipulated if a group is to build up and retain trust and prestige.

Decentralized parties, such as those found in the United States, Japan, sometimes in France, and in several Latin American countries, leave candidates susceptible to interest-group demands at election time. In such parties, candidates often rely on the support of various groups to finance and man the election campaign. Representatives in the legislature carry obligations to interest groups, which must be paid off eventually. These obligations further reduce party cohesion and discipline in a legislature. The most striking example is the United States, where Congress often appears as an every-man-for-himself scramble. Members of Congress vote first of all to satisfy district or parochial interests and concentrate on providing local services to constituents. There is little reason to stress party identification or association with a president if this conflicts with the district connections that a winning candidate has built up and must continue to nurture. Strong, centralized parties, such as the major parties of Great Britain and West Germany, however, are likely to have institutionalized relations with interest groups only at the center of state or national party organizations. Financial support is channeled from the central headquarters, rather given directly to individual candidates as in the United States. Centralized financing increases the disciplinary powers of party leaders and the unity of the party.

It also has been argued that interest groups function as another "circuit of representation" in pluralistic societies. Interest-group membership in a pluralistic society may be relatively low, but the number of individuals belonging to groups is much larger than the number belonging to political parties. One circuit of representation is elections, but these occur every two years at the most, and generally there are intervals of three to five years between elections. New issues arise and party manifestos are vague. Interests groups, to use Samuel Finer's phrase, supply "emotion."[27] They react, communicate opinions, and provide some measure of public response to officials. On the complex application of general statutes, groups can represent their interests to bureaucrats as the administrative implementation is worked out.

In a 1959 study, which has become a classic, William Kornhauser warned against the dangers of **mass society**.[28] Mass society is a potentially dangerous outcome of the industrial, mobile, technologically sophisticated environment of the postindustrial Western world. The end result is that "intermediate relations," which are principally interest groups, break down. A mass society is susceptible to being manipulated by the elites with the technology available to them. One example was Nazi Germany, where the ministry of propaganda under Joseph Goebbels played a key role in brainwashing the masses.

Based on his concern that we avoid the evils of "mass society," Kornhauser lists several positive functions performed by what he terms **intermediate groups**, or interest groups.

1. Independent groups assist in dealing with many local problems. For example, in the absence of such associations as the P.T.A., which provides channels of communication between parents and schools, the individual is less likely to develop or maintain interest and participation in aspects of the school program.

2. Most interest-group leaders, irrespective of their particular aims (unless they seek to transform radically the political system), help to legitimize the larger system of authority within which their authority system is bound.

3. A large number of stable and independent groups result in diverse and competing interests. The opposition and orderly tension among groups restrains each group's power. This discourages concentrations of power dangerous to both decision makers and the masses.

4. Autonomy also prevents a concentration of power. Groups are more or less autonomous in their own spheres because they are not directly determined in their membership and policies by higher authorities.

5. There are some overlapping memberships among groups. Because each group is concerned with only limited aspects of its members' lives, groups generally do not seek total domination over their membership.

6. The presence of many groups places an important responsibility on government. The government should have the capacity, and also assume the responsibility, to protect the individual against domination by any group.[29]

[27]An elaboration of this point and a general and recent discussion of interest groups in Great Britain is on a cassette, "Parties and Interest Groups," by Samuel Finer (New York: Holt, Rinehart and Wilson, 1972), side 2.

[27]See William Kornhauser, *The Politics of Mass Society* (New York: The Free Press, 1959).

[29]Kornhauser, *op. cit.,* pp. 76–78, adapted and condensed.

TACTICS, STRATEGY, AND EFFECTIVENESS OF INTEREST GROUPS

The focus and strategy of interest groups vary considerably. Interest groups do not confine their activities to lobbying public officials and electioneering. They engage in strikes and boycotts on occasion. They also seek to build support through education and information compaigns, attempt to influence the civil service, and, through court action, seek to correct what they consider illegal or inequitable practices. For example, the National Association for the Advancement of Colored People (NAACP) has been especially active in litigation. Much of the civil rights progress in the United States has been achieved by NAACP court-initiated actions, where the organization used the Fourteenth Amendment to argue that many forms of racial discrimination allowed or required by state laws were unconstitutional.

With the federal form of government and separation of powers in the United States there are numerous points of influence for an interest group. A negative response from one agency, one branch, or one level of government will turn the group toward another target. Many interests have found more response from American state legislatures than from the Congress, and vice versa. Interests groups concen-

"All I Want Is Just All The Power There Is"

from *Herblock's State of the Union* (Simon & Shuster, 1972).

trate their government lobbying at the most responsive points in the decision-making process.

The American Congress has been a special target of interest groups, while in Great Britain greater success has been achieved at the cabinet and bureaucratic levels. There also is increased lobbying of the executive branch and the bureaucracy in the United States. The ever-widening scope and technical character of modern economic and social policies has increased the power and responsibilities of the executive/administrative branch. A majority of legislation, even in the United States, is drafted in the executive branch. Bills that become laws tend to be legal frameworks that must be "fleshed out" by administrative interpretation and implementation. Even if an interest group has "lost" and a legislative act has been passed, it may seek to further a relationship with the administering body to secure a congenial interpretation of policy.

Under the British system, the cabinet dominates policy making and the civil service has much latitude in drafting and implementing laws and regulations. Consequently, most British interest groups focus on the executive branch. Moreover, statutes often require such consultation. In 1972 one political scientist counted more than 600 advisory committees that consulted with the British government in specific areas. The groups were legally built into the system to look after the interests of their own members. In his pioneering study of British interest groups, Samuel Finer observed that "on a host of official committees civil servants sit cheek by jowl with representatives of interested associations." For example, The Trades Union Congress is represented on 60 permanent committees, including the Standing Committee on Building Material Prices, the Duty-Free Machinery Imports Committee, and the Joint Advisory Panel for the Decontrol of Fat Stock.[30] It is at these points of contact that much of the influence of interest groups occurs in Great Britain. Not only in Great Britain but in many other countries are there such committees composed of representatives from the government and interest groups.

The French General Confederation of Beet-Growers (GCB) provides an interesting illustration of an interest group that has had to change its tactics. For many years the government-run *Service d'alcools* purchased more alcohol from the farmer than was being used. The alcohol was distilled primarily from beets, apples, molasses, and wine. In more recent years the French government determined to put the *Service d'alcools* on a paying basis. This meant in effect that beet growers and others were going to have to curtail production. For several years after World War II the GCB had been able to influence many legislators in the French National Assembly, but as its power waned it began to concentrate on the civil service. Beets now are used increasingly as a source of sugar. The GCB is expanding its laboratories and research. It now works principally with economists and other groups of civil servants. It concentrates its claims on a sugar law that will establish

[30]Samuel E. Finer, *Anonymous Empire* (London: Pall Mall Press, 1958), pp. 31 and 32.

a production target, a favorable price, and a government program that is committed to a five-year plan or longer and that will provide a predictable market for the beet farmers. With the emergence of the Fifth French Republic in 1958, a new group of leaders dominated the government. Shifts in power in Paris and new ideas about balanced budgets, reducing alcohol consumption, and changing technology as beets became a source of sugar, resulted in a change in tactics and strategy on the part of the beet interest group.[31]

Norway provides a noteworthy example of interest groups focusing their activities on the bureaucracy. One study has emphasized the numerous groups in Norwegian society and the organizability of society reflected in the fact that over 70 percent of the adult population belongs to one or more associations. The largest or peak associations usually consist of smaller organizations over which they maintain considerable control. It is argued that the stability of Norwegian democracy is based on the Norwegians' experiences in one or more of these democratically run groups.[32] A Norwegian political scientist, in studying the same phenomenon, has warned of some of the dangers of the political process in Norway. He concludes that most of the input and bargaining is between government bureaucrats and cabinet officials on one hand and bureaucrats and the peak associations on the other. The political parties and Parliament are bypassed.[33] Political decisions commonly are made in the bargaining process between the administrative/executive level and the interest groups. Consequently, channels are institutionalized and have become regularized procedures for taking action on specific kinds of issues. Essentially, the concerned groups interact with the appropriate departments, and a wider range of viewpoints—such as in the legislative arena—does not occur.

British interest groups function in a manner not unlike the Norwegian case. They attempt to exert influence on those who make most of the decisions: the government (cabinet) or the bureaucracy. Interest groups are so closely interlocked in the decision-making process that frequently they do not have to take the initiative. Prior consultation with affected interest groups is an accepted procedure. Before a bill is introduced into Parliament, the ministry working on the bill will discuss the general principles with relevant groups. This is important because before the Government has publicly committed itself to specific legislation it is more willing to accept requests to modify its proposal. Thus, the principal channels of British interest-group activity lead to the executive branch.

Extensive day-to-day use of administrative channels means that a high proportion of interest-group activities are not readily visible. One specialist on British politics

[31]The discussion of the GCB is taken from Bernard E. Brown, Pressure politics in the Fifth Republic, *The Journal of Politics*, 25:3, 1963, pp. 509–525.

[32]Harry Eckstein, *Division and Cohesion in Democracy* (Princeton: Princeton University Press, 1966), pp. 102–106.

[33]Stein Rokkan, "Norway," in Robert A. Dahl, ed., *Political Opposition in Western Democracies* (New Haven: Yale University Press, 1966).

has labeled this emerging emphasis on functional or interest-group representation with the bureaucracy as the new pluralism. New problems require great technical expertise and ongoing consultation. The result is a **collectivist age** of new group politics whereby interest groups have a continuous impact on government decisions.[34]

The growing phenomenon of interest-group and administrative interaction is the subject of criticism by those who see this as weakening democratic principles and procedures. If the principal representative institution, the legislature, delegates broad responsibilities to the less visible and accountable bureaucracy in administering laws and depends heavily on the executive for drafting bills, broader popular input is eroded. An American political scientist has warned of this policy without law involving diminishing popular control. He sees the growing network of alliances between interest groups and administrative agencies as subverting the legislative role and thus democracy. These alliances favor broad discretionary authority for the bureaucracy so that if problems arise they can be worked out without going back to the legislature. This new concept of representation often restricts input and decision making to those interests directly concerned.[35] Nevertheless, as we noted in our section on pluralism and will discuss later in Chapter Eight, (on the legislative process), legislators still play an important role in decision making, and many issues are too controversial to be handled quietly through interest group/administrative channels.

Strategy, tactics, relations with administrative officials, and the capability of the group's leadership are not the only factors that contribute to the political effectiveness or ineffectiveness of an interest group. Size can be important, but if the membership is not cohesive or does not focus on specific objectives, the group may carry little political influence. The American Medical Association usually has been more politically effective than the much bigger National Congress of Parents and Teachers. The very cohesive 1-million-member-plus National Rifle Association has been highly effective on the single issue of opposition to national gun control legislation. In several close congressional races it has helped to defeat candidates who supported gun control. The political effectiveness, cohesion, and determination of an interest group are affected by the intensity of concern among the members of the group. The size of the NRA membership has been encouraged in fact by executive action. It was only in 1979 that a federal judge ruled that the Pentagon's policy of selling surplus military firearms *only* to members of the NRA was discriminatory on the grounds that this subsidized and thereby bolstered the membership of a private organization.

The first objective of a candidate or a party in a competitive political system is to win elections. Ways that an interest group can have a voice in later policy are by contributing money to candidates, giving key campaigns organizational support, or hav-

[34]Samuel H. Beer, *British Politics in the Collectivist Age* (New York: Alfred A. Knopf, 1965).
[35]Theodore J. Lowi, *The End of Liberalism* (2nd ed.; New York: W.W. Norton & Co., 1979).

ing a substantial membership located in electorally close constituencies. The last assumes that group members will vote nearly "en bloc." Through various means, interest groups can aspire to participate with success in the electoral process.

The indispensability of a group also is relevant. Milk producers, longshoremen, teamsters, or coal miners are relatively small in number, but their role in the functioning of a modern industrial society makes them very important in many countries. These groups will be successful in achieving many goals, especially those of immediate and personal concern to their members. Finally, we might specify what has been implicit—the composition of the total political system is crucial. In a pluralistic environment autonomous input is allowed and even encouraged. Often, the activities of interest groups serve to legitimate the political system. Large numbers of people with various points of view can organize claims and promote their special concerns. In authoritarian systems, this is not the case.

INTEREST-GROUP INPUT IN DEVELOPING AND AUTHORITARIAN/TOTALITARIAN SYSTEMS

Political systems of the **developing world** manifest substantial variation in their tolerance of interest groups. Countries such as Malaysia, Singapore, India, or Venezuela have numerous autonomous interest groups. Other political systems, such as Laos, Burma, Nepal, Paraguay, Saudi Arabia, and many of the African countries have few if any interest groups with any freedom of input in the political system. In authoritarian political systems, where power is concentrated in the hands of a small group (Soviet Union, North Korea, Algeria), some interests are represented by individuals or fractions within the leadership. Inevitably, there also are present the institutional interest groups discussed earlier. Too often though, objectives promoted by institutional interest groups are intended primarily to enhance the position of one segment of an already too-powerful elite.

Interest groups in developing countries, where a degree of autonomous group organization is allowed, can play especially crucial roles. Historically, the rulers in these areas have not been expected to consult or respond to the wishes of their subjects. Reliable information about public concerns and attitudes is not available. The newly independent governments, in order to remain in power for very long, must respond to the more urgent claims and demands of a citizenry conscious of the revolution of rising expectations. There is a danger here because most of the political arrangements are new in the developing countries. Frequently there is serious disagreement over what the political rules of the game should be. Many groups, such as those in Iran, Afghanistan, and Lebanon, do not push specific or particular interests directly related to their group but support, often violently, system issues that they believe will create a political arena generally disposed to favor them. This we call **system conflict**—when people battle over whether there should be a theocratic constitution controlled by religious leaders, a republic, a monarchy, or a Communist system; over who can organize for political purposes; over what groups can be citizens or exercise some local autonomy; or over a free press, an impartial judiciary, or freedom of religion. Where such groups uncompromisingly pursue their objectives without self-restraint, willing to turn to assassination and mob action, pressing for mutually exclusive objectives (which, if successful, restrict the basic values of other groups), the political system is unstable. All groups become suspect, and repression, rather than accommodation, characterizes government policy.

The other type of conflict is called **issue conflict** because the basic institutions and rules of the game in the political system are not the central issues of competition. Issue conflict is limited to the types common in the developed, pluralist systems, on issues such as government subsidies, tax relief, rural uplift programs, housing, industrialization versus pollution, new universities, and so forth.

Third World governments often have great difficulty acknowledging the rights of issue groups while at the same time seeking to control or eliminate the activities of the system-oriented groups. Persistent ignoring of issue groups and failure to initiate responsive programs and policies may lead however, to some form of internal war in the country, or a coup d'etat, as in the case of the fall from power of Emperor Haile Selassie in Ethiopia in 1974. In the latter instance, young military officers placed the emperor under house arrest. The power of decision making was shifted to a younger generation, but power remained concentrated in the hands of a few. A newly independent, developing society with new responsibilities and problems might find useful some form of interest-group development, if for nothing else, to apprise the rulers of the more prevalent concerns of the population.

Authoritarian and totalitarian regimes that are publicly committed to a monolithic conformity reject the existence of autonomous groups and the input of the claims into the decision-making process. So-called interest groups, taken over or created by the state, serve principally to mobilize, regulate, and extend the control of government. Any form of independent, popular expression is prohibited.

One function of a formally organized group in an authoritarian system is to be a government channel, explaining to members what their true interests are and how government is meeting these interests. Interest groups also regiment and monitor individuals and serve as organizations to implement and reinforce government policy.

An example of a totalitarian political system is the People's Republic of China. One method of manipulating the population is to enroll as many persons as possible in one or more state-controlled interest groups. In this case, these groups propagandize and control the most populous nation (1 billion) in the world. One organization, the Women's Federation, has over 80 million members. Much emphasis is placed on equality, and a major objective is to get women out of the home and into production and defense work. The Communist Youth League, with over 25 million members, is the "reserve force of the party" and is open to all young people between the ages of 14 and 25. All members of the central committee and most of its higher officers must be members of the Chinese Communist Party. The Youth League sponsors a junior group, the Young Pioneers, for the 9- to 14-year-olds. During the 1950s these 2 groups were urged to learn and practice the "five loves": love of fatherland, people, labor, science, and public property. Love of parents and family were not mentioned. The Communist Youth League and Young Pioneers mold the minds of the young and reflect ever-changing government policy. These groups support government policy and do not articulate popular demands. They also act as a recruiting device for new party leaders by spotting those with leadership abilities and by striving to create in young leaders an enthusiastic devotion to the party and its goals.[36]

Although formally organized interest groups in authoritarian and totalitarian systems are a mechanism for government control of the population, there is evidence that within the elites (Almond's institutional interest groups) there is some competition.[37] This competition can be over issues, or it may involve leadership and influence disputes, that is, support for one faction, oppose another faction. By faction we mean a group of individuals seeking to increase their influence or power where the principal objective is to serve personal interests and status. Frequently it is difficult to know whether conflict within the elite is issue conflict or whether an issue is simply a means that one faction may use to criticize another faction. We alert the student to this possibility but offer no formula to determine specific cases.

We must assume, however, that sometimes there are genuine policy differences between government ministries or even disagreements within ministries: for example, jurisdiction of the security police versus the military; increased military expenditure versus public housing; expand heavy industry versus more consumer goods; product competition and workers' bonuses versus traditional Marxist industrial policy. One Soviet specialist has summarized the nature of interest groups among those exercising authority in a Communist system: "A striking feature of political interest groups in the Soviet Union is that normally they are not formally organized, but are more often loose groupings of like-minded or like-interested persons."[38]

In recent years a few groups outside the ruling Soviet hierarchy have emerged to call for basic changes in the political system. These groups are generally called dissidents, their numbers are small, and they are frequently arrested, exiled, or otherwise harassed. One example is the human rights movement, which appeared in its present form in the late 1960s with publication of the *Chronical of Current Events*, an anonymous underground journal that had published over 50 issues as of 1980. Though such groups receive international attention, they appear to have scant meaningful input in the Soviet political system. Andrei D. Sakharov, a Nobel Laure-

[36]The material on the People's Republic of China is taken from Richard L. Walker, *China under Communism: The First Five Years* (New Haven: Yale University Press, 1955), pp. 36–42; and James R. Townsend, *Politics in China*, 2nd ed. (Boston: Little Brown, 1980), Chapter VI.

[37]A most useful work on interest groups in a Communist system is H. Gordon Skilling and Franklyn Griffiths, ed., *Interest Groups in Soviet Politics* (Princeton, N.J.: Princeton University Press, 1971).

[38]H. Gordon Skilling, "Groups in Soviet Politics: Some Hypotheses," *Ibid.*, p. 27.

ate physicist now exiled to Gorky, under constant K.G.B. surveillance, is probably the best known leader of this movement.[39]

Interest groups in authoritarian and totalitarian systems are in an early stage of development as compared to pluralistic systems. They only vaguely resemble Western-style interest groups, and the range of their input activities is limited strictly by what an autocratic leadership will allow. As we noted earlier, formal organized groups such as the Academy of Sciences, the Writer's Union, the Lenin-Communist League of Youth, and the Central Council of Trade Unions, are principally instruments of the ruling elite to control the population. These groups possess little autonomy and have little input. Illustrating this point is the fact that one of the most widely used Soviet politics texts does not list interest groups in the index.[40]

SUMMARY

There are obviously many criticisms of interest groups that we have not dealt with in detail. The quiet negotiations through personal contacts between interest-group representatives, government bureaucrats, and political leaders, which take place away from the public limelight, may lead to secret deals. Unfortunately, these decisions too often culminate in payoffs and kickbacks to government officials as a reward for a favorable ruling. Leaving aside the corruption issue, there also is a widespread feeling that a political decision based on the intense pressure of one or two groups means that one "part" benefits to the disadvantage of the "whole" of the general public interest. Producer groups organize more frequently and effectively than consumer groups. Many believe these are narrow, selfish interests intent upon "ripping off" the general public. It is also commonly observed that not all members support the politics of the group with equal zeal. Some members are hardly aware of the group's political positions. Interest-group leaders often are not regularly accountable to their members, and some officers may use funds for their personal benefit.

Nevertheless, autonomous interest groups are a principal means by which to pluralize a political system and to divide power. They frequently provide the citizen with a means to affiliate in an organized and effective manner and voice demands and opinions independent of the government.

Interest groups are objects of much justifiable criticism; nevertheless, they are the life-blood of politics. They are the most effective means to date to prevent the concentration of power in the hands of a single, ruling oligarchy. Autonomous, often-competing activity of many interest groups strengthens democracy and reduces authoritarianism.

[39]For a far-ranging discussion of this movement in a letter smuggled to the West by Dr. Sakharov see "Sakharov: A Letter from Exile," trans. by Raymond H. Anderson, *The New York Times Magazine*, June 8, 1980, pp. 31 ff.

[40]Frederick C. Barghoorn, *Politics USSR*, 2nd ed. (Boston: Little Brown and Company, 1972).

SELECTED READINGS

A short but superior summary of pluralism, pro and con, is in Thomas R. Dye, Lee S. Greene, and George S. Parthemos, *American Government: Theory, Structure and Process* (Belmont, Ca.: Wadsworth Publishing, 1969), pp. 174–76. Pluralism as an approach, or treated as a particular form of democracy, has evolved rather than been presented formally as a theory. Two authors who present a sympathetic and reasoned defense are Robert Dahl, "Further Reflections on the Elitist Theory of Democracy," *American Political Science Review*, 60:2, 1966, 296–305; and William Kornhauser, *The Politics of Mass Society* (Glencoe: Ill.: The Free Press, 1954).

The critics of pluralism are, if anything, more numerous than its proponents. Two representative critical presentations are William E. Connolly, ed., *The Bias of Pluralism** (New York: Atherton Press, 1969); and Jack I. Walker, "A Critique of the Elitist Theory of Democracy," *American Political Science Review*, 60:2, 1966, 285–295.

The standard post-World War II book on interest groups is David Truman, *The Governmental Process: Political Interests and Public Opinion,** 2nd ed. (New York: Alfred A. Knopf, 1971). Also see Harmon Zeigler, *Interest Groups in American Society* (Englewood Cliffs, N.J.: Prentice-Hall, 1964) for a general treatment. Chapter 1 provides a good introductory summary of the literature and major themes. An appropriate introduction to Robert H. Salisbury's theories is his "An Exchange theory of Interest Groups," *Midwest Journal of Political Science*, 13:1, 1969, 1–32. His analysis centers on the hypothesis that, in order for a group to survive, members must derive benefits and leaders "enough return" or "profit." The standard work on British interest groups is Samuel E. Finer, *Anonymous Empire*, 2nd ed. (New York: Humanities Press, 1966). All of the preceding works can be used to develop hypotheses and principles when studying interest groups in other than the Anglo-American systems. Finer's work should be read in conjunction with K. Newton and D.S. Morris, "British Interest Group Theory Reexamined," *Comparative Politics*, 7, 1975, 577–595.

A fact-filled overview of American interest groups, including three chapters on three separate case studies, is Norman J. Ornstein and Shirley Elder, *Interest Groups, Lobbying and Policymaking* (Washington: Congressional Quarterly Press, 1978). Another comprehensive review of American interest-group politics, including techniques of lobbying the three branches of government, electioneering, and group impact on public policy, is Carol S. Greenwald, *Group Power: Lobbying and Public Policy* (New York: Praeger, 1977). A case study of the activities of promotional or citizens' groups is Andrew S. McFarland, *Public Interest Lobbies: Decision Making on Energy** (Washington: American Enterprise Institute, 1977). A provocative work that criticizes the growing power of interest groups and the closeness of groups and bureaucrats in formulating and implementing policy—in the United

*Available in paperback.

States particularly but applicable to most advanced democracies—is Theodore J. Lowi, *The End of Liberalism*,* 2nd ed. (New York: Norton, 1979).

The classic anthology of interest-group activities outside the United States, which includes some theoretical insights, is Henry Ehrmann, ed., *Interest Groups on Four Continents* (Pittsburgh: Pittsburgh University Press, 1958). Two useful case studies of interest groups in Scandinavian political systems are Robert B. Kvavik, *Interest Groups in Norwegian Politics** (Oslo: Universitetsforlaget, 1976); and Christopher A. Wheeler, *White-Collar Power: Changing Patterns of Interest Group Behavior in Sweden* (Urbana, Ill.: University of Illinois Press, 1975). Peter Shipley, ed., *Directory of Pressure Groups and Representative Associations*,* 2nd ed. (New York: R.R. Bowker, 1979) is a comprehensive listing and profile of interest groups that influence British government. It provides some idea of the scope of group activities in postindustrial societies. A well-documented comparative study by a British scholar analyzing the competing demands of groups is Graham K. Wilson, *Special Interests and Policymaking: Agricultural Policies and Politics in Britain and the U.S.A., 1956–70* (New York: John Wiley, 1977). William F. Averyt, Jr., *Agropolitics in the European Community* (New York: Praeger, 1977) is a brief, comparative analysis of agricultural interest groups in France and Germany. A good case study of an institutional interest group in a developing political system is Somboon Suksamran, *Political Buddhism in Southeast Asia: The Role of the Sangha in the Modernization of Thailand* (New York: St. Martin's Press, 1977).

The role of competing interests in authoritarian and totalitarian societies is being studied increasingly, despite the difficulty of acquiring data. In this regard, Gordon F. Skilling and F. Griffiths, eds., *Interest Groups in Soviet Politics** (Princeton: Princeton University Press, 1971) is both theoretically and empirically useful. A study of an institutional interest group in a totalitarian society is Edward L. Warner III, *The Military in Contemporary Soviet Politics* (New York: Praeger, 1977).

Dorothy Smith, *In Our Own Interest: A Handbook for the Citizen Lobbyist in State Legislatures** (Seattle, Washington: Madrona Publishers, 1979) is a useful working guide for individuals wishing to lobby a state legislature or study the legislative process.

A British political science quarterly, *Government and Opposition*, devotes its Autumn, 1978 issue to a series of case studies of trade unions and their relationships to parties in four West European countries.

*Available in paperback.

Chapter Six

Political Parties

POLITICAL PARTIES IN THE CONTEMPORARY WORLD

One of the more succinct definitions of **democracy** states:

Democracy exists where the principal leaders of a political system are selected by competitive elections in which the bulk of the population have the opportunity to participate.[1]

A democratic political system cannot exist without **political parties**. Political parties first emerged in countries which were democratizing. The virtues of popular participation have been debated and fought over since at least the fourth century B.C., when Plato and Aristotle were writing as the Greek city-state system collapsed. It is only in the last 200 years, though, that some variation of democracy has emerged in more than a handful of countries, approximately 30 to 35. When the opinions and desires of a substantial number of citizens began to be taken into account by the political elite—either because of philosophical commitment or practical necessity—political parties were organized. Parties brought organization to mass participation, and were organized originally to win popular support. Enfranchisement was a relatively slow process during the nineteenth century, but the pace increased in this century. In the American presidential elections of 1824, for example, when blacks and women were not permitted to vote and tax and property qualifications still existed in many states, 3.8 percent of the total population voted.[2] A mere 1.1 percent

---

[1] Samuel P. Huntington and Clement H. Moore, "Conclusion: Authoritarianism, Democracy, and One-Party Politics" in Huntington and Moore, eds., *Authoritarian Politics in Modern Society* (New York: Basic Books, 1970), p. 509.

[2] Robert Lane, *Political Life* (Glencoe, Ill.: Free Press, 1959), p. 19.

of the Japanese population was eligible to vote in the first national election held in 1890; subsequent lowering of the tax qualification meant that by 1920 the eligible electorate represented 5.49 percent of Japan's population.[3]

Political parties in a pluralistic system are based ultimately on the assumption that over the long run they are the institution most able to provide the maximum opportunity for popular influence on government. This is done by making it possible for the majority of adults to vote in free and competitive elections. The ultimate justification of a competitive party system is that it is the most effective means by which large numbers of people can have a voice in choosing political leaders and in providing some direction to the policies enacted and enforced by the governing authorities.

Many political scientists have maintained over the last four decades that the most important institution in a democracy is the political party:

> *Political parties created democracy and . . . modern democracy is unthinkable save in terms of the parties. As a matter of fact, the condition of the parties is the best possible evidence of the nature of any regime.*[4]

DEMOCRATIC POLITICAL PARTIES DEFINED

We define democratic political parties first because this is the original type of party. Only in this century have groups called parties emerged as instruments of revolution and control.

A political party in a democracy is a group of voters organized for the purposes of nominating and electing candidates legally to public office in order to influence and/or control personnel and policy. A party is distinguished from an interest group in that a party nominates candidates for public office while interest groups do not. Candidates who win are willing to assume responsibility for the conduct of public affairs generally and do not limit their activities to a few issues, such as gun-control legislation, conservation, pollution control, and so on.

Even if a party wins few electoral victories, it still may have an impact on the political system and attract loyal supporters and members. In the United States, for example, third parties often act as "issue-finders" for major parties. Norman Thomas, the highly respected and leading American socialist of the century, on numerous occasions wryly observed that, though the Socialist Party of America never won an election, many socialist proposals, such as minimum wage laws, unemployment compensation, and a separate Department of Labor, were enacted by the Democrats and Republicans several decades after they were first proposed by the socialists.

[3]Chitoshi Yanaga, *Japanese People and Politics* (New York: John Wiley, 1956), pp. 281–282.
[4]E. E. Schattschneider, *Party Government* (New York: Rinehart & Co., 1942), p. 1.

Democratic political parties that enjoy some electoral successes possess most of the following **organizational** features, though no party exhibits every characteristic or performs each function in a similar way:

1. Associations of leaders and members seeking to win control of and/or influence government decisions.

2. Local organizations, committees, or branches that maintain some relationship (communication, provide election workers, and so on) with the central headquarters. The organization may be highly centralized as the Communist Party in France, or decentralized, as in the United States.

3. Institutionalization or permanency of the party organization, which is only established when there is some means by which party leaders can succeed one another and when in fact a new group or generation of leaders replaces the founding members and the party continues to operate.

4. Institutions regulated in part by government rules; influenced in part by the party's own by-laws and the customs and traditions of the political culture.

Successful democratic political parties also offer some or all of the following **activities**:

5. Campaigning and mobilizing popular support in order to win elective offices.

6. Combining and balancing the views of receptive interest groups and then promoting policy commitments in order to maintain and expand electoral

The 1980 Congress of the Italian Christian Democratic Party.

and financial support for the party, and sometimes manufacturing or blurring issues.

7. Simplifying the issues and emphasizing a few so as to obtain the public's attention and support. Some parties even have their own daily newspaper.

8. Establishing itself as a symbol in the minds of people (or a reference group), providing typical voters with a means to orient themselves to the complex political collage of issues, personalities, and appeals. Simply put: build voter identification. (Reference groups are groups that are important in a person's thinking. They may evoke positive or negative responses. A person need not be a member of a group; even though he positively identifies with it.)

9. Influence the organization of government (personnel) and participate in and influence policy formation.

10. Numerous other functions, some of which are discussed later in the chapter: legitimizing the political system; stabilizing the political system by providing an organization through which the more vocal and compelling claims can influence government (integrating individuals and groups into the political system through participation and avoiding massive alienation, which could lead to sustained violence); acting as a two-way communication process between decision makers and the average citizen outside the more inflexible and impersonal bureaucratic channels; contributing to the orderly succession of political leadership; and recruiting or providing an avenue by which ambitious persons can achieve political elite status.

These 10 points describe the democratically oriented party, which competes for popular support against groups holding divergent opinions and which supports constitutional arrangements that guarantee continued political competition. There are, however, organizations—commonly described as political parties—that are dedicated to the overthrow of a political system and will eliminate competitive elections once they have acquired power, either by working through the electoral system (the Nazi Party at the end of the German Weimar Republic, 1933) or by working outside the existing system (the Bolsheviks as a subversive movement in the 1917 Russian Revolution). If these parties are allowed to compete, as the Nazis were in Weimar Germany (1918–1933), they will adopt electoral strategies designed to disorient and cripple the political system. In the declining years of the Weimar Republic, as Depression conditions increased the ineffectiveness of some of the political leaders, the party system collapsed into street brawls. Uniformed bully boys of the Nazi and Communist parties made it impossible for other political parties to appear in public without the support of a gang of hoodlums. Pitched battles between party militia were difficult to control and systematically weakened party politics to the point where a government could not rule.

Frequently, a **totalitarian** and revolutionary **party** will reject electoral participation or be prevented from electioneering because the rulers prohibit competitive

May Day parade in Prague, Czechoslovakia, 1970.

elections. The party becomes the "organization weapon" to launch a revolution.[5] Such a party has few of the traits typical of a democratic party. V. I. Lenin (1870–1924), the architect of the October 1917 Russian Revolution that brought the Communists to power, first described the principles upon which this type of party is founded, and his prescriptions continue to be mainsprings of action for such groups. As Lenin explained to his followers:

> *And this promise I shall defend no matter how much you instigate the crowd against me for my "anti-democratic" views, . . . 3. that the organization must consist chiefly of persons engaged in revolution as a profession; 4. that in a country with a despotic government, the more we restrict the membership of this organization to persons who are engaged in revolution as a profession and who have been professionally trained in the art of combatting the political police the more difficult will it be to catch the organization. . . .*[6]

If the revolutionary party succeeds, it is the end of competitive politics, and the victorious party becomes an instrument of domination and the elimination of all personal rights. The types of parties that emerge in a country are in large part a result of historical conditions.

[5]Phillip Selznick, *The Organizational Weapon: A Study of Bolshevik Strategy and Tactics* (Glencoe, Ill.: Free Press, 1960).
[6]V. I. Lenin, *What Is To Be Done?* (New York: International Publishers, 1929), p. 116.

Students of Soviet military academies pass in review on Red Square as part of the parade celebrating the 58th anniversary of the October Revolution.

ORIGINS OF POLITICAL PARTIES

Parties in the organized modern sense first emerged in the United States during the late eighteenth century, almost immediately after the 13 colonies achieved independence. Not everyone supported these new organizations. George Washington warned in his Farewell Address on September 19, 1796, "against the baneful effects of parties generally, including opening the door to foreign influence and corruption."[7]

From 1797 onward many political leaders throughout the world, often for less charitable reasons than President Washington's have rejected competitive elections. The presence of one and sometimes two or more political parties in a political system has, nevertheless, become a nearly universal phenomenon in this century. The refusal to permit more than one party usually is based on a twofold need: to preserve domestic tranquility and avoid unnecessary quarreling; and to prevent the infiltration of foreign influence.

The origins of political parties can be traced to five causes, or historical situations, which will be discussed in order of their appearance. Each of the originating conditions occurs in an environment in which traditional institutions and practices are declining and new ideas and techniques are appearing.

TO ENCOURAGE ELECTIONS

Political parties first came into being as a consequence of specific constitutional arrangements and laws that provided for or encouraged competitive elections. Political parties in the United States appeared in the 1790s because state laws encouraged this type of organization by "defining the rules of the game"[8] and providing for election contests.

[7]U.S. House of Representatives, *Washington's Farewell Address to the People of the United States,* House Document No. 504, 89th Congress, 2nd Session, 1966, pp. 15–16.

[8]Paul Goodman, "The First American Party System," in William Nisbett Chamber and Walter Dean Burnham, eds., *The American Party Systems: Stages of Political Development* (New York: Oxford University Press, 1967), p. 65.

Likewise, in other countries, parties evolved because the **suffrage** was expanded and groups of men organized to contest elections. In Great Britain, prior to the Reform Act of 1832, members of Parliament rarely were challenged in an election. Many, if not a majority, came from constituencies under the domination of a wealthy landlord (known as pocket boroughs). The MP (Member of Parliament) was not dependent on constituency opinion but on the goodwill of his wealthy sponsor. One of the most infamous examples of a "rotten borough"—a parliamentary district where the population was virtually nil—was Old Sarum. Old Sarum has been described as "a mound of earth, about two miles from the present city of Salisbury, which at the beginning of the nineteenth century had only seven inhabitants and returned two members of Parliament."[9] The seven voters regularly auctioned their votes to the highest bidder. Prior to 1832 the number of voting constituents per MP averaged 330. The Reform Act eliminated some of the worst inequities, such as providing the city of Manchester—population of 180,000—with representation in the House of Commons for the first time. The Reform Act was a modest effort, increasing the eligible electorate by 50 percent, to between 650,000 and 700,000 people, or about 3 percent of the adult population. This numerical increase in the electorate and the enfranchising of the previously disenfranchised sections of the industrializing North led like-minded groups of MPs to initiate electoral organizations. The development of modern British political parties was set into motion as increasing numbers of individuals gained the vote.

Political parties came into being in Japan in about 1881 as mechanisms of protest. The leadership of these groups was composed largely of ex-*samurai* (warriors) and former members of the government, who resented the domination of the Choshu and Satsuma clans in the government. A political party opposition (marred by assassination and other political acts of violence) began to evolve. The appearance, combining, and disappearance of many organizations was partly a result of the fact that no constitutional or other legal guide provided an appropriate outlet. With the appearance of the Emperor Meiji's constitution in February 1889, party organizations were provided with a logical focus. Chapter III of the new constitution set forth the principles governing the Imperial Diet (the bicameral legislature). Article XXXV described the House of Representatives as "composed of Members elected by the people according to the provisions of the Law of Election." Elections were held first in July 1890, and within 10 years the dominant group in Japanese politics—the Genro, or Elder Statesman—concluded that the most effective way to influence the Diet was to form a political party that could win a majority of seats and organize the House of Representatives. The earlier manipulation and corrupting of individual legislators and party cliques by the executive had brought increasing discredit to the government. The Diet, it was believed, depended on a party system in order to function properly, and the previous techniques could not be relied upon in the future to produce the desired results.

[9]Sydney Dawson Bailey, *British Parliamentary Democracy* (Boston: Houghton Mifflin, 1962), pp. 110–112.

In the fall of 1900, Prince Ito Hirobumi, an Elder Statesman and father of the Meiji Constitution, announced the formation of the Seiyukai party. In a matter of weeks a nonparty man had resigned the premiership, and Ito, president of the Seiyukai, became premier by virtue of the fact that his party had become a majority of the House of Representatives. Japan was moving toward a party government system until the Great Depression and military radicals disrupted the trend. Party government ended in the 1930s and did not appear again until the post-World War II American occupation and the "MacArthur constitution."

The announcement of forthcoming elections to be held (1948) by the British colonial authorities in Singapore led to government-sponsored voter registration drives and the formation of the first legal political party, the Progressive Party. As subsequent constitutions expanded the political powers of locally elected officials, more parties registered. Local self-government and compulsory voting came into being between 1957 and 1959. These measures culminated in a flurry of party activity and intense efforts by a wide range of groups to create effective political organizations to contest the upcoming Legislative Assembly elections in which, for the first time, all assemblymembers were elected. The People's Action Party, which won the 1959 elections, has governed Singapore since 1959.

In his study of Western party systems, Maurice Duverger refers to those who have a "parliamentary origin" and those "externally created" or "extraparliamentary" in origin.[10] In both instances the party seeks to influence or control government because of and through the electoral process. In the first instance are groups of representatives in parliament who have joined together on certain questions over time and established ties with electoral committees as the suffrage is extended and new groups win the right to vote. Examples would be the Conservative and Liberal parties in Great Britain and the American Federalists and Jeffersonian Republicans. The external party usually originates among groups who have not participated in an organized manner in the electoral process and have not participated in the legislature but now see the time as opportune because many potential supporters have gained the franchise. The activities of the Fabian Society and the Trades Union Congress, which led to the creation of the British Labour Party in 1899, are an example.

TO ENCOURAGE UNITY OR DISCOURAGE OPPOSITION

While democratic party systems have emerged as a result of constitutional legal prodding, one-party or authoritarian party systems generally have had different beginnings.

Nationalist movements against a foreign colonial power frequently have led to a single-party system. A successful anticolonial movement was not inclined to tolerate a political opposition after gaining independence. The need for unity in order to

[10]See Maurice Duverger, *Political Parties: Their Organization and Activity in the Modern State*, 2nd English ed., Barbara and Robert North trans., (New York: John Wiley, 1959), pp. xiii–xxxvii.

deal with the numerous economic and political challenges that threatened to overwhelm a poor, economically underdeveloped system, was the reason commonly advanced to justify a one-party system. A less charitable reason given by an individual who studied the West African party systems is that "single party" systems emerged because "it was a goal set by a political elite which then worked self-consciously for its achievement."[11] Political elites presumably were first and foremost concerned with remaining in power, and the means to accomplish this was the single party, which could help control the population. A sure way to stay in power is to prevent effective competition.

Another reason advanced for the creation of one-party states in former colonial territories is that this type of political system is in accord with revered historical–cultural traditions. Rupert Emerson believes that an elite working through a single party is in harmony with traditional practices. He argues that most non-Western traditional societies generally were inclined toward some form of extended deliberation that would result in a consensus, not toward a jarring count of votes with public losers. Majority rule and representative government have no roots in most traditional societies where "the voice of the elders, the wise, and the specially qualified was entitled to extra or even decisive weight"[12] and should not be subject to open, public criticism.

AS REVOLUTIONARY WEAPONS

Beginning with the Russian Communist Party, numerous political parties were founded in this century as revolutionary weapons. Some, such as the Nazi Party, adopted a quasi-constitutional strategy. The Nazis pursued their goal within the existing party system, manipulating and disrupting the system in the name of their totalitarian blueprint for the future. Adolf Hitler proclaimed that the Weimar constitution gave the Nazis "the ground on which to wage our battle." Too many ignored Hitler's warning that when the Nazis captured power, "we shall then mould the state into that form which we consider to be the right one."[13] Most revolutionary parties have, however, preferred or been required to adopt a conspiratorial posture. The Communist Party of the Soviet Union (officially founded in 1898 as the Russian Social Democratic Labor Party), for example, seized power through underground conspiracy, revolution, and finally civil war, which did not end until 1920.

Another revolutionary weapon was the Chinese Communist Party (CCP), founded in July 1921 when the First Party Congress was held in a Roman Catholic girls' school in the French concession at Shanghai—outside the jurisdiction of Chinese

---

[11]Aristide R. Zolberg, *Creating Political Order: The Party States of West Africa* (Chicago: Rand McNally, 1966), pp. 35–36.

[12]Rupert Emerson, *From Empire to Nation: The Rise to Self-Assertion of Asian and African Peoples* (Boston: Beacon Press, 1964), p. 284.

[13]Frederick Mundell Watkins, *The Failure of Constitutional Powers under the German Republic.* (Cambridge: Harvard University Press, 1939), p. 53.

law. Thirteen Chinese, including Mao Zedong, attended this meeting; two Comintern agents—a Soviet citizen and a Dutchman—also attended. The First Congress adopted a hard line and established the party as a revolutionary weapon that refused to cooperate with any existing political group. One document adopted at the Congress urged "aggression" toward existing parties and declared "no relationship with other parties or groups."[14] Today the CCP rules 1 billion people, the largest nation in the world.

IN RESPONSE TO WESTERNIZATION
Political parties also were created as a response to the spread of liberal ideas from the West. Many Japanese parties before the 1890 constitution were partly a consequence of Western ideas and writings, which were widely circulated among the Japanese elites. The overthrowing of the Thai military dictatorship by students in 1973, the formation of political parties, and the January 1975 elections owed much of their inspiration to liberal political ideas. These ideas came primarily from Western books and journals and from Thais trained abroad, mostly in the United States, who returned to their country with a democratic orientation.

AS A MEANS OF CONTROL
A final point of origin for political parties is the need to mobilize and control the growing political consciousness of the masses. Samuel P. Huntington has noted, "Significantly, when authoritarian regimes with weak parties confront crises, the party tends to reemerge as a more important actor."[15] When a new group of leaders, often military officers, seizes power, a political party then is created to penetrate the grassroots to control the population.

In Egypt, for example, after the late Gamal Abdel Nasser led the Free Officers in the July 1952 revolution that overthrew the corrupt monarchy, the new ruler set out to create mass involvement in order to govern Egypt more effectively. Too much influence by the urban intellectuals was to be limited by increasing mass involvement. President Nasser perceived the masses as having few immediate demands, the principal one being that "their government be an Islamic–Egyptian one." Three successive "single mobilization parties" were created, the last being the Socialist Union. The Socialist Union coincided with the adoption of a loudly vocal socialist ideology and was designed to organize and mobilize the masses, to obtain their cooperation.[16]

A second example is Ethiopia. The Emperor Haile Selassie was removed from power by a group of young military officers in September 1974. What has followed

---

[14]Stuart Schram, *Mao Tse-tung* (Baltimore: Penguin Books, 1966). p. 66.

[15]Huntington and Moore, eds., *op. cit.* p. 9.

[16]Leonard Binder, "Political Recruitment and Participation in Egypt," in Joseph LaPalombara and Myron Weiner, eds., *Political Parties and Political Development* (Princeton: Princeton University Press, 1966), pp. 218–219.

is a series of wars against rebel groups and struggles for power within the ruling military oligarchy. The year 1977 was the year of the Red Terror. At least eight persons of the ruling junta were executed, including the man who had been head of state for 26 months. Executions throughout the country may have reached 100,000. The new Ethiopian leader, Col. Mengistu, offered his fellow citizens two choices: "revolutionary motherland or death." After months of intrigue and liquidations, by 1979 what began as five factions within the military-dominated government was reduced to two. These have reached an agreement to collaborate and reduce the self-destructive purges and executions. Col. Mengistu announced in late 1979 that a commission was being formed to organize a Workers' Party, which will replace the military junta. In actual fact, the junta or military oligarchy will rule through the party. The Ethiopian government is aligned closely with the USSR, and the Soviets have urged that a mass-based, Communist-style party be organized to mobilize and control the people. Col. Mengistu's announcement of the new Worker's Party came during a visit by Soviet Prime Minister Alexei Kosygin. The Soviets are not entirely happy, however, as they prefer a civilian-led party as opposed to one manipulated by military officers.

A traditional political system is often a no-party country. But a new, revolutionary government that attempts to bring about fundamental changes in the social and economic systems generally turns into a single, monopolistic party. No party may leave a society out of reach and out of control. A dictatorial government attempting far-reaching and radical new programs must penetrate all of society and harness, persuade, and dominate it. Thus, the creation of a key instrument to accomplish this transformation—a ruling political party. In Egypt, Ethiopia, and many other countries, the single, monopolistic party was or is being created to indoctrinate and control the masses and strengthen the position of the ruling elite.

Party origins profoundly influence the objectives and organization of parties. Parties established to seize power by any available means and/or to harness a population are unlikely to assume a democratic character at a very early date.

TYPES OF PARTIES

Political parties have been classified according to a number of criteria. One of the most ambitious efforts to classify political parties is that of Gabriel Almond, who sets forth a scheme based on party style or behavior in the political arena.[17]

Pragmatic-bargaining or **broker-type** parties are typical of the Canadian and American systems, though this form of party appears to be spreading. This party type is highly voter conscious, is hungry for votes and attempts to respond to the maximum number of interests by policies and campaign statements with the widest appeal. The party appeals to all strata of society and usually attracts support from

[17]Gabriel Almond and James S. Coleman, eds., *The Politics of the Developing Areas* (Princeton: Princeton University Press, 1960), pp. 43–45.

most identifiable social groupings. For example, Britain's Conservative Party attracts upper and middle class voters especially, but approximately one-quarter of British labor union members vote Conservative. Bargaining, compromise, accommodation, reponsiveness, and a marketplace atmosphere dominate party strategy. This type of party functions in a system with a broad political consensus, where intense doctrinal issues do not divide society. The bargaining, broker party has been criticized for failing to present the voters with clear-cut alternatives and for failing to lead on the critical issues of the day. One expert on British parties, writing early in this century, criticized British parties for their overriding concern to win "by picking up votes from every quarter. Parties did not lead, but built blocs of votes and were often obliged to conciliate even the representatives of the fanciful movements and the fads" in order to win votes.[18]

Absolute value-oriented or **ideological parties**, such as the Nazi or Communist party, push a rigid, comprehensive program and usually regard compromise and negotiation as weakness. Unflagging commitment to long-standing principles guides party actions, and party members are recruited from among the most alienated groups in the population. Appeals for support are limited by the fact that potential members must convert to a highly structured party doctrine. Parties that fit into this category usually are revolutionary or reactionary.

Enemies of the party are numerous, and many are killed. A rather extreme but not untypical example is Cambodia. Between 1975 and 1979, Prime Minister Pol Pot's Communists, often called the "*Organization*," deliberately murdered approximately 1 million people in a total population of 7 million. Anyone who had worked with the previous non-Communist government, including all of their family members, were executed. Individuals with a high-school education or above and their families were brutally killed (throat slit, beaten to death, or buried alive). This Asian holocaust occurred because the Communist rulers believed those murdered could never be trusted and it was "safer" and cheaper (in many cases execution squads were ordered not to use bullets) to destroy them rather than attempt to brainwash or imprison them.

Deviation from the "official" ideology is treason or an act of resignation from the party. Challenging the current leadership—and hence party doctrine—can produce fatal results. Leon Trotsky, Lenin's most influential comrade, eventually clashed with Stalin and left the Soviet Union in 1929. After living in several countries and maintaining constant public criticism of the Stalin regime, in 1937 Trotsky settled in Coyoacán, Mexico, where he kept up his attacks against Stalin's leadership. Trotsky was assassinated on August 20, 1940, by a trusted supporter, Jacques Mornard, who drove an ice pick into Trotsky's skull. It was soon discovered that the killer was an agent of the Soviet secret police (KGB).

[18]M. Ostrogorski, *Democracy and the Organization of Political Parties,* Vol. II (New York: Macmillan, 1902), p. 684.

Some parties, such as the Prohibition Party in the United States, are inflexible in only certain policy areas but would negotiate in other matters. Most absolute-value-oriented parties operating in a competitive party system vigorously oppose whatever party or parties are in power. Some Communist parties do become more flexible and bargaining-minded as they come closer to power, particularly after they see an opportunity to form a coalition government with non-Communist parties. This is the case in the Italian Communist Party and other Eurocommunist parties.

Particularistic parties are self-limiting because they combine their appeals to specific ethnic, linguistic, or religious groups, such as the Hindu Maha Sabha, a conservative Indian party that restricts its membership to Hindus. These are communal parties dedicated to traditional values or to what Clifford Geertz has described as "**primordial sentiments**," which are given facts, "such as being born into a particular language or religious community, ethnic or racial group, kinship, geographic region, etc."[19]

At times these particularistic parties are willing to work within the larger political system and pursue a strategy of negotiation and compromise as the best means of protecting the group's interests. Frequently, through, the party's emphasis on traditional identifications intensifies divisions in society to the point that political negotiation becomes unlikely. One of the causes of the Nigerian Civil War (1967–1970) was the fact that political distrusts and misunderstandings were increased after independence. Independence and a new government offer a new prize to be won by ambitious individuals, and often it is the primordial sentiments that are appealed to and politicized by aspiring leaders as they seek to establish a leadership position. For example, one of the best organized Nigerian parties in the pre-Civil War period was the Action Group, whose support was drawn almost entirely from the Yoruba tribe.

ONE-PARTY REGIMES

The first single-party political regime appeared in the Soviet Union in 1917, in Italy in 1922, and in Germany in 1933, when the Communist, Fascist, and Nazi parties, respectively, came to power. Of these original **one-party systems**, only the Soviet system survives today.

Over the years, as other political systems have become dominated by single parties, the variation among one-party systems has been substantial. We are now at the point where to speak of a single-party regime refers to a wide variety of practices. The common factor that most single-party countries share is their authoritarian character. There are regimes, however, that are, in effect, single-party sys-

---

[19]For an analysis of such identifications in contemporary politics, see Clifford Geertz, "Primordial Sentiments and Civil Politics in New States" in *Old Societies and New States; the Quest for Modernity in Asia and Africa* (Glencoe, Ill.: The Free Press, 1963), p. 109.

tems but are not highly authoritarian—in Mexico (Institutional Revolutionary Party), for example, and Singapore, where the People's Action Party controls all 69 seats in Parliament.

One-party systems vary in the amount of power the political leadership allows the party as compared with other institutions in society. In some authoritarian systems preponderant influence may remain with the military, the civilian administrators, the church, and the economic elite, whether it be big business or the landed gentry. The Communist Party dominates in the Soviet Union.

Many one-party systems arise out of a historical experience with severe and prolonged cleavages that have led to internal war. The party's initial objective is to restore order and organize the nation as a productive and self-sustaining unit. In a century when mass political consciousness has become a fact of life, the single-party restrains and organizes this consciousness, in order to control the population. After the seizure of power the victors carry forward the struggle to purge society of the "enemy." Among totalitarian one-party regimes this is a brutal period in the nation's history, as during the first five years (1949–1954) of the People's Republic of China when 10 to 14 million "enemies of the people" were "eliminated."

Samuel P. Huntington[20] has analyzed one-party systems in depth and classified them into two types: exclusionary and revolutionary.

EXCLUSIONARY ONE-PARTY SYSTEMS.

These maintain divisions in society in order to neutralize politically a major segment of the population. In Ataturk's Turkey of the 1920s and 1930s political participation was restricted to the urban, Westernized population. Political leadership in an exclusionary system does not seek to eliminate physically the subordinate group or groups (as did the Nazis) or resocialize it into a single acceptable mold; rather rulers simply want to assure that the excluded group (blacks, peasants) will remain apolitical. Once society experiences economic modernization and the subordinated groups begin to participate in the process of social change, it is difficult to maintain the divisions.

REVOLUTIONARY ONE-PARTY SYSTEMS.

These are not interested in maintaining traditional social divisions but are determined to create a monolithic social and political order. Change, mass mobilization, terror, and absolute loyalty are the hallmarks of a newly established revolutionary one- party system. Those unwilling to convert or those whom the leadership deems unworthy of being converted (for example, Jews or landlords) are destroyed. The revolutionary single party is all-pervasive and its tentacles touch all parts of society and the individual's existence.

[20]Samuel P. Huntington, "Social and Institutional Dynamics of One-Party Systems," in Huntington and Moore, eds., *op. cit.*, pp. 3–47. This section is based on Huntington's chapter.

1.   **Transformation** occurs as the old order or aspects of it are destroyed. This is the most brutal if not the most unpredictable period. Purges, executions, summary imprisonments, and confiscation plague the population. The enemy is identified and destroyed or driven out. The systematic snuffing out of human life on unprecedented scales occurred during the early years of the party dictatorship in Nazi Germany, the Soviet Union, the People's Republic of China, and the Democratic Republic of Vietnam, when millions of people were executed or sent to concentration camps from which they never returned.

2.   In the **consolidation stage**, the old order has been destroyed and the regime legitimizes itself on the basis of the institutions and performance of the new order. Ideology as it was imposed on the population in the revolutionary stage is eroded. Authoritarian and totalitarian ideology previously emphasized the corrupt and degenerate nature of the present in contrast to the future ideal state to be achieved through the party. In the consolidation stage support or tolerance of the regime rests on the institutions and the performance of the system. Ideology becomes rote chant by the ambitious in order to maintain their credibility and career advancement.

The consolidation stage is the period of institutionalization. The most common result is to limit the power of the leader—as in the Mexican presidency—or to establish an oligarchic system in which power is divided among several individuals. Since the death of Stalin, for example, collective leadership has evolved in the Soviet Union as a means of preventing one individual from acquiring the autocratic power that Stalin held.

3.   Assuming that the party has surmounted the succession crisis, that the founding leader is no longer on the scene, and the institutions of the new order have taken hold, the party enters the **adaptation stage.** In this stage the party must relate itself to four social developments: (a) the emergence of highly trained technicians and managers who are, (b) responsible for the operation of an economically modernizing society; (c) the reappearance of intellectuals trained under the new order who, nevertheless, frequently criticize the regime; and (d) various groups in society demanding a role in the decision-making process. Technological development and a growing social pluralism suggest a changing role, if not lower status position, for the party bureaucrat or —to use the Soviet term—*apparatchik.*

As in many industrialized systems in the West, the intellectual and economic–managerial classes in revolutionary one-party systems make day-to-day critical decisions that affect the quality and functioning of society. Economic development and specialization encourage the growth of interest groups, which begin to make claims on the government. Competitive demands by multitudinous groups and interests may provide the party with its principal role—arbitration of competing demands, whether in a factory, a municipal agency dealing with urban transit or housing, or at the highest government level in deciding between those who seek more emphasis on heavy industry and defense versus those who want more and better quality consumer goods.

Even in the more authoritarian regimes there is evidence of a willingness to become more responsive, if not through an opposition party, at least through the occasional inclusion of more than one officially certified nominee per office. This occurs in Hungary and Poland, for example. Such contests enable the party to acquire a more accurate appraisal of the popular mood, respond to those who maintain the need for popular participation in decision making, and provide a means by which a very unpopular candidate or issue can be dealt with in a manner that will gain popular approval and indicate that the leadership is willing to respond to popular dissatisfaction.

Such trends, however, are not always present in the adaptation stage. Still to be determined is what will happen in the People's Republic of China during the adaptation stage that has followed the passing of Chairman Mao in 1976. China now has embarked on a comprehensive development program known as the "four modernizations": modernization of defense, agriculture, industry, and science and technology. A drive has been launched to popularize educational quality. During the Cultural Revolution (1966–1969), teachers who valued knowledge over politics were labeled "bourgeois" and replaced by young, usually uneducated Red Guards. The new campaign has rehabilitated the dismissed teachers and stresses hard study, competitive exams, and discipline in the classroom. Related to this was the emergence in 1977 of the two-block-long "democracy wall" in Peking where those critical of government policies posted their protests. Throughout most of 1979 the government continued to waver on how much criticism could be allowed. The editor of the most popular antigovernment magazine, *Exploration*, was sentenced to 15 years in prison in late 1979. The role of "expert" over "Red" (following the party line but with no technical expertise) now predominates in decision making. Critical groups are demanding more voice in order to avoid past mistakes, but the Communist regime gradually is silencing dissent as the government seeks to mobilize and control all national resources for the four modernizations. Democracy wall, in effect, was closed down in December 1979. A new site in Moon Park was announced, but individuals wanting to put up a wall poster now must register their names and addresses. Every poster will be examined by government officials at a registration center before it is posted. The writer will be held responsible for all legal and political implications. China today is a striking example of the adaptation stage pulling back from the idea of more freedom of political expression. Order is in order in post-Mao China.

POLITICAL PARTIES IN THE DEVELOPING WORLD

Many political systems in the developing world are dominated by a single party and therefore may be expected to move through the stages just outlined. Countries such as Costa Rica, Malaysia, Nigeria, and Venezuela have genuinely competitive elections and cannot be classified as single-party systems. In other political systems, such as in Burma, Egypt, Guinea, and Vietnam, the leaders use the party as an instrument to control and mobilize the population. Newly independent countries must face the fact that two or more parties with substantial support could lead to political divisions that would threaten the unity of the country or weaken a government's attempt to develop and carry out programs.

As political parties emerged in the nineteenth and twentieth centuries in what are now democratic political systems, a principal function was to transmit to a government the wishes of the citizens. In many developing countries the reverse function appears more true: to convey to the citizens the wishes of the government.

One heritage developing political systems share is **avoidance politics**. In colonial political systems, the masses did not participate in policy making and implementation. The best that could be hoped for was a condition in which one could avoid government rules or modify government regulations and requirements through an understanding with local officials. Taxes, peace and order, and military conscripts were the traditional government requirements, which on occasion were brutally enforced. Beyond these, governments limited their involvement in the local community. Participant systems (for example, the United States, Canada, Japan, and Western Europe), on the other hand, have responsive governments that remain in office because they successfully build coalitions of interests that can command an electoral majority. Participation emphasizes input factors at the electoral and policy-making stages.

Transitional policies in the Third World combine the need for nation building (security, stability, economic development, and national integration) with an intellectual movement away from a subject-oriented, toward a participatory, society. This shift in orientation frequently is more verbal than actual. Leaders whose nations are undergoing internal and external stress may believe that only discipline and maintaining a subject political system can build a social and economic base necessary for national development. The overlapping challenges to national stability and development are compounded by international opinion, which often judges a regime by its deviation from democratic-participatory norms—norms that few, if any, developing political systems can now meet.

Subversive involvement by foreign powers, traditional divisions in society, and the limited capacity of the government to solve problems are the ingredients that shape developing party systems. The impact of all these factors pushes a government toward some form of one-party solution. A few developing countries, on occasion, have sought accommodation with opposition groups, despite the fact that popular participation may appear a luxury that the transitional societies cannot afford. In 1945, after the defeat of the Axis powers, Indonesian leaders reacted in this euphoric and democratic atmosphere by adopting the 1945 constitution, which committed them to participatory politics. After a four-year violent struggle against the Dutch, Indonesia became independent in 1949 and the fifth largest country in the world began a democratic experiment. This experiment culminated in the 1955 general elections, in which nearly 38 million Indonesians voted. Four parties—two Muslim, one secular–nationalist, and one Communist—won 78 percent of the vote and captured 198 of the 257 parliamentary seats.[21] The remaining 59 seats were divided among 24 parties and other groupings, such as the two seats held by the Police Employees' Association of the Republic of Indonesia. Coalition governments, preceded by intense bargaining among the parties, continued. Less than 15 months passed before President Sukarno attacked the 1955 elections. Speaking before a youth conference, Sukarno observed:

In November 1945—let us be quite frank—we made a most serious mistake. We suggested the establishment of parties, parties, parties. . . . Just look at the situation. Quite apart from the disease of ethnic and regional loyalties, we are afflicted by the disease of parties which, alas, alas, makes us forever work against one another![22]

By 1959, party government had come to an end in Indonesia. Political parties, so runs the argument of numerous Third World leaders, either increase existing tensions and divisions or create new ones.

SINGLE-PARTY, TWO-PARTY, AND MULTIPARTY SYSTEMS

As the student has seen, political parties can be classified and analyzed according to a number of criteria. One of the most common classifications when considering the political system as a whole is by number of parties: single-party, two-party, and multiparty systems.

SINGLE-PARTY SYSTEMS

An analysis of single-party or one-party systems reveals fundamental variations among these systems. There are monolithic, totalitarian parties, such as the Communist Party of the Soviet Union and the Workers' Party of Vietnam, which penetrate all of society. Parties such as Mexico's Institutional Revolutionary Party and Singapore's People's Action Party (the PAP controls all 69 seats in Parliament) completely overshadow the several legal opposition parties, but they do not monopolize society to the degree the ruling parties in the Soviet Union and the Democratic Republic of Vietnam do.

---

[21]The Communists won 16.4 percent of the popular vote and elected 39 candidates. For an analysis of the 1955 elections and the future implications of the results, see Herbert Feith, *The Decline of Constitutional Democracy in Indonesia* (Ithaca: Cornell University Press, 1962), pp. 424–450.

[22]Sukarno, "Let Us Bury the Parties" in Herbert Feith and Lance Castles, eds., *Indonesian Political Thinking: 1945–1965* (Ithaca: Cornell University Press, 1970), p. 81.

The American South long was described as a single-party system; yet as Hugh Douglas Price has pointed out, this is "a residual category."[23] The term "one-party" in the United States defines a condition where meaningful two-party competition is absent. The South is not a case where a highly authoritarian political organization monopolizes the selection of government officials. "One-party," in the United States, does not imply the existence of a well-oiled monolithic organization that dominates a city or state. The states are required constitutionally to hold elections, and hotly contested electoral battles regularly occur in the primaries, if not in the general elections.[24]

This is not to say that political machines or organizations monopolizing local politics do not exist in the United States. An example of such is former Mayor Richard Daley's Cook County, Illinois, political organization.[25] The gradual disappearance of long-standing political machines is, however, a phenomenon of contemporary American political life, and only a few exist today.

TWO-PARTY SYSTEMS
Two-party systems are limited to a few countries, principally the United States, Great Britain, New Zealand, Austria, and West Germany. (As we note below, no competitive electoral system has **only** two parties.) A two-party system suggests that decisive encounters occur in elections and in the legislature. The opposition is sufficiently united that they can coalesce into a dominant opposition party, which can, if the electoral winds shift, remain united as a governing party. A general mass consensus on the political rules of the game undergird the system, and both parties concentrate on competing for the dominant bloc of the middle-of-the-road electorate. Multiparty systems can tolerate an extremist party, but representative elections cannot continue in a two-party system if one of the two parties is extremist or totalitarian, determined to destroy its competitor when it comes to power.

One of the first two-party systems was the British, where His/Her Majesty's Opposition was, and is, an integral part of the political process. Opposition is regarded as a legitimate public service, and since 1937 the Leader of the Opposition has been paid a special salary by the government. One student of British politics has observed that the two-party system structures and clarifies the issues in a unique manner and that this need for choice and clarity historically gave rise to two-party systems. "The two-party system is a natural concomitant of a political tradition in which government . . . is the first consideration, and in which the views and prefer-

[23]Hugh Douglas Price, "Rise and Decline of Single Party Systems in Anglo-American Experience" in Huntington and Moore, eds., *op. cit.,* p. 77.

[24]A most fascinating, though now somewhat dated, analysis of one-party American states is V. O. Key, *Southern Politics* (New York: Vintage Books, 1949).

[25]A readable, though sometimes inaccurate, description of the Cook County political organization is Mike Royko, *Boss: Richard J. Daley of Chicago* (New York: Dutton, 1971).

ences of voters and members of Parliament are continuously limited to the single alternative of 'for' or 'against.' ''[26]

No functioning two-party system has *only* two parties, but in a two-party system there are only two major parties which have a chance to control elective offices. The smaller third party is common to American national politics. In the 1968 presidential election, George Wallace's American Independent Party garnered 13.6 percent of the popular vote, but no AIP candidate was elected to office. Between 1946 and 1979 in Great Britain, the Liberal Party vote plus the popular votes of several minor parties in general elections have ranged between 2.9 percent and 24 percent. In the 1979 general election, the Liberal Party received 14.1 percent of the popular vote, and the other minor parties received 3.2 percent, yet the Liberals won only 10 of 630 seats in the House of Commons. Never since World War II have the Conservative and Labour parties combined controlled less than 94 percent of the seats in the House of Commons, and the average share of the two major parties has been 97 percent of the seats. Both Great Britain and the United States have single-member districts with plurality election (the election winner is the contestant with more votes than any other candidate, but not necessarily a majority); therefore, unless a party's strength is concentrated in a few districts (as the Liberal's is not) a party may win 20 or even 30 percent of the vote in a district but not elect a candidate.

In the American two-party system, the Democratic and Republican parties are decentralized, with state and even county organizations autonomous of the next higher level in the party hierarchy. Party candidates compete in elections, but the parties do not remain strictly competitive after the elections. Presidents and governments invariably depend on bipartisan support for many proposals, and, almost as inevitably, members of the chief executive's party vote against him or her on major issues.

Great Britain often is described as having a **disciplined two-party system**. The average English voter chooses the party and the candidate he wants to become the next prime minister when voting in the parliamentary election. The personal magnetism and stature of the individual MP candidate usually neither adds nor detracts more than 500 votes per constituency. The competition of the electoral arena carries over into Parliament, and the term "disciplined parties" means that commonly there are no crossovers when the House of Commons votes. The parties usually can depend on the MPs to register unanimously the party position.

We conclude this section by noting that the term "two-party system" is never strictly accurate. There are noticeable differences even within the Anglo-American two-party category.

MULTIPARTY SYSTEMS

Multiparty systems describe a situation in which one party rarely if ever wins an absolute majority of seats in the legislature. Consequently, in a parliamentary re-

[26]L. S. Avery, *Thoughts on the Constitution* (New York: Oxford University Press, 1947), p. 16.

gime, a coalition government must be formed. In multiparty systems parties represent fewer, limited-appeal interests and seek to advance these interests by participating in a coalition government. Parties, at least in their electoral appeal, are more doctrinal or ideological. Party support requires a greater voter commitment and this is unlikely unless the entire party program is acceptable. It may seem surprising, but in trying to build a coalition, only one or two parts of the party program may be accepted by other members of the coalition. The compromises on party doctrine occur in the legislature, after the election. The negotiations are decisive. It is at this time that the critical bargains are struck and ministries divided among the parties.

The number of parties and the amount of party cohesiveness and government stability vary among multiparty systems. The Netherlands has a parliamentary system of government in which five or six parties have dominated the political scene in the post-1945 period. These parties generally receive 80 percent or more of the popular vote. The country becomes a single constituency when national elections are held, and a party's representation in the popularly elected Second Chamber of 140 members is determined by its proportion of the national popular vote.[27]

The continuity of popular support for most parties has been a postwar feature of Dutch politics. A poll taken after the 1956 elections revealed that 85 percent of the persons interviewed had voted for the same party they had supported in 1952. Following the elections held in May 1977, the 4 largest parties controlled 138 of 150 seats (53, 48, 28, and 8 seats, respectively). The government formed in 1977 was composed of 3 parties, representing 110 seats in the Second Chamber. Of necessity, any government must be a coalition government, and while it may require many weeks of negotiation to form the coalition, governments normally remain in office for several years. After the 1977 elections, for example, a 7-month political crisis occurred before a majority coalition government could be formed. However, a multiparty system has not prevented government stability and the capacity to develop and implement policy in the Netherlands, once a coalition has been arranged.[28]

The French Fourth Republic (1946–1958) stands in sharp contrast to the situation in the Netherlands. The French multiparty system was a contributing factor to the *immobilisme* of French politics before 1958. Cabinets or governments were approved and fell with an unhealthy frequency. Between 1946 and 1958 there were 26 different cabinets. Governments ultimately were unable to deal with critical issues, such as Algeria, and important social and economic policies. The Fourth Republic was a parliamentary regime. In 1956, 150 Communist deputies were elected to the 597-member National Assembly. The Communists consistently opposed the government, and cabinets had to be formed from the remaining groups: the Mouve-

[27]The First Chamber is actually the upper house of the Dutch Parliament. It has 75 members elected by the Provincial Councils for six-year terms. The First Chamber does not propose bills and only can approve or reject proposed bills. It has no right to amend bills it considers.

[28]A brief analysis of the Dutch party system is found in Johan Goudsblom, *Dutch Society* (New York: Random House, 1967), pp. 82–94.

ment Populaire Republicain—a social reformist Catholic party with 83 deputies; the Socialists with 95 deputies; and a host of smaller groupings. Some parties other than the Communists, such as the pro-Gaullists and the Poujadists, with approximately 70 seats, also pursued an antigovernment policy. The parties in the middle, which sought to form governments, were limited by the number of parties with which they could realistically negotiate. Throughout most of the Fourth Republic, 350 to 400 of the 597 votes in the National Assembly were available to form a government, but all 400 votes were not available at the same time. Another weakening factor was the absence of party cohesion. On 72 crucial votes between 1946 and 1956 in the National Assembly, only the Communists and Socialists maintained party discipline. On numerous votes, from 10 to 40 percent of the parties' deputies voted against the parties' majority. During this same period, 10 governments were forced to resign because of split voting in parties that originally had voted for installing the cabinet.[29]

In a multiparty system the common denominator is the presence of three or more political parties with substantial and long-term popular support. The ability of the executive branch to govern in a multiparty system varies, depending on the number of parties and party cohesion. There are some political systems, such as Denmark and the Netherlands, where coalition cabinets have a tradition of effective governing once a prime minister and a cabinet have received legislative approval.

PARTY ORGANIZATION

One characteristic a group must possess to be considered a political party is some type of formal organization, even if the organization is as restricted as a few legislators consulting one another under a shared party label. Party organization ranges from the decentralized autonomous, and open-entry arrangements where anyone can join and try to be nominated as a candidate, as found in many parts of the United States, to the hierarchical and centralized pattern common to totalitarian parties.

PARTY AS A STRATARCHY[30]

Samuel J. Eldersveld,[31] in an exhaustive survey of political organization in the Detroit metropolitan area, has pinpointed some of the dominant traits of party organizations, not only in the United States but in other democratic and competitive party systems as well. Many democratic parties have a unique form of organizational ar-

---

[29]David S. McLellon, "Ministerial Instability and the Lack of Internal Cohesion in French Parties," *World Affairs Quarterly*, 28, April 1957, pp. 3–24.

[30]This concept (stratarchy) was developed first by Harold Lasswell and Abraham Kaplan, *Power and Society* (New Haven: Yale University Press, 1950), pp. 219–220.

[31]This section is based on Samuel J. Eldersveld, *Political Parties: A Behavioral Analysis* (Chicago: Rand McNally, 1964), especially pp. 1–13.

rangement called **stratarchy**. In this type of organization there are numerous leaders and power is scattered among several levels of the organization. This scattering of power leads to a reciprocal deference system, whereby the national leaders depend on the goodwill and support of the organization below them, and party leaders at lower levels depend on national leaders for advice, guidance, and rewards. A pattern of accommodation emerges, in which both initiative and indifference at the local and middle party levels are tolerated by the leadership in order to maintain or expand the membership in the party, which is essentially a voluntary organization.

A democratic party is unlike most organizations because it is "greedy" for supporters. If a party consciously seeks to expand its electoral appeal, it attracts the support of various interests, some of which inevitably have conflicting objectives. The effort to manage intergroup rivalries and maintain a broad coalition causes a party to mediate the demands made by the groups that support it. No group gets everything it wants; tension arising from conflicting claims always is present, but there should be enough response on the part of party leaders to retain the support of most, if not all, of the groups. Both the Democratic and Republican parties in the United States receive support from business interests and trade-union members. Neither party can afford to ignore either group, but it requires considerable skill on the part of the party leadership to balance the claims of business and labor so as to satisfy some members from each group and maintain maximum electoral support.

Tension, conflict, and bargaining are ever-present in a democratic, stratarchical party, and most party leaders are unable and unwilling to establish an effective chain of command. This "downward deference" results from the need for votes, the voluntary nature of party support, the few persons interested in working for a party, and the general absence of penalties that can be applied by party leaders to party workers who occasionally are indifferent or recalcitrant. Obviously, over the long run, the top leadership has some rewards to offer the lower-echelon workers, such as moving up in the party organization or the benefits that can be dispensed by a party that enjoys an electoral success, such as jobs, appointments, contracts, and the like. Both the upper- and lower-echelon party workers mutually depend on one another. This reciprocal dependence, combined with the voluntary character of a democratic party, results in a type of organization called stratarchy.

THE IRON LAW OF OLIGARCHY

Robert Michels[32] first elaborated on the dangers of the iron law of oligarchy, which is the opposite of a loosely organized stratarchy. The German Social Democratic Party, the largest socialist party in the world before World War I and presumably committed to democratic principles within its own organization, was the subject of

[32]First published in 1911. Robert Michels, *Political Parties: A Sociological Study of the Oligarchical Tendencies of Modern Democracy*, with an introduction by Seymour Martin Lipset (New York: The Free Press, 1966), pp. 15–39.

Michels' inquiry. His research led him to conclude that the weakness of democracy lay in the nature of organizations. He declared that "who says organization says oligarchy," and that oligarchy was control of the organization by a few people at the top. Political parties, the organizations intended to represent the masses, were controlled by an elite because of a belief in the superior abilities of the leaders. The complexity of modern society leads to specialization, and the skills and knowledge an organization's leaders acquire extend the power of the leaders. The masses become disinterested and society is ruled by an entrenched oligarchy that controls all political parties and interest groups.

Michels argued that the leaders of the German Social Democratic party did not represent the working-class masses. Party leaders eventually became a part of the privileged element in society. Their principal interest became to maintain this privileged status rather than press the interests or claims of their members. Convinced that there was an inevitable conflict of interest between leaders and members, Michels explained that the mass membership actually was unaware of the ever-present exploitation because of the assets held by the leaders, assets that confirmed the oligarchy's power:

1. Access to vital data and "inside" information, which is used to win the support of the masses.
2. Domination over the organization's communication flow, such as control of all party publications and the ability to send party leaders to the branches to justify the leadership's actions.
3. Political occupational skills that leaders but not members have, for example, speech-making, writing articles, and organizing group activities.[33]

The average member often has less education and less time to spend working with and thinking about the organization. Since members attend meetings on a voluntary basis on their own time after work hours, mass participation and knowledgeable interest are minimal.

Few parties are purely oligarchical and hierarchical, or decentralized and stratarchical. Two examples of different types of party organization are the Communist Party of the Soviet Union and Japan's ruling Liberal-Democratic Party.

Japan

Japanese political parties, especially the ruling Liberal-Democratic Party, rest on the ties and loyalties of the **boss–follower** *(oyabun–kobun)* system of traditional Japan. Parties are federations of follower–leader groups—the *ha*, or factions. The electoral strength of the LDP is the association and club affiliated with the faction at the constituency level. These groups are loyal to the individual representative and

---

[33]A summary of Michels' thesis is found in the "Introduction" by Seymour Martin Lipset to Robert Michels, *op. cit.*, pp. 15–39.

his **faction**. It is these associations, rather than the party branch, that provide the decisive electoral support. Political parties per se are the object of only moderate political loyalty. The Japanese voters' commitment to the faction's local associations is the means through which the LDP wins elections. (The Liberal-Democrats, a conservative party compared to the Socialists, have governed Japan since 1955).

Public opinion polls taken in 1958 revealed that less than 33 percent of the electorate was consciously committed to voting on the basis of party affiliation. The candidate and the faction are the key elements in the LDP's organization: "Leaders extend their benevolence, that is they take care of the group interests, and the members reciprocate by accepting the authority of the leader or 'boss.' ''[34]

Traditional affiliations and commitment to group are particularly prevalent in rural areas, where the LDP draws its greatest support. One author reports that in local elections the village community or council usually selects the candidate the village will support, and all villagers are expected to vote for the designated individual. If the campaign heats up, it has happened that "in order to block infiltration from the candidates of other villages, watchers are posted on the roads at the entrances to the village.''[35] Japan is divided into 130 election districts, each returning 3 to 5 representatives, depending on the population size of the district. Each voter has only 1 vote. A party must estimate carefully its vote-getting ability to decide, for example, in a 5-seat district, whether to run 3-, 4-, or 5 candidates, or seats will be lost to another party that concentrates its votes on 1 or 2 candidates. In addition, within the party, factional rivalry is intensified because the most formidable opponent in the district sometimes is an individual from one's own party.

The organizational and monetary support a candidate can expect is drawn principally from the faction leader. Each leader has local associations and, more importantly, has built up a network of financial backers, the only source of adequate funding. The candidate or followers, in turn, are to show loyalty and support to the leader on intraparty and legislative conflicts.

When Kakuei Tanaka (the former Japanese prime minister who was forced to resign because of the Lockheed Aircraft bribery scandal) was Secretary-General of the LDP between 1965 and 1971, each party member running in a general election received $12,000 from the party. More important, from his own pocket and funds collected by him as leader of the Tanaka faction, he also gave an equal or larger amount to members of his faction and numerous candidates of other factions. This explains why there are large numbers of Tanaka sympathizers in other factions. The importance of the money involved is obvious by a comparison with the salary of the individual legislator, which is under $1,000 per month.

[34]Robert A. Scalapino and Junnosuke Masumi, *Parties and Politics in Contemporary Japan* (Berkeley: University of California Press, 1962), pp. 121–122.

[35]Joji Watanuki, "Patterns of Politics in Present-Day Japan" in Seymour M. Lipset and Stein Rokkan, eds., *Party Systems and Voter Alignments: Cross-National Perspectives* (New York: The Free Press, 1967), p. 463.

Having ruled Japan for more than 25 years, the LDP faction leaders have access to substantial funds. It generally is accepted that 90 percent of business contributions are given to the LDP. The bulk of the contributions go to faction leaders who then distribute the money to their followers in the Diet.[36]

The system holds together at the top because party leaders recognize that the various factions forming the party, which in effect is a federation, must receive rewards. For example, in 1973, six major factions were identified in the House of Representatives, each faction identified by the name of the leader, or *oyabun*.

Only 9 LDP Diet members were not associated with a faction. The 6 largest factions ranged between 18 and 53.[37] Factions are organized formally, with a headquarters, regular meetings, and firm discipline. The cooperation of 3 or more factions is necessary for the LDP to nominate a prime minister, but once selected, representatives of all factions serve in the cabinet.

The Liberal-Democrats have an organization that is distinctly not monolithic, with power more collegial than centralized at the top. Within each faction, however, power is centralized. The viability of the party organization is apparent, however, from the fact that it has governed Japan since 1955.

The Soviet Union

Lenin, the founder of the Communist Party of the Soviet Union (CPSU), stressed organization as the "kernel" of his doctrine. Lenin and his successors have accepted the dogma first stated by Lenin that "Marxism is fortified by the material unity of organization which welds millions of toilers into an army of the working class."[38] Without organization, ideology would fail; an army of disciplined communicants was the means to achieve power and then to govern. The term the Communists use to describe their party organization is **democratic centralism**, which in practice means all power is in the hands of a few party leaders, with the democratic component nonexistent. The key features of democratic centralism are:

1. Election of all party executive bodies at all organizational levels from below.
2. Regular accountability of party executive bodies to their party organizations and to higher party bodies.
3. Strict party discipline and subordination of the minority to the majority.
4. The absolutely binding character of the decisions of higher bodies upon lower bodies.[39]

[36]Hans B. Baerwald reports that Japanese reporters estimated a successful Diet candidate had to spend $280,000 on the campaign. A candidate spending only $200,000 was in danger of losing. Spoils or money are the lubricating oil of Japanese politics. Spoils confer power and attract followers. Hans B. Baerwald, *Japan's Parliament* (Cambridge: Cambridge University Press, 1974), pp. 126–127.

[37]*Ibid.*, pp. 62–67.

[38]Selznick, *op. cit.,* p. 8.

[39]Merle Fainsod, *How Russia is Ruled,* rev. ed. (Cambridge: Harvard University Press, 1965), p. 208.

Theoretically, the Party Congress, which is supposed to meet every 5 years, elects the central committee. At the Twenty-fifth Congress of the CPSU held in March 1976, there were 4948 delegates in attendance. A Central Committee of 288 members and 139 candidate members was "elected" and on the last day of the Congress, at a plenary meeting, the Central Committee "elected" a **Politburo** of 16 members and 6 alternatives.

Elections are in fact not competitive because power is effectively centralized in the Politburo. The Politburo, through the 10-member Secretariat, decides who will have Central Committee membership and who will attend the Congresses. This pattern of selection continues down through the organization. Party leaders are co-opted rather than elected. The Politburo is the decision-making body in the Soviet Union. The Central Committee is too large to act as an executive body except on rare occasions, and it meets, on the average, 3 to 6 times a year in plenary session.

The Opening of the 25th Congress of the Communist Party of the Soviet Union in the Kremlin Palace of Congresses in Moscow, February 24, 1976.

Members of the 25th Congress of the Communist Party of the Soviet Union in the process of voting.

Party leaders are inviolable insofar as criticism from below is concerned. The CPSU is a military hierarchy, and subordinates must carry out the decisions of the higher authorities. Discussion and some criticism may be allowed about how best to implement policies or why policies are being poorly implemented, but once a decision has been reached by the Politburo or, occasionally, the Central Committee, the decision is binding. There is a horror of dissent. Criticism organized to the degree that it might represent the statements of an opposition faction is not tolerated. Communist democratic centralism means a monolithic organization in practice.

PARTY MEMBERSHIP
In the eighteenth century, when political parties were just emerging, the British political writer and statesman Edmund Burke defined a political party as "a body of men united for promoting, by their joint endeavors, the national interest upon some particular principle in which they are all agreed."[40]

Dedication to a particular political philosophy or set of political principles is not an important motivating factor for a majority of party members today. In the United States such an individual would be described as an "ideologue" who "weighs policy alternatives posed in a campaign, making his choice on the basis of agreement or disagreement with the candidates' expressed views on the crucial problems of

---

[40]Edmund Burke, *Burke's Works*, vol. I (London: Henry G. Bohn, 1855), p. 375.

the day." This person has "a reasonably self-conscious and overarching view of the good life, usually expressed in the form of a liberal or conservative philosophy."[41]

The data available concerning the number of Americans who are predominantly issue-oriented or "ideologues" indicates that they make up a small minority of the voters. The University of Michigan Survey Research Center concluded that in the 1956 presidential election, which pitted President Eisenhower against Adlai Stevenson, only 4.5 percent of the total sample and slightly under 6 percent of the voters could be classified as "ideologues" or "near-ideology" persons.[42]

The requirements and privileges of party membership are partly determined by the size of the party and the type of party system. The Albanian Communist Party, with a membership of 101,500 represents 4 percent of Albania's population of 2,597,600. This percentage is the lowest ratio of party members to the general population among the Communist-ruled states of Eastern Europe.[43] The opposite extreme is reported for the 2 African countries of Guinea and Mali. In the former, official announcements claimed that the entire adult population—1.6 million—was enrolled in the Parti Democratique de Guinea in 1961. In Mali, party saturation of the adult population was purportedly achieved by 1964. Obviously, membership in the elite Albanian Communist Party is more significant than membership in a party that enrolls every adult. In Mali, for instance, one of the principal reasons for expanding the *Union Soudanaise* was to secure additional revenue. One observer reported that "by 1964, party dues seem to be collected as a matter of course from all adults by government as well as party officials along with annual person taxes."[44]

People join political parties for many reasons. The more apparent motives include promotion of selected political policies or doctrines and securing of economic benefits for a particular stratum or category of the population. People also join parties for reasons that are not immediately obvious from looking at the party and its political orientation.

The desire to exercise power, manipulate people, and receive deference motivates some. Harold Lasswell described **political man** as one who accentuates and demands power and orients himself toward experiences that involve power.[45] All behavior allegedly works toward achieving power. The need for power is the dominant need. Both Robert E. Lane and Harold Lasswell noted later, however, that a person with an overt desire for power is likely to achieve only a minor political status in democratic political systems. A person dominated by power needs will not have the

[41]Fred Greenstein, *The American Party System and the American People,* 2nd ed. (Englewood Cliffs, N.J.: Prentice-Hall, 1970), pp. 29–30.

[42]Angus Campbell et al., *The American Voter* (New York: John Wiley, 1960), pp. 230–231.

[43]Nicholas C. Pano, "Albania," in Richard F. Staar, ed., *Yearbook on International Communist Affairs,* 1979 (Stanford: Hoover Institution Press, 1979), p. 1.

[44]Zolberg, *op. cit.,* p. 105.

[45]Harold Lasswell, *Power and Personality* (New York: W. W. Norton, 1948), p. 57.

interpersonal, broker-type skills that are required of successful politicians in democracies. As Lane has noted, "In adult life the search for the jugular of power may very likely lead to the world of finance, journalism, or industry instead of politics."[46]

Without attempting to provide an exhaustive list of conscious and unconscious personal needs that motivate persons to join a political party, we shall discuss selected motivations in order to give an indication of the needs served by political-party membership.

Social adjustment and social interaction are factors that encourage party affiliation. A survey of political leaders in Detroit, beginning at the precinct level, found that precinct leaders often were disillusioned with the political importance of their jobs, but at least 55 percent remained politically active because of "social contacts and association with friends."[47]

Desire for personal economic gain also prompts some to become party members. It is a political truism that it is not only **what** you know, but **who** you know. The political arena provides the opportunity to make invaluable contracts with influential persons in the world of business and labor. Most of the improper activities that too often make the headlines result from special favors or "inside information" that one may obtain by knowing the right public official at the critical moment. This is not to suggest of course, that all of the economic gain, such as a government contract, is improper or unethical. On occasion, however, the fine line between acceptable and illegal is crossed. One instance was the conviction of the press secretary to Chicago's late mayor Richard Daley. The press secretary was convicted for secretly owning a firm that between 1962 and 1973 held an exclusive contract with the city of Chicago for all advertising and display promotions at O'Hare Airport. More recently, Giscard d'Estang, the President of France was embarrassed by the allegation that while Minister of Finance he accepted diamonds and emeralds valued at $250,000 from the now overthrown Emperor Bokassa of the Central African Republic. French paratroops participated in a 1979 coup against Bokassa, who then was seeking assistance from the Soviets, was accused of cannibalism, and had participated personally in the murder of school children for demonstrating against him. In the years before the coup, France had supported the Bokassa regime with $25 to $50 million in aid annually. French officials may accept foreign gifts, but the French president is having difficulty explaining the source of and reasons for this particular gift. Whether illegal or simply being the right person at the right time in the right place, potential or actual economic benefits attract some to the political arena. Eldersveld's Detroit study confirmed, however, the importance of economic motivation for many active party members.

The career advantages and elite status in a totalitarian political system are even more apparent. Certain jobs are open only to those willing and qualified to join the

---

[46]Robert E. Lane, *Political Life* (Glencoe, Ill.: The Free Press, 1959), p. 127.
[47]Samuel J. Eldersveld, *Political Parties* (Chicago: Rand McNally, 1964), p. 290.

ruling party. A study of party membership in the Soviet Union classified selected occupations as "party restricted," where the number of non-party members was one percent or less: heads of government departments, directorates from the city level up, and the directors of state-owned enterprises. "Virtually party restricted" occupations included those in which non-CPSU members ranged up to five percent: judges, army officers, and probably the police.[48]

Status and ego enhancement also obviously are available to the political activist who has the opportunity to meet various and sundry political personalities of the moment. The "inside information" that swirls throughout any political system enables a party member to stand out among his peers as a person especially knowledgeable and informed and a person to be listened to.

Robert Lane has suggested other needs that are served, including curiosity.[49] Curiosity is a result of the need to come to grips with and understand the environment. For a few, this may include joining a party and comprehending the political world. Lane suggests that the search for meaning may be a "basic" drive to be fulfilled after other basal requirements (temperature, thirst, hunger, sex, security) have been met. Persons with a highly developed curiosity probably will follow events in the political world closely and in some instances will become active political-party members.

Unconscious, neurotic needs also lead some persons to affiliate with a party. This is not a common phenomenon, but it is a fact that one means of working out inner psychic tensions is to join a political party. Furthermore, it is not only the extremist right-wing and left-wing parties that attract this type of person. Parties in the political center also have members who are too intensely, unreasonably, and absolutely committed to party objectives. Such individuals develop their own rigidly structured value system, and their irrational (often neurotic) dedication prompts them to question the motives and credibility of those who politically disagree with them in the slightest way. The liberal–authoritarian or conservative–authoritarian who takes a middle-of-the-road political philosophy and distorts it to alleviate inner tensions is found in most democratic parties.

A study in the early 1950s on the nature of Communist Party membership in the United States, Britain, France, and Italy revealed that, particularly in the United States and Britain, Communist membership appealed to those with psychological needs. The militancy of communism in the 1950s stressed the confronting and striking down of civil opponents. In a majority of cases, resentment and hostility were a result of unhappiness with social conditions, such as racial discrimination, or were a result of party indoctrination. In a substantial number of cases (33 percent in the United States and 34 percent in Britain), however, the incidence of neurotic hostility

---

[48]T. H. Rigby, *Communist Party Membership in the U.S.S.R.: 1917–1967* (Princeton: Princeton University Press, 1968), p. 449.

[49]Lane, *op. cit.,* pp. 112–120.

in party members originated as "a pattern of chronic and unconscious hostility resulting from family and childhood experiences."[50]

After studying the writings of several psychiatrists and psychologists, one eminent political scientist concluded that, in the case of some Communist Party members, the party not only allowed the expression of aggression but also accommodated deviant sex roles.

> *Thus in the Party, dependent and passive men (often with latent or overt homosexual tendencies) were able to profit from a situation where they were told what to do, what to think, and how to live their lives. . . . For women with sexual confusion, the Party offered masculine roles where aggression, dominance, and even masculine clothes and manners were appropriate.*[51]

People join political parties for many reasons. It appears that Edmund Burke's eighteenth-century appraisal of a political party as a group of individuals committed to certain political principles no longer describes the dominant motivation but is only one among numerous reasons. Party membership means different things to different people, and any analysis of active political membership must acknowledge this fact. Whatever the various attractions or need satisfactions of party membership, the functions of political parties are of major importance to the political system.

FUNCTIONS
PARTY FUNCTIONS IN PLURALISTIC SYSTEMS

Political parties in democratic and competitive political systems are first and foremost concerned with controlling or participating in government by electing candidates. Other functions related to this first one include: acting as brokers or mediators/negotiators and balancing competing claims or demands so that conflicting groups resolve their objectives in a peaceful and institutionalized manner; identifying and organizing public attitudes (gun control, reduced property taxes) in order to win votes, with the result that it influences government decisions; educating and informing the citizenry on public issues; simplifying and reducing the number of issue alternatives; recruiting and selecting leaders; establishing and confirming procedural standards for the conduct of government, especially the means by which political leaders are chosen; and providing welfare services and social outlets for party members. Parties out of power provide a constant source of criticism, which should illuminate and influence government policy and contribute to maintaining personal and political liberties. In the American party system and some other party systems such as the French, members of the government party often are as active in criticizing the government as members of the opposition parties.

[50]Gabriel Almond et al., *The Appeals of Communism* (Princeton: Princeton University Press, 1954), p. 261.
[51]Lane, *op. cit.,* pp. 121–122.

A political scientist and former president of Harvard University, A. Lawrence Lowell, observed that brokerage is the most "universal function" of parties in a democracy and that the broker role is "a new profession whose function consists in bringing buyer and seller together."[52]

> *The process of forming public opinion involves, therefore, bringing men together in masses on some middle ground where they can combine to carry out a common policy. In short, it requires a species of brokerage, and one of the functions of politicians is that of brokers.*[53]

Using a term that has become nearly as familiar as broker, Gabriel Almond describes the distinguishing function of parties as **aggregation**, "the function of converting demands by interest groups into general policy alternatives."[54] Aggregation establishes a few policy alternatives in order to build or maintain an alliance of support groups. It presumes the existence of numerous interest groups (trade unions, business organizations) whose claims are balanced, mediated, and combined by parties to gain votes. In competitive political systems, it is at the party level that the inclusive combining process labeled aggregation often occurs.

A critical party function is **electioneering**, although in recent years the ability of parties to sway opinion has been questioned. In the metropolitan Detroit area, where party organization is well-developed and active, it is reported that approximately 60 percent of the adults in Detroit were "completely unexposed to party structure" and 44 percent had **never** been exposed personally to a party organization.[55] If voters are not contacted face-to-face or by phone, it suggests that immediate and significant electoral influence may have to come from another source. Frank Sorauf, who has written extensively on American parties, concludes that "the political party no longer monopolizes the important skills or manpower."[56] The trend today is for candidates to rely on public-relations specialists, who are experts in appealing to the electorate via radio, TV, newspapers, and direct mailings. Ad hoc campaign organizations and a large number of personal volunteers (generally including many college students) for a popular candidate are the more common techniques used today. The importance of **primary elections** in the United States means that most candidates must construct their own organization, at least for purposes of the primary.

---

[52]A. Lawrence Lowell, *Public Opinion and Popular Government,* 2nd ed. (New York: Longmans, Green, 1930), p. 60.

[53]*Ibid.,* p. 62. Lowell first offered this analysis in 1909 in the James Schouler lectures at Johns Hopkins University.

[54]Gabriel A. Almond and G. Bingham Powell, Jr., *Comparative Politics: A Developmental Approach* (Boston: Little, Brown, 1966), p. 98.

[55]Eldersveld, *op. cit.,* pp. 442 and 526.

[56]Frank J. Sorauf, "Political Parties and Political Analysis," in Chambers and Burnham, eds., *op. cit.,* p. 54.

Five Republican presidential primary candidates vie for the voters' attention in Manchester, New Hampshire on February 25, 1980.

If the parties' electioneering function has been modified in democracies, it has not disappeared. The Cook County "organization," or machine, of the late Mayor Richard Daley is but one example of an organization with electoral clout. Mayor Daley had especially strong control over eleven wards, "the automatic eleven" in Chicago. In the 1968 presidential election, for example, he "delivered" 205,000 votes to Hubert Humphrey as opposed to the 21,000 received by Republican Richard Nixon.[57] A British example gives further evidence that the electoral role of party should not be disregarded, especially in close elections. Even though most minds may have been made up weeks or months before election day, parties can encourage those who are so busy they might not vote, stimulate the indifferent, and sway a few. The absentee ballot, or postal vote as it is known in Great Britain, indicates how a party with superior organization can be decisive:

> *What is significant is that in nine most marginally won Conservative seats in 1964 the average postal vote was 1772. . . . On the assumption that they split 2:1 in favor of the Conservatives, they would have been decisive in twelve constituencies; at any other election since 1950 they would have been decisive in at least six constituencies.*[58]

[57]Len O'Connor, *Clout: Mayor Daley and His City* (New York: Avon Books, 1975), p. 212.
[58]Peter G. Pulzer, *Political Representation and Elections: Parties and Voting in Great Britain* (New York: Praeger, 1967), pp. 88–89.

DECLINE OF POLITICAL PARTIES

Finally, we might note that although party as an electoral organization is important, at least in the United States the role of party in elections may be declining. Beginning in the 1970s more people identified themselves as Independents than as Democrats or Republicans. In 1950, 80 percent of Americans voted straight party tickets; by 1970 this had dropped to 50 percent[59] As these figures suggest, party as a guide to electoral behavior has declined noticeably.

In the United States and other advanced countries, the use of mass media is slowly eroding party identification because of the candidates' own actions. When campaigns were conducted principally through personal appearances before partisan audiences and through the efforts of local party workers, party loyalty was stressed. Today, when a candidate appears on national or local television, she or he is speaking not only to party supporters but to supporters of the other party and independents as well. The candidate asks support on the basis of issues and more importantly, on the basis of her or his personal characteristics—capable, trustworthy, and more able to fill the office. Party identification is played down, often not mentioned. Candidates increasingly campaign as individuals and promote themselves in terms of their own talents, rather than join with other office seekers from the same party in a combined effort. Basically, a candidate puts together his or her own organization, often depending heavily on a public-relations firm. If successful in winning office, the official stresses service to the constituents, helping them with myriad and individual problems as they relate to information needs, assistance with government regulation, or intercession with bureaucratic officials. Basically, it is the individual constituency that is of prime concern. If the official can hold its support, he or she can do pretty much as he or she pleases without being penalized by the party.

We might note that the decline of party identity and party loyalty is partly related to the decline of the family in postindustrial society. Party identification, just as one's religion, is inherited in considerable measure from the family environment, as shown in Table 6–1.

Table 6-1   Party Identification and Father's Party Identification

	Recalls Father's Party		Does Not Recall Father's Party	
	France	U.S.A.	France	U.S.A.
Has Party ID	79.4	81.6	47.7	50.7
No Party ID	20.6	18.4	52.3	49.3

Source: Phillip E. Converse, "Of Time and Partisan Stability," *Comparative Political Studies*, Vol. 2, No. 2 (July, 1969), p. 145.

[59]Frederick G. Dutton, *Changing Sources of Power: American Politics in the 1970s* (New York: McGraw Hill, 1971), p. 228.

As the nuclear family declines in importance, often with both parents working, the number of inherited values and attitudes passed from parents to children is reduced. The decline of the family has affected the transmission of party loyalty or identification between generations.

Party reform sometimes has weakened party organization and thus the role of the party. Reforms have been an important influence in the United States and also have affected party organizations in many postindustrial societies. These reforms are carried out to bring in younger and more representative groups of party supporters. The older, dedicated cadre or party workhorses no longer can dominate as much party activity as previously. As one American political commentator observed with reference to reforms in the Democratic Party:

> Who wants to be a party regular, sweating, panting and performing for years, only to be dumped as a [presidential convention] delegate, thus losing a trip to Detroit or New York in 1980? Forlorn were those Democratic Party wheelhorses made to stand outside George McGovern's convention hall in 1972, while the ragtags of political life passed through the security gates like cardinals en route to elect a Pope.[60]

PARTY FUNCTIONS IN AUTHORITARIAN AND TOTALITARIAN SYSTEMS

Parties perform important though changing functions in democracies. In other political systems party functions also are important. In political systems where there are no competitive elections, the ruling political party performs numerous functions: deciding policies and programs, overseeing the government bureaucracy and the implementation of policy, propagandizing and indoctrinating the masses, supervising the behavior of the population, and selecting and approving party leaders and persons in positions of influence at all levels of society.

The North Korean Workers' Party, modeled on the Soviet Communist Party is based on the principle that all government agencies exist as "the faithful executors of the general line of the Party." The party's nerve center is the 20-member Political Committee led by Kim Il-sung, who is both government premier and head of the party. The Political Committee has the task of "policymaking, coordination and supervision" of all activities in totalitarian North Korea.[61]

Joseph Stalin expounded this exclusive position of the Communist Party:

> The Party must stand at the head of the working class; it must see farther than the working class; it must lead the proletariat, and not follow in the tail of the spontaneous movement.[62]

---

[60]Nick Timmesch, "In Retrospect, That Smoke-Filled Room Looks Pretty Good," *Chicago Tribune*, September 18, 1979.

[61]Quotes from Neena Vreeland, Rinn-Sup Shinn, *et al.*, *Area Handbook for North Korea* (Washington, D.C.: United States Government Printing Office, 1976), pp. 158 and 184.

[62]Joseph Stalin, *Foundations of Leninism* (New York: International Publishers, 1934), p. 109, quoted in Merle Fainsod, *How Russia is Ruled*, 2nd ed. (Cambridge: Harvard University Press, 1964), p. 137.

A totalitarian party attempts not only to control the most influential people in society but also to colonize and win their positive support. Academic and professional groups are the most rapidly expanding segments of the Soviet population and the CPSU. The policy-making and supervising functions of the CPSU are the most important, and these functions depend on the allegiance of the academic and professional strata. Table 6–2 shows the concern of the leadership in this regard.

Table 6–2   CPSU Membership Among Major Professional Groups

Profession	Number in Party		Approximate Party Saturation in Percent	
	1947	1964	1947	1964
Teachers	80,000	700,000	16.0	25.0
Doctors	40,000	110,000	19.0	22.0
Engineers	148,000	592,000	38.0	42.0
Agriculture specialists	24,000	118,000	19.0	44.0

Source: Adapted from T. H. Rigby, *Communist Party Membership in the U.S.S.R.: 1917–1967.* Copyright © 1968 by Princeton University Press. Adapted by permission of the publisher.

Recruiting and indoctrinating the highly trained groups is complemented by mobilizing and politicizing the masses. An important means by which the party can accomplish this is through elections, although elections are different from what we regard as normal because generally there is only one candidate per office. Elections are a time for propagandizing and indoctrinating the masses and justifying government policy. Electoral turnout and the percent of valid votes in a district is also an indication of how well the party organization in that district has done its job and of whether any threatening discontent, as expressed through blank or defaced ballots, is present. Some parties claim to be especially successful. If one is to believe official figures, only 4 persons out of 978,161 registered voters failed to vote in the 1966 Albanian elections, (probably the most repressive East European Communist system).[63]

PARTY FUNCTIONS IN DEVELOPING POLITICAL SYSTEMS
Political parties in the Third World perform many of the same functions as in authoritarian and totalitarian systems, especially if there is only one party or if one party overshadows all others. Only a few Third World countries (for example, Costa Rica, Malaysia, Sri Lanka, Venezuela) have competitive elections.

Most developing societies possess only a short political heritage. Such traditional institutions as emperor, king, sultan, or shah, at least at the national political level, are of slight use in the contemporary world. If they do exist they are undergoing substantial modification, as in Thailand, where a once powerful king became a figure-

[63]Julias Birch, "The Albanian Political Experience," *Government and Opposition,* 6:3, 1971, p. 63.

head after the 1932 revolution. The inheritances from the European colonial period, while important, were of short duration because of the rapid and often violent events that led to the withdrawal of colonial governments after World War II. Constitutional and government arrangements generally did not have the time to develop.

Samuel P. Huntington has noted that, in situations where "political institutions collapse or are weak or nonexistent, "stability and the beginning of political integration depend upon a strong party. The party becomes the one institution that can organize and develop the country. It becomes "the distinctive organization of modern politics" whose function is "to organize participation, to aggregate interests, to serve as the link between social forces and the government."[64]

Political parties, like all organizations, are made up of the interaction patterns of human beings and are subject to local customs and social institutions. Constitutions and laws provide the formal guidelines within which parties must operate, but the intraparty behavior patterns—including exercise of influence, the negotiation procedures, rewards and patronage for one's supporters—determine the character of the party or party system.

Whether a party can assume important responsibilities can be answered only by looking at specific countries. Aristide Zolberg's analysis of West African states suggests that the demands on party are often too great. The rapid expansion of party organization in order to undertake the governing functions has, on occasion, made the party a point of conflict between traditional and nontraditional interests. Speaking very candidly to this point, President Touré of Guinea admitted:

> Certain party committees did not represent more than two or three families and the membership was dominated by family discipline or by the family chief who was at the same time the president of the committee.[65]

Few political parties in the developing world are technologically and ideologically capable of achieving the monolithic character of the totalitarian parties in the West. The largest and most notable effort in this regard was made by the Chinese Communist Party. This attempt began to show public signs of failure with the launching of China's **Cultural Revolution** in 1966. The revolution was launched to correct the behavior of party cadre who, after nearly two decades in power, were complacent, bureaucratically sluggish, and often more pragmatic, if not opportunistic, than properly revolutionary. The Cultural Revolution eventually was halted in 1969 when it became clear that the authority system of the Communist regime was being undermined.[66]

The role of the party in a developing country potentially is unlimited, but the problems associated with developing the organization and its responsibilities are of

---

[64]Huntington, *Political Order in Changing Societies,* p. 91.

[65]*Afrique Nouvelle,* November 20, 1964, quoted in Zolberg, *op. cit.,* p. 103.

[66]For a succinct overview of the Cultural Revolution, see John Gittings, "The State of the Party," *Far Eastern Economic Review,* LIX, No. 9 (February 29, 1968), pp. 375–380.

equal magnitude. The struggle to establish government authority patterns that will make possible stability and orderly growth is the history of the developing world since 1945.

CONCLUSION

We should not assume that the emergence of competitive political parties in the 30 to 35 democratic political systems throughout the world has been a natural or easy evolution. It has not. Nor can we assume competitive party systems will emerge inevitably in most countries. The transition from intolerance of opposition to allowing dissent and finally to acceptance of diversity and disagreement has been slow and uneven. It is not easy to manage or nurture a political system in which the activities of most parties do not make effective government practically impossible. One eminent political scientist declares that one of the most serious mistakes Western scholars have made is to assume that democracy, which requires competitive political parties, can be exported very easily.[67]

Competing political parties can be one—if not the most—effective means to reconcile peacefully and in an orderly way private rights and wants and public authority. No democracy exists without two or more healthy and active political parties. Unfortunately, there is no blueprint based on past experiences that can reveal how this can be made to occur in other political systems. One fact that seems to emerge is that only when there is widespread agreement on fundamentals—such as the type of government, religious toleration, minority rights, or a consensus on rules of the game—will there be democracy and competing political parties. Political-party competition requires self-restraint, moderation, and the ability to compromise. It is not surprising that democratic party systems are present in only 20 percent of the world's approximately 170 countries.

In most other political systems, except a few that appear to be making the arduous transition to more open and competitive politics (Taiwan, South Korea, Nigeria, Kenya) political parties are designed to monopolize power. No other party is permitted to exist. The single party is used to strengthen and perpetuate the rule of those who control the government. Regretfully, although parties first emerged to express popular opinion, in a majority of countries they were created and refined to control and penetrate society for the benefit of a small ruling elite.

SELECTED READINGS

The classic American introduction to political parties and interest groups was written by the late V. O. Key, Jr., *Politics, Parties, and Pressure Groups*, 5th ed. (New York: Thomas Y. Crowell, 1964). In a similar vein, a comparative introduction to par-

---

[67]Giovanni Sartori, *Parties and Party Systems* (Cambridge: Cambridge University Press, 1976), p. 14.

ties and interest groups with a European focus is Maurice Duverger, *Party Politics and Pressure Groups,** trans. by David Wagoner (New York: Thomas T. Crowell, 1972).

A well-reviewed major conceptual work on political parties is Giovanni Sortori, *Parties and Party Systems: A Framework for Analysis** (Cambridge: Cambridge University Press, 1976).

There are many studies available on specific party systems. A carefully researched and analytical study of one of the earliest American party systems, first published in 1909, is Carl Lotus Becker, *The History of Political Parties in the Province of New York, 1760–1776* (Madison: University of Wisconsin Press, 1909). Carrying the analysis of American parties into the post-Revolutionary War period are William N. Chambers and Walter Dean Burnham, eds., *The American Party System: Stages of Political Development** (New York: Oxford University Press, 1967). A somewhat dated but excellent analysis of the American party system is by Austin Ranney and Willmoore Kendall, *Democracy and the American Party System* (New York: Harcourt, Brace, 1956). A comprehensive overview is Frank J. Sorauf, *Party Politics in America*, 3rd ed. (Boston: Little Brown, 1976).

A selective sample of studies of political parties other than American includes Samuel H. Beer, *British Politics in the Collectivist Age* (New York: Alfred A. Knopf, 1967); T. McKenzie, *British Political Parties,** 2nd ed. (New York: Frederick A. Praeger, 1964); Thomas J. Bellows, *The People's Action Party of Singapore: Emergence of a Dominant Party System** (New Haven: Yale University Southeast Asia Studies, Monograph Series No. 14, 1970); Leonard Schapiro, *The Communist Party of the Soviet Union* (New York: Vintage Books, 1971); and Nathaniel B. Thayer, *How the Conservatives Rule Japan* (Princeton: Princeton University Press, 1970).

Based on four years of research/observation in Conakray, see Claude Riviere, *Guinea: The Mobilization of a People*, translated by Virginia Thompson and Richard Adolff (Ithica, N.Y.: Cornell University Press, 1977), This discusses, among other factors, the role of the party in building a revolutionary country in Africa.

Three comparative party studies for the more advanced student are Maurice Duverger, *Political Parties,** 3rd ed., trans. by Barbara and Robert North (New York: Methuen, 1964); Leon D. Epstein, *Political Parties in Western Democracies** (New Brunswick, N.J., Transaction Books, 1980); and Seymour M. Lipset and Stein Rokkan, eds., *Party Systems and Voter Alignments* (New York: The Free Press, 1967). The latter book especially is for the advanced student.

The importance of some form of political opposition, either within the ruling party or through the medium of opposition parties, is analyzed in three edited volumes:

---

*Available in paperback.

Samuel P. Huntington and Clement H. Moore, eds., *Authoritarian Politics in Modern Society: The Dynamics of Established One-Party Systems* (New York: Basic Books, 1970); Rodney Barker, ed., *Studies in Opposition* (London: The MacMillan Press, 1971); and Robert A. Dahl, ed., *Political Oppositions in Western Democracies** (New Haven: Yale University Press, 1966).

Opposition generally and opposition factions and parties outside of Western Europe and the United States are discussed in Robert A. Dahl, ed., *Regimes and Oppositions** (New Haven: Yale University Press, 1973).

Western European Communist parties increasingly appear committed to electoral politics and are inclined to participate in coalition governments if the opportunity arises. An insightful discussion of socialism as well as Eurocommunism and its relations with the United States and the U.S.S.R. is William E. Griffith, ed., *The European Left: Italy, France and Spain (Lexington, Mass.: Lexington Books, 1979).*

Two studies that treat the revolutionary and conspiratorial nature of Communist parties are Philip Selznick, *The Organizational Weapon: A Study of Bolshevik Strategy and Tactics* (Glencoe, Ill.: The Free Press, 1960); and Robert Scalapino, ed., *The Communist Revolution in Asia: Tactics, Goals, and Achievements,** 2nd ed. (Englewood Cliffs, N.J.: Prentice-Hall, 1969).

Relatively short but heuristic analyses of the significance of party organization are Samuel J. Eldersveld, *Political Parties: A Behavioral Analysis* (Chicago: Rand McNally, 1964), especially Chapter 1 and Part III; and Robert T. Golembiewski, William A. Walsh, and William J. Crotty, *A Methodological Primer for Political Scientists* (Chicago: Rand McNally, 1969), Chapter XI. Discussions of political party functions are scattered throughout the literature. Anthony Downs, *An Economic Theory of Democracy* (New York: Harper & Row, Publishers, 1957) is especially useful for developing hypotheses. The book analyzes political parties as if they were to follow rationally and consistently a policy of maximizing votes. An introduction to the functional part of the literature is Howard A. Scarrow, "The Function of Political Parties," *The Journal of Politics*, 29:4, 1967, 770–90.

William Crotty, ed., *The Party Symbol: Readings on Political Parties** (San Francisco: W. H. Freeman, 1980) is a basic introduction to the role and scope of political parties in the United States today. One article compares party organizations in the United States, Western Europe, and the rest of the world.

*Available in paperback.

Chapter Seven

Representation and Elections

In political systems where elections actually determine who will have the power to make political decisions, they are one of the most important inputs into the political processes. They provide a link by which the governed can partly control their governors and are a major battleground on which rival interests can fight out their claims. Elections are also the chief institutional mechanism by which representatives are selected. Representation can provide an effective process for making demands and translating them into policy. Though the idea of representation developed independently of democracy, representation and elections are identified closely with modern democratic systems, so closely that many people erroneously think of them as the only means of popular participation and control in large, pluralistic countries. Nevertheless, elections and representation imply that power and authority come from the people, that they flow from the bottom up. Where this condition is missing, elections and representative-type institutions can exist—they are found under almost every form of government—but they do not decide who will govern or how.[1]

THEORIES OF REPRESENTATION

"No taxation without representation" is a well-known battle cry in Western politics. We all are familiar with taxes, but what is **representation**? Representation has many different, even conflicting, meanings. It can mean a typical sample drawn from many similar items; portraying or presenting a likeness of someone or some-

---

[1]We will use the phrase "representative institutions" rather than legislatures to indicate that many agencies may be involved in speaking or defending popular values and interests. Under some circumstances these may include executives, judicial systems, bureaucracies, and even political parties. Legislatures, however, are the major representative bodies.

thing; a symbol; to act the role of someone or play a part; or to stand in the place of someone and act for them or in their name.[2] Politically, representation means having someone act in your place in governmental decision making. Representatives are people who act for or on behalf of other people in the decision-making process. They speak for and commit others to particular courses of action.

There are many different ways in which a person can be understood as representing another politically. Many have nothing to do with either democracy or elections. Throughout history many people have claimed to be representative. Medieval and Renaissance kings claimed to represent or act for their people, regardless of what the masses of people thought. Leninist doctrine creates a role for the disciplined revolutionary party as the representative and embodiment of the proletariat's real interest. According to many Fascists, the leader, or *Führer*, somehow incarnates the will and interest of the people. Other theorists, such as Thomas Hobbes (1588–1679) argued that the people give up all their power to a sovereign whose will is then absolute and unchallengeable but is understood as embodying the will of the people.

Such ideas, however, have nothing to do with liberal, Western concepts of representation. These emphasize that representatives are selected by their constituents and are accountable to them, at least through **elections**. Elections are the key to modern concepts of representation. Linking elections, representation, and responsibility does not, however, tell us what the representative does or what the link or connection is between the representative and the represented. Since at least the eighteenth century, two persistent, conflicting, though plausible, theories have attempted to explain this relation. Variously called delegate versus trustee, mandate versus independent, or delegate versus independent, the argument centers on how much independence a representative can have from the wishes of the constituency. The following answers are typical of a continuing and unresolved debate. This debate is alive today in current American controversies over to what extent members of Congress should mirror their constituents' demands on issues such as busing, inflation, unemployment, foreign aid, and war.

INDEPENDENT OR DELEGATE?
Edmund Burke (1729–1797) best stated the argument that elected representatives should be independent of their constituents' wishes when those wishes conflict with the representative's best judgment on an issue. Burke argued that we elect representatives for their good judgment, not merely as mirror images of our desires. The exercise of judgment requires independence of thought and action. Burke claimed that

---

[2]These and many other meanings are discussed in Hanna Pitkin, *The Concept of Representation* (Berkeley: University of California Press, 1967) pp. 1–13, 241–252, and *passim;* and Hanna Pitkin, ed., *Representation* (New York: Atherton, 1969) pp. 1–23.

it ought to be the happiness and glory of a representative to live in the strictest union, the closest correspondence, the most unreserved communication with his constituents. Their wishes ought to have great weight with him. . . . It is his duty to sacrifice his repose, his pleasures, his satisfactions to theirs. . . . But his unbiased opinion, his enlightened conscience, he ought not to sacrifice to you or any set of men living. . . . They are a trust from Providence, for the abuse of which he is deeply answerable. Your representative owes you, not his industry only, but his judgment; and he betrays, instead of serving you, if he sacrifices it to your opinion.[3]

For Burke the representative's first duty was to look after the national interest. When local interests or opinions clash with national interest or tradition, representatives should ignore local opinion. To do this the representative must have some independence of action. Moreover, elected representatives are at the center of power and deliberation. They are involved in hearing arguments, presenting ideas and weighing and balancing judgments. This argument is amplified greatly in our day by notions of secrecy and exclusive information, with politicians claiming that chief executives should have a larger voice in decision making than legislative bodies since they have access to wider information, especially in foreign affairs, than does Congress. For Burke, representatives could not be bound by local interests or instructions and still perform a deliberative function for the national interest. The representative is, therefore, a trustee, holding the people's power. The people themselves do not hold power. As a trustee it is the representative's duty to work for the constituents' and country's real interest, not for temporary, often mad, opinions that may seize an unreflective and ill-informed public.

Implicit in Burke's argument is the idea that representatives have superior wisdom, information, and expertise. Many have challenged these assumptions and the idea that representatives can best perform their function if independent of their constituency's wishes. Though no single individual sums up this argument as Burke does for independence, many have argued for and accepted the idea that a representative must reflect the expressed interests and desires of his constituency, that he must be a delegate from the local area to the state or country.

In its purest form the representative-as-delegate thesis argues that the representative has no independent function. He or she is merely a proxy, a stand-in, or a pipeline for the constituency. The representative follows only the instructions from the constituency and has no policy-making or deliberative function. His primary duty is to present the constituents' opinions and decisions, defend their interests, and vote according to their instructions. When new situations arise, the representative must return to the local constituency and receive new instructions. If he cannot agree with the constituent's wishes, he must either vote as directed or resign.

Although he did not approve of representative government, Jean-Jacques Rousseau (1712–1778) came closest to expressing the delegate view. In the *Social Con-*

[3]Edmund Burke, "Speech at the Conclusion of the Poll," Bristol, November 3, 1774, many editions. *Works*, Vol. 1 (London: 1854) pp. 446–447.

tract, Rousseau argued that representation was tyranny, control of the sovereign people by their representatives, unless the representatives only conveyed the desires of the people. All they could do was transmit decisions, nothing more.[4]

Without going to this extreme, Thomas Paine, Thomas Jefferson, and John Adams considered that at least one house of the legislature ought to reflect closely the interests and opinions of the people at large. Many European constitutions expressly forbid giving binding instructions to elected representatives but call for proportional representation to insure that many interests will be heard. Common American attitudes indicate a strong belief that representatives should reflect constituent interests, yet reflecting constituent interests is far from serving as a pipeline for constituent wishes. To be effective, the delegate theory would require small and/or homogeneous electoral districts where people would be very much alike. Probably it also would require simple problems and highly informed voters. As such, we have no national examples of the delegate thesis in practice. The U.S. Congress under the Articles of Confederation, when members were instructed by their state legislatures, and the United Nations General Assembly are the closest examples of the delegate thesis in operation.

Obviously, there is a great deal of tension between these different theories. It is not simply a matter of choosing one or the other. There is no unequivocal answer as to which system would be superior. Your own answer must depend on your values, coupled with your expectations about government and interpretation of political traditions. Politicians are of many minds on this question. In Britain members of Parliament see themselves as being concerned with their constituency but vote according to the determination of their party. In the United States,[5] legislators often say they respond to their constituents' interests, particularly in providing services, but rarely find clear statements of those interests. On many issues the public is uninterested or poorly informed on both basic facts and how their representatives voted. Many people, as many as 50 percent in the United States, do not know who their representatives are. Representatives have a great deal of independence of action on issues that have low visibility to the public. On most questions before a legislature, representatives follow their own minds or respond to interest groups simply because the public at large is not deeply interested in or informed about them. On highly visible, often emotional issues, such as busing, foreign aid, inflation, and unemployment, representatives have less room to follow their own inclinations because their constituents have strong opinions on these issues and long memories at the next election. For example, former Senator J. William Fulbright, Democrat from Arkansas, had substantial independence on most foreign policy issues but little on civil rights.

[4]Rousseau's arguments are collected conveniently in Hanna Pitkin, ed., *Representation* (New York: Atherton, 1969), pp. 51–72.

[5]John C. Wahlke, *The Legislative System: Explorations in Legislative Behavior* (New York: John Wiley, 1962), Chapter 12.

In fact, these rival theories represent two ends of a continuum. How close to one or the other end a country or even a particular legislator will come depends on many things that may shift over time. These include the strength of the political parties, laws, customs, and traditions; the legislator's view of duty; the visibility of issues; and the obvious desire for reelection. Weighing these different factors, we can say that one representative is closer to being independent, while another is closer to being a delegate. Each, however, will exercise some elements of these rival theories.

WHAT DOES A REPRESENTATIVE REPRESENT?

Theories of representative/represented relations do not tell us exactly what a representative represents. Burke claimed representatives look after the fixed permanent interests of the nation. Delegate theorists claim representatives defend their constituents' expressed interests. Assuming a fair apportionment and the right of everyone to participate, problems remain; it is useful to point out some of the relevant questions, even though we can give no concrete answers to them.

The larger countries become, the greater the distance and distinction between represented and representative. The more people a representative "represents," the less contact and control each person has over this representative. Representatives become more independent as size and pluralism in districts increase simply because there are more people to respond to. Not only are individual voices lost when many people speak, but in large districts representatives depend less on any single group for reelection than they do in small ones.

If increased size makes contact with individuals more difficult, perhaps it can be said that representatives represent a majority of their constituents. Leaving aside what this means for those who are in the minority, we must ask who or what a majority is. This is neither a flippant nor an easy question to answer. Majorities are rarely fixed and permanent. They shift from issue to issue. A person may be in the majority on one issue, in the minority on another, and in different coalitions on each issue. If the represenative is to carry out a deliberative function, he or she cannot poll the constituency on every issue, even if the members of the constituency could be expected to have opinions and preferences on all issues.

Perhaps interest groups answer our dilemma. Can we say that representatives respond to and represent the expressed interests of organized groups? They do simply because organized groups are better able to offer programs, rewards, and threats than unorganized masses. But the question then becomes, who do the interest groups represent and what do they seek? Moreover, many people are not organized or may never be part of a majority opinion or interest. The theory of representation holds that everyone is represented, but quite often major opinions and wishes are neglected. As will be noted later, proportional representation is one answer to this problem.

Finally, despite our political and institutional focus, representation is not confined to formal political institutions. Large private groups, such as professional organizations and labor unions, often maintain representative mechanisms. The American Medical Association has a House of Delegates, and elected representatives from local medical societies meet yearly to decide basic policy. Most large labor unions have similar mechanisms. Moreover, political parties and interest groups are representative of their members in shaping and influencing governmental policy. Often nongovernmental feedback agencies, such as the press or television, also are involved in "representing" opinions. Bureaucracies often "represent" particular clients or interest groups, but are these representative in terms of democratic values? Many argue that these organizations must be made accountable at least to their members. This demand faces all the problems that formal elected representative institutions face, coupled with the fact that the decision-making process of these organizations tends to be hidden from public view.

What a representative does and how he or she responds, therefore, is not always clear. Despite these problems, representation is still an important key to popular participation in states that are too big for direct decision making by all citizens. Along with interest groups and party activity, representation is one of the most important schemes for including the mass of people in decision making, at least in terms of helping choose who the formal political decision makers will be. Though it does not work perfectly, it provides people with a serious opportunity to influence and set limits to government.

REPRESENTATION IN THE CONTEMPORARY WORLD

The ideas, problems, and tensions discussed previously are peculiar to Western liberal-democratic countries because the concept of effective representation by elected officials is largely nonexistent elsewhere. Elections occur, but they are often more form than substance.

The theory and practice of representation developed in the West before the modern concept of elections. Representation is traceable to the thirteenth century, although only Great Britain has a more or less unbroken record of development. Representative government in secular and church institutions in medieval Europe did not include elections. It was assumed that the nobility, church officials, and burghers spoke for the territories or groups in their realm.[6] It was not until the seventeenth century in England that some theorists began to link representation and responsibility to constituents through elections. Successful institutionalization of this link through widespread adult male participation in moderately honest elections to select representatives did not develop until the late eighteenth and early nineteenth

---

[6]See R. W. Carlyle, *A History of Medieval Political Theory in the West*, vol. 5 (Edinburgh: Blackwood, 1971), pp. 128–140; "Medieval representation in theory and practice, special issue of *Speculum*, 29, April 1954, pp. 347–476; A. R. Myers, Parliaments in Europe: The representative tradition, *History Today*, 5, June and July 1955, pp. 383–390, 446–454.

centuries, first in the United States and then in England. Universal adult suffrage was not achieved until the twentieth century, and even then many people could not participate because of prejudice and social pressures. Nevertheless, the struggle to obtain universal suffrage in the selection of representatives was first fought and won in the West.

Efforts to make representative institutions effective and responsive continue today. In 1962, in *Baker* v. *Carr*, the Supreme Court ruled that reapportionment issues do not constitute "political" questions; therefore, federal courts could hear issues arising in this area. The decision gave rise to several landmark cases. In 1964, in **Wesberry v. Sanders**, the Court declared that the Constitution requires one person, one vote. According to the Court, representatives must be apportioned among the fifty states according to population and be chosen by the people of the states. Wesberry v. Sanders pertained to congressional districts in Georgia. In a subsequent decision the same year, in **Reynolds v. Sims**, the Court ruled that state legislative districts of both houses must be substantially equal in population. These decisions helped to insure that urban and suburban residents would have the same representation as rural voters.[7]

Though decisions such as *Wesberry* v. *Sanders* and *Reynolds* v. *Sims* have led to more equal representation, the significance of representation remains a basic issue. Today many are dissatisfied with the apparent inability of representative institutions to solve fundamental problems. Quite often people complain that representative institutions are in decline, unable to cope with an increasingly complex world. This, however, is a problem for all political institutions everywhere, not only representative ones. Yet this is not a comfort to people concerned with the role and place of representation.

Representative-type institutions exist in the Communist countries of Eastern Europe and the Soviet Union. Their function, however, is different from that in most Western countries. Though the Soviet constitution vests all power in an elected "Supreme Soviet," effective power rests with the Communist Party, which controls both the government and nomination to Local and Supreme Soviets. The Soviets do not control the government in any meaningful sense; rather, they serve to ratify decisions taken elsewhere. Instead of reflecting the flow of power and authority from the bottom up, they serve to socialize people and generate support for government policy.[8] Though the situation varies from country to country—in Yugoslavia political institutions have more power—nowhere in Eastern Europe do political representative institutions have the influence over policy that they have in the West.

There is no single way to characterize representative institutions in the developing countries. In terms of power and success they range from nonexistent in countries such as Saudi Arabia and a few of the one-man-rule countries of Africa to almost

[7]See especially Gordon E. Baker, *The Reapportionment Revolution* (New York, Random House, 1966); and Robert A. Goldwin, ed., *Representation and Misrepresentation* (Chicago: Rand McNally, 1968).

[8]Frederick C. Barghoorn, "Politics in the USSR," in Gabriel Almond, ed., *Comparative Politics Today* (Boston: Little Brown, 1974), pp. 294–297.

thriving as in Singapore. They have been most influential in former British colonies and in Latin Ameria, but even here representative institutions are weak measured by Western standards. Most developing countries have some form of representative institution, but almost everywhere they have little power and are dominated by strong executives. In countries such as Chile and India where a tradition of strong representative institutions appeared to be developing, events of the last decade have virtually eliminated legislatures as effective political voices. As fragile and limited as representative institutions may appear in the West, they have more power and more opportunity to affect policy than anywhere else.

Having discussed the general nature of representation, we shall turn our attention now to the major electoral systems that are used to elect members of the **lower houses** of national legislatures. This will be followed by a section dealing with the selection of members of **upper houses**. Students should keep in mind that not all countries have bicameral legislatures. Procedures for choosing chief executives are discussed in Chapter Nine.

MAJOR ELECTORAL SYSTEMS

Elections in pluralistic societies make it possible for the largest number of persons to participate in politics and permit the largest number of viewpoints to compete for popular support. In authoritarian one-party countries, elections serve a somewhat different function. They provide legitimacy for the regime, create a sense of mass participation in government, and serve to create a democratic facade for the regime.

THE SINGLE-MEMBER DISTRICT SYSTEM

The simplest type of electoral system is the **single-member district system**. This is used in the United States and Great Britain for choosing members of Congress and the House of Commons. The United States, for example, is divided into 435 congressional districts. The people in each of these districts elect only one candidate to the House of Representatives. Thus, a candidate must receive a majority of the votes cast (if there are two candidates for the office) or a plurality (if there are three or more candidates) in order to be elected. This system exaggerates the legislative representation of the winner and gives the second party a near monopoly of the opposition, as will be explained. Minor parties become wasted votes and atrophy. Geographic distribution of electoral support also is crucial.

An American professor, E. E. Schattschneider, was one of the first political scientists to analyze the impact of the single-member district system.[9] As Schattschneider noted:

If for example, one were told merely that a given party received a total of 10,000,000 votes in all of the 435 [American congressional] districts taken together, out of a vote of

[9]See E. E. Schattschneider, *Party Government* (New York: Holt, Rinehart and Winston, 1942), pp. 69–84.

40,000,000 it would be impossible to guess even approximately the number of seats won by the party until something were known of the distribution of the vote.[10]

In a two-party system, votes usually are not evenly distributed geographically. Some districts will be won overwhelmingly; in other districts the popular vote will be extremely close. Each party has its geographical areas of support and is able to survive a major electoral defeat. The second party monopolizes the opposition and accrues support as the inevitable dissatisfaction with the winner occurs. **Third parties** enjoy electoral success only when they have considerable strength in one area of the country and receive a majority or plurality of the votes there. If the third party has no substantial pockets of support it is doomed, as happened in the case of the Liberal Party in Great Britain. During the 1920s and 1930s it became a third party with support distributed throughout the country. Today the Liberal Party holds only a handful of seats in Parliament. In the 1979 parliamentary elections, the Conservatives won 43.9 percent of the vote (as opposed to Labour's 36.9 percent) and 53.4 percent of the seats in the House of Commons. The Liberal Party polled 13.8 percent of the vote but won only 11 seats, less than 2 percent. Under the single-member district system, voters usually are limited to two viable alternatives.

The waning of the British Liberal Party in the 1920s illustrates that the single-member district system does not preclude the emergence of new parties. There were several reasons for the Liberal demise. First, as the party to the left of the Conservatives, the Liberals were more susceptible to the competition of the newly organized Labour Party, whose extraparliamentary origins and organization were quite different from either the Conservatives or Liberals.

Second, divisions and miscalculations among the leadership damaged the party. Lloyd George and one wing of the party joined a Conservative/Liberal coalition. Fifteen years of intraparty quarreling weakened the party and prevented it from reacting vigorously to the electoral challenges of the Conservatives and Labour.

The record of serious third parties in the United States indicates that the single-member district system has been an important factor in their lack of success. The only third party that replaced one of the major parties was the Republican Party in the 1850s, but it was aided by the fact that the Whig Party it replaced was already in a process of dissolution. The Populist Party in the 1880s had some electoral success in electing members of both houses of Congress in the West, but its weakness was that it was largely a sectional party that could not replace the Democrats as the second party. Its failure also was aided by the fact that the Democrats in 1896 endorsed one of its main planks—the free and unlimited coinage of silver. The two major parties in the United States frequently "steal" proposals from minor parties.

The failure of third parties has been most apparent on the congressional level. Theodore Roosevelt's Progressive Party had little success in electing members to Congress, even though Roosevelt was a popular figure who ran second in 1912 in

[10]*Ibid.*, p. 70.

the contest for the presidency. Only for a brief time in the early part of the century were the Socialists able to elect two members, one from a congressional district in Milwaukee, and the other from a district in New York City.

A modification of the single-member district plan is the **runoff ballot**, which is used in elections to the French National Assembly in the Fifth Republic. In France a second election is held for candidates who fail to receive majorities on the first ballot. In some districts only the two highest plurality candidates participate in the runoff. In others all candidates are on the ballot and occasionally even newcomers may enter the race. In all cases the runoff is decided by a plurality vote. Experience in France to date shows that only a minority of candidates receive a majority on the first ballot.

The dual-ballot system was adopted in France principally for two reasons: to encourage the emergence of a majority party in the National Assembly, and to reduce the number of Communist deputies. The law does not work against any particular party, but the final results depend upon the relationships of the parties to one another. The first vote enables each party to secure an accurate reading of its popularity. The one-week interval between elections enables the parties to consolidate their votes and switch their support to the most likely winners in the second vote. If a party is unable or refuses to enter into electoral alliances or trade-offs, the number of deputies it elects is far below its nationwide popular vote.

In 1958, the year Charles de Gaulle became president of France, the French Communist Party (PCF) did not enter into alliances with other parties of the Left. The alliances could have resulted in left support for Communists in some districts, and in turn the Communists supporting the most popular Left candidate in other districts. Thus, while the PCF received 22 percent of the popular vote nationally, it won only 7 percent of the National Assembly seats. By the 1970s the PCF was participating with the Socialists and Radicals in a Union of the Left against the pro-Gaullist Union of Republicans for Progress. In the March, 1979 elections for the National Assembly, only 14 percent of the parliamentary seats were won on the first ballot. The PCF received 20.6 percent of the popular vote in the first round. At the conclusion of the second ballot, 86 PCF candidates were elected—17 percent of the total seats in the National Assembly—a notable improvement over the earlier showing.

PROPORTIONAL REPRESENTATION
Proportional representation is designed to give each political party approximately the same number of legislative seats as the party's voting strength justifies. The two most common forms of proportional representation are the single-transferable vote **(Hare) system** and the **list system**. In the former, each election district generally elects several representatives to the Legislature. The voter indicates the order of preference for candidates by writing in the numbers 1, 2, 3, 4, 5, and so on. The numerical preferences equal the number of candidates to be elected. A quota of votes is worked out that will entitle the candidate to a seat.

The list system is the most common type of proportional representation. Prior to an election, the party draws up lists of candidates, equal to the number of seats contested in the multimember district, rank-ordering the names of the candidates. The larger the percentage of the party vote, the more people are elected from the list. The list system was used in Weimar Germany (1919–1933), The French Fourth Republic (1946–1958), and is employed now in Israel, Italy, and the Netherlands. List- proportional representation reduces popular control—the party, not the voters, selects the names on the list and their rank order. The lower the position on the list, the less likely it is the candidate will be elected. Power is in the hands of the party hierarchy. Also, the list is a simple device. The voters only need to identify with the party or its symbol; however, they may feel isolated from the government because they have no specific representative with whom they can identify and to whom they can turn. The immedite responsibility of the representative is to the party organization, not the voters.

In some countries the voters are allowed some degree of choice in rearranging the list according to their own preferences. Only in Austria are the voters allowed complete freedom in this respect.

Italy is one of the countries using the list system of proportional representation. The country is divided into 32 national election districts. All but 1 of these are multimember districts (i.e., the voters elect several deputies from each district). The names of the party candidates appear on party lists, which are the result of lengthy intraparty bargaining and consultation.

On election day the voters mark on their ballots the party list of their choice with an "X." Furthermore, voters may, if they so desire, write on the ballot the names of their 3 or 4 preferred candidates from among those on the party list. The preference votes help to determine who from among the candidates will be elected. If a party in the first district is entitled to 4 deputies, the 4 list candidates having received the highest number of votes are elected.

After all the votes have been counted, the parliamentary seats assigned to each district are distributed among the parties on the basis of proportional representation. In other words, a district's number of seats is allocated to the parties according to the percentage of votes that each party polled. Remaining percentage fractions and unassigned seats from all districts are transferred to a national electoral pool in Rome and are distributed by that body proportionally to the parties. Thus, each party will receive a number of parliamentary seats generally in proportion to its percentage of the total vote.[11]

To exemplify this procedure, we list in Table 7–1 the results of the 1979 national election in Italy. It should be noted that all parties, with the exception of the New

---

[11]See Raphael Zariski, *Italy: The Politics of Uneven Development* (Hinsdale, Ill.: The Dryden Press, 1972), pp. 194–196.

Table 7-1   Results of the 1979 National Elections in Italy

	Votes	Percent of Total	Number of Seats Won in the Chamber of Deputies
Christian Democrats (DC)	14,007,594	38.3	262
Communists (PCI)	11,107,883	30.4	201
Socialists (PSI)	3,586,256	9.8	62
Neo-Fascists and Monarchists (MSI-DN)	1,924,251	5.3	30
Social Democrats (PSDI)	1,403,873	3.8	20
Radicals (P. Rad.)	1,259,362	3.4	18
Republicans (PRI)	1,106,766	3.0	16
Liberals (PLI)	708,022	1.9	9
Proletarian Unity (PDUP)	501,431	1.4	6
New United Left (N.S.U.N.)	293,443	0.8	—
Democratic Nationalists (Dem. Naz.)	228,340	0.6	—
Alternate List (VARI)	219,658	0.6	2
South Tyrolians (SVP)[a]	206,264	0.6	4
TOTAL	36,553,143	99.9	630

Source: TELITALIA, June 6, 1979, p. 2.

[a]While the total vote of the SVP and the Alternate List was below 1 percent each, these parties, nevertheless, elected 4 and 2 deputies respectively because their voters were highly geographically concentrated.

United Left and the Democratic Nationalists, won seats in the Chamber of Deputies. Had Italy used the single-member district system, as do the United States and the United Kingdom, the two strongest parties (the Christian Democrats and the Communists) would have won nearly all the seats, with the Socialists gaining a handful and the South Tyrolians perhaps obtaining one or two.

Not all countries using the system of proportional representation have as fragmented a party system—and as much political instability—as does Italy. In Austria, for example, only three parties are represented in the *Nationalrat*, the lower house of the legislature.

West Germany, which enjoys political stability, has a modified system of proportional representation. To avoid small splinter parties, the country has excluded from representation in the **Bundestag** (the lower house of the legislature) all parties failing to receive at least 5 percent of the nationwide party vote or 3 seats in one of the states by direct election. West Germany also provides that half of the representatives are to be elected by majority (or plurality) vote in single-member districts, while the other half are chosen by party lists in each state, which is given a certain number of seats to elect. Under this hybrid system, West Germany has approached a two-party system consisting of Social Democrats and Christian Democrats. A small liberal party comparable to the party of that name in Britain often holds the balance of power.

Advantages and Disadvantages of Proportional Representation

The distinguished nineteenth-century British philosopher John Stuart Mill presented the most important theoretical justification of proportional representation.[12] Supporters of this system contend that it gives a more accurate picture of public opinion than the single-member district plan, because it gives minorities representation proportionate to their voting strength. It also is argued that proportional representation is the best method for independent voters to express their views. Another argument is that it will help eliminate lobbying because of the greater variety of interests represented.

Critics reply that although the majority and minority systems have defects, proportional representation may make it impossible for the majority to govern. Excessive representation for minority parties may divide the legislature into interest groups that prevent the enactment of legislation based on a majority consensus. Perhaps the most effective criticism is that the purpose of elections is to create a broad majority consensus in a parliament that will enable the government to act effectively. This cannot be accomplished, it is said, if every minority group is to have exact mathematical representation.

One of the leading scholars on this subject, Carl J. Friedrich, cites the experience in Weimar Germany as a leading cause of the collapse of the Republic in 1933.[13] He feels that the list system stratified party organizations and created new parties because of the ease with which they could be set up. Furthermore, parties were controlled by party bosses who emphasized creed and dogma. At the same time, moderate parties came to be identified with some special interest group. This combination of entrenched interests and radical dogmatism made the organization of stable cabinets very difficult.

On the other hand, Friedrich recognizes the stability of the Scandinavian countries, the Netherlands, and Belgium under proportional representation but attributes this to the moderating influence of the monarchy in those countries. In these countries the monarch still exerts some political influence and the countries' smallness permits a degree of intimacy between the royal Court and Parliament.

No conclusive answer is possible on the merits of proportional representation. It cannot be proved that proportional representation causes multiplication of parties, because most countries that adopted proportional representation already had multiparty systems. Yet frequently the tendency toward political fragmentation is intensified under proportional representation. In view of the political disintegration of the Weimar Republic and the undermining of popular confidence in the Fourth French Republic, the burden of proof would appear to be on the supporters of proportional representation.

[12]See his essay, "Representative Government," in *Utilitarianism, Liberty, and Representative Government* (New York: E. P. Dutton, 1947).

[13]See Carl J. Friedrich, *Constitutional Government and Democracy*, 4th ed. (Waltham, Mass.: Blaisdell Publishing, 1968), Chapter XV, especially pp. 302–306.

SELECTION OF MEMBERS OF UPPER HOUSES

The manner of selecting members of upper houses of legislatures is frequently different from that used for lower houses, and the units of representation in the two houses usually differ as well. Also, the upper houses frequently possess less power. The United States Senate is a notable exception in this respect. In West Germany and the United States the upper house reflects the federal system. The French Senate is selected by an indirect mode of election and the members of the West German *Bundesrat* are appointed. Membership in the British House of Lords is largely hereditary.

The United States Senate is a result of the Connecticut Compromise at the Constitutional Convention, whereby it was agreed that the Senate would represent the states, with two senators from each state. The Senate is a continuing body with one-third of the members elected every two years for six-year terms. Since senators are elected from the state at large, the state serves as a single-member district. The powers of the Senate are substantially the same as those of the House of Representatives.

The British House of Lords is an anachronism as a hereditary second chamber in a progressive democracy. The great majority of its membership of over 1000 hold their seats because each is the oldest son of a nobleman whose ancestor was appointed hundreds of years ago. Its membership also includes princes of the royal blood and 16 peers representing Scotland. There are also members whose seats are not hereditary: the 26 lords spiritual of the Church of England; about 200 members appointed for life under an act of 1958; and the 9 "law lords" who constitute the House of Lords acting as the highest court of the land.

Although once equal to the House of Commons in power, the House of Lords has steadily lost power, especially in this century, by custom of legislative act. Its chief functions today are to relieve the House of Commons of the burden of considering private bills and initiating bills of a noncontroversial nature that can pass the House of Commons with dispatch if previously debated in the Upper Chamber.

The Upper Chamber of the Parliament under the Fifth Republic of France has been renamed the Senate[14] and given limited power. Its life span is 9 years, with 283 members elected indirectly by local electoral colleges consisting largely of local councilors. One-third of the membership is selected every 3 years. In general, the French Senate may block legislation in which the government is not greatly interested.

The West German **Bundesrat** (the upper chamber) represents the territorial units of the West German Republic. Unlike the United States Senate, which represents the people of the states, the *Bundesrat* represents the states or *Länder* as such. The membership of the *Bundesrat* numbers 41, plus 4 nonvoting members from West Berlin. All are officials of and appointed by their respective state governments

---

[14]The influential second chamber of the Third Republic of France (1871–1940) was called the Senate.

and serve for indeterminate terms. Each state casts a single vote determined by instructions from their governments. The *Bundesrat* can be overridden by an equivalent majority of the *Bundestag* (i.e., a bill passed by a simple majority vote in the *Bundesrat* can be nullified by a simple majority vote in the *Bundestag*).

VOTING BEHAVIOR

The significance of voting varies with the importance of elections in determining political decision makers. The percent of people voting, however, does not always reflect the actual importance of elections. Thus, some Communist countries such as Albania report voter turnouts of 100 percent, and typical turnouts in Communist countries are almost invariably in the 95-percent-plus range. Many Western countries report turnouts in excess of 80 percent (see Table 7–2). On the other hand, U.S. congressional elections in nonpresidential campaign years typically draw approximately 45 percent of the eligible electorate (see Figure 7–1). In 1976, 54.4 percent of the voting-age population voted in the United States, although this figure varied from a low of 33.3 percent in the District of Columbia to 71.4 percent in Minnesota.[15]

These differences force us to ask why there is such profound variation, not only among different countries, but also within the same nation-state. Political participation is a learned activity. The processes of political socialization and rewards and punishments for participation help to account for these differences. Yet what lies behind this political socialization? Who participates? Who does not? Why?

Characteristics such as race, age, sex, class, and education are correlated with voting. In the United States (except where noted our discussion will focus on the United States) black people traditionally have had a much lower turnout than white people. In 1972, 52.1 percent of the black population of voting age reported they voted, while in 1976 48.7 percent reported they voted.[16] Comparable statistics for the white population were 64.5 percent in 1972 and 60.9 percent in 1976. The figures for black voting show a rise from previous years. Moreover, black citizens of voting age tend to have a lower rate of registration than white citizens. This record of lower participation does not, however, reflect any racial characteristics but rather the social and political environment of exclusion, threats, and punishments for voting that many black people have experienced. Before passage of civil rights legislation in 1964 and 1965, unequal literacy tests, delay tactics, and intimidation prevented large numbers of blacks from registering to vote. In 1960, before massive

---

[15]These figures are adapted from the U.S. Bureau of the Census, *Statistical Abstract of the United States: 1978* (Washington, D.C.: U.S. Government Printing Office, 1978), p. 523. The 1960 election showed even greater variation, from a low of 25.3 percent in Mississippi to 79.7 percent in Idaho. Unless otherwise noted, all U.S. voting statistics are from this source.

[16]The percentage of people who report having voted is always much higher than the number who actually voted.

Table 7-2   Percentage of Electorate Voting in National Parliamentary or Presidential[a] Elections (Numbers are Rounded Off to Nearest Whole Number)

Country	Percentage	Year
Australia	95%	1975
	95	1977
Austria	93	1975
	92	1979
Canada	77	1979
	70	1980
Denmark	88	1975
	89	1977
Finland	81	1975
	82	1979
France	81	1973
	83	1978
Germany (West)	91	1972
	91	1976
Italy	93	1976
	90	1979
Japan	72	1972
	73	1976
Netherlands	83	1972
	88	1977
New Zealand	83	1975
	80	1978
Sweden	92	1976
	91	1979
Switzerland	57	1971
	52	1975
United Kingdom	73	1974
	76	1979
United States	56	1972
	54	1976

Sources: United States data are from the *Congressional Quarterly*, December 18, 1976; others have been obtained from the Consulate General offices of each country.

[a]The only presidential elections included are those of the United States.

voter registration drives and federal intervention, 23.1 percent of the black population of the 11 southern states that made up the Old Confederacy[17] were registered to vote, as compared to 46.1 percent of the white population. In 1976, 58.5 percent of the eligible black population were registered as opposed to 68.3 percent of the white population. Moreover, North and South, black people tend to have less educa-

---

[17]Alabama, Arkansas, Florida, Georgia, Louisiana, Mississippi, North Carolina, South Carolina, Tennessee, Texas, and Virginia.

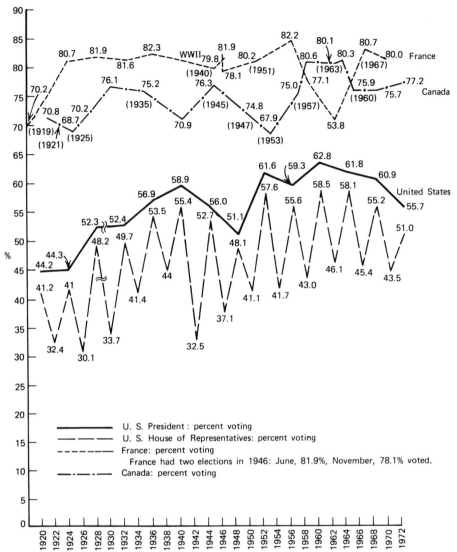

Figure 7-1. Percentage of eligible voters actually voting in national elections. (Canada has been chosen because it is a North American country, France because it is European with a long history of voting. Percentages for the United States, 1920 to 1928, are from U.S. Bureau of the Census, *Statistical Abstract of the United States: 1962* (Washington, D.C.: U.S. Government Printing Office, 1962), p. 373. Percentages for the United States, 1930 to 1972, are from U.S. Bureau of the Census, *Social Abstract of the United States: 1974* (Washington, D.C.: U.S. Government Printing Office, 1974), p. 437. Percentages for the United States, 1974 to 1978, are from U.S. Bureau of the Census, *Social Abstract of the United States: 1979* (Washington, D.C.: U.S. Government Printing Office, 1979), p. 513. Percentages for Canada and France, 1920 to 1972, are based on Thomas T. Mackie and Richard Rose, *The International Almanac of Electoral History* (New York: Free Press, 1974), pp. 75, 81, 133, and 137, adapted by permission of the publisher. Percentages for Canada and France, 1973 to 1980, have been obtained from the consulate general offices of the two countries.

tion and educational opportunities and a lower socioeconomic status than white people. Those less educated and worse off economically tend to participate and vote less than more advantaged groups.[18] This observation holds for minorities in most countries.

As noted in Table 7–3, age and education have a positive correlation with voting. This is true for all races and groups. Here socialization probably accounts for greater participation. As people receive more education, they are exposed to more information about how the system works and their role in it, as well as increased exhortation to participate. People with higher socioeconomic status are more likely to receive more education. Also, as people get older they tend to participate more, probably because they view themselves as having an increased stake in the political system. In the United States in 1976, 38 percent of the eligible 18- to 20-year-olds reported voting, as opposed to 55.4 percent of people in the 25- to 34-year-old category and 68.7 percent in the 45- to 64-year-old category. If present trends continue and if the trauma of war in Southeast Asia, Watergate, and other revelations of governmental corruption do not produce permanent alienation from the political processes, these young voters probably will vote at a higher rate in the future. Lower voter turnout among the young tends to be typical of most Western countries.

If this book had been written 20 years ago, we would now include a somewhat pious and perhaps tongue-in-cheek discussion of how women vote at a much lower rate than do men. Given socialization patterns all over the world, women traditionally have been discouraged from and even punished for participating; "politics is dirty" and "politics is man's work" symbolize this attitude. Moreover, women have been enfranchised only in the twentieth century.[19] Women have had less opportunity to learn participation. This situation is changing now; as Table 7–3 illustrates, the rate of voting for women rapidly is approaching the voting rate of men. New socialization patterns and more out-of-the-home opportunities help account for this convergence. Voting, however, is only one form of political participation, and women still lag far behind men in terms of holding elective offices or participating in political campaigns. Effective resocialization and reform may reduce this difference in the future.

In the United States people with lower socioeconomic status tend to vote less than those with higher status. This is probably the result of less education, less apparent stake in the system, and less reinforcement by other groups that would encourage participation. In European countries with class-based political parties that actively encourage people to vote, there are smaller differences in participation

---

[18]In 1977 the median school years completed were 12.5 for the white population and 11.4 for the black population, though the median school years completed is tending to even out for whites and blacks in the 25- to 34-year-old category. See *Statistical Abstract op. cit.,* ff. 15, p. 143.

[19]Complete franchise equality on a nationwide level: Belgium, 1948; Canada, 1920; France, 1944; Germany, 1919; Italy, 1946; United Kingdom, 1928; United States, 1920.

Table 7-3 Participation in National Elections, by Population Characteristics, 1972 and 1976[a]

	1972				1976			
	Persons of Voting Age	Persons Reporting They Voted		Percent Reporting They Did Not Vote	Persons of Voting Age	Persons Reporting They Voted		Percent Reporting They Did Not Vote
Characteristics		Total	Percent			Total	Percent	
TOTAL:	136,200	85,700	63.0	37.0	146,500	86,700	59.2	40.8
Male	63,800	40,900	64.1	35.9	69,000	41,100	59.6	40.4
Female	72,400	44,900	62.0	38.0	77,600	45,600	58.8	41.2
White	121,200	78,200	64.5	35.5	129,300	78,800	60.9	39.1
Black	13,500	7,000	52.1	47.9	14,900	7,300	48.7	51.3
Spanish Origin	5,600	2,100	37.4	62.6	6,600	2,100	31.8	68.2
18–20 years old	11,000	5,300	48.3	51.7	12,100	4,600	38.0	62.0
21–24 years old	13,600	6,900	50.7	49.3	14,800	6,800	45.6	54.4
25–34 years old	26,900	16,100	59.7	40.3	31,500	17,500	55.4	44.6
35–44 years old	22,200	14,700	66.3	33.7	22,800	14,400	63.3	36.7
45–64 years old	42,300	30,000	70.8	29.2	43,300	29,800	68.7	31.3
65 years and older	20,100	12,700	63.5	36.5	22,000	13,700	62.2	37.8
Median age in years	42.4	44.9	(X)[b]	(X)	41.5	45.1	(X)	(X)
Residence:								
Metropolitan	99,200	63,800	64.3	35.7	99,600	58,900	59.2	40.8
Nonmetropolitan	37,000	22,000	59.4	40.6	47,000	27,800	59.1	40.9
North and West	93,700	62,200	66.4	33.6	99,400	60,800	61.2	38.8
South	42,600	23,600	55.4	44.6	47,100	25,900	54.9	45.1

Table 7-3 Continued

Characteristics	1972				1976			
	Persons of Voting Age	Persons Reporting They Voted		Percent Reporting They Did Not Vote	Persons of Voting Age	Persons Reporting They Voted		Percent Reporting They Did Not Vote
		Total	Percent			Total	Percent	
Years of school completed:								
8 years or less	28,100	13,300	47.4	52.6	24,900	11,000	44.1	55.9
9–11 years	22,300	11,600	52.0	48.0	22,200	10,500	47.2	52.8
12 years	50,700	33,200	65.4	34.6	55,700	33,100	59.4	40.6
More than 12 years	35,100	27,700	78.8	21.2	43,700	32,200	73.5	26.5
Employed	80,200	52,900	66.0	34.0	86,000	53,300	62.0	38.0
Unemployed	3,700	1,900	49.9	50.1	6,400	2,800	43.7	56.3
Not in labor force	52,300	31,000	59.3	40.7	54,100	30,600	56.5	43.5

Source: U.S. Bureau of the Census, *Statistical Abstract of the United States: 1978* (Washington, D.C.: U.S. Government Printing Office, 1978), p. 520.

[a]Persons in thousands. As of November. Covers civilian noninstitutional population. For 1972, persons 18 years old and over in all states. Includes aliens. Figures are based on a population sample and differ from those based on population estimates and official vote counts. Differences in percentages may also be due to overreporting of voting by persons in the sample.

[b]X = Not applicable.

rates between classes than in the United States. In general, strong identification with a political party or candidate tends to encourage participation.

Many other factors affect participation. For some people political participation may seem threatening to their relation with family and friends. Others may feel it is futile due to a sense of personal inadequacy, a feeling that political forces are unmanageable, or that there is a large gap between democratic ideals and political reality. Many have weak spurs to political involvement, being concerned with their families and friends or seeing few links between political activity and satisfaction of their needs.[20] A small number of people may simply be satisfied with their political system and see no need to participate. Others, feeling there is no effective choice between candidates or parties, do not vote.

Electoral procedures also may disqualify people from participating. Voter registration procedures and residency requirements prevent some of the potential electorate from voting in the United States. However, residency requirements are not the deterrent they once were because the Voting Rights Act of 1970 lowered most of them to 30 days. Problems with absentee ballots and difficulties in reaching polling stations disenfranchise some people. Even bad weather or a belief that one's candidate or party will win (or lose) may keep some from voting; in these cases the nonvoters probably have a low motivation to vote based on some other factor.

One additional factor may discourage people from voting: the problem of choosing among candidates or parties. Although it is true that most people do not have well-developed and explicit policy preferences and may have relatively little knowledge about issues, most people do have attitudes about politics. Many express preferred policy outcomes or prefer certain candidate characteristics. The problem is—how should a voter choose when two or more candidates present programs, each program having some policies the voter prefers and some he or she dislikes and rejects? Table 7–4 illustrates this dilemma, common especially in countries with weak party systems.

Table 7–4 Problem of Voter Identification

	Candidate A	Candidate B
Ethnicity of candidate	Yes[a]	No
Religion of candidate	No	Yes
Policy toward Soviet Union	No	Yes
Policy on employment	Yes	Yes
Policy on inflation	No	Yes
Policy on arms spending	No	No
Party identification of candidate	Yes	No
Attitude toward women	Yes	No

[a]Yes indicates the voter approves the candidate's position on the issue; no indicates that the voter disapproves.

[20]Morris Rosenberg, Some determinants of political apathy. *Public Opinion Quarterly*, 18, Winter 1954–1955, pp. 349–366.

Which candidate should the voter select? In such a case powerful cross-pressures are operating because one's vote may be for some issues one favors and others one may oppose. Some voters, unable to choose, may not vote at all.

DETERMINANTS OF VOTING CHOICE

Voting is a complicated act. How a person will vote depends on a number of factors. Some of the more important of these are class identification, education, occupation, parental partisanship, race, region, and religion. Though class identification in the United States has been weaker historically than in Britain and in parts of continental Europe, it has played a role in voting in this country in the sense that the more class- conscious a person is, the more his or her economic position will influence the electoral choices.[21]

Education and occupation are related in the sense that the degree of education a person possesses usually has a close bearing on the occupation the person holds. Table 7–5 might be helpful in explaining some aspects of recent electoral behavior

Table 7–5   Partisan Identification by Occupation, Education and Region in the United States

	% Democratic		% Republican		% Independent	
	1948	1976	1948	1976	1948	1976
BY OCCUPATION						
Professionals, semiprofessionals	29	39	41	27	30	34
Business executives, small businesses	32	37	42	29	26	34
White collar (sales/clerical)	38	42	36	25	27	33
Skilled blue-collar labor	43	49	32	17	26	34
Farm owners, farm laborers	49	45	36	32	16	24
Domestic, protective, and other services	49	53	29	18	23	29
BY EDUCATION						
Less than high school	51	57	29	19	20	24
High school graduate	36	47	38	22	25	31
College graduate	26	37	42	29	31	34
BY REGION						
Northeast	36	46	37	26	27	29
Midwest	35	41	41	24	25	34
South	72	57	15	16	13	28
West	44	46	31	27	25	28

Source: *Public Opinion*, 1:4, 1978, p. 29.

[21]See Gerald Pomper, *Voter's Choice: Varieties of American Electoral Behavior* (New York: Harper & Row, 1975), p. 42ff.

in the United States. It presents data on political partisanship by occupation, education, and geographical region. The table shows two interesting developments: (1) an identification shift in all but one category from the Republicans to the Democrats and (2) a substantial increase in the number of those voters who consider themselves Independents. The percentage of Independents is smallest among the oldest voters and largest among the youngest voters. Gerald Pomper shows a range of 19.6 percent Independents among members of the pre-New Deal generation to 50.9 percent for new voters in 1972.[22]

Table 7–5 shows clearly that as of 1976 a larger percentage of people in each occupational category considered themselves Democrats rather than Republicans, with the latter showing their best strength among farmers and businesspeople. Democrats, too, led in all three educational categories, their smallest percentage of support coming from college graduates. Finally, Democrats showed a lead in all four regional categories. Only in the South, where the former Democratic one-party system is changing slowly into a modified two-party system, did Republicans experience a slight increase.

Religion and ethnic considerations are 2 factors that have had more significance in some presidential elections in the United States than in others. While John F. Kennedy received 82 percent of the Jewish vote and 78 percent of the Roman Catholic vote in 1960, according to some experts, the religious issue has become muted in American politics in recent years.[23] Nevertheless, religioethnic differences have deep roots in American political history. Jews and Roman Catholics are more likely to vote for Democratic candidates than are Protestants. There is more support for Democrats among Roman Catholics of Irish and Polish ethnic background than among Catholics of German and Italian ethnicity.[24]

There are similarities and differences among the voting patterns in the United States and the other democratic countries of the world. Economically well-to-do voters in Western Europe, Australia, New Zealand, and Japan are more likely to vote for political candidates and parties to the right of the center than their counterparts in the United States. On the left, a number of West European countries, as well as Australia and New Zealand, traditionally have had strong social-democratic-type labor parties, such as the Social Democratic parties in Austria and West Germany and the Labour Party in Britain. These have garnered the labor vote in their countries more completely than the Democratic Party ever has been able to do in the United States. Much of this holds true also for Scandinavian electoral politics, with the addition that politics in these countries has been influenced considerably by rural/urban contrasts and considerations, as evidenced by the presence of strong Agrarian parties in Norway and Sweden.

[22]*Ibid.*, p. 236.

[23]See especially Albert J. Menendez, *Religion at the Polls* (Philadelphia: Westminster Press, 1977).

[24]Norman H. Nie, Sidney Verba, and John R. Petrocik, *The Changing American Voter* (Cambridge, Mass.: Harvard University Press, 1976), p. 213 ff.

Religion as a factor in voting has been more prominent in some European countries than in others. The electoral support for the Christian Democratic movements in Belgium, Italy, the Netherlands, Switzerland, and West Germany cuts through the whole range of occupational groups in these countries, though more in some provinces than in others. For example, a substantial number of blue collar workers in Bavaria (West Germany) are staunch supporters of the conservative Christian Social Union.

Some of the preceding criteria, such as the tendency to vote for the political forces to the left or the right of the center depending upon one's economic and class standing, apply also to those developing countries that have viable two- or multi-party systems, such as Barbados, Jamaica, or Venezuela.

One interesting but partially disturbing feature of European electoral politics has to do with intergenerational changes of value. Students of American politics have shown that in this country most of the children adopt the voting preferences of their parents. In regard to electoral orientation in particular and value systems in general, there has been a greater intergenerational change in some of the European democracies than in the United States. This change is most substantial in those democracies that have suffered most during World War II. Here, a sizable number of children of economically well-to-do and conservative-voting parents have forsaken their families' political and economic values, have taken on what Ronald Inglehardt calls a "post-bourgeoisie" system of values, and have moved politically far to the left of their parents.[25] This trend has been most pronounced in France, Italy, the Netherlands, and West Germany. Some of the "switching" young people have moved to the extreme left. As one examines the socioeconomic profiles of contemporary political terrorists in Italy and West Germany, one finds that nearly all of them stem from well-to-do families whose political preferences are to the right of the center of the political spectrum. The intergenerational change between those young people who have become terrorists and their parents is astounding.

THE SIGNIFICANCE OF ELECTIONS

WESTERN DEMOCRACIES

Free elections perform a crucial but limited role. They do not mathematically reveal popular sentiment about a long list of controversial public issues. At best, competitive elections are only a rough approximation of popular feeling. No electoral system goes beyond this indispensable yet restricted function, but in the absence of some type of election and a legislature, free or manipulated, few governments today believe the public will accept them as legitimate.

[25]See Ronald Inglehardt, The Silent Revolution in Europe: Intergenerational Change in Post-industrial Societies. *The American Politican Science Review*, 65:4, 1971, pp. 991–1017.

Bigger Than Either

(Reg Manning/McNaught Syndicate, October 31, 1968.)

Elections can strengthen legitimacy.

Even in competitive elections, voters are not knowledgeable about all aspects of a party's program. A vote for a candidate or a party cannot be interpreted as support or even awareness of each item in the electoral program. For example, in the 1962 Wisconsin gubernatorial race, taxes were a major issue. The Democrat supported a higher income tax instead of a sales tax. A voter survey revealed that the percentage of Democratic voters favoring the sales tax was greater than the percentage of people who switched to the Democrat because of his pro-income-tax policy.[26]

[26]See Peter G. J. Pulzer, who summarizes the paradoxical role of issues in British and American elections in *Political Representation and Elections: Parties and Voting in Great Britain* (New York: Frederick A. Praeger, 1967), pp. 131–137.

Survey research in the United States reveals the impressionistic and unstructured view of politics common to a majority of people. The University of Michigan Survey Research Center concluded that presidential elections in the United States do not decide policy but at most determine *"who shall decide* what government shall do."[27] There is substantial lack of familiarity with even the most important political issues of the time. There is also considerable confusion in the public mind about what effect the election of one party over another would have on specific policies. As a result, according to the study, it may be implied that the electoral outcome is necessarily ambiguous as to what specific policies government should pursue. Also, as a consequence of the public's limited understanding of issues, interpretations as to the meaning of elections are speculative.

As to why the party vote oscillates between the two major parties, political scientists have suggested that a negative public response to the record of the party in power is more likely to influence the electorate than a positive appeal of the party out of power.

> *A majority party, once it is in office, will not continue to accrue electoral strength; it may preserve for a time its electoral majority, but the next marked change in the party vote will issue from a negative response of the electorate to some aspect of the party's conduct in office, a response that tends to return the minority party to power.*[28]

Electoral systems never equitably represent every element in the community. Neither are they as revealing of specific popular feeling as reformers in the nineteenth century had hoped. Despite these qualifications, competitive elections are the best means for the largest number of qualified persons to influence government. Popularly chosen legislatures are the institutions that include the bulk of elected officials; where the widest range of groups have a voice; and where interaction with, and accountability to, the public most frequently occurs.

COMMUNIST SOCIETIES

Democratic societies are not the only political systems that have elections and provide some form of legislative representation. Many authoritarian political systems also believe elections are important. Elections in the Soviet Union, for example, have several purposes.[29]

1. Elections provide legitimacy. The claim to be "democratic" must be substantiated, at least in part. Electoral support of 98 to 99 percent reassures an elitist ruling party, focuses attention on the supposed popularity of the regime, and offers some evidence of "democracy" to the rest of the world.

[27]Angus Campbell et al., *The American Voter* (New York: John Wiley, 1960), p. 541. This work is an excellent study of voting behavior.
[28]*Ibid.*, p. 288.
[29]This section on Soviet elections is drawn from Vernon V. Aspaturian's succinct analysis in Roy C. Macridis, ed., *Modern Political Systems: Europe*, 4th ed. (Englewood Cliffs, N.J.: Prentice-Hall, 1978).

2. Electioneering imparts a sense of mass participation and involvement and contributes toward building a sense of Communist civic awareness and responsibility. And, in some of the Eastern European countries (for example, Poland), there may be more than one official party candidate for the same seat, thus providing a minimal competition and increasing the sense of participation.

3. Limited signs of dissatisfaction are detected. Even a slight percentage of abstentions or *nyets* signals an early warning that there is discontent and trouble in certain districts.

4. Electioneering provides occasions to meet the people, to explain and defend government policies, and to announce new programs. Western observers have noted the "political" personalities of Soviet figures, such as Party Secretaries Khrushchev and Brezhnev. They had or have the ability to communicate and interact with the population and adopt an "on the campaign trail" political style. Campaigns can strengthen bonds of identification between rulers and the ruled and bring government to the grass roots, if only sporadically.

Elections in a one-party country provide minimal popular input. They demonstrate, though, the ambivalent attitude modern authoritarian regimes have toward representative government. Some effort must be made to establish a democratic facade in order to acquire legitimacy. Elections and legislatures are common institutions in modernizing authoritarian political systems.

DEVELOPING COUNTRIES

Depending on the nature of the political system, the functions of elections in developing countries range from some of those just listed under "Western Democracies" to the manipulated elections of Communist countries.

Some political leaders contend that elections are an integral part of the "democratic" process, even in one-party countries. For example, President Julius Nyerere of Tanzania writes and speaks frequently on democracy in Africa.[30] Tanzania has only **one** political party, the Tanzanian African National Union, and seats rarely are contested in an election. President Nyerere, nevertheless, claims Tanzania is a democracy. He maintains that a national movement open to every segment of population has nothing to fear from discontented and excluded factions because no such faction exists. If a country has two or more parties, each represents only a segment of the population, but a single party is identified with the country as a whole. Elections confirm that one party is a **genuine** national movement, representing the whole country and excluding none. President Nyerere suggests that frequently

[30]A cogent presentation by President Nyerere is "African Democracy," in Frank Tachau, ed., *The Developing Nations: What Path to Modernization?* (New York: Dodd, Mead, 1972), pp. 173–180.

there are vigorous debates and the input of grassroots opinion at party meetings. He appears to argue for free debate in private party conferences, but once a policy is decided party discipline prevails. Debate and input occur before elections, but elections are a necessary part of the policy-making cycle and affirm decisions that supposedly have been debated freely within the party.

Elections are also sometimes a means of psychologically reinforcing a leadership or, after a change in government, of ratifying the new leaders. These carefully controlled elections are intended to demonstrate the success of efforts to achieve national harmony and integration. Often elections are an effort to legitimize a political system by demonstrating that a government has popular support, even when some opposition groups are allowed to compete. Beginning in 1967, there were two major elections in South Vietnam before it fell to the Communists in 1975. The Americans pressured the South Vietnamese government to hold both elections so that the Saigon government could demonstrate legitimacy, both by showing how many Vietnamese were willing to vote despite Communist opposition to voting and by proving that despite a number of opposition groups the government could win a majority in relatively free elections. A government that in some way can achieve a popular electoral majority is reinforced in its own sense of legitimacy and by the mandate it can hold before world opinion. In a few developing countries, such as Sri Lanka (formerly Ceylon), elections are genuinely competitive, relatively honestly administered, and occasionally result in the incumbent party being turned out of office. Elections can provide voters with the most direct and available means of molding policy, and the Sri Lankans use them accordingly.[31]

A particular electoral problem in developing countries is the mobilization of people who have had little or no electoral experience and retain strong traditional ties. Electoral mobilization sometimes inflames existing social cleavages. Clifford Geertz, who has studied this problem, warns of the danger of politicizing "primordial sentiments."[32] Primordial sentiments are the givens of biological and social inheritance, such as family, tribe, caste, language, religion, and ethnic group. Most of the new countries of Africa and Asia are multilinguistic, multiethnic, and multireligious. Once a country has achieved independence, there is a new and important prize— the new government. If one seeks to mobilize supporters through elections or other means, the most obvious identifications and groups to which to appeal are the primordial groups. Self-rule actually may lead to increased splintering, self-awareness, and suspicion of others, based on traditional ties and obligations. Latent primordial hostilities can be aroused that will lead to bloody and cruel confrontations. Elections may provide a mechanism by which to channel some of these emotions, or they may provide an opportunity to arouse these attachments. Consequently, elections

[31]See, for example, the case study by Janice Jiggins, Dedigama 1973: A profile of a by-election in Sri Lanka. *Asian Survey*, 14:11, 1974, pp. 1000–1010.

[32]Clifford Geertz, ed., *Old Societies and New States: The Quest for Modernity in Asia and Africa* (Glencoe, Ill.: The Free Press, 1963), pp. 105–157.

may be rejected or manipulated so as to give the voter no opportunity to identify with and be stimulated by disruptive, centrifugal forces.

There are many reasons for developing countries to reject elections. The wonder is that at this stage of development elections with various degrees of competition are still held in several developing countries.

SUMMARY

Elections, voting, and representation are extremely important political inputs but are not the only means of political participation. As we saw in the two previous chapters, people also participate through interest groups, political parties, and campaigns. Nevertheless, elections and voting provide the most common form of mass participation.

Electoral systems never represent equitably every element in the community. Neither are they as revealing of specific popular feeling as reformers in the nineteenth century had hoped. Despite these qualifications, competitive elections are one means for the largest number of persons to influence government. Popularly chosen legislatures provide a place for the widest range of groups to have a voice and for interaction with, and accountability to, the public. Whether voting, elections, and representation have a major impact on political outcomes varies from country to country. Where they do, they provide one of the most effective means for people to influence decision making.

SELECTED READINGS

For brief selections from various theorists who have dealt with representation see Hanna F. Pitkin, ed., *Representation** (New York: Atherton Press, 1969). See also her *Concept of Representation** (Berkeley: University of California Press, 1967) for an excellent analysis of the conflicting theories of representation. J. Roland Pennock and John W. Chapman, *Representation* (New York: Atherton Press, 1968) and Robert A. Goldwin, ed., *Representation and Misrepresentation** (Chicago: Rand McNally, 1968) provide superb introductions to the broad range of issues involved in defining and implementing representation.

There are suprisingly few general histories of the development of representative institutions. See J. A. O. Larsen, *Representative Government in Greek and Roman History* (Berkeley: University of California Press, 1955) for an analysis of the origins of representative institutions, though these were different from the ancestors of modern representative institutions. A. R. Myers, "Parliaments in Europe," *History Today*, 5 (1955), pp. 383–390, 446–454, is an accurate and readable account of the

*Available in paperback.

development of European representative institutions from the Middle Ages to the eighteenth century.

Comparative analysis of voting is important to understanding its contemporary significance. Douglas W. Rae, *The Political Consequences of Election Laws* (New Haven: Yale University Press, 1971) examines the impact of proportional representation, and other electoral arrangements, on participation. For an informative analysis of different electoral systems and their impact on political integration within Western, Communist, and developing countries see A. J. Milnor, *Elections and Political Stability** (Boston: Little, Brown, 1969). Two important cross-national studies of participation and voting are Richard Rose, ed., *Electoral Behavior: A Comparative Handbook* (New York: The Free Press, 1974); and Stein Rokkan *et al., Citizens, Elections, Parties* (New York: David McKay, 1970). Gabriel A. Almond and Sidney Verba, eds., *The Civic Culture Revisited** (Boston: Little Brown, 1980), offer insights into patterns of participation in Germany, Great Britain, Italy, Mexico, and the United States.

Two informative country studies on electoral behavior are David Butler and Donald Stokes, *Political Change in Britain,** 2nd ed. (New York: St. Martin's Press, 1976); and Giorgio Galli and Alfonso Prandi, *Patterns of Political Participation in Italy* (New Haven: Yale University Press, 1970).

There are a number of "classic" studies of political behavior, which, while somewhat dated in terms of data, offer a bonanza of insights into and information about participation. See especially Robert E. Lane, *Political Life** (New York: Free Press, 1959). Seymour Martin Lipset, *Political Man: The Social Bases of Politics,** (New York: Anchor Books, 1960) examines participation in a very wide perspective. Angus Campbell et al., *The American Voter: An Abridgement** (New York, John Wiley, 1964) is still basic reading for anyone interested in voting in the United States. Paul Lazarsfeld et al., *The People's Choice** (New York: Columbia University Press, 1968), though originally published in 1944, is still enlightening reading. Its successor book, Bernard R. Berelson, Paul F. Lazarsfeld, and William N. McPhee, *Voting: A Study of Opinion Formation in a Presidential Campaign** (Chicago: University of Chicago Press, 1954) provides much basic information for understanding American electoral behavior. More recent informative publications on the same subject are Gerald Pomper, *Voters' Choice: Varieties of American Electoral Behavior** (New York: Harper & Row, 1975); Norman H. Nie, Sidney Verba, John R. Petrocik, *The Changing American Voter* (Cambridge, Mass.: Harvard University Press, 1976); and Bruce A. Campbell, *The American Electorate: Attitudes and Action** (New York: Holt, Rinehart and Winston, 1979).

Hugh A. Bone and Austin Ranney, *Politics and Voters* (New York: McGraw-Hill, 1971) is a basic introduction to the analysis of why people participate. Angus Camp-

*Available in paperback.

bell et al., *Elections and the Political Order* (New York: John Wiley, 1966) focuses mainly on the United States, with some excellent comparative data from other countries.

For an enlightening discussion of religion and voting behavior, see Albert J. Menendez, *Religion at the Polls* (Philadelphia: Westminster Press, 1977).

Penn Kimball, *The Disconnected* (New York: Columbia University Press, 1972) analyzes the psychological and political factors leading to nonparticipation in the United States and some of the efforts to increase participation.

Reapportionment is much less of an issue today than after the *Baker* v. *Carr* decision. Nevertheless, it still involves basic questions of representation and government. See Gordon E. Baker, *The Reapportionment Revolution,** (New York: Random House, 1966) and Royce Hanson, *The Political Thicket: Reapportionment and Constitutional Democracy* (Englewood Cliffs, N.J.: Prentice-Hall, 1966).

*Available in paperback.

Part Three

The Output Agencies

Chapter Eight

The Legislative Process

INTRODUCTION

Legislatures popularly are regarded as less important today than 50 years ago, but the student should not ignore the special contributions of legislative institutions.

Whenever a society is larger than an extended familial network, many objectives and values can be achieved only through authoritative rules applying to everyone in society. The legislature is the institution that makes rules for the whole society. The numerically and geographically larger a society, the more complex lawmaking and law-enforcing functions become. Legislatures, especially in pluralistic systems, have a key role in the lawmaking process.

During the twentieth century, groups and organizations have turned increasingly to government to solve a problem or oppose a proposed solution. Contemporary political systems are more politicized because of a tendency to regard government as having responsibilities in most areas of human concern (environment, inflation, defense, education, retirement benefits, and so forth). In **participatory political systems** governments devote a majority of their time to negotiating and balancing the claims and counterclaims of diverse ideas and groups demanding an official response or opposing a proposed response. The volume and complexity of political issues and interests continue to expand.

A democratically elected legislature is directly and frequently accountable to the people. Electoral accountability to citizens is the best means to facilitate and organize the flow of claims from the population. Legislatures are unique because they are the only political institutions providing both broad avenues of access and regular popular accountability. They also are the political body whose members maintain close contact with the general population. Legislature and representation, as discussed in the preceding chapter, are inseparable concepts. A legislature, more than any other government institution, includes among its members individuals **representing** the broadest range of interests. Such legislatures provide a breadth of representation and normally include persons articulating a wide range of viewpoints.

THE EVOLUTION OF THE DEMOCRATIC LEGISLATIVE INSTITUTION

Contemporary representative legislatures trace their origins to the U.S. Congress, American state legislatures, and the British House of Commons, as they developed in the eighteenth and nineteenth centuries.

The Greek *boule* was the first—but only brief—attempt at a popularly chosen, representative legislature. Throughout the Middle Ages the notion of representation and legislative assemblies was nurtured in Europe, but in practice the resemblance to modern legislatures was slight. Nevertheless, a strain of thought persisted among medieval theorists that the king should be limited in his power, though usually it was not clear how this was to be implemented.

Medieval political theorists such as Thomas Aquinas (1227–1274) and William of Occam (1280–1349) sought an ordered society and a government with limited powers. The restraints on government were reason and equity. Rulership was a trust, and rulers were justified because of their contribution to the common good. Justifiable resistance to tyranny was acknowledged as a possibility, but the writers did not lay out a blueprint for popular control of government.[1]

The concept of groups of people consulting and limiting the rulers or monarch never disappeared in Europe, but it was several centuries before effective institutions emerged. Nobility and, later, commoners were called first for consultation to approve new taxes. Subsequently, those called together would submit a list of grievances that the monarch often was compelled to acknowledge before taxes were voted. These assemblies did not originate as a method of popular control but were called into being as a means of strengthening the central government by raising taxes. The various groups and classes required to attend these meetings, however, gained political information and skills that ultimately undermined the monarchy.[2]

There was ebb and flow in the influence these councils or assemblies had on monarchs. By the fourteenth century the Commons (referring to knights and burgesses from communities, rather than commoners) and the Lords were groupings the English monarch felt compelled to deal with, and the maturation of the **Mother of Parliaments** was beginning. The English Parliament was the symbol and visible

[1]A standard discussion of medieval theorists is found in George H. Sabine, *A History of Political Theory*, 4th ed. (New York: Holt, Rinehart & Winston, 1973), especially Chapters 12–16.

[2]Charles A. Beard and John D. Lewis, Representative government in evolution. *The American Political Science Review*, 26:2, 1932, pp. 238–239.

embodiment of the English people, but it was not an elected or popularly account-able legislature. Nevertheless, toward the end of the centralizing and often authori-tarian period of the Tudor dynasty, an English historian could write about Parliament in 1583 that "every Englishman" was regarded as represented and the consent of Parliament was regarded "to be every man's consent."[3]

The turning point came with the expulsion of the Stuart dynasty in the Glorious Revolution of 1688. It affirmed the ascendancy of Parliament over the monarchy, though the monarchy remained an important institution in the decision-making proc-ess until the middle of the nineteenth century. The 1689 Bill of Rights required that Parliament meet regularly and that parliamentary consent was necessary for all laws involving taxation. Twelve years later, the Act of Settlement limited the mon-archy to Protestants. It was no longer possible for a strong monarch to reject a law passed by both houses of Parliament. During the next 100 years constitutional prac-tice (not law) established that the prime minister and cabinet should have the confi-dence of the House of Commons. The last effort of a king to appoint a prime minis-ter who did not have majority support in Parliament occurred in 1834 when William IV dismissed Melbourne and appointed Peel to form a cabinet. Peel's repeated re-buffs by Commons ultimately forced the king to withdraw the appointment. The "golden age" of parliamentary influence and primacy in the British political system had begun.

Overlapping the assertion of **parliamentary supremacy** was the movement to democratize Parliament by expanding the suffrage. The great British electoral re-form bills were those of 1832, 1867, and 1884. Prior to these the number of voters was small and sometimes almost nonexistent in a district. Inequitable districts, pub-lic voting, and the buying and selling of districts were not uncommon. Occasionally a member of Parliament took what we today would regard as a very corrupt view of his legislative role and responsibilities. The following excerpt is from an MP's letter in the first part of the eighteenth century, in which he refused a constituent petition:

> You know, and I know, that I bought this constituency. You know, and I know, that I am now determined to sell it, and you know what you think I don't know, that you are now looking for another buyer, and I know, what you certainly don't know, that I have now found another constituency to buy.
>
> About what you said about the excise [tax]: may God's curse light upon you all, and may it make your homes as open and free to the excise officers as your wives and daughters have always been to me while I have represented your rascally constituency.[4]

Parliamentary supremacy preceded democratization of that august institution, but by the end of the nineteenth century universal male suffrage was established in

---

[3]Sir Thomas Smith, quoted *ibid.*, p. 225. Westminster, begun as the monastery for the west part of Lon-don, became the monarch's palace in the tenth and eleventh centuries and maintained the monastery as well. Parliament was called (to Westminster) to consult with the King. By 1550 St. Stephan's Chapel in the Westminster had become the permanent home of the House of Commons.

[4]P. G. Richards, *Honorable Members*, 2nd ed. (New York: Praeger, 1964), p. 157.

Britain; Commons, the dominant house, was elected and accountable to the popular will. Representative government was secure, and the most corrupt legislative practices were eliminated in the face of competitive elections.

American legislative experience is briefer, except to the degree that our representative institutions are an offshoot of the British experience. Pre-Revolutionary War events in America had made the colonists distrustful of a strong executive. The Articles of Confederation (1781–1789) declared Congress supreme at the national level, though actual power was held by the states, through their legislatures. Each of the 13 states had 1 vote in Congress, but a state could have several members in a congressional delegation. States could withdraw delegates from Congress at any time. All important measures required 9 votes, and amendments to the Articles required unanimity. In the states, legislatures held power, with governors often elected for only 1 year at a time with minimal powers. Legislatures were the dominant government institutions in the United States during the nineteenth century, and the right of Americans to participate in elections expanded rapidly in that century.[5]

In summary, limitations on the power of the monarchs and the existence of councils and assemblies in some manner representative have a tradition dating back to classical Greece. The first modern elected legislatures were the English Parliament and American legislative institutions as they have evolved since the eighteenth century. The oft-described Anglo-American political tradition has a representative, democratically elected legislature as one of its principal features.

LEGISLATURES IN PARLIAMENTARY AND PRESIDENTIAL SYSTEMS

PARLIAMENTARY GOVERNMENT

Under a parliamentary system, sometimes called cabinet government, a popularly chosen legislature selects the prime minister who chooses the cabinet. The prime minister and cabinet constitute the executive branch of government. The legislature controls the government through debate, discussion, and voting on government proposals, and changes the government if it loses the confidence of the legislature. Generally, parliaments have a maximum life of five years, though new elections may be called at any time. Usually parliaments are dissolved by the government before the term of office is up, at an auspicious moment when the majority party or parties believe they will enjoy maximum popularity at the forthcoming election. As our following discussion of France indicates, it is unusual for a coalition government

---

[5]Suffrage, except for slaves and women, expanded more rapidly even than in England, and property tax qualifications were abolished by all but one state (Massachusetts) before the Civil War. See Figure 2.1 in Robert E. Lane, *Political Life* (Glencoe, Ill.: The Free Press, 1959), p. 10.

to dissolve a legislature simply because it loses a vote of confidence and must resign.

Under a parliamentary system the policy-determining members of the executive—prime minister and cabinet—are, with few exceptions, members of the legislature. In contrast to separation of powers under a presidential system, formal supreme political authority resides with the legislature, and the cabinet depends on continuing legislative support.

Parliament in Great Britain

The prototype of parliamentary systems is the bicameral British Parliament, with power in the popularly elected House of Commons, and the House of Lords exercising minimal influence. One becomes Prime Minister by being the leader of the victorious party in the House of Commons. Because of the close relationship between the British Parliament and the Cabinet, it is not surprising that prime ministers have considerable legislative experience. Of the 17 individuals who have become Prime Minister in this century, the least anyone had served in Parliament was 14 years and the average length was 25 years. By contrast, 9 of the 15 men who became President of the United States in this century had never served in Congress.

A distinguishing feature of the British Parliament is the highly disciplined two-party system in the House of Commons. Policy innovation, formation, and implementation emanate from the cabinet, not the legislature. The role of the cabinet has grown considerably in the last century. The phenomenon of disciplined party voting in Commons means that once a government is chosen and is committed to a particular policy, there is little likelihood that the members of Parliament will break ranks and defeat the government.

Parliament rarely makes or breaks governments. The selection of a prime minister is decided at the general elections when the leader of the winning party becomes prime minister. Party discipline and government stability are depicted in Table 8–1, where a unanimous party vote would be a coefficient of cohesion of 100.

Under a disciplined two-party system such as this, party leadership, (i.e., the prime minister and his cabinet) dominates. The cabinet, not the legislature, is the center of power. By and large, Parliament today does not possess a choice of governments during a session. Between 1846 and 1860 Commons was supreme and governments suffered eight major defeats. The power to change governments has declined steadily ever since. The last time a government resigned because of a negative vote in Commons was in 1923.[6]

Formal voting is not, however, the only way to bring about changes in government personnel or policy, and a ruling party is able to select new leaders in critical political circumstances. Events in 1940 and 1956 demonstrate that a prime minister will resign if a policy erodes the confidence of his party colleagues. In May, 1940,

[6]Samuel H. Beer and Adam B. Ulam, eds., *Patterns of Government*, 3rd ed. (New York: Random House, 1973), p. 207.

A view of the House of Lords at the opening of a parliamentary session. Queen Elizabeth II reads the Opening Speech to the joint meeting of Parliament.

Prime Minister Neville Chamberlain was sharply attacked for his previous diplomatic compromises with Nazi Germany (Munich, 1938) and the deteriorating war situation, signalled by Norway's falling to the Germans. When the division bells rang and the vote of confidence was taken, Chamberlain's normal majority of 200 slipped to 81. Sixty Conservative MPs abstained and 33 supported the opposition. Within the

The House of Commons in session.

Table 8–2   Representation in the French National Assembly (Fourth Republic)

	1946		1951		1956	
	Deputies	Percent	Deputies	Percent	Deputies	Percent
Communists	182	29.4	101	16.1	150	25.2
Socialists	102	16.5	107	17.1	100	16.8
MRP	166	26.9	97	15.5	83	14.1
Radicals and RGR	71	11.5	91	14.5	94	15.8
Conservatives	67	10.8	98	15.7	121[a]	20.3
RPF (Gaullists)			120	19.1		
Poujadists		4.9			42	7.0
Misc. and unaffiliated	30		13	2.1	6	1.0
	618		627		596[b]	

Source: Walter H. Mallory, ed., *Political Handbook of the World* (New York: Harper & Brothers; for the Council on Foreign Relations); 1947, p. 61; 1952, p. 68; 1957, p. 69.

[a]Troubled conditions in Algeria made it impossible to hold elections for the 30 representatives from that area in 1956.

[b]The Conservatives in 1956 included the remnants of the RPF, the Social Republicans.

week Chamberlain had resigned and the House of Commons elected Winston Churchill, a Conservative, to lead a national government.

Anthony Eden was prime minister in 1956 during the Suez Crisis. An Israeli attack on Egypt in October/November 1956, was supported by the British and French, in large part because of Egyptian President Nasser's nationalization of the Suez Canal. Eden subsequently resigned for reasons of health, several weeks after a Middle Eastern ceasefire. There were many pressures on Eden, international pressures from the United States, the Soviet Union, and the United Nations, and also the physical and mental strain in dealing with those dangerous and complicated circumstances. Numerous interpretations of the Suez affair have appeared. One factor leading to Eden's resignation was a revolt in the Conservative Party. There were reports that 40 Conservative MPs were prepared to vote against the prime minister, though on a Suez vote following the ceasefire only 8 opposed the government.[7] R. T. McKenzie, a leading authority on parties and Parliament in Great Britain, has described succinctly the mix of discipline and deference in the House of Commons: "Once the Conservatives have chosen their Leader he can stay in office . . . until he himself decides to retire or, as has happened on at least three occasions in this century, he is forced from office by a revolt among his followers."[8] The Chamberlain and Eden cases reveal the measure of leadership autonomy and perceived political failure a British ruling party in Parliament will tolerate. In this and similar cases, the ruling party selects a new prime minister who also becomes the party leader.

The ultimate constraint of a forced resignation describes unique situations and must be balanced against the fact that the cabinet presides on a day-to-day basis. One indication of the cabinet's dominant position is interest-group lobbying. Most British interest groups concentrate their activities on administrative officials and ministries. A case is won if a ministry can be convinced to take or reject a particular action. MPs are approached only as a second or third step in strategy, when the response from the executive has been unsatisfactory.[9]

The size of the executive also has increased, and it has been charged that patronage inherent in this expansion further reduces MP independence and influence.

With over a hundred members of the ruling party holding ministerial positions, Mr. Wilson [Labour Prime Minister between 1964 and 1970, and 1974 and 1976] has assuredly dispensed patronage with a liberality which even George III or Lord North might have blushed. Patronage and party discipline have eroded the independence of the members of the legislature . . .[10]

The House of Commons has 630 members; there are 20 or 21 ministries in the

[7]R. T. McKenzie, *British Political Parties*, 2nd ed. (New York: Frederick A. Praeger, 1964), pp. 555–556.
[8]*Ibid.*, p. 579.
[9]K. C. Wheare, *Legislatures* (New York: Oxford University Press, 1963), especially Chapter 3.
[10]Richard Middleton, The problems and consequences of parliamentary government: A historical review. *Parliamentary Affairs*, 23:1, 1969, p. 57.

cabinet. If one takes into account noncabinet senior ministers and junior ministers (usually with the title parliamentary secretary), there are approximately 100 ministerial appointments to be filled by a government. Thus, 25 to 30 percent of a majority party can anticipate receiving an executive appointment. Appointments balance and mend differences within the party, but appointments are also reward, control, and "patronage" instruments.

In a constitutional monarchy such as Great Britain, the cabinet does not exercise unlimited power. Not the least of the limitations is the requirement of consultation and negotiation, so party leaders may maintain the confidence of their fellow MPs and present a favorable image to the electorate. British parties are not monoliths, and the spirit of compromise and negotiation permeate the party organizations as well as the entire political system.[11]

One example is the **1922 Committee** composed of Conservative backbenchers (the less prominent MPs, not holding any ministerial posts). The chair of the committee has access to cabinet ministers, to whom he conveys backbenchers' opinions. The committee members are organized into functional committees corresponding to government departments, thus permitting detailed review and impact on party and government policy. While formulating policy, British parties are guided by the principle of anticipated response. Policy is drafted and discussed in a manner that takes into account the views of MPs not holding ministerial positions.

Parliament in France
Parliament during the French Fourth Republic (1946–1958) had several features missing in Great Britain, but not uncommon in parliamentary systems. The National Assembly, the popularly elected lower house, was a multiparty chamber, with no party ever controlling more than 29 percent of the seats. Except for the Communists, the parties were loosely disciplined, and it was common for a party to have some deputies supporting a bill and others opposing it. The Assembly overshadowed the Cabinet, not the Cabinet the Assembly.

The multiparty nature of the Fourth Republic is apparent in Table 8–2.

Certain political parties were unwilling to participate in a government unless the political system was amended drastically. Governing parties in the Fourth Republic did not include the Communists or Gaullists, who controlled approximately 33 percent of the Assembly seats. Coalition governments were a necessity, but the range of potential partners was circumscribed. An essential component of government making was *replâtrage* ("replastering"), whereby there was continuity of personalities and parties in the cabinet, with political leaders simply occupying different min-

---

[11]In his concluding remarks on the British party system, Allen Potter declares: "Great Britain is, socially and politically, a pluralistic society, in which the government no more than any other group or institution is outside the interaction of social forces that constitute the society. British politics is by nature the politics of compromise." "Great Britain: Opposition with a Capital O," in Robert A. Dahl, ed., *Political Oppositions in Western Democracies* (New Haven: Yale University Press, 1966), p. 33.

Table 8-1   Party Unity in the House of Commons

Year	Coefficient of Cohesion		
	Conservatives	Labour	Liberals
1860	63.0	—	58.9
1871	74.0	—	75.5
1881	87.9	—	83.2
1899	97.9	—	82.5
1906	91.0	88.4	96.8
1914–1928	99.2	99.8	88.8
1945–1946	99.0	99.9	—

Source: Adapted from Samuel H. Beer and Adam B. Ulam, eds., *Patterns of Government*, 3rd ed. Copyright © 1958, 1962, 1973 by Random House, Inc. Adapted by permission of the publisher. Original data source: Samuel H. Beer, *British Politics in the Collectivist Age*, rev. ed. (New York: Knopf, 1965), pp. 123, 257, 262. Beer states: "Starting from the assumption that a fifty-fifty split in a party signifies zero cohesion, we calculate the coefficient of cohesion by dividing by fifty the difference between fifty and the percentage of party members voting on one side. Thus when 90 percent of the members of a party are on one side, the CoC is 80 percent. . . . Abstainers are not counted."

isteries in successive governments. There was stability of a sort, at least among ministers. One authority has observed that between January 1946 and December 1952, 16 ministries were held by 66 persons in France (this period includes 6 cabinets that lasted less than 6 weeks). During the same period in Great Britain, the 16 counterpart ministeries were occupied by 58 persons.[12]

Policy innovation and implementation were inhibited, however. Coalition governments were formed on the lowest common denominator of agreement. When a pressing new issue arose, the government would lose a **vote of confidence**, be forced to resign, and a new coalition was formed. Governing parties were the reservoirs of the *ministrables*—deputies who had achieved or were eligible for a ministry. On occasion ministers would leave or "abandon" a government at a strategic moment in order to maximize the chances of participating in a subsequent government. A premier always was on the alert to mollify restless coalition partners; moreover, he could not be certain that his own party would continue to support him. Coalition mending and dealing with the smaller, daily questions meant that major problems such as German rearmament and the Algerian revolution did not receive a policy mandate at an election. Governments did not form because of direct electoral choice, as in Great Britain, but because of bargains struck among minority parties over matters which, in some instances, were only minor issues at the previous election.

The power to dissolve the legislature and thus require new parliamentary elections is a potential weapon in the hands of the executive, but one that may backfire. Dissolution as a means to discipline recalcitrant opponents and increase sup-

---

[12]Philip Williams, *Politics in Post-War France* (London: Longmans, Green, 1954), p. 375.

porters in the legislature was used only once during the Fourth Republic, and it was unsuccessful. Premier Edgar Faure dissolved the National Assembly in December 1955. His government was divided over the correctness of a dissolution, and the 1956 election failed to increase the number of pro-Faure deputies. Following the elections, Guy Mollett, a Socialist, formed a government. Faure, a leader of the Radical Party, was expelled from the party in January 1956, for failing to consult with the party while he was premier.

A principal difference between parliamentarianism in Great Britain and France is that the British system is premised on the need to make and execute policy, while an enduring theme in French political cultures is the politics of defense—parliament restrains government to protect individual or group interests. A French political essayist in the last decade of the Third Republic (1875–1940) expressed an attitude also characteristic of the Fourth Republic when he declared that "the executive is inherently monarchic" and that democracy is "a perpetual struggle by the ruled against the abuses of power."[13]

The constitution of the Fifth Republic (adopted in 1958) includes several changes that increase the executive's authority. The Fifth Republic is a parliamentary/ presidential hybrid. The president is popularly elected for a seven-year term; he or she symbolizes national popular choice and, depending on the election issues, carries some type of policy mandate. The president nominates the premier, who must resign only if she or he loses a vote of confidence in the Assembly. France has had three strong presidents under the Fifth Republic, Charles de Gaulle (1958–1969), Georges Pompidou (1969–1974), and Giscard d'Estaing (May 1974, to date). The Gaullists and their allies have controlled the Assembly and Senate since 1958. The president has exerted great influence on the premier. Resignations were issues between the president and premier and did not result from a no-confidence vote in the Assembly.

The *ministrable* phenomenon, which previously had led some ambitious deputies to bring about a change in government in the hopes of a ministerial appointment, has diminished. A legislator now must resign his seat if he accepts a ministerial appointment. In addition, the government (president, premier, and cabinet) has control of the parliamentary agenda, which was not true in the Fourth Republic. The government decides which bills will be considered and in what order and determines which, if any, committee amendments will be debated and voted on by parliament. A decisive control is the "package requirement," which enables the government to require a vote on the entire bill. Thus, the government need not compromise on technicalities or amendments.

The Fifth Republic provides for executive leadership, and de Gaulle's presidency tipped the balance further in this direction, to the point that even the cabinet had only a minor voice in policy making. Since de Gaulle resigned in 1969, however, the poli-

---

[13]Suzanne Berger, "The French Political System," in Beer and Ulam, eds., *op. cit.* p. 361.

tics of negotiation and accommodation are now important elements in parliamentary/executive relations. The president is chosen popularly, and this means he must appeal to many different groups in building a national majority. Once elected with a majority mandate, the President under the Constitution of the Fifth Republic holds considerable power. When the President has named a premier and cabinet (the Government), it is not necessary to secure the approval of the National Assembly (the popularly elected lower house). The Government has ultimate control over parliament's timetable, thus avoiding prolonged debates that often delay or prevent enactment of government policy. Should the executive wish to push an essential bill, the premier can stake the life of the cabinet on the issue. If the opposition hopes to defeat the government, it must make a motion of censure, which can only pass if a majority of the *total* membership of the National Assembly supports censure. A bill will pass and the censure motion fail even if a majority of those voting, but not 50 percent plus one of total membership, supports the censure motion.

Parliament does have the power, and the president and premier must work with it. The constitution facilitates executive action if there is goodwill between parliament and the executive. Should the two branches find themselves in irresolvable conflict, France could return to the *immobilisme* of the Fourth Republic. The need to avoid this had led the executive to become increasingly receptive to legislative input. A slight majority in the National Assembly (Gaullists and pro-Gaullists had a 65 seat majority in the 491-seat National Assembly following the March 1978 elections) means the executive must respond to factions and interests within the Assembly majority, as well as acknowledge or preempt politically popular opposition arguments. Prior to the 1978 Assembly elections, the moderate conservative President Giscard d'Estaing indicated he would accept a popular vote that brought a Left Front (Socialists and Communists) to power and he would work with a left-wing majority. However, the narrow defeat of the left did not make this necessary.

In summary, we can say that the French and British Parliaments maintain an important role, particularly in facilitating inputs and mediating political conflict through negotiation and bargaining.

THE LEGISLATURE IN A PRESIDENTIAL SYSTEM

The distinctive feature of a presidential system is **separation of powers**: the chief executive and the legislature are elected independently of one another; each holds office for a definite period of time, which ordinarily cannot be altered by the other; and both the legislature and the executive are not readily controlled by the other.

The American national government is the prototype of **presidential government**. The president is elected for a four-year term by national popular vote via the electoral college and can be removed legally by one of two methods, both of which involve Congress. He may be impeached by majority vote in the House of Representatives, followed by conviction by a two-thirds vote in the Senate. (One president, Andrew Johnson (1865–1869), was impeached; he was adjudged not guilty by one vote in the Senate.) The Twenty-Fifth Amendment also provides that if the vice-president and a majority of the cabinet inform Congress that the president cannot discharge his duties, the vice-president will become acting president. If the president subsequently declares no inability exists, Congress must decide the issue within 21 days. Other than these two unique circumstances, the presidential term of office is not controlled by the legislature. Periodically, however, the majority in either the House of Representatives or the Senate does not represent the same party as the president. Between the 80th Congress, which took office in 1947, and the 96th Congress, elected in 1978, the House of Representatives has been controlled by the opposition party (not the President's party) 16 of those years, and the opposition has controlled the Senate for 14 years. Even when the opposition party controls one or both houses of the legislature, the president completes his or her term.

Both the legislative and executive branches share broad spheres of power; policy is a compromise between the two branches. The separation of powers associated with presidential government is actually a system of checks and balances. Powers held by one branch are shared in selected but decisive ways with another branch.

President Carter delivering the 1980 State of the Union Address to Congress.

Congress has the law-enacting responsibility, but the president holds the veto power, which requires a two-thirds majority of those present and voting in both houses to override. Between 1913 and May 1971, for example, only 37 of 1303 vetoes were overriden by Congress.[14] If Congress is at a disadvantage vis-à-vis a presidential veto, it possesses considerable control through the authority of the Senate to confirm—"advise and consent to"—major presidential appointments. A majority of appointees serve in the executive branch, but a number also involve the judiciary, the third branch of government. The president nominates, but the Senate confirms. Headlines are made when the Senate rejects a nomination (for example, when the nominations of Carswell and Hainsworth to the Supreme Court by President Nixon were rejected in 1969 and 1970). A continuing dialogue is maintained to avoid an embarrassing rejection. A government acquaintance told one of the authors how the names of "six persons were run by" the Armed Services Committee recently before a nomination to the Department of Defense was submitted. One of the important bargaining tools held by Congress, through the Senate, is the power to confirm, or reject executive nominations. In a similar vein, the power of the purse, the power to raise taxes and appropriate money, is a restriction the executive branch cannot readily overcome.

A major point at issue, as in parliamentary government, concerns whether or not the legislature is coequal with, or overshadowed by, the executive branch. The president, through public messages (State of the Union, Budget Message, and so forth) and through bills drafted by the administration, has the principal role in recommending and innovating policy. The bulk of the expertise resides in the executive. Congress in recent years has attempted to increase its pool of expertise, but is still overshadowed by the executive and his bureaucracy. Between 1977 and 1979, the personal and committee staff tripled from 4489 in 1957 to 13,000 in 1979. Each committee has a professional staff and members of Congress have their own personal staff aides paid out of their office budgets.[15]

The Congressional Research Service has been of minor help to Congress in ferreting out new facts. The CRS reports are well-drafted but depend almost entirely on published sources. Unless Congress were to erect a bureaucratic behemoth, it could not have immediately available to it the necessary technical resources and dispassionate experts responsible only to Congress. Congress is unable, even if it so desired, to monopolize the initiation of programs and legislation; it must share this with the executive and frequently defer to the president on this first step. However, policy incubation and modification through bill-drafting and amending are fundamental roles enabling Congress to retain important lawmaking duties.

[14]Nelson Polsby, *Congress and the Presidency*, 2nd ed., (Englewood Cliffs, N.J.: Prentice-Hall, 1971), p. 81. See also, *Congressional Quarterly's Guide to Congress: 1971* (Washington: Congressional Quarterly Service), p. 583.

[15]Harrison Fox, Jr. and Susan Webb Hammond, *Congressional Staffs* (New York: Free Press, 1977), p. 171

Active politicians are prone to propose solutions to what they perceive to be important issues with popular support or potential support.[16] Much legislation that is subsequently regarded as a "presidential program" actually has its origins in Congress. President Johnson's promotion of consumer protection, pollution control, and auto safety legislation in 1965 and 1966 preempted legislative hearings and bills originating at the congressional level. These happened to be popular issues that lent themselves to preemption by the executive. President Nixon, on the other hand, proposed and got a consumer protection agency in the president's Executive Office. The president preferred this to proposals first made in Congress to create a cabinet-level post or establish a new independent regulatory agency.

Executive preemption can cause executive/legislative rivalry, even when persons involved are from the same party. The late Senator Kefauver, a liberal Democrat from Tennessee, initiated a series of committee hearings in December 1959 on abuses in the drug industry. The hearings gained wide popular attention and roused indignation at apparent abuses. Legislation eventually emerged from the Kefauver Committee in 1962, and the senator requested administration support to push for final passage. The story is complex, but President Kennedy's message and legislative recommendation succeeded in transferring the policy-initiation role to the executive. The law that ultimately came into effect omitted several Kefauver items, but the legislation took its origin and essential framework from Senator Kefauver's hearings and the resulting draft bill. John R. Johannes, who has described this case in detail, concludes that as President Kennedy was signing the bill into law and taking most of the credit, Senator Kefauver remained convinced "that it was Congress,

("The Small Society" by Brickman © Washington Star Syndicate, permission granted by King Features Syndicate 1973.)

Government by compromise

[16]The following two paragraphs draw heavily from the excellent analysis by John R. Johannes, *Policy Innovation in Congress* (Morristown, N.J.: General Learning Press, 1972).

and not the Administration, which had initiated the bill and should receive the plaudits."[17]

The period from proposal to law in a presidential system requires negotiation, trade-offs, and compromising. An important contribution to policy making by Congress is sometimes overlooked. This influence does not always take the form of an amendment or a competing draft bill. Daily contacts between members of congress and congressional staff and administration officials, frequent conferences and briefings, and visits and inspection tours all contribute to an exchange of views. This continual interaction constrains executive actions and reveals on a day-to-day basis legislation that can reasonably be expected to originate in Congress or be accepted by Congress. Many committee staffs and members of congress hold office much longer than any presidential appointee in the executive (cabinet officers, department heads, undersecretaries) can hope to, and this longevity and network of contacts is a legislative advantage. This informal and partially concealed network of legislative associations has not received the study it deserves.

Government in a presidential system is essentially compromise government. Many elected officials in Congress, and also the president, must approve if policy is enacted. The U.S. Constitution gave the House of Representatives, the Senate, and the President fixed but different terms of office (two, six, and four years, respectively). The heart of the system under these conditions is continuous bargaining, accommodation, and compromise; and, despite its label, the role of the legislature remains important in a presidential system.

BICAMERAL AND UNICAMERAL LEGISLATURES

In many countries the division of legislatures into two houses (**bicameral**) is a result of historical precedent. Bicameral or even tricameral (the three estates under the ancient regime in France) legislatures were first organized by estates or principal classes in the country. As democratic choice and representative government evolved, the lower chamber—for example, the House of Representatives or the British House of Commons—was based on adult suffrage and popular representation, while the "upper" chamber usually was appointed or indirectly elected. The upper chamber was supposed to be a moderating, conservative influence, that would check a potentially tyrannical popular majority. It also might represent certain groups in the community that a government, yielding before the claims of mass participation in the lower chamber, hoped would retain a special voice in the political process.

The British House of Lords in the nineteenth century was nearly coequal with Commons, although the selection of a prime minister rested exclusively with the latter body. Today, the House of Lords has only slight power. The Lords have no bud-

---

[17]*Ibid.*, p. 15.

getary powers. They do have a suspensive veto, rarely implemented, that permits them to reject a bill, which Commons then must repass in a subsequent session.[18] The most important function of the Lords is that of discussion and revision. Technical errors and other flaws, substantive or minor, can be ironed out during the debate in the House of Lords. Broad questions of public policy and new solutions or approaches can be initiated in the Lords, especially since life peers (who are in office only for the lifetime of the individual, as instituted in 1958) are to be distinguished persons, such as journalists, lawyers, trade unionists, academics, and scientists. The Lords certainly is not an historical anachronism, but its role is substantially diminished. Under a parliamentary government, where the principal executive officers are chosen by the popularly elected lower chamber, it is inevitable that the cabinet and the elective house dominate.

Second chambers also are sometimes devised to provide for a different type of representation, even though selection may be by popular vote. Japan's House of Councillors exemplifies this principle. The House of Councillors has 250 members who serve 6-year terms, half elected every 3 years. One hundred and fifty are chosen from prefectural districts (Japan has prefectures rather than provinces or states) and 100 are chosen from the nation at large. The voter has 2 votes, 1 for the prefectural level and 1 for the national level. The House of Councillors was to combine territorial representation with the selection of distinguished persons who had achieved eminence in their chosen careers. The latter hope was not realized. Tightly organized interest groups and minority parties are able to elect some candidates at the national level (for example, the Small Business Political League and the Expropriated Farmer's League), and the party organizations of the bigger Japanese political parties play a paramount electoral role. Few independent candidates are elected. Winning candidates often lack the stature envisaged by the drafters of the postwar constitution. In 1962, for example, the largest number of votes was won by a panelist on the Japanese TV program, "What's My Line?" who ran as a Liberal Democrat.

The Councillors' power is not coequal to Japan's 492-member House of Representatives. On matters such as the budget and treaty ratifications, the House of Representatives can override Councillors' opposition by a simple majority; in other matters it requires a two-thirds majority. Except for a few special interests and minor political party representation, the partisan composition of the Councillors is similar to the House of Representatives. The wisdom of eminent persons and the calmer and more studied deliberation that were to take place in the House of Councillors has not occurred. The primary difference between the two houses today is the term of office and the size of the electoral district. If, however, a party other than

---

[18]The Parliament Act of 1911 prohibited the House of Lords from rejecting any financial bill and reduced the power of delay the Lords could exercise over other bills passed by the House of Commons. The Act of 1949 states a bill could become law over the House of Lords' opposition if Commons passed the bill in two consecutive sessions and a year had elapsed between the first reading and final passage.

the Liberal Democrats (who have ruled Japan since 1955) should win control of the House of Councillors, the political status of the Japanese upper house would increase perceptibly.

A frequent reason for a bicameral legislature is a federal political system in which power is distributed through a written constitution between the national government and the states or provinces. The upper house, representing territorial units, is organized differently from the lower house. The territorial chamber may represent a different balance of interests, assuming the federal units have special interests or concerns that are a minority at the national level (such as the French-speaking culture of Quebec).

The upper house in West Germany, the *Bundesrat*, or Federal Council, is made up of delegations from the 10 states. Each state has 3 to 5 representatives, depending on the size of its population, although the 2 largest states include 47 percent of the West German population, exluding West Berlin. Members of the *Bundesrat* are selected by the state governments. Each state delegation must vote as a unit. Constitutional amendments must be approved by a two-thirds vote in both the *Bundesrat* and the lower chamber, the *Bundestag* (federal parliament). Approximately half of the legislation enacted annually involves what the West German constitution or Basic Law describes as "consent" law, requiring approval by the *Bundesrat*. The *Bundesrat* has many political interests: first is to represent the special needs and interests of the state government and maintain the position of the states under West German federalism. Perhaps because its members are not directly elected, West Germans are only slightly aware of the *Bundesrat's* purpose. The percentage of West Germans who were roughly aware of "what the *Bundesrat* is here for" rose slowly from 8 percent in 1951 to a mere 14 percent in 1956.[19] The *Bundesrat's* special concern with sustaining state government interests, and its indirect representative character, have given it a significant political role but have failed to attract much public interest.

The upper house under American federalism has, however, achieved a great deal more popular attention than its West German counterpart. The U.S. Senate is organized along state lines, 2 senators per state elected for 6-year terms. Since the Seventeenth Amendment (1913) all senators have been elected by popular vote (before 1913 Senators were chosen for 6-year terms by the state legislatures). The Senate shares most powers with the House of Representatives. The Senate alone, however, confirms presidential appointments (majority vote) and ratifies treaties (two-thirds majority). Because the Senate has only 100 members, the individual senator has more visibility than the typical representative. The Senate generally is regarded as the more prestigious and august body. Senators represent their electors and make no claim to watch over state government interests, as do *Bundesrat* delegates.

[19]Karl Deutsch and Eric Nordlinger, "The German Federal Republic," in Roy C. Macridis and Robert E. Ward, eds., *Modern Political Systems: Europe*, 3rd ed. (Englewood Cliffs, N.J.: Prentice-Hall, 1973), p. 402.

Countries such as Denmark, Finland, Israel, and Sweden have adopted **unicameral** legislatures (one house) because they believe them to be more efficient due to the concentration of the legislative process into one chamber or because they believe bicameralism is less democratic when the upper house is indirectly chosen or election is not based on one person, one vote. In some cases there are no compelling reasons for bicameralism: no historical precedents, such as the House of Lords, need be continued; no special interests require representation; the possibility of calmer and more extended discussion or the presence of eminent but nonpolitical persons is not regarded as mandatory for popular government; or they have a nonfederal system.[20]

FUNCTIONS OF LEGISLATURES

Legislative functions involve interaction between legislators and other political actors, such as constituents, lobbyists, political leaders, presidential representatives, and bureaucrats. Legislatures will be regarded as legitimate in a political system because of their representative quality and their willingness to interact with many interests. Figure 8–1 shows the legislative system, which includes the legislature and the interaction process.

The functions listed below are not exhaustive, but they give the student an awareness of the multifunctional character of legislatures:

1. Legislatures share with other institutions and groups the power to initiate, enact, and modify policy through lawmaking and other means. The individual legislator's role in this area is often informal and not open to public view, yet the role is very real. In the British Parliament, for example, disciplined party voting and the cabinet's preeminence suggest that the average MP contributes little to policy making. In practice, though, the MP has considerable leverage with ministers, through the party committee in Commons. Legislative whips in Britain officially are given the duty of "whipping" MPs into line on a vote but, as in many legislatures, spend more of their time apprising the government of MP opinions than "whipping" the legislative party.

The core of the legislature's policy-making functions conflicts with management principles of quick, decisive action. The legislature provides the arena where competing demands can struggle, negotiate, compromise, and it is hoped, be at least minimally accommodated. Compromise and, often, delay are institutionalized in the legislative process in a democratic system, and legislative negotiation often provides a stability or balance otherwise difficult to achieve. Speaking about the American system, one study recognized that the demands of some interests might not be met even partially, but that legislatures "can grant these interests a hearing—per-

---

[20]J. Blondel reports that in 1971 there were 52 bicameral legislatures out of 108 countries having legislatures. *Comparative Legislatures* (Englewood Cliffs, N.J.: Prentice-Hall, 1973), p. 32.

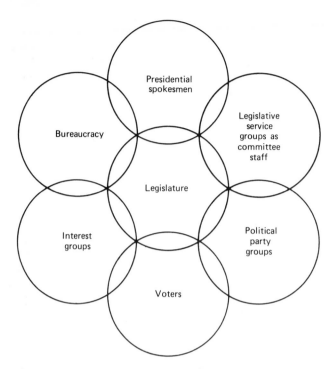

Figure 8-1. A legislative system. Adapted from Malcolm E. Jewell and Samuel C. Patterson, _The Legislative Process in the United States._ Copyright © 1966 by Random House. Adapted by permission of the publisher.

haps not obtainable elsewhere—and this hearing can be an important factor in the management of conflict.''[21]

A legislature generally will not have among its members individuals with the depth of technical expertise as those who serve in the executive or interest groups, but it possesses a perspective that the experts will not have. En masse, legislators have a range of knowledge and experience in terms of class, ethnic, religious, and geographic origin and an awareness of constituent views that make them exceptionally sensitive to public opinion and demands and most able to judge the acceptability and feasibility of policy. Legislatures' size may inhibit efficient procedure, but size also has its attributes.

2. Legislatures usually influence the composition of the chief executive officers. Under a parliamentary system the prime minister and the cabinet are responsible legally to the legislature. British practice provides that the prime minister

[21]Malcolm E. Jewell and Samuel C. Patterson, _The Legislative Process in the United States_, 2nd ed., (New York: Random House, 1971), p. 12.

invariably is the leader of the party that won the election. Even in Great Britain, though, the composition of the cabinet is decided by negotiation and bargaining with various elements of the majority party. The House of Commons no longer makes and unmakes governments during a parliamentary term, but it can make or cripple reputations. A minister must be a "good House of Commons man" and be able to hold his own in parliamentary debate, else he falter and feel compelled to resign. One Conservative minister, in describing his first months in office, observed "the remorseless interest of the House of Commons in seeing a man brought down."[22] Commons provides a setting in which ministers must regularly justify their actions and show competence.

When choosing his cabinet and making apppointments, a president of the United States must give consideration to the temper and anticipated reaction of the Senate. The Senate does not make a habit of rejecting presidential nominees, but the occasional refusal to confirm an appointment makes it clear that the president should consult with senators prior to announcing a key appointment.

3. While performing a lawmaking function, committee hearings may perform a valuable role in discovering and/or making public new information. The United States has the most developed legislative committee system.

A case study of the Kefauver hearing on prices and practices in the drug industry (conducted by the Antitrust and Monopoly Subcommittee of the Senate Judiciary Committee) shows that they began in a situation where "practically no data on the

The U.S. Senate Banking Committee holds a hearing on New York City's financial problems.

[22]*Economist*, February 27, 1971, p. 17, quoted in Beer and Ulam, eds., *op. cit.*, p. 238.

subject were available in usable form, and the staff commenced a laborious research job."[23] Not only did the hearings make nationwide headlines, they also publicized facts that only a few insiders had been aware of up to that time. Similarly, the Watergate hearings conducted by the Senate Select Committee on Presidential Campaign Activities brought together and organized information in a situation when most if not all participants themselves had knowledge that was restricted to only small segments of the affair. Committee hearings serve many purposes, including preparation of legislation and supervision of other branches of government. In doing so, they make public and organize information that might not be revealed under any other circumstances.

   4.   Legislatures legitimize government actions and in turn serve to legitimize the political system. In following accepted procedures, legislatures reassure the public of the rightness and propriety of the policy process. The legitimizing functions include outputs as well as procedures followed. Legitimacy, however, is determined principally by the output and the success in responding to the most pressing demands and accommodating a diverse range of interests.

   Transitional political systems that are moving from authoritarianism to a limited pluralism focus on procedures. At the beginning of the transitional stage, the legislature barely is involved in formulating laws and policy. The Supreme Soviet, which is the bicameral Soviet legislature, illustrates this first step in the legitimizing function. One of the Supreme Soviet's functions is to enact laws and thereby bestow a certain legality and acceptability on the lawmaking process. This adherence to proper procedure is a significant first step. Important policy is no longer simply party or administrative directive. The rule of law, legitimacy, and authority are at a very early—though developing—stage in the Soviet Union. The Supreme Soviet is one institution through which procedural norms will evolve if this transition continues.

   5.   Democratic legislatures should oversee other branches of government and thereby uphold freedom to criticize and evaluate programs and officials. In the United States a majority of the supervisory functions occur in committee hearings. It would be hard to find an American high-school or college student who is unaware of at least one congressional investigation that has turned the glare of publicity on some government agency or official. In Great Britain the most telling public overview takes place during the Question Hour, which occurs the first four days each week when the House of Commons convenes at 2:30. Ministers must respond to questions (written and then followed up orally) submitted by an MP. Individual responsibility and explanation are rigorously and regularly enforced during the Question Hour. Many ambitions have been lofted or deflated during this grilling period.

   6.   Educating and informing the public are functions best performed by democratic legislatures. This is a corollary to the previously cited functions, but is of sufficient importance to be included in a separate category. The educative/informational function occurs in legislative debates, committee hearings, and elections, and dur-

---

[23]John R. Johannes, *op. cit.*, p. 14.

ing the period between elections when legislators attempt to maintain ties with constituents by interpreting major issues in newsletters, in TV and radio talks, and through back-home visits.

7.   Legislatures can be a bulwark of democracy. Some also function as a transitional institution to a more open society. Legislatures can be a forum for promoting diverse viewpoints not always in harmony with the government of the moment, such as in Taiwan, South Korea, and Nigeria. In political systems that are making an effort to be more tolerant of differing political viewpoints, legislatures will play an essential role in the movement toward liberalization. Throughout the world a majority of political systems limit political competition. Where there is an effort to expand the boundaries of political expression, the legislatures will be among the first arenas in which political discussion and criticism are allowed, first during the elections and then in the legislative sessions.

8.   Legislatures function as electioneering forums, particularly during the period between elections. The publicity and controversies generated are relevant to the winning and losing of popular support. This is true of both developed and developing political systems. In one sense, governing is a protracted election campaign. At a news conference on the day following the 1972 parliamentary elections, Singapore's prime minister was asked when the next election would take place. He replied that the next election began the day after election day. The British Parliament has been described as "the agreed arena in which most of the campaign is fought." The parliamentary sessions are the place where the political parties "obtain something like equal access to the ear of the electorate in the long formative period between official campaigns."[24]

In developing countries, where parties are relatively new and party organization is at an embryonic state, action in the legislature can be the most important way to win attention and build electoral support. In Singapore, for example, the period between 1955 and 1959, when the country was moving toward self-government, was critical. The People's Action Party, which has governed Singapore since June 1959, had only four members in the 1955–1959 Assembly. Several factors accounted for the PAP's electoral victory in the May 1959 elections. One was the ability of the future prime minister, Lee Kuan Yew, through his incisive rhetoric, to dominate a good portion of the legislative debate. His statements and proposals also won support from some of the English-educated people in Singapore and convinced most of the English-educated community (30 to 35 percent of the voters at that time) that PAP leaders, as distinct from the PAP grassroots organization, were not pro-Communist.[25] The legislative forum was critical to building up mass support and wooing key segments of society.

9.   Individual service to constituents looms increasingly large as a function of legislators in postindustrial society. This is particularly true in the United States but

---

[24]Bernard Crick, *The Reform of Parliament* (Garden City, N.Y.: Anchor Books, 1965), pp. 25–26.
[25]Thomas J. Bellows, *The People's Action Party of Singapore: Emergence of a Dominant Party System* (New Haven: Yale University Southeast Asia Studies, Monograph Series No. 14, 1970).

also is a trend in other democracies. Voters often evaluate legislators on the basis of service to constituents and the district, rather than on policy positions. For example, a 1978 survey of American newspapers revealed that legislators in their campaign speeches, tended to separate themselves and the job they were doing from Congress and its performance. There is a growing distrust of such political institutions as legislatures, but thus far this has not spilled over into high distrust of individual legislators. Illustrating this was a 1978 survey in which a mere 20 percent said Congress is doing a "good job," while 65 percent gave their own representative in Congress "high ratings."[26] Thus, the legislator emphasizes serving the district but is critical of the job the legislature as a whole is doing. If one function of elections is to

Call of the Open Road

(Shanks in the Buffalo Evening News.)

[26]*Institute for Social Research Newsletter*, Autumn 1979, p. 4.

"throw the rascals out" and move policies in a new direction, voters have been disappointed. In most democracies the problems have persisted—high inflation, energy shortages, heavy defense spending, and so forth. Elections often have not produced changes, and voters are beginning to change their expectation that politicians can deliver on their promises. A principal reason most legislators have assumed an increasing service function is that they can emphasize this role in contrast to a negative and even cynical attitude people have toward Congress as a formulator of policy. One political scientist concluded that, in this era of increased government activity, representatives and senators are overloaded with "case work." This refers to activities in legislative offices directed toward coping with problems of individual constituents. Frequently the case results from administration of a federal program or regulation. It often is resolved by a congressional staff member going to an agency to get favorable action such as speeding up approval of a grant application.[27] This type of service function, which absorbs a majority of a legislator's worktime, has become the primary reason legislators are reelected.

10. The nine functions discussed thus far characterize democratic legislatures, or those where the political system is transiting toward a more open and competitive situation. Legislatures in authoritarian systems fulfill functions much the same way as one-party elections (discussed earlier in Chapter Seven, on representation and elections.) Authoritarian legislatures function as a recruiting device, to reward the upwardly mobile regime faithful or, in some cases, to take a closer look at an ambitious individual. The Supreme Soviet is careful to represent major vocational and national groups. The legislative overseeing function is minimal, if not nil. The Supreme Soviet is sometimes a device permitting the government to educate the members on objectives and policies, who in turn will represent these views to the masses. The Soviet legislature functions as a sounding board for party proposals and provides one method to reach the masses. More recently the Supreme Soviet, through its committee system, has provided some input in drafting laws.

LEGISLATIVE DYNAMICS

Legislative dynamics and policy making are important subjects, but space limitations prevent a detailed discussion here; therefore, only two aspects will be discussed, in order to provide the student with some appreciation of the influences that affect the workings and output of a legislature.

THE U. S. CONGRESS AND LEGISLATIVE COMMITTEES

The American system disperses power. Congress has been described as a conglomerate of little legislatures—the **congressional committees** (22 in the House,

[27]Charles O. Jones, *Introduction to the Study of Public Policy*, 2nd ed. (North Scituate, Mass.: Duxbury Press, 1977), p. 140.

Representatives of the opening meeting of the USSR Supreme Soviet.

The Soviet of the Union (lower house of the USSR Supreme Soviet) in session.

21 in the Senate). Once a bill is introduced into either the House of Representatives or the Senate, it is referred to a committee; to *which* committee it goes sometimes can be extremely important. Civil rights bills in the Senate have been sent to either the Judiciary Committee or the Commerce Committee. The membership of the latter is more liberal and more likely to result in a favorable vote for the bill. The most common way to kill a bill is to table it or simply not bring it up for consideration, the agenda being determined by the committee chair. If a bill is reported out (positive vote) in the House of Representatives, it must then go to the Rules Committee, which decides when or if it shall appear on the House agenda, the nature and extent of debate that will be allowed, and whether or not amendments can be offered.

We might note that proliferation of subcommittees designed to encourage Congressional specialization has also further decentralized power and opened up even more input opportunities for interest groups of all hues and persuasions. The flow of legislation, consequently, often is hindered. The House of Representatives has over 140 subcommittees. A recent news analysis reported that one reason Congress could not agree on an energy bill was that "too many cooks spoil the broth."[28] The House has 78 committees and subcommittees dealing with energy. This means that innumerable interest groups have a wide choice of access points at which to push their particular proposal. Consequently there is no comprehensive energy policy as a result of the legislative "disarray."

More than 4,000 bills are introduced in Congress annually. (See Figure 8–2) Without a division of labor, these bills would never be reviewed even superficially. The

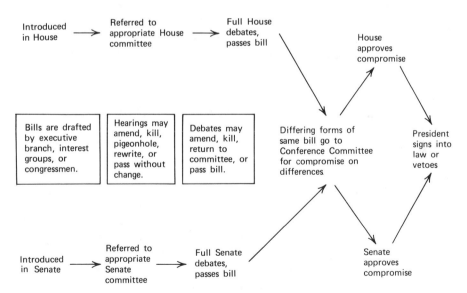

Figure 8–2. How a bill becomes law in the United States.

[29]Robert Bendiner, *Obstacle Course on Capitol Hill* (New York: McGraw-Hill, 1964), p. 15.

political system would be buried under a landslide of legislation if the reviewing, sifting, and culling process did not, as it does now, eliminate 80 percent of the bills introduced. After a bill has cleared subcommittees and each chamber, there usually are differences between the bills approved in the House and Senate. This requires a Conference Committee composed of members from both houses. The Conference Committee usually can work out a compromise bill, but in the event that the committee cannot or Congress adjourns, the bill is dead and must be reintroduced and go through the entire procedure again. Congress has been called an obstacle course: "For sheer difficulty the way of a serious legislative proposal through Congress is equalled only by that of a camel through the eye of a needle or a rich man into the Kingdom of God."[29]

Three facts stand out: First, the committee system is a key to the American congressional process. Legislative committees are the only way a large and great nation can handle the many issues and proposals that must be considered. The need for specialization is juxtaposed by the fact that pockets of power are controlled by a few persons—committee members and, notably, committee chairs—and the range of widespread representative input necessarily is reduced.

Second, guiding a bill to law requires procedural expertise. Wooing of majority support occurs at several points and involves different persons. Not one vote but many are involved. Actors and conditions change during the legislative gamut; negotiation and adjustment are a continual process for the bill's sponsors, up to the point the bill reaches the president's desk, to be signed or vetoed.

Third, the legislative road is complex, and there are many points where the bill can be amended or defeated. Supporters of the bill must win each vote; those who wish to amend or kill the legislation can focus on one or two votes. Few bills arrive on the president's desk in their original form or one nearly identical to it.

BRITISH PARLIAMENT

While a thousand bills may become law during a U.S. congressional session, the British Parliament enacts only about 200 (see Figure 8–3). Bills originate in the ministries in discussions involving ministers, the civil service, and, oftentimes, interest groups. The Future Legislation Committee of the cabinet reduces the proposals to a manageable number, and these become the basis for the government's program. Individual MPs cannot introduce bills involving taxation or expenditure. A "private" bill involves primarily minor subjects with a narrow focus, and if it is to be enacted the government must be sympathetic or at least neutral. (Private bills are included in the 200 figure.) Backbenchers have some influence, as do the arguments of the opposition, but a legislative proposal is highly developed before the government introduces it. Further, since a government regards each bill as a vote of confidence, a test-of-strength showdown will fall to the government.

[28]*Christian Science Monitor*, September 25, 1979.

"Next I want to sing a song about the House Rules Committee and how the legislative functions of Congress are tyrannized over by its procedural calendar, dominated in turn by an all-powerful chairman hamstringing the process of democracy."

(Drawing by Koren; © 1964 The New Yorker Magazine, Inc.)

Legislatures have their critics.

There are only 6 **standing committees** in the House of Commons. A, B, C, D, E, and the Scottish Committee. All except the last consider bills without regard to subject. Committees have from 20 to 50 members, they do not call in outside experts, and as soon as they have reported on one bill they receive another, in order of consideration, not according to subject matter. Following a Second Reading, one of the first 5 committees considers the bill. The bill cannot be tabled, because the cabinet ultimately determines the order of business before the House. The standing committee goes through the bill line by line, noting any discrepancies or ambiguities. The government usually accepts only technical amendments at this stage. It is at this point that MPs, speaking for various points of view or interests, can seek modifications, though the policy guidelines are definitely settled at the Second Reading.[30]

[30]The First Reading is a formality; only the title is read. The bill is printed subsequently and within three weeks, at the Second Reading, general policy is affirmed by a vote after the bill is debated by the government party and opposition.

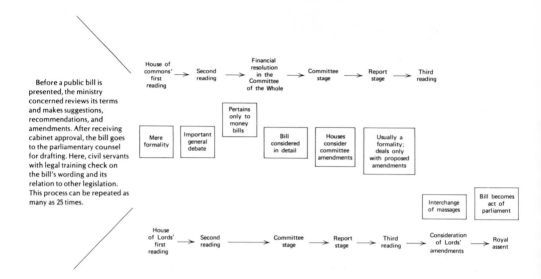

Before a public bill is presented, the ministry concerned reviews its terms and makes suggestions, recommendations, and amendments. After receiving cabinet approval, the bill goes to the parliamentary counsel for drafting. Here, civil servants with legal training check on the bill's wording and its relation to other legislation. This process can be repeated as many as 25 times.

British bills are categorized as either public or private. Public bills are almost always government-sponsored and affect the entire nation. Private members' bills are introduced by individual members and have a personal or local application only. A private bill, distinguished from a private member's bill, usually deals with minor questions, but on rare occasions involves controversial issues that a party does not wish to sponsor

Figure 8-3.   How a public government-sponsored bill becomes law in the British parliament.

Congressional committees in the United States and some legislative committees in continental Europe have much broader policy authority than do committees of the House of Commons, which do not have the power to table a proposal or substantially amend bills. Nevertheless, as we have seen, there can be some policy input at this stage, though under a disciplined parliamentary system the decision to accept amendments rests with the executive or cabinet. The principles of accommodation and negotiation that undergird British politics make the process more democratic than it might otherwise be. In authoritarian systems with a weak or nonexistent committee system, legislators find that they have negligible influence on policy formation.

INSTITUTIONAL BEHAVIOR AND RULES OF THE GAME

The formal structure of a legislature—the committee system—can be critical in the policy process. The rules of behavior discussed in this section are not written down formally, but they are understood generally within the institution itself and exemplify another key aspect of legislative policy making.

Legislative role requirements shape a legislator's actions by virtue of membership in a specific institutional context. Role is a concept that assumes regularized interaction patterns, guides the actor's behavior, and inclines the individual to be conscious of, and responsive to, the reactions of significant others—in this case, legislative colleagues.

Role defines what should be done and what cannot be tolerated. Depending on the length of time the role has existed, the specific behavior patterns that have evolved, and the flexibility and adaptability that have developed during the evolution, a role can be specific down to the most minute behavioral and ceremonial detail, or it can simply define behavior limits in broad and general terms. Role requirements in modern legislatures tend toward broad guidelines, rather than specific details. In a modernizing, democratic context roles adapt and change and allow more variation in behavior patterns as compared to a traditional, status quo, or authoritarian system, which stresses rigid, highly structured behavior patterns covering nearly all aspects of behavior.

Legislators must relate to their colleagues in an acceptable way or they will not achieve maximum influence. Unwritten rules, customs, rules of the game, or folkways may tolerate several behavior patterns, but the institutional setting determines the limits of appropriate behavior. What we have said thus far assumes, of course, that the institution (in this case, the legislature) is viable, performs relevant functions in the political system, and does not include a substantial number of persons determined to destroy or radically transform the institution.

A perceptive analysis of legislative role behavior was done by Donald R. Matthews in his study of U.S. Senators.[31] Senatorial folkways facilitate the operational efficiency and effectiveness of the U.S. Senate. These norms discourage verbosity in an institution that seldom formally limits debate. Specialization and expertise are encouraged and a senator is discouraged from publicly debating each issue of the moment. Toleration, mutual respect, and friendship guide personal relations. Senators are encouraged to be "compromisers and bargainers" and to use their powers in a restrained and careful manner.

The most generally accepted rule is apprenticeship. Freshmen senators receive the less attractive committee assignments. For two years, and even more, freshmen are discouraged from speaking frequently, if at all, on the Senate floor. Respect for senior members bordering on deference makes a senator acceptable to many of his or her colleagues. As one new senator explained; " 'Keep on asking for advice, boy,' the committee chairman told me. 'That's the way to get ahead around here.' "[32]

[31]Donald R. Matthews, *U.S. Senators and Their World* (Chapel Hill: The University of North Carolina Press, 1960), see especially Chapter 5. The information on senatorial rules of the game is drawn from this book.
[32]*Ibid.*, p. 93.

Senators must specialize if they want to influence their colleagues. If most senators spoke on each issue, Senate work would move considerably slower. Specialization provides a necessary division of labor, encourages more action and less talk, and builds senators' reputations and effectiveness among their colleagues. "The really effective senators are those who speak only on the subjects thay have been dealing with at close quarters, not those who are on their feet on almost every subject all the time."[33]

Courtesy fosters the civility that 100 important people must have if they are daily expected to function as a decision-making body on controversial issues—issues that often are the center of intense popular feelings. Conflicts inevitably exist, but debate usually is restrained by the underlying courtesy rule. A colleague's motives are never questioned, nor are other states criticized. Less personal address formalizes debate and reduces personal emphasis; for example, Senator X is not referred to by name on the Senate floor, but as the "Senator from State Y." Courtesy allows strong personalities and potential competitors to achieve a necessary degree of cooperation. Courtesy is absolutely necessary in order to muffle the rivalries and potential personal conflicts in a problem-solving institution like the Senate.

Institutions cannot expect 100 percent commitment to the unwritten rules of conduct by members, and the U. S. Congress is no exception. The political novice may not understand immediately that there is time to accept a deferential apprenticeship of several years. The Appropriations Committee is a highly valued assignment in the House of Representatives. Members of the committee consider themselves among the hardest working group in the House. There is also consensus in this large committee (40 to 50 members) that it is the guardian of the federal budget and there is an obligation to hold spending down to the minimum. New committee members go through an acute socialization experience in which they learn the norms and learn to compromise. Speaking too often, or even speaking much at all during the first couple of years on the committee, or being abrasive and contentious can lead to punishments—"raised eyebrows, not being sent on a trip to Europe, a change in subcommittee assignment, or not being given anything to do."[34] Most members who wish to continue on the Appropriations Committee and be effective absorb the committee's folkways. One example of the reverse side of the coin is the case of the senator who has loftier political ambitions, especially the presidency. This individual speaks on many issues, appeals to many national groups and potential constituencies, and of necessity disregards the axiom of specialization and limiting public exposure to specific issues. Presidential ambitions are nurtured by groups outside the Senate, and Senate norms become secondary. One example was the late Senator Kefauver from Tennessee. Once a vice-presidential nominee of the Democratic Party, and nearly a presidential nominee, he had, however, limited influence in the Senate, partly the result of his disregard for some Senate norms.

[33]Edward G. Milne, "Mr. Pastore in Washington," *Providence Evening Bulletin*, February 8, 1956.
[34]Donald R. Matthews, *op. cit.*

Unwritten rules, by their very nature, do not specify penalties; but diminished status in the institution is the obvious result, and penalties are tangible. Rules of the game socialize newmembers into the institution, influence the decision-making process within the institution, and affect the legislative output. These rules are an integral component of the legislative process of most legislatures.

SUMMARY

The diminished role or status of legislatures remains a debated question. Clearly, during the last few decades in even pluralist systems, the executive and the courts have initiated policy and engaged in rule making to the point that they frequently overshadow legislatures.

Complex crises also seem to work against the importance of the legislative process. Extended consideration, negotiation, and compromise, which characterize democratic legislatures, sometimes appear to neglect public opinion and encourage a sluggish response to issues that require quick decisions. Those who stress the necessity of clear-cut and speedy decisions because they honor rationality, efficiency, and an immediate response as supreme virtues, or who identify themselves as strict majoritarians, find the legislative process cumbersome and in violation of the public will.

Nevertheless, legislatures are the single institution that can give public voice to the widest range of claims and groups in the rule-making process. Democratic legislatures provide the continuous maximum breadth of representation in society and are also regularly accountable through elections. No other institution has this type of representativeness or accountability. In authoritarian systems that are becoming more pluralistic, it is often in the legislature that the pluralism is manifested and nurtured mostly effectively. Participation in the rule-making process is only one of several valuable functions performed by legislatures.

As we have seen, legislatures perform many other functions. A principal function of viable legislatures is rule making. Rule executing, discussed in the next chapter, is an executive administrative function, but the executive branch also performs more than the single function of rule executing.

SELECTED READINGS

A classic and not difficult introduction to the role and importance of democratic legislatures is K.C. Wheare, *Legislatures*,* 2nd ed. (New York: Oxford University Press, 1967). An equally readable and helpful overview but one focusing on rule making as a function rather than legislatures as institutions, is Gabriel A. Almond and G. Bingham Powell, Jr., *Comparative Politics: System, Process, and Policy*,* 2nd ed. (Boston: Little, Brown, 1978), pp. 128–142.

*Available in paperback.

One of the first efforts to collect similar data systematically on the 108 existing legislatures throughout the world today is J. Blondel, *Comparative Legislatures** (Englewood Cliffs, N.J.: Prentice-Hall, 1973). For an early effort that has continuing theoretical implications and that studied characteristics and behavior of legislators mostly at the state level, see John C. Wahlke et al., *The Legislative System* (New York: John Wiley, 1962). Still valuable today because of the theoretical and method-ological issues raised is John C. Wahlke and Heinze Eulau, eds., *Legislative Behavior: A Reader in Theory and Research* (Glencoe, Ill.; Free Press, 1959).

The idea of rule making by legislatures is more than 2500 years old. The some-times successful efforts to establish representative institutions in the classical world are described by J. A. O. Larsen, *Representative Government in Greek and Roman History* (Berkeley: University of California Press, 1966). A good overview of what representation and assemblies meant in the Middle Ages is found in the symposium sponsored by the International Commission for the History of Representative and Parliamentary Institutions, "Medieval Representation in Theory and Practice," *Speculum*, 29:2, 1954, pp. 347–476 Covering some of the same period is a histori-cal description of representation until the seventeenth century by A. R. Myers, "Par-liaments in Europe: The Representative Tradition, I and II," *History Today*, 5:6&7, 1955, pp. 383–390 and 446–454.

The functions of legislatures and individual members are widely discussed. Two collections that provide various viewpoints on the importance or decline of legisla-tive functions are Elke Frank, ed., *Lawmakers in a Changing World** (Englewood Cliffs, N.J.: Prentice-Hall, 1966); and Gerhard Loewenberg, ed., *Modern Parlia-ments: Change or Decline?** (Chicago: Aldine-Atherton, 1971).

There are a number of good case studies or collections of case studies of specif-ic legislatures or legislative systems. The most extensive writing has been done on American legislatures. Malcom E. Jewell and Samuel C. Patterson, *The Legislative Process in the United States*, 2nd ed. (New York: Random House, 1977) is a basic introduction to American legislative systems. Robert Bendiner, a journalist, de-scribes the difficulties, equal to passing "a camel through the eye of a needle," of getting a proposal through the congressional committee system in *Obstacle Course on Capital Hill* (New York: McGraw-Hill Book Company, 1964). Randall B. Ripley, *Congress: Process and Policy* 2nd ed. (New York: W. W. Norton, 1978) presents a wide-ranging analysis of Congress in the belief that Congress plays an important policy-making role. The book includes an extensive and helpful bibliography on the American Congress. Following a similar though briefer format and also including a good bibliography is Lawrence C. Dodd, *Congress and Public Policy* (Morristown, N.J.: General Learning Press, 1972), showing through a series of case examples that, despite arguments to the contrary, Congress retains considerable policy initia-

*Available in paperback.

tive. A critical study of Congress written for the popular market emerged from the Ralph Nader Congress Project: Mark J. Green, James M. Fallows, and David R. Zwick, *Who Runs Congress?* rev. ed. (New York: Bantam Books, Grossman Publishers, 1975).

Roger H. Davidson and Walter J. Oleszek, *Congress Against Itself* (Bloomington, Ind.: Indiana University Press, 1977) is an excellent study of how Congress works, the role of committees, and the importance of compromise in the legislative process.

Much also has been written on the British legislative process. The history of parliamentary reform in Great Britain is traced by Bernard Crick, *Reform of Parliament** (Garden City, N.Y.: Anchor Books, 1965). Ronald Butt argues that critics have overestimated the extent to which the role of Parliament is being undermined in his *Power of Parliament: An Evolutionary Study of the Functions of the House of Commons in British Politics* (New York: Walker, 1968). As the qualifications of members of Parliament appear to have increased, it is paradoxical that the status of the average MP seems to have decreased. A volume of readings, almost half of which were contributed by MPs, indicates that the backbencher has more influence than commonly assumed: Dick Leonard and Herman Valentine, eds., *The Backbencher and Parliament* (London: Macmillan Press, 1972).

Two highly regarded studies of European parliaments are Gerhard Loewenberg, *Parliament in the German Political System* (Ithaca, N.Y.: Cornell University Press, 1967); and Philip M. Williams, *The French Parliament: Politics in the Fifth Republic* (New York: Praeger, 1968). One early contribution of elected legislators in a developing country is that they can help to link the government with the people. David Morrell analyzes such a situation in "Legislative Intervention in Thailand's Development Process: A Case Study," *Asian Survey*, 12:8, 1972, pp. 627–646.

A symposium of case studies that focuses on the problem of political integration is Albert F. Eldridge, ed., *Legislatures in Plural Societies: The Search for Cohesion* (Durham, N.C.: Duke University Press, 1979). Lloyd D. Musolf and J. Frederick Springer, *Malaysia's Parliamentary System* (Boulder, Colo.: Westview Press, 1979) discusses how an ethnically diverse developing country has evolved a functioning legislative system. Focusing on how a legislative system operates and why certain individuals are influential are Allan Kornberg and William Meshler, *Influence in Parliament: Canada* (Durham, N.C.: Duke University Press, 1976). Peter Vanneman, *The Supreme Soviet: Politics and the Legislative Process in the Soviet Political System* (Durham, N.C.: Duke University Press, 1977) is a careful discussion of the expanding though still limited functions of the Soviet legislature. A useful review of six books on various legislative systems is Samuel C. Patterson, "The Emerging Morphology of the World's Legislatures," *World Politics*, 30:3, 1978, pp. 469–481.

*Available in paperback.

Three major efforts to carry forward legislative research on a comparative basis are Herbert Hirsch and M. Donald Hancock, eds., *Comparative Legislative System* (New York: The Free Press, 1971); Allan Kornberg and Lloyd Musolf, eds., *Legislatures in Developmental Perspective* (Durham, N.C.: Duke University Press, 1970); and Samuel C. Patterson and John C. Wahlke, eds., *Comparative Legislative Behavior: Frontiers of Research* (New York: John Wiley, 1972). A new journal, *Legislative Studies Quarterly*, published by the University of Iowa's Comparative Legislative Research Center, intends to include theoretical and conceptual articles as well as studies of specific representative assemblies.

*Available in paperback.

Chapter Nine

Executive Leadership and Administrative Organization

The **executive branch** is the second of the "output" agencies. It includes the executive government and the **bureaucracy**. Both agencies are charged with implementing policies made by the legislative branch but partake, as we shall see, in the policy-making process too. We would like to begin our discussion of the executive branch by recalling a major event that occurred a few years ago.

On August 9, 1974, newspapers in many countries of the world featured on their front pages an unprecedented happening—the resignation of Richard M. Nixon from the presidency of the United States. For two years Mr. Nixon had tried to stymie an increasing number of charges made against him, such as his alleged knowledge and coverup of the Watergate burglary, his alleged misuse of governmental agencies, his alleged acceptance of illegal campaign contributions, and his allegedly illegal income-tax deduction. Faced with the certainty of impeachment, Mr. Nixon resigned the evening of August 8. Because part of this chapter will deal with the presidential and the parliamentary executive, the following statement by Louis W. Koenig is of some relevance:

> *In a parliamentary system, Nixon, after only a few of his infractions, would have been swiftly ousted from office. But the cumbersome impeachment machinery and a fixed term of office enabled Nixon to dodge and parry for more than two years while the nation suffered and drifted.*[1]

Though the orderly succession of Mr. Ford gave proof "that the American system works," the Watergate crisis left a deep scar in American society.

Was Watergate just a historical accident or does it reflect other trends, such as a decline of executive **leadership**? Some analysts point out that the contemporary

[1]Louis W. Koenig, *The Chief Executive*, 3rd ed. (New York: Harcourt Brace Jovanovich, 1975), p. 73.

world does not have any of the "great leaders" of the caliber of a Churchill, Roosevelt, or de Gaulle. While this may be true, one needs to add that there has been a steady growth in the complexities of government and the issues that leaders need to deal with. At no time have the strains and stresses on executive leadership been greater than they are now. With the preceding in mind, let us examine the evolution of the executive and its role in various contemporary political systems. Our emphasis will be primarily on the national executive.

THE EVOLUTION OF THE MODERN EXECUTIVE

All political units (villages, towns, cities, states, and countries) have had and now have some form of central leadership in the form of one person or a small group of people. This central leadership has become known as the executive. Prior to the establishment of viable legislative and judicial institutions, the executive virtually constituted the government, and even in recent decades its role often has gone substantially beyond that of simply executing policy. Throughout most of history executive leadership has been in the form of hereditary kingship, with such brief exceptions as Athenian democracy in ancient Greece and the republican governments of the Roman Republic. Feudal kings ruled in Europe from the Dark Ages until the Reformation. Modern nation-states developed in Western Europe during the sixteenth and seventeenth centuries, and these were ruled by absolute monarchs. One of the last rulers of this type was perhaps Haile Selassie of Ethiopia, who was overthrown only a few years ago.

England was the first country to move toward a constitutional monarchy when Parliament in 1689 placed specific constitutional limitations on the crown, a step that became known as the "Glorious Revolution." The next important development occurred again in England when in the early eighteenth century Sir Robert Walpole established himself as the first prime minister, thereby giving rise to the dual executive consisting of a **chief of state** and a **chief executive**. Finally, the founders of the United States provided for a president, that is, a nonhereditary "king," as chief executive, thus establishing the system of a single nonhereditary executive.

In the nineteenth century in some countries the role of the strong king was taken over by strong prime ministers, such as Metternich in Austria, Bismarck in Prussia, and, after 1871, those of the German Empire.

During the first few decades of the twentieth century, some Western legislatures gained enough power to challenge effectively their executive counterparts. In the United States, for example, in early 1920, Congress defeated President Wilson's quest for American membership in the League of Nations. In 1937 Congress defeated President Roosevelt's "Court-packing" proposal, a plan designed to shift the Supreme Court's viewpoint. More specifically, President Roosevelt had introduced legislation that would permit him to appoint additional Supreme Court justices equal in number to those incumbents who had reached the age of seventy. The President hoped that this new Court would rule more favorably on the items of his New Deal legislation. A short-lived ascendancy of parliamentary power can be noticed in continental Western Europe during the 1920s, too.

A number of strong leaders came to office during World War II and during the subsequent decade to cope with the complex issues at hand. Is it a historical accident that Churchill became British Prime Minister after Dunkirk, or that de Gaulle took over the leadership of the Free French forces after Petain's surrender in 1940? Tito emerged as the leader of the Yugoslav partisans during his country's occupation. After World War II, De Gasperi became Prime Minister of Italy and Adenauer became Chancellor of the new West Germany. Were these historical accidents? Did Ghandi and Mao Zedong rise to leadership by sheer chance? According to Max Lerner:

> Often the great leaders have arisen after great catastrophes, to meet the crisis of spirit that follows. . . . The qualities of greatness must be there in the man before he can rise to his stature. But the demands of the occasion and the need and receptiveness of the people are what bring the qualities out.[2]

In the meantime, all the great and strong leaders of the post-World War II era have died.

The steady growth in the real role and power of the chief executive, however, has continued worldwide. Reasons for this development can be found in the growing

[2]Max Lerner, "Where Is Strong Leadership in the World Now That We Need It Most?" *The Providence Journal,* January 1, 1975.

Four eminent West European statesmen who were most influential in shaping the post-World War II setting of their countries. Winston Churchill (United Kingdom), Alcide DeGasperi (Italy), Konrad Adenauer (West Germany), and Charles deGaulle (France).

complexity of economic issues and the many political and military crises throughout the world. The tremendous technological advances of recent decades, especially in the areas of armaments, communications, and transportation have produced a setting that often requires quick and knowledgeable governmental decisions. Much of this needs to come from the executive because it is the central collection and evaluation source of important information and it can act much more speedily than legislative bodies, which are by nature deliberative.

The Watergate incident, however, clearly illustrates the growth of distrust of executive leaders. While this noticeable lack of trust may have arisen first in the United States in conjunction with our military involvement in Southeast Asia and with Watergate, it has spread to other Western countries, too. It seems that the people of these countries are rather ambivalent toward their executive leadership. On the one hand, they distrust strong leadership. On the other hand, however, they do look to the president (or prime minister, premier, or chancellor) to come forth with speedy answers to the monumental economic and other problems that confront Western societies. This ambivalence is found in its strongest form in the United States because of the Watergate trauma.

Looking at the Communist countries, we see a growing desire among the intelligentsia for their leaders to rule in a more restrained, humane fashion and desire for a greater degree of civil liberties. The writings of such eminent Russian spokesmen as Andrei Sakharov and Alexander Solzhenitsyn give ample proof of the presence of this quest.

Frequent coups d'etat provide short executive tenure in many of the developing countries. One aspect of interest in regard to executive leadership in developing countries is that, during the initial years following independence, some indigenous people rose meteorlike to power. A good illustration is Joseph Mobutu. He had been a sergeant in the Belgian forces in the Congo, the highest rank a Congolese could obtain. Following the Belgian withdrawal in 1960, Mobutu advanced within a few months to the rank of general and commander-in-chief of the Congolese forces. He became President of the Congo (now Zaire) in 1965. The point is that, as more young people from developing countries are being trained for professional positions, their rise to power will be substantially slower and more tedious than that of present incumbents.

The political executives of today have many different titles, and their range of duties differs from country to country. A number of countries, such as the United States, have a presidential type of executive, with the president serving as chief of state and chief executive. Others, such as Britain, have a parliamentary system of government, which provides for a dual executive. Here the chief of state may be a hereditary ruler (the British Queen) or an elected president (as in France or West Germany). In most parliamentary systems the chief of state serves as a symbolic ruler, having very little political power. Exceptions to this are the presidents of France and Zaire, and a few other chiefs of state who wield considerable power. But in many societies the actual decision-making process is directed by the chief executive, who may carry the title of prime minister (in English-speaking countries), premier (in French-speaking countries), or chancellor (in German-speaking countries).

An important point to note is that the degree of industrialization and the political culture of a given society have considerable bearing on the scope of power a chief executive may wield in his society. For example, presidents and prime ministers in the countries of the postindustrialized Atlantic community are subject to substantially more restrictions than many of the leaders in developing countries and the Communist nation-states.

A PROFILE OF EXECUTIVE LEADERS

James MacGregor Burns, in his seminal work, *Leadership*, defines the concept as follows:

> *Leadership is the reciprocal process of mobilizing, by persons with certain motives and values, various economic, political, and other resources, in a context of competition and conflict, in order to realize goals independently or mutually held by both leaders and followers.*[3]

Similarly, William A. Walsh speaks of leadership as "the ability to mobilize human resources in pursuit of specific goals."[4]

Who are the people who, as chief executives of their countries, provide this leadership? They belong to the group of the "powerful," which can be found on top of any political society. They are people who possess, as Robert A. Dahl points out, considerable resources in the form of charisma, desire for power, influence, motivation, skill, and wealth.[5]

In terms of their socioeconomic background, most of the leaders of Western countries, including Latin America, have come from middle- or upper-class families. The "log cabin" heritage has been the exception to the rule. British prime ministers usually have been graduates of Cambridge or Oxford University. This thesis also holds true for most leaders in the continental European democracies and for Japan. The case of Willy Brandt, who came from a rather poor background, is one of the few exceptions. We do find a difference, however, when we look at the Communist countries. Lenin came from an upper-class family and graduated from law school before becoming a professional revolutionary. Stalin, the son of a cobbler, attended a theological seminary. Khrushchev, in contrast, was an illiterate coal miner during his late teens. He received all his formal education under party auspices. Several other Communist leaders have made their way from blue-collar ranks to the top ex-

[3]James MacGregor Burns, *Leadership* (New York: Harper & Row, 1978), p. 425.
[4]William A. Walsh, *Leaders and Elites* (New York: Holt, Rinehart and Winston, 1979), p. 18.
[5]See Robert A. Dahl, *Modern Political Analysis*, 3rd ed. (Englewood Cliffs, N.J.: Prentice-Hall, 1976), p. 101.

ecutive office in their respective countries. The large majority of the leaders in the developing countries of Africa and Asia, too, come from fairly well-to-do family backgrounds. This obviously holds true for the kings of Saudi Arabia, Jordan, and Morocco, but it applies also to many of the nonhereditary rulers in Africa and Asia.

Looking at the leaders' professional training, we find that a considerable number of them, especially in the developing countries, have come from the military. This group includes President Mobutu of Zaire, Colonel Qaddafi of Libya, and a number of others. In the United States, we may recall, some military officers ascended to the presidency—Washington, Grant, and Eisenhower, for example. Many of the top leaders in the advanced countries are professional politicians. British prime ministers, for example, usually have spent between 15 and 25 years in the House of Commons before gaining the office of chief executive. All chancellors of the Federal Republic of Germany (Adenauer, Erhard, Kiesinger, Brandt, and Schmidt) have been full-time politicians before becoming chief executives. All the top political leaders in the Communist countries were full-time party officials and/or administrators in their earlier career years. A number of presidents in the United States have served in Congress or as governors prior to being elected to the highest office. A few top political leaders in the advanced countries have had extensive training in business before moving into politics and ultimately gaining the top office. One example in this category would be Georges Pompidou, second President of the Fifth French Republic.

Additional common features, but also differences between generations of executive leaders, can be found within political regions. Victor T. Le Vine, in his discussion of political leadership in Africa in the late 1960s, stated that

> Political leadership in most independent African states is still in the hands of a generation of "elder statesmen"—men who carried the fight against colonialism, who founded the principal political parties, and who developed nationalist ideologies and doctrines. These are men whose backgrounds, political styles, and ideological commitments often seem more appropriate to the winning of independence than to its consolidation or to the establishment of a legitimized political order.[6]

Turning to the second generation of African leaders, Le Vine remarked:

> At the same time a new generation of leaders—usually a group of men who have become politically important since independence—is concerned with the attainment of political goals much different from those that constituted the horizons of the older generation: instead of independence, the elimination of the foreign presence, and greater measures of political freedom and participation, the newer goals are more directly relevant to the post-independence situation—various kinds of economic development, the establishment of effective central government, and the satisfaction of specific political, economic, and social demands.[7]

[6]Victor T. Le Vine, *Political Leadership in Africa* (Stanford, Cal.: Stanford University Press, 1967), p. 1.
[7]*Ibid.*

Le Vine's observations regarding first- and second-generation leaders in Africa could be applied, at least in part, to first- and second-generation leaders in Communist regimes. For example, Stalin was much more set on building "communism in one country" than Lenin, and there were also considerable differences in leadership between Khrushchev and Stalin. Other similarities are found as we look at other Communist countries, such as Hungary, Poland, and Romania.

In terms of their effectiveness, rulers have differed widely. Some political historians in this country have ranked American presidents, according to their performance, as "great presidents" (George Washington, Thomas Jefferson, Andrew Jackson, Abraham Lincoln, Theodore Roosevelt, Woodrow Wilson, and Franklin D. Roosevelt); near-great presidents (Harry Truman); average presidents (Dwight D. Eisenhower); and weak presidents (as typified by James Polk and Warren G. Harding). A good comparison of leadership stature among British prime ministers would be the contrast between the soft-spoken Neville Chamberlain, who let himself be "hoodwinked" by Hitler at the Munich Conference (1938), and his successor, Winston Churchill, who led Britain successfully through World War II. Churchill undoubtedly would be ranked as one of Britain's great prime ministers. In recent French political history, the charismatic and strong performance of President Charles de Gaulle differs starkly from the weak leadership rendered by his predecessors of the Fourth Republic.

In a broader sense, history depicts many different kinds of rulers. Some have exercised strong leadership, others have been weak, and many others have been moderate in their role as leaders. The reigns of some rulers have been more beneficial to the masses than the reigns of others. Some rulers have been outright cruel to their subjects, indicating clear mental deficiencies. Among twentieth-century rulers, Hitler and Stalin would fall into the category of "sick personalities." Certainly the world would have been better off without them. Fortunately, the cases of Caesar and Ghengis Khan, as well as Hitler and Stalin, constitute the exception to the rule. In most instances rulers have been and still are substantially more sane and responsible than these four men. In addition, modern rulers have advisers who can exercise a moderating influence if needed. Nevertheless, it is imperative in our times that "sick personalities" be kept from obtaining high political and military office. In the age of nuclear weaponry there exists the danger that a number of countries will obtain atomic warheads. Accordingly, the number of political leaders who potentially could cause substantial harm will increase correspondingly.

In summary, we find that the top political executives throughout the world have certain attributes and traits in common, and it is on the basis of these attributes and traits that these leaders have arrived at the top positions. The large number of people who do not become chiefs of state or chief executives also may have some of these attributes and traits, but they will have them to a lesser extent and/or will maximize them less than those who become chief executives.

The study of leadership phenomena is one of the more recent areas of academic inquiry. Much still needs to be learned about the factors and variables that are responsible for elevating a person to a leadership position.

MAJOR VARIETIES OF EXECUTIVE GOVERNMENT

The two major kinds of the executive are the presidential and the parliamentary forms. The only exception to these two major forms are the transitional military regimes, presently found in Chile and Ethiopia, for example. As we shall see in the following, the parliamentary and presidential executives exist in many different varieties, leading some writers to use other classification schemes, such as democratic executives, restrictive executives, and totalitarian executives.[8] We believe, however, this approach involves a fallacy, since the categories are variations or perversions of either the genuine presidential or parliamentary executive. Any executive branch, as well as the other parts of the government, will reflect the political culture and heritage of a society, including its democratic, authoritarian, or totalitarian tradition. Let us examine the presidential and parliamentary types of the executive and the functions each performs.

THE PRESIDENTIAL EXECUTIVE

Some 50 countries have presidential executives. Among them are the United States, most Latin American countries, and some in Africa and Asia. A basic characteristic of the presidential type of executive is that the offices of chief of state and chief executive are held by the same person. A president serves as the ceremonial and symbolic leader of a nation-state, but also has to attend to the day-by-day issues of governmental business. Thus, he or she often will become involved in party politics, unlike the chief of state in a parliamentary system.

In some ways the president is the modern counterpart to the king of ancient days: the central point of power in a society. How does a president arrive at this highest political position a country has to offer? Some are popularly elected for a specific term of office, such as the president of the United States. Let us examine the process by which U.S. presidents are chosen.

Since the time of Andrew Jackson, candidates for president and vice-president are selected by political conventions called by the respective political parties every four years. The number of delegates from each state are roughly in proportion to the size of their electorates. Delegates are chosen by state party conventions or committees and state presidential primaries or a combination of the two methods. In some primaries delegates may be pledged to specific candidates. The national party

---

[8]See D. George Kousoulas, *On Government and Politics*, 2nd ed. (Belmont, Cal.: Duxbury Press, 1971), pp. 228–233.

convention meets in the summer preceding the election. Sometimes no candidate has a majority of delegates, in which case a number of ballots may be necessary and party leaders may intervene to break a deadlock. The presidential nomination is followed by the selection of a vice-presidential candidate, which is usually accomplished quickly. The interim between the conventions and the election is devoted to campaigning.

When the voters go to the polls on the first Tuesday after the first Monday in November, they are technically voting for a slate of presidential electors chosen by the respective party organizations. The electoral role of each state is equal to the number of representatives in the House of Representatives plus the two senators. A party may require electors so chosen to cast the state's electoral vote for the presidential and vice-presidential candidate selected by the party's national convention. Only on rare occasions in the absence of a pledge have one or more electors cast a vote for any but the authorized candidates. The electors assemble at their respective state capitals to formally cast the state's electoral vote on the first Monday after the second Wednesday in December.

Thus, the voters do not actually vote for the presidential candidates of their choice, but for presidential electors selected by a political party. To be elected, the candidate must receive a majority of the electoral vote. Almost always the candidate with a majority of the popular vote has a majority of the electoral vote. But this is not so every time, as the popular vote is distorted in the electoral college. The winning candidate receives the entire bloc of the state's vote even if his winning plurality is very small. Thus in 1888, Benjamin Harrison defeated Grover Cleveland, even though Cleveland had a popular plurality in the country as a whole. But Harrison received a majority of the electoral vote since he carried New York with its big electoral vote by a small plurality.

The intention of the framers of the Constitution was that electors would exercise independent judgment in performing their task. With the rise of political parties and the selection of electors by popular vote, rather than state legislatures, the original plan broke down. Thus, the form rather than the substance of the electoral procedure is observed.

The greatest weakness of the present system is that if no candidate wins the necessary majority of electoral votes, the president will be picked by the House of Representatives from among the three candidates with the highest number of electoral votes. Each state has one vote and the members vote by states. The vice-president is to be selected by the Senate from between the two highest candidates. These procedures open the door to the selection of a president by a process of crude political bargaining.

Only once, in 1824, was a president—John Quincy Adams—chosen by Congress. In two elections in the present century the shift of a comparatively small number of votes would have thrown the election into the lap of Congress. In 1948, due to the Dixiecrat party of dissident Southern states, the loss of a few close states by President Truman to his Republican opponent would have meant the absence of an electoral college majority for any candidate. A similar situation almost occurred in 1968 due to the sizable electoral vote in the South amassed by Governor Wallace of Alabama running as a third-party candidate against Republican Richard Nixon and Democrat Hubert Humphrey. As this manuscript is being prepared for publication, questions are being raised whether any of the three present presidential candidates (Anderson, Carter, Reagan) will receive a majority of electoral votes in 1980. If not, whom would the House of Representatives pick?

In countries where democratic elections are less established or less meaningful, presidential hopefuls often obtain the presidency through a coup d'etat and stay in the office until they are overthrown. The latter practice is still widespread in Latin America and the developing countries of Africa and Asia.

Presidents in democratic societies are subject to greater limitations and restraints than their counterparts in more authoritarian countries in Latin America, Africa, and Asia. The president of the United States, for example, may make treaties only with the advice and consent of the U.S. Senate, and while the president may nominate candidates for high federal positions in the executive and judiciary, the final appointment of these persons, again, requires Senate approval. Moreover, the Vietnam and Watergate affairs have shown that public opinion and the mass media have become important watchdogs on the actions of U.S. executives. The strong presidents of authoritarian Latin American or African societies, as typified by General Stroessner of Paraguay or Mobutu of Zaire, face substantially less internal restraint.

Presidential Functions

The functions and powers of a president perhaps can be explained best by examining the responsibilities of the president in the United States. The presidential system in this country has served as a model for many other nation-states.

1. The president serves as **chief of state**, a symbolic and ceremonial function. In this capacity he is expected to exhibit and symbolize the glory, greatness, and values of the United States. He will receive and entertain leading officials from other countries and award medals and other tokens of recognition. The citizenry expects him to be above reproach in his manners and personal life. It is this expectation that, among other things, Mr. Nixon grossly violated during the episode that became known as the "Watergate crisis."

2. The president is the **chief executive** of the country. He carries final decision-making power and ultimate responsibility. President Truman had the famous "THE BUCK STOPS HERE" sign on his desk. President Kennedy went on nationwide television to take full responsibility for the abortive Bay of Pigs invasion in 1961. The president provides leadership for his cabinet and attempts to direct the bureaucracy. Finally, he needs to maintain open channels of communication with the people and inform them of major steps taken by the government. Franklin D.

Roosevelt used his radio-broadcast "fireside chats" for this purpose; more recent presidents have addressed the people via television during prime-time hours.

   3.   The president serves as the **chief legislator** of the country. He will keep pressure on Congress to have it perform according to the charge contained in his State of the Union address. He must cajole and persuade congressional leaders and other influentials to do the things he believes need to be done in the interest of the country. As President Truman put it at one time:

> I sit here all day trying to persuade people to do the things they ought to have sense enough to do without my persuading them. . . . That's all the powers of the President amount to.[9]

The point is that the assertion of presidential leadership in legislative matters is very important; however, the president must lead in a positive and constructive fashion so as not to annoy those whose action and support he seeks. Since legislative assemblies are still in a formative stage in many of the developing countries, their presidents have considerably more leeway in dictating terms than does a president of the United States.

   4.   The president is the **commander-in-chief** of the armed forces in his country. The philosophy underlying this role is that of civilian control of the military. Presidential command of the armed forces, coupled with congressional fiscal control of military expenses, was intended by the founders of the United States to forestall military coups d'etat. However, not all countries that have a presidential executive also provide for civilian control of the military. In Africa, Asia, and Latin America, presidents often have been brought to power by the military and they may wish or are forced to retain the military as their main arm of support, thereby creating "a state within the state."

   5.   The president serves as the **chief diplomat** of the country. The U.S. Constitution stipulates presidential leadership in foreign relations by stating that the President "shall have the power, by and with the Advice and Consent of the Senate, to make Treaties, provided two-thirds of the Senators present concur," and "he shall nominate, and by and with the Advice and Consent of the Senate, shall appoint Am-

HOO-BOY! THE PRESIDENT PROMISED TO DELIVER... BUT HE DIDN'T GIVE A DELIVERY DATE —

Washington Star Syndicate, Inc.   BRICKMAN

The Small Society by Brickman © Washington Star Syndicate, permission granted by King Features Syndicate.

[9]Quoted in Richard E. Neustadt, *Presidential Power: The Politics of Leadership From FDR to Carter* (New York: John Wiley, 1980), p. 9.

bassadors.'' The president can bypass the consent of the Senate provision by concluding an **executive agreement**, instead of a treaty, with the leader of another country. A famous example of this is the agreement concluded between President Roosevelt and Prime Minister Churchill in 1940, whereby the British received 50 outmoded American destroyers in return for leases on British territories along the east coast of the American continent, for the purpose of constructing air bases on some of these islands. An increasing number of executive agreements have been concluded since World War II. Some U.S. presidents have been more active in the making and execution of foreign policy than others. Some have delegated most of the duties in this area to the Secretary of State, as, for example, President Eisenhower did with John Foster Dulles. The increasing use of summit meetings since World War II, generally speaking, has enhanced further the role of the U.S. President and other chief executives in foreign relations.

These five are the major constitutional duties a president of the United States performs. Since 1789, his roles have expanded to include three others, as follows.

6. With the rise of political parties in this country, the President has become the leader of his party. In this capacity he is expected to play an active role in directing the overall affairs of the party and to speak at party gatherings. The president's role

President Carter campaigning in Nashville, Tennessee in support of Jake Butcher, Democratic nominee for Governor and Jane Eskind, Democratic nominee for U.S. Senator.

as party leader is a difficult one. As President of the United States he is the spokesman of all people in this country, but on partisan issues his role as leader of his party may limit his capacity to perform his spokesman role in full. According to Louis W. Koenig:

> The President's uneasy party role is aggravated by the continual tension between his responsibilities to his office and the claims of his party. His office, and therefore its duties and problems, presumably exceed any obligation the party can impose upon him. He is a politician who must also be a statesman. Yet the party often insistently violates this assumption.[10]

7. Starting with the Great Depression of the late 1920s and early 1930s, the president of this country has played an increasing role in economic affairs as "manager of prosperity." Examples of this function are found in the New Deal programs of President Roosevelt, in President Truman's efforts to convert the country's economy from a war-time setting to a peace-time economy in the late 1940s, and in President Carter's attempts to deal with the energy problem and with inflation. The importance that people assign today to presidential leadership in the economic area can be seen readily in opinion polls judging presidential performance. Shortages in gasoline, domestic increases of oil prices, a rise in the rate of inflation—all these automatically trigger a decline in presidential popularity as shown by the polls.

8. A final role performed by the president of the United States, one that is mentioned rarely and perhaps conceived of less by the people of this country than by people abroad, is that he serves informally as the leader of the Western democracies. This role was placed on the shoulders of the president of the United States in 1945, when this country emerged from World War II as the most powerful nation-state. Surely there have been changes in the power relationships of countries since 1945, but even today the president of the United States is looked upon by people and governments of many countries to provide the foremost leadership in dealing with the crucial issues of our time. This expectation has been made known to this author at many occasions during his travels abroad. This is not an easy leadership function, but it is one that neither our president nor the people of this country can abrogate.[11]

The roles performed by chief executives in other countries with presidential systems are more limited. There exist, of course, a number of variations. In some of the developing countries, for example, the single dominant political party has been

---

[10]Louis W. Koenig, *op. cit.,* p. 116.

[11]For a detailed discussion of the functions of the U.S. president see Koenig, *op. cit.;* Neustadt, *op. cit.;* and Richard M. Pious, *The American Presidency* (New York: Basic Books, 1979). Shorter treatments of the subject are found in Fred R. Mabbutt and Gerald I. Ghelfi, *The Troubled Republic: American Government, Its Principles and Problems* (New York: John Wiley, 1974); Peter Woll and Robert H. Binstock, *America's Political System,* 3rd ed. (New York: Random House, 1979); and James T. Myers, *The American Way: An Introduction to U.S. Government and Politics* (Lexington, Mass.: D. C. Heath, 1977).

Prime Minister Begin, President Carter and President Sadat at the press conference following the signing of the Peace Treaty between Egypt and Israel in March, 1979 on the White House lawn in Washington.

created by the incumbent president, and his role as party leader still is integrated more closely with his larger role as chief executive than would be the case in the United States. An example of this is the relationship between President Nyerere, the TANU movement, and Tanzanian socialism in Tanzania.[12] The more autocratic a society, the more all-embracing the real powers of a president will be. Recent examples of extreme dictatorial presidential rule are the cases of Francois ("Doc") Duvalier of Haiti and Idi Amin of Uganda.

THE PARLIAMENTARY EXECUTIVE

The parliamentary system, characterized by its fusion of power of the executive and legislative branches, has one person holding the office of chief of state and another, of chief executive. The former may be a hereditary ruler (as for example, in Belgium, Morocco, Thailand, or the United Kingdom) or an elected president (such as in Austria, France, Italy, Israel or West Germany). The latter is usually the leader of the country's majority party or of a coalition government and may carry the title of

[12]His ideology is expressed cogently in Julius K. Nyerere, Freedom and Unity (London: Oxford University Press, 1966).

prime minister, premier, or chancellor. The power of the chief of state has declined considerably in most countries during the past century. A leading exception is France. The writers of the Constitution of the Fifth Republic (adopted in 1958) shifted sizable powers from the office of the premier to that of the president.

With a few exceptions, the chief of state performs primarily symbolic and cere-monial functions. He or she personifies the nation-state and, by taking care of the official ceremonial functions, relieves the chief executive of many time-consuming duties. The political influence wielded by the British queen or president of the Feder-al Republic of Germany, to cite two examples, depends to a large extent on the po-litical circumstances as well as the ability, intelligence, personality, and wisdom of the incumbent; however, the presence of the office adds stability to the parliamen-tary system. Many of the chiefs of state in advanced Western countries have made it a point to stand above domestic politics. Queen Elizabeth has no clear association with any of the political parties in Britain. Neither do the monarchs of the Benelux or Scandinavian countries. President Heuss, the first president of the Federal Republic of Germany, resigned his membership in the Free Democratic Party when he was elected to his office in 1949. He thought that party membership was incompatible with holding the office of president. Even Charles de Gaulle, after becoming presi-dent in 1958, declined to partake in the party work and leadership of the "Gaullists," a political movement he had helped to establish in 1947. He felt that his office re-quired him to stand "above" the squabbles of French party politics.

The prime minister (premier or chancellor), as found in the Western democratic countries, is usually a person of considerable political experience, having served for a number of years as party official, legislator, and as a minister in a previous admin-istration.

How are prime ministers chosen? In Britain, the prime minister is selected by the sovereign after a national election has taken place. In practice, however, there is lit-tle choice in this selection. If, as it usually happens in British elections, one political party has obtained a majority in the House of Commons, the leader of the victorious party will be asked by the sovereign to take over the office of prime minister and to form a new government. The British model applies, with some variations, to most of the other Western parliamentary democracies, too. A major exception is France, which has a hybrid presidential–parliamentary system. Here the premier is ap-pointed directly by the President of France.

The prime minister's duties differ somewhat from those of the president of the United States, who makes ultimate decisions and carries final responsibility. We would like to explain the functions of a prime minister by using its prototype, the Brit-ish example.

The Prime Minister's Functions

The main statutory responsibilities of the British prime minister are as follows:

1.   The prime minister serves as the **chief executive** of the country. He or she recommends (to the monarch) the appointment and dismissal of all ministers. The

Margaret Thatcher, British Prime Minister.

prime minister directs the day-to-day work of the government. He or she presides over the Cabinet, the inner policy-making and policy-directing body of the government. The prime minister of yesteryear used to be labeled a *primus inter pares* ("first among equals") within the Cabinet. Major decisions were made collectively by that body, with the prime minister serving as the chair of the meetings. However, most students of British politics maintain that the contemporary prime minister is substantially more powerful than the Latin phrase indicates. According to Humphry Berkeley:

> The Prime Minister is not, and has not been for a long time, primus inter pares. . . . If the Cabinet discusses anything it is the Prime Minister who decides what the collective view of the Cabinet is. A Minister's job is to save the Prime Minister all the work he can. But no Minister could make a really important move without consulting the Prime Minister, and if the Prime Minister wants to take a certain step the Cabinet Minister would either have to agree, to argue it out in Cabinet, or resign.[13]

[13]Humphry Berkeley, *The Power of the Prime Minister* (London: George Allen and Unwin, 1968), pp. 23–24.

Despite the growth of the prime minister's power, the ultimate responsibility for major governmental decisions rests with the whole Cabinet, rather than with the prime minister alone.

2.   The prime minister is the **chief legislator.** He or she provides leadership in the House of Commons. The prime minister is the chief government spokesman and leader of the majority party in the House. With the exception of the budget debate, during which the opposition is statutorily in control, the prime minister directs all business in the House of Commons.

3.   The prime minister is the **leader of his or her political party.** He or she directs the over-all affairs of the party, plans strategy and chooses the date of an election. When either one of the two major political parties in Britain chooses a new party leader it, in fact, potentially chooses a future prime minister.

4.   The prime minister serves as the **link between the government and the Sovereign.** The prime minister informs the monarch weekly of the proceedings in the Cabinet and in Parliament, as well as on major national and international developments. Even though Queen Elizabeth plays largely a symbolic role as chief of state, it is important for the well-being of the British system that she remains well informed.

5.   The prime minister functions as the **chief diplomat** in Western parliamentary societies. The only exception to this is in France, where the President performs this role. International relations in the atomic age often call for speedy decisions, which must be made by the person at the helm of the government. Further, a good deal of diplomacy since the end of World War II has been conducted in summit meetings. The prime minister serves as the country's leading representative at these important meetings.

6.   Finally, the prime minister serves as the country's "**manager of prosperity.**" Recent British prime ministers, for example, have taken a special interest and have played an active part in treasury and budget policy making. The state of the economy has great bearing on the popularity or unpopularity of the prime minister and his or her government.

THE PRESIDENTIAL AND PARLIAMENTARY EXECUTIVES COMPARED

A brief comparison of the real powers of the U.S. president and the British prime minister shows a mixed bag of similarities and dissimilarities. Both have extensive powers of **patronage**, although major appointments in the United States are subject to Senate confirmation. Both are leaders of their party, but the British prime minister is in a stronger position vis-à-vis the party than the president in the United States. The president serves a fixed term of office, while the prime minister's tenure is not constitutionally set but depends on retention of majority support in the House of Commons. More generally speaking, the president of the United States has substantially broader constitutional powers than does the British prime minister. Lastly, because the president is chief of state as well as chief executive, his office portrays the incumbent as a person of greater prestige than the British prime minister.[14]

The power relationship between the president and the chancellor in the Federal Republic of Germany is in many ways similar to that of the British monarch and prime minister. The president performs largely ceremonial functions and the chancellor serves as the political leader of the nation-state. Similar statements can be made about the relationship between the chief of state and the chief executive in most other postindustrial societies having a parliamentary system, with the exception of France because of its strong president and appointed (rather than elected) prime minister in the Fifth Republic.

What types of countries have a parliamentary, rather than a presidential, system of executive leadership? As we have indicated, the United Kingdom can be considered the prototype of the parliamentary system. Many countries in the British Commonwealth have followed its example. They have been joined by all the democratic countries of Europe, as well as Israel and Japan.

Most Communist countries, according to their constitutions, have some kind of parliamentary system too. The Soviet Union, for example, has a prime minister (the chairman of the Council of Ministers) and a chief of state (the chairman of the Presidium of the Supreme Soviet). The latter performs a number of the ceremonial duties exercised by chiefs of state in other societies. There is a substantial difference, however, between the functions performed by the executive in the Communist countries and those of the executive in Western parliamentary systems. The highest decision-making body in the Soviet Union (and other Communist countries) is not the prime minister's cabinet but the Politburo of the Communist Party. Furthermore, the secretary general of the Communist Party often performs duties rendered by either the chief of state or the chief executive in Western countries. The Soviet prime minister executes the policies passed down from the Politburo. Thus, while the Soviet constitution provides for a parliamentary system with a dual executive, its functions differ from those performed by parliamentary executives in Western countries.

ADVANTAGES AND DISADVANTAGES OF THE PARLIAMENTARY AND THE PRESIDENTIAL EXECUTIVES

The parliamentary executive (resembling the British type) is found in most of the postindustrialized societies. In order to function satisfactorily, the parliamentary system requires a well-developed and well-functioning political party system—a level of political sophistication found presently only in the more advanced countries. The presidential executive, in turn, is found in the United States and in many of the developing countries.

[14]See Berkeley, *op. cit.* For a discussion of the Cabinet system, see John P. Mackintosh, *The British Cabinet,* 2nd ed. (London: Stevens & Sons, 1968).

The fusion of executive and legislative powers under the parliamentary system provides for a much closer and smoother working relationship between these two branches of government than does the prevailing practice under the presidential system. In turn, one of the advantages of the presidential form lies in the fixed term of office of the incumbent (assuming that he does a satisfactory job). The prime minister, in order to stay in office, must maintain majority support in the lower chamber of the legislature. Does either system provide for better executive leadership? The answer, we think, depends very much on the circumstances. One could argue that the presidential stature and prestige of Lincoln, Wilson, and Roosevelt increased their eminence as wartime leaders. To achieve a similar effect, Churchill, when appointed prime minister in the early days of World War II, established a coalition government, which included all parties represented in the British Parliament. This move created a base of united support for him at home, made him a kind of "super-prime-minister," and put him on a more equal footing with the president of the United States.

In turn, however, the Watergate dilemma shows that the president and the office of the presidency can suffer inordinate loss of popular respect if the incumbent involves himself—or gets drawn into—the kind of nefarious activities that Mr. Nixon did. The parliamentary system offers a better setting for handling crises of this nature. If a prime minister loses his credibility, he can resign or be forced to resign. When a prime minister resigns, the presence of the chief of state may lend continuing stability to the system, a kind of stability that was not present in the United States during the later phases of the Watergate crisis.

Let us cite an example to illustrate this theory. The Federal Republic of Germany experienced a type of "Watergate crisis" in May of 1974, which involved the rather popular Chancellor Willy Brandt. Intelligence sources had discovered that a member of the chancellor's immediate staff, Gunter Guillaume, was a spy in the pay of the Communist German Democratic Republic. Mr. Brandt reacted quickly and resigned from his office. A new chancellor was elected within 10 days, and the transition was very smooth. The office of chancellor suffered little loss of prestige on account of the crisis. The important point is that the presence of a chief of state, separate from the chancellor (as the chief executive), provided some stability to the West German government during the crucial days because the executive was not completely void of leadership. It must be added, however, that Mr. Brandt's quick resignation—in contrast to the drawn-out struggle fought by Mr. Nixon—helped to keep the problem within manageable limits. In terms of seriousness, however, the Guillaume case, though quite different from Watergate, was probably as dangerous a matter as the wrongdoings that occurred in Washington during the Watergate crisis.

Both systems, the presidential and the parliamentary executive, may be perverted. Hitler and Mussolini rose from parliamentary settings, while many of today's semideveloped and developing countries are ruled by autocratic or dictatorial presidents.

A last item that deserves mention has to do with the workload of the incumbents. Observers of the presidency of the United States have found that, especially in more recent years, the president's obligation to perform both ceremonial and executive functions places an ever-increasing burden on the shoulders of the incumbent. In this setting political analysts have raised the question of whether the duties of the presidency have become too large to be performed by one person. The split responsibilities of the British dual executive certainly reduce the performance demands each executive must face in that country, possibly contributing to better executive performance.

PUBLIC ADMINISTRATION AND NATIONAL BUREAUCRACIES

Modern governments provide a large number of services and regulate a variety of activities. Many of these either did not exist in years past or were left to the individual or the free market economy. Furthermore, rapid advancements in technology call for more and more expert knowledge at governmental levels. The implementation of public policy is handled by public administration, a part of the executive branch of government that goes back to antiquity, but it has taken on in recent years an increasingly significant role in the governing process of many countries.

While there may be some difficulties in defining public administration precisely, we would like to present two widely used definitions. According to one eminent student of the subject, public administration consists of "all those operations having for their purpose the fulfillment or enforcement of public policy."[15] Another scholar defines the area as follows:

> The process of public administration consists of the actions involved in effecting the intent or desire of a government. It is thus the continuously active "business" part of government, concerned with carrying out the law, as made by legislative bodies (or other authoritative agents) and interpreted by courts, through the processes of organization and management.[16]

Public administration covers an enormously wide scope of activities, ranging from the negotiation of a treaty to the delivery of mail. It includes the many governmental activities in such areas as health, welfare, public works, and conservation. Administrative agencies are deeply involved in the preparation of the national budg-

[15]Leonard D. White, *Introduction to the Study of Public Administration*, 4th ed. (New York: Macmillan, 1955), p. 1.

[16]Dwight Waldo, "The Study of Public Administration," in Richard J. Stillman II, ed., *Public Administration: Concepts and Cases* (Boston: Houghton Mifflin, 1976), p. 4.

ets, but more so in the developed countries than in developing societies. In Britain, for example, about 80 percent of the national budget is prepared by members of the **civil service**.[17] In the United States, 3 administrative agencies, the General Accounting Office (GAO), the Congressional Budget Office (CBO), and the Office of Management and Budget (OMB) are instrumental in the formulation of the national budget and perform pre- and postauditing functions.

Public administration takes place at all levels of government—international, national, state, and local. Our discussion will focus largely on the national aspects of public administration.

Quite often the terms "administration" and "bureaucracy" are used interchangeably. People speak of the national bureaucracy when referring to the administrative part of our federal government. The classic description of bureaucracies, one that still is accepted widely today, comes from the German social scientist Max Weber. He defined bureaucracies as

> *Organizations with a pyramidal structure of authority, which utilize the enforcement of universal and impersonal rules to maintain that structure of authority, and which emphasize the none-discretionary aspects of administration.*[18]

Obviously, some public agencies are more loosely organized than others, and Weber's definition may apply more directly to some than to others. We will use the labels administration and bureaucracy in an interchangeable fashion.

A good deal of the public administration process takes place within the various executive departments; however, the growing need for specialization has led, in recent decades, to the creation of **regulatory boards, commissions,** and **agencies** here and abroad. These bodies have been authorized to issue rules within their sphere of jurisdiction, to supervise the implementation of these rules, and to settle disputes originating from the implementation of the rules. Domestic examples of regulatory agencies are the Federal Trade Commission (FTC), the Interstate Commerce Commission (ICC), the Federal Power Commission (FPC), the National Labor Relations Board (NLRB), and the Federal Aviation Administration (FAA). There are a large number of regulatory-type public corporations in Britain that oversee the nationalized industries in that country. The better-known of these are the British Broadcasting Corporation (BBC); the London Passenger Transport Board; the corporate agencies in charge of the coal, electricity, and gas industry; and the public corporation directing British civil aviation. The Soviet Union has a large number of State Committees; which correspond loosely to the regulatory agencies in the United States. The areas of jurisdiction of these committees range from cinematography to

---

[17]See Hugh Heclo and Aaron Wildavsky, *The Private Government of Public Money: Community and Policy in British Political Administration* (Berkeley, Cal.: University of California Press, 1974).

[18]Quoted in B. Guy Peters, *The Politics of Bureaucracy: A Comparative Perspective* (New York: Longman, 1978), p. 3.

vocational education and include such important areas as economic planning (Gosplan), publishing, state security (KGB), and television and radio broadcasting.

Can public administration be carried on in a politically neutral setting, or do public administrators become involved in policy making and in politics? A famous political scientist and a president of the United States, Woodrow Wilson, stated in 1887:

> Administration lies outside the sphere of politics . . . it is a part of political life only as machinery is part of the manufactured product.[19]

Today Woodrow Wilson's account is looked upon as wishful thinking. It is widely recognized these days that public administrators are involved in policy making and are drawn into political struggles. According to B. Guy Peters:

> Administration and policy, instead of being discrete phenomena, are actually interrelated. In both an objective and a subjective manner the nature of the administrative system can influence the policy outputs of the political system. Administration does make policy, although these policies are not always written and promulgated in the same manner as the rules made by the legislatures and executives.[20]

Public administrators become involved in policy making in at least two areas: (1) in the budgetary process, the administrator's input will help to build the foundation for future policy outputs and (2) most statutes, as promulgated by legislatures, are general prescriptions and often need to be interpreted by administrators before they can be applied to specific situations; this interpretation may add new substance to a law, and thus constitute a kind of policy making. In turn, members of the administration may initiate new legislation by way of reporting difficulties they have encountered in the process of implementing existing laws. A number of complaints regarding a particular rule will lead legislators to enact improved legislation.

National bureaucracies in all countries have a tendency to grow in size and complexity. They range in size from a few hundred national employees in the smallest countries to a number of millions in the largest countries. The People's Republic of China and the Soviet Union have by far the largest and most complex national bureaucracies.

In terms of classification, members of the bureaucracies fall into one of the following categories: political appointees; noncivil service career officials; and civil servants. Members of the first group are appointed to office by political officials for one of many reasons, ranging all the way from particular qualifications to nepotism. The second category encompasses professional governmental officials in countries that do not have a standardized civil service system. The third group consists of career governmental employees recruited and employed under a (civil service) merit

---

[19]Quoted in William L. Morrow, *Public Administration: Politics and the Political System* (New York: Random House, 1975), p. 4.

[20]Peters, *op. cit.*, p. 13.

system. The basic concept underlying the civil service system is that people employed under its auspices are politically neutral and will carry out faithfully the policy instructions of their superiors. Their jobs are tenured, in contrast to those of political appointees, who come and go with individual administrations.

In order to discuss national bureaucracies in more detail, we would like to examine and compare the administrations of the United States, the United Kingdom, the Federal Republic of Germany, and the Soviet Union, and then complete our discussion with a more generalized discussion of the bureaucracies in the developing countries.

THE BUREAUCRACY IN THE UNITED STATES

The federal administration in this country consists of approximately 3 million civilian employees. It is divided into 13 departments[21] and, as mentioned earlier, includes a number of regulatory commissions, and some independent agencies, such as the Postal Service. The personnel at the top of the federal bureaucracy consists of nearly 3000 political appointees, such as the secretaries of the 13 departments and, within each department, undersecretaries, assistant secretaries, as well as the deputies and assistants of those just listed. All these political appointees are nominated by the president, and their appointment requires the consent of the Senate. They serve at the pleasure of the president. Each incoming administration ultimately will select its own people for the appointive positions, even if the same party stays in power with a new president. For example, when President Johnson took office, he kept the Kennedy appointees in office during the transition period but then replaced many of them with his own people. Secretary of State Dean Rusk was one of the few who served in his position from the start of the Kennedy administration through the end of the Johnson administration.

Customarily, an incoming president will select the nominees to head departments and they, in turn, will propose to the president candidates for the subordinate political positions in their departments. The candidates are usually members of the president's party. Mr. Kennedy's nomination of Robert McNamara, a Republican, for secretary of defense, and Mr. Nixon's nomination of a democrat, John Connally, for secretary of the treasury, are exceptions to the rule.

What is the professional background of these political appointees?[22] Some have served in the executive branch during a previous administration of their party. Others are recruited from business, as in the case of Mr. McNamara. In more recent years some candidates for high executive office have come from among academicians, as for example Secretary of State Henry Kissinger. Defeated candidates

---

[21]Departments of State, Treasury, Defense, Justice, Interior, Agriculture, Commerce, Labor, Health and Human Services, Housing and Urban Development, Transportation, Energy, and Education.

[22]An excellent profile study of federal executives is W. Lloyd Warner, et al., *The American Federal Executive* (New Haven: Yale University Press, 1963). The study examines the profiles of nearly 13,000 civilian and military executives, ranking from GS 14 (or equivalent) through cabinet secretary.

for gubernatorial office, if they belong to the president's party, may be offered an appointive position in the federal executive. John Chafee, after having been defeated in the 1968 gubernatorial election in Rhode Island, was appointed secretary of the navy by Richard Nixon.

The Civil Service in the United States

Most federal employees below the rank of the political appointees in the Cabinet departments and independent agencies are under the merit system. Their recruitment and employment has been handled by the United States Civil Service Commission or the civil service programs of particular agencies, such as the State Department's foreign service. The United States Civil Service Commission was abolished, under a governmental reorganization plan, on December 31, 1978. Its functions now are performed by three agencies: (1) the Office of Personnel Management, (2) a bipartisan Merit System Protection Board, and (3) a bipartisan Federal Labor Relations Authority. The system of a civil service was established in the United States with the passage of the Pendleton Act in 1883.[23] Today more than 90 percent of all federal employees hold civil service status.

The civil service in the United States uses two types of classification systems for its employees: the CPC (Crafts, Protective, and Custodial) grouping encompasses all the blue-collar jobs—about one-fifth of all the positions; and the large majority of all federal employees under the merit system, those holding white-collar jobs, are under the GS (General Schedule) system, which ranges from grade GS 1 to grade GS 18. College graduates are recruited at the GS 5 or GS 7 level, depending on their previous experience and performance on the **PACE** (Professional and Administrative Career Examination). Information about the test and employment matters can be obtained from the nearest federal civil service office. The United States government is the largest employer in the United States. Its range of employment involves thousands of job categories. Its pay scale, as well as conditions of employment, have been steadily improved and are presently competitive with comparable private occupations.

THE BRITISH BUREAUCRACY

The British have perhaps the most professional administration in the Western world. It is professional in the sense that there are few (substantially fewer than in the United States) political appointees and nearly all of these have been members of

[23]A classic source on the development of the civil service in the United States is Paul P. Van Riper, *History of the United States Civil Service* (Evanston, Ill.: Row, Peterson, 1958). See also Herbert Kaufman's chapter "The Growth of the Federal Personnel System," in the American Assembly, *The Federal Government Service*, 2nd ed. (Englewood Cliffs, N.J.: Prentice-Hall, 1965). His table on pp. 41–43 lists the number of federal employees under the merit system from 1884 to 1963. For an analysis of the competitive position of the federal government as an employer see the excellent but dated study by Franklin P. Kilpatrick, Milton C. Cummings, Jr., and M. Kent Jennings, *The Image of the Federal Service* (Washington, D.C.: The Brookings Institution, 1964).

Parliament for years and, quite often, have had previous administrative experience in the executive branch. The number of ministers (i.e., the people in charge of executive departments—called ministries in Britain) customarily ranges between 40 and 50, with approximately 20 of them being members of the prime minister's cabinet. A ministry may have from 3 to 6 political appointees at the top of its hierarchy. They are ranked in the following order: minister (or secretary), minister of state, undersecretary, parliamentary secretary, and parliamentary private secretary. These officials are appointed by the prime minister and serve at his or her pleasure. Most ministers are long-term members of the House of Commons. A few department heads customarily are members of the House of Lords. In these instances the second-ranking political appointee must be a member of the House of Commons, in order that he can represent the ministry in the lower house. Most ministers of state, under-secretaries, and parliamentary secretaries are members of the House of Commons. All in all, there are some 200 political appointees at the helm of the British bureaucracy. Their small number, as well as the presence of civil servants at the highest level of government, has led one British scholar to comment:

> The great advantage of having permanent officials at the highest levels is that they make available to new Ministers an unrivalled fund of experience. The American practice whereby the equivalents of our Permanent Secretaries, Deputy Secretaries and Under-Secretaries, are political appointments have corresponding disadvantages.[24]

As suggested by Stacey, the obvious advantage of this particular British system is far more continuity at the highest levels of the ministries.

The British Civil Service

As implied previously, the British civil service reaches higher into the top-level administration than its counterpart in the United States. The highest-ranking British civil servant, the permanent secretary, would about equal a GS 21 or, in other words, an assistant secretary in the United States.

The British civil service is the oldest in the Western world. It was started in the 1780s, and its merit system now covers nearly all the civilian employees of the British national government. Until the early 1970s the British civil service consisted of four distinct parts: the administrative class (the top echelon administrators); the executive class (the middle-level administrators); the professional, scientific, and technical class (this category was added during the 1950s and encompassed professional specialists such as engineers, physicians, and scientists); and a two-tier clerical class. Each category had its own entrance route.

Britain's civil service has been subject to periodic reviews, the most important and most recent being the inquiry by the Fulton Committee (1966–1968). Its proposals included a strong recommendation to abolish the strict quadripartite division

---

[24]Frank Stacey, *The Government of Modern Britain* (Oxford: Clarendon Press, 1968), p. 343.

with the separate entrance routes, replacing it with a single hierarchical structure similar to the system in the United States, which would cover all civil servants in one system. This proposal was accepted by the government and the changeover to the new system began in 1971. According to the Fulton Committee, a single-structure civil service would do away with the "caste system" and could increase considerably the mobility within the ranks. In the past, promotions from the executive class to the administrative class took place in very exceptional cases only and each class had become "a small world of its own." Members of one group had little contact with members of the other. One of the particular features of the administrative class has been its exclusive educational background. Approximately two-thirds of its members have been graduates of Oxford or Cambridge University.[25]

The responsibilities of the British bureaucracy are broader in scope than those of its counterpart in the United States because of its administration of the nationalized industries. Government intervention in the economy has taken place on a much larger scale in Britain than in the United States. Presently, the British government controls in full or in major part the following industries: electricity, gas, radio and television, civil aviation, coal, and steel, among others. Some of the nationalized industries are under the direct control of a minister, while others are governed by public corporations.

PUBLIC ADMINISTRATION IN THE FEDERAL REPUBLIC OF GERMANY

The number of federal ministers in West Germany is considerably smaller than in Britain, having ranged between 14 and 19. They are appointed by the chancellor and, as in Britain, serve completely at his pleasure. In contrast to Britain, all West German ministers are members of the chancellor's cabinet. They do not have quite an equal footing in the cabinet, however. Some play a more important role than others. The minister's importance in the government depends on the particular department he heads, his standing as a party leader, and his personal relations with the chancellor. In regard to the first point, the ministers of foreign affairs, defense, interior, and finance enjoy an elevated position in the cabinet because of the great importance of their departments. The ministers are usually members of the *Bundestag,* the lower house of the West German legislature. Their length of parliamentary experience, however, is often less than that of their counterparts in Britain.

Most West German administrations have been coalition governments consisting of two parties. One of the coalition arrangements has been the practice, since 1966, that the position of minister of foreign affairs be held by the parliamentary leader of the junior party in the coalition. Thus, Willy Brandt of the Social Democratic Party served as foreign minister from 1966 to 1969; Walter Scheel served from 1969 to 1974 and, since 1974, Hans-Dietrich Genscher has served, both of the Free Democratic Party.

[25]An excellent study of the social structure of the former administrative class is R. K. Kelsall, *Higher Civil Servants in Britain* (London: Routledge & Kegan Paul, 1966).

Formerly, all administrative positions below the rank of minister were staffed with civil servants. More recently, however, one or two positions in each ministry analogous to that of an undersecretary in the United States or parliamentary secretary in Britain have been made appointive. The appointees are members of the *Bundestag* and carry the title of parliamentary state secretary. They are primarily responsible for maintaining liaison between their ministry and the legislature.

The West German Civil Service

The roots and traditions of the German civil service system were formed in early nineteenth-century Prussia and perpetuated in the German Empire and the Weimar Republic. During those years the civil service developed into a kind of caste or "state within the state," known for its efficiency and loyalty to the government. During the Third Reich, efforts were made to politicize it in the sense that those who joined the Nazi Party were promoted over those who did not. Some modernization of the civil service has occurred in the post-World War II era, but efforts to make it more similar to the civil service in the United States largely have failed. According to a leading West German political scientist:

> The main problem of the German administration is its lack of open personnel policy and the fact—seen from the point of view of the citizen—that the federally organized administration is too complex to understand. The tendency of the administration to be autonomous towards the political decision-makers by referring to a pressure exerted by the logic of facts has made the problem of the technocracy acute in the Federal Republic too. The civil service as the supposed neutral authority of the state interest tends to be a power factor with a strong dynamic of its own that is politically difficult to keep under control, a bureaucracy in the strictest meaning of the word.[26]

During the 1960s and the 1970s, a number of proposals to reform the civil service were examined in the *Bundestag*. Finally, in 1979, a civil service college, similar to the **Ecole Nationale d'Administration** in France, was established. All future members of the higher civil service will be trained at this college. A hindrance to any large-scale reform of the civil service in the Federal Republic of Germany, however, is the provision in Paragraph 5, Article 33 of the West German constitution stating that "law regarding the public service shall be regulated with due regard to the traditional principles concerning the status of professional civil servants."

In terms of structure, the West German civil service is divided into three major categories, which are similar to the former British system.

1. On top of the hierarchy is the higher service, the most important and influential category. Its members are customarily graduates of law schools. They receive their initial appointment after passing a competitive examination. After a three-year training period a second examination must be passed

[26]Kurt Sontheimer, *The Government and Politics of West Germany,* trans. by Fleur Donecker (New York: Praeger, 1972), pp. 145–146.

before the candidate receives life-term tenure in the higher civil service. *Beamte* (the general label for tenured civil servants) have enjoyed an extraordinarily high social status in German society, but that seems to be declining today. Personal connections have had some bearing on promotions within the ranks. Graduates of the "right" university and the "right" fraternity of that university have been looked after favorably by their older fraternity brothers in the upper ranks.

2. The second category of the West German civil service is the salaried service, consisting of the clerical employees. Most of them also enjoy a high degree of job security but less prestige than the members of the higher service.

3. The third category is that of wage earners, essentially blue-collar workers whose jobs may be of either a temporary or permanent nature.

One substantial difference between the West German civil service and those of the United States and Britain is that while West Germany has a unified civil service structure (encompassing federal, state, and local employees in the executive and judicial branches of government), the number of civil servants in the employment of the federal government (approximately 15 percent of the total) is substantially smaller than in Britain or the United States. About 53 percent of the West German civil servants are employed at the state level, and the remaining 32 percent with local governments. These figures reflect a main feature of West German federalism: no ministries, with the exception of defense and finance, have field offices at the state or local level. Consequently, the federal ministries depend on state and local agencies for the implementation of federal policies at these levels, which explains the large number of civil servants employed with state and local governments.

In terms of scope of responsibility, the West German bureaucracy is broader than its counterpart in the United States but not as broad as the British. In addition to the comparable areas under public control in the United States, the West German government administers—under the Ministry of Transport, Posts and Telecommunications—radio, television, telegraph, and telephone service, as well as civil aviation and railroads—areas that are basically in private hands in the United States.[27]

ADMINISTRATION IN THE UNION OF SOVIET SOCIALIST REPUBLICS

The Soviet bureaucracy differs substantially from its counterparts in the United States, Britain, and West Germany. The scope of responsibility of Soviet administra-

[27]There are relatively few primary English-language sources dealing at length with the bureaucracy of the Federal German Republic. Two early studies are John H. Herz, "Political Views of the West German Civil Service," in Hans Speier and W. Phillips Davison, *West German Leadership and Foreign Policy* (Evanston, Ill.: Row, Peterson, 1957); and Karlheinz Neunreither, Federalism and the West German bureaucracy, *Political Studies* (October, 1959), pp. 233–245. A more recent publication of interest is Renate Mayntz and Fritz W. Scharpf, *Policy-Making in the German Federal Bureaucracy* (New York: Elsvier Scientific Publishing Co., 1975).

tion is vast because it directs and supervises nearly all areas of societal endeavors: the traditional areas of public responsibility, such as foreign affairs, defense, finance, justice; as well as agriculture, civil aviation, communication, culture, education, all industries, public health, and transportation. The Communist Party is dominant over governmental agencies. Decisions on all major issues are made by the highest council of the party, the Politburo. The government's executive branch, therefore, becomes largely a tool for implementing policy, being less involved in the policy-making process than its counterparts in non-Communist countries. There is no Western-type civil service in the Soviet Union; however, most of the bureaucratic officials are career people. Those just listed are some, but by no means all, of the differences between Western bureaucracies and those of the Soviet Union (which has served as a model for the bureaucracies of other Communist countries).

At the top of the Soviet administrative structure is the Council of Ministers, directed by the chairman (prime minister), who is a member of the Politburo of the Communist Party. The members of the Council are appointed by the Supreme Soviet (the national legislature), an automatic procedure after their names have been proposed to the legislature by the party leadership. According to the 1977 Constitution, the Council of Ministers "shall be the highest executive and administrative organ of state power in the USSR. . . . The Council . . . shall be responsible and accountable to the Supreme Soviet of the USSR. . . . The Council . . . shall be empowered to deal with all matters of state administration that come within the jurisdiction of the Union of Soviet Socialist Republics in so far as they do not, by force of the Constitution, come within the competence of the Supreme Soviet of the USSR and the Presidium of the Supreme Soviet of the USSR."

The primary function of the Council of Ministers is to supervise the huge administrative apparatus and to implement all the basic party decisions that pertain to the vast area of executive/administrative jurisdiction in the Soviet Union, including the allocation of resources in the economic realm, the overall direction of economic and social affairs, and the execution of defense and foreign policies. The Council of Ministers is very large. In its present composition it consists of the chairman of the Council of Ministers, 2 first vice-chairmen, 9 vice-chairmen (the above 12 form the presidium and serve as a kind of cabinet), and approximately 90 other members, including ministers of functional departments, chairmen of state committees, and the 15 chairmen of the Republic Councils of Ministers. The components of the Council of Ministers have been subject to frequent change.[28]

The national ministries in the Soviet Union are of two kinds: all-union and union-republic. All-union ministries are in complete charge of their sphere of administration throughout the Soviet Union. For example, civil aviation is administered by an

---

[28]A detailed chart depicting all the components of the Council of Ministers as of 1971 can be found in Frederick C. Barghoorn, *Politics in the USSR*, 2nd ed. (Boston: Little, Brown, 1972), pp. 340–341. See also the slightly less detailed diagram in Robert J. Osborn, *The Evolution of Soviet Politics* (Homewood, Ill.: The Dorsey Press, 1974), pp. 268–269, depicting the composition of the council as of July, 1973.

all-union ministry, which has its main office in Moscow and field offices in the 15 republics and their local districts. Union-republic ministries, in contrast, have a central ministry in Moscow and corresponding ministries in the 15 republics. Agriculture is such a ministry. Its national programs are administered at the republic and local level through the officials of the republic ministry rather than those of the national office.

The vast Soviet bureaucracy employs a large number of officials at the national, state, and local levels. Estimates of their number range from 10 to 15 million. These employees can be classified loosely into 3 categories: party officials whose job it is to see that party policies are properly implemented in the administrative realm; administrators who put into practice the governmental programs (as distinguished from party policies) and managers who direct the work in agriculture and industry; and specialists, such as architects, artists, biologists, chemists, dentists, educators, physicians, physicists, and so forth. Recruitment to positions in the bureaucracy and promotions within the ranks are supervised by the party and based on capability, performance, and political loyalty. The last criterion is often the most important consideration. According to Barghoorn:

> The tightly centralized Soviet recruitment system tends to protect the mediocre and exclude much talent from participation in public life. Nevertheless, from the Kremlin's point of view it has compensatory advantages. Perhaps the most important is that it tends to assure the filling of all strategic posts in party, state, and other areas by politically reliable personnel.[29]

In addition to political loyalty, membership in the Communist Party is practically a must for those who wish to advance in the administration.[30]

One of the astonishing features of the Soviet higher administrative elite has been the extraordinary longevity of people in office, despite the severe purges that occurred under Stalin and, to a lesser degree, under Khrushchev. Mr. Kosygin is only the 8th prime minister in the history of the Soviet Union. Still more remarkable is the longevity at the ministerial and subministerial levels. Some ministers have been in charge of their departments for 20 and more years. Andrei Gromyko is the world's most senior foreign minister, having been promoted to that position in 1957.

Perhaps the greatest shortcoming in the Soviet bureaucracy is that its complexity—resulting from size and duplications caused by the existence of concurrent party and governmental agencies in nearly all areas of administrative endeavors—has given rise to an inordinate amount of red tape. Reports from visitors to the Soviet Union and accounts in major Soviet newspapers abound with complaints about the prevalent administrative inefficiency, apathy, and nepotism. While the Soviet leader-

[29]Barghoorn, *op. cit.,* p. 174.
[30]An interesting in-depth study of the bureaucratic elite in the Ukraine is John A. Armstrong, *The Soviet Bureaucratic Elite: A Case Study of the Ukranian Apparatus* (New York: Frederick A. Praeger, 1959). See also Ronald J. Hill, *Soviet Political Elites: The Case of Tiraspol* (New York: St. Martin's Press, 1977).

ship has tried to remedy the more flagrant abuses and shortcomings, it has made little headway in its attempts to make the bureaucracy more efficient. The larger a bureaucracy, the more difficult it is to reform it. The monstrous size of the Soviet bureaucracy makes any kind of reform difficult. Moreover, some possible reforms, such as eliminating the duplication caused by overlapping party and administrative agencies would run counter to basic principles of the Soviet system and obviously are not desired by the ruling elite.

BUREAUCRACIES IN THE DEVELOPING COUNTRIES

Since the late 1940s a large number of countries in Africa, Asia, and Latin America have achieved independence. Prior to independence, these countries were ruled by an administrative structure centered in the colonizing country and the governor of the colony. The administration under the governor customarily was patterned and structured along the lines of the colonizing country's bureaucracy. The colonial administrative personnel consisted of a small number of Europeans (such as Britishers in British colonies) in the higher positions and indigenous officials in the middle and lower ranks. In the British colonies, for example, Britishers filled about four or five percent of the administrative positions. But since these were the higher positions, the European administrators in fact controlled the bureaucracy.

When the colonies became independent, most of them had fairly well-established administrative systems with built-in civil services, but little in terms of other political institutions. A resulting problem has been described by Fred Riggs:

> *A phenomenon of the utmost significance in transitional societies is the lack of balance between political policy-making institutions and bureaucratic policy-implementing structures. The relative weakness of political organs means that the political function tends to be appropriated, in considerable measure, by bureaucrats. Intra-bureaucratic struggles become a primary form of politics. But when the political arena is shifted to bureaucracies—a shift marked by the growing power of military officers in conflict with civilian officials—the consequences are usually ominous for political stability, economic growth, administrative effectiveness, and democratic values.*[31]

The point made by Riggs is that in many new countries the administrations are far more developed than the fledgling legislatures and therefore play an inordinately large role in the policy-making process.

Let us now examine the impacts that the transition period from colony to independent country has had on Third World bureaucracies.

The first generation of chief executives in the new countries usually have been composed of people who either moved up from an administrative position held under the old order or who came from the military. They appointed some of their own people as ministers and other immediate subordinates, but also retained the serv-

---

[31]Fred W. Riggs, "Bureaucracy," in Frank Tachau, ed., *The Developing Nations: What Path to Modernization?* (New York: Dodd, Mead, 1972), p. 115.

ices of a number of European administrative experts who had been present under the colonial order. The speed with which the foreigners have been replaced by indigenous experts has varied from country to country and, obviously, depended on the availability of trained natives; there were more, for example, in India, Pakistan, and the West Indies than in Africa. As Henry L. Bretton points out:

> Few of the first-generation African leaders possessed the skills, though many possessed the intelligence, to understand let alone manage and direct complex ministries in the crucial sectors of finance, foreign and domestic trade, industry, the central banks, and the sensitive areas of telecommunications. The potential of high-level civil servants increased in direct proportion to the lack of experience, know-how, and expertise of the African heads of ministries.[32]

In the former British colonies of Africa, the degree of Africanization of the civil service at the time of independence differed considerably from country to country and, in the case of Nigeria, from region to region. Moreover, there were interesting differences in the subsequent further Africanization. According to J. F. Maitland-Jones:

> The degree to which the public services in ex-British Africa have been Africanized/localized, and the speed with which it had taken place, clearly varied very greatly. . . . Ghana and Uganda, which were relatively speaking always the most advanced countries, kept British permanent secretaries for longer than the other countries—because. . . . an Africanization policy had been seen by the public to be in operation for so long they could believe in it, and they did not therefore need to exert pressures experienced elsewhere to Africanize speedily at the expense of efficiency.[33]

The new leaders of the developing countries have changed little in their countries' administrative systems. By and large these bureaucracies today have the structure they had during colonial time.[34] The replacement of foreigners with indigenous administrators went ahead more rapidly in ex-British colonies than in ex-French colonies, because Francophone Africa had, relatively speaking, substantially fewer indigenous administrators at independence than Anglophone Africa, and the Francophone countries generally have maintained closer ties with France than the Anglophone countries with Britain. Most Britishers were phased out of the bureaucracies of African countries within the first 10 years of independence, although a number of British advisers have been retained in such countries as Kenya, Malawi, Nigeria, Sierra Leone, and Zambia. In contrast, the reduction of French personnel has been rather slow in ex-French Africa, with the exception of Algeria and

---

[32]Henry L. Bretton, *Power and Politics in Africa* (Chicago: Aldine Publishing, 1973), p. 177.

[33]J. F. Maitland-Jones, *Politics in Africa: The Former British Territories* (New York: W. W. Norton, 1973), p. 99.

[34]For a detailed discussion of the civil service in Anglophone Africa, presented by an eminent African administrator, see A. L. Adu, *The Civil Service in Commonwealth Africa: Development and Transition* (London: George Allen & Unwin, 1969).

Tunisia. During the 1960s, the number of French civil servants leaving Africa was matched easily by the arrival of French technicians and agricultural experts. Rubin and Weinstein report that:

> Even though French civil servants in the states of West Africa, Equatorial Africa, and Madagascar decreased from 10,278 in 1960 to 8,423 in 1966, 1,500 more military men arrived to work as technicians, and 3,800 agricultural specialists were sent. Those Frenchmen still in administrative post rose in rank, to have control over a greater number of African civil servants than in the past.[35]

Several Francophone African governments have maintained themselves in office with the help of French troops. As late as 1980 French military units were stationed in Chad, Gabon, and Senegal.

The previous discussion indicates that the bureaucracies of many developing countries are still in a transitional phase, in the sense that the transfer of administrative responsibilities to a completely indigenous staff has not yet been completed. Some of these countries will depend on the help of foreign administrative experts for some years still.

SUMMARY

This has been a survey discussion of the executive branch of government. We described the parliamentary and presidential forms with their similarities and differences. It is important to be aware that there exist many varieties of the single and the dual executive. Some of them may differ considerably from our two models, the British parliamentary executive and the presidency in the United States.

The primary constitutional function of the executive is to implement policy, but we have noted that chief executives also participate in the policy-making process. The degree of involvement will vary from country to country, depending on the viability of legislative bodies (especially in the developing countries) and the role of party leadership, especially in the Communist countries. Generally speaking, the increasing complexities of societal and worldwide problems have contributed to the growth of the *informal* powers (as distinguished from the constitutional powers) of chief executives in recent years.

Presidents and prime ministers preside over vast bureaucracies. We compared briefly the administrations of the United States, the United Kingdom, the Federal Republic of Germany, the Union of Soviet Socialist Republics, and concluded the section with a more general discussion of the bureaucracies in developing countries. The number of political appointees at the top of the administrative hierarchy differs from country to country. Likewise, the features of the civil service may vary. One common characteristic of nearly all bureaucracies is their continual growth. Since

[35]Leslie Rubin and Brian Weinstein, *Introduction to African Politics: A Continental Approach* (New York: Praeger, 1974), p. 201.

people look increasingly to their national governments for help of one kind or another, there are no easy ways to arrest the trend of bureaucratic growth.

SELECTED READINGS

A superb analysis of political leadership is James MacGregor Burns, *Leadership* (New York: Harper & Row, 1978). Other books providing suitable discussion of the subject are James D. Barber, *The Presidential Character: Predicting Performance in the White House* (Englewood Cliffs, N.J.: Prentice-Hall, 1972); William A. Welsh, *Leaders and Elites* (New York: Holt, Rinehart and Winston, 1979); John D. Nagle, *System and Succession: The Social Bases of Political Elite Recruitment* (Austin, Tex.: University of Texas Press, 1977); Lewis J. Edinger, ed., *Political Leadership in Industrial Societies: Studies in Comparative Analysis* * (New York: John Wiley, 1967); R. Barry Farrell, ed., *Political Leadership in Eastern Europe and the Soviet Union* * (Chicago: Aldine, 1969); and Victor T. Le Vine, *Political Leadership in Africa* (Stanford, Cal.: Stanford University Press, 1967).

A number of biographies provide valuable information on an individual's rise to power and political leadership. Some of the better biographies of recent political leaders are Lewis Broad, *Winston Churchill*, 2 vols. (New York: Hawthorn, 1958); Alexander Werth, *De Gaulle: A Political Biography* (New York: Simon and Schuster, 1966); Terence Prittie, *Adenauer* (London: Stacy, 1971); and by the same author, *Willy Brandt: Portrait of a Statesman* (New York: Schocken, 1974). The best book on Stalin is Issac Deutscher, *Stalin: A Political Biography,* * 2nd ed. (New York: Oxford University Press, 1967). A well-written biography of his successor is Edward Crankshaw, *Khrushchev: A Career* * (New York: Viking, 1966).

Among the more useful discussions of the U.S. presidency are Thomas E. Cronin, *The State of the Presidency* * (Boston: Little, Brown, 1975); Richard M. Pious, *The American Presidency* (New York: Basic Books, 1979); Louis W. Koenig, *The Chief Executive,* * 3rd ed. (New York: Harcourt Brace Jovanovich, 1975); Richard E. Neustadt, *Presidential Power: The Politics of Leadership from FDR to Carter* * (New York: John Wiley, 1980); Two helpful sources on the office of the British chief executive are Humphry Berkeley, *The Power of the Prime Minister* (London: George Allen and Unwin, 1968); and Andrew Alexander and Alan Watkins, *The Making of the Prime Minister* (London: Macdonald, 1970).

The classic study of the Cabinet in the United States is Richard Fenno, *The President's Cabinet* (Cambridge: Harvard University Press, 1959). Another study that provides a detailed discussion of the federal executive is W. Lloyd Warner et al., *The American Federal Executive* (New Haven: Yale University Press, 1963). The stan-

*Available in paperback

dard work on the U.S. Civil Service is Paul P. Van Riper, *History of the United States Civil Service* (Evanston, Ill.: Row, Peterson, 1958). For a more recent survey, see Herbert Kaufman, "The Growth of the Federal Personnel System," in the American Assembly, *The Federal Government Service*, 2nd ed. (Englewood Cliffs, N.J.: Prentice-Hall, 1965).

For insights into the federal bureaucracy provided by a former chairman of the U.S. Civil Service Commission, see John W. Macy, Jr., *Public Service: The Human Side of Government* (New York: Harper & Row, 1971).

Two informative studies of public administrators in Western Europe are John A. Armstrong, *The European Administrative Elite* (Princeton, N.J.: Princeton University Press, 1973), and Mattei Dogei, ed., *The Mandarins of Western Europe: The Political Role of Top Civil Servants* (New York: John Wiley, 1975).

The classic study of the British Cabinet is John P. Mackintosh, *The British Cabinet*, 2nd ed. (London: Stevens, 1968). Useful works on the British civil service include R. A. Chapman, *The Higher Civil Service in Britain* (London: Constable, 1970); and R. K. Kelsall, *Higher Civil Servants in Britain* (London: Routledge & Kegan Paul, 1966).

There are no English-language books dealing exclusively with the West German executive. The Adenauer and Brandt biographies cited previously provide some insight. For a brief discussion of the subject, see Arnold J. Heidenheimer and Donald P. Kommers, *The Governments of Germany*,* 4th ed. (New York: Thomas Y. Crowell, 1975). Various aspects of the bureaucracy are discussed in John H. Herz, "Political Views of the West German Civil Service," in Hans Speier and W. Phillips Davison, eds., *West German Leadership and Foreign Policy* (Evanston, Ill.: Row, Peterson, 1957); and Renate Mayntz and Fritz W. Scharpf, *Policy-Making in the German Bureaucracy* (New York: Elsevier, 1975).

Chapter 7 of John S. Reshetar, Jr., *The Soviet Polity: Government and Politics in the U.S.S.R.*, 2nd ed. (New York: Harper & Row, 1978) provides some general information on the national administration in the Soviet Union. Post-Khrushchev reforms are analyzed by Jerry F. Hough in "Reforms in Government and Administration" in Alexander Dallin and Thomas B. Larson, eds., *Soviet Politics since Khrushchev** (Englewood Cliffs, N.J.: Prentice-Hall, 1968). An informative study of state and local administration is John A. Armstrong, *The Soviet Bureaucratic Elite: A Case Study of the Ukranian Apparatus* (New York: Frederick A. Praeger, 1959).

The best source on political leadership in Africa is Le Vine's book, cited previously. Another useful publication is Henry L. Bretton, *Power and Politics in Africa** (Chicago: Aldine, 1973). The most authoritative study of the civil service in Africa is A. L. Adu, *The Civil Service in Commonwealth Africa: Development and Transition* (London: George Allen and Unwin, 1969). His discussion focuses on Anglophone Africa. For an Asian comparison, see C. P. Bhambhri, *Bureaucracy and Politics in India* (Dehli, India: Vikas, 1971).

Chapter Ten

The Judicial Process: Law and the Courts

LAW AND JUSTICE

The judicial branch constitutes the third governmental output agency. It entails law, judges, and courts. These forces play a role in all political systems. It is difficult to think of the state without law because when people live in great proximity they require rules and regulations to define their respective rights and obligations as members of society.

Law generally is regarded as one of the greatest achievements of civilization. It is concerned with basic rules of conduct that reflect to some degree the concept of **justice**. These rules concern the relationships of the individual with government and with other people.

An ideal of justice frequently expressed is that government should be a government of laws and not of men. Whether this goal can be achieved is questionable, as laws are made and administered by men, but in practice this ideal generally is interpreted to mean a legal system that treats everyone equally and is not subject to change through the arbitrary acts of a dictator, or even the whim of transient majorities.

There are many kinds of law and no single definition of the term is possible, as scholars are not in agreement on the nature of law. The rules of law are based on custom or legislation and court decisions, but the language of the law is technical and not easily understood, and the proceedings through which the courts function are frequently complex.

POSITIVE LAW AND NATURAL LAW

Positive law is associated with the nineteenth-century English utilitarian philosopher, John Austin, who defined law as consisting of well-defined rules of human conduct, enforceable by appropriate sanctions of government.[1] Law, in this sense, is man-made and is essentially a relationship between ruler and ruled. This conception of law does not exhaust the meaning of that term, but it does describe the aspect of law with which political scientists are most concerned.

To many there is another type of law, one traditionally called **natural**—a law more basic than man-made law and one that is based on fundamental principles of justice. A human law that conflicts with natural law is void. The idea of natural law was developed first by the Greek and Roman Stoic philosophers. The Roman jurist Cicero (106–43 B.C.) defined the law of nature as "right reason" implanted in nature, which is the basis of measuring justice and injustice. This concept was adopted by the Christian church and incorporated into the philosophy of the great medieval thinker Thomas Aquinas. In more modern times it became part of the philosophy of John Locke, the seventeenth-century English philosopher who derived the idea of natural rights from the concept of natural law. When Thomas Jefferson spoke of "life, liberty, and the pursuit of happiness" in the Declaration of Independence, he was stating in new language Locke's ideas of natural rights.[2]

CIVIL AND CRIMINAL LAW

Civil law, in its most widely used sense, is concerned with the relations between individuals and their legal rights. A typical civil suit would be for breach of contract, a divorce action, or tort action (an injury to one's person or property) such as a suit growing out of an automobile accident. Usually civil actions are between private individuals, but it is possible for the government to be party to a civil suit. For example, the U. S. government might sue a corporation for breach of contract.

All crimes are offenses against society, and the state as the representative of society charges the individual or corporation with a violation of law. A penalty for such violation usually is provided by statute. Crimes may be serious, such as murder or arson, or petty, such as violation of a traffic law. Punishment ranges from death or imprisonment to a fine.

INTERNATIONAL LAW

International law consists of a body of rules and principles regulating the behavior of countries, international organizations like the United Nations, and the rights and obligations of individuals as they are affected by differences in the legislation of different states. International law lacks the effective sanctions of the governments of national states, as international organizations possess limited or no enforcement power.[3]

---

[1]See John Austin, *Lectures on Jurisprudence*, vol. 1, 3rd ed. (London: J. Murray, 1869), pp. 182–183.

[2]See George H. Sabine and Thomas L. Thorson, *A History of Political Theory*, 4th ed. (Hinsdale, Ill.: Dryden Press, 1973), Chapters 9, 14, and 27.

[3]See J. L. Brierly, *The Law of Nations*, 6th ed., rev. by Sir Humphrey Waldock, (New York: Oxford University Press, 1963) for a good, brief introduction to international law. The subject is discussed in more detail in Chapter 14.

CONSTITUTIONAL, ADMINISTRATIVE, AND STATUTORY LAW

A constitution is the fundamental law of a country. It may be unwritten in the sense that it is not limited to a single document. The British constitution, for example, consists of historic documents such as the Great Charter of 1215, which the English barons forced King John to sign at Runnymede; acts of Parliament of extraordinary importance such as the Great Reform Act of 1833, which enfranchised much of the middle class; important judicial decisions; and custom and tradition. Even the United States, with its written Constitution, has a supplementary "unwritten Constitution" growing out of judicial decisions, important acts of Congress and the president, and custom and tradition. American political parties, for example, had their origin in custom and tradition and are not part of the written Constitution.

Constitutional law consists of interpretations of a nation's constitution by the courts. In the United States, for example, the Supreme Court may decide the meaning of congressional power over interstate commerce.

Somewhat similar to constitutional law is **administrative law**, which is concerned with the legal accountability of government officials in carrying out government policy as expressed in statutes. This branch of law also consists of the rules and regulations written by bureaucrats after Congress delegates this authority to them. In the United States, for example, Congress has delegated to administrators extensive rule-making authority. The federal courts may review the rules and regulations of the Federal Trade Commission concerning "unfair and deceptive" trade practices to determine whether the administrators have acted within the scope of the law.

Legislatures inevitably must state the rules embodied in statutes in general terms, for they cannot anticipate all the problems that will arise over specific provisions. **Statutory law** is the interpretation Courts give to statutes, which determines their meaning. An important standard the courts employ in this respect is "legislative intent."

LAW AS SOCIAL ENGINEERING

Some social scientists, especially sociologists, believe law to be not primarily a body of rules but a dynamic process involving all aspects of state action. This school of thought stresses the need to study law in action as well as law in the books. It regards as a central myth the belief that the norms or principles of the written law represent the actual operation of the legal order. A corollary to this myth is the idea that the state as represented by the courts and the police is a neutral framework in which the struggle of interest groups takes place.

This philosophy is similar in some respects to the Marxist concept of law. It believes that control of the state itself is the principle goal in the constant conflicts of groups in society. The legal order is considered nothing more than a self-serving system that is not impartial, as can be seen in different treatment of blacks and whites.

This school of thought regards social engineering as the means by which a good society can be achieved. Conscious control over the legal system will be a type of social engineering by which social processes can be controlled to some extent; however it is admitted that social changes to improve society are difficult to achieve, due to deeply engrained habits, resistance of entrenched interests, and other factors.[4]

ANGLO-AMERICAN LAW

THE COMMON LAW

The basis for the legal system of Great Britain, the United States, and most of the English-speaking countries is the **common law**. The common law is judge-made law. Its roots go back to the twelfth century in England when the king sent itinerant justices throughout the realm to settle local disputes on the basis of general customs. Gradually a body of legal precedents was developed from the various decisions of the royal judges.

In hearing disputes, the judges consider previously decided cases. In determining the relevance of a previous decision, they reason by analogy to reach a decision. They determine whether an earlier case of a similar nature is sufficiently comparable to the case at hand to constitute a binding precedent. If so, it becomes the basis for deciding the case. This process of following earlier precedents is known as *stare decisis*. On the other hand, judges may distinguish the controversies before them from an earlier precedent. This is no simple, mechanical process, however, as no two cases are exactly alike and judges ordinarily have considerable latitude in reaching their decisions. **Stare decisis** leads to both stability and flexibility in the law. It also permits judges to modify old law to meet new social conditions. Regulations of public utilities, for example, grew out of old common-law doctrines regulating innkeepers.

The common law was carried to English colonies in various parts of the world. When many of these countries became independent, they continued to apply the common law. In the United States, the states generally apply the common law to varying degrees but, as in Great Britain, it has been modified considerably by statute. Common-law marriages, for example, are not usually recognized by statute.

EQUITY

Another source of Anglo-American law is **equity**, which developed because the early common law courts did not always insure justice. These courts, for example, usually allowed only monetary damages as a remedy in most civil cases. Litigants who could not get justice in the regular courts appealed to the chancellor, the king's legal adviser, who frequently provided relief on the basis of general principles of jus-

---

[4]See William J. Chambless and Robert B. Seidman, *Law, Order, and Power* (Reading, Mass.: Addison-Wesley, 1971) for a thorough discussion of law as social engineering, especially Chapters 1 and 24.

tice. Eventually, a complementary system of law was developed by a new court known as a Court of Chancery. The primary difference between the justice administered by the two systems of law was in the remedy. A Court of Equity or Chancery would issue, for example, an injunction to prevent irreparable harm to property. Under the common law a person whose property rights were threatened could take no action until the injury occurred, in which case he could sue for damages. An injunction, on the other hand, prohibits a person or persons in general from committing acts that would result in injury to the property. For violations of an injunction, the judge may summarily punish by fine or even imprisonment in some instances. Injunctions frequently have been used in labor disputes. Another difference between common law and equity is that juries are not used in equity cases.

Equity, like the common law, was carried overseas into new English-speaking settlements, but in England and most of the American states today the same courts administer both common law and equity. The American federal courts have jurisdiction in all cases in law and equity involving the Constitution, laws, and treaties.

THE JUDICIAL SYSTEM IN GREAT BRITAIN

The British court system (see Figure 10–1) is headed by a lord chancellor, who is a member of the cabinet. He presides over the House of Lords and advises on all judicial appointments. The highest court is the House of Lords, but only a small group of appointed law lords, headed by the lord chancellor, act as a court in the name of the

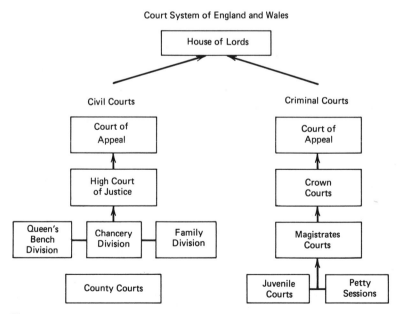

Figure 10-1.   The Court System of England and Wales.

House of Lords. The British courts are known for the outstanding legal qualifications of their judges.

The legal profession in Great Britain is divided into two categories—**solicitors** and **barristers**. The former are office lawyers who handle legal problems before the trial stage. Unlike barristers, solicitors are not required to have university training. They become members of the Law Society by passing special examinations. The barristers, who have greater prestige, are exclusively trial lawyers who are trained in one of the four famous Inns of Court, which are both law schools and guild associations and which enforce very high standards on their members. Judges are chosen from the more outstanding barristers.[5]

Unlike the United States, England maintains a separate system of civil and criminal courts except at the highest level, the House of Lords, which serves as an appellate court hearing cases on appeal from lower courts. The appellate jurisdiction of the House of Lords is limited to civil and criminal cases involving important points of law.

The highest civil court is the Court of Appeal, which hears appeals from the High Court of Justice and County Courts. There are three divisions of the High Court of Justice, as shown in Figure 10–1.

The highest criminal court is the Court of Criminal Appeal. The trial courts for all criminal cases except those of a petty nature are a group of courts known as the Crown Courts. At the bottom of the judicial structure are the Magistrate Courts, for juvenile offenses and minor crimes.

THE AMERICAN JUDICIAL SYSTEM

Because the American governmental system is federal in nature, this country possesses a dual court system of federal and state courts (see Figure 10–2). Although there are variations among the state court systems, typically the lowest courts are police magistrates or **justices of the peace**. Usually there are general trial courts based on a county or combination of counties, which are courts of general jurisdiction. As such they hear a variety of cases. These courts also hear appeals from police magistrates and justices of the peace. Above the general trial courts, appellate courts are common. Usually each appellate court hears appeals from general trial courts within its district. At the top, every state has a court of appeals with statewide jurisdiction, usually called the supreme court.

Very few cases originate in the U. S. Supreme Court, which is primarily a court of appeals. The two primary procedures for reaching the U.S. Supreme Court for review are appeal and the writ of **Certiorari**. Examples of the right of appeal are where a lower federal court or a state court hold an act of Congress unconstitutional.

---

[5]See William Martin Geldart et al., *Elements of English Law* (London: Oxford University Press, 1975) for an excellent introduction to English law.

The Judicial Process: Law and the Courts

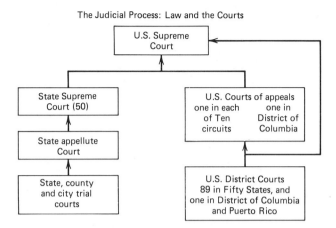

United States Court System
[with special and Legislative Courts omitted]

Figure 10-2. The United States Court System (with special and legislative courts omitted).

The writ of Certiorari is used more frequently, and the issuance of the writ is up to the discretion of the court. Technically, Certiorari is a writ issued by a higher court, such as the U.S. Supreme Court, calling up the record of a lower court for review. The writ is limited to cases of constitutional importance involving actions of government officials, such as the denial of a fair trial or the denial of a constitutional right such as trial by jury.

State courts are not inferior to federal courts, despite a common opinion to the contrary. State courts have exclusive jurisdiction of all cases not within the constitutional grant of power to the national government. Only in certain limited areas may the U.S. Supreme Court review state court decisions.

State judges are chosen by a variety of methods.[6] Until recently, election for a term of years, commonly on a party basis, was the prevailing method. In five states the legislature selects judges with considerable gubernatorial and party influence. In a few states the Governor appoints judges.

Election of state judges has been subject to considerable criticism on the ground that the quality of the state judiciary has suffered. The most frequent criticism is directed at police magistrates and justices of the peace, who frequently are nonprofessionals with little knowledge of the law. Municipal-court judges or other local judges frequently are indebted to a local political machine. State supreme court

[6]See Henry Robert Glick and Kenneth N. Vines, *State Court Systems*, Foundations of State and Local Government series, Wallace Sayre, ed. (Englewood Cliffs, N.J.: Prentice-Hall, 1973), pp. 39–47, for a good discussion of methods of electing judges.

judges rarely are appointed to the U.S. Supreme Court. Notable exceptions were Oliver Wendell Holmes and Benjamin N. Cardozo, both of whom were not only distinguished jurists but also well known as philosophers of the law.

A new trend toward a mixed elective-appointive system divorced from parties or politics began in Missouri and California in the 1930s. In these states, judges go before the voters at the end of their terms or after a fixed number of years to determine whether or not they should be retained in office for another term. The essence of this plan is that judicial vacancies are filled by the governor from a list of nominees submitted by a nonpartisan commission.[7]

Today, 25 states have adopted some variation of the Missouri and California plans. In these states there are nonpartisan elections and little party influence in the selection of judges.

The only court required by the Constitution is the U.S. Supreme Court. Since 1789, however, Congress has provided for a system of lower federal courts. Today, there are 87 district courts within the 50 states and territories. While each state has at least 1 district court with at least 1 judge, some districts have more than 20 judges and many states have more than 1 district court. These are courts of general jurisdiction, where most lawsuits originate.

Above the district courts are the 11 judicial circuits, each one of which has a court of appeals. Most cases never get beyond the court of appeals. The minority of cases that reach the U.S. Supreme Court usually do so through the writ of certiorari, which may be granted at the discretion of at least 4 judges of the U.S. Supreme Court from the highest state court if a federal question is raised.

All federal judges are appointed by the President, subject to confirmation by the Senate. Most judicial appointments are of the same political party as the President. U.S. Supreme Court appointees are usually men, who reflect the same philosophy of government as the president, even when they are chosen from the opposite party. Other judicial appointments, especially district court judges, are subject to "Senatorial courtesy." This means that the president, in filling appointments for judicial vacancies, must consult with the state's senator or senators if they are of his own party. "Senatorial courtesy" is a custom that permits a senator of the President's party to block the confirmation of an objectionable appointee from his own state. In effect, the President does not have a free hand. Where there is no senator from the President's party in a given state, his range of choice is greater.

ANGLO-AMERICAN CIVIL AND CRIMINAL PROCEDURE

Courts generally will take jurisdiction over a civil question only if there is a real controversy of a legal nature between two or more parties and not simply an abstract question of law to be decided. Thus, in a civil case a typical justiciable issue would

---

[7]See Charles Aiken A new method of selecting judges in California, *American Political Science Review*, 29, June 1935, 412–414; and Thomas E. McDonald, Missouri's ideal judicial selection law. *Journal of American Judicial Society*, 24, April 1947, pp. 194–199.

be a suit by party *A* against party *B*, alleging that *A* was injured by *B* who, while negligently driving his automobile, ran into *A*, who was crossing the street. *A's* attorney would file a complaint alleging the above facts. *B* would respond with an answer. If *B* in his answer, denied any negligence, the issue before the court would be whether *A's* injury was due to *B's* negligence.

Criminal procedure begins with the law-enforcement process. Six steps are involved in this process: arrest of law violators, preliminary hearing, preferring of charges, **arraignment**, trial, and punishment of convicted persons.

On the local level law enforcement is primarily the function of the police or, in rural areas, the sheriff. Persons arrested for violating the law are brought before a minor magistrate for a preliminary hearing, the purpose of which is to decide whether the evidence against the accused is sufficient to hold him or her for action by the prosecutor or **grand jury**. If the accused is held for further action, the magistrate would set bail unless the offense is a nonbailable crime punishable by death. Traditionally, the next step is action by the grand jury, a body of 5 to 23 persons summoned by the prosecutor to determine whether the evidence against the accused justifies returning an **indictment**, a simple statement describing the essential ingredients of the crime. The local prosecutor is usually an elected county official, whereas in the federal courts there is a district attorney, appointed by the President with the consent of the Senate, for each district court.

In Great Britain there is no official comparable to either the United States federal or state district attorney. There is a director of public prosecutions, who may direct the prosecution in such serious criminal cases as murder. In England and Wales the police initiate and conduct most prosecutions. This arrangement is possible only because of the lower crime rate in Great Britain.

Great Britain also has abolished use of the grand jury. Some American states virtually have discontinued use of the grand jury. A majority of our states permits some use of an alternative procedure known as prosecution by information for lesser crimes. This differs from the traditional indictment only in that it is filed by the prosecutor without a grand jury. After the charges are filed, the accused is arraigned before the trial court where a plea of "guilty" or "not guilty" is entered.

The Anglo-American court system is based on the **adversary system**. Each side in a law suit, whether civil or criminal, presents evidence to support its case. The trial jury, if one is used, is traditionally a body of 12 competent citizens who must render a unanimous verdict on the basis of the facts and the law. Today, in some states in civil cases and trials for lesser crimes have relaxed the unanimity rule and provided for juries of less than 12 members. It is assumed that the jury can arrive at the truth from the testimony presented by each side. The role of the judge is essentially that of an impartial referee, who is responsible for observance of the rules of evidence and procedural safeguards. If there is no jury, the judge performs the function of the jury. In a criminal action the state must prove its case beyond a reasonable doubt, whereas in a civil case the plaintiff, the party who institutes the suit, need only present a preponderance of the evidence in his behalf.

(Editorial Cartoon by Paul Conrad©Los Angeles Times, Reprinted with permission.)

Equal Justice?

If a verdict of guilty has been returned by the trial jury in a criminal case, the court pronounces the sentence.

THE CIVIL LAW OF EUROPE

In countries of Western Europe the law is based on Roman law and generally tends to be codified in contrast to common law. Its origins go back to the code prepared for the Roman Emperior Justinian in 533 A.D. During the Middle Ages the Roman Catholic church based its canon law on Roman law. In the French and Italian universities of the twelfth and thirteenth centuries, Roman law was rediscovered. It had great appeal to the educated and rising mercantile classes and to many European monarchs who in particular liked its authoritarian features. In more modern times the law codes of Napolean I have been of great importance. They have influenced not only the legal systems of European countries and Latin America, but the Canadian province of Quebec and the state of Louisiana as well.

The **codes** assume that the fundamentals of the nation's law can be stated in comprehensive statutes. The codes, of course, require interpretation and elaboration. This task is more the responsibility of law teachers than of the judges. Typical subjects of a code are civil and criminal procedures, property, commercial law, and the like.

The differences between code and common law should not be overstated. The code law is more the work of the legislature than the courts. Although the judges tend to see the law as written reason in code law countries, common-law systems also rely on statutes and have legal commentaries and some codification, but to a lesser degree. Even in interpreting a statute, Anglo-American judges refer to prior relevant decisions. Under the code law judges are supposed to follow the code alone.

Another difference between the two systems of law is found in criminal procedure.[8] In a typical code-law country such as France the first step in a criminal case is a preliminary examination of the accused and chief witnesses by an investigating judge, who determines whether the accused should be tried formally. The trial itself repeats this "inquisitorial" procedure to get at the truth. The role of the judge is that of an active participant in the procedure and there is little emphasis on procedural safeguards for the defendant. The French system however, gives the judge complete control of the trial and permits him and the prosecutor to develop the case against the accused on the basis of the *dossier* resulting from the preliminary examination.

By the time a suspect has undergone this thorough preliminary examination and is standing trial, the general assumption is that he is probably guilty. This is unlike the Anglo-American law, which, through its many safeguards for the defendant, seeks to minimize the possibility of an innocent person being found guilty. French code law lays more stress on preventing a guilty person from escaping punishment.

In France, the jury system plays only a minor role. There is nothing comparable to the grand jury, and the trial jury is used only in cases of serious crimes tried by the local trial courts. When used, the jury consists of nine local citizens who sit with one or more judges. No unanimity is required. In France, the jury frequently is regarded as an instrument for confusing the issues in a case.[9]

---

[8]See Henry J. Abraham, *The Judicial Process*, 3rd ed. (New York: Oxford University Press, 1975), pp. 97–102, for a comparison of the Anglo-American adversary system with the accusatorial practice of code countries.

[9]Henry J. Abraham, *op. cit.*, pp. 110–114.

The French legal system seeks to provide justice economically and to make it readily available to the French people. Although the French have a separate system of civil and criminal courts, the separation is in many respects more apparent than real. First, the two highest courts, the Court of Cassation (supreme court of appeal) and the Appeal Court, review both civil and criminal cases. Secondly, civil and criminal courts on the lower level have the same judges and use the same buildings (see Figure 10–3).

The Court of Cassation limits its jurisdiction to interpretations of law in civil and criminal cases.

The French Court system was streamlined under President Charles DeGaulle in 1958. The highest civil courts are the 172 Courts of **Grand Instance**, which have unlimited civil jurisdiction and appellate jurisdiction over the Courts of First Instance, which are limited to minor civil cases. The Assize Courts have jurisdiction over most serious crimes, while the Criminal Courts decide lesser offenses. For minor offenses there are local Police Courts. Certain special courts are not shown in Figure 10–3.

An important feature of the French judicial system, as well as those of most continental European democracies, is that judges and prosecutors are part of the same public service. Prosecutors are under the Ministry of Justice, but judges have seniority of tenure and are not subject to government discipline by the ministry. Another difference is that in France an individual decides at the beginning of his or her career whether to become a lawyer or a member of the judiciary.

Another important feature of French law is the separate system of administrative law, which utilizes special administrative courts. There are no comparable courts in England and the United States. These tribunals hear complaints and law suits against the state itself and afford the citizen protection against arbitrary decisions of

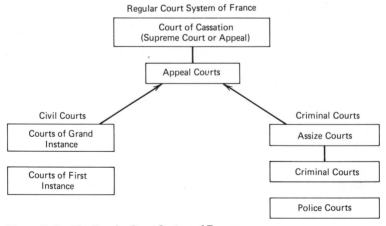

Figure 10–3.   The Regular Court System of France.

government officials. The function of the administrative courts is the annulment of rulings where officials have exceeded their power. The highest administrative court is the Council of State, which has an excellent reputation both in France and abroad. The Council frequently has awarded generous damages to individuals injured by the government. It also has protected civil servants wrongfully dismissed by the government.

In Anglo-American countries the state may not be sued without its consent for the actions of government employees committed in the discharge of their duties. In the United States and Great Britain the public official personally is charged with dereliction, not the state, and is sued in the regular courts. Other code-law countries follow the French practice in having a separate system of administrative law.

COMMUNIST LAW AND LEGAL SYSTEMS

THE MARXIST CONCEPTION OF LAW

The Marxist, Communist, conception of law is fundamentally different from that of Western democratic states. The latter assume that law is binding upon the governors and governed alike and that individuals should be guaranteed certain rights that protect them against state action.

Marx and Engels assumed that law is a tool of the state and that the state in turn is the instrument of the ruling class. Judges in capitalistic states, according to Marx, because of their training and background, would favor the interests of property in their decisions. He felt that even guarantees of equality before the law were of little value to the poor because they could not afford the best lawyers and the high cost of legal proceedings.

In his views of a Communist state, Marx was utopian. He believed that coercion ultimately would become unnecessary and the power of public opinion would be sufficient to maintain an orderly and peaceful society. Marx, however, recognized that there would be a short period of transition between the Communist revolution and the attainment of this ideal state. During this interim period it would be necessary to revise bourgeois law so that it no longer would protect property rights against justice for the masses. The selection of judges sympathetic to communism also would be necessary.

THE SOVIET CONCEPTION OF LAW

Needless to say, the Soviet Union, although it came into existence in 1917, has not attained the condition of pure communism where law is unnecessary. In fact, law is very much a part of the Soviet system; however, Soviet law assumes that, as the Soviet state is the product of the type of revolution Marx and Lenin predicted, it embraces all the interests of its citizens. Thus, according to this assumption, there can be no conflict between the interests of the state and the rights of the individual. Because the Soviet Union is a state presumably based on the welfare of the proletariat, or working class, its law and court decisions always reflect the interests of the working class in theory.

In practice, law plays a greater role in the Soviet system than in Western democratic states because all spheres of life are subject to government control. For example, there are commercial courts that have jurisidiction over state enterprises and organizations that buy or sell from each other.

Whenever the interests of the regime are affected, law is simply an instrument of state policy. This explains the lack of procedural safeguards in criminal procedure

"Guilty Of Revolutionary Activities! Take Him Away"

(From The Herblock Gallery, Simon & Schuster, 1968.)

and the fact that the bill of rights in the Soviet Constitution of 1977 is a mere declaration of intention, of no legal significance and not enforceable in the courts. The law codes aver that the state is supreme over the individual and that the conduct of a criminal trial reflects this fact. The defense attorney, who is a state employee, is chosen from a lawyers' collegium that is subsidized by the state. Neither the defense attorney nor the defendent is shown the state evidence until the day before the trial. The judge, as in countries with code law, questions the defendant and witnesses. Furthermore, the defendent must prove his innocence, and cases may be reopened by a higher court after acquittal in a trial court.

The structure of the Soviet courts is in many respects like that of Western European countries (see Figure 10–4). At the bottom of the regular court system are regional courts, with a supreme court in each of the union republics. At the top of the pyramid is a supreme court of the union, which is primarily an appellate court. There are also peoples' courts, which are quite informal. These are organized in neighborhoods and places of work and are administered by nonprofessionals. Minor cases, such as drunkenness and petty theft, are tried in these courts, which consist of one lay judge and two lay assessors. Their jurisdiction is limited to the simplest of disputes. Judges are elected, but candidates always are politically reliable.

The formal court structure of the Soviet Union reflects the theoretical federalism of that nation. The Supreme Court of the USSR has jurisdiction over serious political crimes and disputes between republics, as well as limited appellate jurisdiction. Judges and lay assessors of the courts are chosen by the Soviets (legislative bodies) of their respective areas, except in the Peoples' Courts, in which they are popularly elected. Courts outside of the regular system are not shown in Figure 10–4.

During the Khrushchev era (1953-1964) the government issued new and less harsh rules of both civil and criminal law. For example, in criminal law, punishment by analogy was abolished. Under this doctrine, in force since the revolution, an act that was not a crime but similar to a criminal act, could be made punishable as a

Structure of the Courts of the Soviet Union

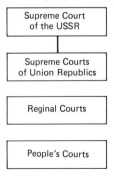

Figure 10–4.

crime by a judge. Nevertheless, Soviet criminal law is still harsher than that of Western democratic states. Political crimes usually are still tried in military courts, which exist in every military district. The courts are conducted in secret. Civilians convicted for treason, espionage, and assassination of a public official abroad, to name some of the more serious crimes, can be sentenced to death.

An important post in the Soviet legal system is that of the **Procurator General of the Soviet Union**. There are also procurators in each of the republics and districts as well. The procurator's duties extend to the organization of the courts and execution of the rules of law in use, as well as the traditional duties as prosecutor for the state. The Procurator General of the Soviet Union is one of the most important officials in the country and is always a high-ranking member of the Communist Party.[10]

LAW IN DEVELOPING COUNTRIES

INFLUENCE OF WESTERN LEGAL SYSTEMS

The term "developing states" is used to refer to those nations that differ from modern Western societies in a number of ways, including a low rate of literacy, low per capita income, a basically rural economy, and little technological development. Some of these countries have primitive economies with no food reserves, a limited cultural and artistic life, and limited political development. The newly independent nations of Africa and Asia are typical of this Third World, but the older political societies of Latin America also share many of the characteristics of developing nations.

Western legal systems generally were introduced in the developing states of Africa and Asia prior to independence, but the impact of Western law was negligible, since colonial rulers generally permitted much of customary law and practice to remain in force on the village level. One of the important problems facing the newly independent governments has been to reconcile Western legal standards with existing customary practices.

The new governments of the developing nations frequently have looked upon Western law as an obstacle to desirable new programs. This often has resulted in disregarding established legal procedures. In some instances ruling ethnic or racial groups have used established law to dominate minorities. The result has been that the role of law continues to be in a state of flux.

AFRICAN LAW

A brief survey of the judiciary in a few of the new African countries will illustrate some of the problems of these countries. Many changes have been made in the

---

[10]For excellent studies of Soviet law see the following: George Feifer, *Justice in Moscow* (New York: Dell Publishing, 1964); Eugene Karneuba, The Soviet view of law, *Problems of Communism*, March–April 1965, 8–16; John A. Hazard, "Soviet Law and Justice," in John W. Strong, ed., *The Soviet Union under Brezhnev and Kosygin* (New York: Van Nostrand, 1971); Alfred C. Meyer, *The Soviet Political System: An Interpretation*, (New York: Random House, 1965), pp. 300–355.

legal systems imposed by former colonial rulers, because the African leaders believed the inherited system did not reflect contemporary needs and aspirations. Customary law based on tradition also has been modified in many ways. For example, in some African countries, the giving of gifts at a time of marriage or a feast at baptism is limited, to minimize the impoverishment of African families, and marriage has been secularized and arranged marriage forbidden.

As to the new legal codes, Marxist influence appears to be minimal. The French governmental structure is retained in the former French colonies. Although the old courts administering customary laws are abolished, specialists in the old law are advisers in the new courts.[11]

LATIN AMERICAN LAW

The civil law of Spain and Portugal was carried over to the New World and became firmly established. Since countries achieved independence the civil law of other European countries has had considerable influence, but the influence of the United States has not been absent. The writ of habeas corpus, for example, has had widespread adoption in Latin America.[12] Latin American countries also have adopted many laws that are responses to their own local problems. Examples are the mining codes of Peru and Mexico's agrarian reform laws.[13]

Judicial procedure in Latin America is quite unlike that of the United States and Great Britain. In Argentina procedures are fairly typical of Latin America. A trial of a civil action is usually a private hearing in which a secretary presides over the proceedings and keeps a detailed record of everything that takes place. The judge usually does not bother to attend the hearing. Instead, he bases his decision on the written record.

Argentine criminal procedure offers the defendant fewer safeguards than Anglo-American practices. A person arrested and charged with a criminal offense is brought before a judge who combines the functions of a committing magistrate and grand jury. He decides whether the accused will be held for trial and under what circumstances, if any, he will be released on bail. Pending trial, the accused may be held incommunicado for a number of days. During this time the police attempt to obtain criminal evidence. When the trial takes place, it is held without a jury and usually behind closed doors. The trial judge frequently is absent during part of the proceedings. Sometimes he bases his judgment to a large extent on written evidence prepared by a secretary. It is said that justice often depends on the accuracy of a secretary's notes. Another variation from Anglo-American practices is that the public prosecutor, as well as the accused, may appeal the verdict. This makes it

[11]See John H. Hazard, Law and social change in Marxist Africa. *American Behavioral Scientist*, 13:4, 1970, pp. 575–584.

[12]In the United States, a person who claims to have been imprisoned unjustly may apply to a federal court for a writ of **habeas corpus**. If the court finds that the imprisonment is contrary to some provision of the Constitution or laws of the United States, the writ will be issued and the person released.

[13]Alexander T. Edelmann, *Latin American Government and Politics*, rev. ed. (Homewood, Ill.: The Dorsey Press, 1969), p. 465 ff.

possible for a person found innocent in a lower court to be adjudged guilty in a court of appeals.[14]

JUDICIAL INDEPENDENCE

In the newly independent African countries, judges generally are appointed by the executive, often without requiring approval by the legislature. Judges usually serve for life, subject to removal from office for high crimes and misdemeanors.

Sometimes removal power is vested in the president, as in Ghana, where, under former President Nkrumah, the constitution provided that the President could remove the chief justice at will and judges of the lower court if two-thirds of the assembly concurred. Since a one-party system prevailed in Ghana, Nkrumah was able to get the necessary legislative majority to remove three supreme-court justices after the court failed to convict three persons of plotting to overthrow the President. A special court was then selected to retry the case. The defendants were convicted and sentenced to death. This action of Nkrumah's led the International Jurists Commission to condemn him for violating the independence of the judiciary. Other African countries have created special courts to try cases involving threats against the government.

Since most African countries do not have judicial review, their Parliaments can override court decisions under the doctrine of legislative supremacy. This has been done on several occasions and usually does not involve any great difficulties, for government majorities are typically large. Even where judicial review formally exists, as in Tanzania and Nigeria, judicial decisions have been overruled.[15]

It would be incorrect to assume from the preceding illustrations that the judiciary always lacks independence in developing countries. The courts of many countries in southeast Asia frequently have shown a high degree of independence. In Burma, for example, the government, believing the existence of the state was threatened, invoked a preventive detention act in the 1960s. The higher courts, however, frequently released detained persons because of insufficient grounds for holding them. The Philippine supreme court, during the presidential campaign of 1965, unanimously upheld an injunction preventing the national board of censors from banning a movie that portrayed the opposition candidate for president, Ferdinand Marcos, as a man of destiny. The judges, several of whom had been appointed by the incumbent, President Macopagal, resisted strong pressures to support the government, which wished to prevent showing of the movie.[16]

Clearly, relatively independent courts can and do exist in developing countries. The commonly accepted view that internal political pressures undermine judicial independence, as exemplified in Ghana and other countries, requires reservations.

[14]Alexander T. Edelmann, *op. cit.*, pp. 480–482.

[15]Dorothy Dodge, *African Politics in Perspective* (Toronto: D. Van Nostrand, 1968), pp. 136–138.

[16]See Theodore L. Becker, *Comparative Judicial Politics: The Political Functioning of Courts* (Chicago: Rand McNally, 1970), pp. 159–160.

JUDICIAL REVIEW

Judicial review is the process by which courts determine whether the legislative and executive branches, especially the former, have exceeded their power. Judicial review is most likely to exist in a federal system such as the United States and in countries with written constitutions. In a federal system, with power divided between the central government and the member states, the courts are the logical branch of government to determine the power boundaries between the two levels of government.

Although judicial review exists in a number of countries, its scope is broadest in the United States. In nations where judicial review exists, the judiciary usually plays a more significant role in the governmental process than in countries where the courts do not exercise this power. In the United States both federal and state courts have held federal and state laws invalid under the federal Constitution. The United States Supreme Court has the last word on the constitutionality of a federal or state law. Judicial review is important not only because of its use, but also because of the threat of the judicial veto. Congress and the president, in making policy, always must consider the possible unconstitutionality of their acts.[17]

Judicial review is not granted specifically in the Constitution, but it has been exercised since 1803 with respect to acts of Congress.[18] Many more state laws have been held unconstitutional, however, than acts of Congress or the president. Since 1789, about 80 congressional laws have been held unconstitutional. The instances where executive acts have been held beyond the power of the president are relatively few. One of the more recent examples occurred in 1952, during the Korean War, when the Supreme Court held that President Truman did not have authority to seize the steel industry to avert a strike.[19] Although originally the subject of controversy, judicial review generally is accepted today.

After **Marbury versus Madison**, no act of Congress was held unconstitutional until 1857, more than 50 years later. It was in the period from about 1890 to 1937 that the Supreme Court acquired the reputation of being a "super legislature" by striking down many federal and state laws. Since the Supreme Court during this period generally reflected conservative economic and political values, many of the laws held unconstitutional were regulations of property rights. Following the "constitutional crisis" of 1937, provoked by President Franklin D. Roosevelt's unsuccessful attempt to enlarge the Supreme Court's membership to make the liberal minority of judges a majority, the Supreme Court generally has deferred to the judgment of Congress and the states with reference to laws regulating property rights.

---

[17]See Loren P. Beth, *Politics, the Constitution, and the Supreme Court* (Evanston, Ill.: Row Peterson, 1962), pp. 58–61, for a succinct discussion of judicial review.

[18]*Marbury versus Madison*, 1 Cranch 137 (1803). The opinions of the Supreme Court are now published by the U.S. government. Until 1875 the reports were cited according to the name of the reporter, in this instance Cranch. The first number refers to the volume and the second to the page.

[19]*Youngstown Sheet and Tube Co.* versus *Sawyer*, 343 U.S. 579 (1952).

This shift in the Court's position is explainable in that two of the "middle-of-the-road" judges joined the liberal minority after 1937 to constitute a new majority and in the replacement of the conservative members of the Court following their retirement or death. Since the mid 1950s the Court has used judicial review actively to promote civil rights. This trend is discussed later, in the sections on "Civil Liberties" and "The Judicial American Process."

Judicial review exists in some European countries, but in no country has it existed as long as in the United States, nor does the judiciary in these countries play a role comparable to the United States courts.

In France, under the Fifth Republic, the constitutional council is a body consisting of all ex-presidents of France and nine other appointed individuals. The council, which is not part of the regular judicial system, may hold unconstitutional certain laws of Parliament if they are referred to it by the president of the republic, the premier, or the presidents of both Houses of Parliament. This is very limited judicial review, for no individual can challenge the constitutionality of a law. The weakness of the council is illustrated by its refusal to rule on President de Gaulle's referendum on direct election of the president of France in 1962, despite the fact that the French constitution did not authorize such action.[20]

West Germany has a special constitutional court, which may decide the validity of any federal or land (state) law and which protects the fundamental rights of citizens. This court has assumed a role of importance in the West German governmental system. Among its important decisions were two that declared both the Communist Party and neo-Nazi party to be unconstitutional as organizations detrimental to a democratic state.[21]

The postwar Japanese constitution, as a result of the American occupation and influence, allows the review of all laws, ordinances, administrative regulations, and official acts of government. The final authority rests with the Japanese Supreme Court. In practice, however, the Japanese court has not exercised this power to any great extent.[22]

Judicial review is also common in Latin America, due to the influence of Anglo-American law. Mexico has a unique form of judicial review in the form of the writ of *amparo*, which permits a citizen to apply to a federal court for redress if a law or act of a government official impairs any right guaranteed by the constitution of Mexico. This writ, however, is less than real judicial review, since the judges do not grant relief to each petitioner who files a complaint.[23]

[20]Henry J. Abraham, *op. cit.,* pp. 296–299.

[21]*Ibid.,* pp. 311–312.

[22]See Warren M. Tsuneishi, *Japanese Political Style* (New York: Harper & Row, 1966), Chapter 10. See also *Law in Japan: The Legal Order in a Changing Society*, ed. by A. T. Van Hebren (Cambridge: Harvard University Press, 1963).

[23]See Alexander T. Edelmann, *op. cit.,* pp. 483–484.

JUDICIAL INTERPRETATION OF STATUTES

Interpretation of statutes by the courts, as well as judicial review, is important in analyzing the role of the courts in making national policy. In the United States, the country where judicial review is most important, statutory interpretation and development of doctrines growing out of the common law substantially enhance the power of the courts. Many acts of Congress are complex and their meaning is not always clear. Ultimately, a federal statute means what the U.S. Supreme Court says it means.

For example, Congress in 1940 enacted the **Smith Act**, which made teaching and advocacy of the overthrow of the government by force a criminal offense. What is the meaning of this provision? It presumably would not prevent the teaching of the revolutionary doctrines of Marx and Lenin in a college class; but on the other hand, is there a distinction between abstract advocacy of violent overthrow of the government and incitement to violence now or as soon as practical? In **Yates versus U.S. (1957)**, Justice Harlan, speaking for the U.S. Supreme Court, gave the Smith Act a narrow interpretation by holding that to convict under the act the government would have to prove advocacy of violent action now or in the future. Mere belief in the desirability of violent overthrow of the government as an abstract doctrine is not enough to convict.[24]

What is true of the United States also would be true in other countries where the courts play an important role in judicial interpretation.

CIVIL LIBERTIES

The courts frequently play a leading role in the preservation of **civil liberties**. The U.S. Supreme Court, under Chief Justice Warren (1953–1969), lent support to the "civil rights revolution" through its interpretation of the "equal protection" clause of the Fourteenth Amendment as a prohibition of segregation laws.

In general, the U.S. Supreme Court has furthered the cause of civil liberties by **"nationalizing civil rights."** Since the 1920s, the Court has held that the First Amendment freedoms (speech, press, assembly, and religion) are incorporated into the "due process clause" of the Fourteenth Amendment, which restricts the states from abridging the rights of citizens. In recent years more and more of the **Bill of Rights** has been incorporated into the Fourteenth Amendment by judicial interpretation. Since the Bill of Rights restricts Congress, the result of the "nationalizing of civil rights" has been to make much of the Bill of Rights indirectly binding on the states through the Fourteenth Amendment. Today the result is that the Supreme Court not only protects the First Amendment freedoms from violation at the state level, but also extends the application of procedural rights, such as the right to

[24]355 U.S. 66 (1957).

counsel and protection against self-incrimination, to the state level. In **Escobedo versus Illinois**, the court held in a five-to-four vote that in criminal prosecutions the right to representation by counsel extended back to the time a suspect is subjected to questioning.[25] Two years later the Court, in another five-to-four decision, **(Miranda versus Arizona)** ruled that in order for a conviction to stand—if obtained by evidence introduced at the trial as a result of "custodial interrogation"—it would be necessary to show that the suspect had been told he could remain silent, informed that any information volunteered could be used against him, told that he may have an attorney present during interrogation, informed that any attorney would be furnished if he could not afford one, and, lastly, allowed to end police interrogation at any time.[26]

The purpose of these rules is to protect the prisoner against self-incrimination and preserve his right to counsel. Not only is the Supreme Court divided on the wisdom of extending procedural safeguards this far, but so is public opinion. Critics claim that the Court is discouraging the use of voluntary confessions and making the conviction of criminals difficult. Defenders of the Court point to the unquestioned fact that in the past the procedural rights of suspects frequently have been violated, especially on the state level. Probably an important factor in polarizing opinion on this issue is that the Court has acted at a time when the public is understandably concerned about the rising tide of crime in our cities.

In Great Britain the primary responsibility for the preservation of civil liberties rests upon alert public opinion. It is part of the "unwritten constitution" of that country that Parliament shall pass no law infringing upon the traditional civil liberties of the realm. Nevertheless, as we have seen, while the courts cannot hold an act of Parliament unconstitutional, judges in Great Britain do have the authority to restrain executive officials from depriving people of their rights. Any invasion of civil rights usually is raised in Parliament. Any British citizen who believes his rights have been violated usually can find a member of Parliament to cross-examine an appropriate member of the ministry to get all the facts. Evidence of a violation of basic rights may lead to extended debate in Parliament. Even without the power of judicial review, the courts are effective in protecting civil rights. They make certain that the executive branch, in carrying out its functions, adheres to the rules of procedure laid down by law. Through judicial interpretation, the courts also have construed seditious conspiracy narrowly. Although violence may not be used to change the constitution or the laws, any type of agitation that does not include violence may be used.[27]

The preservation of civil liberties is of particular importance in West Germany today. The Nazi regime (1933–1945) not only destroyed the independence of the judi-

[25]378 U.S. 478 (1964).

[26]384 U.S. 436 (1966).

[27]See Sydney D. Bailey, *British Parliamentary Democracy*, 2nd ed. (Cambridge, Mass.: Houghton-Mifflin, The Riverside Press, 1966), pp. 97–100; and Gwendolyn M. Carter and John H. Herz, *Major Foreign Powers*, 5th ed. (New York: Harcourt, Brace & World, 1967), pp. 52–53.

ciary but also established special courts not bound by any law. Fortunately, the West German regime has shown an awareness of the importance of civil liberty. The Bonn Constitution restored the principle that punishment must be inflicted only according to law after a fair trial. Furthermore, the establishment of extraordinary courts is forbidden and double jeopardy (more than one prosecution for the same offense) is prohibited. The Constitutional Court of West Germany is authorized to hear all complaints by individuals against any violation of their constitutional rights. The Court's record is generally considered to be progressive.[28]

In Japan the concept of basic civil rights has not become firmly rooted in Japanese constitutionalism. The pre-World War II Japanese constitution authorized basic civil rights "subject to the limits of the law." In practice this meant little, as few rights were allowed. The postwar constitution grants a wide range of specific rights, including freedom of the press, assembly, speech, and academic freedom. In addition, a variety of procedural safeguards are included—such as protection against self-incrimination, the right to speedy trial, and the writ of habeas corpus. The last is a court order to any official holding a person in custody, directing him to bring the prisoner before the court to explain why he is confined. If the court finds the person unlawfully detained, he is released. In Japan the only restriction is that these rights may not be used so as to jeopardize the public welfare. The Japanese supreme court has interpreted the scope of civil rights narrowly. The constitutionality of every law challenged as a limitation of freedom of expression has been upheld as necessary to preserve the public welfare.[29]

There are no civil liberties, in the Western sense, in the Soviet Union. Although the constitution of 1977 contains a **bill of rights**, the emphasis is on social and economic rights, such as the right to work and the right to a free education, rather than freedom from interference by the government. The social and economic rights are merely declarations of intention, not enforceable by the courts. Even such political guarantees as freedom of association and the press are only for those who support the regime.

Neither procedural rights, such as habeas corpus, nor bail are allowed. A Soviet citizen who is arrested can be detained in jail for nine months while the charges against him are investigated. He cannot have an attorney until the day before his trial.[30]

Many African constitutions provide for substantive civil liberties, such as freedom of the press, speech, and religion. In these countries, however, there is less emphasis on procedural rights, such as right to counsel and jury trial. In Nigeria during what was known as the Action Group crisis of 1962, which grew out of a split in the leadership in the western region of that country, the governor removed the prime

[28]See Arnold V. Heidenheimer, *The Governments of Germany*, 3rd ed. (New York: Thomas Y. Crowell, 1971), Chapter 7, for a discussion of the constitutional court.

[29]Tsuneishi, *op. cit.,* pp. 185–187.

[30]Ellsworth Raymond, *The Soviet State* (New York: Macmillan, 1968), pp. 211–212 and 240.

minister and a struggle developed over control of the office. The leader of the opposition party and others were charged with treason, felony, and conspiracy against the government. The defendants were not allowed to use counsel brought from England in their defense. When the late Tom Mboya was minister of justice in Kenya, he indicated jury trial was foreign to Africans. On issues of evidence, some African courts have ruled that they would make a presumption in favor of the government.[31]

Ghana's postindependence republican constitution had no bill of rights. In its place the president, upon assuming office, was required to declare his adherence to certain fundamental principles, but the Ghana Supreme Court held that this was of moral significance only and did not restrict either the president's or the legislature's legal powers.[32]

What are the future trends likely to be? Professor L. C. B. Gower of Lagos University believes that it is likely that if African courts apply provisions of bills of rights frequently, civil rights will either be abolished completely, whittled away, or the bench will be packed with judges who will do the government's bidding.[33]

In the United States considerable progress has been made in advancing civil rights, especially through court decisions outlawing segregation and imposing the procedural guarantees of the Bill of Rights of the U. S. Constitution on state courts as well as national. In Great Britain civil rights continue to be protected, despite the absence of judicial review. Communist nations reject the Western conception of civil rights. On the other hand, progress has occurred at least in a formal sense in Japan and many of the developing nations, which have included bills of rights in their new constitutions.

THE AMERICAN JUDICIAL PROCESS

When attorneys are appointed to the judiciary, they carry with them their social and political philosophies. Most judges seek to be objective in deciding a case and to avoid prejudices, but all judges possess basic attitudes that are outgrowths of social background, legal training, professional experience as lawyers, and political affiliation. Attitudes toward what are commonly called "liberalism" or "conservatism" frequently will be reflected in judicial opinions, especially where questions of social policy are involved. As we have seen, American presidents, when they appoint judges, usually are influenced by what they consider to be a judge's social philosophy. President Nixon, in appointing Chief Justice Burger, sought someone who

[31]Dorothy Dodge, *op. cit.,* pp. 138–140.

[32]L. C. B. Gower, *Independent Africa: The Challenge to the Legal Profession* (Cambridge, Mass.: Harvard University Press, 1967), p. 79.

[33]*Ibid.,* pp. 82–83.

would be a **strict constructionist** and less of a **judicial activist** than his predecessor, Chief Justice Warren.

In deciding cases, judges make law. Obviously, they do not do so in the sense that a member of the legislature does, but they do make policy. Today the traditional idea that judges "discover" the law generally has been discarded. This "slot machine" idea of the law assumed that judges arrived at their decisions by applying the correct rule or principle to the case at hand. If the case involved the constitutionality of an act of Congress, the U. S. Supreme Court supposedly would merely lay the law alongside the Constitution to see if there was a conflict. If Congress, for example, passed a law making income-tax rates higher in Illinois than elsewhere, its invalidity would be obvious, for the Constitution provides that national taxes shall be uniform throughout the United States. The type of controversy that comes before the Supreme Court is far more complex and cannot be resolved by such a simple test.

To state that American courts do not decide cases by a process of logical deduction is not to suggest that they act in an arbitrary manner. Courts generally take precedents seriously, but frequently there are competing judicial doctrines available with respect to open-ended clauses of the Constitution, such as interstate commerce. Precedents are not always consistent and can be interpreted narrowly or broadly, as the decision demands. At times the Court specifically will overrule an earlier precedent, but most judges usually try to decide cases on the basis of sound legal reasoning and to provide some continuity to the law.

The recent decision of the Supreme Court in *Oregon* versus *Mitchell* illustrates the operation of the judicial process.[34] In this case the Court, by a five-to-four opinion, held that, by statute, Congress could reduce the voting age to 18 in federal elections but that Congress lacked the power to reduce the voting age to 18 in state and local elections.

Contrary to popular belief of recent years, there is no specific provision of the Constitution granting Congress the power to fix voting qualifications. In fact, the determination of who shall vote has been considered a state function. Article I, Section 2 of the Constitution states that the electors for the House of Representatives "shall have the qualifications requisite for electors of the most numerous branch of the state legislature." The Seventeenth Amendment, providing for direct elections of senators, has identical qualifications for voters. Article II provides that presidential electors shall be chosen in the manner the state legislature directs. The two suffrage amendments, however, require that in fixing qualifications, the states cannot discriminate on account of race or sex. (The Fifteenth and Nineteenth Amendments are worded in the negative.) Article I, Section 4, moreover, grants to state legislatures the power to determine the "times, places and manner of holding elections"

[34]400 U.S. 112 (1970).

for Congress, subject to such alterations as Congress may make. Lastly, the "equal protection" clause of the Fourteenth Amendment also has a bearing on the problem, in the opinion of four of the U. S. Supreme Court justices.[35] This clause states that no state may deny to anyone within its jurisdiction the equal protection of the laws. The Fourteenth Amendment grants Congress the power to enforce its provisions by appropriate legislation.

The act of Congress authorizing 18-year-olds to vote in federal, state, and local elections was an amendment to the Voting Rights Act of 1965. The primary constitutional argument advanced on behalf of the law was that Congress, in exercising its enforcement powers under the Fourteenth Amendment, could determine that the denial of suffrage to 18-year-olds was a denial of "equal protection."

What is novel about the constitutional argument is the broad interpretation of congressional power to enforce the equal protection clause. Generally, the equal protection clause has been used to hold invalid state legislation that was alleged to be unconstitutional because of its discriminatory nature. An example would be **Brown versus Board of Education**, which held that segregation in education was a denial of equal protection.[36]

Actually, the court in **Oregon versus Mitchell** was even more deeply divided than the five-to-four decision might indicate. Justice Black, who wrote the official opinion, held that Congress, on the basis of Article I, Sections 2 and 4, had general supervisory power over congressional and presidential elections but not state or local elections; however, no other member of the court agreed with his reasoning or conclusions. Four of his colleagues—Douglas, Brennan, Marshall, and White—believed the equal protection clause gave Congress power to determine age limits for voting in all elections, in the interests of equal protection. On the other hand, Justice Stewart, Blackmun, Harlan, and Chief Justice Burger held that the states had exclusive authority over age limits for voting. Justice Stewart contended that the "manner" of holding elections does not include the qualifications of voters, as Section 2 of Article I spells out what these qualifications are. As to state and local elections, Stewart held that the power to decide on qualifications for voting, if it means anything, must include the power to select 21 as a reasonable voting age.

The dissenting judges' views reflected a conservatism that laid greater stress on earlier precedents and the importance of preserving a constitutional balance between the nation and the states. The issue, according to Justice Stewart, was not whether it was good policy for 18-year-olds to vote, but whether Congress had the

[35]The relevant portion of the Fourteenth Amendment states: "No state shall make or enforce any law which shall abridge the privileges or immunities of citizens of the United States; nor shall any state deprive any person of life, liberty or property, without due process of law; nor deny to any person within its jurisdiction the equal protection of the laws. . . . The Congress shall have power to enforce, by appropriate legislation, the provisions of this article. . . ."

[36]347 U.S. 483 (1954).

power to decide the issue in this way, rather than through the slower and more complex process of a constitutional amendment.[37]

In *Oregon versus Mitchell*, the U. S. Supreme Court made important public policy by upholding part of a controversial act of Congress. Sometimes the court breaks new ground by dealing with a problem that Congress refuses to act on for political reasons. For many years, segregated public schools were common in the South and parts of the North. In 1896, the court, in the case of **Plessy versus Ferguson** had set forth the "separate but equal" doctrine, which allowed segregation in public facilities as long as facilities were "equal."[38] By holding that southern segregation laws did not violate the equal protection clause of the Fourteenth Amendment, the justices encouraged segregation as a policy.

By the 1930s and 1940s there was growing criticism of this policy by blacks and many whites. At first the U. S. Supreme Court responded by "tightening up" the requirement of equal facilities for blacks. The best solution would have been for Congress to outlaw state segregation by passing a law under its enforcement powers under the Fourteenth Amendment. This was politically impossible due to southern opposition and the possibility of a filibuster in the Senate. Finally, in 1954, as we have seen, the Court repudiated segregated education in *Brown* versus *Board of Education*, by holding it a form of "invidious discrimination."[39] This was followed by cases holding other forms of segregation unconstitutional. This policy gave a boost to the "Negro Revolution" and ultimately (despite southern opposition) contributed to the creation of a climate of opinion that forced Congress to act by passing the various civil rights laws between 1957 and 1968.

More recently the court has had to deal with the problem of **affirmative action** programs. These programs are designed to aid members of minority groups who have suffered past discrimination in employment and education. As this is an area where public opinion is deeply divided, the court is proceeding with caution.

A divided court in the well-known case of **Board of Regents versus Bakke** ruled unconstitutional a quota system for disadvantaged minority students at the University of California Medical School at Davis but approved race as a factor in admissions programs designed to select a diverse student body.[40] In the area of employment the court has approved a retroactive award of seniority to a group of black truck drivers who had been victims of past discrimination by the employers.[41]

The activism of the Warren Court in ending school segregation and the granting of civil rights to black people has won general approval outside of segregationist cir-

[37]Since this decision, the Twenty-Sixth Amendment has been added to the Constitution. This grants suffrage to those 18 years old and over, in both federal and state elections.
[38]163 U.S. 537 (1896).
[39]347 U.S. 483 (1954).
[40]*Regents* versus *Bakke*, 438 U.S. 265 (1978).
[41]*Franks* versus *Bowman Transportation Co.*, 424 U.S. 747 (1975).

cles, but other aspects of the court's activism have been more controversial, as will be recalled from our discussion of civil liberties earlier in this chapter.

The appointment of four "conservative" judges by President Nixon led to the expectation that the judicial trend would be reversed. Except for some changes in criminal procedure in a conservative direction, the Burger court seems to be as activist as the court under Warren. In some areas it even has broken new ground, such as in the 1973 ruling on abortion that held invalid virtually all state laws on that subject. The court decreed that state laws must treat each third of the pregnancy period by different standards. Previously, state abortion legislation was considered a legislative rather than a judicial question.[42]

Yet, despite criticism, especially in law-enforcement circles, of such cases as *Miranda* and *Escobedo*, and criticism of the abortion decisions by many religious groups and some scholars, the court has not become the subject of political controversy comparable to that of the 1930s, when it ruled on the constitutionality of the New Deal. Up to now at least, the court has avoided the great danger of allowing judicial activism to get ahead of public opinion and of making decisions that are not enforceable.

SUMMARY

There is a variety of legal systems in the world. The two systems generally associated with democratic regimes, the Anglo-American common-law system and the code law of Western Europe, differ in numerous ways. The former is based to a greater degree on judge-made law and stresses procedural safeguards for defendants in criminal cases, limiting the role of the judge to that of an impartial referee in the conduct of a trial. Judicial review, so important in the American legal system, is not found in the British system, but is provided for in some code-law countries.

The Communist legal system reflects to varying degrees the authoritarian nature of the Communist governmental systems. Japan and the developing nations are influenced by both the Western legal systems and indigenous factors.

It is clear that courts make policy. In a sense in the United States, the Constitution is what the judges say it means. In the short run there may be a conflict between the ways in which a majority of the U. S. Supreme Court justices interpret the Constitution and the manner in which the majority of the people desire the Constitution to be interpreted; however, in the long run, the Supreme Court is likely to interpret the Constitution in the way the majority desires. This is because presidents are likely to appoint judges who reflect dominant policy values. Also, failure on the part of the Court to reflect such values over a period of time is likely to undermine its prestige.

[42]Nathan Glazer, Toward an imperial judiciary? *The Public Interest*, 41, Fall 1975 (New York: National Affairs Inc.).

Except in Communist countries, courts generally try to exercise independence from political pressures and to maintain objectivity. That this is not always possible in developing states is illustrated by Ghana, to name only one example. It is likely that there is some relationship between the relative independence of the courts and the countries whose judicial system is based on the common law. Perhaps, as Theodore L. Becker has suggested, "Where judges can rely, in a common law system, on norms *they* produce, they need rely less on other norm-producing structures, that is, the legislature, the administrative agencies, etc."[43]

SELECTED READINGS

Henry J. Abraham, *The Judicial Process,** 3rd ed. (New York: Oxford University Press, 1975) is an excellent comparative introduction to the judicial process and administration of justice of leading Western states, with emphasis on the United States, England, and France. A study that emphasizes judicial politics and the role and function of the courts of various judicial systems is Theodore L. Becker, *Comparative Judicial Politics* (Chicago: Rand McNally, 1970).

There is a number of good studies of the judicial systems of particular foreign countries. For a study of Soviet law, see Harold J. Berman, *Justice in the U.S.S.R.: An Interpretation of Soviet Law** (New York: Vintage Press, 1963). A. T. Van Meren, *Law in Japan: The Legal Order in a Changing Society* (Cambridge: Harvard University Press, 1963) is a study of Japanese law. An introduction to African law is found in L. C. B. Gower, *Independent Africa: The Challenge to the Legal Profession** (Cambridge: Harvard University Press, 1967). Delmar Karlen et al., *Anglo-American Criminal Justice* (New York: Oxford University Press, 1967) is a study of criminal justice in the United States and Great Britain, from the role of the police to post-sentence remedies.

There are several specialized works dealing with various aspects of the American judicial system. Charles Warren, *The Supreme Court in United States History*, rev. ed., 2 vols. (Boston: Little, Brown, 1935) is still a valuable study, although outdated in some respects. Oliver Wendell Holmes, Jr., *The Common Law* (Boston: Little, Brown, 1948) has become a classic study of the common law. This work was published first in 1881, written by one of the most distinguished justices of the U. S. Supreme Court. An early study of the judicial process by a distinguished legal scholar and U. S. Supreme Court justice is Benjamin N. Cardozo, *The Judicial Process* (New Haven: Yale University Press, 1921).

Edward H. Levi, *An Introduction to Legal Reasoning** (Chicago: University of Chicago Press, 1948) is an excellent introduction to legal reasoning in the field of con-

---

[43]Becker, *op cit.,* p. 161.
*Available in paperback.

stitutional law. Professor Levi was formerly Attorney General of the United States, President of the University of Chicago, and Dean of the University of Chicago Law School. For an excellent beginners' book on American law for college students whose interests center in the social sciences, see C. Gordon Post, *An Introduction to the Law** (Englewood Cliffs, N.J.: Prentice-Hall, 1963).

C. Herman Pritchett, *The American Constitution*, 2nd ed. (New York: McGraw-Hill, 1968) is an analytical summary of what the American Constitution means. Professor Pritchett begins with the Constitutional Convention and its background and presents analytical summaries of leading U. S. Supreme Court decisions, under such topical headings as the executive, interstate commerce, and the various amendments.

A good introduction to the behavioral approach to American constitutional law is found in Glendon Schubert, *Judicial Policy Making** (Glenview, Ill.: Scott, Foresman, 1965). Professor Schubert approaches constitutional law through the analytical framework known in social science as "systems analysis."

Alexander M. Bickel, *The Supreme Court and the Idea of Progress** (New York: Harper & Row, 1970) is a friendly criticism of the U. S. Supreme Court under Chief Justice Warren. The late Professor Bickel of Yale believed that the Warren Court was inclined to read its liberal philosophy into the Constitution, just as conservative courts of an earlier day "found" the economic philosophy of *laissez-faire* in the Constitution. Another commentary on the Warren Court is Philip B. Kurland, *Politics, the Constitution, and the Warren Court** (Chicago: University of Chicago Press, 1970). Professor Kurland of the University of Chicago Law School has written this series of lectures examining the significance of the Warren Court, both historically and in its relationship to other branches of government. Like Professor Bickel, he is a friendly critic.

A commentary on the American judicial system that is challenging but not in the mainstream of thinking is Macklin Fleming, *The Price of Perfect Justice* (New York: Basic Books, 1974). A California judge, he argues that the current quest for "perfect justice" has resulted in an overemphasis on procedural rights, which has led frequently to needless and costly litigation.

*Available in paperback.

Chapter Eleven

Public Policy and Political Economy

The political processes, activities, and institutions analyzed in the previous chapters are directed toward influencing, controlling, or managing **public policy**. In this chapter we will examine the public policy process, drawing our examples from **political economy**—those issues and policies where politics and economics overlap. At all levels of government public policy results from political conflict and is the major output of the political system. As a cause of feedback and as a focus for debate and new demands, public policy is also an important input into the political system. Thus, public policy has a deep impact on public welfare; on the distribution of goods, services, and power among groups; on the functioning of the economic system, political processes, and social relations; and on support for the political system.

At its simplest public policy refers to all the laws, decisions, rules, and regulations produced by the political processes of a country. These aim at dealing with or eliminating problems through use of public—governmental—means. Thus, public policy is *"A purposive course of action"* by government actors *"in dealing with a problem or matters of public concern."*[1] It defines common problems, the means to solve them, and the ends to be achieved by the policy. Public policy is goal oriented, even if that goal is not always clear. It involves more than simply deciding to do something such as curb pollution, but includes regular patterns of action that attempt to achieve that goal. It may encourage or require people to carry out specific actions, such as conserving energy or hiring the handicapped, or policy may forbid them to do something such as driving more than 55 mph or practicing race or sex discrimination in hiring. Always it aims at achieving an end or purpose that the public, government, or ruling groups consider should be achieved through collective ac-

[1]James E. Anderson, *Public Policy-Making* (New York: Praeger, 1975), p. 3.

tion. It is based on authoritative decisions and the purposive behavior and actions necessary to carry out those decisions.[2]

Political scientists are increasingly becoming concerned with the causes and consequences of public policies. It is important to study public policy because it focuses on what governments do, as opposed to what they say. The study of public policy enables us to describe, analyze, and explain the origins, sources, and impact of government actions. It enables us to understand why specific policies have been adopted or ignored, who benefits from these and who pays for them. At a higher level of sophistication, the study of public policy may enable us to analyze policy prescriptions and perhaps even to participate in making policy. Participation requires knowing how policy is made, what causes issues to develop, and how policy and environment affect each other.

Political economy may be defined as the study of the mutual impact and interrelation of politics and economics. Usually political economy is discussed in terms of the relation of government and economics. Political and economic, government and business processes overlap and mingle. Many important policies are affected, even shaped by both political and economic considerations and concerns. There is a close and constant interaction of politics and economics in many important issues; examples include tax policy, domestic spending on defense, international trade, farm policy, and welfare policy. Political decisions inevitably affect seemingly economic questions such as energy pricing, supply or allocation, rates of employment, and the relative prosperity of agriculture and industry. Economic decisions such as product pricing, plant location, and personal spending patterns affect political debate over such issues as class and ethnic relations, defense spending, and regional relations ("snowbelt" versus "sunbelt," north versus south in Italy and Brazil, the Greater London Area versus the old industrial northwest in Britain). Whether the government is interventionist or adopts a "hands-off" policy toward the economy, that policy affects economic relations. Examination of specific public policies is one of the best ways to study political economy. Policies having **both** political and economic components, often inextricably united, or involving the interaction of government and business, are extremely important and will grow in importance in the foreseeable future. Simple slogans about the proper roles of polity and economy, whether by pure capitalists or pure socialists, do not reflect reality accurately. To understand the contemporary world we must understand that economics often involves power relations and conflict over decision making and that politics often involves decisions about who will pay and who will benefit from production and distribution, whether from defense or highway policy. Apparent economic issues develop into political issues, and governments and businesses increasingly find it in their interests to cooperate in dealing with these issues.

[2]*Ibid.,* pp. 3–4. See also James E. Anderson, David W. Brady, and Charles Bullock III, *Public Policy and Politics in America* (North Scituate, Mass.: Duxbury Press, 1978), pp. 4–5.

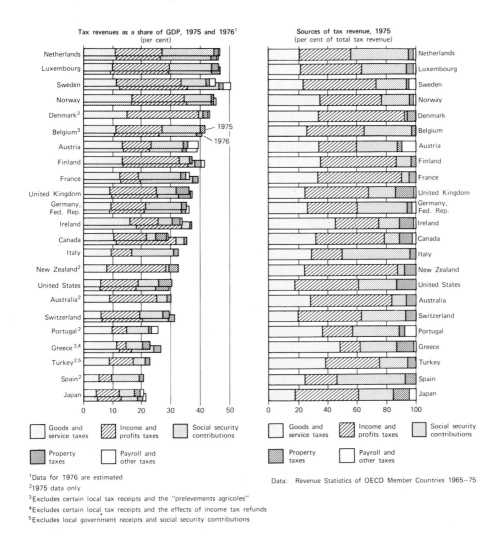

Figure 11-1. The varying impact of taxation in countries with market economies (Source: *IMF Survey*, January 23, 1978, published by the International Monetary Fund, Washington, D.C. 20431).

There are many areas of public concern and many types of public policy (See the last two chapters for a discussion of foreign policy.). Recent headlines include such issues as inflation, unemployment, health care costs, civil rights, aid to industry, abortion, welfare reform, assistance to agriculture, foreign policy, energy, defense, interest rates, education, affirmative action, tax reform, regulation of industry, pollution control, health and safety regulations, auto safety, and the balance of payments. In each of these public policy areas, intense political conflict occurs over what government should or should not do. Rather than attempt a brief and incomplete overview of each of these areas, this chapter will focus on those important and controversial policy issues where political and economic considerations mix together at all stages of the policy process. Though the general processes of public policy making are similar for all policies, we will focus on political-economic policy because this area of public policy is now particularly important and visible. It affects the domestic and international relations, welfare, and even the survival of tens of millions of people and is expected to grow in importance during the rest of this century.

We will examine the connection between political economy and public policy in the remainder of this chapter. First, we will argue that popular expectations and ideologies deeply affect what is considered to be a legitimate policy issue and legitimate tools for dealing with that issue. Second, we will examine the reasons why the scope of public policy has expanded everywhere in this century. Third, we will review some of the major historical and existing political-economic systems, thereby noting the major ways in which governmental-business-economic relations are or have been organized. Fourth, we will look at the general process of policy making, a process that is always and everywhere essentially political rather than merely technical or administrative. Finally, we will examine three cases of political economy in public policy: energy, agriculture, and development.

POPULAR EXPECTATIONS AND THE POLITICAL ECONOMY OF PUBLIC POLICY

Some readers may not agree with all of the analysis in this chapter because they have values and expectations different from those of the authors. If you disagree with some of the conclusions, ask why. Such disagreement lies at the heart of policy debate. Public policy is deeply affected by popular values and ideologies. We often interpret policy through our preferences and values. As we have already seen in Chapters Three and Four, political beliefs color how each of us views the world, having an impact on each stage of the policy process. For example, most people probably have an opinion about what public policy should be on issues such as the energy crisis or lower taxes. These issues involve conflict over the role of government and politics in significant areas of economic and social life. Public policy debate, especially over political economic issues, is in the first instance debate over the proper role of government—what government may or may not and should or should not do in terms of regulation of, support for, or intervention into economic and social affairs. A person's answer to these questions depends heavily on his or her empirical and normative beliefs. **Empirical** evaluation always is colored by a person's values and ideology. It includes judgments about the capacity of government to deal with a problem, available resources, the impact of government intervention in other areas, past successful policies, and the efficiency of government.

Normative judgments include personal values, ideology, assumptions about human nature or proper political conduct, and acceptance of common values from the political culture. People rarely examine their values and assumptions, even though they affect judgments. Thus, a person who accepts values such as freedom, individualism, and private enterprise may reject proposed solutions to the energy crisis involving increased centralization, rationing, or bureaucratic growth.[3]

The effect of values and value preferences on public policy is important because it helps set limits to what people define as a problem, accept as legitimate tools to deal with a problem, and consider a desirable outcome. This perception may change with time. Many currently accepted public policies were considered illegitimate 50 years ago. At the start of the Great Depression in the early 1930s, many people assumed that poverty was due to personal failing or laziness and that government had no role in alleviating it; that business cycles and depression were natural and government had no role in regulating them. Popular attitudes had to change before governments could intervene actively in these areas, whether with unemployment compensation or a "War on Poverty." Though the structure of government, its resources, existing social conditions,[4] the available policy models, and the international system deeply affect public policy, so do the values, assumptions, and preferences of the mass public and major power holders. These values provide important clues to group and party policy differences. You should always ask how a person's or group's ideologies and preferences affect what they define as a public problem or an acceptable solution to a problem.

THE INCREASING ROLE OF GOVERNMENT AND PUBLIC POLICIES IN ECONOMICS

Everywhere, governments are expected to carry out policies to protect, promote, or regulate the economy.[5] In the developing countries governments are generally expected to guide and encourage economic development and a more just distribution of resources. In the **developed market-economy** systems, governments are expected to manage the economy to avoid such major shocks as depression or massive unemployment. In **developed nonmarket systems**, governments attempt to control all investment and demand. Leaving these nonmarket systems aside for now, there are many reasons why the role of government in the economy is increasing.

---

[3]For a good discussion of values and public policy see Charles W. Anderson, The place of principles in policy analysis, *American Political Science Reveiw*, 73, September 1979, pp. 711–712. See also James E. Anderson, *Public Policy-Making, op. cit.,* pp. 15–16.

[4]See Arnold J. Heidenheimer, et al., *Comparative Public Policy* (New York: St. Martin's Press, 1975), pp. 258–259.

[5]For an alternative, though supplementary analysis, see Robert Eyestone, *Political Economy* (Chicago: Markham, 1972), pp. 85–101.

In general terms, change is the catalysis for governmental involvement in the economy. Very often it generates conflicts and demands that only governments can deal with. Because an economic system is so important and pervasive, because people spend such a large part of their lives in it, and because it provides much of the material base for such other activity as social status and leisure, changes in production can have a profound impact on social and political institutions and activities. These changes also may form a new input into or arena for political conflict.[6]

One of the simplest and most plausible models of the impact of change on politics was developed by Emmanuel Mesthene.[7] Mesthene admits that we simply do not know the mechanisms by which technology induces social change; however, he argues that new tools or technologies create new possibilities to solve old problems or meet old or new goals. Because of the initially instrumental quality of new tools or technology some people will want to use them. Use of new tools and technology to realize goals or solve problems necessitates changes in social organization to take full advantage of the innovations. Although Mesthene does not discuss this, work, institutional and group specialization often result from adopting new technology. New organizations or work patterns replace older ones that had solved social-economic problems based on older technologies. This in turn causes conflicts "between the old values and new technique" that may not be compatible. In turn this generates conflict between different groups who support either the old or new values. When such conflict becomes very intense, the only way to solve it is through the political processes. If successful, new tools and organizations—and groups based upon them—will replace older groups, technologies, and values: national markets replace local ones, large farms replace small ones, industry becomes more important than agriculture, new energy sources are developed or are exhausted, all causing regional disagreements. In this process of challenge and replacement, it is inevitable that some will benefit and others be injured, encouraging both to turn to politics for protection.

Specifically, "economic intervention on the part of government, even though it uses an almost endless number of devices, serves a few simple purposes."[8] We now may review some of these purposes.

REGULATION OR INTERVENTION REQUESTED BY BUSINESS

Quite often, business has asked for government regulation or intervention to end what it considered to be "ruinous" or unfair competition or to provide a set of industry-wide standards. In the United States, first state governments, as with the Texas Railroad Commission, and then the federal government agreed in the 1920s and

[6]Wilbert E. Moore, *The Impact of Industry* (Englewood Cliffs, N.J.: Prentice-Hall, 1965), pp. 16, 45, 83–84 and briefly throughout.

[7]Emmanuel Mesthene, *Technological Change: Its Impact on Man and Society* (Cambridge, Mass.: Harvard University Press, 1970), pp. v–viii, 28ff.

[8]Eyestone, *op. cit.,* p. 8.

1930s to regulate and **limit** petroleum production because competition had forced the price of oil as low as 10¢ a barrel. Initial government intervention was to **raise** the price received by producers. Farm price support and crop-limitation programs, **tariffs**, quotas, government-enforced cartel agreements, subsidies (to shipping companies and airlines), licensing of lawyers and physicians, allocation of broadcasting frequencies, and enforcement of contracts are a few of the many types of government intervention often demanded by business.

There are many other regulations and interventions designed to aid business; most are not controversial. These include copyright and patent laws, the census, gathering and disseminating information about economic and crop conditions, and occasionally tariffs.

HEALTH AND SAFETY

Demands that government regulate unsafe or unhealthy conditions, especially in industry, date back at least to the Middle Ages. In the modern period, Britain instituted the first laws regulating industry. In 1802, government began to regulate factory working conditions of pauper children; in 1833 it instituted the first factory inspections for health and safety; in 1842 it passed a law regulating employment of children and women in mines; and in 1847 it passed an act limiting workers to a 10-hour day. In 1970, the United States Congress passed the Occupational Safety and Health Act (OSHA) in response to "The fact that during the period 1960 through 1969 more than 140,000 workers were killed on the job, and nearly 21 million are known to have been injured. . . . " in addition to many made sick by job health hazards.[9] This is among the most far reaching legislation on health and safety in the world.

Every country attempts to regulate health and safety hazards. Areas of regulation include pure food and drug laws; mine, transportation, and industrial safety conditions; minimum requirements for doctors, nurses, and pharmacists; regulation of such unsafe or hazardous products as explosives, radioactive materials, and poisons; and limitations on the number of hours worked. Such laws are based on the assumption that society has other goals than merely maximum profits. Legitimate social goals also include health and fair distribution of all the costs of production. Many manufacturing processes have **externalities**: costs of production that are passed on to someone other than producers or consumers. These costs often are not reckoned into the price of a product. Unsafe working conditions that reduce production costs can be such an externality if the industry or consumer does not have to pay for injuries or deaths. Unsafe cars may be cheaper to produce and buy but surely cost the larger society more in terms of deaths, injuries, lost production, and higher insurance rates. Pollution is one of the most important externalities. It is the

[9]U.S. Congress, Subcommittee on Labor of the Committee on Labor and Public Welfare, *Legislative History of the Occupational Safety and Health Act of 1970* (Washington, D.C.: U.S. Government Printing Office, 1971) p. iii. This total greatly exceeds U.S. casualties during the Vietnam War of the same period.

focus of intense policy debate in Europe, Japan, North America, and some of the developing countries. The cost of pollution often is ignored if someone else pays for it in the form of illness, dirty clothes, acid rain, ruined paint, difficulty in breathing or dirty air, fouled water, and polluted soil. Random dumping of dangerous chemicals may be cheap initially for those doing the dumping in the Love Canal area in New York, the Rhine River and Mediterranean Sea in Europe, and Tokyo Bay in Japan, but very costly to society in the long run. Increasingly, public policy is attempting to impose cleanup costs on those who violate the environment. Policies requiring pollution control equipment on industrial plants, or those requiring industries to reduce solid and thermal pollution of water, or those limiting strip mining, are under regular attack. Businesses often complain that government regulation is hurting profits and productivity because public policy is starting to require that they and consumers pay the costs that previously were passed on to society in the form of pollution.

Policy debate over health and safety regulation is becoming more acrimonious and pervasive as we begin to compute the real costs involved. Very few people

A man sits on the front porch of his home in the Love Canal area, which he will have to leave because of chemicals seeping into the basement from the nearby chemical landfill.

deny the necessity of regulation in this area. Debate centers on much more philosophical, even ideological, questions: can a democratic society legislate in the area of welfare and economics? Who should prove the safety of a new food product or drug: government or industry? Who should pay the costs of dealing with pollution or nuclear wastes? Can governments ban products that **may** be unsafe, as Canada did with saccharin? What kinds of tradeoffs will we allow between health and safety on one side and increased or cheaper production on the other? These are not questions of one or the other, but questions of how much. As some economists are fond of saying, there is no such thing as a free lunch, so the questions are who will pay, who will benefit, and in what kind of currency will we choose to make these payments.

REGULATING NATURAL MONOPOLIES

Competition in a free and open market is the key principle of modern capitalism; however, markets are not always free and open, nor is competition always possible. Natural monopolies develop when the nature of an enterprise does not allow competition. Then customers may not have any alternatives to choose from . Typical examples include broadcasting; utility and telephone companies; sometimes bus, airline, railroad, and pipeline companies; perhaps even some enterprises with an important social component, such as large defense contractors. Some countries have nationalized part or all of these industries. In Canada, the Canadian Broadcasting Corporation, Air Canada, and one of the two major rail systems are nationally owned. In Britain, broadcasting is partly a government monopoly and transportation and utilities are wholly government owned. Similar patterns are found on the European continent. In spite of some local government ownership of utilities, the United States has tended to regulate natural or semimonopolies. Close regulation includes supervision, having a voice in rate setting and determining routes, and minimum standards of performance. In such cases regulation takes the place of competition, attempts to protect public welfare, ensures good service, protects investors, and acts as an alternative to public ownership. The recent deregulation of airlines in the United States has allowed them greater flexibility in fare and route determination but has led many people to complain about reduced service. Opposition by the trucking industry to deregulation of trucking rates illustrates how some industries welcome regulation that reduces competition.

REGULATION TO AID AND PROTECT THE ECONOMY

Some forms of regulation, intervention, and control are designed to promote economic growth and stability, whether or not specific businesses request aid. Promotion of economic growth is a major governmental activity in developing states. In developed Western countries, regulation attempts to strengthen the framework within which the economy functions, ensure that competition takes place, and prevent abuses that may be harmful to business and the public.

As early as 1776, Adam Smith, in *The Wealth of Nations*,[10] argued that defense, protection of justice, and provision of public works such as harbors was necessary to support the economy. Today, regardless of ideology, most persons accept such things as road building as legitimate governmental economic activities. The overwhelming majority of decision makers also have accepted the basic assumptions of Keynesian public policy and economics, developed in the 1920s and 1930s by the English economist John Maynard Keynes (1883–1946). He attempted to rethink the basis of modern economics. Keynes argued that massive unemployment, stagnation, and eventually the Great Depression proved that classic *laissez-faire* policy (to be discussed) did not work well. Keynes argued that capitalism could survive only if government accepted the responsibility for stimulating consumer demand during depressions and (while writing during World War II) reducing demand when inflation threatened. In addition to demanding basic changes in the way people viewed the relation of politics and economics, Keynes suggested interventionist policies to aid the economy. Many of these have become important to the mixed market-economy state (to be discussed). The politically easiest policies have been adopted by all Western industrialized countries. Keynes suggested public planning; fiscal and monetary policy to encourage investment, employment, consumption, or reduced consumption; some public works; limited control of investment; and international cooperation. The tax cut of 1964 to stimulate the economy and the surtax of 1968 to slow it down during the Vietnam War are examples of Keynesian policy in the United States. Though many businesspeople and conservative economists reject Keynes, he represents the intellectual justification of increased government involvement in the economy.[11]

In the United States, antitrust policy is designed to foster competition if artificial monopolies develop, in order to make capitalism work. Policy includes breaking down large companies when they act as monopolies, forbidding rivals from acquiring each other's stock, and forbidding price control and restraint of trade agreements. Enforcing competition is seen as an alternative to nationalization. This policy is based on the Sherman Antitrust Act of 1890 and the Clayton Act of 1914. Though enforcement of these laws has varied and many businesses oppose them, they represent a public commitment to ensuring the competitive conditions necessary for a free economy. Policy debate centers on the ever-shifting area of determining when enforcement of competition begins to undermine free enterprise.

REGULATION TO ACHIEVE A COMMON SOCIAL GOAL
Governments often regulate behavior or business to ensure that a noneconomic goal will be met. This type of regulation often is inherently controversial. Except for

---

[10]Adam Smith, *The Wealth of Nations* (New York: Modern Library, 1937), pp. 653–716.

[11]John Maynard Keynes, *The General Theory of Employment Interest and Money* (New York: Harcourt, Brace and Company, 1936); and "How to Pay for the War" (1940) in *Collected Writings, Vol IX, Essays in Persuasion* (London: Macmillan, 1972), pp. 367–439. See also *Essays in Persuasion*.

the desirability of defense, Western societies often are deeply split over the purpose of public policy or the meaning of common interest. Though European and North American countries are dedicated officially to promoting justice, equality, and fairness, there often is basic disagreement over what is a legitimate public economic and business policy to promote these goals. In the United States, there has been severe conflict over policies designed to ensure equal access of all citizens to housing and jobs. Efforts to apply antidiscrimination policies to private industry have proven exceedingly difficult. European countries are beginning to face similar problems due to the influx of a large number of "guest workers" and citizens from former colonies. Arguments over whether business has any social responsibilities other than profit making, efforts to develop alternative energy sources much faster than can be done through exclusive reliance on the market, and efforts to reduce medical costs, are all politically difficult questions with which public policy in Western nations is attempting to deal.

Many economic demands and conflicts can be settled only through politics and public policy. This includes disagreements over both economic inputs (land usage, labor conditions, and regulation of capital) and outputs (such as distribution and competition). All are affected by, and exist in a framework of, public policy and protection. Intervention is usually in response to group demands for aid and protection: tariffs; legalization of labor unions; mandatory collective bargaining; unemployment compensation; assistance when economic changes make some skill obsolete; protection of cherished values, social patterns, and aspirations in the face of change; and guarantees of safe water and working conditions. Most regulation is directed to someone's benefit, often to remove "undesirable side effects" of other's actions.[12] This does not mean that some, or even much, regulation or intervention is inefficient, wasteful, or poorly enforced. It does mean we must keep the different purposes of regulation in mind when we analyze political-economic policy. Thus, if a policy does not make sense in narrow profit-and-loss terms, ask what it attempts to achieve and who supports it. In debating policy this will help us keep our values and preferences clearer and should help us keep in mind tradeoffs between one preference and another.

THE MAJOR POLITICAL ECONOMIES

Despite important differences, every country in this century has been forced by technological and economic change to decide what values and institutions will regulate political/economic relations and conditions. ". . . [T]he fundamental politico-economic alternatives open to man make up only a very short list. One is social organization through the authority of government. One is social organization through

---

[12]Eyestone, *op. cit.*, p. 91.

exchange and markets."[13] Though there is virtually an unlimited number of possible combinations of government and market, 4 political/economic systems have been dominant in the last 300 years. These are **mercantilism**; **laissez-faire** or the free market; various types of **mixed economies**, often associated with the welfare state; and **command economies**. Traditional economies including peasant agriculture, which are disappearing, and cooperative or worker owned systems are theoretically important but have had much less impact on policy.

MERCANTILISM
This refers to a bundle of theories and ideas that began to develop in the sixteenth and seventeenth centuries. It is linked to development of the modern state and represents an effort to control, regulate, and foster economic growth for the purpose of increasing national power. Highly nationalistic, mercantilist theorists argued that economic power was the basis for political power. Public policy was directed to building domestic industry, often through monopoly and exclusive trading provisions. It tried to create an export surplus, a favorable balance of trade, and a steady flow of gold and other precious metals into the home country. As wealth and power were both legitimate ends, and each was a means to the other, governments had a right to control labor and domestic industry, as well as attempt to acquire colonies. Colonies would provide both raw materials and a captive market for finished domestic products. At the same time, exclusion of rivals from colonial trade would weaken potential enemies.[14] This policy was based on the belief that what benefited one nation harmed another, and vice versa. Mercantilism's policies created a maze of rules and regulations that advocates of a market economy, such as Adam Smith, ridiculed as slowing growth. Today most major nations have rejected the basic purposes of mercantilism, if not all its policies.

LAISSEZ-FAIRE OR THE MARKET ECONOMY
This was a conscious and deliberate reaction to mercantilism. It represents the ideal of modern capitalism. Adam Smith spelled out its basic assumptions in *The Wealth of Nations*,[15] first published in 1776. Smith argued that there is a tendency toward natural harmony among people if each person is allowed to pursue his or her own interest. Smith emphasized "natural liberty," freedom from restraint, and freedom to seek one's own interest. Government interference and excessive public

---

[13]Charles Lindblom, *Politics and Markets* (New York: Basic Books, 1977), p. 4. See also p. ix, where he argues that "Aside from the difference between despotic and libertarian governments, the greatest distinction between one government and another is in the degree to which market replaces government or government replaces market." Analysis of both market and government is necessary to understand either one.

[14]There are many excellent sources about mercantilism. For a good summary see Jacob Viner "Economic Thought: Mercantilist Thought" in *International Encyclopedia of the Social Sciences,* vol. 4 (Macmillan Co. and the Free Press), 1968, pp. 435–442.

[15]Adam Smith, *op. cit.*

spending retard the natural progress of society toward wealth and improvement, waste wealth, interfere with the natural workings of the economy, and destroy liberty. Government has only a very limited policy role. Restraints and regulations of any kind, such as aid to some groups or control of some sector of the economy to pursue social goals, produce waste and inefficiency.

Free exchange is the key to a market economy. Modern supporters assume that a self-regulating competitive market is the essential and **only** legitimate device for allocating goods, services, and resources among individuals. Each good, service, product, and person's labor is offered for sale on this market. Prices depend solely on unregulated supply and demand. In the ideal self-regulating market individuals are assumed to be able to bargain equally with each other, with no one having an inherent advantage over anyone else or such a large share of the market that he could arbitrarily affect price. Both monopoly and government restrictions are seen as interferences with the right and ability of individuals to bargain freely with each other. In this free bargaining, each individual seeks his own advantage. Seeking one's own advantage naturally leads to competition and an effort to gain more by increasing one's share of the market. Under free competition and the discipline of an open, unregulated market, one can gain more of the market only by improving one's product, lowering its price, or both. This requires greater efficiency, and efficiency, achieved solely for personal gain, benefits everyone. Freedom creates plenty. Government is banished from this system because it introduces unnatural and disruptive influences into a natural process. Government has no active role in deciding distribution or in helping anyone harmed by economic processes.

Laisse-faire philosophy was dominant in Britain and the United States in the nineteenth and early twentieth centuries. Many modern supporters argue that government regulation of economic relations is inherently wasteful and disruptive and that no one should attempt to achieve social goals through management of the economy. Even in the nineteenth century, business received massive governmental aid in the form of tariffs on foreign goods, land grants for building railroads, patent protection for inventions, and determined efforts to maintain a stable money supply. Though the market economy has been tremendously liberating in allowing people to seek their own interest it has created a number of problems. The major problem of existing market systems is a tendency toward economic instability, especially recession and depression. The Depression of the 1930s caused shock and disturbance, accelerating public demands for government regulation.

MIXED ECONOMY OR MODIFIED MARKET SYSTEM

This is the major answer to economic instability. It has confounded Marxist predictions that capitalism inevitably will collapse and has encouraged a more equal distribution of goods and services. It is the prevalent form of political economy in the West and usually is associated with liberal-democratic political systems. It has grown in a haphazard manner. Though the Depression encouraged development of the modified market economy, its beginnings may be found in the demands of nine-teenth-century reformers for health and safety regulation of the industrial market-place. Active government intervention in economics is the basis of the modified market economy.

Intervention or direct involvement in economic affairs, and regulation, the crea-tion of rules which business must follow, are conceptually distinct but produce a similar result: increased government involvement in economic decisions and af-fairs. This involvement is based on the view that the market is not self-regulating. Large corporations are freer of market forces than small family businesses. A tend-ency to monopoly is common in many areas. Market imperfections, undesirable side effects such as unemployment, recession, inflation, and other economic dislo-cations, are not natural and inevitable. They can be modified and corrected. Policy makers have developed many tools, often policies suggested by Keynes, to inter-vene in the economy. These include indirect controls, such as regulation of the money supply, changes in interest rates, increases or decreases in taxes, changes in government borrowing or spending, tax credits for desirable investment, unem-ployment compensation, and demonstration projects. Direct controls include gov-ernment purchases of private goods, wage and price controls, public works pro-jects, and regulations requiring a specific kind of behavior. Since increasing taxes or decreasing spending is more difficult to achieve in the political arena than de-creasing taxes or increasing spending, modified market systems have found it easier to deal with the problems of recession than those of inflation.

Business regulation is also important. On the assumption that a pure market is an imperfect instrument for allocating resources in an era of national and multinational business and complex interdependent problems, supporters of an active govern-ment role in the economy have accepted all the previously noted reasons for regu-lation. Regulation also demands an increase in planning. "Planning is one of government's major methods of promoting business. . . ."[16] Planning includes eco-nomic forecasting, tax reductions for desired investments, and, in some countries such as France, creation of a national economic plan to encourage and guide pri-vate investment. Intervention includes some direct provision of goods and services, such as medical care and welfare payments, and outright ownership of some indus-tries, such as the Tennessee Valley Authority in the United States and the steel in-dustry in Great Britain. In each of these areas supporters of the mixed economy argue that regulation and intervention can increase the public's real freedom and opportunities.[17]

[16]Lindblom, op. cit., p. 111.
[17]The modern welfare state, which seeks to establish a minimum floor below which no citizens will be al-lowed to fall, is related to but distinct from the mixed-economy system. Theoretically it is compatible with a laissez-faire system in that it attempts to guarantee a minimum amount of income and services through unemployment insurance, old age insurance, perhaps medical services, free or cheap education, and so forth. These kinds of individual benefits are not necessarily linked to regulation of business or other eco-nomic intervention.

Some examples will help explain the functioning of the modified market system. Britain and France began to develop a mixed system before the United States. In Britain, government aid to and involvement in the economy was common, even in the nineteenth century. Legislation made possible development of large farms, railroad building, and some protection for workers in mines and factories. Today public policy is deeply involved in attempting to make the economy work.[18] The British government employs all the common policy tools to aid the economy: fiscal and monetary policy, public expenditures, incentives for investment, provision of some services, limited planning, and public ownership of some industries.

A Department of Industry and a National Development Council have responsibility for aiding industry; bringing government, management, and labor together to discuss problems; and for making policy recommendations. Economic imbalance due to different rates of regional growth is a major problem in Britain, and the government is employing tax incentives, grants, loans, and location regulations to encourage investment in depressed and rural areas. In addition, the National Health System provides inexpensive medical care for people who choose not to use the services of the parallel private system; the majority use the national public system. As in the United States, primary and secondary education is free, although more elitist, and a wide range of welfare services is provided. Moreover, the government owns a large number of public corporations that once were private industries. These include coal, electricity, most steel, transportation, and the Bank of England. Most of these basic industries were in grave financial trouble (some still are). They were technically obsolescent and in need of reorganization when they were nationalized (i.e., taken over by the government). Other concerns, such as the British Broadcasting Corporation and the British National Oil Corporation (formed to exploit North Sea oil), were publicly owned since their creation. Each is governed by a managing board appointed by the government for a limited time. Each theoretically is responsible to Parliament but usually has had a great deal of autonomy. Intense political debate over the legitimacy of government ownership has slowed down this type of involvement in recent years.

Historically, France has maintained a strong central government.[19] Government aid to, control over, or ownership of parts of the economy was widespread before the French Revolution. Mercantilist policy was stronger and *laissez-faire* sentiment weaker than in Britain or the United States. France has a long tradition of a strong, professional, national administrative system, a system that sometimes literally has governed and managed France during political crises. The French government employs most policy tools already noted for Britain. It, too, owns a number of indus-

[18]This section is based mainly on *Britain, An Official Handbook* (London: Her Majesty's Stationery Office, published yearly). See also A. H. Hanson and Malcom Walles, *Governing Britain* (London: Fontana, 1970), pp. 192–241.

[19]The economic parts of this section are based on T. Ridley and J. Blondel, *Public Administration in France* (New York: Barnes and Noble, 1969), pp. 193–205, 233–249; and on the periodical, *France* (New York: French Embassy, Press and Information Division, various issues).

tries, most nationalized soon after World War II: electricity, gas, mines, railroads, and Air France. In 1970 the government formed Aerospatiale to build aircraft. More importantly, the French have developed a system of planning that encourages cooperation among industry, labor, and government.[20]

French economic planning is more extensive than in other Western nations, emphasizing long-range growth and development. The *Commissariat du Plan* (Planning Commission) is at the heart of French long-range planning. Its members direct the development of a national plan that sets guidelines and goals for each sector of the economy as well as the economy as a whole. The Commission supplements normal policy processes; it does not replace them. It provides a forum for private firms and government agencies to meet and discuss their programs. Though it has little formal power and a small staff, the Commission can draw on other government agencies for help and has a great deal of influence. It coordinates the planning of government departments and encourages these departments and private enterprise to settle differences. Government agencies are required to show that their own proposals fit into the goals set by the Commission. Once a plan is drawn up, execution depends primarily on voluntary compliance. Though the nationalized industries should follow the plan, actual control over them lies with the Finance Minister and other relevant ministries. In most areas, private industry—especially small firms— may ignore the plan, though the government attempts to encourage compliance through granting tax benefits. Large industries that have a voice in drawing up the plan tend to follow the guidelines. The planning process itself was designed to supplement the market and has increased the participants' profits and productivity. France is an example of a country with extensive planning coupled to a parliamentary democratic system.

The United States has the world's largest national economy. Government involvement in the economy never has been as pervasive as in Europe or Canada.[21] Except for government sponsored medical care, most welfare measures employed in Europe also are found in the United States, although they tended to be implemented in the United States at much later dates. Social security legislation is now over a century old in Germany and dates to 1911 in Britain; it was not passed in the United States until 1935. Direct ownership of industry is much rarer than in Europe; the Tennessee Valley Authority and direct governmental operation of some railroads through Amtrak are rare exceptions. Ideological opposition to government intervention also extends to planning. The Council of Economic Advisors is a pale reflection of the *Commissariat du Plan*. Created in 1946, the Council consists of three prominent economists who advise the president on economic matters. It has no power to create a national plan nor any means to enforce policy. It does not even have direct contact with the Board of Governors of the Federal Reserve system.

---

[20]Lindblom, *op. cit.*, p. 318.

[21]For example, government spending as a share of the GNP is approximately 28 percent in the United States and over 50 percent in Sweden. This includes a much larger defense budget in the United States. See Lindblom, *op. cit.*, p. 109.

Nevertheless, the U.S. government is and always has been involved in the economy. Most of this involvement has been for defense, health and safety, and aid to business. Involvement began soon after the U.S. Constitution was signed. (The Constitution itself was seen by many as creating a framework of conditions conducive to growth.) In 1791, Alexander Hamilton, in his *Report on Manufactures*[22] to the new Congress, suggested massive aid to create a powerful industrial and commercial America. In the nineteenth century the states were more active in regulation and intervention, but such federal tariffs and subsidies as those given to the railroads and shipping lines, the Homestead Act of 1862, and control of labor unions greatly aided industry. The federal government accepted responsibility for maintaining a stable economy with the Full Employment Act of 1946. The major policy tools for maintaining a stable economy include Federal Reserve interest-rate policies, tax cuts or increases, and spending policy. These, along with antitrust policy, are designed to make the market function more smoothly. Regulation to make capitalism work— done by such agencies as the Civil Aeronautics Board, Federal Deposit Insurance Corporation, Interstate Commerce Commission, and Securities and Exchange Commission—is much more acceptable ideologically than more direct government intervention or ownership. Americans also tend to accept defense contracting and massive federal aid for research, as with nuclear energy, as legitimate aids to capitalism.

Economic policy in the United States is fragmented among more levels of government and different agencies than in Europe. The U.S. government tends to depend much more on "Financial inducement rather than direct control."[23] That is, it tends to rely on tax incentives and cash grants to encourage states and private businesses to follow federal policy. Compliance brings financial rewards from the government. There are many more points where powerful groups are able to veto a proposed policy. Major policy changes usually occur only under severe pressure. In the late 1970s and early 1980s increasingly large and vocal groups were demanding that the central government reduce its regulatory role. The debate over aid to Lockheed Corporation (1970–1971) and to Chrysler Corporation (1979–1980) reveals that many people believe that direct federal aid to business is questionable and even illegitimate.[24] The future of the modified market in the United States will depend on ideology and the pressures generated by the emerging energy crisis.

Many other Western industrialized countries directly control business. Canada, Italy, the Netherlands, Sweden (where the state owns 10 percent of the industry), and many more countries have moved to control or influence their economies. Contemporary Western countries seem committed to the mixed economy. It seemingly

[22]Alexander Hamilton, "Report on Manufactures" in *Papers on Public Credit, Commerce and Finance,* Samuel McKee Jr., ed., (New York: Columbia University Press, 1934) pp. 175–276.

[23]Heidenheimer et al., *op. cit.,* p. 260.

[24]Americans seem much more willing to allow local and state governments to aid business through such subsidies as direct cash grants, low-interest loans, reduced taxes, and so forth. See Ralph Nader and Jerry Jacobs, "The Subsidy Snowball," *The Nation,* 229, October 6, 1979, p. 289ff.

has solved the worse problems of recession but today is faced with other problems, such as limited energy, inflation, and increasingly complex governments.

COMMAND ECONOMY

The command economy is characterized by government economic sovereignty, rather than consumer sovereignty. The political leadership makes all major economic decisions. It determines inputs and outputs (prices, labor conditions, what will be produced, how resources will be allocated), thereby determining consumption patterns. Command economies are based on the belief that central planning and central control can achieve increased productivity and reduced inequalities more efficiently than a market system. Advocates of the command economy argue that competition is inherently wasteful and that markets respond to what it is profitable to produce, not what is most useful or necessary. Though no system has eliminated the market completely, market relations are secondary to planned production. At best, markets are seen as useful for distributing what is produced, not for deciding what ought to be produced. Ideologically, command economies are based on the belief that competition is selfish and wasteful, that man is basically cooperative.

Socialism or communism and a command economy are not necessarily synonymous. Theoretically, private ownership and state determination of production are possible. Nazi Germany approximated this scheme in some respects. In fact, most countries that have attempted to replace the market with central-government direction also have emphasized state ownership of the means of production. Markets have proven too flexible, however, to eliminate competition entirely. Yugoslavia has succeeded in introducing a modified market that has a large role in determining production. Czechoslovakia appears to have intended to introduce more market determination of production before the Soviet invasion of 1968 destroyed that experiment. Poland allows a semifree market for small businesses. All so-called socialist and communist countries allow peasants to sell some products privately, yet the overriding fact of command economies is that government determines the direction and nature of production and consumption.

Stalin's efforts to modernize the Soviet Union illustrate the command economy at its worst and in its purest form. Stalin determined that the Soviet Union must equal and then surpass Europe and the United States. He emphasized central planning and control. Local control was eliminated. The Soviet planners squeezed agriculture to provide the resources to build heavy industry. The output of heavy capital intensive industry then was reinvested in producing more heavy industry. Production of consumer goods was held to a low minimum. Central control of labor and extensive use of forced labor eliminated worker autonomy. Production targets or quotas, rather than profits or consumer demand, were and largely still are employed to determine what will be produced. Often, those who exceeded quotas were rewarded with bonuses and those who failed were removed from their position. Plant managers often ignored the quality of their products simply to meet quotas; thus, huge quantities of unusable products often were produced. In the 1960s the Soviet Union began to experiment with some limited decentralized decision-making. Within limits, factory managers were and are allowed production and pricing choices. These reforms have had only limited success. Though the system today is much less repressive, the basic pattern of central determination of production remains.

THE POLICY PROCESS

How have these different policies developed? The stages of policy making are similar from country to country although what is considered a policy problem, who will participate in the policy debate and at what stages, who has influence, how demands are made, and what policies will be adopted vary greatly. The policy debate is colored by ideology, self-interest, normative and empirical assumptions, political culture, real problems, perceptions of problems, and the type of issue involved (economic or civil rights policy, domestic or foreign policy). Nevertheless, the general process of policy making is remarkably similar.

Policy making is a continuous, complex process. Everywhere, it involves coalition building, creating support, and majorities of relevant decision makers at every step of the decision-making process. This is very obvious in the United States Congress, where pluralism, decentralized power, weak party structure, strong interest groups, the impact of **federalism**, and the separation of powers create a complex decision-making process. Yet a similar process occurs in parliamentary systems. In those countries with a disciplined two-party system, as in Britain, negotiation and compromise go on within the majority parliamentary party before a vote is taken. In multi-party systems coalitions of parties must agree on a common policy in order to create legislative majorities. Even in authoritarian systems or in command economies, conflict goes on within the dominant party. Leadership must satisfy at least its major supporters and the bureaucracies that will carry out and modify policy.

Who is involved in policy making varies from country to country and from issue to issue. Obviously the formal institutions of government discussed in previous chapters are involved. Legislatures, executives, bureaucracies, and—especially in the United States—courts may and often do have different policy preferences. Informal power holders also are involved in pluralistic, nonauthoritarian countries: interest groups, political parties, and sometimes the mass public through demonstrations or direct action. Occasionally a single individual has major influence in deciding policy issues. Ralph Nader started much of the policy debate regarding automobile safety in the United States when he published *Unsafe at Any Speed*.[25] Because of growing economic interdependence, foreign interests and actors often will be involved. For

[25]Ralph Nader, *Unsafe at Any Speed* (New York: Grossman, 1965).

example, the United States cannot implement an energy policy without considering the reaction of multinational corporations, petroleum-exporting countries, and importers who are also major allies. Moreover, policy conflict between levels of government is common. In federal systems such as Australia, Canada, and the United States, local government units have real autonomous power. There is constant negotiation between levels of government over jurisdiction and cost sharing. Quite often the national government does not have the power to order a province or state to conform but instead must offer financial incentives to gain cooperation. On any complex policy one or more of these actors may act as a veto group; that is, a group that, because of its influence, position in the decision-making process, or manipulation of symbols and ideology, is able to prevent consideration, passage or implementation of policies with which it disagrees. The policy process is, therefore, characterized by competition, struggle, and compromise, much of it far from public view.

PROBLEM DEFINITION
The first stage is **problem definition**. It is not always obvious what the problem is. Was treatment of black citizens a problem requiring public solution? Until the 1950s most Americans said no. Are unemployment, health care, pollution, gasoline shortages, huge profits for oil companies, low profits for small farmers, domestic surveillance of American citizens, and poor schools problems requiring a public solution? "A policy problem, in short, is a political condition that does not meet some standard."[26] Definition depends on values, preferences, assumptions, and what we are aware of. People and groups have many wants. Policy initiation begins when they attempt to convince the public and the decision makers that one of these wants or demands is important and legitimate. Groups constantly fight over these attempts because defining a problem is part of the political process. You cannot have a solution until you agree that there is a problem. Groups with high prestige and/or access to mass media or government officials usually will find it easier to have their demands defined as legitimate problems than those groups who are poor or despised.

AGENDA SETTING
Agenda setting is the next stage. It involves getting your problem or issue on the agenda of public debate. Every country has an agenda of issues that people consider important enough to warrant discussion. Most potential issues never receive serious consideration from policy makers. Even if people agree with your definition of a problem, they may consider your demand too complex, too difficult to meet, untimely, or too volatile to be considered. In the 1950s many people argued that the growing demands of black citizens were legitimate but should be postponed because most people were not yet ready to accept policies guaranteeing justice to

[26]Charles W. Anderson, *op. cit.*, p. 712.

this minority. No matter how vital a problem may be to the group articulating it, if they are unable to schedule it for government and public debate, they automatically lose. Leadership, protest, crises, and publicity all help move items onto the public agenda. Veto groups and opponents attempt to convince policy makers to keep policy demands they consider undesirable off the public agenda.

POLICY FORMATION

Policy formulation is logically distinct from, but often goes on simultaneously with, problem definition and agenda setting. **Formulation** is the process or action of proposing and developing alternative policies or courses of action for dealing with public problems. It includes determination of basic policy goals and principles, as well as determination of policy actions that may carry out these principles.[27] This process includes suggesting policies, testing if they may work, and starting to build a coalition of supporters. Many formal and informal actors typically are involved, though with unequal effect. Courts have a smaller impact at this stage than legislatures and executives. Interest groups are very active, but the mass public usually has little impact. Success of one or another alternative depends on the public's and policy makers' perceptions of an actor's legitimacy, the legitimacy of the proposals, available resources, and compatibility of new proposals with previously adopted ones. High-prestige actors, viewed as having a legitimate interest in a policy, who make incremental proposals that appear to have little cost and are considered legitimate and not requiring major deviations from previous policies, are likely to win. Costly proposals that require major changes in policy or the institutions that carry out policy are less likely to succeed. Innovations requiring significant changes in thinking and in the carefully built up coalitions of supporters and beneficiaries surrounding existing public policies are always the most difficult for which to find support.

ADOPTION

Formulation of a policy does not guarantee its **adoption.** Policy adoption by legislatures, executives, bureaucracies, and courts means choosing from the alternatives. This stage is intensely political. Actors modify proposals to build or weaken support or opposition. Generally major actors will not be completely satisfied but will see adoption of a policy as the first step in getting what they want. Quite often decision makers will not act positively on a proposal; in effect, they make a nondecision, leaving existing policy essentially unchanged.

IMPLEMENTATION OR EXECUTION

Few policy decisions are self-executing; therefore, the next stage, **implementation** or **execution**, is necessary. Implementation is complex and often subject to intense debate, conflict, and compromise. No major policy is complete when adopted.

---

[27]James E. Anderson, *Public Policy-Making, op. cit.,* p. 70.

Many important details must be worked out. Administrative agencies that usually have a voice in determining alternatives will be selected to implement the policy. Implementation often modifies it. Winning coalitions must be careful that their policy will be administered or carried out by a friendly or "sympathetic" agency. This may involve creation of a new agency, such as the Department of Education in the United States in 1979. Losers often attempt to move implementation to unfriendly agencies. These attempts are important because administrators have a good deal of discretion in interpreting and applying exceptions and in enforcement. For example, if gasoline rationing is approved, someone must write specific rules and decide how rationing legislation will be interpreted, who gets how much gasoline, and so forth. An agency that is opposed ideologically to rationing or swamped by other demands will not be capable of doing this successfully. One that favors such a policy, is on good terms with major actors, and understands the political problems of rationing still will fail to satisfy some actors but has a better chance of successfully implementing rationing. Such power extends to most decisions. The United States Department of Justice has discretion to determine how and against whom it will prosecute antitrust suits. Rival actors constantly attempt to convince administrators to adopt one policy interpretation rather than another. Moreover, agencies differ in organization, political skill, and operating policy, all characteristics that affect implementation.

FEEDBACK AND EVALUATION

There is overlap between implementation and the next stage, **feedback and evaluation**. Feedback refers to the flow of information and proposals back to decision makers about the impact or outcome of a policy. The major sources of feedback are the mass media, interest and client groups, political parties, and administrative personnel charged with day-to-day policy implementation. Based on their preferences and criteria, they decide whether or not a policy is working the way it was intended to work. Are costs too high? How do we measure costs? Is the agency carrying the policy out correctly? Does the policy have undesirable consequences? Undesirable consequences from whose perspective? Groups may claim that a new highway is not capable of carrying large volumes of traffic safely, that a program designed to increase employment is not meeting that goal, that minimum wage laws lead to teenage unemployment, or that price support programs harm family farms. The list is endless. These new demands may restart the entire policy process. At minimum they probably will also lead decision makers to evaluate the program in response to this feedback.

Evaluation requires criteria and guidelines in order to determine what is successful. These too are subject to intense debate. Some guidelines are legislatively mandated, with a stipulation of goals to be achieved, such as a 5 percent unemployment rate or an average of 20 miles per gallon for all new cars. Others are based on fairly technical criteria, such as the minimum requirements to keep an airplane flying or to reduce automobile pollution. Many criteria of evaluation are heavily value laden. Safety is a key component in the current debate about nuclear energy. How much safety is enough? What is an acceptable risk? Purely technical criteria cannot answer such questions. They require a normative judgement. The same is true of a wide range of other issues: What is equal opportunity? How much unemployment is acceptable? What tradeoffs should we accept between environmental pollution and cheaper production processes? Sometimes goals will be symbolic, unclear or diffuse, making evaluation very difficult.

CONTINUATION, MODIFICATION, OR TERMINATION
Evaluation of the relative success or failure of a policy and its relation to other policies leads to the final stage, **decisions to continue, modify or terminate the policy program**. Opponents of a policy always demand modification or termination; supporters ask for continuation or expansion. Legislatures often are involved in this debate. In recent years the U.S. Congress has debated whether to forbid use of federal money for abortions and whether the government should continue to subsidize and perhaps expand grants for public transportation. This stage of the policy process also is open to major disagreement. In a real sense demands or decisions to modify a program restart the entire policy process.

There is overlap among all stages. They are more distinct conceptually than in real policy debates. We can see this overlap, as well as pressure for policies, when we examine specific case studies of the public policy process.

THREE CASE STUDIES OF PUBLIC POLICY AND POLITICAL ECONOMY
Case studies enable us to see how politics and economics interact in policy making. In this section we shall examine three policy areas: energy, and, briefly, agriculture, and modernization. These areas are interdependent and cannot be separated easily. Each is the subject of intense political debate. Each problem area—for these topics are bundles of related problems and policies—will be with us for a long time. They are too complex to be solved easily; all possible solutions are costly. In examining these cases we shall look at the problem, demands, decision makers, policy alternatives, and what policies are being implemented.

ENERGY
Energy illustrates the tremendous difficulty of making public policy when high political, social, and economic stakes are complicated by ideological differences. Energy is a problem that can only be understood if we look at all of its relevant aspects. We may view the current energy debate as a case study still in the first

stages of the policy process outlined previously. We can easily **define the problem** in broad terms, but there is much disagreement over the exact content and meaning of the problem and still more conflict over possible solutions. Though there is a long history to energy policies, the 1973 Arab oil boycott, in response to the Arab–Israeli War, changed the basis for all previously existing energy policies. Many of these, such as those that encouraged private cars and dispersed housing, actually encouraged energy consumption based on the assumption that cheap Mideastern petroleum would always be available. The oil boycott and the many subsequent price rises for all forms of energy after the boycott demonstrated that energy prices can be manipulated. The resultant shock to the world financial and industrial system, and the growing realization that there is a long-term energy shortage symbolized the need for new energy policies. Despite this, the high stakes surrounding energy and the technical difficulties inherent in shifting energy use patterns have slowed the entire policy process. Energy is such an important policy issue that we have felt compelled to include it, even though the policy process is far from complete. The following discussion closely follows the systems (input-output) model developed in Chapter Two.

Energy is the key to this chapter. In attempting to **define the problem**, we realize that energy is the most important and complex technical/ethical policy issue today and is a perfect example of the interdependence of politics and economics at the domestic and international levels. It involves debate over what is the issue and what is the role of government and the market, questions of who will pay what, and a shift in the world balance of power. Energy affects agriculture because modern agriculture is an energy intensive industry. American, Canadian, and European agricultures consume much energy. Plentiful energy is a key to economic growth for the developing countries and essential to continued growth, even survival, for the developed countries. Expensive energy has slowed growth, increased inflation, generated unemployment, upset the balance of payments for many countries, and weakened the entire international economic system. The energy debate affects more people, involves more resources, and has a graver potential for future instability than any issue except the threat of nuclear war, and even that latter threat is related to energy in terms of nuclear proliferation—the spread of nuclear weapons. Proposals to expand nuclear power production may allow more countries to develop nuclear weapons from the byproducts of atomic plants. Moreover, there is a real possibility of conflict over energy resources.

These problems seem clear, but in a significant sense we are still at the stage of defining the problem. We cannot solve a problem until we decide what the problem is. Is there an energy shortage? The answer depends in part on your time scale—5 years or 25. Are prices too high? Probably. Will they come down? That is unlikely. What can be done? That is the heart of the current energy debate. Every area of our social, political, and economic values, as well as personal and public goals, is affected by energy. Most people find it difficult to understand all the ramifications of energy policy. It is easy to see how high prices and supply shortages affect our immediate daily needs. It is much harder to understand how energy will affect us in the next years or decades. It is extremely difficult to understand how energy will affect the larger society, nations and international political economy.

Consumption patterns are one problem. World consumption is increasing faster than production. In the United States, production of petroleum and natural gas, which accounts for 75 percent of consumption, has decreased since 1970. One can see the dimensions of the energy question by noting that the United States, with 6 percent of the world's population, consumes nearly one-third of the world's energy, including petroleum (Table 11-1). No country except Canada, which has a much greater potential and capacity for energy independence, approaches America's per-person levels of energy use. Per capita consumption in the United States is nearly 6 times greater than the world average. It is nearly twice that of the Soviet Union, 2½ times that of Western Europe, and 5 times that of Japan. On a per-person basis, it is nearly 30 times greater than Africa. At present the United States imports approximately 50 percent of its petroleum, the equivalent of one-fourth of its total energy consumption. Half of American energy consumption is for transportation needs, one-seventh of the world's total consumption.[28]

Dependence on an imported source of energy began in the 1950s when petroleum sold for $2 or less a barrel and there seemed no limits to its availability. Cheap petroleum literally fueled the great post-World War II economic expansion and encouraged the shift to petroleum. No one made a deliberate decision to become dependent on imported oil. Western governments largely allowed private companies to make energy policy decisions. Dominant values dictated that government involvement was undesirable. There was little or no strategic planning even though some people in the 1950s had begun to predict a future energy shortage.

Availability of energy is less an **immediate** problem than growing dependence on the Middle East and increasing prices. The Middle East has approximately three-quarters of the proven petroleum reserves outside China and the Soviet Union. The United States, Western Europe, and Japan have become dependent on continued sales of this oil to maintain their industrial economies. We are now in a situation of "asymmetrical interdependence and vulnerability."[29] Western countries depend on oil-exporting countries more than they depend on their Western Allies. This is politically dangerous. The Middle East is undergoing modernization, with all its inevitable political and social turmoil. The West depends most heavily "on Saudi Arabia, a nation of 5 or 6 million people—a highly traditional society."[30] Revolution, war and

[28]Barbara Ward, *Progress for a Small Planet* (New York: W.W. Norton, 1979), p. 50.

[29]Leon N. Lindberg, Energy policy and the politics of economic development. *Comparative Political Studies*, 10, October 1977, p. 355

[30]Robert Stobaugh and Daniel Yergin, eds., *Energy Future* (New York: Random House, 1979), p. 55

Table 11–1   World Primary Energy Consumption (Million Tonnes Oil Equivalent)

Country/area	1974 Oil	1974 Natural Gas	1974 Solid Fuels	1974 Water Power	1974 Nuclear	1974 Total	1973 Oil	1973 Natural Gas	1973 Solid Fuels	1973 Water Power	1973 Nuclear	1973 Total
U.S.A.	785.4	560.4	331.9	76.9	28.8	1,783.4	818.0	572.3	335.0	75.6	21.8	1,822.7
Canada	88.1	64.1	15.0	59.4	4.9	231.5	83.7	63.8	16.4	55.5	4.4	223.8
Other Western hemisphere	178.9	48.0	14.0	31.3	0.3	272.5	169.9	42.5	16.4	28.5	—	257.3
Total Western hemisphere	1,052.4	672.5	360.9	167.6	34.0	2,287.4	1,071.6	678.6	367.8	159.6	26.2	2,303.8
Belgium & Luxembourg	27.5	10.0	11.6	0.1	—	49.2	31.5	8.2	11.0	0.1	—	50.8
Netherlands	35.4	32.9	3.3	—	0.8	72.4	41.3	32.2	3.1	—	0.3	76.9
France	120.1	17.0	27.0	12.6	3.0	179.7	127.3	15.7	26.3	10.6	3.0	182.9
W. Germany	134.4	32.1	82.9	5.0	2.7	257.1	149.7	27.0	87.9	3.0	2.9	270.5
Italy	100.7	15.9	9.2	11.0	0.9	137.7	103.6	14.4	7.6	10.1	0.8	136.5
U.K.	105.8	30.8	68.9	1.3	7.3	214.1	113.4	26.1	78.5	1.2	5.9	225.1
Scandinavia	51.1	—	7.3	36.7	0.4	95.5	55.9	—	7.0	32.6	0.5	96.0
Spain	38.2	1.0	12.3	8.2	1.9	61.6	36.3	1.0	11.7	7.5	1.7	58.2
Other Western Europe	86.0	6.4	39.4	25.4	1.5	158.7	90.0	5.2	38.7	23.6	1.6	159.1
Total Western Europe	699.2	146.1	261.9	100.3	18.5	1,226.0	749.0	129.8	271.8	88.7	16.7	1,256.0
Japan	261.1	5.1	58.8	19.0	4.1	348.1	268.3	4.8	59.8	15.8	2.1	350.8
Australasia	33.9	4.1	26.1	2.4	—	66.5	32.8	3.9	29.4	2.2	—	68.3
U.S.S.R.	341.8	216.6	369.1	38.7	4.0	970.2	317.7	200.4	361.8	36.9	3.0	919.8
Eastern Europe	78.3	43.5	225.1	5.7	0.3	352.9	74.8	39.4	218.7	5.3	0.1	338.3
China[a]	48.8	4.4	331.5	9.5	—	394.2	41.7	4.0	316.3	9.0	—	371.0
Other Eastern hemisphere	227.4	42.0	134.8	21.1	1.0	426.3	220.0	37.9	127.5	19.5	1.0	405.9
Total Eastern hemisphere	1,690.5	461.8	1,407.3	196.7	27.9	3,784.2	1,704.3	420.2	1,385.3	177.4	22.9	3,710.1
World	2,742.9	1,134.3	1,768.2	364.3	61.9	6,071.6	2,775.9	1,098.8	1,753.1	337.0	49.1	6,013.9

Source: Robert L. Loftness, *Energy Handbook* (New York: Van Nostrand–Reinhold Co., 1978), p. 123

[a]Includes Albania, N. Korea and N. Vietnam.

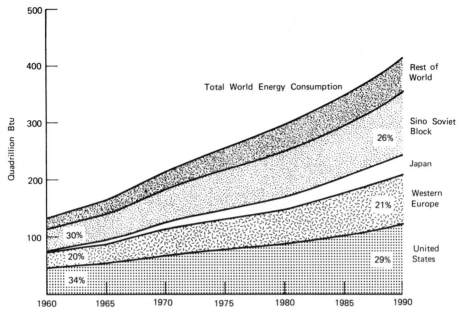

Figure 11–2. World energy consumption by region, 1960–1990 (Source: *Energy Perspectives*, U.S. Department of the Interior, February 1975; reprinted in Robert L. Loftness, *Energy Handbook* New York: Van Nostrand–Reinhold Co., 1978, p. 122).

assassination can cut off the nearly 10 million barrels of petroleum the Saudis sell each day. It is highly unlikely that this dependence can be reduced significantly, much less ended, in this century.

The economic and political problems caused by this dependence are staggering, compounding the difficulty of formulating workable policies. We can list some of these. The Organization of Petroleum Exporting Countries (OPEC) controls enough petroleum to virtually determine world prices, at any level its members choose. Between 1973 (when OPEC imposed the first successful price rise in response to an Arab-producer oil boycott during the 1973 Arab–Israeli War) and 1979, OPEC oil revenues went from $23.1 billion to an estimated $185 billion per year.[31] This has caused severe balance-of-payments problems for all importing countries. The United States alone spends nearly $200 million per day for imported oil. Massive arms sales and food exports have become necessary to pay for this. Still, the U.S. balance-of-payments deficit, at the time of writing, is nearly $2 billion per month. This deficit, in turn, has helped cause the decline in value of the U.S. dollar, further undermining international trade. Domestically, increased prices have fueled both recession and inflation, reducing the Gross National Product of the developed countries by esti-

[31]Embarrassment of riches. *Time*, November 5, 1979, p. 37.

mates that range from 1 to 5 percent per year. (In the U.S., a 2 percent reduction is approximately equal to the yearly budget deficits of the late 1970s.) Some of this money now is being recycled, invested back in the importing countries, leading to fears that oil exporters will be able to gain control of important parts of the banking, industrial, and agricultural systems of the developed nations.

Politically, the oil crisis has caused many problems. These include competition for supply; export drives to pay for imports, thus increasing economic and political competition between the United States and its allies in Europe and Japan; weakening of the European Economic Community and NATO; weakening of the international monetary system; disputes over ownership of potential producing areas in the East China Sea, the Eastern Mediterranean Sea, and elsewhere; efforts to use oil as a weapon; dangers of supply interruption; pressure to change U.S. and European foreign policy from support for Israel to support for the Arab cause; and, possibly, a reduction in foreign aid from the developed countries. Even the ability of the U.S. and Europe to respond to the Soviet Union is weakened by oil dependence. Domestically, political conflict has increased in the developed and developing countries due to the price increases and the growing danger of supply shortages from political causes and the genuine problem of not enough energy being available to meet all demands. Regional conflicts, disagreement over pricing policies, conflict over development of alternatives, and increasing labor and class conflict over redistribution as growth slows down are becoming common.

The developing countries especially have been hurt by price increases. Petroleum is the major commercial energy source in Africa and Latin America. As a group, the developing countries need both imported petroleum and foreign currency to develop. At a time when their foreign debts are over $200 billion, they too must pay 10 times or more the amount they paid for petroleum in 1973.[32] As most developing countries are petroleum importers, and few have easily available alternative energy sources, they face 2 possibilities. One is to import less oil, thus reducing their potential for growth. The other is to consume the scarce foreign currencies that are necessary for importing capital goods for economic development by spending them on the petroleum that also is necessary. Despite OPEC pledges of aid to the developing countries, there is a much greater flow of real resources from the poorer nation-states of the world to OPEC than from OPEC to the poorer countries.

These problems point to the kinds of **demands** and **policy recommendations** that are being made by domestic and international actors. People making demands differ over whether the energy crisis requires a political or economic solution. Various identifiable demands and policy goals include: cheap energy, plentiful energy, rapid growth, better distribution, protection of the environment from pollution, reduction of inflation, improvement in the balance of payments, and long-term availability

---

[32]In 1979 the poorest countries were spending an extra $15 billion per year for oil imports. Use less oil, *The Economist,* June 30, 1979, p. 71.

of energy. Different groups make different policy demands. Consumers want low prices and plentiful energy. Energy companies demand that the rate of profit remain the same even though prices increase drastically. Traditional political alliances fall apart. In the United States, civil rights groups found it hard to support the Democratic Party over President Carter's energy program because they felt that it would reduce the rate of growth. This would increase racial conflict as white people attempted to secure the best jobs for themselves. Moreover, reduced growth means there will be fewer resources to meet the policy demands of the disadvantaged and more conflict over how to spend the national budget. In Canada, the six-month-old Conservative government fell from power in late 1979 because it was not able to maintain its majority coalition in Parliament on a vote to raise gasoline taxes.

Clearly, many of these demands and goals are incompatible. In the short run of 10 to 20 years we cannot simultaneously use more coal cheaply **and** reduce pollution. We cannot improve the balance of payments **and** import more oil at the same time, even if more oil were available. These and other alternatives require us to choose, but choice requires a criterion, and the nature of that criterion is part of the current policy debate. Someone will pay. The question is who and how evenly costs will be shared. As there are few supports for any single policy option, we must expect that conflict will continue making agenda setting and policy formulation very

(Auth © 1977 The Philadelphia Enquirer. The Washington Post Writers Group.)

difficult as groups that oppose a specific policy know that if they can keep it off the agenda for debate they will have won. Under these circumstances efforts to adopt or implement a specific policy are often frustrated by the inability to put together a winning coalition of supporters at each stage of the policy process. Construction of a majority coalition is often hampered by fragmentation among relevant decision makers.

The energy decision-making system is highly fragmented affecting our ability to formulate, adopt and implement consistent energy policies. No single group, level of government, or nation has sufficient resources to impose its policies without making major compromises with others. This fragmentation makes policy adoption and implementation very difficult. To understand why, we must distinguish domestic and international, official and unofficial actors. Domestically, not a single government has yet developed a consistent energy policy.[33] In the United States, Presidents Nixon, Ford, and Carter presented elaborate energy programs, none of which proved popular with Congress. In countries with parliamentary systems, efforts to reduce energy imports and provide alternatives have proven equally difficult. So much money and the stability of established social-political-economic patterns is involved that all major interests have a vital stake in policy outcomes. Energy policy requires coalition-building among many different groups and interests. The energy debate has added many new groups, such as consumers and environmentalists, to the policy debate. Within a pluralist system no single interest is powerful enough to get all that it wants. Many, such as oil companies and states or provinces with large energy reserves, are powerful enough to veto policies they oppose. With such a diversity of demands it is very difficult to find any meaningful policy that a significant number of interests is able to agree on, and it is easy to see why policy is stalemated. Thus, we find conflict between groups, between legislatures and the executive, and between and within bureaucratic agencies. Until we find a common denominator, or until disaster strikes, these divisions probably will remain. Lest we assume the energy crisis is only a problem for democratic countries, all available evidence indicates the Soviet Union also is headed for an energy crisis, despite the fact it has large energy reserves.

Decision makers also are split along local central lines, further complicating the policy process. In a country such as the United States, state and local governments have a large role in energy policy. Implementation of some existing policies, such as the 55 mph speed limit, requires the cooperation of all levels of government. Much significant policy is made at the local level: housing costs that affect energy use, enforcement of speed limits, zoning policies that affect population density and distribution patterns, utility rate regulation, public transportation, even decisions about eliminating nonreturnable cans and bottles. The state and federal governments have been involved in debates over revenues from windfall profits and in le-

[33]Lindberg, *op. cit.,* p. 357. "Capitalism or communism, central planning or market-oriented economies, indicative planning or authorative planning, the similarities prevail and differences are only marginal."

gal suits over oil drilling in tidelands and the continental shelf. California has tougher antipollution laws than does the Federal government. In Canada, most mineral policy is set at the provincial level. Most of Canada's oil is in the west, particularly Alberta, while most of the population is in the east, in Ontario and Quebec. Federal-provincial splits over rates of exploitation and taxes are more severe than in the United States. In Great Britain, discovery of large oil deposits in the North Sea has encouraged a resurgence of Scottish nationalism, even separatism.

External actors, both multinational petroleum companies and individual countries, are very important participants in energy policy. Producing nation-states have an impact on policy. Mexico would like the United States to modify its immigration policy as part of any deal to sell petroleum or natural gas. Libya and Saudi Arabia attempt to change U.S. policy toward Israel. In late 1979 newspapers reported that the Saudi government, the major foreign supplier of oil to the United States, was angry and upset that the United States had not yet developed an energy policy and had allowed oil-company profits to increase as much as 200 percent. The Saudis wanted a windfall profits tax imposed on oil companies at the same time that powerful interests in Congress opposed such a tax.

American allies—Canada, Europe, Japan—form a seond powerful external decision-making group, even if their demands are not always the same. Canada is reducing petroleum sales to the United States because of its own growing needs. At the same time it wants the United States to control domestic recession and inflation because Canada's economy is so closely tied to that of the United States that American economic problems are exported automatically to Canada. Europeans and the Japanese make the same demands on the United States. Moreover, they consistently have argued that as long as the United States continues to import nearly one-third of the oil sold in international trade, prices will remain high. Based on the fact that European per-person consumption is much lower (little more than half of American consumption) and that the United States has more energy resources than Europe, they have argued that the United States must take the lead in conservation and development of alternatives. Less American consumption will leave more oil for Europe, reducing Western dependence on OPEC.

The United States also makes energy-related demands on Europe and Japan. These are primarily for support for the U. S. dollar, which is still the major currency employed in international trade. The Europeans also make energy demands on each other. Great Britain and Norway, the main beneficiaries from the discovery of North Sea oil, are determined to use this oil first for their own national needs. The European Economic Community (the EEC or Common Market) has not developed a common energy policy, yet Europe imports a larger part of its energy needs than does the United States. Common Market energy policies are tied to policies on agriculture and creation of a common monetary policy.

Within this interdependent web of rival demands and decision makers, adoption and implementation of effective policies require more cooperation than has so far occurred. Decisions in one area may have unforseen or undesirable consequences in other areas. For example a decrease in petroleum imports could increase unemployment. An increase in imports could worsen the balance of payments, which could also increase unemployment. Energy *policy decisions* are thus complex and intensely political. Moreover, policy decisions involve a series of other vital questions. One is, what is our time horizon? Will we focus on the next few years, or the next several decades? Long-range decisions are difficult because political payoffs are far distant in coming. Different solutions become feasible or not depending on your time frame. Secondly, what kinds of social, regional, or political changes are acceptable? Changes in energy policy can affect social and personal mobility, regional prosperity, even class and racial relations. Thirdly, what kinds of interventions are ideologically acceptable? Which activities could harm basic political and social values, such as liberal democracy and individualism?

To date, the energy debate has focused on a very narrow range of policy alternatives. Ideology, inertia, old policy decisions that limit current options, customs, high costs of developing alternatives, and limited learning experiences narrow policy in any area.[34] Changes in policy also are limited by disbelief that change is necessary and by faith in high-cost, complex, technological solutions. The huge sums invested in areas depending on cheap and plentiful energy—highways, private cars, wasteful manufacturing processes, dispersed housing—make major changes difficult despite much pressure to modify policy in these areas. Simply because something is necessary does not mean it will be translated into policy. Technology will not easily and cheaply solve our policy problems without hard choices from the public. Each of the many policies that has been suggested has a different coalition of supporters; requires different means to carry it out; and has different social, economic, and political costs. Each one, even conservation, will alter some relations and long-established social–economic patterns; policies may increase or decrease centralization or make suburban life more expensive. In all probability, a workable policy requires balance, but the current debate is dominated still by wishful thinking and insistence on accepting one alternative to the exclusion of all others.

In spite of these obstacles to policy formulation, some governments have started to deal with energy. Many **policy proposals** have been formulated. Proposals to overcome the energy crisis fall into four general categories: do nothing, emphasize market mechanisms, develop energy independence through alternative sources, and create a new value system. The last three proposals are not mutually incompatible, but supporters of each proposal tend to be suspicious of each other. Acceptance of any of these policies requires termination of such older policies as price limits, inexpensive leases of energy deposits on public land, and tax policies that encouraged energy use. Quite often, ideology colors the view that rival policy proposers have of each other. Let us now review some of the proposed policies.

Although all governments, on the surface, appear to have done little or nothing about energy problems, this is due to the complexity of the crisis and of the deci-

---

[34]See Lindberg, *op. cit.,* for a good discussion why energy policy is unlikely to change.

sion-making process. Each one has rejected inaction as a viable policy. To do nothing in the hope that there is no crisis or, if there is one it will go away, invites disaster now and for the future. All are agreed, therefore that **something** must be done. But what?

Market solutions are one answer. These propose allowing the market to determine price and consumption and are really a form of rationing by price. Most western countries have adopted some form of market solution. Traditionally, most European countries have allowed energy prices to be regulated by world prices and have discouraged energy use through very high taxes. The United States has decided to end regulating energy prices, a policy originally designed to protect producers' profits, thereby allowing prices to rise. This should decrease consumption to a limited extent and presumably increase domestic production. It is doubtful that all the needed energy can be produced domestically, at least in the United States,[35] as most of the easily recoverable petroleum and natural gas appear to have been discovered. Canada is also moving to decontrol prices and remove consumer subsidies, allowing domestically produced energy to rise to world price levels.

Feedback against implementing these market solution policies has been intense. These policies will drastically redistribute income between consumers and producers. Many consumers have begun to demand government aid to pay for energy for those too poor to afford higher prices. Some have resisted decontrol of prices or are demanding that controls be reimposed. Many people are demanding higher taxes on energy producers. At the same time, rival groups may be able to unite to frustrate policies they oppose in common, but not to formulate or implement a common policy. For example, the U.S. Congress, on June 6, 1980, overwhelmingly passed a bill, over President Carter's veto, to forbid the President from imposing a 10 cent per gallon tariff or import fee on petroleum. Although the tariff was designed to curb consumption by raising prices, increase revenues to balance the budget, and demonstrate the willingness of the United States to adopt an energy policy, producers and consumers united to defeat it. Consumers opposed the tariff because it would raise prices. Producers opposed it because it could have lowered profits. Other market proposals include voluntary reductions in consumption; additional taxes on consumption; grants, tax write-offs, and other incentives to encourage private businesses to conserve or develop additional energy sources; and some form of rationing where consumers who did not use their gasoline ration could sell it to drivers who needed more fuel than had been allotted to them. Each policy is opposed by groups who might have to change their current activities if the proposal was implemented.

---

[35]See Stobaugh and Yergin, *op. cit.,* p. 46: ". . . there is no domestic oil solution to the problem of increasing U.S. oil imports, no way that production from American oil wells can close the gap of 9 million barrels daily between what the U.S. produces and what it consumes." Only alternative energy sources can do that. Elsewhere they note that more oil wells have been drilled in the United States than in the rest of the world.

Decision makers in many countries have decided to supplement the market through government policies directed toward achieving energy independence through conservation and development of alternative fuels. Independence implies a drastic reduction or elimination of foreign energy imports. In the early 1970s, President Nixon proposed Project Independence but was unable to generate sufficient support to have his recommendations implemented. The United States has the potential for independence, but implementation of this project failed because of opposition generated by its high environmental, political, and economic costs; underestimation of the time required to develop alternatives; and violent disagreement over proposed options, especially nuclear power to generate electricity. Current American policy aims at reducing import dependence through conservation, development of alternatives, and creation of a petroleum reserve in salt caverns along the Gulf coast. This last program currently is running behind schedule and ahead of estimated costs.

Other countries are attempting to reduce dependence. Canada, a nation-state that has great energy potential, hopes its vast tar sand deposits can be mined successfully, but costs are very high, as much as $2½-billion for one fully producing plant. Britain's North Sea oil could give it relative independence until the end of the century, when alternative sources might begin to have a major impact. The Common Market countries attempt to maintain a minimum 90-day supply of petroleum to reduce the impact of supply interruptions. Japan, which of all major industrial nation-states imports the largest percent of energy, attempts to maintain large petroleum stocks. Stockpiling, however, is only an expedient to overcome temporary supply disruptions, not an energy policy.

Development of alternative energies is costly, difficult, and time consuming. All alternatives require a substantial public commitment. Supporters talk about a hard path and a soft path.[36] The "hard" alternative emphasizes massive technological solutions: coal and coal gasification and liquification, with its environmental and social problems; shale oil, which is expensive to develop and requires large amounts of water to produce; natural gas, which is in short supply; combination fuels, such as gasahol; nuclear power, which raises questions of safety now and into the foreseeable future; and, in the next century, fusion power. "Soft" energy solutions emphasize renewable and often smaller-scale policy options: solar power, which includes wind, hydro, and direct heating by the sun, all of which could, given the policy decision, meet 20 percent of American energy needs by the year 2000[37]; conservation, which does not necessarily reduce production or jobs; small-scale hydro; geothermal projects; biomass conversion, including trees, crops, manure and trash; and use of ocean currents.

Each proposal, hard or soft, requires serious public commitment. Supporters of some proposals find it hard to imagine others. Each alternative competes for scarce

[36]Amory B. Lovins, *Soft Energy Paths* (Cambridge, Mass.: Ballinger Publishing Company, 1977).
[37]Stobaugh and Yergin, *op. cit.*, pp. 211–212.

time, resources, and technological skills. Adoption and implementation of each of these policies have been stymied by massive opposition from those who will pay the most costs. Each proposal requires major changes in investment patterns, regional relations, and probably the role of government. Public policy is slowly, painfully moving toward some choices, but policy decisions are only the first step. Implementation of any policy except immediate conservation or rationing will take a decade or longer before having a major impact.[38]

Finally, there is the alternative of creating a new value system. For generations, critics have argued that the Western emphasis on conquering nature and expanding production is doomed to ultimate disaster. Such philosophy they argue, leads to resource depletion, pollution, emphasis on quantity not quality, control over others, and authoritarian centralizing technology. Rather, we need to create a new life style, one that will be more harmonious with nature in the sense that it will consume fewer nonrenewable resources that future generations also will need. Such an alternative life style could maintain a relatively high standard of living but would deemphasize consumption and growth as ends in themselves. Rather, it would focus on human use of resources, smaller-scale technology, and use of renewable resources.[39]

Energy remains an issue in search of agreement on the nature of the problem or problems and possible solutions to these problems. Individuals, private businesses, and governments are attempting to create and follow policies beneficial to them, and are often working at cross-purposes. Implementation of some policies has begun: higher prices to reduce consumption, pilot projects for synthetic fuels, conversion to coal, limited sales of gasohol, limited research on solar energy, and many more. Much remains to be done. Energy is one of the largest and most complex issues facing contemporary public policy. The eventual disposition of this issue, assuming that is possible, will require massive debate and commitment. It will take years, perhaps decades to understand and evaluate the full impact of these alternative policies.

AGRICULTURE

The nature of food and agricultural policy varies from country to country. In a basic sense the fundamental problems are similar: everywhere, whether the United States or Africa, small farmers find it very difficult to make a living; production is often inadequate to meet domestic and perhaps export demands; compensation to producers is often inequitable; and somehow consumers must be guaranteed relatively low prices. Within these broad outlines there is no single agricultural problem or policy but rather a series of problems the exact nature of which depends on the technical, economic, and social levels of the nations involved. In dealing with these

[38]This argument forms the basic theme in *ibid.*

[39]E.F. Schumacher, *Small is Beautiful* (New York: Harper & Row, 1973), was a leading advocate of this position.

problems, countries have employed a similar set of policy tools: tariffs, quotas on imports, bounties for exports, price supports, and storage and price guarantees. In this century, no major government has felt that it was possible to allow a pure market solution to agricultural problems. Economically, farming has been viewed as too important to allow prices and output to fluctuate freely. Politically, farmers are usually well organized and willing to vote their economic interests. In this century, European and North American farm organizations have been among the most successful interest groups, able to attain a large amount of public support to maintain prices. In this section we will focus on agriculture in the developed countries, looking at the major policy outcomes that farm groups have succeeded in convincing their governments to implement.

Since 1940, U.S. agricultural output has more than doubled, providing abundant, inexpensive food for domestic consumers and large surpluses for export. This growth in output is related to growth in farm size and a biological, mechanical, and chemical revolution that has reduced drastically the number of persons employed in agriculture. At the same time American and Canadian agriculture has become highly energy intensive. In the United States only the steel and petrochemical industries consume more energy than agriculture and food processing; the latter consume 3.5 percent of all U.S. energy. This includes direct usage as well as fertilizers and chemicals.[40] This expansion in production and the accompanying expense to farmers has been catastrophic for traditional farming.

Technical and scientific change, as well as growth in the scale of farming, is undermining the family farm. As farming becomes more complicated and expensive, as new machines and chemicals become available, as the size of markets grows beyond the local community or region to the world, small farmers in the United States and elsewhere find it exceedingly difficult to compete with large, often corporate farms. These trends encourage more specialization; specialized farmers are very sensitive to price changes in their commodity. Food production is the closest we can find to a process that operates on the approximation of a pure market. Typically, high prices encourage farmers to produce more; increased production drives prices down; low prices often encourage more production to overcome financial losses due to low prices. Unlike most of the rest of the world, American and Canadian agriculture is plagued by problems generated by their efficient output: low prices, often low farm income, and frequent overproduction. Agricultural interest groups sometimes find policy agreement difficult because a problem of overproduction for one farmer may mean cheap inputs for another; thus, a surplus of corn or grain may drive prices down but also reduce feed costs for poultry and cattle raisers.

Until the early 1900s, government agricultural policy in the United States focused on increasing production. In 1787 the vast majority of the population lived on farms. Jefferson justified the Louisiana Purchase in part as providing more cheap farm

---

[40]Richard C. Dorf, *Energy, Resources and Policy* (Reading, Mass.: Addison Wesley Publishing, 1978), p. 189.

land. Inexpensive sales of government lands eventually resulted in the Homestead Act of 1862, giving settlers 160 acres of land in exchange for living and working that land for 5 years. The Morrill Act of 1862 started the land-grant colleges; states received public lands to support colleges of agriculture and engineering. Public policy supported low-cost mail delivery, research into crop development, extension services, conservation, cooperatives, and, in the 1930s, rural electrification. All these policies, and more, continue to support agriculture, but since the 1950s public policy has changed to cope with problems generated by a farming system that produces more food than the market can absorb.

The Depression of the 1930s began for farmers in the 1920s. The Roosevelt administration in response to low prices and farmer's demands commenced active intervention to raise farm prices and reduce production. The Agricultural Adjustment Act of 1938, still the basis for contemporary agricultural policy, introduced the idea of an "ever-normal granary"; that is, the idea that public policy should aim at stable food supplies and stable prices. Between 1933 and 1973, policy emphasized planting restrictions or quotas and price supports to stabilize farm income. Price supports occasionally included direct purchase but more often involved a loan program that established minimum prices for such major products as corn and wheat. This program gave loans to farmers who used their crops as collateral. If prices rose above the value of the loan, farmers could repay the loan and sell their crops. If prices fell below the value of the loan, the government took control of the crop, in effect purchasing it above the market price. This led to massive government-owned surpluses; in the late 1960s and early 1970s these surpluses were costing the public up to $4 billion a year. In 1954, Congress enacted Public Law 480, the Food for Peace Program, to give or sell surplus food to the developing countries. At its inception, PL 480 was primarily a domestic disposal program that used foreign policy as its means of execution. Today, with reduced surpluses and growing foreign markets, Food for Peace is a more limited program, designed to help the poorest nations. In 1979 and 1980 it provided about $1.2 billion in food aid each year.

New laws in 1973 and 1977 created a system of "target prices," which are minimum prices for such crops as wheat. Under a complex formula, the government computes the cost of production to farmers. If the price of a product falls below this level, the government pays farmers the difference between the market price and the target price. Farmers have complained that the target price is much too low and it does little to assist small farmers; however, it has greatly reduced the cost of aid to farmers something demanded by many consumers. In addition, programs such as the food-stamp program (which pays out over $5 billion a year) and PI 480 provide indirect price support. The U.S. government also actively promotes and aids foreign food sales, providing further indirect aid to agriculture. Many people have argued the United States should use the threat of withholding these sales as a foreign policy weapon, but such a policy is opposed actively by exporters.

The United States currently is exporting approximately $25 billion in farm products a year. American consumers pay one of the lowest proportions of income in the world for food. The United States increasingly is building one of the world's few large reserves of surplus food. American farmers have serious problems, but they are the most successful agriculturalists in the world. This paradox is due to public agricultural policy.

The large increase in population that accompanied industrialization in Europe far outstripped the ability of European farmers to meet domestic food needs. Imports became necessary, and by World War I Britain imported half of its food. Other countries less dedicated to free trade protected and aided domestic farmers with tariffs, import quotas, and subsidies. With war Britain also subsidized food production. Even with government aid, European farms still failed to meet all domestic food needs. Less agricultural land per capita than in North America, smaller farms, and large agricultural populations all contributed to this crisis.

In an effort to make Europe more food independent and in response to farmers' demands for higher prices, the Common Market countries have created a Common Agricultural Policy (CAP) that has encouraged both production and efficiency.[41] Along with increased mechanization and use of fertilizers and other agricultural chemicals, CAP has dramatically increased the amount of food produced in Europe. CAP regulates trade with other nations by establishing a price for food inside the EEC. It creates a common external tariff that slides up or down along with EEC needs and prices. Tariffs go up if EEC farmers produce a large surplus, down if there is a shortage. Under the CAP farmers may receive subsidies from their own national government and the Common Market. Aid to farmers is financed jointly by EEC members.

Though CAP has encouraged increased production, the cost has been high. In addition to higher food prices for consumers, the EEC paid over $15 billion in farm subsidies in 1979.[42] Unfortunately, in Europe as in the United States, large farmers receive most of the subsidies because aid is based on production. Thus, at the same time that the United States is reducing the cost of agricultural aid, the EEC is increasing its aid. This aid is building up huge surpluses of food. Europeans refer to a "butter mountain" and a "wine lake" of unsellable surpluses. In addition, there are large surpluses of sugar and other commodities. The EEC has found it very impolitic to reduce subsidies, because of strong farmer opposition. Farmers are organizing on a Common Market level, presenting the first case of international organization by interest groups. Moreover, agriculture is an important part of bargaining within the EEC because governments trade support in areas such as monetary policy for support from other countries for their farmers. Dispute over agricultural policy has pitted Britain against France and France against West Germany; it has slowed admission membership applications of other countries, including Spain. In Europe

---

[41]John Marsh, Europe's agriculture: Reform of the CAP, *International Affairs,* 53, October 1977, pp. 604–614; Denis Bergmann, Agricultural policies in the EEC and their external implications, *World Development,* 5, May-July 1977, 407–415

[42]Use less oil. *The Economist,* June 30, 1979, p. 72.

as in the United States, debate over agricultural policy involves very high political and economic stakes.

MODERNIZATION

Growth presents policy problems for all countries, but especially for the poorer nations of the world. Many of the specifics of development policy will be discussed in the chapter on political development. Here we will limit ourselves only to an outline of major policy issues. Development policy is a problem because poverty and relative lack of industrialization and modern agriculture characterize the developing countries. The gap between rich and poor nations is not decreasing. Everything needs to be done. Decision makers face a series of basic policy choices that must be made before the actual process of modernization can begin.

The first choice is deciding on a model for development. What system works "best" given limited economic, political and decision-making resources? Most developing countries accept some form of modified market economy. Many have attempted to implement welfare policies immediately; developed countries took centuries to produce their social security and universal education programs. A small number, in particular China, have adopted a command economy. Most argue that it is necessary to combine elements from each of the major political/economic systems in order to develop an alternative to mixed and so-called socialist models. The basic question often becomes what should be the investment split between government and private enterprise, not whether development should be left to one or the other. India combines government ownership of some basic industry, aid to agriculture and industry, regulation, welfare policy, and a vigorous capitalist system. Mexico owns the petroleum industry but encourages capitalist development of most other industries.

Resources are always limited and the developing countries have a second series of hard policy choices: What segment of the economy should be emphasized? How can capital be accumulated and utilized best? Should the authorities emphasize infrastructure—the building of communication and transportation networks necessary to a modern economy—or agriculture, or industry? If industry, should it be heavy industry, that is industries that produce steel, machine tools, and the like? All these areas must be changed, but where does one start? Twenty-five years ago the answer was simple—industry. That has not worked well, however, in countries with large rural populations. Industrial development consumes great amounts of scarce capital, especially labor-saving Western technology that often requires tremendous imports of petroleum. Agricultural productivity is low and more output is necessary to feed industrial workers and growing cities. Massive rural to urban migration is a fact in all developing countries, leading to severe strains on food and urban services. If the rural area were more attractive fewer people might move, but how does government make it more inviting? It could change agriculture, but that is costly and may cause additional severe dislocations. Agricultural growth requires much more than simply new seeds and a few machines. It requires heavy investment in education and rural health, to allow farmers to use new opportunities; investment in roads and markets; changes in land tenure systems, to guarantee that farmers will benefit from improvements they institute; extension services; cheap credit; fertilizers that will be imported or will require imported petroleum for their production; storage facilities; and many other factors.[43] Simply increasing output without altering the rural social and political system may force landless laborers, tenant farmers, and small holders off the land, increasing unemployment and urban growth. Any policy requires balance, but balance, too, is costly.

Developing countries also must decide if they will emphasize production for export or domestic use. One goal of development is an improved standard of living, but growth requires foreign imports. These must be paid for with exports into the already heavily competitive world market. The developing nations are unable to pay for their import needs, including oil, and their foreign debt grew by $40 billion in 1979.[44] They also are faced with the cruel choice of increased consumption now or forced savings out of meager production in order to build capital goods that will increase future consumption. It is necessary to balance these competing claims, but the point of balance is part of the policy debate.

Finally, the developing countries must deal with the inevitable social-political change generated by economic growth. There is not a single recorded case of a country undergoing major economic change without social-political change. European, American and Japanese industrialization illustrate that Iran typifies the pressures faced by developing countries. Under the Shah, a modernizing autocracy attempted to impose economic growth on a largely traditional society. The Shah pushed industrialization at a rapid rate but opposed political concessions to the rising bureaucratic and technical middle class produced by and needed to continue modernization. Nor was he willing to make concessions to traditional groups who opposed modernization since it undermined traditional social relations and religious practices. At the same time, high inflation, insufficiently trained personnel, and inadequate infrastructure encouraged discontent. Unlike Stalin, the Shah could not control opposition. Groups hostile to each other, having incompatible pictures of Iran's future, could agree on one thing: the Shah must go. Iran's future depends on which of these rival groups will be able to seize power and keep it, Iran's revolution against its modernizing autocracy could happen in any country where leaders attempt to impose rapid change without considering its impact on other areas of life or without the necessary tools to put down opposition effectively. The basic problem is to encourage change at a pace fast enough to improve living conditions but slow enough to avoid overly rapid social change.

[43]Max F. Millikan and David Hapgood, *No Easy Harvest* (Boston: LIttle, Brown, 1967).
[44]*New York Times,* "Business and Finance" Section, June 10, 1979, p. 1.

SUMMARY

It is possible to study many public policies. This chapter emphasized those policies dealing with political economy. (Other chapters look at schools, development, and foreign policy.) Public policy analysis focuses on what governments attempt to accomplish. There is great pressure for governments to deal with the economic, social, and political problems generated by economic and technological change. Though governments differ in form, ideology, and who is influential, policy follows a similar series of stages from recognition of a problem to evaluation of the success of policies designed to deal with the problem. Though all governments face a similar series of problems, actual policy responses differ greatly. Ideology, available resources, and available problem-solving models all affect the outcome.

SELECTED READINGS

James E. Anderson, *Public Policy-Making** (New York: Praeger, 1975) is an excellent, highly readable introduction to policy-making. It is a very good place to start further reading on this topic. See also James E. Anderson, David W. Brady, and Charles Bullock III, *Public Policy and Politics in America** (North Scituate, Mass.: Duxbury Press, 1978). This book examines a wide variety of policies, including energy, the environment, intervention in the economy, and agriculture. Robert Eyestone, *Political Economy: Politics and Policy Analysis** (Chicago: Markham, 1972) is a very good discussion of many of the issues discussed in this chapter. Douglas E. Ashford, ed., *Comparing Public Policies: New Concepts and Methods* (Beverly Hills: Sage Publications, 1978) analyzes some of the tools and perspectives available for analysis of public policy. Arnold J. Heidenheimer, Hugh Heclo, and Carolyn Teich Adams, *Comparative Public Policy: The Politics of Social Choice in Europe and America** (New York: St. Martin's Press, 1975) is an excellent analysis of such public policies as health, schools, transport, and taxation in the United States and several West European countries. Its comparative approach adds an essential perspective for analyzing and understanding public policy. Barbara N. McLennan, *Comparative Political Systems: Political Processes in Developed and Developing States* (North Scituate, Mass.: Duxbury Press, 1975) gives a cross-cultural comparison of nine countries. Richard Rose, ed., *Policy Making in Great Britain: A Reader in Government* (New York: The Free Press, 1969) examines the full range of public policies. Albert O. Hirschman, *Journeys toward Progress: Studies of Economic Policy-Making in Latin America** (New York: Doubleday, 1965) is a classic in the field of public policy. Barbara Ward, *Progress for a Small Planet* (New York: W.W. Norton, 1979) is an excellent popular discussion of the policy and values surrounding the threat of scarcity for developed and developing nations. She discusses all of the pol-

*Available in paperback

icy issues in this chapter. Ward argues we need to develop a conserving strategy on a world-wide basis. Christopher Freeman and Marie Jahoda, eds., *World Futures: The Great Debate* (New York: Universe Books, 1978) analyzes and discusses basic policy issues, including food and energy, in terms of possible future developments. Thomas R. Dye, *Understanding Public Policy* (Englewood Cliffs, N.J.: Prentice Hall, 1978) analyzes important American case studies.

There are a number of good journals that deal with public policy. *Philosophy and Public Affiars* analyzes some of the ethical and philosophical aspects of contemporary public issues. More empirically oriented journals include *Policy Analysis, Policy Review, Policy Sciences,* and *Policy Studies Journal.* It is necessary to read periodicals regularly to keep informed on public policy and political economy. Any good newspaper and news magazine will do, but we have found *Congressional Quarterly Weekly Report, The Economist,* and the *New York Times* especially useful.

Public policy has a very large ethical component. See Tom L. Beauchamp, ed., *Ethics and Public Policy* (Englewood Cliffs, N.J.: Prentice Hall, 1975) for discussion of such issues as discrimination, abortion, and biomedical technology. Fred M. Frohock, *Public Policy: Scope and Logic* (Englewood Cliffs, N.J.: Prentice Hall, 1979) analyzes the normative aspects of complex public policies. Charles W. Anderson, *Statecraft: An Introduction to Political Choice and Judgement* (New York: John Wiley, 1977) is an excellent discussion of the operational and ethical problems of decision making. See also his ''The Place of Principles in Policy Analysis,'' *American Political Science Review,* 73, September 1979, pp. 711–723.

Politics and Markets: The World's Political–Economic Systems, by Charles E. Lindblom (New York: Basic Books, 1977) is one of the finest analyses of the contemporary interrelation of politics and economies. He examines market economies, government-controlled economies, variations on these, and possible alternatives, while always being concerned with democracy. Leon N. Lindberg, ed., *Politics and the Future of Industrial Society** (New York: David McKay, 1976) analyzes the political problems of change in the highly developed countries. Everyone interested in political economy and public policy should become familiar with some of the classics of this field. Adam Smith's *An Inquiry into the Nature and Causes of the Wealth of Nations,* (New York: Modern Library, 1937) first published in 1776 and available in many modern editions, provides the basic description and defense of a *laissez-faire* political-economic system. It still makes excellent reading after more than 200 years. John Maynard Keynes, *The General Theory of Employment Interest and Money,** (New York: Harcourt, Brace and Company, 1936) first published in 1936 and available in many editions, is difficult but rewarding. This is the classic intellectual justification for government involvement in economic relations. At the least, read Chapter 24, ''Concluding Notes on the Social Philosophy Towards Which the

*Available in paperback

General Theory Might Lead." For good studies of the impact of Keynesian economics on public policy, see Robert Lekachman, *The Age of Keynes* (New York: Random House, 1966) and *Economists at Bay: Why the Experts Will Never Solve Your Problems* (New York: McGraw-Hill, 1976). See also Donald Winch, *Economics and Policy: A Historical Study* (London: Hodder and Stoughton, 1969).

Because the issue is so important, and debate is so intense, there is a huge number of books and articles on energy. Those listed here are a tiny sample. Newspapers, newsmagazines, and scholarly journals regularly publish important pieces on energy, and we suggest you sample these for yourself. Robert Stobaugh and Daniel Yergin, eds., *Energy Future: Report of the Energy Project at the Harvard Business School* (New York: Random House, 1979) is one of the most important books to date analyzing the American energy situation within its political and economic context. The authors conclude that for the rest of this century public policy must emphasize and encourage conservation and solar energy to reduce dependence on foreign oil. Expanded production of natural gas, coal, oil, and nuclear energy is not possible due to resource shortages and technical constraints. See also Richard C. Dorf, *Energy, Resources and Policy* (Reading, Mass.: Addison-Wesley, 1978). Robert L. Loftness, *Energy Handbook* (New York: Van Nostrand Reinhold, 1978) contains superb charts and statistics on energy. Leon N. Lindberg "Energy Policy and the Politics of Economic Development," *Comparative Political Studies,* 10, October 1977, 355–382, is essential reading for anyone seriously concerned with energy policy. Thomas H. Tietenberg, *Energy Planning and Policy: The Political Economy of Project Independence* (Lexington, Mass.: Lexington Books, 1976), analyzes a very important policy episode. *The Geopolitics of Energy* by Melvin A. Conant and Fern Racine Gold (Boulder, Colo.: Westview Press, 1978) and Mason Willrich et al., *Energy and World Politics* (New York: The Free Press, 1975) give important analyses of the political issues involved with energy policy. *Myth, Oil and Politics: Introduction to the Political Economy of Petroleum* (New York: Free Press, 1977) by Charles F. Doran, examines and refutes some of the popular misconceptions about petroleum politics, including the myth that Israel is the cause of high oil prices and that OPEC is highly cohesive. Amory B. Lovins, *Soft Energy Paths: Toward a Durable Peace** (Cambrdige, Mass.: Ballinger, 1977) is one of the most influential books discussing alternative energy policies to reduce dependence on high-technology, nonrenewable energy sources. Lovins argues that it is possible to use technologies that employ renewable energy sources, increase production and productivity, and reduce conflict over energy. See also his "Energy Strategy: The Road Not Taken?" *Foreign Affairs,* 55, October 1976, 65–96.

The Great Economic Debate: An Ethical Analysis* (Philadelphia: The Westminister Press, 1977) by J. Phillip Wogaman examines contemporary political economic

*Available in paperback

ideologies, from *laissez-faire* capitalism to Marxism, from a religious value perspective. Wogaman insists that economics and economic decisions are morally relevant. E.F. Schumaker, *Small is Beautiful: Economics as if People Mattered** (New York: Harper & Row, 1973) argues that technology must serve people first, not systems, and that a more humane world is possible only if we change our values.

The Summer 1978 issue of *Policy Studies Journal* is devoted to analyzing most of the policy issues confronting U.S. agriculture, such as who is involved in making policy, water problems, and foreign sales. There are many good books dealing with world food shortages. From among many sources see George R. Lucas, Jr. and Thomas W. Ogletree, eds., *Lifeboat Ethics: The Moral Dilemmas of World Hunger* (New York: Harper & Row, 1976) and Joseph W. Willett, compiler, *The World Food Situation: Problems and Prospects to 1985* (Dobbs Ferry, N.Y.: Oceana Publications, 1976) 2 volumes. These volumes bring together United States, United Nations and scholarly examinations of world hunger. Georg Borgstrom has written extensively about food problems; see especially *Too Many: A Study of Earth's Biological Limits* (London: Macmillan, 1969) and *Harvesting the Earth* (New York: Ableard-Schuman, 1973). For good discussions of the political, economic, and environmental problems of agriculture in the developing countries, see Max F. Millikan and David Hapgood, *No Easy Harvest: The Dilemma of Agriculture in Underdeveloped Countries** (Boston: Little, Brown, 1967) and Theodore W. Schultz, *Transforming Traditional Agriculture* (New Haven: Yale University Press, 1964). Vilho Harle, ed., *The Political Economy of Food* (Westmead, England: Saxon House, 1978) is an excellent, thorough series of discussions of the political and political-economic environment of food, especially in the developing nations. Vernon W. Ruttan, et. al., eds., *Agricultural Policy in an Affluent Society* (New York: W.W. Norton, 1969) and Ross B. Talbot and Don F. Hadwiger, *The Policy Process in American Agriculture* (San Francisco: Chandler, 1968) provide very good reviews of the history and content of agricultural policy. Stanley Johnson, *The Green Revolution* (New York: Harper & Row, 1972) reviews one of the most important policy outcomes of this century: expansion of agricultural output in the developing countries.

A number of books on technology and change are available. See George M. Foster, *Traditional Cultures and the Impact of Technological Change* (New York: Harper and Brothers, 1962). See also Emmanuel Mesthene, *Technological Change: Its Impact on Man and Society** (Cambridge, Mass.: Harvard University Press, 1970). The literature on development is growing and often well written. Jason L. Finkle and Richard W. Gable, eds., *Political Development and Social Change** (New York: John Wiley, 1971) is especially valuable. It intelligently covers the full range of development policy. See also Dankwart A. Rustow, *A World of Nations* (Washington, D.C.: Brookings Institution, 1967).

*Available in paperback.

Part Four

Political Change and International Politics

Chapter Twelve

Dynamics of Political Change and the Developing World

The developing world, or Third World, includes Africa, Asia, Latin America, and the Middle East. This is in contrast to the postindustrial democratic countries of Western Europe, the United States, Canada, Australia, New Zealand, and Japan; and the Second World, the Communist countries of Europe. Depending on the speaker and the context, the People's Republic of China (PRC), with a population of approximately 1 billion, sometimes is included in the Communist world, but more often in the Third World. We include the PRC in the developing-country category. Altogether, the developing world accounted for 71 percent of the world's population in 1975 and at current growth rates will contain 78 percent of the world's population in 2000. It is a majority of the world we *cannot* ignore (see Figure 12–1).

The Third World often includes Latin America. In several ways, however, Latin America is unique and is not identified always as a Third World region. Almost all of the Latin American countries achieved their independence by 1824. For the rest of the developing world, independence came generally after World War II. Latin America also has a shared inheritance, which many developing countries, even those that border one another, do not have. Most of Latin America was a Spanish colony. Its social, political, and economic backgrounds are similar. These countries shared common religious, political, and economic structures for many years before independence. When one looks at other developing countries, one sees contiguous countries where one colony was ruled by Great Britain and neighboring colonies by France, Belgium, Portugal, or the Netherlands. The colonial heritages and traditions are much more diverse in Asia, Africa, and the Middle East than in Latin America.

There are some 160 sovereign nation-states in the world today. More than half of these have come into existence since World War II. These new countries that emerged from colonial rule after 1945 commonly are referred to as developing countries or developing political systems. United States government publications

394

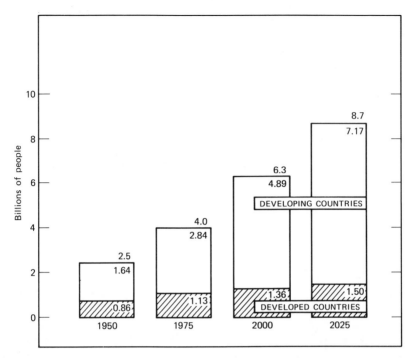

Figure 12-1.   World population growth, 1950–2025. *Source: Concise Report on the World Population Situation in 1977.* United Nations, New York, 1979, page 8. *Population Studies*, No. 63 ST/ESA/SER. A/63. Projected growth for developing world is 2.2 percent annually and 0.7 percent annually for the developed world.

refer to these countries as LDCs, or Less Developed Countries. We do not use that term in this book because it suggests that countries labeled LDC have an inferior status.

These new developing political systems share certain characteristics:

1. Their formal independence is relatively recent. Most are less than 30 years old.

2. The government and constitutional structures are new and still evolving, as are the organization and responsibilities of the executive branch; the organization, training, and functioning of the administrative service; and the organization and functioning of legislative and judicial institutions. These structures are just beginning to institutionalize, and their organization and duties are often subjects of intense political disputes. A rather extreme case occurred in late 1979, when the head of the Korean CIA shot and killed President Park Chung Hee.

3. Many political organizations, such as political parties, are unsure of their objectives (whether to participate in government or overturn the political system), have weak organizations, and are searching for an effective style of participation (electioneer, demonstrate, or be bought off by the ruling elites).

4. There are few autonomous interest groups, such as trade unions and business organizations, that have a history of making claims on government or have an input in policy making and are not controlled by government.

5. There is a tradition of avoidance politics, where the village head, village council, or religious or clan leaders seek to minimize the impact of government. The masses had no opportunity to influence policy making, but they were concerned with avoiding or mitigating more arbitrary or demanding government requirements, such as taxes, conscription, or "voluntary" labor.

6. Government usually limited itself to providing security, transportation facilities, and occasionally irrigation and flood-control projects. It required taxes, military conscripts, and the corvée (unpaid contributed labor for public works projects). Governments could be and often were oppressive, but their functions were limited.

7. A number of easily quantifiable characteristics are present, such as low per capita income; limited distribution of technology; a predominantly rural society, with often as high as 80 to 85 percent of the population living in rural areas; a small percentage of the population working in manufacturing; lower levels of caloric consumption; limited medical and health facilities, with fewer doctors or nurses per 1000 population; limited educational opportunities and high unemployment for those who do earn a college degree; relatively low literacy, often below 50 percent; high birth rate; limited social mobility; and so on.

8. Exports are largely primary products, such as bauxite, copper, oil, rubber, wood, rice, copra, spices, coffee, tea, and other agricultural products. It has been estimated that 80 percent of the developing world's foreign earnings come from such sales. There is little local processing of these goods, and it is the processing and manufacturing that provides more jobs, profits, and tax revenue. The processing and distribution of the final product usually occurs in the developed, industrialized countries.

Each of the more than 80 developing countries will not have all of the traits listed. This is simply a summary of some characteristics common to most of them.

MAJOR PROBLEMS IN DEVELOPING COUNTRIES

Problems facing the developing countries are numerous, sometimes overwhelming. In many ways they seem even greater when compared to the situations new countries were facing 50 or 100 years ago. A simple listing gives one some indication of the unprecedented demands that are being made on these countries and particularly on the governments, which are regarded as responsible for responding to most of the challenges:

1. Rapid urbanization, since there are no jobs in the countryside or there is rural violence, but with only limited increase in employment in the urban centers. The result is millions living in squatter slums.

2. The challenge of communism, either as an insurgency movement or through organized and sustained demands for revolutionary change and reform.
3. A popular revolution of rising expectations with regard to the material standard of living. The communications revolution, which brings to many an awareness of the fruits of modern society, stimulates consumer appetites. It also provides an entry for revolutionary ideologies.
4. Encouraging economic development, with an effort to improve productivity in the rural areas and industrialization to provide jobs and offset dependence on the often-impoverished agricultural sector.
5. Population growth, which can reach over 3.5 percent annually.
6. Social mobilization (discussed later).

Population growth, a young population, hunger, spiraling oil prices, and unemployment are interlocking problems that seem to continue without end. Even in oil-rich Iran, there is massive unemployment because of political turmoil; moreover, the job problem is compounded by the growing need to find employment for a young population: 65 percent of Iran's population is under 21, with national unemployment at 20 percent. Turkey, which lies between Europe and Asia and is a neighbor of Iran, has similar problems. Nearly 55 percent of the Turks are under 19. Unemployment is 20 percent (higher at the threshold ages as youths attempt to enter the job market) and inflation averages 100 percent annually. It is a tribute to Turkey's leaders that they are striving hard to maintain a democracy, but as one U.S. State Department official understated it, they "have significant problems."[1]

One-half of all the deaths in the developing world are of children under age 5. Most of these deaths are caused by a combination of infection and malnutrition. Each year there are 200 million cases of malaria, a similar number of snail fever cases, and 40 million cases of river blindness.[2] The World Bank estimates more than 1 billion people are permanently malnourished. Hunger and starvation are tragic problems for children. A Stanford University food expert calculates that in 1978 some 12 to 13 million children died of easily preventable diseases associated with malnutrition.[3] In India, for example, 30 percent of the children die before their fifth birthday. Not included in this figure of 13 million are the 200,000 to 300,000 people who starve to death each year. One reporter analyzing United Nations documents noted that in 21 African countries life expectancy is under 40 years and that 90 percent of Africans live in countries where food production is declining. One in 4 Africans has insufficient food and 1 in 2 cannot find a job.[4] A government's ability or willingness to respond to something as extreme as famine often is limited. In 1979 a drought followed by flood brought starvation to 500,000 people in Zaire. Private

[1]Matthew Nimetz, State Dept. Speaker, in House of Representatives Subcommittee on Europe and the Middle East, *Foreign Assistance Legislation for Fiscal Years* (Part 3). (Washington, 1979), pp. 325–326.

[2]A basic summary of the dramatic statistics is in "The Growing Crisis," *War on Hunger: A Report from the Agency on International Development*, No. 2, September 1975, pp. 1–9.

[3]Walter P. Falcon, *Agenda* (Agency for International Development, December 1979), p. 16.

[4]David Lamb, "Africans Find Independence a Hard Road," *New York Times*, February 16, 1979.

relief agencies were unwilling to channel food through the government because of theft and corruption. As one relief worker put it, "not much would get to the users."[5]

Despite the absence of adequate medical and health care, conditions are at least no worse than they were at the beginning of this century. The percentage of people killed in local wars in the developing world is reduced as compared to the eighteenth century. The result, despite the earlier depressing statistics, is that the birth rate, survival rate and life expectancy have increased to the point that today the population growth rate (birth minus death rate) for the developing world is more than 3 times that of the developed world. For example, at present high growth rates, South Asia (Bangladesh, India, Nepal, Pakistan, and Sri Lanka) will double its population in 29 years. It will take the United States and Canada 110 years to double their populations and Europe 147 years! An annual population growth rate of 2.0 percent will double a country's population in only 35 years.

The number of people increases, but there is not a corresponding growth in food production. There are real possibilities that the food shortfall may increase, since even some "developed" countries, such as the Soviet Union, import large quantities of foodstuffs because their grain production is below consumption needs. South Asia's 1975 food grain production was 150 million tons or 192 kilograms per person, about 45 percent of the world average. Grain consumption in this region is 202 kilograms per person, or approximately 5 percent more than the production.[6]

South Asia presents the most serious crisis, but other regions of the Third World face similar problems. Food production has not shown any noticeable increases in most of the developing world since 1970, and the Third World does not have the money to import more fertilizer and equipment to accelerate production.

During the 1960s there occurred what is popularly known as the Green Revolution, making available "miracle rice" and "miracle wheat" hybrid strains. Production jumped in the late 1960s (for example, from 105 million tons of food grain in South Asia in 1966 to 148 million tons in 1970), but this increase leveled off in the 1970s. There were many problems. The wealthier, middle-sized and large farmers had the money and the larger-sized farms to buy and effectively use fertilizer and farm equipment. The wealthier farmers could build and maintain the necessary irrigation and drainage systems. The small farmer did not have the surplus to invest and in too many cases lost his land as his production and profits fell behind. In some ways, what was to be a humanitarian breakthrough created more economic inequality. Now, even the wealthier farmers are finding it more difficult to purchase fertilizer and other needs from abroad to maintain production levels.

Acting as a unit, the **Organizaton of Petroleum Exporting Countries** quadrupled the price of oil during the last three months of 1973.[7] The cost of this price in-

---

[5]Charles Mohr, "Famine Perils the Western Region of Zaire," *New York Times*, February 15, 1979.

[6]Data from Shahid Javed Burki and Shahid Yusuf, Population: Exploring the food-fertility link. *Finance and Development*, 12:4, 1975, p. 32.

[7]A readable analysis of petroflation and its consequences is the Committee for Economic Development, *International Economic Consequences of High-Priced Energy* (New York:; CED, 1975).

crease to the developing world was approximately $10 billion in 1974, an amount equal to almost all forms of development assistance the developing countries received from industrialized, donor nations. By 1980, oil was selling at between $30 and $40 per barrel, an increase of 1000 to 1400 percent since 1973. This is an intolerable burden on most Third World countries that do not produce oil. The non-oil-producing Third World needs oil not only as a fuel but for many other products as well, such as commercial fertilizer, most of which is petrochemical in origin. Well over half of the developing countries have annual per capita incomes of under $200. These countries with the least money are hurt most by skyrocketing oil prices, which then leads to price increases on almost all other imported items.

As discussed earlier, the exports of most developing countries are primary products. Paradoxically, as oil prices and the prices of manufactured goods inflate, the prices received by developing countries for other primary products drops (copper, for example, sold at $2,200 a ton in early 1974, at $1,500 a ton in early 1979). It is estimated that the combined trade deficit for the developing world, excluding oil-exporting countries, was $35 billion in the mid 1970s.[8] The peoples of the developing world are caught in a vicious cycle just to survive physically until the year 2000. Medical and health improvements, though limited, have contributed to high population growth. To increase food availability, which now is perilously close to a mass-starvation level, requires extensive imports. Most of these countries do not have the hard cash earned through exports to purchase the necessary items to increase

(Editorial cartoon by Pat Oliphant © Washington Star. Reprinted with permission of Universal Press Syndicate.)

"Tell me more about this energy crisis of which you speak"

[8]*New York Times*, December 18, 1975, p. 1.

agricultural and industrial production. A difficult situation is complicated tragically by increased oil prices, which penalize the developing world most. The problems confronting the political leaders of the Third World are as great in the 1980s as they have ever been. As you read this book, you are aware that no one has an answer to the population/food production/petroflation crisis.

Even under the best of conditions, where the government is making a reasonable effort to solve major problems and is not being subjected to a local or externally supported insurgency, it is obvious that government resources are overtaxed. Governments are confronted with responsibilities that most governments in these areas have not been required to respond to in the past. The new governments have limited resources in terms both of finances and of a trained public service that can analyze problems, draw up a policy response, and then have access to the necessary materials and skills to implement the policy.

Some of these problems, for analytical purposes, can be broken into two general categories: control of the environment and political integration.

CONTROL OF THE ENVIRONMENT

Control over and efficient use of the environment refers to the physical, economic, and social aspects of the environment. This has been one approach used to summarize the principal tasks of governments in the developing countries. Often the

Famine in the Sahel: People collect and eat animal fodder dropped by French military planes for livestock.

emphasis is on the technological, but of course technology has important implications for social and political control of human resources. A historian, Karl Wittfogel, has shown that in China the development of complex hydraulic (irrigation and flood control) systems along the Yellow River and other major Chinese rivers resulted in a highly organized, hierarchical, and authoritarian society. In order to maintain the hydraulic system for hundreds of miles, it was necessary to regulate the populations and to create a complex bureaucratic system to supervise and administer the geographic and human environment. Traditional Oriental government was semimanagerial. It possessed total political power, but it exerted only limited social and intellectual control over its subjects. The result was, in Wittfogel's terminology, "Oriental despotism."[9]

The development of a public policy to meet the essential economic and political needs of a country may result in a population so organized and regimented that it will lose all essential political liberties. Society may be harnessed to achieve what government officials believe should be the maximum use of the environment, but the consequence can be an authoritarian political system. The latest in technological development, as Karl Wittfogel warned us, does not necessarily increase personal freedom.

Samuel P. Huntington points out that the one common denominator of **political development** (or **political modernization**) is the weakening of what we call a traditional political system. Events are not always a coordinated series of changes moving toward modernization in the social, economic, and political systems. What is common is the initial weakening of traditional practices or patterns. Urbanization and industrialization may occur, industrialization may lead to a larger Gross National Product, and the Green Revolution in agriculture may increase total agricultural output. Literacy and the exposure to newspapers and radio may spread. Social and political inequalities can, however, be intensified as a few wealthy businesspeople and officials reap the benefits of economic change. Economic production figures of the country may climb as the result of industrialization policy and new technology in the rural areas, but the urban worker may suffer for many years while new industries are established. The small farmer may be unable to take advantage of the latest technology and expensive fertilizers, resulting in the loss of land to the more affluent landowner who has access to credit and can adopt the new agricultural technology. Even though some progress may be occurring in the economic system and there may be pockets of economic and social change, positive political and social changes may be restricted to a small middle class. Advances in one aspect of society may actually lead to setbacks in other parts of the social system. Control of the environment can place unusual if not impossible strains on the polit-

[9]See Karl J. Wittfogel, *Oriental Despotism* (New Haven: Yale University Press, 1957); and The historical position of Communist China: Doctrine and reality. *The Review of Politics*, 16, No. 1, January, 1954, pp. 463–474.

ical system, to the point that there occurs regression or, as Huntington describes it, "decay."[10]

It is obvious that one aspect of development or modernization is to effect more rational and effective exploitation of the natural resources these new countries possess. Will the development of these resources lead to further social and economic inequity in society? How much investment of resources and management skills is required and who will bear the burden of this investment? Only a relatively small percentage of the population—10 to 20 percent—may benefit for many years, while the majority may find that conditions are worse for several decades. European experiences are not encouraging. The British industrial revolution began in 1760 and continued for over a century. The average English citizen actually was worse off as industrial development took place than in the preindustrial period. Charles Booth's *Life and Labor of the People of London* shows that 30 percent of London was at or beneath the level of base subsistence at the end of the nineteenth century.[11] Joseph Chamberlain, a Conservative Party leader, quoted scholarly sources to the effect that the English working class was worse off in the nineteenth century than it was at the close of the fifteenth century.

Inequitable distribution of income is a depressing fact in many Third World countries. Too often the poor seem to get few of the economic benefits the wealthiest 20 percent of the population obtains. Table 12–1 reveals how little of the nation's spendable income the poorest 40 percent of the population receives annually in selected developing countries. In all the countries listed, the wealthiest 5 percent receives 40 to 50 percent of the national income annually!

Part of the reason for the disparity is that in the effort to industrialize, countries invest in highly technological industry that employs few people at high investment costs of $200,000 per job or more. There is too much emphasis on the latest technology, involving heavy use of capital investment and energy. The use of older equipment, smaller enterprises, and labor-intensive industry frequently is rejected. Those who are employed benefit, but there are far too few jobs necessary to em-

Table 12-1   Percentage of Income Received by Poorest 40 Percent

Colombia	7.3%
Iraq	8.0
Libya	.5
Mexico	10.5
Peru	8.8

Source: Irma Adelman and Cybthia Taft Morris, *Economic Growth and Social Equity in Developing Countries* (Stanford, Cal.: Stanford University Press, 1973), p. 152.

[10]Samuel P. Huntington, Political development and political decay. *World Politics*, 17:3, pp. 386–430.

[11]See O. F. Christie, *The Transition to Democracy:1867–1914* (London: George Rutledge & Sons, Ltd., 1934), p. 287.

ploy all those needing work; moreover, as we discussed earlier in this chapter, the Green Revolution and mechanization of agriculture often have benefited only the wealthy landowner and further impoverished the small farmer.

Substantial changes in the economic and social systems can place responsibilities on governments in the developing countries that sometimes appear insurmountable. Development or control of the environment may require sacrifices that only regimentation can enforce. Coordination of resources can lead quickly to authoritarian and arbitrary government policies by a government beset with innumerable claims and pressures.

As we have noted earlier, the People's Republic of China is a good example. For a few months in 1978 and 1979, Chinese officials permitted political dissent. The most famous example being the two-block-long "democracy wall" in Peking, where people could paste up posters criticizing government policies. Now this has been stopped as China pursues a vigorous industrialization policy. All resources including human ones must be harnessed, and political dissent is forbidden.

POLITICAL INTEGRATION

Some form of **political integration** is necessary if a country is to survive. This is true if only to prevent the twin problems of **separatism**, where a segment of the community, usually geographically concentrated, wishes to break away as an independent nation (Bangladesh from Pakistan); and of **irredentism**, where a segment of the community, again usually geographically concentrated, wishes to become part of a neighboring political system and separate from the nation they are currently a part of, such as some Irish Catholics in Northern Ireland.

Political integration implies a relationship and a feeling of community among people within the same geographic-political boundary. There are social, economic, psychological, and political ties existing that give the population a feeling of identity, self-awareness, and exclusiveness, a sense of belonging to a common nation or political system. Political integration occurs when government contributes to the material and psychological cohesion of the political system. A sense of interdependence and cooperation exists. Citizens come to believe that their personal well-being depends in part on membership in the national unit, and, at least in some ways, personal well-being can be advanced by government policies. A minimum requirement is that government provide the individual with an acceptable degree of security while political integration is occurring. If political integration is taking place, the bulk of the population will not be inclined to respond to irredentist or separatist appeals. There also will be little popular support for rapid, drastic, and violent changes in the political system.

The colonial experience often complicates political integration. The political boundaries of many of the new nations were decided by outside, European powers in response to the creation of colonies by other expanding colonial powers in the same general area. The African country of Gambia, a former British colony that became independent in 1965, is a rather extreme example of a national boundary that has scant relationship to previous identities. Gambia "defies all principles of boundary making. There are no geographical features or other lines of demarcation, whether economic, cultural, or racial, separating it from the country surrounding it."[12]

Another, more violent example involves the Kurds. After World War I and the dismemberment of the Ottoman Empire by the victorious allies, a number of mandated territories emerged (administered by European powers on behalf of the League of Nations, preparatory to independence). The drawing up of political boundaries ignored the independent statehood demands of 16 million Kurds living in Iran, Iraq, Turkey, and what is today Soviet Armenia. By late 1979, a vigorous insurgency was being directed against the Iranian government. The Kurds in Iraq have fought the Baghdad government since the 1960s, sometimes with Soviet help and sometimes with American assistance, depending on the political leanings of the Iraqui leaders. As one Iraqui Kurd told an American correspondent: "Of course, we dream of an independent Kurdistan. Your own President Woodrow Wilson gave us the idea when he supported it in 1919. If we controlled Iraq's Kirkuk oil fields, we could have a strong, influential state."[13] The two-decade-old war continues in Iraq. In Turkey, where Kurds are not recognized oficially as such and cannot teach their language, they reportedly are receiving Soviet assistance. Initially, the Kurds sought autonomy in their respective countries, but now, through such organizations as the Kurdistan Action Commmittee, they are insisting on a separate Kurdish nation-state.

A newly independent government, then, must promote policies that will foster social, economic, and psychological interdependence and will begin the process of political integration. As in the case of those governments dealing with the Kurds, this may be very difficult to do. Political integration does not assume that tensions, conflicts, and policy disagreements will cease. It does suggest, however, that most of the public issues be handled within a broad framework of rules of the game so that the fundamental existence of a particular political system is not challenged. Otherwise, simple survival instead of problem solving becomes the paramount concern of government officials.

TRADITIONAL AND TRANSITIONAL SOCIETIES: SOME MISPERCEPTIONS

The study of developing political systems frequently is complicated by incorrect assumptions. Four examples are discussed so that students will be aware of some of the pitfalls to avoid.

---

[12] E. W. Evans, *Britannia Overseas* (London: Thomas Nelson, 1946), pp. 55–56.

[13]John K. Cooley, "Memories of an Old Dream: A Future Independent Kurdistan," *Christian Science Monitor*, September 20, 1979.

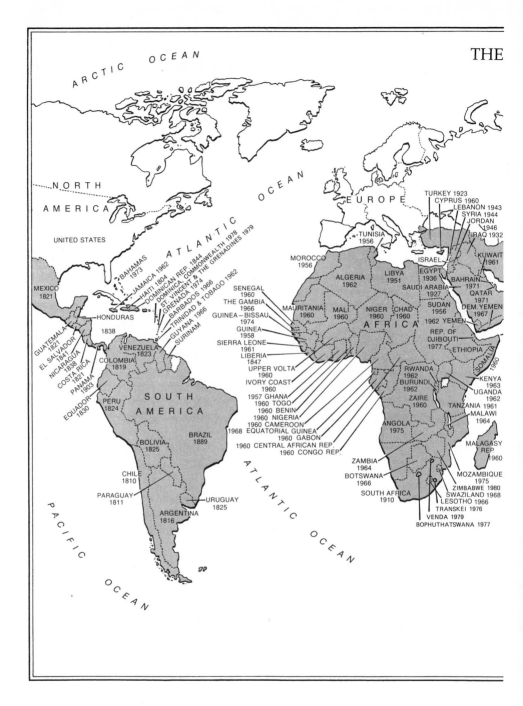

THE

ARCTIC OCEAN

NORTH AMERICA

UNITED STATES

ATLANTIC OCEAN

EUROPE

TURKEY 1923
CYPRUS 1960
LEBANON 1943
SYRIA 1944
JORDAN 1946
IRAQ 1932

TUNISIA 1956

MOROCCO 1956

ISRAEL

KUWAIT 1961

EGYPT

BAHRAIN 1971

MEXICO 1821

BAHAMAS 1973

JAMAICA 1962

HAITI 1804

DOMINICAN REP. 1844

DOMINICA COMMONWEALTH 1978

ST. VINCENT & THE GRENADINES 1979

GRENADA 1974

BARBADOS 1966

TRINIDAD & TOBAGO 1962

HONDURAS

1838

GUYANA 1966

SURINAM

SENEGAL 1960

THE GAMBIA 1966

GUINEA–BISSAU 1974

GUINEA 1958

SIERRA LEONE 1961

LIBERIA 1847

UPPER VOLTA 1960

IVORY COAST 1960

1957 GHANA

1960 TOGO

1960 BENIN

1960 NIGERIA

1960 CAMEROON

1968 EQUATORIAL GUINEA

1960 GABON

1960 CENTRAL AFRICAN REP.

1960 CONGO REP.

MAURITANIA 1960

MALI 1960

NIGER 1960

CHAD 1960

ALGERIA 1962

LIBYA 1951

SAUDI ARABIA 1927

QATAR 1971

DEM. YEMEN 1967

SUDAN 1956

1962 YEMEN

AFRICA

REP. OF DJIBOUTI 1977

ETHIOPIA

SOMALIA 1960

RWANDA 1962

BURUNDI 1962

ZAIRE 1960

KENYA 1963

UGANDA 1962

TANZANIA 1961

MALAWI 1964

ANGOLA 1975

MALAGASY REP. 1960

GUATEMALA 1821

EL SALVADOR 1841

NICARAGUA 1838

COSTA RICA 1821

PANAMA 1903

EQUADOR 1830

VENEZUELA 1823

COLOMBIA 1819

PERU 1824

SOUTH AMERICA

BRAZIL 1889

BOLIVIA 1825

ZAMBIA 1964

BOTSWANA 1966

SOUTH AFRICA 1910

MOZAMBIQUE 1975

ZIMBABWE 1980

SWAZILAND 1968

LESOTHO 1966

TRANSKEI 1976

VENDA 1979

BOPHUTHATSWANA 1977

CHILE 1810

PARAGUAY 1811

URUGUAY 1825

ARGENTINA 1816

ATLANTIC OCEAN

PACIFIC OCEAN

Adapted from Robert P. Clark, *Power and Policy in the Third World*, John Wiley and Sons, 1978, pp. 24–25.

404

THIRD WORLD

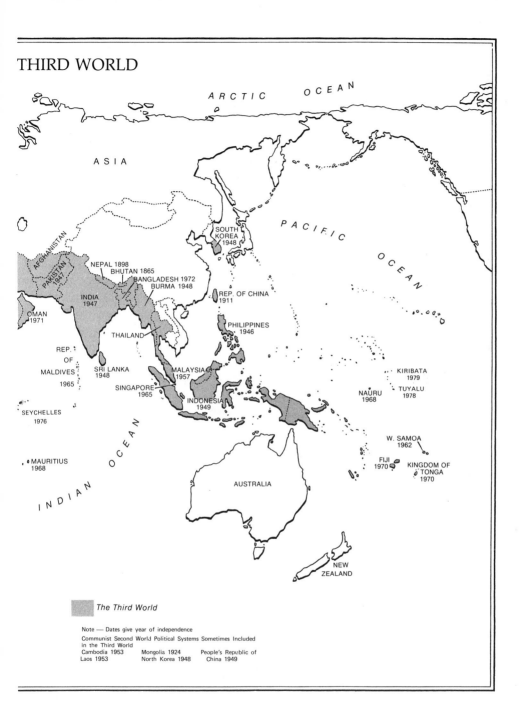

A R C T I C   O C E A N

ASIA

P A C I F I C   O C E A N

AFGHANISTAN

PAKISTAN 1947

NEPAL 1898
BHUTAN 1865
BANGLADESH 1972
BURMA 1948

INDIA 1947

SOUTH KOREA 1948

REP. OF CHINA 1911

OMAN 1971

THAILAND

PHILIPPINES 1946

REP. OF MALDIVES 1965

SRI LANKA 1948

MALAYSIA 1957

KIRIBATA 1979

SINGAPORE 1965

INDONESIA 1949

NAURU 1968

TUYALU 1978

SEYCHELLES 1976

INDIAN OCEAN

W. SAMOA 1962

MAURITIUS 1968

FIJI 1970

KINGDOM OF TONGA 1970

AUSTRALIA

NEW ZEALAND

The Third World

Note — Dates give year of independence

Communist Second World Political Systems Sometimes Included in the Third World

| Cambodia 1953 | Mongolia 1924 | People's Republic of China 1949 |
| Laos 1953 | North Korea 1948 | |

THE STATIC–STABILITY ERROR

Traditional societies often are described as stable and experiencing slight or no change in social and political patterns. Traditional societies are usually farming, hunting, fishing, gathering, and sometimes nomadic. There are few inventions, technological changes, or innovations. Trade is minimal and often by barter. There is little economic specialization and most of the labor force is in primary (agricultural, fishing) production. Loyalty is to the family, clan, tribe, or village. Rule is usually by one man or a few (oligarchy). The masses do not participate and their freedom of action usually is limited because society is hierarchical, with a ruling and a subject class, the latter far more numerous. Landowning is often the single source of wealth and power. Custom dominates most of day-to-day living, with limited need to respond to new circumstances. An article written by the sociologist F. X. Sutton in the 1950s contrasted "intensive agricultural" (traditional) and "industrial" (modern) societies. A distinguishing feature of traditional society is stability, both with regard to work patterns within the village and spatial mobility or migration away from the village. The status of groups is constant, determined by such things as birth, age, and sex. "Access to facilities and rewards" is continuous and unchanging. People are familiar with and committed to the locality and the status quo. Change is minimal.[14]

Traditional, non-Western, or historically older societies do undergo fundamental changes, though. Non-Western societies should not be treated as inevitably rigid and static. When British colonial officials began to assert control over northern Burma, they encountered a group of hill peoples known as the Kachin, who lived adjacent to the Chinese border and near the Assam area in India. E. R. Leach, a British anthropologist who has studied the Kachin in detail (300,000 people in an area of 50,000 square miles), describes a revolutionary political transformation occurring as late as 1870, shortly before the British arrived.[15]

Typically, Kachin villages had been ruled by an hereditary leader called a *sawbwa*. Villagers had to cultivate the *sawbwa's* land without compensation and were required to pay various taxes to him. During the latter part of the nineteenth century a series of village "revolutions" occurred. Many *sawbwas* were killed and were replaced by popularly responsible leaders.

The revolutionary villages, those without *sawbwas*, were called *gumlao*, or "rebel villages." At one point Leach speaks of the "spontaneous" emergence of the rebel villages. It is clear that among the Kachin, at that time little affected by Western, British contacts, fundamental changes occurred in the political system. The spread of *gumlao* villages either was the result of new settlements (three or more "original" houses of equal status that intermarry) or of political revolt.

[14]F.X. Sutton, Representation and the nature of political systems. *Comparative Studies in Society and History*, 2, October 1959, pp. 1–10.

[15]E. R. Leach, *Political Systems of Highland Burma* (Boston: Beacon Press, 1965; first published in London, 1954). Material for this section was taken principally from pp. 197–207.

There is a tradition of revolution in which the former gumsa chiefs were either driven out or reduced to the status of lineage headman having no special rights.[16]

Interestingly, British officials, who might be said to represent modernization, opposed the republicanism of the rebel villages. It was much easier to deal with a *sawbwa*-owned village where the *sawbwa* was friendly and could control his subjects. The newly emergent "representative" form of rebel village government developed by the Kachin was inconvenient in the eyes of British officials and they opposed it. Revolution, not stability, took place in this "traditional" society, and not as a consequence of Western colonial contacts. British colonial officials eventually succeeded in reversing the trend toward "representative" village government among the Kachins and actually discouraged change.

ADAPTABILITY OF TRADITIONAL INSTITUTIONS

Sometimes traditional institutions are treated as hindering political change. It is assumed they either attract a loyalty that contradicts efforts to establish a national identity and loyalty, or they impede the growth of more open, participatory political processes. This is not always so.

One example of a traditional institution that assumed a new democratic function is the Indian caste association. Over the centuries the Indian caste system was an indispensable feature of India's repressive and stratified social system.

Membership in a caste is completely ascriptive: once born into a caste, a man has no way to change social identity insofar as the social structure and cultural norms recognize caste. Caste norms prescribe the ritual, occupational, commensal, marital and social relationships of members, and caste organization and authority enforce these norms. . . . The unit of action and location of caste has been, until recently, the sub-caste in the village or group of villages.[17]

The caste association in postindependence India (1948) has been described as "one of the chief means by which the Indian mass electorate has been attached to the processes of democratic politics."[18]

Today, caste associations are most influential at the state level in the Indian federal system, rather than at the national level. Caste organizations with specific objectives emerged in the nineteenth century with the spread of communications, transportation, and a market economy during the British colonial period. At first the lower caste associations concentrated on upgrading their position in the social hierarchy by encouraging members to adopt the behavior of the higher castes: for example, vegetarianism, abstention from liquor, and preventing widows from remar-

[16]*Ibid.*, pp. 206–207.
[17]Lloyd I. Rudolph and Susanne Hoeber Rudolph, The political role of India's caste association. *Pacific Affairs*, 33:1, 1960, p. 6.
[18]*Ibid.*, p. 5.

rying. The associations also began to turn to the state to correct grievances, such as assigning caste members more administrative positions and greater access to university education through scholarships and quotas. After independence, the local associations supported members for elective office, either through existing parties or by forming new parties. The intention of the caste associations is to maximize caste influence and representation in governing bodies at the state and local level. The adaptability and performance of new functions by the caste associations have been rather successful. The associations have been praised for their capacity "to organize the politically illiterate mass electorate, thus making possible in some measure the realization of its aspirations and educating large sections of it in the methods and values of political democracy."[19] Castes, then, have participated in and even facilitated India's political development process.

MODERNIZATION AND POLITICAL DEVELOPMENT

Modernization and political development are terms that have been used interchangably. Both terms are used widely in the literature. We have discussed political development. This section questions the assumption that modernization is usually an integrated process moving all elements of a society in a single direction, reducing differences in society through a homogenizing process. Daniel Lerner, in his study of Middle Eastern societies, concludes that "urbanization, industrialization, secularization, democratization, education, media participation do not occur in a haphazard and unrelated fashion." They seem to be "highly associated" and "went together so regularly because, in some historical sense, they *had* to go together."[20]

We have discovered, however, that components of "modernization" (or of political development) do not interact in the same way or move uniformly in the same direction. Some parts of society may change while others remain isolated and unaffected by the changes. Interaction between "modernizing and traditional" segments of society may be delayed, the cause of interaction uncertain, the stimulus and reasons for interaction unclear, and the results unpredictable.

The case of Iran dramatically illustrates these tensions. Since the late Shah was forced into exile in early 1979, Iran has become a theocratic regime, ruled by a religious leader, Ayatollah Khomeni. The 3-decade-long modernization process, confined principally to the urban centers and one-quarter of the population, is being purged because of its corruption of the Islamic life. The Iranian "revolution" is a rejection of what are regarded as the least attractive features of Western-style modernization: alcohol, movies, materialism or conspicuous consumption, relaxing of dress codes, disinterest in religious life, and so forth. To a majority of Iranians,

---

[19]*Ibid.*, p. 8.

[20]Daniel Lerner, *The Passing of Traditional Society: Modernizing the Middle East* (Glencoe, Ill.: The Free Press, 1958), p. 438. Samuel Huntington has listed nine characteristics that various writers on modernization assign to this concept. See "The Change to Change," *Comparative Politics*, 3:3, 1971, pp. 288–290.

Ayatollah Khomeni is a man of God, a miracle worker with special appeal to a country where 60 percent of the population cannot read. The Koran (Muslim holy book) and the mosques are their education. Islam makes no distinction between religion and government, and in its struggle to reassert itself the sword of Islam is attacking what it sees as atheistic Western influences.

Iran is only one example where compartmentalized change occurred, affecting only certain parts of the population or limited segments of one's lifestyle. Some segments of society may remain largely unaffected for a long time in other political systems, without a revolution breaking out as in Iran. A perceptive study of Sicily, one of the more traditional regions in Europe, further illustrates these observations.[21]

The Sicilian case shows that modernization and development are not identical concepts and that change can affect some groups in the population but not others. The case study of Sicily defined modernization as imported change: attitudes, behavior patterns, institutions, commodities, expectations, and the like, which are stimulated by contact with established industrial-developed centers. The example of Sicily suggests that as a modernizing region becomes dependent on urban-industrial centers, it imports indiscriminately those items that are easier to acquire and that have more appeal. Development is defined as being more difficult—a region's efforts "to acquire an autonomous and diversified industrial economy on its own."[22] During modernization, some incomes may rise, fewer people will be employed in agriculture, urbanization and mass communications will expand, but the changes will occur primarily in a few urban areas that have economic linkages with distant industrial-urban centers (in Sicily's case, Western Europe). Some changes take place because of foreign investment, although these often are isolated pockets of economic change that do not spill over on the rest of society. Frequently workers leave the region for employment in distant, prosperous areas, such as Germany, Switzerland, and France, and remit portions of their salaries to their home, increasing purchasing power and consumption. Between 1950 and 1961, for example, more than 400,000 men left Sicily for employment in Western Europe. A third source of funds that changes life styles is tourism. One town near the Sicilian coast is a case in point. The local youth soon equated the behavior and possessions of the American, British, French, and Scandinavian youth with the "desirable and modern."

Coca-Cola and Scotch became prestigious drinks, juke boxes in glossy new bars blared hard rock music, and sexual standards of local maidens were threatened by comparison with the reported conduct of foreign girls on the coast. This too is modernization.[23]

[21]The Sicilian data is taken from Peter Schneider, Jane Schneider, and Edward Hansen, Modernization and development: the role of regional elites and noncorporate groups in the European Mediterranean. *Comparative Studies in Society and History*, 14, June 1972, 328–329.

[22]*Ibid.*, p. 341.

[23]*Ibid.*, p. 343.

Regions exposed to modernization through tourism or limited economic ties with affluent industrial centers—and there are hundreds of such regions with tens of millions of people in the Third World—are in a dependent position. The prosperity they enjoy is tied closely to the economic well-being of the metropolitan industrial centers. Modernization may bring change that does not develop and benefit most of society. In some cases, of course, modernization has set in motion fundamental, interrelated, and far-reaching changes, as Karl Deutsch suggested would happen in his theory of social mobilization. Sicily and Iran are examples of instances where modernization has not brought about such changes. A middle class emerges, but it invests for short-range profit. It does not invest in industrial or agrarian enterprises, which require a slower profit return. The principal investments of the Sicilian middle class

> include real estate speculation, commerce appropriate to the new consumer markets which modernization engenders, and perhaps agricultural or light industrial production, cautiously capitalized because of its vulnerability to fluctuations on world markets. . . . If anything, modernization implies either the fragmentation and dispersal of money, or its waste.[24]

We would add that modernization implies a third option regarding money: placing profits and income in Swiss banks, rather than investing it in the local economy.

Modernization and development are not two different words to describe the same phenomena. One interpretation of modernization, which has some basis in fact, is that it is contemporary, often superficial, and does not automatically lead to progressive changes throughout most of society. One means of distinguishing between development and modernization is to regard development as an evolutionary process in which local institutions adapt and control change and are not simply caught up in imitating and reacting to outside forces. Modernization often is contemporary, imported, and creates a dependency on the technologically advanced urban/industrial centers, without helping local political and social institutions to grow and adapt. Development means that a system has some ability to be selective in the type and pace of changes and does not haphazardly import what is appealing and affordable, whether it be high-priced liquor or unnecessary computers.

Second, modernization is not, as Daniel Lerner described it, a "consistent whole," a unifying set of changes and responses. Modernization is not always associated with general social improvement that benefits most of the population. Modernization may sometimes be only the most current in personal life-styles. Often its impact on society is haphazard, limited to a wealthy elite in the urban areas. The modernization process can lead to the introduction of serious tensions rather than laying the groundwork for a series of interrelated changes moving toward the objective of a transformed and prosperous society.

[24]*Ibid.*, p. 344.

WESTERN-STYLE DEMOCRACY

A fourth misconception assumes that unless a political system has free-wheeling, competitive, national elections, with one or more major opposition parties, it is not "politically developed."

The movement toward individual freedom need not necessarily be led, symbolized, or guaranteed by a competitive party system at the national level. This was often the case in Anglo-American experience, but there are other potential patterns of change. An anthropologist, Clifford Geertz, has argued persuasively that competitive elections in some of the newly independent societies may have negative consequences. Part of the reason for this is that many people in these new, heterogeneous countries believe that their individual identities and basic values are tied to primordial attachments, such as kinship, race, ethnic group, religion, language, and region of birth. These attachments are combined with a growing awareness in this century that government can, depending on which group is in control, protect and enhance these values. Competitive politics may arouse and organize these primordial attachments as the surest and easiest way to attract popular support. Universal suffrage and competitive elections can temporarily place intolerable strains on governments with limited resources and a host of other problems.[25]

A rule of law, with protection of civil liberties and the increasing autonomy of individuals and groups in society, may be another approach to nurturing political pluralism in a developing country. The opportunity for individuals to involve themselves in those choices that most directly affect them might provide a better strategy than instant national elections, which are soon abolished or become transformed into one-choice plebiscites to ratify government leaders. Two examples that appear to be working are Yugoslavia and the Republic of China (Taiwan). There are 571 communes or county councils in Yugoslavia. Their job is to plan and carry out functions similar to local governments in the United States. These activities include such things as roads, education, city planning, building codes, and local social services. The local communes have some taxation powers and also receive funds directly from the national government. The commune councils have the power to make decisions within a general framework of national policies established by the central government in Belgrade.

Council members are elected and hire their own administrative staffs. At one time the councils had authority over industrial development within their commune, but this responsibility has been transferred to the workers' councils. One student of the Yugoslav political system has spoken of local self-management and direct democracy in the sense that "wide participation among the populace" is encouraged. As a result an "impressive variety of committees, commissions, citizens' councils,

[25]For an overview of primordial attachments and some political implications, see Clifford Geertz, "The Integration Revolution: Primoridal Sentiments and Civic Politics in the New States," in Clifford Geertz, ed., *Old Societies and New States: The Quest for Modernity in Asia and Africa* (Glencoe, Ill.: The Free Press, 1963).

public boards, and other bodies now exist." There are also "voters' meetings," which allow the individual citizen to express opinions on local government issues. There is widespread participation as long as there is no direct challenge "to central authority and socialist foundations." Decentralization in this Communist country has led to substantial and increasing participation by individual citizens in matters that directly affect their livelihoods, their environment, and their living conditions.[26]

In the case of Taiwan, there are 22 county farmers' associations and 324 township farmers' associations.[27] The effective level of operation of the farmers' association is at the township. Each association has an elected board, which is the policy-making instrument of the local organization. This board selects the administrative staff, somewhat analogous to our county agents, as well as budget officers, managers of the cooperative store, and so forth. Approximately 6 percent of the regular members of the farmers' association hold elected positions in the association. Another 3 percent are members of village extension committees, while other villagers hold office in the local government, irrigation associations, farmer tenancy committees, credit unions, and the like. The elections and decision making by local farmers at this level are not controlled by the central government except in terms of such general policies as encouraging greater use of fertilizer and encouraging sugar-cane production.

The farmers' associations were developed in conjunction with a far-reaching land-reform campaign in Taiwan in the 1950s. The associations have been effective in increasing production and making available marketing arrangements for the rural economy. The various office-holding opportunities opened up by the development of the associations have created a large number of new leadership positions in society, beyond the number of traditional, village elder leadership positions that existed in pre-World War II, Japanese-occupied Taiwan. Two foreign-aid specialists who have studied Taiwan and a number of other developing countries concluded that new leadership positions

> are a way of subjecting traditional leaders to competition. But most important of all, the application of this principle confronts the traditional leaders with a choice. Either they must become leaders of development or run the risk of losing their positions.[28]

The new local institutions have not been taken over by the traditional elites or officials from Taipei, the capital. The central government insists that farmers' associa-

---

[26]M. George Zaniovich, *The Development of Socialist Yugoslavia* (Baltimore: Johns Hopkins Press, 1968), pp. 119–121.

[27]For a historical analysis of Taiwan's changing rural society, see Martin C. Yang, *Socio-Economic Results of Land Reform in Taiwan* (Honolulu: East-West Center Press, 1970).

[28]Edgar Owens and Robert Shaw, *Development Reconsidered* (Lexington, Mass.: D. C. Heath, 1972), pp. 27–28.

tions prepare annual work programs and budgets, assisting them and making sure that these programs are carried out. They also assist the associations in obtaining budgeting information, financial aid, and general information about production and marketing. In such a way, the potential abuse and power at the local level by traditional elites or the more wealthy farmers is controlled. Individual villagers not only are concerned with carrying out decisions affecting their personal livelihood but also have the opportunity to have a voice in making these decisions. One sees a form of representative politics emerging at the grassroots level in Taiwan. The local cooperatives involve the farmers in participating in rural change and using the most efficient agricultural techniques. They also provide an opportunity for independent decision making that has been carried forward to local township government councils, where there is growing freedom of political choice in electing members.

The importance of self-conscious participation and a growing feeling of being effective and of identification with the political system are affirmed in *The Civic Culture*, a book that studies the political cultures of five countries: West Germany, Great Britain, Italy, Mexico, and the United States:

> *Organizations in which there is some opportunity for the individual to take an active part may be as significant for the development of democratic citizenship as are voluntary organizations in general. . . . Democracy depends upon citizen participation, and it is clear that organization membership is directly related to such participation. . . . Membership in a politically oriented organization appears to lead to greater political competence than does membership in a nonpolitical organization, and active membership in an organization has a greater impact on political competence than does passive membership.*[29]

Participation is a crucial aspect of political development. Participation may be initiated more effectively at the local level, evolving upward, than at the top, in national elections. Habits and skills of participation often do not percolate downward very rapidly, if at all, but the introduction of local participation can contribute to building a more open political society.

THEORIES OF POLITICAL DEVELOPMENT

There is no universally accepted theory of political development. Many of the definitions various authors have drawn up overlap and share several features. There are also differing emphases, and some characteristics are unique to a definition. Three representative theories discussed are the development syndrome and those of Karl Deutsch and Samuel P. Huntington.

---

[29]Gabriel A. Almond and Sidney Verba, *The Civic Culture: Political Attitudes and Democracy in Five Nations* (Boston: Little, Brown, 1965), pp. 262–263.

THE DEVELOPMENT SYNDROME

One of the first widely used terms, "development syndrome" suggests a linear movement whose ultimate objective seems to be a pattern similar to what has been achieved in the Western world.[30] The result, the emergence of a "world culture":

> But at an ever-accelerating rate the direction and volume of cross-cultural influences has become nearly a uniform pattern of the Western industrial world imposing its practices, standards, techniques, and values upon the non-Western World.[31]

The development syndrome (a syndrome is a pattern of interrelated traits) included three general characteristics. The first was **equality**, which as an ultimate political goal anticipated universal adult electoral participation, with popular interest and involvement. Interestingly, also included was totalitarian mobilization such as one-party-only elections in the Soviet Union, as one possible type of participation that supposedly would provide a "pretense" of popular rule. Equality also meant a general system of laws that would apply to all citizens equally. General opportunity for social mobility was an aspect of equality, particularly as related to political office or the public service. Achievement standards were introduced, rather than a spoils system or a system that emphasized ascriptive or inherited status qualities, such as ethnic group, religion, kinship, nobility over commoner, or region of the country. Demonstrated merit was the principle for hiring and advancement.

A second feature of the development syndrome referred to the **capacity** of a political system in terms of the types and range of activities government was undertaking and its effectiveness in making and implementing public policy. A high capacity government would achieve high professional standards including such things as professional training, technical skills, and rational approaches to policy.

The third characteristic, **differentiation and specialization**, drew heavily on anthropology and sociology. We assume that as society and government become more complex and specialized, political pluralism will emerge. Specialization or expertise are considered important. Each agency will perform specialized and limited functions; therefore, it can be more responsive and capable in its activities. Unfortunately, there has been little thought given to the coordination of the various specialized, government departments. A hundred subdepartments approaching a problem from multiple angles can, as we have learned, impede effective and responsive public policy.

The development syndrome recognized that there would be inherent tensions between various groups, some making demands for equality, others emphasizing capacity or a strong government, and still others stressing technological innovation. The particular mix of these demands and the way the political system reacted

---

[30]This definition represented the thinking of the Committee on Comparative Politics of the Social Sciences Research Council and was set forth in Lucian W. Pye, *Aspects of Political Development* (Boston: Little, Brown, 1966).

[31]*Ibid.*, p. 9.

would result in patterns of development. Advocates of the development syndrome also emphasized five "crises" that every developing political system must confront and deal with if it is to evolve as a developed state.[32] The crises as listed will not necessarily be followed in sequence by each country though it is obvious that the order in which they are presented is based on British experience:

1.   The **identity crisis** is surmounted when a people within a given territory feel a sense of group identity, recognizing that this is their national territory. It can be described as a sense of togetherness and the absence of significant separatist or irredentist pressures. It is similar in many respects to the political integration problem discussed earlier.

2.   The **legitimacy crisis** refers to popular acceptance of the constitutional nature of the political system or the commonly accepted rules of the game. Legitimacy also is related to the responsibilities or functions of a government and the popular feeling about whether government is effectively doing what it should be doing, that is, taking care of internal security, land reforms, new jobs, and health care.

3.   The **penetration crisis** concerns the ability of government to influence basic policies and decisions throughout the country. A government that is restricted to the major towns and a few of the main roads during the daylight hours will not be able to penetrate society effectively, carry out its work, and develop feelings of confidence and rapport between government officials and citizens.

4.   The **participation crisis** is concerned with the number of people participating in the political system and the range of alternatives the individuals may consider when making political input. The participation crisis is worked out principally through the evolution of competitive elections, interest groups, and a political party system. Participation requires choice in terms of numbers of alternatives that can be popularly discussed and the opportunity to select between competing candidates in an election. In most developing countries if universal suffrage is bestowed almost immediately after independence, there is no question of formal participation. We might question, however, if this participation is really effective or whether voting is simply a controlled election with no choice arranged by the political elite.

5.   The **distribution crisis** occurs as government attempts to encourage the distribution of goods and services throughout society, eliminating the more flagrant inequities and equalizing the benefits received by the population. Such undertakings as unemployment legislation, social welfare, and public parks tend to reduce gaps between the wealthy and the poor. Government may be active in providing opportunities for groups that previously had been at a disadvantage, such as through job quotas or scholarships. An industrialization program that provides help, even modestly, for the under- and unemployed is a form of distribution response.

---

[32]The seventh volume of the Committee on Comparative Politics, which discusses these crises in detail, is Leonard Binder et al., *Crises and Sequences in Political Development* (Princeton, N.J.: Princeton University Press, 1971), parts of which are used in this discussion.

These five crises were based on the British experience. In the British case each crisis took decades, if not centuries, to solve. The appearance of these "crises" occurred in the order they have been discussed. Frequently, generations of people were involved in dealing with a particular "crisis."

Many of the developing countries face a situation where several crises are occurring simultaneously. An unbearable strain may be placed on government. An insurgency, which generally is a legitimacy crisis, can make it impossible for a government to deal with other "crises," such as penetration, participation, and distribution. The inability of the government to deal with other pressing issues in turn makes its legitimacy even more suspect and unstable. As a result, the government is in the untenable situation of not being able to respond to some of the problems that might strengthen its legitimacy. An administrative apparatus, systematically subjected to a war of attrition, cannot perform even the minimal output functions that are necessary to build legitimacy in a new political system. A tragic example is the former nation of South Vietnam, where figures reveal that there were 6700 deliberate political assassinations between 1957 and 1963.[33]

> The common characteristic of this activity against individuals is that it was directed at the village leader, usually the natural leader—that individual who, because of his age, sagacity, or strength of character, is the one to whom people turn for advice and leadership. Many were religious figures, schoolteachers, or simply people of integrity and honor. Since they were superior individuals these persons were more likely to stand up to the insurgents when they came to the village and thus most likely to be the first victims. The assassination rate declined steadily from 1960 to 1965 for the simple reason that there was only a finite number of persons to be assassinated. Many villages by 1966 were virtually depopulated of their natural leaders, who are the single most important element in society.[34]

Political systems cannot survive this systematic terrorism against a government infrastructure over a period of many years. Legitimacy in the developing countries requires young governments to win popular support by delivering outputs. Without an administrative service, no government can do more than survive for a few years. Public policies cannot be developed and implemented because of the day-to-day need for physical survival. Political development becomes impossible under such circumstances. Too many developing countries face a brutal and extended internal war, which is an intolerable drain on already limited resources.

SOCIAL MOBILIZATION

Patterns of political development also have been studied as sets of **dependent variables**, as political responses to changes that occur in society generally and that in turn require reactions by government if the political system, those particular political leaders, and the existing rules of the game are to survive. Implicit in this inter-

[33]Douglas Pike, *Viet Cong* (Cambridge, Mass.: The M.I.T. Press, 1966), p. 102.
[34]*Ibid.*, p. 248.

pretation is the notion that many of the social changes that occur are not directed or inspired by government policies, but evolve as the society responds and adapts to complex environmental pressures. Karl Deutsch, who was one of the first to interpret political development in this way, developed a widely quoted approach known as **social mobilization**.[35]

Deutsch maintained that social mobilization increases the probability of political tensions and demands in society and brings about fundamental changes in the nature of the political system because of the "changing range of human needs that impinge upon politics." People expect their government to do more. Social mobilization occurs as more people move to the cities and as more people are exposed to political events through newspapers and radios, both in the cities and in the rural areas. People come to believe that there are needs the villages no longer meet, either because they have new concerns for better schools, better water supplies, the introduction of a partial cash economy, and so forth, or because they have left the village and moved to a new location usually to seek jobs and economic betterment. The result is that more people take part in political discussions, possibly in riots and demonstrations, in strikes, in insurgencies, and in various organizations that speak to government officials, demanding more services and benefits.

Militants of the Republican Moslem People's Party, who support Shariatmadari, demonstrate in Tabriz, Iran on January 1, 1980 against the Khomeini regime.

[35]Karl Deutsch, Social mobilization and political development. *American Political Science Review*, 55, September 1961, p. 495.

The variables that Deutsch identifies as part of social mobilization are empirically measurable, and most are available in various statistical data books, such as *The United Nations Statistical Yearbook* or the *World Handbook of Political and Social Indicators.*[36] The traits are considered to go together, but no single trait is related to a specific effect on the political system. Social mobilization politicizes individuals who previously did not play an active role in the political process. The number of claims on government increases in scope and intensity. Government is held responsible for the changes and their effects on society, or it is regarded as the only institution capable of responding to the new and diverse challenges. Some of the characteristics or measures of social mobilization are:

1. Increase in Gross National Product and per capita Gross National Product.
2. Decreasing percentage of labor force in agriculture and an increasing percentage in manufacturing.
3. Increasing percentage of population in cities with 100,000 or more inhabitants.
4. Growing percentage of population over age 15 that is literate.
5. Increasing number of radios and television sets and newspaper circulation per 1000.
6. Population growth (the lower the rate the better).
7. Increasing voting participation as percent of adult population.
8. Increasing number of persons who have changed residence locality since birth.

Social mobilization exposes people to "modernity" and makes them want change. It encourages or makes it possible for them to change their residences, occupations, communication patterns, reading habits, peer groups, aspirations, political outlooks, levels of political information, general attitudes toward the political system, and expectations about what the political system should do. These various traits increase or decrease at different speeds, but they all supposedly move in the direction of "modernity," which includes expecting government to do more and do it better.

It is implicit that the final outcome in terms of literacy, birth rate, life expectancy, exposure to mass communication, and so forth will approach contemporary Western standards. A "world culture" bias is apparent in social mobilization analysis. Also apparent is the belief of a general "forward" movement in society, which affects most groups more or less equally. Changes in the political are more a result than a cause of the social mobilization process. We believe there is a certain weakness in an approach that overlooks the fact that political actors and institutions usually influence the social system more than any other single cause.[37]

[36]The latter is edited by C. L. Taylor and M. C. Hudson, *World Handbook of Political and Social Indicators*, 2nd ed. (New Haven: Yale University Press, 1972), and parts of it are used in this discussion.

[37]For an elaboration on this point, see Giovanni Sartori, From the sociology of politics to political sociology. *Government and Opposition*, 4:2, 1969, pp. 195–214.

INSTITUTIONALIZATION AND POLITICAL CHANGE
Samuel P. Huntington has written on political development and political change for many years.[38] He is a political scientist who has changed his perspectives over the years and has acknowledged this change in his own writings. He was one of the first to point out that we cannot assume that all political systems will be moving together in a progressive, linear development pattern. There is also a possibility that some political systems will regress or "decay."

Huntington believes that one should distinguish between political development and political modernization. To use the terms interchangeably artificially restricts one's focus. It would be very difficult to analyze modernization in the time of the Roman Empire or the Middle Ages because these periods are not modern by our standards. Political development, on the other hand, **has** occurred over the centuries and is not a term that should be applied only to recent events.

In *Political Order in Changing Society*, Huntington presents his institutionalization thesis. Here he is concerned with interaction between the demands of political participation and the necessity of political institutionalization in order for day-to-day governing to occur. The pressure for political participation is nearly universal in the contemporary world and can be set into motion by a multitude of historical experiences. Political institutionalization is regarded as a means by which societies respond to this single most important demand—the striving for some form of political participation. It is assumed that traditional or colonial political systems that have experienced a high level of institutionalism (for example, a bureaucracy, a governing council, or a partly elected legislature) would be more capable of responding to pressures for political participation and input claims. He also suggests that certain leadership groups drawn from the traditional aristocracy, the military, or a revolutionary leadership, might be able to either adapt or create new institutions that would allow a political system to respond to or control pressures in an orderly fashion. Stability and the ability to survive by responding to the most intense demands would be achieved through working political institutions in the society. One difficulty is that a highly institutionalized political system, such as the Soviet Union, could be classified as politically developed. This would be true in terms of institutionalization but not true in terms of civil rights, personal and group autonomy, and some freedom of political choice. The "participation crisis" might be averted by prohibiting it. A second difficulty is that by stressing political participation as a catalyst, the focus remains on the modern or contemporary. This was an orientation Huntington had previously criticized.

Huntington later expanded his thesis and argued that two modifications should be made: there were factors other than political participation that should be taken

---

[38]A superior overview of the political development literature, including summaries of his own works, is found in Samuel P. Huntington, The Change to Change, *op. cit.*, pp. 283–322. Most of the references to Huntington are taken from this article. Huntington documents all of his previous political development writings in this essay.

into consideration, and political development more properly should be called political change.[39] There should be an effort to relate changes in one part of the system to changes in another part, to begin to establish some cause-and-effect relationships. Political scientists should concentrate on the most important institutions and processes in the political system, those that seem to have the predominant impact at the moment. There should be some effort to measure the rate, direction, and scope of change and recognize that one part of the political system has an effect on other parts. Huntington suggested five items as particularly useful for persons interested in political change in any given political system:

1. **Culture**—the values, attitudes, orientation, myths, and beliefs relevant to politics and dominant in the society.
2. **Structure**—the formal organizations through which the society makes authoritative decisions, such as political parties, legislatures, executives, and bureaucracies.
3. **Groups**—the social and economic formations, formal and informal, that participate in politics and make demands on the political structure.
4. **Leadership**—the individuals in political institutions and groups who exercise more influence than others on the allocation of values.
5. **Policies**—patterns of government activity that are designed consciously to affect the distributions of benefits and penalties within the society.

SUMMARY OF THEORIES OF POLITICAL DEVELOPMENT

The advantage of stressing change as does Professor Huntington is that it has universal application, since every political system is experiencing change. Analysis is not restricted to a particular time period. A single political system can be studied over a period of time such as the French 4th and 5th republics, or one can compare two or more political systems during a given period of history. Our concern is back to the political, where it should be for political scientists. Political institutions and political leaders are independent factors that shape the natural and social environment. Intervening social and economic factors often are more a result of political decisions than many writers have acknowledged. Industrial parks, the commitment of resources to hydroelectric or nuclear power plants, defense expenditures, increasing literacy through more schools, the availability to basic medical facilities, birth control programs, government-assisted foreign trade programs—all influence the intensity and scope of demands made on governments. But these factors are usually the result of decisions made in the first instance by political leaders. A focus on change recognizes the important role of political decisions and their consequences for the country.

[39]This proposed analytical approach is discussed *ibid.*, pp. 315–319.

POLITICAL DEVELOPMENT: AN OUTMODED TERM?

In recent years we have witnessed a shift in emphasis away from the term political development because many believe it implies that the ultimate objective is some type of Anglo-American democracy based on a two-party system, underpinned by a popular political consensus. Early writings on political development went so far as to divide the world's political systems into Western and non-Western and to speak of a unique non-Western political process. One political scientist drew up a "generalized model" of 17 traits that were "dominant and distinctive characteristics of a non-Western political process."[40] Non-Western countries were fundamentally different. These differences would affect the way these societies moved toward a more rational, prosperous, and Western-style political system.

Almost immediately a lucid rejoinder by another political scientist appeared in the same journal in which the first article was published. The rejoinder said the distinction between a Western and a non-Western or Third World political process was not valid. The problems of rapid change and the efforts to industrialize rapidly are not new. Western Europe in the nineteenth century experienced similar political, social, and economic problems as it sought to deal with the French revolution, the industrial revolution, capitalism, and the revolutionary claims of Karl Marx.[41]

A seminal work, Almond and Coleman's *The Politics of Developing Areas*, published in 1960, argued convincingly that all political systems were "mixed." For analytical purposes one might draw a continuum, with traditional at one pole and modern at the other. Almond insisted that the "dualism" of political structure was "characteristic of modern Western political systems [and] non-Western and primitive" political systems.[42] Every political system is in some degree of transition and each has a mixture of modern and traditional elements. Almond illustrated this "mixed" character of modern political systems with an American example.

During and immediately after World War II, several studies of the impact of mass communications (radio, newspapers, and movies) in the United States suggested a situation whereby the electorate was composed of "atomized individuals" linked "to a system of mass media which were assumed to monopolize the communication process." Further research revealed that this model of modern political communications was inaccurate. The studies indicated media information was filtered to individuals through opinion leaders. The opinion leader was commonly "a trusted individual whose political influence was often a diffuse consequence of other roles," who might be listened to and respected by virtue of being the landlord, a

---

[39]This proposed analytical approach is discussed in *ibid.*, pp. 315–319.

[40]Lucian Pye, The non-Western political process. *The Journal of Politics*, 20, August 1958, 468–486.

[41]Alfred Diamant, Is there a non-Western political process? *The Journal of Politics*, 21, February 1959, pp. 123–124.

[42]Gabriel A. Almond and James S. Coleman, eds., *The Politics of the Developing Areas* (Princeton, N.J.: Princeton University Press, 1960), p. 23.

well-liked and respected friend in the peer group, a religious leader in the village or parish, or a vigorous and extroverted personality. There was a "mixed" (modern/traditional) two-step communication process. The opinion leader was often the intermediary who made a group of associates aware of significant political information and interpreted this information. Awareness, cues, and interpretation were mediated through the traditional, informal opinion leader. The opinion leader in turn was influenced more by other people than the mass media. The opinion leader was considered traditional when compared with "modern" political parties:

> The modern, mass, bureaucratically organized, political party has not supplanted the informal coteries of notables which preceded it, but combines with this "more primitive" type of structure [local organization leaders] in what amounts to a mixed system.[43]

This recognition that political systems in all parts of the world share fundamental features led some to reject the notion of political development as artificially dividing Western and non-Western systems. Nevertheless, the concept of political development still is applied principally to non-Western countries, which are or should be purposively acquiring the chief features of their older, more mature, and successful Western counterparts. This underlying theme, often present in political development literature, also presumes a movement toward a "Western" objective and does not consider seriously the possibility of regression or decay. If a military junta or a Communist-led insurgent group takes over a country, it frequently is seen as an unpleasant necessity on the road to rationality, efficiency, and maximum use of national resources.

Reacting to the political scientists' concern with modernization, transition, and non-Western versus Western societies, Samuel Huntington, as we have seen, foresees a more general interest in political change emerging, not limited to particular parts of the world or to specific periods in history. Nevertheless, this recognition of change and transition as the essential focus for political science should not discourage us from studying something called political development. Political change with special reference to the problems of the developing or emerging countries is an appropriate focus; in fact, the term political development is now so widespread that it is used even by Third World officials to describe the deliberate construction of a more open political system. The individual who became president of Korea after the 1979 assassination of the autocratic President Park spoke of a historic mission and promised his country: "I will be the cornerstone in achieving political development amid stability and Constitutional order."[44]

We listed at the beginning of the chapter certain characteristics shared by most Third World countries that set them apart from Western countries. Most were under colonial rule until well into this century. Third World countries are geographically separate from the Western world, do not share the Judeo–Christian heritage, and are technologically less advanced. Their political institutions are newer and more in-

[43]*Ibid.*, pp. 20–21.
[44]"Peaceful Transfer of Rein Mission," quoted in an article in *The Korea Herald*, November 25, 1979.

clined to be unstable, and these countries are usually behind the West in terms of per capita GNP, persons employed in manufacturing, literacy, health care, and the like. The study of developing countries does not rule out study and appreciation of the Western experience. The recognition that political change is universal and that there are discernible stages of development or regression in political systems, and that all political systems are "mixed" in nature allows for comparisons that draw on Western examples to comprehend better underlying changes, "crises" or major problems, and contemporary government responses in developing countries. Many of the same problems or stages occurred in the West decades or even centuries ago.

It is clear that political development as a subfield in the discipline has shed its non-Western exclusiveness. In the future, political development will refer to challenge, response, and change, with a bias toward stable, nonrevolutionary, and nonviolent adjustments. Political development does not have an Anglo-American democratic model as its objective. Its essence is innovative responses by political leaders that make possible orderly adjustments. It is committed to the optimum degree of social, economic, and poitical freedoms, recognizing that each country has unique qualities. Therefore, no single pattern will emerge. Political development also presumes that new political institutions will emerge or there will be substantial modifications in existing institutions. The burden of performance is on the leadership of these new countries. They must live within political boundaries that often were drawn by colonial powers more concerned with avoiding disputes among competing colonial countries than with drawing boundaries in accord with the ethnic and geographic realities of the local situation. Problems of village parochialism; primordial sentiments such as first loyalty to religion, language group, region, and so on; and the need to create employment and reduce the population growth rate are juxtaposed against government leadership with only limited resources. There is an inadequate tax base, a shortage of motivated and skilled labor and, all too frequently, an externally supported insurgency that may force a government to concentrate on military and physical survival, passing over important social and economic problems. At this moment in time the burdens and capacities of the developing countries differ in important ways from those of the Western nations. A central problem is to distinguish between threats to the security of the country and threats to the security of the ruling group. Ruling elites tend to define challenges to national security. The result is that political reform is even more difficult to achieve. The developing countries are a separate category of countries. We believe it is appropriate to concentrate on them in terms of their political development.

AUTHORITARIANISM AND SYMBIOSIS
This section is concerned with two divergent approaches to directing political change in developing countries: the authoritarian which maintains a naive faith in the unique integrity, capacity, and wisdom of the ruling elite; and the symbiotic,

which recognizes aggregation and accommodation as critical in effective nation building, assumes that policy is not simply rule and administration but includes a broad range of inputs, and favors "organic" rather than imposed uniformity.

The attraction of an elitist government is not limited to those who perceive government as an authoritarian and pervasive institution. Whenever a society is composed of more than an extended family network, most members believe that certain objectives and values can be achieved only by authoritative rules applicable to everyone in society. As society becomes numerically and geographically larger and more complex and impersonal, citizens regard government as the most promising way of enforcing laws binding on everyone in the social system. Disagreement over who will make the laws, what the laws should be, and how they shall be applied is political conflict. The amount of participation and discussion allowed and the administration of enforcement procedures locate a political system on a scale between authoritarian and pluralistic.

Many assume that a strong, authoritarian, flexible government is the most appropriate institution to confront the challenges of the 1980s. This is especially true in the Third World where the demands made on new governments are cumulatively greater than demands made at similar points in Western political development, when problems such as national identity, industrialization, population growth, social mobilization, Communist subversion, elections, and the revolution of rising expectations were sequential rather than simultaneous.

Renewed interest in the achievements of the People's Republic of China (PRC), reported throughout the world press but instantly observable via satellite television, has strengthened the association of such terms as development, order, and authority. Rosy and myopic analyses of mainland China's accomplishments and weaknesses result.[45] Some China visitors apparently are overwhelmed by a political system that can create order, cleanliness, discipline, smiling faces, overt consensus, and a sufficient—albeit plain—food supply for 1 billion people who had experienced increasing degrees of political chaos and anarchy since the nineteenth century. If a harsh, even totalitarian system is necessary for the PRC, the lessons drawn from this case are appropriate for other developing nations.

We often ignore the psychological and human suffering that have occurred on the Chinese mainland since 1949. Some overlook the fact that thousands of Chinese continue to flee the mainland. Hong Kong has absorbed more than 1.8 million refugees since 1950, and illegal immigrants from the mainland continue to arrive regularly. Recent modifications in PRC policy responded to serious mistakes made by overly ambitious, authoritarian policies. The late Premier Chou En-lai had several times rebuffed foreign visitors whose sycophantic compliments overlooked the stresses still present in the system. The appeals of authoritarian, reformist, modernizing governments have not had their source in the PRC experience, but renewed in-

---

[45]See, for example, Harrison E. Salisbury, *To Peking—And Beyond: A Report on the New Asia* (Chicago:Quadrangle Books, 1973).

terest in and awareness of the PRC's political system has lent support to those who maintain that a firm hand is the means to political, economic, and social progress.

A government that seeks to control everything through centralized planning, however, runs into serious problems. The Chinese Communist Party newspaper, *People's Daily*, recently went so far as to discuss overcentralization. A small, isolated, mountainous county printed over a million pages of documents in 1978. The county's party chief had to study an average of 16 daily reports from superiors, while the 360 county officials spent over one-third of their time traveling to the county seat to attend meetings. The determination to enforce a policy of absolutely following the government/party line has led in the PRC to what is called the "three evils": too many meetings, too many documents, too many inspections.[46] We tend to overlook, or be shielded from through censorship, the inefficiencies of authoritarian governments.

The number of authoritarian governments in the Third World, the successes of disciplined Communist insurgents, and the imposition of martial law in countries such as the Philippines may suggest that the practical turn of events is a reasonable justification for authoritarian political systems. This is reinforced by academics who analyze and evaluate political development in the Third World. Since people first made tools, weapons, and laws, a principal theme in Western tradition is humanity's struggle to master nature and history. Behind the Enlightenment of the eighteenth century and subsequent events is the belief that reason, progress, and modernization are measured by the degree to which we control our natural and social environment. Absolute commitment to reason and change can lead soon to a dogmatic rationalism that judges human progress by the amount of order and control in a system.

Even those with a personal liberal philosophy sometimes urge developing nations to adopt authoritarian solutions because it will be easier to bring about orderly change. A sympathetic overview of the emancipation of African and Asian peoples, written two decades ago by a Harvard University scholar, declared:

> For a backward people precariously moving out from under colonialism with all the problems of economic development still ahead of them, it is highly doubtful that the sovereign remedy is a full-scale installment of democracy. . . . [T]he prime requirement is not more freedoms but for discipline and hard work, not for opposition but for a national consolidation of all forces and talents.[47]

A few weeks after the end of World War II, the New York-based Social Science Research Council undertook to sponsor a Committee on Comparative Politics. One of its main tasks was to publish a series entitled *Studies in Political Development*, which we have referred to earlier. The seventh volume in this excellent collection appeared in 1971. It summarized and reconsidered conclusions in the previous

[46]Reported by Fox Butterfield, "China Posts a New Target: Bureaucratic Ossification," *The New York Times*, February 17, 1979.

[47]Rupert Emerson, *From Empire to Nation* (Boston: Beacon Press, 1962), pp. 289–290.

volumes. Progressively, the series and published spinoffs by persons associated with the committee emphasized the crucial role of a strong (if necessary, authoritarian) government for developing nations. In writing on the need for governmental capacity, the authors discussed "penetration" as indispensable:

> *Penetration means conformance to public policy enunciated by central government authority. The degree of penetration may be viewed as the probability that governmental policies regarding the polity as a whole, or any of its subdivisions will be carried out. . . . Penetration refers to whether they, the governing authorities, can get what they want from people over whom they seek to exercise power. Such power clearly refers to areas of governmental policy that go considerably beyond taxation, conscription, and control of deviant behavior.*[48]

We would like to suggest that the values of national political integration and respect for the autonomy of the individual spirit usually can be achieved better through less authoritarian political arrangements. In part, this is because of our bias against authoritarian regimes. Practically, we believe that better results can be achieved via a more democratic form of politics. Developing nations are usually heterogeneous—multiethnic, multitribal, multilinguistic, multireligious, having valley and hill peoples, and so forth. Authoritarian, or "strong," governments have a disturbing tendency to represent only one community in the country; consequently, other groups become increasingly alienated and grievances lead to various degrees of insurrection, leading to more authoritarian government responses.

Nonauthoritarian solutions are not without their advocates. Emile Durkheim (1858–1917), one of the first modern social scientists, investigated conditions in the Third French Republic similar to those facing much of the developing world today. During the latter part of the nineteenth century, France experienced a multitude of social and economic changes; the empire had just been replaced by a republic, but in the transition France had escaped narrowly a return to military rule. Durkheim's discussion of mechanical and organic solidarity was both a description of, and a prescription for, the Third Republic. It remains equally incisive today as we evaluate political policy in the developing nations.

Symbiosis is a related though not identical term describing the organic solidarity Durkheim advocated. Symbiosis describes the interdependence of dissimilar components. Mutual benefits encourage cooperation, although factors inducing cooperation may be dissimilar for each actor. For example, Singapore became a part of Malaysia because it believed this would lead to economic, common-market benefits, while the central government in Kuala Lumpur saw the union as a means to constrain Communist elements on the island and prevent Singapore from becoming Malaya's Cuba. The eventual separation in 1965, with Singapore achieving independence, occurred because the symbiotic relationship had not evolved. Sing-

---

[48]Leonard Binder et al., *Crises and Sequences in Political Development* (Princeton, N.J.: Princeton University Press, 1971), pp. 208–209.

apore's Communists were in disarray, but the economic benefits were slow in coming.

Emile Durkheim was one of the first to recognize that there was such a problem as nation building. He theorized that orderly change and a minimal national consensus built on a monolithic and imposed set of values was less satisfactory than a society based on the accommodation and aggregation of diverse and legitimate interests. Successful modern societies are based on a broad range of mutually beneficial symbiotic relationships.

Durkheim sought to discover laws that would explain social development. Development meant individual differences, autonomous groups, economic complexity, and specialization, rather than standardization of thought and behavior.

National integration or "solidarity" could be achieved "mechanically" or "organically." Under mechanical solidarity, beliefs and values are to be common to all members. Mechanical solidarity and individual choice are opposed. Mechanical solidarity typifies traditional societies or contemporary authoritarian and totalitarian systems where there is little freedom of choice.

Organic solidarity describes a more open, pluralistic society, one that has achieved specialization and a division of labor or is moving in that direction. Durkheim stated that individualism, innovation, and independence increased in society as organic solidarity evolved. Further, he argued that the human potential could be realized only in a society based on organic rather than mechanical solidarity. An individual's specialized and creative functions are possible only "if each one has an individual sphere of action, consequently a personality." Each unit "has its special physiognomy, its autonomy. Yet as the unity of the organism increases the more marked is the individuality of its parts."[49] Political development requires autonomy and creativity, as well as effective government, diversity, and unity.

We do not advocate a return of the night watchman state, which confined itself to external and internal security and maintaining a communications and transportation network. The numerous crises telescoped into a narrow time span in the developing nations require active, efficient, rational, and honest governments to deal with problems ranging from external subversion to rice shortages caused by drought or flood. Simultaneously, we must realize that the capacity of governments in the developing world is limited. One Third World dilemma is that as more demands are made on governments, the demands must be balanced against a rather narrow resource base upon which these governments can draw for taxes, technicians, and so forth. In addition to all their internal problems, there are external forces that impinge on the functioning of developing political systems.

---

[49]These quotes are taken from Book 1, Chapter 3 of Emile Durkheim's *Division of Labor* (Paris: F. Alcan,) first published in 1893. For a succint interpretation of Durkheim's writings, see George Simpson, *Emile Durkheim: Selections from his Work, with Introduction and Commentaries* (New York: Thomas Y. Crowell, 1963).

INTERNATIONAL FACTORS

Political development cannot be studied simply as a result of forces and decisions operating **within** the boundaries of a particular nation. The majority of the developing countries have a history of being influenced significantly by pressures outside the country, over which they have little or no control. Students also should note, however, that the Western or developed nation-states also are influenced by groups not readily subject to national control. Study of the international environment as a source of factors influencing internal stability, development, and decay generally has been neglected. While there are many examples we could discuss, such as the need for foreign markets and foreign investment, we offer two examples of international influence to illustrate the types of problems facing the Third World. One example is political, the other economic.

INSURGENCY AND INTERNATIONAL INTERVENTION

The case of the Tho, concentrated in the mountainous Vietnam–China border area, illustrates the problems of nation building from both a historical and international perspective.[50]

When the French took control of various parts of what is now Vietnam in the nineteenth century, it was a time of vigorous territorial expansion. This territorial spreading out of the lowland Vietnamese threatened the non-Vietnamese hill tribes who had been the only inhabitants of the sparsely populated highlands. The French separated uplanders, or *Montagnards*, from Vietnamese administration and ruled these peoples directly or through local tribal officials whom they appointed. There was general acceptance of this policy by the Montagnards, except in the case of the 400,000 Tho. The Tho had supported an unsuccessful Vietnamese rebel in the sixteenth century. Determined to avoid this in the future, the victorious Vietnamese emperor sent Vietnamese officials to intermarry with the Tho and to administer them. The descendants of the resulting intermarriages—the Tho-ti—became the ruling elite, were accepted as rulers, and became the political link with the lowland Vietnamese. The Tho-ti were alienated because they were passed over by the French as the French colonial rulers appointed local officials. A major Tho tribal rebellion against the French occurred in 1940. The scattered remnants of the Indochinese Communist Party, which had been weakened by an unsuccessful revolt against the French in 1930–1931, now fled from the lowlands and delta to the Tho area. They promised equality and autonomy to the Tho. The Tho mountain area became the first major Communist base, as both groups joined against the common French enemy. When the first Vietnam war, against the French, ended in 1954, 20 percent of the anti-French insurgents (Vietminh) were composed of Tho tribesmen.

---

[50]See John T. McAlister, Jr., "Mountain Minorities and the Viet Minh: A Key to the Indochina War," in Peter Kunstadter, ed., *Southeast Asian Tribes, Minorities, and Nations*, Vol. 2 (Princeton, N.J.: Princeton University Press, 1967), pp. 780–788.

The international aspects of this Tho–Vietminh alliance is summarized by a political scientist who has studied this situation in detail:

> *But possession of a base area in the Tho homeland was more important to the Viet Minh for another reason. The Tho homeland provided the all-important supply route to China through which the Viet Minh obtained external assistance—thereby internationalizing the Viet Minh war.*[51]

Before the Communists seized all of China in 1949, the Vietminh and Tho had traded opium for guns. After 1949, political motives were the source of Chinese support for the insurgents. One writer has said that if it were not for the weapons from China, the Vietminh insurgency would have failed.[52]

The results of the protracted Vietnamese Communist insurgency are self-evident. In April and May of 1975, South Vietnam fell to the insurgents, and Saigon became Ho Chi Minh City. One factor that influenced the continuation of the Vietnam wars for 29 years (1946–1974) was the outside assistance contributed by the Chinese, the Russians, the French, and the Americans. The United States alone spent more than $150 billion between 1960 and 1975. This "international aid" was a crucial factor influencing political development and political decay in Vietnam.

After Vietnam fell to the Communists, the next area of big-power involvement became the Angolan Civil War. Angola was given independence by Portugal in 1975. The victorious Peoples Liberation Movement of Angola was supported by the Russians, Cubans, and Nigerians. Two other political–military movements that lost the civil war received support from the United States, the People's Republic of China, South Africa, and Zaire, among others.

The relatively weak internal condition of many developing countries makes them turn to outside political forces that wish to influence specific policies or the type of political system that will endure.

MULTINATIONAL CORPORATIONS

The nation-state and the **multinational corporation** (MNC) have been described as the "two dominant institutions in the world in the late twentieth century."[53] One way to show the impact of MNCs is to draw up two lists: a list of countries ranked according to their Gross National Product and a list of corporations ranked according to their gross annual sales, with the countries having the highest GNP at the top of the one list and the companies having the highest gross annual sales at the top of the other list. If these lists then are merged and the 100 names at the top are separ-

---

[51]Gary D. Wekkin, "Tribal Politics in Indochina: The Role of Highland Tribes in the Internationalization of Internal Wars," in Mark W. Zacher and Stephen Milne, eds., *Conflict and Stability in Southeast Asia* (Garden City, N.Y.: Anchor Press, 1974), pp. 129–130.

[52]David Feingold, "Opium and Politics in Laos," in Nina S. Adams and Alfred W. McCow, eds., *Laos: War and Revolution* (New York: Harper & Row, 1970), pp. 335–336.

[53]Lester R. Brown, The multinationals and the nation-state. *Vista: The Magazine of the United Nations Association*, 8:6, 1973, p. 15.

ated, 59 names on the list are nation-states and 41 are multinational corporations. General Motors' gross annual sales are higher than the GNPs of Switzerland, Pakistan, and South Africa. Ford Motor Company's sales are higher than Austria's GNP.[54]

An MNC is a corporation that has operations in several countries. Firms are duplicating their activities or dispersing essential parts of their operation among several different states.[55] One of the first MNCs was Bata, which was founded in Czechoslovakia and later transferred to Canada during World War II. In 1968 Bata was manufacturing shoes in 79 countries and selling them in 89 countries.

An IBM Corporation executive has summarized IBM's overseas operations as follows:

1. We operate in 126 countries overseas with some 125,000 employees.
2. We do business in 30 languages, in more than 100 currencies.
3. We have 23 plants in 13 countries.
4. We have 8 development laboratories in as many countries.
5. And we have a very healthy offshore growth rate, going from $51 million in gross income in 1950 to $5.14 billion in 1973. In fact, since 1970 our overseas business has accounted for more than half the corporation's net income.[56]

Developing countries seek outside investment to provide jobs, to introduce technology, as a source of loans and investment dollars, and to be affiliated with a worldwide marketing network. Much of this investment in the developing countries comes through multinational corporations. If one looks at the total world product (WP), that portion dominated by the multinational corporations accounts for 14 percent of WP, and the percentage increase in MNC sales has steadily grown faster than WP. Jobs, economic development, urbanization, unemployment, and equitable or unreasonable distribution of profits and wages often are important factors contributing to the stability of a political system. Not only will the local economic condition help to prevent widespread discontent, it also may provide important taxation resources for a new government faced with numerous demands. Many of the economic decisions that then have political implications are not solely or even principally within the jurisdiction of the developing country, as the following hypothetical case shows:

Many decisions once considered the province of the nation-states are now being made by externally based MNCs, particularly in such matters as the nature, timing, and loca-

[54]U.S. Senate, Committee on Finance, *Multinational Corporations, Hearings* (U.S. Government Printing Office, 1973), p. 404. Testimony given before a subcommittee on International Trade and Finance, 93rd Congress, 1st Session (February 26, 27, 28, and March 1 and 6).

[55]For a review tracing the development of the term multinational corporation, see Howe Martyn, "Development of the Multinational Corporation," in Abdul A. Said and Luiz R. Simmons, eds., *The New Sovereigns: Multinational Corporations as World Powers* (Englewood Cliffs, N.J.: Prentice-Hall, 1975), pp. 30–43.

[56]Jacques Maisenrouge, "How a Multinational Corporation Appears to Its Managers," in George W. Ball, ed., *Global Companies: The Political Economy of World Business* (Englewood Cliffs, N.J.: Prentice-Hall, 1975), p. 15.

tion of investment. These decisions may affect the employment level, the rate of economic growth, the balance of payments, or whether a given natural resource is developed. A planning commission sitting in Accra, the capital of Ghana, may make certain decisions concerning, say, the creation of additional employment, but critical decisions influencing the number of new jobs to be created in Ghana may be made in the executive offices of the MNCs headquartered in New York, Amsterdam, or Osaka.[57]

Important economic and social decisions to which older governments and nation-states previously were able to respond without considering external forces now must carefully operate within the parameters of outside interests. The political system is concerned, among other things, with poverty, overpopulation, rising unemployment, and the taxation base, but these factors do not occupy a prominent position in terms of corporate strategies of MNCs. Each MNC's global strategy is concerned with such decisions as where to secure raw materials, which components will be manufactured in what factory in which particular country, where the assembling of various components will occur, in which countries or with which banks one should seek capital for financing, and where assembly plants, manufacturing plants, employee training, research plants, management offices, and research laboratories should be located most efficiently and most cheaply. These types of problems continue to impinge upon the public policy decisions of many of the developing countries, particularly because of the size and range of activity of many of the MNCs active in the developing world.

One indicator of sovereignty or national independence is the number and scope of decisions influenced by forces outside the country. In important ways many economic decisions are by MNCs in circumstances under which the local government has little control. On occasion, however, the MNC may become directly involved politically in order to continue operating in a country.

One example is a disclosure by Gulf Oil Corporation that it "donated" $4 million over a 5-year period to South Korea's Democratic-Republic Party is an unpleasant reminder of the political role a wealthy MNC can play in a developing country. Gulf Oil has a $350-million investment in South Korea in oil, fertilizer, petrochemical, and shipbuilding facilities. The Democratic-Republicans won only 51 percent of the vote in the 1971 Korean general elections. The party's finance chief, who was described by a Gulf executive as being "as tough a man as I ever encountered," explained his request in 1971 to Gulf as follows: "Here we are, a struggling young democracy, and as you know it takes money to run an election. We therefore are appealing to business people to accomplish this."[58] In the Korean case, Gulf apparently was a reluctant political contributor. The company official, testifying before the Senate Foreign Relations Committee, did admit, however, that the $3 million contribution to the 1971 election campaign was "an unwarranted interference" in Korean internal politics though such donations often are required if a company is to continue doing

[57]Lester R. Brown, *op. cit.*, p. 50.
[58]Richard D. Lyons, "Gulf Oil Admits it Illegally Gave 5-Million Abroad, " *New York Times*, May 17, 1975, p. 37.

business in a country. The Gulf–Korean episode is one example of how MNC policy and the local government's actions may influence one another in important political ways.

SUMMARY

Unity, national integration, political development, political modernization, or political change are phenomena that affect most of the world's population, but are of special importance to people living in the developing world. The developing countries include over 70 percent of the world's population and more than 110 political systems. The Third World confronts most of the problems the developed countries face as well as additional ones such as substantial and long term unemployment, low income, inadequate food production, insurgencies, and numerous other problems discussed earlier. Unfortunately most of these countries fall far short of the necessary resources, such as trained personnel and tax revenue, to deal effectively with even most of the problems they face. Theories of political development help us to understand better what the major problems are, but they provide no clear solutions, except that with limited resources priorities must be established.

We believe, however, that political and economic improvement are better achieved by accommodation of diverse claims, recognizing that much of the impetus for change, evolution, and improvement can be achieved by social and economic decisions and innovations not dictated by government. An evolving political integration is superior to an imposed political uniformity. History shows that authoritarian regimes seldom maintain a spirit of reason, efficiency, and charity. In general, some degree of political and social freedom is the surest way to proceed toward political, economic, and social development. The problems that confont developing systems oftentimes seem insurmountable. Authoritarian solutions are too frequently adopted for purposes of short-run survival, but do not lead to better decisions more efficiently implemented.

SELECTED READINGS

The literature abounds and there are many ways for students to introduce themselves effectively to the major issues that confront a large majority of the world's population. Sometimes rather detailed, but among the most stimulating books written, is Samuel P. Huntington, *Political Order in Changing Society** (New Haven: Yale University Press, 1968). Huntington's book should be read in conjunction with Gabriel A. Almond and G. Bingham Powell, Jr., who use a functional approach: *Comparative Politics: System, Process, and Policy*, 2d ed. (Boston, Little, Brown, 1978). A work that emphasizes becoming modern and political leadership is Dank-

*Available in paperback

wart A. Rustow, *A World of Nations* (Washington, D.C.: The Brookings Institution, 1967). Well-organized overviews of many of the characteristics associated with the developing world are: John H. Kautsky, *The Political Consequences of Modernizaton** (New York: John Wiley, 1972); Fred R. von der Mehden, *Politics of the Developing Nations** 2nd ed. (Englewood Cliffs, N.J.: Prentice-Hall, 1969); and Monte Palmer, *Dilemmas of Political Development** 2d ed. (Itasca, Ill.: F. E. Peacock Publishers, 1980).

Most of the writing on political development has been by American writers. A good collection of British authors is Colin Leys, ed., *Politics and Change in Developing Countries* (Cambridge, Eng.: University Press, 1969). For recent trends in the developmental literature as it applies to Latin America, see Ronald H. Chilcote and Joel C. Edelston, eds., *Latin America: The Struggle with Dependency and Beyond** (New York: John Wiley, A Halstead Press Book, 1974). Finally, for a superior review of the literature and the various approaches that have emerged, see Samuel P. Huntington, "The Change to Change: Modernization, Development and Politics," *Comparative Politics*, 3:3, 1971, pp. 283–322.

There are available numerous introductory readers on political development. Three of the better ones are Jason L. Finkle and Richard W. Gable, eds., *Political Development and Social Change,** 2nd ed. (New York: John Wiley, 1971); John H. Kautsky, ed., *Political Change in Underdeveloped Countries* (New York: John Wiley, 1962); and Claude E. Welch, Jr., *Political Modernization: A Reader in Comparative Political Change,** 2nd ed. (Belmont, Cal.: Wadsworth Publishing, 1971).

The Committee on Comparative Politics of the Social Science Research Council has sponsored the excellent Studies in Political Development Series, which includes conceptual works as well as individual country works. The case studies are drawn from both Western and non-Western countries. The following books in the series all are published by Princeton University Press: Joseph LaPalombara, ed., *Bureaucracy and Political Development,** rev. ed., 1967; Robert E. Ward and Dankwart A. Rustow, eds., *Political Modernization in Japan and Turkey,** 1964; James S. Coleman, ed., *Education and Political Development,** 1965; Lucian W. Pye and Sidney Verba, eds., *Political Culture and Political Development,** 1965; Joseph LaPalombara and Myron Weiner, eds., *Political Parties and Political Development,** 1966. The seventh published volume in the series, Leonard Binder et al., *Crises and Sequences in Political Development,** 1971, does not include any case studies and is rather esoteric in places.

Political pluralism is not achieved easily in the developing countries, but we should not discount it as an objective. Robert Dahl, *Polyarchy: Participation and Opposition,** (New Haven: Yale University Press, 1971) considers on a worldwide

*Available in paperback

basis the possibility and problems of authoritarian political systems becoming more pluralistic. One of the few works that argues that there are sound, practical reasons for a developing country to become more pluralistic is William A. Douglas, *Developing Democracy* (Washington, D.C.: Heldref Publications, 1972). Competitive elections are relatively rare in the Third World. Internal war and insurgency make it even more difficult to hold elections that provide some choice. Surprisingly, major elections held in South Vietnam in 1967 and 1971 provided more choice and were fairer than is popularly assumed. A thoughtful analysis is Howard R. Penniman, *Elections in South Vietnam** (Washington, D.C.: American Enterprise Institute for Public Policy Research, 1972).

Forrest McDonald, *E. Pluribus Unum: The Formation of the American Republic, 1776–1790,** rev. ed., (Indianapolis: Liberty Press, 1979) argues that the special feature of the years after the American Revolution was that the political leaders produced a government system to check the forces that had been unleashed, unlike most postrevolutionary governments today.

Two publications that argue for autonomy and innovation at the local level as a basis for effective socioeconomic development and as an impetus to a widening political pluralism are Thomas J. Bellows, "Political Development, Authoritarianism and Symbiosis," *Journal of Thought*, 8:2, 1973, pp. 123–130; and Edgar Owens and Robert Shaw, *Development Reconsidered* (Lexington, Mass.: D. C. Heath, Lexington Books, 1972).

An effort to explain why bureaucratic elites dominate in so many developing countries is Gerald A. Heeger, "Bureaucracy, Political Parties, and Political Development," *World Politics*, Vol. 25:4, 1973, pp. 600–607. A thorough case study of a bureaucracy's role and importance in a developing political system is Robert O. Tilman, *Bureaucratic Transition in Malaya* (Durham, N.C.: Duke University Press, 1964).

Big-power involvement in the destinies of the developing world is a matter of continuing discussion. Alvin Z. Rubinstein has edited a volume that suggests that in many instances the two big Communist powers have not achieved their objectives: *Soviet and Chinese Influence in the Third World* (New York: Praeger, 1975).

Authoritative reviews of Communist Party activities throughout the world are available in Richard F. Staar, ed., *Yearbook on International Communist Affairs* (Stanford, Cal.: Hoover Institution Press, published annually).

Political development and political change are not confined to non-Western countries. The processes also occur in the West. Two works that include numerous case studies from Western Europe are the eighth volume in the SSRC Studies in the Polit-

*Available in paperback

ical Development Series, Charles Tilly, ed., *The Formation of National States in Western Europe** (Princeton, N.J.: Princeton University Press, 1975); and Gabriel Almond, Scott C. Flanagan, and Robert J. Mundt, eds., *Crisis, Choice, and Change: Historical Studies of Political Development* (Boston: Little, Brown, 1973).

A good introduction to the multinational literature is a review article of 15 recent publications on the topic by a World Bank specialist, Paul Streeton, "Multinationals Revisited," *Finance and Development*, June 1979, pp. 39–42. Kenneth S. Templeton, Jr., ed., *The Politicization of Society** (Indianapolis: Liberty Press, 1979), is a collection of essays that warns against the continual and growing involvement of government in society.

At different times in this chapter we have referred to the impact of political violence. The following works provide a good introduction to this phenomenon. An excellent study of revolutionary behavior, as well as theory, by a British army veteran giving due regard for the more primitive forces of tribalism and racialism is Anthony Burton, *Revolutionary Violence: The Theories* (New York: Crane Russak & Company, 1978). A classic discussion of revolution that argues for economic causes as well as discussing other theorists is James C. Davies, "Toward a Theory of Revolution," *American Sociological Review*, 27:1, 1962, pp. 5–19. A comparative discussion of political decay in totalitarian revolutionary societies is found in C.W. Cassinelli, *Total Revolution: A Comparative Study of Germany under Hitler, the Soviet Union under Stalin, and China Under Mao** (Santa Barbara: Cleo Press, 1976). An excellent case study of terrorism adopted as a calculated tactic is Martha Crenshaw Hutchinson, *Revolutionary Terrorism: The FLN in Algeria* (Stanford, Cal.: Hoover Institution Press, 1978). A periodical dealing with political violence throughout the world is *Terrorism: An International Journal.* A book that addresses itself to policies governments should adopt to thwart domestic and international violence is Robert Kupperman and Darrell Trent, *Terrorism: Threat, Reality, Response* (Stanford, Cal.: Hoover Institution Press, 1979).

*Available in paperback

Chapter Thirteen

Components of International Politics

We believe that it is highly appropriate to conclude our survey of politics with a discussion of politics on the international scene. As mentioned in the first chapter, the phenomenon of politics extends from the smallest group of people to the international community.

The need to know more about the larger world around us has grown steadily because of rapidly increasing international interaction. Figuratively speaking, the world has shrunk considerably in recent decades. Today a person can travel around the globe by jet plane in a matter of some 20 hours, in contrast to the 3 years needed by the adventurer sailors of the sixteenth century. Via telephone, one can contact people in Africa, Asia, and Europe in a few minutes. Formerly, mountains and oceans helped to protect **nation-states**. Today, airplanes and missiles defy these barriers. Technological revolutions have been accompanied by a substantial expansion in international trade. Our supermarkets and department stores feature goods from many different countries, while some of our goods are sold around the world.[1]

The growing interchange on the international scene has not been accompanied by a commensurate educational growth. How much do we know about the people in other parts of the world? How much do they know about us? The need to have as much information as possible about the people abroad is especially crucial for the policy makers of the nation-states. In order to make wise decisions regarding another country, a government needs to have a high degree of accurate information and knowledge about that society.

[1]The energy crisis clearly illustrates the crucial nature of economic interdependence. For a lucid discussion of the growing economic interdependence of nation-states, see Lester R. Brown, *World Without Borders* (New York: Random House, 1972), pp. 183–208.

The technological discoveries of recent decades have not been unilateral blessings. In addition to their merits, they have encouraged the production of weapons capable of destroying humanity. Scientific discoveries **appear** to have outstripped our capability to control them permanently. Today the United States and the Soviet Union possess enough nuclear weapons to kill each other's populations many times over. Will the world community succeed in establishing sufficient social and political counterbalancing forces to nuclear weaponry? We believe that man has the ability to control and correct the ecological, economic, military, and social problems of our time.

PROGRESS OF MAN

(Parrish, reprinted courtesy of The Chicago Tribune.)

SIMILARITIES AND DIFFERENCES BETWEEN DOMESTIC AND INTERNATIONAL POLITICS

In some points **international politics** is similar to domestic politics. Political actors in both settings try to achieve their desires, and some succeed more than others. The actors on the domestic scene are individuals or groups of people in private or public organizations. In international politics the primary actors are the representatives of nation-states (that is, the leaders of the United States, the Soviet Union, France, Japan, Nigeria, and so on). Moreover, in both spheres the more powerful customarily will wield more influence on economic, military, and political processes than those with less power.

The main point of difference between domestic and international politics has to do with the degree of authority and order, in the sense of law, that prevails in each sphere. Domestic governments, by and large, have a preponderance of authority and power in their societies. This means that these governments will have enough military and police support to make their decisions stick and to squash internal unrest. In addition, a national government is the source of final sanction in the judicial sphere. Should a government lose its preponderance of power, it will be overthrown by coup d'état or revolution. The Russia Revolution (1917), the Spanish Civil War (1936–1939), the Cuban Revolution (1958–1959), and the multitude of coups d'etat in the developing countries serve as examples. By and large, however, the domestic scene has been substantially more peaceful than the international scene. According to Quincy Wright, only 70 out of 244 wars in which European countries participated between 1480 and 1941 were civil wars.[2] Since 1945, however, the number of civil wars has increased to equal the figure of wars among countries. These figures indicate that there has been more anarchy on the international than on the domestic scene. The reason is that internationally there is no institution having a preponderance of power. The Security Council and the General Assembly of the United Nations are at best weak facsimiles of domestic governments. War is still the ultimate method of sanction on the international scene, and conflicts among nation-states often are settled on a "might makes right" principle, rather than on the basis of what is right according to international law. History abounds with examples of an action successfully executed by the stronger party becoming "the just decision" in the minds of the victors and their supporters.

THE ACTORS IN INTERNATIONAL POLITICS

We have said that the representatives of nation-states or countries are the principal political actors on the international scene, along with international and regional organizations (discussed in the following chapter), multinational corporations, and political terrorists.

[2]Quincy Wright, *A Study of War*, 2nd ed. (Chicago: The University of Chicago Press, 1965), p. 651.

Nation-states have certain common characteristics. They are political entities separated from other countries by boundaries that are usually officially recognized. In some instances, however, boundaries of a country, or even the existence of a country, may be disputed by some other countries. The Indian–Pakistani conflict is an example of the former, while the Chinese claim to Taiwan exemplifies the latter.

Nation-states have central governments and maintain diplomatic relations with other countries depending upon their standing in the world community. For instance, the United States, Canada, and Sweden maintain diplomatic relations with many other nation-states, while Taiwan and Albania have diplomatic relations with relatively few countries. Nation-states are said to be sovereign according to international law. Sovereignty implies equality with other nation-states and independence from outside interference in the pursuit of domestic and international affairs. In reality, however, no country enjoys absolute sovereignty. The policies and pursuits of one country frequently will have bearing on the actions of others. Powerful countries often will limit the foreign policy range of weaker nation-states or even interfere directly with their domestic affairs. An example of the first type can be seen in the relationship between the Soviet Union and its European allies and has been spelled out in the Brehznev doctrine.[3] The United States committed actions of direct interference in Guatemala in 1954, in Laos in 1962, in the Dominican Republic in 1965; the Soviet Union in East Germany in 1953, in Hungary in 1956, in Czechoslovakia in 1948 and 1968, and in Afghanistan in 1980.

The present world community consists of some 160 nation-states. They range in size from the Soviet Union (8,649,489 square miles) and Canada (3,851, 809 square miles) to such minute entities as the Vatican (109 acres) and Monaco (600 acres). In terms of population, the nation-states vary from the People's Republic of China (with a population of 894,749,000) and India (with 647,840,000 people) down to the Vatican (with a population of 810) and Nauru (with 8,940).[4]

Obviously, these nation-states differ greatly in terms of power. By power we mean the capability to make one's influence or will prevail over others. Some are labeled superpowers, while others are ranked in a second, third, or fourth category. What are the ingredients that help to make one country more powerful than another? The following are some of the major elements that contribute to power:

1. The Geographic Element (size, climate, location, and terrain). Much of human history has been made between 25° and 60° North Latitude, in the temperate zone. Size lends itself to power in that it provides flexibility for retreat and relocation of labor and industry. The vast size of Russia presented an insurmountable problem to Napoleon and Hitler. In turn, countries like Andorra or Liechtenstein have not be-

---

[3]This doctrine was promulgated by the Kremlin after the 1968 occupation of Czechoslovakia and, in essence, holds that the Soviet Union has the right to intervene in a Warsaw Pact country if the Communist system there is in danger of being overthrown or radically changed.

[4]These data are from *Political Handbook of the World: 1979* (New York: McGraw-Hill, 1979) and *The 1979 World Almanac and Book of Facts* (New York: Newspaper Enterprise Association, 1978).

THE WIZARD OF ID   by Brant parker and Johnny hart

("The Wizard of Id" by permission of Johnny Hart and Field Enterprises, Inc.)

come great powers. Certain locations and terrains have constituted advantages in the premissile age. For example, the British Isles have not been invaded by a conquering force since the eleventh century, while the mountains have protected Switzerland. In World War II Hitler's High Command refrained from invading either of the two, primarily because of logistical considerations.

2.   The Demographic Element (population). A large population will lend power to the country, provided that the people are adequately nourished, well trained in industrial and professional skills, and highly motivated in supporting the aims of the incumbent power elite. Without these ingredients, a large population may be a deterrent to power. For example, the Soviet government found itself greatly weakened during the early 1930s because of the widespread famine leading to substantial starvation in many areas of the country, including the Ukraine—the primary breadbasket of the USSR. Likewise, the government of the People's Republic of China was occupied during the 1950s largely with raising enough food for its many millions of people. The Chinese intervened militarily in Korea only after United Nations Forces came close to its border at the Yalu River, and even then the Chinese limited their involvement. India, with the second largest population of any country in the world, still struggles to meet the basic necessities of its people.

3.   Natural Resources, Technology and Transportation. Extensive natural resources readily accessible for exploitation and an adequate plant system to transform the natural resources into commercial and military goods add considerably to the power of a country. Essential to the production process and the maintenance of domestic unity are up-to-date and well-functioning systems of communication and transportation. Keeping in mind the confusion and chaos an occasional brown-out, black-out, or strike by airline employees causes, the results of a complete breakdown of communication and/or transportation facilities would be infinitely more chaotic and confusing and could render a postindustrial society completely helpless. Technological superiority customarily will give a nation-state an advantage over those who are less developed. The perpetuation of the power potential depends on the continuous allocation of resources (labor and money) for further research. A society that calls a halt to scientific and technological developments soon will come to a technological standstill. The vicious arms race between the United States and the Soviet Union since World War II is, among other factors, a sign of the perpetual technological–military competition between the two superpowers. While efforts have been made to curtail this race, both societies will continue their technological–military research in order to protect their **national interests**.[5]

4.   Military Power and Preparedness. The presence of a strong and well-trained military establishment equipped with up-to-date weaponry is perhaps the most obvious element of national power. There is some difficulty in calculating actual military power. How many infantry battalions, how many tanks, how many pieces of artillery equal a 5-megaton nuclear bomb? To what extent does the tremendous manpower potential in the People's Republic of China equal Soviet nuclear strength? Another question pertains to the speed with which the resources in manpower and weaponry can be mobilized.

Whatever system of calculation is used, the United States and the Soviet Union are substantially ahead of all other countries in military power. Both have vast quantities of nuclear weapons and the delivery systems for short-, medium-, and long-range missiles. The other members of the "nuclear club" are France, the People's Republic of China, and the United Kingdom. Furthermore, India has tested nuclear devices, and it generally is assumed that Israel and the Republic of South Africa have a nuclear capacity, too. A number of other countries have the capability to produce nuclear weapons but have refrained from producing them. An expansion of the **nuclear club** would make international relations more complex and more dangerous. At this time the governments of the United States and the Soviet Union are vitally interested in preventing an expansion of the "nuclear club," in order to forestall international complications.

5.   Governmental Leadership. Last but not least, the quality of governmental leadership has considerable bearing on the power of a nation-state. The leaders in the national government set the priorities and determine the allocation of resources for the armed forces, foreign aid, and domestic purposes. It is of paramount importance for society that the top leaders in the national government keep fully informed about the happenings at home and abroad. Furthermore, it is extremely important that these leaders make wise decisions, wise in terms of short-term and long-term implications. History abounds with examples of leaders who have fumbled and have led their societies into catastrophes, such as those committed by Napoleon, Mussolini, the Japanese military oligarchy of World War II, and Hitler.

Strength and wisdom in leadership help to produce a stronger country, and it is a rare quality of a society to develop the kind of political system that brings the most

[5]The term national interest is rather elusive and difficult to define precisely. One of the more thoughtful definitions is that of Frederick Hartmann, who speaks of national interests "as those things that states could or do seek to protect or achieve vis-a-vis other states." Frederick H. Hartmann, *The Relations of Nations*, 5th ed. (New York: Macmillan, 1978), p. 7.

able leaders into the top national positions and supports and sustains their decisions.

The five elements just cited are some of the main criteria of national power. Obviously, they are not all-inclusive, and exceptions to the rule as well as special circumstances need to be taken into consideration when examining a particular case.[6]

THE NATURE OF INTERNATIONAL POLITICS

The origin of the modern nation-state system dates back to the sixteenth century. The Italian writer and diplomat Niccolò Machiavelli (1469–1527) provided an early analysis of and justification for leadership and centralized power at the national level in *The Prince*. Since those days the number of existing nation-states has increased considerably. Many of the 100-plus countries customarily classified as "developing nation-states" have become independent only in recent years, since World War II. A large number of nation-states have been born in a revolutionary or semirevolutionary setting. The people in the United States declared their independence from Britain during their revolutionary war. Other colonies were granted independence from their mother countries under more peaceful settings. An example would be that of Britain granting independence to the Bahamas in 1973.

The community of nation-states exists in a setting of constant change. While some new countries are being born, others are being swallowed up by more powerful ones. For example, the former Baltic countries of Estonia, Latvia, and Lithuania were annexed by the Soviet Union during World War II. Still other countries have been divided and temporarily swallowed up by adjacent nation-states. A good example of this would be Poland, which was divided three times during the eighteenth century and again during World War II. Germany and Korea were divided at the end of World War II, and in both instances two quite different political units have developed. Because of perpetual shifts in the power relationship among countries, the process of change in the nation-state community will exist as long as the nation-state remains the primary unit of the international community.

THE VIABILITY OF A NATION-STATE

Which nation-states are likely to remain in their present geographical form and which will experience losses of territory, divisions, or will disappear completely? The perpetuation of a nation-state in its present geographical make-up is based on external and internal considerations. External factors include the nation-state's power

[6]The main points of this discussion were drawn from Vernon Van Dyke, *International Politics*, 3rd ed. (New York: Appleton-Century-Croft, 1972), pp. 223–242. Related discussions of the elements of national power are found in Hans Morgenthau, *Politics Among Nations*, 5th ed. (New York: Alfred A. Knopf, 1973), pp. 112–149; and Hartmann, *op. cit.*, pp. 45–68. Hartmann's discussion includes some very useful tables comparing the labor force, production of vital materials, and armed forces of selected countries.

position vis-à-vis its neighboring countries and other potential adversaries, the presence of natural frontiers, and the ubiquity of enlightened leadership. The power of a country (as defined in our earlier discussion) will exercise restraints upon the ambitions of other governments. Natural frontiers, such as the Pyrenees between France and Spain, are unlikely to lead to boundary disputes. Finally, enlightened statesmen will try to resolve their disputes with other leaders in amicable rather than belligerent ways, thereby refraining from endangering the existence of their country.[7]

The opposite example would be the story of the Third Reich, where the policies of the super-belligerent and paranoid Hitler regime led to the destruction of Germany and the death of many millions of people. One could conjecture that if German leaders had continued the enlightened Stresemann spirit as exhibited in the Locarno Treaties (1925) during the 1930s and 1940s, there still would be a Germany today with the boundaries of 1937. The above presupposes, of course, that the leaders of the surrounding countries also would have continued their enlightened spirit of 1925.

Internal factors are very important to the viability of a country. For a nation-state to remain viable, there must exist a high degree of national integration, including enough nationalism to bind society together,[8] sufficient ethnic homogeneity, preferably a uniting language, and wise leadership. Nationalism, as related to the viability of a nation-state, refers to the public loyalty put forth by the citizenry. The large majority of citizens must extend their public loyalty in the first instance toward their nation-state, rather than a subunit thereof or a foreign country. Ethnic homogeneity and a unifying language serve as helpful ingredients. Countries such as Iceland, Norway, and Sweden are leading examples of these requirements, and the homogeneity of their societies has reinforced their viability as nation-states considerably. In contrast, the Austro-Hungarian Empire, which was a conglomerate of national groups and languages, fell apart in 1918 because the individual national groups desired to achieve independence. The people in former East Pakistan, having little in common with the people and government in West Pakistan, fought successfully for independence and established their own country, Bangladesh, in 1971. In contrast, some years earlier, the Ibos fought for independence from Nigeria and lost.

African countries have been especially beset by internal divisions, and boundary changes and efforts toward tribal independence can be expected in Africa in years and decades to come. The present boundaries, drawn arbitrarily by the colonial powers in the nineteenth century, frequently fail to reflect tribal locations and language considerations. A case in point would be Nigeria, where the population consists of a number of tribes— the largest ones being the Hausa, the Ibo, and the

---

[7]For an extensive treatment of the issues of national integration, see Karl Deutsch, *Nationalism and Its Alternatives* (New York: Alfred A. Knopf, 1969), pp. 3–91.

[8]See Hans Kohn, *The Idea of Nationalism* (New York: Macmillan, 1961).

Yoruba. The Hausa are the most populous tribe in Nigeria, but they also overlap into neighboring Niger. The Yoruba, in turn, overlap into Dahomey. Most likely, some of the tribal aspirations will be contained through domestic power struggles (such as the violent conflicts between the Hutu and Tutsi in Burundi and Rwanda) and others through civil wars (as the Ibo case illustrates). Some other ethnic conflicts undoubtedly will lead to boundary changes in the years to come.[9]

An Asian example of geopolitical complexity is India. The country features about a dozen major languages and several hundred dialects. Various efforts to make Hindi, the most widely spoken language, the official language of the country have been opposed by measures that at times included demonstrations, violence, and bloodshed. As a consequence, the Indian government has seen no choice but to retain English as the official language of the country. Only about 30 percent of the Indian people speak Hindi.[10] Would a future imposition of Hindi as the national language lead to separatist movements by the non-Hindi-speaking groups?

FOREIGN POLICY AND INTERNATIONAL POLITICS

The term international politics embraces the sum total of the nation-states' foreign policies. A nation-state's **foreign policy** consists of its government's relations with other countries. More specifically, these relations are based on considerations of national interest and may involve political, economic, cultural, and military measures. The basic element underlying the foreign policy of all countries is the quest for security. Foreign policy involves sets of objectives and strategies, often conceived over a period of time, involving three ingredients—conception, content, and implementation. In the words of Frederick Hartmann:

> Because a foreign policy consists of selected national interests presumably formulated into a logically consistent whole that is then implemented, any foreign policy can be viewed analytically in three phases: conception, content, and implementation. Conception involves the strategic appraisal of what goals are desirable and feasible. Content is the result and reflection of that appraisal. Implementation looks to both the coordinating mechanisms within a state and the means by which it conveys its views and wishes to other states. Although inefficiencies and failures can be very costly in any of these three phases, it is apparent that the most critical phase is conception.[11]

Hartmann's three-step formula can be applied to the foreign-policy-making process of all countries. What differs, however, are the goals pursued by the individual countries. These differences have to do with the power capabilities of a country, its needs, location, and so forth. The Soviet Union and the United States, our present-day superpowers, pursue worldwide interests and have these reflected in their

[9]A good source for ethnic information and country profiles of sub-Saharan Africa is Donald G. Morrison, ed., *Black Africa: A Comparative Handbook* (New York: The Free Press, 1972).

[10]See A. H. Hanson and Janet Douglas, *India's Democracy* (New York: W. W. Norton, 1972), p. 2.

[11]Hartmann, *op. cit.*, p. 69.

foreign policies. Botswana or Paraguay, in contrast, are underdeveloped and land-locked countries with rather limited foreign policy aims and pursuits.

THE CONDUCT OF INTERNATIONAL POLITICS

CHANNELS OF COMMUNICATION

Once foreign policy has been formulated, by what means is it put into effect? How do nation-states deal with each other? The range of possible relations is wide, stretching from friendly diplomatic acts on the one hand to warfare on the other. **Diplomacy**, according to Nicolson, who is quoting from the *Oxford English Dictionary*, is

> the management of international relations by means of negotiation; the method by which these relations are adjusted and managed by ambassadors and envoys: the business or art of the diplomatist.[12]

Diplomacy is the means by which governments conduct business with each other. In order to facilitate the conduct of diplomacy, nation-states customarily establish some degree of diplomatic relations with each other. For example, country A may have a trade mission in country B and use this trade mission for conducting trade and diplomatic matters. A case in point would be the East German trade mission in Bonn. Or, a country may maintain a special office or legation in another country, headed by a *charge d'affaires* or minister. For example, the United States was represented in some of the Arab countries by *charges d'affaires* after the 1967 war. Some countries maintain only consular relations (i.e., less than full diplomatic relations) with each other. The Republic of South Africa, for example, has only consular relations with Denmark and Japan. While the South African government would like to maintain full diplomatic relations, the two countries prefer for political reasons to keep relations at a less conspicuous level.

Countries that have full diplomatic relations with each other exchange ambassadors.

All diplomats are employed by the state department or foreign ministry of their home country. They enjoy certain privileges, such as diplomatic immunity. Should a diplomat violate the laws of the host country, he may not be tried there; rather, he would be declared *persona non grata* and asked to return to his home country. Governments customarily adhere to the international rules obliging the host government to protect consulates and embassies, as well as the immunity privileges of foreign diplomats. The 1979 takeover of the U.S. Embassy in Tehran by Iranian militants and their further action of holding those diplomats as hostages—steps taken with the approval of the Iranian government— constitute gross violations of international law and were condemned as such by all civilized governments.

[12]Harold Nicolson, *Diplomacy* (New York: Oxford University Press, 1963), p. 15.

How are diplomatic relations established? As a new country comes into being, the governments of other countries will decide whether to establish diplomatic relations or not. Various political considerations are involved in this decision-making process. For example, will our establishment of diplomatic relations with country X offend country Y, a friend of ours? What will be our economic and political gains in establishing these relations? For instance, when Bangladesh became independent in December of 1971, the U.S. government temporarily held back extending diplomatic recognition to that new nation-state in order not to offend our ally, Pakistan. After a number of other countries had recognized Bangladesh, however, the United States followed suit. The U.S. government did not recognize the Communist regime in Russia until 1933,[13] and some degree of diplomatic relations with the People's Republic of China, was established only after President Nixon's 1972 visit to that country.

Disputes between countries will lead at times to a reduction in diplomatic relations or a complete severance. For instance, the United States government severed diplomatic relations with some of the Eastern European countries after they had been taken over by Communist regimes at the end of World War II. Following the abortive Hungarian Revolution of 1956, our government reduced its diplomatic representation in Hungary by recalling the ambassador and leaving a *chargé d'affaires* in control of our embassy. Full restoration of diplomatic relations occured some years later, after a considerable improvement in United States–Hungarian relations had taken place. The United States and most Latin American countries broke diplomatic relations with Cuba after the Castro takeover, but in recent years a number of them have begun to move toward reconciliation. The point is that diplomatic recognition is used often as an instrument of political expediency and a means of reward or punishment. Generally speaking, however, governments will find it more convenient to maintain diplomatic relations with other countries than not to do so. In the absence of diplomatic relations, other sources have to be found to negotiate existing issues. For example, during the late 1950s and most of the 1960s, our ambassador in Warsaw met on a fairly regular basis with his Communist Chinese counterpart to negotiate matters of interest to both countries.

Before a government appoints a person as ambassador, inquiries will be made regarding whether he or she is acceptable (*persona grata*) to the host country. If not, a more suitable person will be selected. Diplomats serve two primary functions: they represent the home government in the host country and they keep the home government informed about the cultural, economic, military, and political happenings in the host country in order that the state department or foreign ministry at home can formulate intelligent policies toward the other country. The diplomats stationed abroad attend to the day-to-day items of business. Issues of great concern

[13]The issues surrounding the late U.S. recognition of the USSR are discussed in detail in Edward M. Bennett, *Recognition of Russia: An American Foreign Policy Dilemma* (Waltham, Mass.: Blaisdell Publishing, 1970).

are more likely to be dealt with by special negotiators appointed to conduct a particular conference, by secretaries of state or foreign ministers, or by the leaders of the countries themselves.

In addition to the embassy, a country may maintain one or more consulates in the host country. The consular staff attends to matters such as issuing visas, assisting citizens traveling abroad, promoting trade, and providing public information.

Since World War II a number of **summit meetings** have been held between the leaders of the major countries, as well as those who are still in a developing stage. For such meetings to be successful, a great deal of preliminary work needs to be done at the professional diplomatic level. Three important summit meetings took place during and at the end of World War II: Tehran, 1943 (Churchill, Roosevelt,

The "Big Three" at the Potsdam Conference, from left to right: Prime Minister
Winston Churchill, President Harry S. Truman, and Marshal Josef Stalin.

Stalin); Yalta, 1945 (Churchill, Roosevelt, Stalin); and Potsdam, 1945 (Churchill, At-tlee, Truman, Stalin). At these three meetings the Allies' war aims, the fate of the vanquished countries, and the creation of the United Nations were discussed, and important final decisions were made on these subjects. In 1955 Bulganin, Eden, Eisenhower, and Faure met in Geneva to consider the future of Germany and Euro-pean security. The meeting between Kennedy and Khrushchev in Vienna in 1961 served as an exchange of United States' and Soviet views on confrontation issues in Europe and Southeast Asia. Nixon's 1972 visit to the People's Republic of China, leading to the establishment of partial diplomatic relations between the United States and China; Nixon's subsequent visit to Moscow; Brezhnev's 1973 visit to Washington, D.C.; the 1974 conference between Ford and Brezhnev in Vladivostok; and the 1979 meeting of Carter and Brezhnev in Vienna regarding SALT II are more recent examples of big-power summit meetings.

METHODS FOR CONDUCTING INTERNATIONAL RELATIONS
The previous discussion has centered on the **channels** used by nation-states to conduct their official affairs with each other. The following discussion deals with the **methods** used by governments in the pursuit of their foreign relations. International problems can be solved through amicable political or judicial methods, or through nonamicable means, including retortion, reprisal, or even war. The main amicable

A history-making foursome, from left to right: Premier Nikolai Bulganin, President Dwight D. Eisenhower, Premier Edgar Faure, and Prime Minister Anthony Eden at the Geneva Conference, 1955.

Contemporary summitry: Leaders of developed countries meet in June, 1980, in Venice, Italy, for a major politico-economic conference. They are from left to right, Prime Ministers Okita from Japan and Trudeau from Canada, Chancellor Schmidt from West Germany, President Giscard d'Estaing from France, Prime Minister Cossiga from Italy, President Carter, Prime Minister Thatcher from Great Britain, and EEC President Jenkins.

political instrument is that of **negotiation**. Representatives of two or more countries will meet with the purported purpose of achieving agreement on a given issue. The process of negotiation is based on the assumption that the parties involved have some interest in solving the problem at hand. Fred Charles Iklé classifies the objectives of governments in international negotiations into four types. The first three are: extension or renewal of an existing agreement with perhaps slight changes of the former; the normalization of relations, such as the negotiations that led to U.S. recognition of the Soviet Union in 1933; a redistribution of territory and/or political power. This latter type of negotiation is conducted between an offensive and a defensive party, with the offensive side trying to acquire something from the other. For example, in 1958, the Icelandic government claimed a 12-mile offshore zone for native fishery exclusively. The British, having fished previously in that area, began to comply with the Icelandic demand in order to forestall future difficulties, which developed anyway. Of greater politico-military importance were Khrushchev's repeated demands during the late 1950s for a change in the status of West Berlin. In this instance, the West did not acquiesce. The fourth type of negotiation includes innovation agreements that serve to establish a new relationship between the parties involved. The Treaties of Rome (1957), which set up the European Economic Community and Euratom, serve as a good example.[14]

Do leaders always negotiate to achieve agreement on an issue of concern? According to Iklé:

> Side-effects—that is, effects not concerning agreement—may be an important part of the outcome, even if all parties negotiate primarily for the purpose of reaching agreement. They may arise either by accident or by design of one party or all parties involved. When diplomacy produces agreements only rarely—as between East and West—the objective of producing side-effects, in fact, often dominates.[15]

Iklé lists six major points of negotiating for side effects:

1. The purpose of one or both negotiators may be plainly that of maintaining contact with each other to keep open the channels of communication. An example of this would be the negotiation between the Soviet Union and the United States regarding the German question and, more specifically, the status of West Berlin during the 1950s and early 1960s. Though the parties had arrived at a stalemate on these issues, the leaders in Moscow and Washington decided that the negotiations should be continued to prevent a worsening of the situation, which could have had dire consequences for both.

2. Negotiations can serve as a substitute for violent actions. The argument made in support of this thesis is that the process of negotiation can be so pleasing to one's adversary or catalyze in him the feeling of obligation to see the negotiations through that he will refrain from taking the violent action he otherwise would have. Iklé goes on to say that the thesis holds true in some instances, while it does not apply to others. For example, contrary to Neville Chamberlain's hopes, the Munich Conference did not keep Hitler from starting World War II; neither did the United States–Japanese negotiations in 1941 forestall Japan's attack on Pearl Harbor.

3. Negotiations may be used to gather intelligence information about the adversary. During the process of negotiation the opponent may reveal some of his intentions, long-term aims, or range of negotiability—that is, the minimum and maximum desires. There is some evidence that President Nixon's talks with the Chinese and Russian leaders served in part to get a reading of their views regarding Southeast Asia, and that the President developed his subsequent policies accordingly.

4. The major purpose of a particular negotiation may be deception—to deceive the opponent about one's aims. An example of deception took place during the Hungarian Revolution in 1956. During the first four days of the uprising the Soviet ambassador in Budapest negotiated with the leaders of the new Hungarian govern-

[14]Fred Charles Ilke, *How Nations Negotiate* (New York: Frederick A. Praeger, 1967), pp. 26–42.
[15]Ikle, *op. cit.*, p. 43.

ment about their political aims and the withdrawal of the Russian troops. This period gave the Soviet Politburo enough time to plan its counterattack to overthrow the Nagy government.

5. Negotiations sometimes are used for propaganda purposes. In this setting one or both sides will set forth proposals, knowing that they are unacceptable to the other side. The prime aim is to gain favorable publicity. Important forums, such as summit meetings and the rostrums of the Security Council and the General Assembly of the United Nations, lend themselves well to gaining publicity and prestige. Presidential speeches, here and abroad, are filled with statements favoring peace and the well-being of mankind. While there may be some true intention in these comments, the point is that often one side tries to outdo the other in order to score points with the rest of the world by making the other side look hypocritical. One case in point is the publicity during the disarmament conferences of the past eight decades and, in particular, the Russian proposals, commencing with Lenin, for complete disarmament. In addition, it appears that past Soviet and United States proposals concerning the unification of Germany contained a good deal of farce, too.

6. Negotiations may be for the purpose of influencing third parties—to intimidate a third country. During the 1960s some governments of developing countries tried to play Washington against Moscow and vice versa in order to obtain favorable economic deals.[16]

In summary, negotiations often have been used for purposes other than those purported. Nevertheless, negotiations are far preferable to less amicable alternatives, but in order for negotiations to make sense, there must be a negotiable issue and the parties involved must have some desire for agreement and must show some flexibility, because the outcome of successful negotiations is usually a compromise solution.

Sometimes the process of mediation is employed. Here a third party is called upon to disentangle the problem between two parties and to help to bring about an agreement. Most likely, this third party will be an outside government or an international forum such as the Security Council of the United Nations. In 1966 Premier Kosygin invited the leaders of India and Pakistan to Tashkent in order to help them delineate a ceasefire line and to improve relations between the two countries. Kosygin's efforts were of some success and contributed to a temporary easing of tensions between India and Pakistan.

A more recent example of high-level mediation occurred in 1978, when President Carter invited the leaders of Egypt and Israel, President Sadat and Prime Minister Begin, to Camp David and, in the process of lengthy and difficult discussions, helped considerably to improve the relations between the two countries. President

---

[16]For a more detailed discussion, see Ikle, *op. cit.*, pp. 43–58.

Carter continued his mediation efforts until the Egyptian-Israeli peace treaty was finalized.

While a number of international problems have been settled through negotiations in a fairly amicable fashion, other conflicts have led to nonamicable measures, customarily involving a good deal of coercion. Vernon Van Dyke identifies four types of nonamicable methods: retorsion, reprisal, intervention, and war.

Retorsion is a deliberate, unfriendly but legal act that has a retaliatory purpose. For instance, government *A* may be displeased by an action taken by government *B* and, to show its indignation, may reduce or sever diplomatic relations with the latter. A less severe step would be a temporary curtailment of trade or trade privileges. For example, in December 1979, President Carter expelled 183 Iranian diplomats from the United States, thereby reducing their number in this country to 35. This was one of several actions taken by the U.S. government to show its extreme displeasure concerning the take-over of our embassy in Tehran by Iranian militants.

The term **reprisal** refers to a deliberate, unfriendly, and illegal action taken in response to a prior violation of international law by the other country. It usually involves some kind of military action. One case in point is the Gulf of Tonkin incident of 1964. While even today very few facts about this affair are known to the public, the point is that as a consequence of North Vietnamese action the President of the United States ordered an all-out air attack on North Vietnamese oil storage facilities and PT-boat bases, thereby substantially escalating our military involvement in Southeast Asia.

Intervention means direct interference by one country in the affairs of another. This type of interference is usually of broader scope than an act of reprisal and may result without a provocation by the other country. Intervention is an act committed by governments for one of several purposes. Intervention may involve meddling in the electoral process of another country to insure the election of a candidate favorable to the intervening country, or it may lead to pressure on the other government to pursue or not to pursue a certain foreign policy. Intervention may involve the sending of troops into another country to force that government and for segments of the population "to fall into line;" for example, in the early decades of this century the U.S. government sent marines into several Latin American republics. In more recent years, the U.S. intervention in 1965 in the Dominican Republic, the Soviet reoccupation of Hungary in 1956, the Soviet occupation of Czechoslovakia in 1968 as well as the Soviet invasion of Afghanistan, commencing in late 1979, are obvious examples of intervention.

In the absence of an international authority that has a preponderance of power, **war** remains the ultimate means for settling a conflict on the international scene. History abounds with examples of countries having gone to war against each other after they had exhausted the existing political and judicial means for settlement, or even before they had tried some or all of them. Thus, war still plays an important

function in international politics. It remains the ultimate method for settling a problem. This fact makes it more difficult to reduce or to outlaw war successfully on the
international scene.[17]

The previous discussion of methods used in international relations does not include such judicial means as arbitration and adjudication. They will be explained in
the next chapter having to do with international law. The choice of method used by
governments to solve a given problem will depend very much on the circumstances
at hand, the objectives pursued, the attitudes of the leaders (reasonable and rational or belligerent and revengeful), the power ratio between the nation-states involved,
the willingness of both sides to compromise, and other factors. Suffice it to say that
it is better to talk with each other than to shoot at each other. It is hoped that in the
years to come more and more leaders will be able to solve their disputes by amicable means rather than through warfare.

INTERNATIONAL POLITICS IN THE
POST-WORLD WAR II ERA
Having examined the elements of international politics and the methods employed
by nation-states in their relations with each other, it may be worthwhile to scrutinize
briefly the major international developments since World War II.

THE BRIEF PERIOD OF BIPOLAR DEVELOPMENT
The United States and the Soviet Union emerged from World War II as the two
global powers. Clearly, in 1945 the United States was substantially stronger than the
Soviet Union, which had suffered considerably from the effects of the war; but the
immense size of the Soviet army, its presence in most of the Balkan states, in
Poland, in the heart of Germany, in Manchuria, and in the northern part of Korea,
plus the strength derived from the dictatorial government of the country, compensated for some of the points of Russian weakness and gave the Soviet Union an important power position in world affairs.

In comparison to the two giants, other major World War II allies had become, at
best, secondary powers. The United Kingdom emerged economically weakened
from the war. Its hold over its vast colonial empire began to crumble, and with the
independence of the Indian subcontinent in 1947 a movement was set into motion
that in the next 15 years led to the independence of most of the British colonies.
France after World War II was economically weak and politically divided. A major
general strike in 1948 led the country to near chaos. In addition, domestic political
instability and the Indochina crisis, as well as the problem in Algeria, kept France
from playing any influential role in foreign affairs until the return to office of de
Gaulle in 1958. In the Far East, the end of World War II signaled the resumption of

---

[17]Van Dyke, *op. cit.*, pp. 294–296.

the civil war between the Communists, led by Mao Zedong and the government forces under Chiang Kai-shek. In 1949 the Communists won the war and Chiang Kai-shek fled with the remnants of his forces to Taiwan. These developments and others left the Soviet Union and the United States temporarily the uncontested global rulers.

The governments of both powers set out to consolidate their areas of influence and, by doing so, established a **bipolar** order. The major line between these two spheres cut through the center of Europe. As Sir Winston Churchill stated so appropriately in his famous May 5, 1946 speech at Westminster College, Missouri:

> From Stettin in the Baltic to Trieste in the Adriatic, an iron curtain has descended across the Continent. Behind that line lie all the capitals of the ancient states of Central and Eastern Europe. Warsaw, Berlin, Prague, Vienna, Budapest, Belgrade, Bucharest and Sofia, all these famous cities and populations around them lie in what I must call the Soviet sphere, and all are subject in one form or another not only to Soviet influence but to a very high and, in many cases, increasing measure of control from Moscow.[18]

Churchill's classic statement points at the **Iron Curtain** as the man-made division between the two spheres of interest and alludes to the commencement of the Cold War era, an epoch that continued, with a varying degree of severity, until after the Cuban missile crisis.[19]

The only Western enclave behind the Iron Curtain has been West Berlin, the part of the city occupied by British, French, and United States' troops since the summer of 1945 and governed by the Western Allies. During the late 1940s and 1950s, the Soviet government made several attempts to eliminate Western presence in Berlin, the more serious ones being the 1948–1949 blockade and Khruschev's demands in 1958 and 1959 to turn West Berlin into a "free city" after the withdrawal of the Western troops. All these attempts failed, and the status of West Berlin has not been changed.

The new types of order established after the end of World War II under the **hegemonic** control of the two superpowers in Eastern and Western Europe differed considerably from each other. In Western Europe, democratic systems were reestablished and soon gained a strong momentum of their own. In contrast, the imposition of Soviet-type communism in the East European countries required considerable force. One feature of this difference can be seen in the large number of people who fled to the West from the countries under Soviet control. There is clear evi-

[18]Randolph S. Churchill, ed., *The Sinews of Peace: Post-War Speeches by Winston S. Churchill* (London: Cassell and Company, 1948), p. 100.

[19]For perceptive analyses of the Cold War, see Lynn Etheridge Davis, *The Cold War Begins: Soviet–American Conflict Over Eastern Europe* (Princeton, N.J.: Princeton University Press, 1974); Herbert Feis, *From Trust to Terror: The Onset of the Cold War* (New York: Norton, 1970); Walter Lefever, *America, Russia, and the Cold War, 1945–1966* (New York: Wiley, 1967); Paul Seabury, *The Rise and the Decline of the Cold War* (New York: Basic Books, 1967); and Daniel Yergin, *Shattered Peace: The Origins of the Cold War and the National Security State* (Boston: Houghton Mifflin, 1977).

dence that as early as 1949, in the absence of foreign military intervention, the Adenauer government in West Germany and its democratic order could have sustained itself quite readily without the presence of British, French, and United States' troops in the country. In contrast, evidence shows that during the same time period the incumbent regimes in Czechoslovakia, East Germany, Hungary, and Poland were kept in power only with the help and as a result of the presence of Soviet troops.

CHALLENGES TO SOVIET AND UNITED STATES' HEGEMONY

Over the years, both major powers have faced difficulties in maintaining hegemony in their respective area. A general assessment of the developments in Europe and Asia shows that the Soviet Union clearly faced the greater difficulties. Let us examine these developments in some detail.

The first open conflict in the Soviet empire occurred in 1948, when Marshal Tito of Yugoslavia asked Russian advisers to leave his country and commenced a course of policies independent of Moscow. In 1953 widespread demonstrations against the Ulbricht regime occurred in East Germany. This uprising threatened to overthrow the incumbent Moscow-loyal power elite and was suppressed only by large-scale intervention of Soviet troops. Further unrest in the German Democratic Republic led to the building of the infamous Berlin Wall in 1961. A revolutionary type of uprising occurred in Hungary in 1956 and led temporarily to the withdrawal of Russian troops from that country and the installation of a popular government under Imre Nagy. A few days later, however, Russian troops reinvaded Hungary and forcefully replaced the Nagy government with Hungarian Communists loyal to Moscow. During the same year demonstrations in Poland led to a change in leadership and brought Wladyslaw Gomulka into office. On the basis of subsequent negotiations between Gomulka and Khrushchev, the Soviet power elite decided against a military intervention in Poland. A similar situation occurred in Poland in late 1970, when fairly widespread demonstrations forced Gomulka out of office and brought Edward Gierek to power, who, in turn was replaced by Stanislaw Kania during the widespread strikes in the summer of 1980.

In the Balkans, Albania shifted its allegiance from Moscow to Peking in the early 1960s. In 1963, the government of Romania began to pursue a foreign policy semi-independent of that of Moscow and the Warsaw bloc, although the Romanian leaders did maintain a rigidly Soviet-style policy course in domestic affairs. The Soviet government refrained from intervening directly into the separate pursuits of the governments of Yugoslavia, Albania, and Romania.

The developments in Czechoslovakia in 1968 were a different story. We may assume that to the members of the Soviet Politburo, the liberal Communist government under the leadership of Alexander Dubček constituted a threat to the Russian national interest. As in the Hungarian episode of 1956, Soviet leaders feared in 1968 that Dubček's experiments with a high degree of freedom of speech and of the press would become contagious—they might affect the thinking of people in Poland and, especially, East Germany. Moreover, there was fear in Moscow that Dubček, in his foreign policy, might align himself with the West, thereby exposing a stretch of the Russian border to the West. The same would have occurred, according to Soviet reasoning, if Nagy had remained in government in Hungary. Both the Hungarian and the Czech cases threatened to blow a hole into the *cordon sanitaire* (buffer zone) that the Russians had established so carefully since World War II between their western boundary and the U.S. sphere of influence.

The ultimate Soviet reaction to Dubček's policies was a logistically smooth, large-scale military intervention by Warsaw Pact troops, the occupation of the country, a forced change in the Czech leadership, and the declaration of the Brezhnev Doctrine, which in fact states that the Soviet Union has the right to intervene in any Warsaw Pact country where the Communist system is in danger of being overthrown.

Finally, in our discussion of difficulties that the Soviet power elite has experienced in maintaining control of its "bloc," some mention needs to be made of the Sino-Soviet dispute. When Mao initially came to power, he accepted quite readily Moscow's leadership in the bloc and, in turn, received extensive economic and technical aid from the Soviet Union. The deterioration of relations began in about 1960 and gained momentum during and after the Chinese–Indian border war (1962). The 1960s abounded with serious verbal clashes between the Chinese and the Soviet leaders, growing to such momentum that the Chinese seriously challenged Moscow's leadership of the Communist bloc. The conflict did not stay in the realm of rhetoric: in March of 1969, Chinese and Russian troops engaged in two military clashes on the Ussuri River, resulting in hundreds of casualties on each side.[20] The rapprochement between the United States and the People's Republic of China during the 1970s, without a doubt, has strengthened China's position vis-à-vis the Soviet Union. The Sino-Soviet dispute is intense and complex. It will be with these two countries in one form or another for some years to come. The dispute not only is over doctrine but more basically has to do with the substantial differences in the national interests as conceived by the power elites of both countries.

While the Soviet Union has had its share of problems, the United States did not remain unscathed either. The post-World War II U.S. sphere of influence—the Americas and Europe west of the Iron Curtain—has been subject to a number of economic and political developments that have catalyzed changes in the relations between these countries and the United States. In comparison with the Soviet Union, however, the United States has experienced substantially fewer traumatic experiences with its allies.

[20]A perceptive English-language analysis of the March 1969 clashes is found in Thomas W. Robinson, The Sino-Soviet border dispute: Background, development, and the March 1969 clashes. *The American Political Science Review*, 66, Decembere 1972, pp. 1175–1201. See also Tai Sung An, *The Sino-Soviet Territorial Dispute* (Philadelphia: Westminster Press, 1973).

Generally speaking, the nation-states of the American continent have become more independent of the United States. Castro established a Communist-type government in Cuba and associated that country with Moscow. In Chile a socialist-type of system gained control in legitimate elections in 1970, but was overthrown three years later. The relations of other American nation-states with the United States differ from country to country. Some relations are closer, others are less so. The main point is that the era in which the United States dominated these countries politically and U.S. business and industry exploited these countries is (more or less) over, and a new relationship is in the making. This relationship is, in the case of some American nation-states, a new partnership; in the case of others it is a somewhat strained relationship.

Turning to Western Europe, the countries there have changed colossally since 1945. At the end of the war, they were war-torn, devastated, and prostrate. Their relationship with the United States at that time could be compared to the relationship between very small children and an all-powerful parent. In the meantime, however, these European countries have grown to adulthood; they have recovered economically and politically and require a much more equal relationship with the United States than years ago. The required change in relations has been an agonizing experience for the policy makers in Washington. Their reaction has been slow. Confessedly, it is much easier to leave a policy as it is than to change it, but history does not stand still.

The primary West European challenge to U.S. foreign policy came from France during the 1960s. For some years, President de Gaulle pursued the plan to weld Western Europe, under French leadership, into a third superpower that would serve as a balancing force between the Soviet Union and the United States.

The termination of U.S. military involvement in and pre-occupation with Southeast Asia provided an opportunity for this country to reexamine relations with Western Europe, and it is no coincidence that former Secretary of State Kissinger called 1973 "the year of Europe" and recommended the negotiation of a new Atlantic Charter: a new set of economic, political, and military objectives to be pursued by and to govern the relationship of the democratic alliance. Progress in this direction has been slow. The growing economic strength of the countries of the European Economic Community, especially West Germany, has had some dire consequences for U.S. foreign trade and the stability of the dollar. The energy issue has created some problems among the Western allies. There have been disputes over standardization of NATO military equipment. Quite importantly, our European allies have raised questions from time to time about the willingness of the United States to defend the European allies in the case of attack. All these isssues and questions have increased the need for our government to establish, jointly with our Canadian and West European allies, a new framework to meet more adequately the needs of the Atlantic community in the 1980s. Similar considerations apply to our relations with Japan. Now and in years to come, the countries of Western Europe need the alliance with the United States, and in turn the United States needs the alliance with Western Europe.

The previous discussion has alluded from time to time to the critical international issues of the 1980s; however, before we can examine these, a discussion of the rise of the Third World is in order.

THE GROWTH OF THE THIRD WORLD

Following World War II the colonial empires remaining in the control of the British, Dutch, and French disintegrated rapidly. After the British had granted independence to the Indian subcontinent, some 70 countries in Africa, Asia, and Latin America achieved independence within the next 3 decades. The new countries, and others which have been independent for some time but are still in the developmental state (such as Ethiopia and Liberia), customarily are referred to as the Third World, to distinguish them from the postindustrial societies of the West and the Communist countries. This division, however, is more academic than real. For example, the leaders of Yugoslavia and of the People's Republic of China have played important roles at Third World meetings.

The countries of the Third World have several important features in common. They are still in an early stage of industrial development and are trying to industrialize their societies as quickly as possible. Their governments are putting forth considerable efforts to build cohesive nation-states. This applies especially to sub-Saharan Africa, where substantial tribal differences still need to be overcome. Common to almost all these countries is a strong spirit of nationalism and the desire not to be dominated or manipulated by either of the two superpowers. As a consequence, most of the developing countries try to remain as nonaligned and uncommitted as possible. The initial tenets of the doctrine of nonalignment were first stated in the form of the doctrine of *Panch Sheel* (Five Principles of Peaceful Coexistence) in the Sino-Indian Agreement on Tibet of 1954 and reiterated by Nehru at the Bandung Conference in 1955.[21] While the members of the conference ascribed to the five principles, the members of the Third World have not always adhered to the doctrine in later years. The border clash between India and the People's Republic of China, the repeated military conflicts between India and Pakistan, Nasser's intervention in Yemen, and a number of conflicts between African countries are obviously in violation of the spirit of Bandung.[22]

The developing countries have become an important element for the superpowers. The Third World makes up about two-thirds of the membership of the

[21]The five principles are: (1) mutual respect for each other's territorial integrity, (2) mutual nonaggression, (3) peaceful coexistence, (4) mutual noninterference in each other's internal affairs, and (5) equality and mutual benefit. A detailed discussion of the significance of the Bandung Conference is found in Michael Brecher, *The New States of Asia* (New York: Oxford University Press, 1966), pp. 153–215.

[22]See I. William Zartman, *International Relations in the New Africa* (Englewood Cliffs, N.J.: Prentice-Hall, 1966); and Adda B. Bozeman, *Conflict in Africa: Concepts and Realities* (Princeton, N.J.: Princeton University Press, 1976).

United Nations. In addition, some of these countries have large resources of oil, minerals, and other materials of great importance to the industrially advanced societies. This has been illustrated vividly by the rapid growth of influence and power of the OPEC members. The governments of the People's Republic of China, the Soviet Union, the United States, and some European powers have put forth considerable efforts to gain and increase their influence in the Third World countries via foreign aid, the Peace Corps, information offices, and other methods. Neither of the great powers or other developed countries has gained—or will gain—a monopoly of influence in the Third World. Rather, the competition for influence will continue in the future.[23]

In recent years, the phrase the **north–south split** has become popular among many students of international relations. The term refers to great cleavages in living standards of the postindustrial societies on the one hand and many of the developing countries on the other. The point is that now and in the years to come the developing countries need various kinds of help from the postindustrial societies, but they want it on their own terms, with no strings attached. The desire to remain independent of outside influence is a natural desire but does not always jibe with the pursuits of the great and near-great powers in their dealings with the developing countries. While the latter need the help of the former in some areas, the same holds true in reverse; however, as the developing countries become more viable, their leaders will insist still more strongly on receiving equal treatment in the family of nation-states. The governments of the People's Republic of China, the Soviet Union, and the United States, as well as others, will have to adjust their foreign policy dealings with the developing countries accordingly and at all times will have to learn to cope with temporary behavior patterns that are enigmatic at best.[24]

THE CRUCIAL INTERNATIONAL ISSUES OF THE 1980s

Having surveyed the major international developments since the end of World War II, let us examine now the present-day relations and major policy schemes of the global powers, as well as the primary international issues of the 1980s as we see them at this time. While there have been considerable changes in world politics since 1945, the Soviet Union and the United States have retained their position as great powers primarily because of their immense military power. The governments of both countries, however, have realized over the years that their countries cannot

---

[23]For discussions of the interrelationship between foreign aid and foreign policy, see John White, *The Politics of Foreign Aid* (New York: St. Martin's Press, 1974); Judith Tendler, *Inside Foreign Aid* (Baltimore: Johns Hopkins University Press, 1975); John F. Copper, *China's Foreign Aid: An Instrument of Peking's Foreign Policy* (Lexington, Mass.: Lexington Books, 1976), and Robert S. Walters, *American and Soviet Aid: A Comparative Analysis* (Pittsburgh, Pa.: University of Pittsburgh Press, 1970).

[24]The previous discussion of "International Relations in the Post-World War II Era" is an expansion of a brief part of a former publication of Winter in Bellows, Erikson, and Winter, eds., *Political Science: Introductory Essays and Readings* (Belmont, Cal.: Duxbury Press, 1971), pp. 456–458.

play the role of world police in perpetuity. In the case of the United States, our large-scale military involvement in Southeast Asia in the 1960s and early 1970s raised a number of questions and has led ultimately to a large-scale reappraisal of U.S. foreign policy on a global scale. The beginning of a new approach was enunciated by President Nixon in his Guam speech of July 1969. As stated in a Department of State publication, the policy—known as the Nixon Doctrine—calls for a more restrained style of conducting foreign affairs:

> We will attempt, consistent with protection of our own interests, to reduce our official presence and visibility abroad. We will emphasize mutuality and multilateralism. We will encourage others to assume a greater share of the responsibilities for the security and economic development of the area.[25]

The two superpowers are basically in agreement on several crucial issues of world politics. The most important of these is an understanding that the governments of both countries must do their utmost to prevent a war between themselves. Such a war, and both sides are fully aware of the consequences even though this awareness may not always be reflected in the official Soviet position, would be mutual suicide and would mean the annihilation of the Northern Hemisphere. Both superpowers are also in agreement that the United Nations (which will be discussed in the next chapter) serves a worthwhile purpose and deserves continuing support. This is not to say that the governments of the Soviet Union and the United States always see eye to eye in the United Nations and on matters pertaining to it, but both countries will refrain from wrecking that foremost international organization. Finally, the Soviet Union and the United States would like to keep the "nuclear club" limited as much as possible. A proliferation in the number of nuclear powers would increase the chance of nuclear war, be it by accident or by intent. Whether the superpowers can prevent secondary powers (other than China, France, and the United Kingdom) from developing such weapons is one of the crucial questions of our decade.[26]

It is difficult to categorize the major current international issues in terms of priority. Some of them are equally important, and most of them are interrelated. The following is not an exclusive list of all crucial issues. Some issues, such as the energy issue and world hunger, have been discussed in Chapter II; the problem of reformulating U.S. relations with its NATO allies has been mentioned earlier in this chapter; and the problem of making the United Nations a more effective force for maintaining world peace will be examined in Chapter 14.

---

[25]From *United States Foreign Policy 1969–1970: A Report of the Secretary of State* (Washington, D.C.: U.S. Govt. Printing Office, Department of State Publication #8575), p. 36. The implications of the Nixon Doctrine are discussed in some detail in subsequent pages of this publication.

[26]For a more detailed discussion of the proliferation issue, see William C. Davidon et al., *The Nth Country Problem and Arms Control* (Washington: National Planning Association, 1960); Alastair Buchan, ed., *A World of Nuclear Powers?* (Englewood Cliffs, N.J.: Prentice-Hall, 1966); and David C. Gompert et al., *Nuclear Weapons and World Politics* (New York: McGraw-Hill, 1977).

Major efforts should be directed in the 1980s toward reducing the arms race between the Soviet Union and the United States; preventing the spread of nuclear
weapons to further countries; reducing the military confrontation between East and
West in Central Europe; diminishing the tensions in the Middle East; and helping to
improve the standard of living in the developing countries.

The arms race between the superpowers has been going on since 1945, and
thousands of billions of dollars have been spent in military pursuits. During the early
years of the arms race, the United States had a four-year lead over the Soviet
Union. For example, the United States had its first operational atomic bomb in 1945
and the hydrogen bomb in 1949. The respective years for the Soviet Union are 1949
and 1953. During the following years, which saw the development of missiles, the
sophistication of warheads, and the production and employment of MIRVs (Multiple
Independent Reentry Vehicles), the Soviet Union succeeded in slowly but surely
narrowing the gap. Both sides have continued to sophisticate their missile weaponry in recent years and have added new types of weapons and weapon carriers to
their inventory. Recent items include the Soviet Backfire bomber and the American air-launched Cruise missile. At the time of this writing, our Congress is debating
the question of whether we should produce and install a new land-based missile,
the MX.

The governments of both superpowers in recent years have come under increasing pressure at home to allocate more resources for domestic improvements and
less for military efforts. The disarmament conference of the 1960s produced the
1963 Nuclear Test Ban Treaty (banning nuclear tests in the atmosphere) and the
Nuclear Nonproliferation Treaty of 1968. The Strategic Arms Limitation Talks (SALT)
between the Soviet Union and the United States commenced in 1969. Meeting al-
ternately in Helsinki and Vienna, the two negotiation teams worked out the details of
the treaty, which was signed by President Nixon and General Secretary Brezhnev in
May of 1972. Salt I consists of two parts: (1) the ABM Treaty and (2) the Interim
Agreement. The ABM Treaty deals with the **defensive** part of the two countries' nuclear weaponry systems. In essence, the treaty limits the Soviet Union and the
United States to the construction of two ABM (Anti-Ballistic Missile) sites only, thus
preventing both from building nationwide ABM systems.[27] The number of ABM sites
subsequently was reduced to one for each side by the ABM Protocol of 1974. The
Interim Agreement deals with the **offensive** part of the two countries weapons systems. It limits the number of ICBMs for the United States and the Soviet Union to
those deployed or under construction at the time of the signing of the document.

Salt II was signed by President Carter and General Secretary Brezhnev in Vienna
in 1979. Preliminary discussions of the treaty took place in the U.S. Senate during
the Autumn of 1979, and it was then hoped that ratification would be forthcoming.
On January 3, 1980, however, President Carter urged the Senate to postpone fur-

[27]The text of the Anti-Ballistic Missile Treaty is published in *The Department of State Bulletin*, 66, June
1972.

"Basically, of course, we've got to pull together."

(Le Pelley in The Christian Science Monitor © 1966 TCSPS.)

ther debate of the treaty because of the flagrant invasion of Afghanistan by Soviet military forces. SALT II tries to limit strategic offensive missile systems further. Specifically, each country will be limited to 2400 strategic nuclear delivery vehicles, with sublimits for each category of delivery systems (such as MIRVed ICBMs). SALT

II includes the stipulation that the initial ceiling of 2400 delivery vehicles be reduced to 2250 by the end of 1981.[28]

The main hindrance in disarmament and arms control discussions in general, and in the negotiations between the United States and the Soviet Union in particular, has been the psychological element of suspicion. Each side fears that the other side may not comply in full with the provisions of the agreement. In the case of the nuclear treaties between the two superpowers, the Russians' constant refusal to permit on-site inspection and verification in their country used to be a hindrance to the negotiations. In recent years, however, the development of satellite surveillance has decreased significantly the importance of on-site inspection. Nevertheless, the

ARMS WRESTLING

(Jim Dobbins, The Boston Post.)

[28]For the text of the SALT II Treaty, see *The Department of State Bulletin*, 79, July 1979.

growth of reciprocal good will—that is, an improvement in political relations—remains very important for success in arms control and disarmament negotiations.

Regarding the **nonproliferation** of nuclear weapons, mention should be made of the fact that perhaps a dozen countries in addition to the nuclear powers have the know-how to produce such weaponry. Others will gain the capability in years to come. The Nuclear Nonproliferation Treaty of 1968 forbids signatories in the nuclear club to supply nonnuclear countries with nuclear weapons or weapons technology. In addition, the treaty prohibits nonnuclear signatories to use their nuclear facilities for military purposes. A majority of the members of the United Nations have signed the Nuclear Nonproliferation Treaty. The nonsignatories include France and the People's Republic of China, two members of the nuclear club.[29]

The issue of bringing about a partial military disengagement in Central Europe has received considerable attention in recent years. Since 1945 the Soviet Union and the United States, supported by their respective allies, have maintained vast military establishments along the Iron Curtain. The Cold War of yesteryear has given way to a new set of relationships between East and West, which foreshadows the possibility of some degree of disengagement. Recent statements from both sides have indicated some interest in discussing the possibility of balanced force reductions. At the Moscow summit of 1972, the governments of the Soviet Union and the Unites States agreed that

> the goal of ensuring stability and security in Europe would be served by a reciprocal reduction of armed forces and armaments, first of all in Central Europe. . . . Agreement on the procedures for negotiations on this subject should be reached as soon as practicable between the states concerned.[30]

The military balance of power in Europe has been very delicate since the start of the Cold War—delicate in the sense that a small incident along the Iron Curtain has the potential to trigger a nuclear holocaust. The time is ripe for taking a fresh look at this potential Pandora's box. Unfortunately, East-West negotiations regarding the reduction of armed forces in Central Europe are clearly stalled at this time and are unlikely to progress in the near future.

The Middle East has been one of the world's major problem areas for some time. While the rapprochement between Egypt and Israel, achieved with President Carter's help, has improved the situation, the over-all problem is far from being solved. Somehow an agreement has to be achieved under which all Arab countries give legal recognition to the existence of the nation-state of Israel. Concurrently, the problem of the Palestinian refugees has to be solved in a humane fashion. A better way of living and a future has to be provided for these people. The two issues are deeply intertwined. Israel has the potential to contribute considerable know-how to the development of its Arab neighbors, and both sides would benefit from better relations.

[29]For an extensive treatment of the Nuclear Nonproliferation Treaty, see Mason Willrich, *Non-Proliferation Treaty: Framework for Nuclear Arms Control* (Charlottesville, Va.: Michie, 1969).

[30]Department of State, *Foreign Policy Outlines*, 24–31, June 1973, p. 1.

(From The Herblock Gallery, Simon & Schuster, 1968.)

The final issue mentioned has to do with the developing countries, populated by about two-thirds of the world's people. Most of these people are poor and illiterate. A "revolution of rising expectations" is sweeping the Third World. Generally speaking, the leaders of the developing countries would like to move their societies into modernity as quickly as possible—to industrialize and increase the general welfare. These societies need aid and advice in many areas. The postindustrial societies have the means to render help. Ways should be found to reduce more successfully than in the past the cleavage between the rich and the poor nation-states.

Many other current problems—and problems in the making—are not only of national but of international scope. Pollution, disease, and food scarcity transcend national boundaries. These problems lend themselves more readily to international collaboration than politico-military issues. Some degree of international cooperation already has been established to examine these problems. It is hoped that, in years to come, more and more leaders and their citizens will realize that there exist problems that threaten the survival of humanity and that out of this realization stronger international ties of fellowship will grow to serve the well-being of all of humanity.

In this chapter we have examined the nature of international politics, its actors, the characteristics of the nation-state system, the methods used for interaction on the international scene, the major developments in international politics since World War II, and the major issues of our time. Collective efforts toward peace through collective security, and international and regional organizations, as well as through international law, will be the subject of the final chapter.

SELECTED READINGS

Good, general treatments of the subject of international politics are, among others, Frederick H. Hartmann, *The Relations of Nations*, 5th ed. (New York: Macmillan, 1978); John G. Stoessinger, *The Might of Nations: World Politics in Our Time*,* 6th ed. (New York: Random House, 1979); Werner J. Feld, *International Relations: A Transnational Approach* (Sherman Oaks, Cal.: Aflred Publishing, 1979); Theodore A. Couloumbis and James H. Wolfe, *Introduction to International Relations: Power and Justice* (Englewood Cliffs, N.J.: Prentice-Hall, 1978); Norman J. Padelford, George A. Lincoln, and Lee D. Olvey, *The Dynamics of International Politics*, 3rd ed. (New York: Macmillan, 1976); and Vernon Van Dyke, *International Politics*, 3rd ed. (New York: Appleton-Century-Crofts, 1972).

A highly readable examination of contemporary worldwide issues and problems is Lester R. Brown, *World Without Borders** (New York: Vintage Books, 1972). For a contrasting study that explores the force of nationalism and the potential for developing international loyalties, see Karl W. Deutsch, *Nationalism and Its Alternatives* (New York: Alfred A. Knopf, 1969). An interesting psychological discussion of international problems is Otto Klineberg, *The Human Dimension in International Relations** (New York: Holt, Rinehart and Winston, 1964).

The foreign policies of eight leading countries are examined in Roy C. Macridis, ed., *Foreign Policy in World Politics*,* 5th ed. (Englewood Cliffs, N.J.: Prentice-Hall,

*Available in paperback.

1976). A more recent discussion of the foreign policies of key European countries is Wolfram F. Hanrieder and Graeme P. Auton, *The Foreign Policies of West Germany, France, and Britain** (Englewood Cliffs, N.J.: Prentice-Hall, 1980). Two excellent analyses of the relations between major powers are Adam B. Ulam, *The Rivals: America and Russia Since World War II** (New York: Viking Press, 1971); and John G. Stoessinger, *Nations in Darkness: China, Russia, and America,** 3rd ed. (New York: Random House, 1978).

An excellent analysis of U.S. foreign policy is Frederick H. Hartmann, *The New Age of American Foreign Policy* (New York: Macmillan, 1970). Of some interest are the more recent writings of Henry A. Kissinger, namely, *American Foreign Policy,** 3rd ed. (New York: W. W. Norton, 1977) and, especially, *White House Years* (Boston: Little, Brown, 1979). For an analysis of Kissinger diplomacy, see John G. Stoessinger, *Henry Kissinger: The Anguish of Power** (New York: W. W. Norton, 1976). Another very fine book by Stoessinger, which focusses on the twentieth century "movers" of this country's foreign policy, is *Crusaders and Pragmatists: Movers of Modern American Foreign Policy** (New York: W. W. Norton, 1979). Three useful discussions of the process of U.S. foreign policy making are: Charles W. Kegley, Jr. and Eugene R. Wittkopf, *American Foreign Policy: Pattern and Process** (New York: St. Martin's Press, 1979); John Spanier and Eric M. Uslaner, *How American Foreign Policy is Made,** 2nd ed. (New York: Holt, Rinehart and Winston/Praeger, 1978); and Marian Irish and Else Frank, *U.S. Foreign Policy: Context, Conduct, Content** (New York: Harcourt Brace Jovanovich, 1975). The public influence on foreign policy making is analyzed in Bernard C. Cohen, *The Public's Impact on Foreign Policy** (Boston: Little, Brown, 1973).

A standard work on the development of organized diplomacy and recent changes in diplomatic practice is Harold Nicolson, *Diplomacy,** 3rd ed. (New York: Oxford University Press, 1963). See also William Macomber, *The Angels' Game: A Handbook of Modern Diplomacy* (New York: Stein and Day, 1975). Two informative treatments of the activities of diplomats are Humphrey Trevelyan, *Diplomatic Channels* (Boston: Gambit, 1973); and Eric Clark, *Diplomat: The World of International Diplomacy* (New York: Taplinger, 1973). The practice of international negotiations is analyzed superbly in Fred C. Iklé, *How Nations Negotiate** (New York: Frederick A. Praeger, 1967); and Arthur Lall, *Modern International Negotiations: Principles and Practice* (New York: Columbia University Press, 1966).

Helpful sources analyzing and discussing the economic component of international politics are Joan Edelman Spero, *The Politics of International Economic Relations** (New York: St. Martin's Press, 1977); Dennis Pirages, *The New Context for International Relations: Global Ecopolitics** (North Scituate, Mass.: Duxbury Press, 1978); and Mason Willrich, *Energy and World Politics* (New York: Free Press, 1975).

*Available in paperback.

The classic study on warfare is Quincy Wright, *A Study of War*,* 2nd ed. (Chicago: University of Chicago Press, 1965). For a comprehensive treatment of the potential implications of the nuclear arms race, see Herman Kahn, *On Escalation: Metaphors and Scenarios* (New York: Frederick A. Praeger, 1965). A highly readable case study of war is John G. Stoessinger, *Why Nations Go to War*,* 2nd ed. (New York: St. Martin's Press, 1978). Recent data on worldwide military expenditures and on arms trade are compiled in *World Military Expenditures and Arms Transfers: 1968–1977** (Washington, D.C.: U.S. Arms Control and Disarmament Agency, 1979).

The following publications are informative treatments of arms control and disarmament issues: Alva R. Myrdal, *The Game of Disarmament: How the United States and Russia Run the Arms Race* (New York: Pantheon, 1977); William Epstein, *The Last Chance: Nuclear Proliferation and Arms Control* (New York: Free Press, 1976); John Newhouse, *Cold Dawn: The Story of SALT* (New York: Holt, Rinehart and Winston, 1973); and Mason Wilrich and John B. Rhinelander, eds., *SALT: The Moscow Agreement and Beyond* (New York: Free Press, 1974). The texts and histories of the arms control and disarmament agreements concluded in the twentieth century are published in *Arms Control and Disarmament Agreements** (Washington, D.C.: U.S. Arms Control and Disarmament Agency, 1975).

*Available in paperback.

Chapter Fourteen

Collective Means for Cooperation and Integration in the International Community

On December 4, 1979, the Security Council of the United Nations unanimously adopted a resolution urgently demanding that Iran release the American hostages in Tehran. The Council's resolution reflected a rare degree of unity, one that depicted the common views and interests of all countries represented on the Council: Western allies, developing countries, as well as the Soviet Union and the People's Republic of China. Eleven days later the International Court of Justice ruled unanimously that Iran should release all its American hostages and return the U.S. Embassy compound in Tehran to U.S. control.

Both resolutions condemn the violations of international principles committed by Iranian militants with the approval of the Khomeini government and urge the restoration of law and order. Only time will tell whether and when the Khomeini forces will follow suit.

This illustrates a major facet of the history of humanity, namely, the presence of violence on the one hand and attempts toward peaceful settlement on the other. International lawlessness has existed since antiquity, but so have efforts toward establishing a greater degree of order, both by formulating international rules applicable to all people, and by establishing international organizations to maintain peace and order. We have pointed out in the previous chapter that the international community has faced a greater degree of anarchy than domestic society because there is no single international government having a preponderance of power.

This chapter attempts to examine briefly the nature of international law, international and regional organizations, and the role these play in international politics today.

International law and organizations are collective in the sense that they are supposed to apply to and serve all countries and all of mankind, rather than one group of people or one country. These forces are means that can and do place limitations on the behavior of countries in their relations with each other. Let us first look at international organizations.

INTERNATIONAL ORGANIZATIONS: THE HISTORICAL PERSPECTIVE

International organization is a response to insecurity in the multinational system. The **League of Nations** was established after World War I to prevent another worldwide war. In 1945 the **United Nations** was created "to save succeeding generations from the scourge of war."[1] The underlying aim of international organization is to increase cooperation among the nation-states and to decrease friction and violence on the international scene.

Attempts at international organization date back as far as the League of Greek City-States at the time of Plato and Aristotle. The modern era of international conferences commenced with the Treaty of Westphalia (1648), when hundreds of envoys, representing nearly every European country, met and catalyzed a new era of European relations. A number of interesting plans toward international federation and organization were proposed during the seventeenth and eighteenth centuries. For example, the Frenchman Emeric Cruce advocated a world union of independent states; the "Grand Design" of Henry IV of France called for converting Europe into a Christian Republic to be composed of 15 equal units; William Penn and Abbe de Saint-Pierre proposed related plans for a "Parliament of Europe."

The Congress of Vienna (1815) set the stage for the Quadruple Alliance and its periodic congresses—a system that became known as the "Concert of Europe," which in essence was a system of balance of power maintained by the four great continental powers of that time.

In 1899 and 1907 two international conferences were held in The Hague, Holland. The professed aim of these meetings was to bring about general disarmament and to develop means for the peaceful settlement of disputes. While these conferences were far from being successful, they had some importance for the development of international organizaton because representatives of a number of non-European countries joined their European colleagues at these gatherings, and the principle of one country–one vote (as found in the voting procedure of the General Assembly of the United Nations) was put into operation.

The prevalent political climate at the end of World War I led to the establishment of the first nearly universal organization, the League of Nations. Its permanent headquarters were located in Geneva, Switzerland. The major bodies of the League were the Assembly, in which all member countries were represented, and the Council, which was made up of the great powers. The day-to-day staff work was handled by a permanent Secretariat under the direction and supervison of the Assembly and

---

[1]This passage is taken from the Preamble to the Charter of the United Nations.

Council. The organizational structure of the League, as well as its practices and experiences, had, as we shall see later on, a considerable influence on the shaping of the United Nations in the 1940s.

While the existence of the League of Nations lent itself to improved international relations during the 1920s, it did not fulfill the Wilsonian hopes of preventing another world war. By the late 1930s the League, for all practical purposes, had become a defunct organization. While a number of reasons could be cited for this, the two most important ones are that the major powers never showed a concurrent, full commitment to support the League and its principles. The United States, whose President had been the prime mover in establishing the League, did not even become a member of the organizaton. Related to this, the principle of collective security, written in rather loose language into Articles 10 and 11 of the League Covenant, never became operative. The concept of collective security denotes a security arrangement wherein all members pledge themselves to common retaliatory action in the case of an attack against a member country. In the 1930s, beginning with Japan's invasion of Manchuria in 1931, the League consistently failed to invoke such retaliatory action against aggressors and so lost its credibility as a force for international order.

One of the greatest long-range values of the League of Nations lies perhaps in the fact that the founding fathers of the United Nations were able to learn from the League experience and, accordingly, write a United Nations Charter that was substantially superior to the League Covenant.[2]

THE UNITED NATIONS

Representatives of 51 nation-states met in San Francisco in the spring and early summer of 1945 to draft and discuss the charter for a new international organization—the United Nations. The final document was signed on June 26, 1945. The name "United Nations" was coined by President Roosevelt and Prime Minister Churchill during their Arcadia Conference in 1941. During the early 1940s the governments of the United Kingdom and the United States spearheaded the drive toward establishing this new international organization. The Soviet Union, having become a wartime partner of the Western allies, was kept informed about the initial developments. In September 1944, a meeting of representatives of the 3 allies was held in Dumbarton Oaks, an estate in Washington, D.C., and dealt exclusively with United Nations matters, centering around the issues of membership, security provisions, and the veto (explained in our discussion of the Security Council). Different

[2]For readings on the League of Nations, we suggest M. E. Burton, *The Assembly of the League of Nations* (Chicago: University of Chicago Press, 1941); D. F. Fleming, *The United States and the League of Nations* (New York: Putnam, 1932); Francis P. Walters, *A History of the League of Nations* (New York: Oxford University Press, 1952); Alfred Zimmern, *The League of Nations and the Rule of Law* (New York: Macmillan, 1939); and George Scott, *The Rise and Fall of the League of Nations* (New York: Macmillan, 1974).

views regarding the veto between East and West continued to exist until an agreement was arrived at in Yalta (February 1945).

In contrast to 1919, public opinion in the West (especially in the United States) was rather favorably disposed toward a United Nations, and it was a forgone conclusion that the United States would play a leading role in creating the organization and would be one of the major members of it.

The other original charter members, including France and China, who were to become permanent members of the **Security Council**, played peripheral roles in shaping the United Nations prior to the San Francisco conference. By the end of June 1945, the participants of the conference had completed the United Nations Charter, and the document came into force on October 24, 1945, after the necessary number of nation-states had ratified it. Since 1945 the charter has been amended twice. Amendments adopted in 1963 enlarged the membership of the Security Council and of the **Economic and Social Council** and adjusted the voting procedures of these two organs to reflect the larger membership. The second adoption of an amendment occurred in 1965 and relates to provisions having to do with the review of the charter.

The first meeting of the United Nations was held in London in January 1946. In the next few years, a permanent headquarters was built along the East River in New York City and became operative in early 1950.

THE FUNCTIONS OF THE UNITED NATIONS
The functions and purposes of the United Nations are stated clearly in Article I of the charter:

1. To maintain international peace and security, and to that end: to take effective collective measures for the prevention and removal of threats to the peace, and for the suppression of acts of aggression or other breaches of the peace, and to bring about by peaceful means, and in conformity with the principles of justice and international law, adjustment or settlement of international disputes or situations which might lead to a breach of peace.
2. To develop friendly relations among nations based on respect for the principle of equal rights and self-determination of peoples, and to take other appropriate measures to strengthen universal peace.
3. To achieve international cooperation in solving international problems of an economic, social, cultural, or humanitarian character, and in promoting and encouraging respect for human rights and for fundamental freedoms for all without distinction as to race, sex, language, or religion.
4. To be a center for harmonizing the actions of nations in the attainment of these common ends.[3]

[3]The full text of the charter is published in, among other sources, the *Yearbook of the United Nations* (New York: United Nations Office of Public Information, published annually). A helpful and popular source of information about the United Nations and its affiliated agencies is *Everyman's United Nations* (New York: United Nations Office of Publicatons).

**A general view of the permanent headquarters of the United Nations in New York.
The 39-story Secretariat is flanked by the General Assembly building and the
Library (foreground).**

THE STRUCTURE OF THE UNITED NATIONS

Article 7 of the United Nations Charter delineates six principal organs of the organization (see Figure 14–1): (1) the General Assembly, (2) the Security Council, (3) the
Economic and Social Council, (4) the Trusteeship Council, (5) the International Court
of Justice (located in The Hague and discussed in the later part of the chapter), and
(6) the Secretariat.

A number of specialized agencies are affiliated directly with the United Nations
and also are shown in Figure 14–1. The following listing gives the date of their es-

476

THE UNITED NATIONS SYSTEM

The United Nations

United Nations Truce Supervision Organization in Palestine (UNTSO)

United Nations Military Observer Group in India and Pakistan (UNMOGIP)

United Nations Peace-keeping Force in Cyprus (UNFICYP)

Main Committees

Standing and Procedural Committees

Other Subsidiary Organs of General Assembly

United Nations Relief and Works Agency for Palestine Refugees in the Near East (UNRWA)

United Nations Conference on Trade and Development (UNCTAD)

Trade and Development Board

United Nations Development Programme (UNDP)

United Nations Capital Development Fund

United Nations Industrial Development Organization (UNIDO)

United Nations Institute for Training and Research (UNITAR)

United Nations Children's Fund (UNICEF)

United Nations High Commissioner for Refugees (UNHCR)

Joint United Nations -FAO World Food Programme

Disarmament Commission

Military Staff Committee

SECURITY COUNCIL

INTER-NATIONAL COURT OF JUSTICE

GENERAL ASSEMBLY

SECRETARIAT

TRUSTEESHIP COUNCIL

ECONOMIC AND SOCIAL COUNCIL

Regional Economic Commissions

Functional Commissions

Sessional, Standing and Ad Hoc Committees

The Specialized Agencies and IAEA

IAEA — International Atomic Energy Agency

ILO — International Labour Organisation

FAO — Food and Agriculture Organization of the United Nations

UNESCO — United Nations Educational, Scientific and Cultural Organization

WHO — World Health Organization

IMF — International Monetary Fund

IDA — International Development Association

IBRD — International Bank for Reconstruction and Development

IFC — International Finance Corporation

ICAO — International Civil Aviation Organization

UPU — Universal Postal Union

ITU — International Telecommunication Union

WMO — World Meteorological Organization

IMCO — Inter-Governmental Maritime Consultative Organization

GATT — General Agreement on Tariffs and Trade

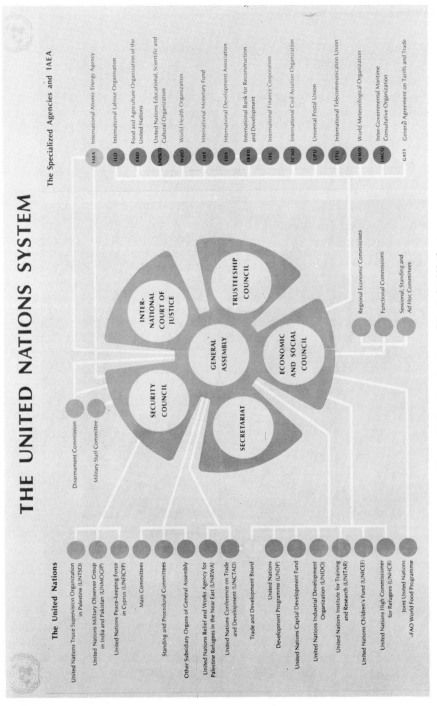

Figure 14–1.   The structure of the United Nations.

tablishment and their place of headquarters in parentheses: Universal Postal Union (1875, Berne); International Telecommunications Union (1865, Geneva); International Labor Organization (1919, Geneva); Food and Agriculture Organization (1944, Rome); International Monetary Fund (1944, Washington); International Bank for Reconstruction and Development (1944, Washington); United Nations Educational, Scientific, and Cultural Organization (1945, Paris); World Health Organization (1946, Geneva); International Civil Aviation Organization (1947, Montreal); World Meteorological Organization (1950, Geneva); International Finance Corporation (1956, Washington); Intergovernmental Maritime Consultative Organization (1958, London); and International Development Association (1960, Washington).

The General Assembly: An Approximation of a World Forum

The **General Assembly** is the basic forum of the United Nations in that all member nation-states are represented in it. Voting in the Assembly emphasizes the principle of equality, with each member country having one vote in its decisions. The only exception is the Soviet Union, which has three (one for the Soviet Union at large, one for the Ukraine, and one for Belorussia—a compromise forced by Stalin at Yalta). The General Assembly holds annual sessions that start in September and may continue until the early spring of the following year.

The functions and powers of the General Assembly are very broad. According to the charter:

The General Assembly may discuss any questions or any matters within the scope of the present Charter or relating to the powers and functions of any organs provided for in the present Charter, and, except as provided in Article 12 [which states that the General Assembly shall not make any recommendation on a dispute while it is being discussed by the Security Council], may make recommendations to the Members of the United Nations or to the Security Council or to both on any such questions or matters.

In size, the General Assembly has grown from its original 51 members to 151 in 1979. It has served as a valuable forum for debate and exchange of views. In the decision-making area, it by and large has left specific actions on security matters

("The Small Society" by Brickman © Washington Star Syndicate, permission granted by King Features Syndicate, 1973.)

and peace-keeping functions to the Security Council. It should be pointed out, however, that in this area the General Assembly has become a backstop of the Security Council with the passage of the Uniting for Peace Resolution in 1950. This resolution grew out of the experience derived from the early part of the Korean conflict—the recognition that a permanent member of the Security Council could block easily a majority-approved U.N. peacekeeping action. To circumvent this, Article I of the Uniting for Peace Resolution provides that in emergencies, when the Security Council is prevented from acting (on account of a veto or the threat of a veto), the General Assembly is authorized to meet on short notice and to recommend any appropriate collective measures, including the use of armed force. The resolution enabled the General Assembly to deal with several important security problems during times of a deadlock in the Security Council, such as periods of the Korean conflict and the Congo crisis.

The rapid increase in membership has given the General Assembly a near universal flavor and representation. Over the years its function as a forum for discussion and debate of regional and worldwide economic, military, political, and social issues has been of considerable value to the world community.

The Security Council: An Approximation of an International Presidium

Underlying the composition and the voting procedure in the Security Council is the concept of big-power control or "world sheriff" as embodied in the Concert of Europe. The Council, as created in 1945, consisted of 11 members. Five of these were permanent members: China, France, the Soviet Union, the United Kingdom, and the United States. The remaining and nonpermanent 6 members were to be elected for 2-year terms by the General Assembly. In 1963 the number of nonpermanent

"We've just been admitted to the United Nations."

(OFF THE RECORD by Ed Reed, reprinted courtesy The Register and Tribune Syndicate.)

members was increased to 10, in recognition of the growing membership of the United Nations.

Some mention needs to be made of the voting procedure in the Security Council. Each member country has 1 vote. Decisions on procedural matters (recommendations that do not include sanctions) require the affirmative vote of any 9 of the 15 members. Substantive decisions, however, require the affirmative votes of 9 members including those of all 5 permanent members. It is here that the veto may occur. The negative vote of a permanent member on a substantive issue constitutes a veto and will block Security Council action.[4]

According to Article 24 of the United Nations Charter, the member-states "confer on the Security Council's primary responsibility for the maintenance of international peace and security, and agree that in carrying out its duties under this responsibility the Security Council acts on their behalf." The particular powers granted by the charter to the Security Council to discharge its duties are laid down in Chapters VI (Pacific Settlement of Disputes), VII (Action with Respect to Threats to Peace, Breaches of the Peace, and Acts of Aggression), VIII (Regional Arrangements), and XII (International Trusteeship System). In essence, the actions of the Security Council will involve one or several of the following: it may suggest methods of reconciliation; it may offer specific resolutions (this was done, for example, in the Congo crisis); it may order a provisional truce (as on Cyprus in 1964 and 1974); it may invoke nonmilitary sanctions (in 1965 the Security Council invoked economic sanctions against Rhodesia); and finally it may resort to military sanctions, as it did in Korea and in the Congo.

Over the years the Security Council often has been handicapped by the quarrels among its permanent members and has not been fully able to mobilize the United Nations as intended by the founders. Its best area of success has been—and is—in disputes where the aggressor is not a permanent member of the Security Council and is not being directly supported by a permanent member. The presence of the veto usually prevents the Security Council from taking action against a permanent member or another country actively supported by a permanent member.

The peacekeeping capability of the United Nations was enhanced in 1956 when the General Assembly passed a resolution creating the United Nations Emergency Force (UNEF), an international military force with the task of supervising armistice arrangements decreed by the United Nations. The members of this military force were to be drawn from member countries, with the exception of the permanent members of the Security Council. Since 1956 UNEF has served in its capacity in the Congo (where it was known as ONUC) and several times at critical places in the Middle East (in Cyprus, near the Suez Canal, and in the Golan Heights). A number of

---

[4]Both the governments of the Soviet Union and the United States insisted during the preparatory stage that the veto principle be built into the United Nations Charter. For an excellent discussion on the use of the veto, see Sidney D. Bailey, Veto in the Security Council, *International Conciliation* No. 566 (January 1968), pp. 5–66.

countries have contributed troops to UNEF; for example, Finland, Sweden, Canada, Austria, Ireland, India, and several African countries sent troops during the Congo operation. The United Nations Emergency Force is the first step in modern history toward establishing an international military force.

By and large the actions taken by the Security Council mirror the particular state of international relations. Any change in its composition, functions, and powers will continue to require the consent of its permanent members. Of these the United States and the Soviet Union have remained superpowers. The United Kingdom and France have lost some of their former influence in world affairs and are second-rate powers. The fifth permanent seat, for a long time held by the Chiang Kai-shek government, was turned over to the People's Republic of China in 1971.

Could the Security Council be made more viable by further additions and/or changes in membership? The 1963 amendment, enlarging the number of nonpermanent members from 6 to 10, was designed to give more voice in the Security Council to the rapidly growing membership of the United Nations; but, as of 1979, no nation-state from Latin America, Africa, or the Middle East held a permanent seat.

The Secretariat: An Approximation of an International Civil Service

The Secretariat performs the day-to-day administrative tasks of the United Nations. It is directed by the secretary-general, who is appointed by the General Assembly upon recommendation by the Security Council. The functions of the **secretary-general** are spelled out in Chapter XV of the United Nations Charter:

He shall be the chief administrative officer of the Organization.

The Secretary-General shall act in that capacity in all meetings of the General Assembly, of the Security Council, of the Economic and Social Council, and of the Trusteeship Council. . . . The Secretary-General shall make an annual report to the General Assembly on the work of the Organization.

The Secretary-General may bring to the attention of the Security Council any matter which in his opinion may threaten the maintenance of international peace and security.

As the highest administrative officer, he oversees the work of thousands of international civil servants, recruited from many of the member countries. Most of the Secretariat's employees work at the headquarters in New York, but others are in Geneva or at one of the several field offices the United Nations maintains throughout the world.[5]

The present secretary-general, Dr. Kurt Waldheim (Austria), is the fourth person to hold this position. He was preceeded by Trygve Lie (Norway), 1945–1952; Dag

[5]For an examination of some of the complexities of international administration, see Robert S. Jordan, ed., *International Administration: Its Evolution and Contemporary Applications* (New York: Oxford University Press, 1971).

Hammarskjold (Sweden), 1952–1961; and U Thant (Burma) 1961–1971.[6] All four have been persons of high ability and have contributed considerably to the viability of the United Nations. Their major problem has been that the concept underlying their position, namely to act as the leading international representative, is still relatively new. The job of the secretary-general has an unavoidable problem—most of the time they have to "walk a tightrope." If in fulfillment of their duties they speak out too loudly and forcefully, they may incur the wrath of one or several of the permanent members of the Security Council; yet if they do not speak out at all, they would doom their office to sterility. It takes a most talented person to play, under the strains of this dilemma, a forceful and productive part in the work of the United Nations.

The Economic and Social Council: The Promotion of Economic and Social Welfare

One of the main purposes of the United Nations, as stated in the charter, is "to achieve international cooperation in solving problems of an economic, social, cultural, or humanitarian character." The Economic and Social Council was established to serve as the key agency for coordinating the United Nation's activities in the economic and social realms. The functions of the council are spelled out in Chapter X of the charter and include the initiation of studies and reports on international economic, social, cultural, and educational matters; preparation of recommendations for the General Assembly, and giving assistance to the Security Council on economic and social matters when so requested. The Economic and Social Council consists of 27 members, of whom 9 are elected each year by the General Assembly for 3-year terms.

The founders of the United Nations had hoped that the organization's activities in the economic and social realms could be kept out of the arena of political conflict, which, as they correctly envisaged, might trouble the General Assembly and the Security Council from time to time. Moreover, they hoped that the habit of peaceful collaboration in the economic and social realms could later be extended to the organization's political and military activities. In the composite perspective, the Economic and Social Council has become a very important organ of the United Nations and a stimulant of international cooperation.

The Trusteeship Council: Protecting the Rights of Non-Self-Governing Societies

This is the successor to the League of Nations Mandate System, which was established after World War I to render some degree of international control over former

[6]For a useful discussion of the office of secretary-general and the experiences of the first two incumbents, see Trygve Lie, *In the Cause of Peace* (New York: Macmillan, 1954); Brian Urquart, *Hammarskjold* (New York: Alfred A. Knopf, 1972); and Rajeshwar Dayal, *Mission for Hammarskjold: The Congo Crisis* (Princeton, N.J.: Princeton University Press, 1976).

German colonies and the territories once held by the defunct Ottoman Empire. With the establishment of the United Nations, those former League mandates that had not yet achieved independence were turned into trusteeships of the United Nations and placed under the supervision of the Trusteeship Council. The only former mandate dealt with directly by the General Assembly and the Security Council has been former South West Africa, now Namibia, which appears to be on the way toward independence.

The Trusteeship Council consists of the permanent members of the Security Council, other countries administering trust territories, and enough additional member countries (elected by the General Assembly) to insure an equal balance on the council between countries administering trust territories and those that do not.

Chapter XII of the charter declares that the basic objectives of the Trusteeship Council are "to promote the political, economic, social, and educational advancement of the inhabitants of the trust territories, and their progressive development toward self-government or independence." Since 1945 most of the former trust territories have become independent. As of 1980, only the Carolines, Marianas, and Marshall Islands in the Pacific (administered as a strategic trust territory by the United States) remain under the jurisdiction of the Trusteeship Council. If these Pacific Islands become independent in 1981 as scheduled, the Trusteeship Council will have no further duties to perform and thus will cease to function.

A BRIEF EVALUATION OF THE UNITED NATIONS

The shortcomings of the United Nations mirror the problems of today's world. Its strength and productivity rest, in essence, on the support given by the member countries, especially by the great powers. The major problem of the United Nations was stated candidly by Secretary-General Waldheim in 1973:

> *At the present there does not appear to be a clear agreement between member-countries on the way the organization should proceed, and there are times when it is hard not to feel that not all governments fully accept the consequences that arise from their membership of [sic] the United Nations. . . .*[7]

The major powers, especially the United States and the Soviet Union, have found it expedient to bypass the United Nations on many occasions and have negotiated most of their bilateral issues outside the international organization. But this should not be interpreted to mean that the two global powers have forsaken the United Nations and that they do not care about it at all. The viability of the United Nations was threatened on several occasions, especially during the Congo crisis in the early 1960s and the fiscal impasse during the Nineteenth General Assembly (1964), which was created by the refusal of the Communist countries, France, and some other non-Communist members to pay their part of the expenses of United Nations

[7]*Frankfurter Allgemeine Zeitung*, September 17, 1973, as translated and reprinted in *The German Tribune*, October 4, 1973.

peacekeeping operations in the Congo and the Middle East. At these two in-stances—and at many other times—the governments of the United States and the Soviet Union have exercised enough flexibility to insure the continuation of the United Nations. While the two global powers may not agree about the kind of United Nations they like to see in operation, they are in fundamental agreement that the United Nations serves a useful purpose and must continue to exist.

Over the years the United Nations has undergone a great deal of change. Its membership has tripled. Its discussion has shifted to many new issues. After rapid growth in membership during the 1950s and 1960s, the United Nations has arrived at a consolidation stage, which may provide the basis for striking out toward new horizons in the future. According to John G. Stoessinger:

> Political institutions pass through periods of growth and periods of consolidation. The United Nations is no exception, and, in the overall assessment, it is vital to bear in mind this time dimension. In this fundamental sense, it is not true that the United Nations has fallen so low as many fear; it has merely not yet been permitted to rise as high as many had hoped.[8]

To cope with the changing fortunes of international politics, the United Nations has exercised flexibility in various ways. First, it has amended the charter to enlarge the membership of the Security Council and the Economic and Social Council in recognition of the organization's growing membership. Second, it has reinterpreted the charter on several occasions. For example, it has established the United Nations Emergency Forces in such a way that the global powers are excluded from partaking in the actual peacekeeping operations. Third, it has shifted, depending upon the need, the initiation of action between the Security Council, the General Assembly, and the Secretariat. This has been made possible through the passage of the Uniting for Peace Resolution and initiatives taken by the secretary-general, such as the actions taken by Dag Hammarskjöld during the Congo crisis. Finally, the secretary-generals have succeeded in maintaining, at all times, enough political consensus within the United Nations to insure the internal stability of the organization.

Any evaluation of the United Nations will leave the observer with mixed reactions. It has not met the founders' hopes in some areas, while meeting or surpassing them in others. The plain fact is that the United Nations cannot be much stronger than it is because of the limitations imposed by the present-day nation-state system. The member countries are neither ready nor willing at this stage to surrender their rights of national sovereignty to the United Nations.

The United Nations has helped to bring representatives of the various people of the world closer together. The General Assembly constitutes the only permanent worldwide forum where the representatives of the many member countries can meet, exchange opinions, and publicly voice their views on regional and worldwide

[8]John G. Stoessinger, *The United Nations and the Superpowers: China, Russia, and America*, 3rd ed. (New York: Random House, 1973), p. 209.

HARASSED NURSEMAID

(Justus, The Minneapolis Star.)

Frankfurter Allgemeine Zeitung, September 17, 1973, as translated and
reprinted in The German Tribune, October 4, 1973.

problems. The importance of this forum should not be underestimated. In the area of economic and social development the United Nations renders important help to many of the developing countries and has contributed, beyond original expectations, to the improvement of the general welfare. Finally, the United Nations helps to maintain peace throughout the world. While its intended role as mediator and conciliator has not borne fruit at every occasion, its partial results have been of help to the world community. Any composite and realistic evaluation of the United Nations must lead to the conclusions that the international institution has made a positive contribution to international order and well-being. The global community has been in need of the United Nations and will need its services in the future.

REGIONAL INTEGRATION

Since World War II a number of regional organizations have been created. These systems may be defined as groupings of three or more nation-states that have formed distinct international arrangements for the purpose of economic, military, and/or political integration at the regional level. Regional integration denotes the establishment of common goals by the member countries, increasing cooperation in joint endeavors, and the voluntary surrender of certain aspects of national decision-making to the authoritative organs of the regional organization.

Regionalism, according to some theorists, can serve as "a steppingstone toward universalism." Advocates of this theory emphasize that the present world is too diverse culturally, economically, ideologically, and psychologically to develop global common loyalties. Integrating commonalities could be established more readily within regions. The building blocks created by regional integration can serve in the future for the creation of a greater degree of worldwide order. Some supporters of regionalism support the "federal approach" and others the "functional approach." The first calls for the establishment of supranational agencies within regional organizations. The members would surrender part of their sovereignty to the supranational bodies. The "functionalists," in contrast, have encouraged the development of broad-scale intergovernmental collaboration in lieu of supranational agencies. According to their view, economic, social, and cultural cooperation is a paramount prerequisite to political integration. The regionalism that has developed in recent decades appears to contain aspects of both theories.[9]

Articles 52 through 54 of the Charter of the United Nations give international recognition to regional arrangements and define the relationship between such bodies and the United Nations. According to Article 52:

Nothing in the present Charter precludes the existence of regional arrangements or agencies for dealing with such matters relating to the maintenance of international peace and security as are appropriate for regional action, provided that such arrangements or agencies and their activities are consistent with the Purposes and Principles of the United Nations.

The Members of the United Nations entering such arrangements . . . shall make every effort to achieve pacific settlement of local disputes through such regional arrangements before referring them to the Security Council.

The Security Council shall encourage the development of pacific settlement of local disputes through such regional arrangements . . . either on the initiative of the states concerned or by reference from the Security Council.

In addition, Article 51 provides legitimacy for the collective security provisions found in the treaties establishing military regional alliances. This states:

Nothing in the present Charter shall impair the inherent right of individual or collective self-defense if an armed attack occurs against a Member of the United Nations, until the Security Council has taken the measures necessary to maintain international peace and security.

[9]For a theoretical discussion of regional integration, see Ernst B. Haas, "International Integration, the European and the Universal Process," and Amitai Etzioni, "The Dialects of Supranational Unification," in *International Political Communities, An Anthology* (Garden City, N.Y.: Doubleday, 1966), pp. 93–147.

The important point is that, according to the United Nations' Charter, regionalism is compatible with the United Nations and should be utilized to help the Security Council in its peacekeeping function. Have regional organizations developed along these guidelines?

Some degree of "regionalism," in the sense of grouping a number of nation-states together for the pursuit of a common policy, existed prior to the United Nations. The defense alliances, formed before and after World War I, and the British Commonwealth serve as examples. Regional organization gained considerable momentum in the late 1940s and during the 1950s, leading to the establishment of a large number of military, economic, and political arrangements, which will be discussed later. The move toward regional association was spearheaded by arrangements in the Atlantic community area and in the Americas. They were countered in the 1950s by regional arrangements among the Communist countries. Other regional organizations were established in the Middle East, Africa, and Southeast Asia.

Generally speaking, the multitude of regional organizations developed after World War II can be divided into three categories: (1) multipurpose organizations, (2) security organizations, and (3) economic organizations.

MULTIPURPOSE ORGANIZATIONS

The major post-World War II regional organizations that fall into this category are the League of Arab States (commonly known as the Arab League and established in 1945), the Organization of American States (OAS, 1948), the Council of Europe (1949), and the Organization of African Unity (OAU, 1963).

Of these four, the Council of Europe has maintained perhaps the most limited profile. Over the years its activities have been overshadowed by questions and issues relating to NATO and European economic integration. The Organization of American States was established as a follow-up to the Rio Pact (1947). Under the active leadership of the United States, OAS has been used to coordinate hemispheric American politics. In contrast to the Council of Europe, OAS has occupied itself with a number of broad issues involving political, economic, and military matters. For example, the Alliance for Progress program was carried on, at least technically, under the auspices of OAS. Generally speaking, the Alliance for Progress was based on the U.S. commitment to Latin American countries to help them to raise their standard of living. The most notable military action of the OAS occurred in 1965 in conjunction with a governmental crisis in the Dominican Republic. Civil war and the threat of an apparent Communist takeover in late April and early May of that year led the U.S. government to send troops to the Dominican Republic. After a ceasefire had been achieved between the warring factions, an Inter-American Peace Force was established under OAS auspices, consisting of U.S. troops plus contingents from Brazil, Costa Rica, El Salvador, and Nicaragua. The force was directed by a Brazilian general and remained at the scene until the fighting was stopped and a new, viable government was established.

The Arab League is the oldest of the four multipurpose regional organizations. Its espoused purpose has been to foster and increase cooperation among the Arab countries. While its first aim was essentially to seek the liberation of all Arab countries from colonial rule, it soon became involved in military actions when it sought to prevent the establishment of the nation-state of Israel. Integrated economic pursuits were added to the Arab League's responsibilities in later years. Perennial divisions of interest among some of the Arab countries have limited the effectiveness of the Arab League over the years.

The Organization of African Unity is the newest of the multipurpose regional organizations. It is the only regional organization combining the black and Arab African countries. Established in 1963, it has sought to unite under its framework the divergent groupings of African nation-states. The charter of the Organization of African Unity calls for achieving the aspirations of the African people through economic and political development. The members of OAU have pledged themselves to coordinate their policies, to defend their sovereignty, and to eradicate colonialism in Africa. Some of OAU's major accomplishments have been related to the prevention or settlement of disputes between members. The most successful achievement occurred in 1963, when OAU officials achieved a ceasefire in the border dispute between Algeria and Morocco. Subsequent OAU meetings helped in bringing about a settlement.

More than the other regional organizations, OAU has been subject to various internal strains; however, the organization has endured all crises during the past and has succeeded in achieving international importance. Perhaps one of its greatest problems in recent years has been the growing division between the Arab member countries on the one hand and the black countries on the other. Requests for financial aid made by several of the sub-Saharan countries to counter the rising cost of oil have not yet been met with an adequate response by the newly rich oil-producing countries of the north. It appears that this problem and the rivalry over black or Arab leadership in OAU will continue for some time to come. Thus, while OAU has had some success as a regional arbitrator, it has done little to further "pan-African unity."

SECURITY ORGANIZATIONS

Regional arrangements whose primary function is that of security include the **North Atlantic Treaty Organization** (NATO, established in 1949); the Australia, New Zealand, United States Security Treaty Organization (ANZUS, 1952); the **Warsaw Treaty Organization** (WTO, 1955); and the Rio Pact (1947, which became one of the two basic documents of the Organization of American States established one year later).

Underlying all of these security-oriented regional arrangements is the principle of collective security; that is, the concept that an attack upon one member of an association should be considered as an attack on all members, and all shall rally to the defense of the attacked nation-state. For example, Article 3 of the Rio Pact states:

> *The High Contracting Parties agree that an armed attack by any State against an American State shall be considered as an attack against all American States, and, consequently, each one of the said Contracting Parties undertakes to assist in meeting the attack in the exercise of the inherent right of individual or collective self-defense recognized by Article 51 of the Charter of the United Nations.*[10]

Similar provisions are found in the treaties that serve as the constitutional foundation for the North Atlantic Treaty Organization; the Australia, New Zealand, United States Security Treaty Organization; and the Warsaw Treaty Organization.

Let us look briefly at the specific purposes of some of these security arrangements. The Rio Pact was designed to provide an inter-American treaty of military assistance and to establish a system of collective security in the Americas. The North Atlantic Treaty Organization was created to contain the perceived Communist threat to Western Europe. To counter the Western military alliance system, the Soviet government converted in 1955 its bilateral military treaties with other East European countries into a multilateral agreement, the Warsaw Treaty Organization, commonly referred to as the Warsaw Pact.

The North Atlantic Treaty Organization and the Warsaw Pact are more structurally developed than the other military alliances. NATO and WTO each consist of semi-integrated military systems that have been commanded perpetually by United States and Russian officers respectively. The large-scale development of nuclear weaponry in recent years has rendered questionable some of the basic premises upon which the two military alliances (and the others, too) were built. For instance, will the United States come to the defense of its allies in the case of *any* Soviet military attack on Western Europe, including West Berlin? Increasingly, West Europeans have growing doubts as to whether or not the United States would come to their defense. In essence, how much credibility does the assumption of collective security carry in a time when warfare in the Northern Hemisphere could lead to nuclear annihilation? This credibility gap was, allegedly, one of the primary reasons that de Gaulle took France out of NATO.

The move toward reform has been stronger in NATO than the other military regional organizations. A number of conferences have been held in recent years on how to reinvigorate NATO and to make it more relevant to present-day issues. Its endeavors have been broadened to include political, economic, and environmental issues. In the composite, however, the reform of NATO is still far from satisfactory completion.[11]

---

[10]The text of the Rio Pact is reprinted in M. Margaret Ball, *The OAS in Transition* (Durham, N.C.: Duke University Press, 1969). For the text of the North Atlantic Treaty, see, among others, A. H. Robertson, *European Institutions* (New York: Frederick A. Praeger, 1958). The English-language text of the Warsaw Treaty is published in Robin A. Remington, *The Warsaw Pact* (Cambridge, Mass.: The MIT Press, 1971).

[11]One evaluation of NATO is Edwin H. Fedder, *NATO: The Dynamics of Alliance in the Postwar World* (New York: Dodd, Mead, 1973).

NATO, ANZUS, Rio Pact, and Warsaw Pact are basically defensive military alliances established to protect the hegemonical interests of the United States and the Soviet Union. Depending upon the circumstances, these interests may be opposed potentially to those held by a majority of the members of the United Nations. This being the case, the pursuits of military regional organizations do not necessarily jibe with the expectations as set forth in Article 52 of the United Nations Charter.

ECONOMIC ORGANIZATIONS

The largest number of regional organizations have developed in the economic realm. Some of them have achieved substantially more structure and organizational viability than others. They differ also in size, ranging from the macrosized Organization of Economic Cooperation and Development (OECD) (which includes 24 developed countries) to such microsized organizations as the Nordic Council (which consists of the 5 Scandinavian countries). The basic effort underlying the economic regional groupings has been to decrease trade barriers between the member countries and to increase commerce between them. This pursuit has led to substantially increased economic cooperation in some parts of the world. The most important strides toward economic integraton have taken place in Europe: in Western Europe under the auspices of the European Economic Community (the Common Market) and in Eastern Europe under the Council for Mutual Economic Assistance (COMECON or CMEA).

The **European Economic Community** was established in 1957 for the purpose of integrating the economic policies of Belgium, the Netherlands, Luxembourg, France, the Federal Republic of Germany, and Italy. These were joined in 1973 by the United Kingdom, Denmark, and Ireland and in 1981 by Greece. In 1951, the original six countries mentioned above, also known as the "Inner Six," had established the European Coal and Steel Community to provide a common market in coal and steel and its byproducts among the six members. The European Economic Community provided a still broader scope and aimed to integrate the entire economies of the member countries. A European Atomic Energy Community (Euratom), with the purpose of establishing a basis for the joint exploitation of atomic energy, was created simultaneously with the Common Market.

The ostensible purpose of the moves toward West European economic integration was to increase the economic well-being of all the member countries. In actuality, however, the major impetus came from French leaders, especially Robert Schuman, who sought integration as a means of eliminating the danger of armed conflict between France and Germany. It is in this aspect that one of the major rationales underlying West European integration differs considerably from those of economic integration in other parts of the world.

While there has been considerable economic integration among the Common Market countries, progress has been faster in some specific areas than in others. Accomplishments include the creation of a Customs Union, which became operative in 1968; the establishment of a common agricultural policy, which by 1974 encompassed most of the community's agricultural production; the creation of a community-wide Monetary Cooperation Fund; and endeavors toward common policies in environmental, scientific, and technological affairs.

West European economic integration showed its greatest momentum during the early and mid-1960s and has leveled off in more recent years. Among other problems, the oil crisis of late 1973 led to divisive tendencies among the Common Market countries and policies that were based on an "each for his own" attitude rather than constructive, joint endeavors. In a larger sense, current inflation and questions of how to cope with it present a formidable challenge today to economic unity within the Common Market. Despite all these problems, however, the European Economic Community has achieved more economic integration among its members than any other regional economic organization in the non-Communist part of the world.

The **Council of Mutual Economic Assistance** (COMECON or CMEA) is the regional economic organization of Communist countries. In 1980 the members were the Soviet Union, Poland, the German Democratic Republic, Czechoslovakia, Hungary, Bulgaria, Romania, the Mongolian Republic, Vietnam, and Cuba. (Albania, one of its original members, left COMECON in 1961.) Its creation came as a reaction to the Marshall Plan and subsequent West European economic integration. Over the years a close system of economic interdependence has been developed, under the auspices of COMECON, between the Soviet Union and the other members. During the 1950s and 1960s COMECON members conducted most of their foreign trade within the organization and a considerable portion thereof with the Soviet Union. A leveling-off tendency in this trade pattern has occured in recent years, however, with Romania, for example, increasing its trade with the West. Other countries pursuing a similar pattern, though at a smaller level, are Poland and Hungary.

Two unique COMECON projects are the construction of an oil pipeline linking the Soviet Union with Poland, Hungary, Czechoslovakia, and the German Democratic Republic and an electric power grid system connecting the Soviet Union with these same countries plus Bulgaria and Romania. One may deduce from these examples that integration within COMECON, at least in some areas, has gone still farther than among the Common Market countries.

One of the basic differences between the Common Market and COMECON is that in the latter the Soviet Union, because of its power and influence, has played a dominant role. No such great predominance has been exercised by any country within the Common Market. The Soviet leadership has been able to utilize COMECON to increase, at least temporarily, its control over the member countries, despite occasional setbacks such as the departure of Albania and the defeat in 1963 of Khrushchev's plan to introduce a still greater degree of specialization among the industries of the COMECON countries.

AN EVALUATION OF REGIONAL ORGANIZATIONS

What has been the success of regional organizations in the post-World War II era? What has been their contribution to peace? Have they performed according to the expectations of the founding fathers of the United Nations, as stipulated by Article 52 of the charter? The composite picture of regional organizations shows a "mixed bag" situation, in that some regional organizations have been much more successful than others. Regional organizations dominated by one or the other superpower, such as NATO, OAS, the Warsaw Pact, or COMECON, have been used extensively and perhaps understandably to protect and perpetuate their spheres of influence. According to Nye:

> *Regional organizations are not a major cause of spheres of influence, but to some extent they help to perpetuate them. One can argue that these spheres of influence have been useful no-trespassing signs that help to prevent miscalculation by the superpowers and thus help to avoid nuclear holocaust.*[12]

An alternate argument, however, is that regional spheres are "likely in the long run only to provoke rather than prevent further conflict both within and without."[13]

In any case, regional organizations have made some constructive contribution to world peace. They have helped in varying degrees to create a greater sense of commonality among the populations of the member countries. Good examples are the Council of Europe and the Common Market. Both organizations have contributed much toward overcoming the historic national rivalries between France and Germany. The regional consciousness in Western Europe—the feeling of belonging together—is greater today than ever before. Regional organizations have helped in curtailing conflict among member countries. Admittedly, the disputes settled by regional organizations were cases of low intensity in terms of their seriousness for the global community.[14]

The composite evaluation of the roles played by regional organizations shows that while they do not constitute a panacea for world order, they have made a definite contribution to peace and have complemented the work of the United Nations in a number of instances.

INTERNATIONAL LAW

Our concluding discussion in the international area deals with law among the nation-states. We would like to explain its nature, sources, and role in contemporary international politics.

THE NATURE OF INTERNATIONAL LAW

Queries about the existence of **international law** are of a rhetorical nature, because the body known as international law is of a somewhat different nature than

---

[12]J. S. Nye, *Peace in Parts: Integration and Conflict in Regional Organization* (Boston: Little, Brown, 1971), pp. 179–180.

[13]Evan Luard, *Conflict and Peace in the Modern International System* (Boston: Little, Brown, 1969), p. 167.

[14]See Nye, *op. cit.*, for his analysis of the OAS, OAU, and Arab League and their performance in controlling conflicts.

domestic law. The governments of nation-states, usually having a preponderance of power in their respective societies, enforce domestic law. On the international scene, however, there is no world government and therefore no agency that can consistently and effectively enforce international law. Definitions of international law usually recognize this important difference between the roles of domestic and international law. According to J. L. Brierly, "The Law of Nations, or International Law, may be defined as the body of rules and principles of action which are binding upon civilized states in their relations with one another."[15] A still more pointed definition comes from Charles Hyde, who states:

> The term international law may fairly be employed to designate the principles and rules of conduct declaratory thereof which states feel themselves bound to observe and, therefore, commonly observe in their relations with each other.[16]

Hyde's definition stresses the aspect of voluntarism in international law, the fact that nation-states "feel themselves bound to observe" the law for common-sense reasons and thus do so voluntarily usually.

Governments of nation-states will adhere to certain aspects of international law for various reasons. First, many countries follow international law simply because it is customary to do so. This would apply, for example, to the field of diplomatic practices. Second, governments may adhere to some parts of international law out of a belief that it is morally right to do so. Third, some governments may obey international law out of expediency. They will refrain from violating international principles out of the consideration that otherwise other countries would do likewise. An example of this would be the general adherence of Western countries to the Prisoner of War rules as stated in the Geneva Convention of 1929 and revised in 1949. In World War II, for example, the authorities of the United States, Britain, and Germany treated their respective prisoners more humanely, as compared with the treatment of German POWs in the Soviet Union and Russian POWs in Germany. Finally, governments may adhere to international law out of fear of sanctions, which may take the form of condemnation by other governments and outside public opinion or the threat of or initiation of retaliatory actions, such as severing diplomatic relations, instituting economic sanctions, or taking military actions. These economic or military actions may be pursued against the perpetrator by one or several countries, a regional organization, or the United Nations. Examples of the last would be the economic sanctions imposed by the United Nations against Rhodesia and the application of military sanction to combat aggression in Korea.

International law deals with many aspects of international behavior and developments. It includes, for example, the principles and rules having to do with the estab-

---

[15]J. L. Brierly, *The Law of Nations*, 6th ed., rev. by Sir Humphrey Waldock (New York: Oxford University Press, 1963), p. 1.

[16]Charles Cheney Hyde, *International Law Chiefly As Interpreted and Applied by the United States*, Vol. 1 (Boston: Little, Brown, 1945), p. 1.

lishment of nation-states and their recognition by other countries, as well as the privileges accorded to diplomats. International law deals with the rules that have been developed in regard to the conduct of military hostilities and the treatment of prisoners and enemy civilians. Contemporary international law places certain restrictions on countries concerning their resort to war. Such stipulations are found in the Kellogg–Briand Pact (1928) and the Charter of the United Nations. A substantial part of international law deals with commercial relations between countries.

THE DEVELOPMENT OF INTERNATIONAL LAW AND INTERNATIONAL LEGAL ORGANIZATIONS

When the Dutch scholar Hugo Grotius, commonly known as "the father of international law," published his famous work, *De jure belli ac pacis* ("On the Law of War and Peace"), in 1625, he categorized and codified in his book all aspects of international law that had been developed in the previous centuries of Western civilization. He placed into a modern setting the interstate rules and principles that had been developed by the Greeks, the Romans, and subsequent Western cultures. His book was the first comprehensive treatment of the subject and has served as the basis for further study and growth.[17]

In the modern nation-states era, which began roughly with the Treaty of Westphalia (1648), international law has grown in a fashion similar to the growth of common law, and this process of growth is continuing steadily. New features were added in recent decades in the form of international forums and agencies rendering decisions on disputes between two or more nation-states.

The first permanent International Court of Arbitration was established by the First Hague Conference (1899). A second international judicial body was established in 1920 as part of the League of Nations. It became known as the Permanent Court of International Justice. In 1945 the founders of the United Nations established the **International Court of Justice** as successor to the Permanent Court of International Justice. The International Court of Justice is one of the 6 principal organs of the United Nations. Located, like its predecessors, in The Hague, it consists of 15 judges who are elected by the General Assembly and the Security Council of the United Nations. The members of the court are elected for 9-year terms on a staggered basis (5 every 3 years) and may be reelected.[18] The court deals with legal cases (that is, questions having to do with what the law is in a particular case), rather than political cases (questions about what the law should be). Issues of the latter category cannot be adjudicated by the court. They have to be dealt with by

[17]For an English-language translation of Grotius' writings, see A. C. Campbell, *The Rights of War and Peace Including the Law of Nature and the Law of Nations Translated from the Original Latin of Grotius* (Washington and London: M. Walter Dunne, Publisher, 1901). A useful biographical discussion of Grotius is Hamilton Vreeland, *Hugo Grotius* (New York: Oxford University Press, 1917).

[18]The United Nations has published an informative handbook on the court. See United Nations Office of Publications, *The International Court of Justice* 5th ed. (New York: United Nations, 1965).

methods producing peaceful change (diplomacy) or, if these fail, by means of violence (such as war or threat of war).

Only nation-states may be parties in cases before the International Court of Justice. The court can try only those cases that parties in dispute submit voluntarily. It does not have any enforcement powers enjoyed by domestic courts. Even if two countries agree to submit their dispute to the International Court, they do not have to adhere to its judgment. An exception to the foregoing statement is that in conjunction with Paragraph 2 of Article 36 of the Statute of the International Court of Justice a number of countries have pledged themselves to accept compulsory jurisdiction of the court.[19] By 1977, 47 countries had pledged themselves to this "optional clause," some, however, with various kinds of reservations that limit their cooperation with the International Court of Justice.

All in all, the role of the International Court of Justice is different from and weaker than that of domestic courts.

THE SOURCES OF INTERNATIONAL LAW

As domestic law has grown from the needs of people living within societies, international law has grown out of the needs of nation-states. The following are some of the major sources of international law.

International Conventions

This refers to treaties concluded on a multilateral basis. Bilateral treaties rarely create a new rule of international law. They usually are built upon and are declaratory of existing rules. Treaties constitute an important part of international law. As an international practice, they date back as far as written records have been found. In our century a number of multilateral treaties and agreements have come into existence. While none of them have obtained universal ratification, they have achieved the support of enough nation-states to be considered part of international law. The Covenant of the League of Nations of 1919, the Kellogg–Briand Pact of 1928, the Charter of the United Nations of 1945, the Nuclear Test Ban Treaty of 1963, and the Non-Proliferation Treaty of 1968 are examples of multilateral treaties.

While bilateral and multilateral treaties are considered binding on the signatories, history shows a number of examples of the governments of some participant countries having broken their promises and having either partially or fully terminated their respective international obligations. This, obviously, decreases the force of in-

---

[19]The states that are party to the present statute may at any time declare that they recognize as compulsory ipso facto and without special agreement in relation to any other state accepting the same obligation, the jurisdiction of the court in all legal disputes concerning:

    1. The interpretation of a treaty.

    2. Any question of international law.

    3. The existence of any fact which, if established, would constitute a breach of an international obligation.

    4. The nature or extent of the reparation to be made for the breach of an international obligation.

ternational law. The Nazi German government, for example, unilaterally terminated several treaties with the questionable assertion that the other party had violated them.

In recent years copies of some multilateral treaties have been deposited with the United Nations, in order to give them a greater degree of international legal standing. This practice was followed by the United States and the Soviet Union after their ratification of the Nuclear Test Ban Treaty and the Nuclear Non-Proliferation Treaty. We may assume that this practice will be followed by these countries and others in the future.

International Customs

Established customs among the nation-states constitute an important part of international law. These are rules of behavior that were introduced decades or even centuries ago by one or some countries in dealing with each other and slowly were adopted by others because they found them useful. Once an adoption of this kind has become nearly universal, a new international law has been established. A great number of customs that now are accepted universally have developed over the centuries in the area of diplomacy and the rights and privileges of diplomats. A good example is the principle of diplomatic immunity enjoyed by accredited diplomats throughout the world. Violations of this principle, as, for example, that committed by Iranian militants with the approval of the Khomeini government against U.S. diplomats in Tehran in 1979, have been condemned by all civilized governments.

General Principles of Law

A third source of international law is made up by generic principles of law, which are recognized by "the civilized nation-states" of this world. What are these general principles? While there is some disagreement among students of international law on the exact nature of these principles, a number of them point out that Article 38 of the Statute of the International Court of Justice refers to the general principles of justice and reason as found in natural law as being rationally understood and applied to modern society. How are these principles applied to present-day cases? According to Frederick H. Hartmann:

> The "general principles" of law, to be applied at all, must be applied in a particular case to specific facts that are the corollaries of those principles. The question asked is: what does the principle mean in this case? The answer is the result of the use of reason and, where necessary, analogies from principles pervading the municipal law of nations in general.[20]

It appears from this that the "general principles" stated in Article 38 constitute an element of international law that is less defined and more difficult to apply than the principles originating from treaties and customs.

[20]Frederick H. Hartmann, *The Relations of Nations*, 5th ed. (New York: Macmillan, 1978), p. 118.

Judicial Decisions and Writings of Scholars

Both are indirect and subsidiary sources of international law. Decisions rendered in domestic courts may help international jurists here and there in forming their opinions. More important are the decisions rendered by international tribunals. The growing body of these decisions will serve as precedents for international jurists in years and decades to come.

The writings of experts were very important during the formative stage of modern international law; however, with the formation of a body of modern international law and the establishment of international tribunals, the publicist has become a commentator and interpreter, rather than a maker of international law.[21]

THE ROLE OF INTERNATIONAL LAW IN CONTEMPORARY TIMES

Because of the lack of universal executive enforcement powers, international law has not taken on the effectiveness of domestic law, nor has the International Court of Justice achieved the important role of national supreme courts. According to Stanley Hoffmann:

The nature of the international system condemns international law to all the weaknesses and perversions that it is so easy to deride. International law is merely a magnifying mirror that reflects faithfully and cruelly the essence and the logic of international politics. In a fragmented world, there is no "global perspective" from which anyone can authoritatively assess, endorse, or reject the separate national efforts at making international law serve national interests above all.[22]

Modern international law has developed essentially within the framework of the Western countries. The rise of the Communist countries and the developing nation-states of the Third World has brought about a high degree of pluralism on the international scene, which, in turn may call for the revision of some formerly accepted international principles in order to make them universally applicable. One may assume that this adjustment will continue for years to come. All countries, whether postindustrial Western, Communist, or developing, engage in similar basic activities. They all have certain interests in common. It is in the area of commonality that universal principles can be achieved first. As stated by Oliver J. Lissitzyn:

The conflicts of interest do not prevent mutually acceptable regulation of transnational activities in the areas of international relations where there is some community of interest, however limited. Since all states engage in such activities, there is a basis for the existence of "universal" international law in the sense of a number of concepts and norms understood, invoked, and honored by all states, as well as of "particular" interna-

[21]For more extensive discussions of the sources of international law, see Gerhard von Glahn, *Law Among Nations: An Introduction to Public International Law*, 2nd ed. (London: The Macmillan Company, 1970), pp. 10–22; Charles A Fenwick, *International Law*, 4th ed. (New York: Appleton-Century-Crofts, 1965), pp. 84–97; Brierly, *op. cit.*, pp. 56–68; and Ahmed Sheikh, *International Law and National Behavior* (New York: John Wiley, 1974), pp. 62–69.

[22]Stanley Hoffmann, in Lawrence Scheinman and David Wilkinson, eds., *International Law and Political Crisis: An Analytic Casebook* (Boston: Little, Brown, 1968), p. *xvii*.

tional law-norms that apply to some but not all states. Both universal and particular international law may be expected to grow in scope and complexity as the volume and variety of transnational activities increase.[23]

The governments of all nation-states have common interests (though there may be a difference in degree) in internationally accepted rules pertaining to the exercise of diplomacy, the issue of maritime jurisdiction, traffic on the high seas, regulation of outer space, treatment of enemy nationals and their property during wartime, as well as the rights and obligations of neutrals. In this context, it is of some interest that two adversary countries, Cuba and the United States, were able to conclude a reciprocally beneficial agreement against skyjacking.

The presence of international law exercises a moderating influence on the foreign policy activities of governments. It provides basic norms of conduct governments can use for their communication with each other. It furnishes means for channeling conflict so that issues can be decided by peaceful means instead of force. It serves as a moral force in that international condemnation can be directed against the violator of universally established norms.

The problematic nature of international law will continue for some time. Its plight, in the words of Stanley Hoffmann,

> *is that, now as before, it shows on its body of rules all the scars inflicted by the international state of war. The tragedy of contemporary international law is that of a double divorce: first, between the old liberal dream of a world rule of law, and the realities of an international system of multiple minidramas that always threaten to become major catastrophes; second, between the old dream and the new requirements of moderation, which in the circumstances of the present system suggest a down-playing of formal law in the realm of peace-and-war issues, and an upgrading of more flexible techniques, until the system has become less fierce.*[24]

In the complete absence of international law, this world of ours would be much worse off than it is now. One only can hope that the world community will make speedy headway in transforming traditional international law into the norms and principles that can be accepted universally by the multiple world we live in. Moreover, it is hoped that governments will use increasingly the existing body of international law to settle disputes by peaceful means, so that the world can become a more lawful community.

SELECTED READINGS

A very informative discussion of the creation of the League of Nations and its years of growth, stability, and demise, written by a former deputy-general of the League, is

---

[23]Oliver J. Lissitzyn, "International Law in a Divided World," *International Conciliation* (March, 1963), pp. 3–69. The author examines very incisively the impact that the rise of the Communist bloc of countries and the developing nation-states have had on existing international law.

[24]Stanley Hoffmann, *op. cit.*, pp. *xvii* and *xix*.

Francis P. Walters, *A History of the League of Nations* (New York: Oxford University Press, 1952). The best source on the structure, functions, and activities of the United Nations and its related agencies is *Everyman's United Nations** 8th ed. (New York: UN Office of Public Information, 1968).

Good texts on international organizations are, among others, A. LeRoy Bennett, *International Organizations: Principles and Issues*, 2nd ed. (Englewood Cliffs, N.J.: Prentice-Hall, 1980); Philip E. Jacob, Alexine L. Atherton, and Arthur M. Wallenstein, *The Dynamics of International Organization*, rev. ed. (Homewood, Ill.: The Dorsey Press, 1972); and Inis L. Claude, Jr., *Swords into Plowshares: The Problems and Progress of International Organization*, 4th ed. (New York: Random House, 1971).

Three books that provide considerable insight about the United Nations are the autobiography of the first secretary-general, Trygve Lie, *In The Cause of Peace* (New York: Macmillan, 1954); the discussion, by a close associate, of Hammarskjold's years as secretary-general in Brian Urquart, *Hammarskjold* (New York: Alfred A. Knopf, 1972); and *View from the U.N.*, written by the third secretary-general, U Thant (New York: Doubleday, 1978).

For informative discussions of various agencies and activities of the United Nations, see Sidney D. Bailey, *The Procedure of the U.N. Security Council* (New York: Oxford University Press, 1975); Andrew Boyd, *Fifteen Men on a Powder Keg* (New York: Stein and Day, 1971); Richard Hiscocks, *The Security Council: A Study in Adolescence* (New York: Free Press, 1974); Hayward R. Alker, Jr. and Bruce M. Russet, *World Politics in the General Assembly*, rev. ed. (New Haven, Conn.: Yale University Press, 1965); Theodor Meron, *The United Nations Secretariat* (Lexington, Mass.: Lexington Books, 1977); and Indar Rikhye et al., *The Thin Blue Line: International Peacekeeping and its Future* (New Haven, Conn.: Yale University Press, 1974).

Two good treatments of U.S. foreign policy and the United Nations are Lincoln P. Bloomfield, *The United Nations and U. S. Foreign Policy,** rev. ed. (Boston: Little, Brown, 1967); and Robert E. Riggs, *U.S./U.N., Foreign Policy and International Organization** (New York: Appleton-Century-Crofts, 1971). A superb comparative analysis of the roles of the United States, the Soviet Union, and the People's Republic of China in the United Nations is John G. Stoessinger, *The United Nations and the Superpowers: China, Russia, and America,** 4th ed. (New York: Random House, 1977).

For a good, comprehensive treatment of regional organization, see J. S. Nye, ed., *Peace in Parts: Integration and Conflict in Regional Organization** (Boston: Little, Brown, 1971). A standard work on European integration is A. H. Robertson, *European Institutions* (New York: Frederick A. Praeger, 1958). A more recent publication of similar style is Michael Palmer, John Lambert, et al., *A Handbook of European Or-*

*Available in Paperback

ganizations (New York: Frederick A. Praeger, 1968). Other informative discussions of European integration are Werner J. Feld and John K. Wiedgen, *Domestic Political Realities and European Unification* (Boulder, Col.: Westview Press, 1977); Roy Pryce, *The Politics of the European Community* (Totowa, N.J.: Rowman and Little-field, 1973); and Christoph Sasse, ed., *Decision Making in the European Community* (New York: Praeger, 1977).

The creation of NATO is examined in Escott Reid, *Time of Fear and Hope: The Making of the North Atlantic Treaty, 1947–1949* (Toronto: McClelland and Stewart, 1977). For a good analysis of the North Atlantic Treaty Organization, see Edwin H. Fedder, *NATO: The Dynamics of Alliance in the Postwar World** (New York: Dodd, Mead, 1973). The best comprehensive discussion of its Communist counterpart is Robin A. Remington, *The Warsaw Pact* (Cambridge, Mass.: The MIT Press, 1971). The evolution, principles, structure, and activities of the Organization of American States are treated extensively and competently in M. Margaret Ball, *The OAS in Transition* (Durham, N.C.: Duke University Press, 1969).

For an informative and detailed analysis of political integration in Africa, see Zdenek Cervenka, *The Organization of African Unity and Its Charter* (New York: Praeger, 1969). More recent informative sources on the OAU are Yassin El-Ayouty, ed., *The Organization of African Unity after Ten Years: Comparative Perspectives* (New York: Praeger, 1975); and Berkanykum Andemicael, *The OAU and the UN* (New York: Africana, 1976). For a study of the Arab League, see Robert W. McDon-ald, *The League of Arab States* (Princeton, N.J.: Princeton University Press, 1965).

The classic introduction to international law is J. L. Brierly, *The Law of Nations*, 6th ed., rev. by Sir Humphrey Waldock (New York: Oxford University Press, 1963). For a more recent and broader study, see Gerhard von Glahn, *Law Among Nations: An Introduction to Public Law*, 3rd ed. (New York: Macmillan, 1976); or Michael Bar-ton Akehurst, *A Modern Introduction to International Law*, 3rd ed. (London: Allen & Unwin, 1977). An important contribution to this area is the work of a former member of the International Court of Justice, Philip C. Jessup, *The Price of International Justice* (New York: Columbia University Press, 1971). An excellent behavioral interpre-tation of contemporary international law is Ahmed Sheikh, *International Law and National Behavior** (New York: John Wiley, 1974). Several good case studies are featured in Lawrence Scheinman and David Wilkinson, eds., *International Law and Political Crisis** (Boston: Little, Brown, 1968).

*Available in paperback

Glossary

Absolute Value-Oriented Parties   Follow a rigid, comprehensive program, usually very ideological. Unwilling to negotiate or compromise except as a tactic to gain power. Examples are Fascist and Communist parties.

Adaptation Stage   The third stage of revolutionary one-party systems. Technicians and managers have a greater role and less dependence on party bureaucracy. Sometimes characterized by a slowly evolving pluralism.

Administrative Law   The type of law that is concerned with the legal accountability of government officials in carrying out policy such as rules and regulations based on statutes.

Adversary System   The practice in Anglo-American law whereby each side presents its case, with the judge or jury determining the truth of the facts and reaching a decision for one side or the other.

Affective Socialization   Learning and accepting feelings values, loyalty, support, and affection vis-a-vis the political system.

Affirmative Action   A program or policy to correct past racial or sexual discrimination usually in reference to admittance to an institution such as school or trade union, hiring, promotion, and equal pay. A part of the American equal rights movement legislated under federal law.

Agenda Setting   The second stage of the policy process. This involves getting the problem or issue on the agenda of public debate.

Aggregation   Occurs when demands/claims are brought together into a smaller number of policy alternatives. A principal function of political parties.

Alienation   Marx in his early years developed the idea that the worker under capitalism is alienated because he becomes nothing more than an extension of the machine. Communist writers of Eastern Europe have argued that the worker in the Soviet Union during the Stalin era was as alienated as under capitalism because of the inhumane policies of the Soviet bureaucracy.

Anomic Interest Groups   Spontaneous, immediate action oriented. Participants are alienated. Strikes, riots, and demonstrations are characteristic of their tactics.

Anti-Trust Policy   A policy designed to foster competition and make capitalism work. This includes forbidding monopolies, price controls, and competitors from acquiring each other's stock.

Apathy   Lack of interest in politics. Is a support when an individual is relatively satisfied. Sometimes based on a sense of hopelessness. As a reservoir of frustration, can be mobilized against a regime when there is a sudden, revolutionary turn of events.

Appellate Court   A court that reviews decisions of a lower court; for example, the federal courts of appeals to which cases are brought from federal district courts.

Arraignment   A proceeding in Anglo-American law before a court whereby the criminal charge is read and the accused enters a plea of guilty or not guilty.

Articulation   Occurs when individuals or groups request/demand that government change or continue or reject a policy or policies. In developed societies often a principal function of interest groups.

Ascriptive Recruitment   Achieving government office because of lineage and status, such as blood descent and membership in a particular tribe or ethnic group rather than because of merit or achievement.

Associational Interest Groups   Specialized organizations that have interest articulation as a principal function. They are well organized with full-time professional staff. Examples are trade unions, farm organizations, and business associations.

Authoritarian Regimes   Rule by a small elite with very limited popular input and few civil rights. Some authoritarian regimes are striving to become more pluralistic such as Brazil, the Republic of China, the Republic of Korea, and Yugoslavia.

Authority   A type of power generally regarded as rightful or legitimate. The more authority, the less the need to use force.

Avoidance Politics   Traditional, subject political system in which the average individual had no political input. All one could do was avoid government rules or hope to modify them as they were enforced. Has characterized most political systems throughout history.

Barrister   A trial lawyer in Great Britain who is trained at the famous Inns of Court. See Solicitor.

Behavioralism   Movement within political science that began in the 1920s. It intended to make the discipline more scientific by focusing on the individual and using new research techniques such as survey research. Initially emphasized quantitative methods almost exclusively.

Bicameral   A two-house legislature such as the United States Congress, which is composed of the Senate and the House of Representatives, or the British Parliament, composed of the House of Commons and House of Lords.

Bill of Rights of the American Constitution   The first ten amendments that set limits to governmental actions and powers by putting basic civil rights beyond the powers of Congress. Protected are the basic rights of the First Amendment and many procedural rights. Today most of the Bill of Rights restricts the states through the Fourteenth Amendment. See "Nationalizing Civil Rights."

Bill of Rights of the Soviet Union   The Soviet Constitution contains a bill of rights similar in form to the American Bill of Rights. But the emphasis is on social and economic rights such as the right to work. All rights are merely declarations of intention and not enforceable by the courts.

Bipolarity   An international condition that existed for several years after World War II. There were two overwhelming global powers, the United States and the Soviet Union, that dominated much of international politics.

Board of Regents* versus *Bakke   The United States Supreme Court decision holding the quota system for minority groups at the University of California Medical School at Davis unconstitutional but approving the admissions policy of taking race into account as part of a plan to have a diverse student body.

Boss–Follower System   The Japanese oyabun-kobun system. An aspect of the traditional Japanese social system that influences contemporary Japanese parties. Parties are federations of follower–leader groups.

Brown* versus *Board of Education   The Supreme Court decision of 1954 holding segregated schools to be a form of "invidious discrimination" violating the equal protection clause of the Fourteenth Amendment.

Bureaucracy   The staff of large, complex organizations in both the public and private sectors. Ideally, organizational characteristics include specialization, merit, impersonality, hierarchy, and a system of rules.

Certiorari   A writ issued by a higher court such as the United States Supreme Court calling up the record of a lower court for review.

Chief Executive   The chief decision-making and administrative official of a government, such as the British and Japanese Prime Ministers, the West German Chancellor, and the American President. The American President also serves as chief of state.

Chief of State   The principal role is symbolic or ceremonial, holding limited power, such as the British Monarch, or the West German, Indian, and Singapore presidents.

Chinese Communism   The Chinese Communists under Mao Zedong developed some ideological characteristics that differed from the revolutionary leaders of the Soviet Union. The Chinese based their revolutionary techniques on the peasants rather than the proletariat and developed the concept of guerrilla warfare as both a military and political principle.

Civil Law   The branch of law that in its widely used sense refers to the relations between individuals and their legal rights. See also Civil Law of Europe.

Civil Law of Europe   The system of law in countries of Western Europe that grew out of Roman law and tends to be codified, in contrast to common law. Sometimes called Code Law.

Civil Liberties   The freedoms individuals enjoy such as those guaranteed by the Bill of Rights in the American Constitution.

Civil Procedure   The procedure followed in suits between private individuals or groups such as suits for compensation for past wrongs or for breach of contract.

Civil Service   All non-military persons employed by government in non-profit-making departments or agencies. (A pilot on a government-owned international airline would not be a civil servant.) Today civil service usually refers to positions in which one is recruited and promoted on the basis of one's abilities (the merit system).

Classical Democratic Theory   Political theory of the eighteenth and nineteenth centuries that stressed individual responsibility and individual choice based on rational evaluation of all the factors involved. Did not stress group identifications or influences.

Code Law   See Civil Law of Europe.

Cognitive Socialization   The transmission of political knowledge and information. The information may be acquired either formally or informally, but is specifically political in content.

Collectivist Age   Term applied by a Harvard political scientist to describe the current British political system. Most government decision-making is a result of consultation on specific, relatively narrow issues involving interest groups and administrative agencies.

Command Economy   The political leadership makes all major economic decisions. There is government economic sovereignty rather than consumer sovereignty.

Common Law   A system of judge-made law that has its roots in Medieval England and is used by most English-speaking countries.

Communications Revolution   Rapid increases in mass communications (radio, television, newspapers) in which one or all are increasingly available to almost all the population.

Communism   Term applied to followers of Karl Marx who believe that the aims of Socialism as they interpret them—the common ownership of the means of production and exchange—can be achieved most effectively through a violent revolution. Communism is distinguished from Democratic Socialism, which favors attaining its objectives through democratic means. See Soviet Communism, Chinese Communism, Eurocommunism, Marxian Socialism, and Democratic Socialism.

Confederation   A loosely organized political entity in which final power resides in the parts and some power is delegated to the center. The United States Articles of Confederation (1781-89) is one example. Today confederal arrangements are principally economic such as the European Common Market.

Congressional Committee   Permanent or standing committees in the U.S. Congress—18 in the House of Representatives, 15 in the Senate, and 4 joint committees. They exercise a great deal of power.

Conservative   The movement originally associated with Edmund Burke against the French Revolution. It initially drew support from the European aristocracy and stressed support of established institutions such as churches and the monarchy. Conservatives are not opposed to all social change but wish orderly change with due regard for what is good and beneficial in traditional practices and institutions.

Consolidation Stage   Second stage of revolutionary one-party systems. The old order has been destroyed and the regime legitimizes itself on the basis of its new institutions and performance. A period of institutionalization.

Constitutional Law   The system of law interpreting a nation's constitution.

Conversion   A function of government that transforms or converts inputs into outputs.

Council of Mutual Economic Assistance (COMECON)   Regional economic organization of European Communist countries plus Mongolian Republic, Cuba, and Vietnam.

Criminal Law   The branch of law that treats offenses of individuals or corporations against the state.

Criminal Procedure   The steps involved in the law enforcement process beginning with the arrest of the law violator, followed by a preliminary hearing, preferring of charges, arraignment, trial, and concluding with punishment or acquital.

Cross-Cutting Identifications   Identifications in the form of a grid. The vertical are often inherited (e.g. religion, ethnic group, male–female) while the horizontal (e.g., education, and income) vary in degree and quantity. These identifications sometimes conflict over a particular political issue or candidate. Thus, they reduce intensity and facilitate compromise.

Cultural Revolution   Occurred in the People's Republic of China between 1966-1969. The political system almost ceased to function as various leadership groups mobilized mass support to struggle against one another. Mao Zedong led the movement that was especially critical of the unrevolutionary attitudes of many members of the civil service and the Communist Party.

Culture   The widely shared rules, values norms, cognitions. and ways of life of members of a social group.

Demands   Efforts of people urging government to undertake or reject certain actions, for example, to oppose or support gun control. Includes voting, personal contact, writing letters, petitions, and demonstrations. The greatest range and number of demands or claims are in democratic political systems.

Democracy   A political system where political leaders are chosen in competitive elections and the bulk of the adult population is enfranchised. Basic civil rights are protected, usually in a constitution.

Democratic Centralism   Organizational basis of Communist parties. Each level is elected by the next lower level. In practice the higher level directs the lower level to choose selected individuals. Decisions made by higher levels of organization are absolutely binding on the lower levels.

Dependent Variable   A characteristic or trait that is considered a consequence rather than a cause. For example, the more education one has the more likely one is to vote. Voting is the dependent variable in this case.

Developed Market Economy   Governments are expected to manage the economy to avoid major shocks such as depression or massive unemployment.

Developed Nonmarket Systems   Governments attempt to control all investment and demand.

Developing World   Most political systems in Africa, Asia, Latin America, and the Middle East. Often associated with, for example, low literacy, low per capita income, and rural and agricultural situations. Political organizations and processes that are relatively new and often unstable.

Development   Suggests deliberate selective adaptation of outside techniques in terms of controlled change with conscious social and political objectives in mind.

Dialectical Materialism   The doctrine based on a transformation of Hegel's dialectical philosophy that asserts that all ultimate reality is matter in motion. Economic forces working themselves out in history determine the character of the state and its institutions including the cultural and religious ideas of any given period.

Dialectical Philosophy   The doctrine of the German philosopher, George Wilhelm Friedrich Hegel, which deals with the way truth is discovered. A doctrine is advanced, which by its nature is partial and one-sided. Consequently, an opposite doctrine is put forth to correct the errors in the initial doctrine. But this is only a partial truth and will lead to a third doctrine embodying the true elements in the first doctrine or thesis and its opposite antithesis. However, as the synthesis or third doctrine is only a partial truth, the dialectical process will start again. See Marxian Socialism.

Diplomacy   The formal and official means by which governments conduct business with one another. Customarily involves full diplomatic recognition and exchange of diplomatic personnel.

Disciplined Two-Party System   One first thinks of Great Britain. Discipline in Parliament is almost invariably maintained because no party member votes with an opposition party on a bill or issue.

Economic and Social Council (of United Nations)   Key agency to develop and coordinate U.N. activities in the economic and social areas. Twenty-seven members; nine elected each year for three-year terms.

Electioneering   Participating in elections whether running as a candidate or supporting a candidate or party.

Elections   The chief institutional mechanism by which representatives are selected. In democracies this is done through the secret ballot with competitive candidates for the same office.

Eminent Domain   The right of government to acquire private property for public use. Fair compensation must be paid to the property owner.

Empirical   Scientific, based on observation and experience. Value-free.

Entrepreneur (Organizer)   Individual(s) who offers potential members benefits if they join the organization. Often the moving force behind the creation of the organization.

Equity   A supplement to the English common law that provides judicial remedies not allowed by the common law, such as the injunction.

Escobedo* versus *Illinois   The United States Supreme Court decision holding that in criminal prosecutions the right to representation by counsel extends back to the time a suspect is subjected to questioning.

Eurocommunism   A demand by the Communist parties of both Eastern and Western Europe for a degree of independence from Moscow that would give each party the right to develop its own road to socialism.

European Economic Community (EEC)   Also known as the Common Market. Established in 1957 to integrate the economic policies of France, West Germany, Italy, Belgium, the Netherlands, and Luxembourg. Great Britain, Denmark, and Ireland joined in 1973. The most successful of the regional economic organizations.

Evaluation Judgments   These combine both factual information and values. They express judgments and opinions about the political system.

Exclusionary One-Party Systems   Such parties maintain traditional social divisions in order to exclude some groups from the political process, such as South Africa where Blacks are excluded.

Executive Agreement   An agreement between the President of the United States and a foreign government that, unlike a treaty, does not require Senate approval. Sometimes these agreements are secret. The President can do this under his constitutional power as commander-in-chief or his authority in foreign affairs under Article II. Congress may nullify such agreements.

Executive Branch   One of three branches of government; the others are the legislative and judicial. Includes the head of government (prime minister, premier, president), the cabinet, and the bureaucracy. Implements laws; is also as responsible for major policy input and decision making.

Externalities   Costs of production that are passed on to other than producers or consumers such as pollution.

Fabian Socialism   Name applied to British socialists in the late nineteenth and early twentieth centuries who favored socialism by gradual means. To them socialism was a system by which means of production would be under the supervision of the civil service.

Factions   Groups within a party, usually organized around an individual rather than an issue. Numerous factions means a party cannot be highly centralized.

Fascism   The philosophy of the dictatorships in Italy under Mussolini and Germany under Hitler. It is characterized by belief of the supremacy of the state over the individual, the leadership principle, and a totalitarian one-party state. The German version, known as National Socialism, was more extreme than Italian Fascism and stressed the doctrine of the supremacy of the "Aryan race" and inferiority of Jews and other races.

Federalism   A distribution of powers within a political system in which the subdivisions (states, provinces, or cantons) have certain powers and the national government has other powers, and sometimes concurrent powers. This distribution is usually achieved through a written constitution. Examples include Canada, India, Malaysia, Nigeria, and the United States.

Feedback   Results from the changing opinions and actions of citizens in response to government output. May only affect attitudes, or how a person will vote in the next election, or in some situations may lead to revolutionary action. All governments need some type of feedback to assess reaction to government actions.

Foreign Policy   A nation's official relations with other countries involving economic, cultural, military, and political interaction. Efforts to protect and promote the national interest in the international arena.

Formal Political Socialization   The deliberate efforts by schools, parents, groups, or government to teach information, values, and attitudes they feel may affect the political system.

Franks **versus** *Bowman Transportation Co.*   The United States Supreme Court decision approving a retroactive award of seniority to a group of Negro truck drivers who had been victims of past discrimination by the employers.

Functionalism   Often called structural functionalism. All societies must perform requisite functions if they are to survive. In political science this has usually meant when studying institutions or political actors we should consider the functions performed.

Future Shock   The idea that information and values acquired during childhood are inadequate to the new social, political, and economic realities of an altered world during adulthood.

General Assembly (of United Nations)   Major forum of the United Nations. Each country has one vote except for the Soviet Union which has one vote plus one each for the Ukraine and Belorussia. Majority vote decides most policy questions, which generally are recommendations only.

General Will   The concept of the French philosopher Rousseau that the common good is expressed in the general will, which is more than the will of the majority. It is possible that the general will may be expressed by a minority or even one man, although usually it is an expression of the will of the majority.

Government   The institution that successfully upholds a claim to the exclusive use of physical force in enforcing its rules within a given territorial area. It is the most inclusive institution in society. Sometimes refers to the executive political leadership, that is, the President and the cabinet or the prime minister and cabinet. For example, "the government is proposing an additional gasoline tax."

Grand Instance   French courts of general jurisdiction in civil cases and of appellate jurisdiction over minor courts.

Grand Jury   A body of from five to 23 persons, originating in England, which is summoned by the prosecutor to determine whether the evidence against a person accused of crime is sufficient to return an indictment.

Green Revolution   Occurred in the 1960s when strains of wheat and rice were developed that dramatically increased output per acre. These strains require substantial increases in terms of fertilizers, flood and irrigation control, mechanization and storage facilities.

Habeas Corpus   A writ that permits a person who claims that he is unjustly imprisoned to apply to a federal court for a hearing. If a court finds that the imprisonment is contrary to some provision of the Constitution or laws of the United States, the person will be released.

Hare System   A complex form of proportional representation proposed by an Englishman, Thomas Hare, in 1857. Candidates are listed alphabetically without party label. The voter numbers preferences. If the vote is not needed to elect his or her first choice, the vote is transferred to the second, third, or fourth choice as appropriate. Also known as "single transferrable vote." During this century it was used in a few American cities.

Hegemony   When country A exercises hegemony over country B it does not legally exercise control of that country but maintains preponderant influence in the domestic and foreign affairs of the subservient country.

Ideology   An extension of political theory in simplified form so as to arouse the masses in order to win popular support. Ideology consists of a political plan including emotionally charged doctrines for curing some political or social evil.

Individualism   One of the characteristics of the modern age that began about 1500. The result was a new humanism centering on man as the "measure of all things." The new individualism was a revolt against existing restraints of the social order and religion and a movement toward personal autonomy. One result was the social contract theory of government that began with the individual who voluntarily created government. See Social Contract Theory of the State.

Indoctrination   The manipulation and control of public norms, attitudes, and behavior in a particular political system. The term has a negative connotation, and should be distinguished from socialization.

Influence   Related to power. The outcome is less predictable because penalties for noncompliance are less severe and the rewards are fewer and smaller.

Informal Political Socialization   Political learning that is incidental to other activities. Often absorbed in unstructured form and sometimes subconsciously. Frequently as a result of remarks by parents, teachers, friends, etc.

Inputs   Functions of the political system that include claims or demands, supports, apathy. Democratic political systems allow for the greatest freedom of citizen inputs.

Institution   Regularized patterns of human relationships, evolving over time, formalized by custom and/or written rules and regulations.

Institutional Interest Groups   Came into being to perform functions other than interest articulation. They are often government departments or agencies. Examples are the army, a university, bureaucracy, and church.

Interest Groups   Organized groups of people concerned with specific interests. Usually part of their activities occur in the political system. They do not have candidates for public office; they do have lobbyists to represent their needs.

Intermediate Groups   Another term for interest groups. Used by William Kornhauser in discussing dangers of mass society.

International Court of Justice   Established in 1945 and located in the The Hague, a successor to the Permanent Court of International Justice created in 1920. Fifteen judges, elected by the U.N. General Assembly and the Security Council. Hears only cases voluntarily submitted by the parties (nation–states) and has no enforcement power.

International Law   The rules and principles regulating the behavior of countries, international organizations like the United Nations, and the rights and obligations of individuals as they are affected by differences in the legislation of different countries.

International Politics   Politics among countries; the principal actors are spokesmen of nation-states, international and regional organizations, and often revolutionary organizations. In domestic politics government usually has the preponderant authority and power. There is no final or sovereign authority in the international setting.

Iron Curtain   Term coined by Winston Churchill in a 1946 speech at Westminster College, Fulton, Missouri. As the Soviet Union consolidated its influence in Eastern Europe, Churchill said this man-made, political division descended across the European continent.

"Iron Law of Oligarchy"   Concept identified with Robert Michels. All groups eventually dominated by the leadership. The average member has little interest in, knowledge about, or influence on the group's policies.

Issue Conflict   Characterizes pluralistic or democratic systems. Conflict over narrower, specific issues. Less intense, often willing to compromise.

Judicial Activist   A U.S. Supreme Court Justice who interprets the Constitution and the powers of the U.S. Supreme Court broadly so as to bring about social changes he deems desirable.

Judicial Independence   The independence of courts in developing countries, especially Africa, is frequently compromised by various means, such as parliamentary or executive overriding of judicial decisions.

Judicial Interpretation of Statutes   Courts play an important role in making policy through the interpretation of statutes because legislative acts are frequently complex and unclear.

Judicial Process   The various factors entering into a court's decision in a legal controversy such as a judge's social background, legal training, professional experience as a lawyer, political affiliation, and legal reasoning.

Judicial Review   The process by which courts determine whether the legislative and executive branches, especially the former, have exceeded their authority with the power to declare a law or act unconstitutional. The scope of judicial review is broadest in the United States.

Jury Trial   A body of competent men and women, traditionally consisting of 12 members, which unanimously renders a verdict based upon the facts and the law in criminal and civil cases.

Justice   The ideal that a legal system should strive to maintain the equal treatment of everyone and protect freedom from change through arbitrary acts of a dictator.

Justice of the Peace   A local officer originating in England and continuing in some American states who has authority to try petty cases.

Laissez-Faire or the Market Economy   The ideal of modern capitalism. Government should have very limited policy role or intervention in the economy.

Latent Functions   Often important functions of an institution but were not originally intended as the institution was founded and has evolved. For example, India's caste associations now are important means by which to organize and appeal to voters.

Leadership   The ability to mobilize human and other resources, often in a competitive situation, to achieve determined objectives.

League of Nations   Created at the end of World War I, headquartered in Geneva, Switzerland. The moving force behind its creation was Woodrow Wilson, but the United States did not join. Through principles of collective security it was designed to prevent a second world war. It failed in this notable endeavor.

Legislature   Formal lawmaking institution in most political systems.

Legitimacy   An objective of political rulers because it increases support and stability in the political system. A relative concept involving widely accepted procedural norms in acquiring and exercising power, as well as government which produces the outputs generally expected of it by the population.

Liberal   A liberal is in a position midway between socialism and conservatism. A liberal believes in democratic and constitutional government as opposed to dictatorship of any kind.

Early liberalism was identified with John Locke, laissez-faire economics, and the social contract theory of government that put the individual before the state. In the late nineteenth century as a result of the evils of the industrial revolution and the philosophy of T. H. Green, liberalism abandoned laissez-faire and adopted a policy that favored state intervention in the economy to remove social evils, such as poverty, that hindered the development of the individual.

List System   The most common type of proportional representation. The party draws up a list of candidates equal to the number of contested seats in the multimember district. The larger the percentage of the party vote, the more people are elected from the list.

Lower House   In a bicameral legislature the elected house or the one most regularly responsible to the electorate. Examples: In Great Britain the popularly elected House of Commons that elects the Prime Minister; in the United States, all members of the House of Representatives are elected biennially.

Manifest Functions   Functions that were intended when the institution or organization was created.

Marbury* versus *Madison   The first decision of the United States Supreme Court holding an act of Congress unconstitutional.

Marxian Socialism   The Socialist doctrines advocated by Karl Marx. Marx took Hegel's dialectic and transformed it into "dialectical materialism," which assumed the ultimate reality is matter in motion. The dialectic works itself out in history through economic forces and relationships that determine the culture and religious ideas of an era. History is a record of class struggles and Capitalism tends to destroy itself. As economic conditions worsen, the proletariat or working class becomes more class conscious and a revolution more likely. Marx was not always clear about whether the revolution must be violent or peaceful. The revolution would be followed by the dictatorship of the proletariat that would continue until the attainment of the classless society and the "withering away of the state."

Marxist Conception of Law   The assumption of Marx and Engels was that law is a tool of the state and the state is an instrument of the ruling class.

Mass Media   Communication media capable of reaching large audiences nationwide. Includes newspapers, national magazines, radio, and television.

Mass Socialization   Learning common political attitudes, values and behaviors that are considered appropriate to all the people of a particular political system. Involves attitudes and behavior that should characterize overwhelming majority of people. Content and method of learning often heavily influenced by government agencies.

Mass Society   Concept developed by William Kornhauser. A highly technical society where autonomous interest groups have a diminished role. This type of society can be manipulated by elites using advanced technology such as in Nazi Germany or the Soviet Union.

Material Benefits   The tangible-personal rewards, such as higher wages-benefits, that interest group members receive from an organization

Mercantilism   An effort to control, regulate, and foster economic growth for the purpose of increasing national power. Mercantilists argue that economic power is the basis for political power. Theory that emerged in the sixteenth century.

Miranda **versus** *Arizona*   The United States Supreme Court decision that held that for a conviction based on custodial interrogation to stand it is necessary to inform the suspect in advance of the questioning of his right to remain silent and to be represented by counsel.

Mixed Economy   The prevalent form of economy in the West. Its basis is active governmental intervention in the economic system to promote growth and equity.

Modernization   Suggests utilizing the most modern technology to control and develop the environment. Sometimes suggests the contemporary, imported, superficial attributes and life-styles of a relatively few people confined to urban areas, such as conspicious consumption.

Mother of Parliament   The British legislature whose institutional history goes back to the twelfth century. The first parliamentary legislature.

Multi-Issue Interest Groups   Promote the specific self-interests of members as well as the broader interests they believe will benefit most of society and their members. The AFL-CIO and the National Association of Manufacturers are examples.

Multinational Corporation   Corporation that duplicates or divides up essential parts of its productive operation in two or more countries.

Multiparty Systems   One party rarely wins a majority of seats. Usually two to five parties win over 10 percent of the seats. In a parliamentary form of government, two or more parties must form a coalition to form a government.

Multipolarity   An international condition that began to evolve in the late 1950s. There emerged several sources of power and influence and the international arena was no longer dominated by American–Soviet rivalry.

Nation-State   Political entities with officially recognized boundaries. Sovereignty is within each political system and supposedly not subject to outside interference. Country, nation, nation-state are terms popularly used interchangeably.

National Interest   A basic premise is that each nation-state is required to protect and promote certain basic interests if the country is to survive physically and its basic political, economic, and social values are to be maintained. Usually within each political system there are disagreements on the indispensable or national interests. A national interest supposedly benefits everyone and is more than the sum of individual or group interests.

"Nationalizing Civil Rights"   The incorporation by the United States Supreme Court of the First Amendment of the American Constitution and most of the remaining Bill of Rights into the due process clause of the Fourteenth Amendment. This makes most of the Bill of Rights binding upon the states through the Fourteenth Amendment.

Natural Law   The concept originating with the Stoic philosophers of Greece and Rome that there is a law of reason in agreement with nature above and beyond human law. This doctrine was developed by Thomas Aquinas and carried into modern time by John Locke.

Natural Rights   The doctrine that men inherently possess natural rights that can be asserted against the state. This concept is an important part of the philosophy of John Locke who believed that government was a trustee of society's rights.

New Left   A movement in the United States and Western Europe composed primarily of students and young intellectuals that represents a new type of radicalism. Although non-Communist, it is Marxian in a general sense. The New Left is very critical of the basic values of

Western society and advocates a new society to be brought about by revolution. All, however, do not favor a violent revolution. The leading philosopher of the movement is the late Herbert Marcuse. In the United States the New Left is an outgrowth of such traumatic events as the Viet Nam War and the opposition it aroused.

Nineteen Twenty-Two (1922) Committee   British members of the Conservative Party who do not hold ministerial rank. Organized to study issues and communicate to the government when the Conservatives are in power.

Nonassociational Interest Groups   Groups of people who share one or more characteristics in common but are not formally organized as such. Examples include ethnic, kinship, religion, sex, and age groups. Spokesmen speak for these groups, often in informal settings such as at country clubs and religious meetings.

Nonpolitical Learning   The political results or side effects, often unintended, of other learning. In the family or at school children learn attitudes about authority, order, and obedience that may have an impact on their political attitudes.

Nonproliferation   Efforts by most members of the nuclear club to prevent the spread of nuclear weapons and effective delivery systems to other countries.

North Atlantic Treaty Organization (NATO)   Major security organization, established in 1949. Based on collective security principle. Includes the United States, Canada, and thirteen European countries.

North–South Split   Refers to the difference in the living standards and social and economic development between the advanced countries in the northern hemisphere and the developing countries, most of which are in the southern hemisphere.

Nuclear Club   Countries with substantial quantities of nuclear weapons and extensive delivery systems: United States, Soviet Union, France, Great Britain, and the People's Republic of China.

One-Party System   Originally totalitarian regimes but now includes regimes that overwhelmingly dominate a country but allow some opposition such as Mexico and Singapore. Sometimes referred to as single-party systems.

OPEC Organization of Petroleum Exporting Countries.   The thirteen members are Saudi Arabia, Iran, Iraq, Kuwait, Nigeria, Algeria, Libya, Indonesia, Venezuela, Ecuador, United Arab Emirates, Gabon, and Qatar.

Oregon* versus *Mitchell   The United States Supreme Court decision holding that by statute Congress could reduce the voting age to eighteen in federal elections but that Congress lacked the authority to reduce the voting age to eighteen in state elections.

Outputs   Government decisions such as laws, executive-administrative orders, court decisions, or a conscious government decision not to take action.

PACE   Professional and Administrative Career Examination in the United States for entry into a wide range of federal job areas. Usually requires a B.A. or B.S. degree. An important opportunity for graduating seniors.

Parliamentary Government   The prime minister/premier is elected by the legislature, or the popularly elected lower house, and remains in office only if he or she has a legislative majority. The prime minister selects the cabinet.

Parliamentary Supremacy The legislature is not subject to or controlled by a hereditary monarch. The premier or prime minister is in office only if he has a majority in the legislature or at least the popularly elected lower house.

Participatory Political System A type in which a significant number of the citizens have legal means, usually through elections, to influence or determine important political decisions.

Particularistic Parties Self-limiting because they appeal to a specific ethnic, linguistic, or religious group such as an Islamic Revolutionary Party. Sometimes willing to compromise but speak for only one segment of the population.

Patronage Appointments to government service or the distribution and assignment of favorable economic opportunities or benefits to faithful political supporters. Used to build a political organization or insure that individuals in a government agency are strong supporters of the elected officials.

Peer Groups People with similar status and often similar interests, such as close friends, colleagues, neighbors, small clubs, and informal associations.

Penetration An aspect of government capacity referring to the ability to enforce conformance and obedience to public policy. Often argued it is the *sine qua non* without which political development cannot occur.

Petroflation Economic inflation whose principal cause is believed to be the continuous and apparently never-ending increase in the per-barrel price of oil.

Philosopher–King Advocated by Plato. A near-perfect ruler who would rule to achieve justice, harmony, and stability in a political system.

Plessey versus Ferguson The 1896 decision of the United States Supreme Court that set forth the separate but equal doctrine allowing segregation in public facilities.

Pluralism Extensive participation in the political process through competing and autonomous groups.

Policy Formation The third stage of the policy-making process, developing alternative policies for dealing with public problems.

Policy Implementation Carrying out of government decisions. Usually implemented through civil or military bureaucracies.

Policymaking Rule-making process carried on in every political system.

Polis The ancient Greek term for the most sovereign and inclusive political association.

Politburo Decision-making body of most Communist parties. The political bureau membership ranges between 15 and 25.

Political Analysis Studying a problem or question, organizing the data into categories or elements and relating the parts to one another. Inductive, empirical research.

Political Culture Those aspects of our social heritage that involve attitudes, values, and behavior patterns affecting the way people perceive and behave in the political system.

Political Development Innovative responses to challenge and change by political leaders with a bias toward nonrevolutionary, nonviolent, and orderly adjustments. Working toward optimum degree of social, economic, and political choice and freedom. Every country has unique features, and the end objective is not necessarily some form of the Anglo-American model.

Political Economy   The study of the interrelationships of politics and economics and the influence each has on the other. Often discussed in terms of the relationship between government and economics. For example, mortgage rates increase as government policies reduce the amount of money available for loans.

Political Integration   The population in a country develop relationships and a feeling of community. Social, economic, psychological ties evolve that give a population feelings of identity, self-awareness, and exclusiveness. Political integration refers to the efforts of government to foster this cohesiveness.

Political Learning   The acquisition of information, attitudes, and evaluations about politics. The learning can be formal, as in the schools, or informal, as from family or friends.

Political Man   Term used by Harold Lasswell to characterize an individual who seeks power, is fascinated with it, and seeks experiences that involve power.

Political Modernization   Sometimes criticized because as a concept restricted to contemporary societies only. Some authors associate it with sudden increases in mass participation when the political system has no institutions into which to channel this participation.

Political Party   In a democracy a group of voters organized to nominate and elect candidates to political office in order to influence and/or control personnel and policy.

Political Science   A discipline within the social sciences. Deals with the political behavior and characteristics of individuals, groups, institutions, and societies as well as the influences that affect this behavior.

Political Socialization   The gradual learning of the norms, attitudes, and behavior accepted and practiced by the ongoing political system. Its goal is to train individuals so they will become well-functioning members of the political society.

Political System   An approach to studying politics that places government at the center of the system with due consideration given to inputs, outputs, conversion, and feedback. A political system has many parts that interact, in varying degrees are interdependent, and has boundaries.

Politicized   Politics increasingly touches on an individual's life with the expansion of government activities. More and more disagreements in which groups or individuals turn to government.

Politics   Activities in the public realm in which individuals and groups pursue conflicting objectives over the allocation of scarce resources by government.

Positive Law   The philosophy of law associated with the nineteenth century Utilitarian philosopher, John Austin. Law consists of well-defined rules of human conduct enforceable by appropriate sanctions of government.

Postindustrial Society   Characterizes the democratic political systems of Western Europe, North America, Japan, Australia, and New Zealand. Society is highly complex, technologically advanced, and interdependent. This stage emerged after World War II. The service sector rather than industry dominates the economy, and white collar jobs are more numerous than blue collar jobs. Political implications somewhat unclear and contradictory.

Power   A relationship that affects in a predictable way the actions of another individual, group, society, or political system.

Power Base   Includes some or most of the following assets depending upon the situation: wealth, social status, preponderance of physical force, formal office, skills (e.g. legal, managerial, and technical), personal magnetism, friendships, affiliation or extended relationships such as family, ethnic group, and religion.

Power Motivated Change   The amount of change an individual, group, state must expend that it would not do except in order to exercise power or influence in a given situation.

Pragmatic-Bargaining Parties   Also called broker-type. Most common in Great Britain and the United States. Hungry for votes, these parties attempt to appeal to most segments of society to attract support. They emphasize bargaining, compromise, and accommodation.

Presidential Government   First emerged in the United States. Head of government popularly elected and cannot ordinarily be removed from office by the legislature. (Contrasts with parliamentary government.)

Pressure Group   A group that deliberately seeks to influence the public authorities. Often created just for that purpose. The term is often used interchangeably with interest groups.

Primary Elections   A largely American phenomenon that evolved in this century. An election in which party members or supporters select the party nominee who will run in the general election. Reduces the influence of party leaders and the party organization.

Primordial Sentiments   Basic attachments and identifications with which one is born such as race, language, religion, kinship, or tribal group.

Problem Definition   The first stage of the policy process. This involves defining the problem.

Procurator General of the Soviet Union   The highest judicial official of the Soviet Union who is prosecutor and supervises the organization of the courts and executes the rules of law in use. There are also procurators in each republic and district.

Promotional Groups   These groups are not organized to promote primarily the special positions of their members. They support positions they believe will improve society in general. Examples are the League of Women Voters, the Sierra Club, and the British Royal Society for the Prevention of Cruelty to Children.

Proportional Representation   Designed to give each political party approximately the same number of legislative seats as the party's electoral vote justifies.

Public Administration   Organized group effort to carry out official (government) policy. In practice it is concerned with management techniques as well as the influence of government employees on shaping policy as it is developed and implemented.

Public Policy   All the laws, decisions, rules, and regulations produced by the political processes of a country. It is a course of action for the purpose of dealing with a problem of public concern.

Purposive Benefits   Suprapersonal benefits—such as saving the environment or opposing the spread of nuclear power plants—that motivate some members to join an organization.

"Reciprocal Deference System"   Opposite of the "iron law of oligarchy." Leaders depend heavily on support of members. Members and leaders defer to one another on various issues. Characterizes many local party organizations in the United States.

Recruitment Filling new roles or jobs, replacing individuals, and promoting individuals.

Regime The overall constitutional process including the major political institutions and the rules of the game that determine procedures with reference to demands, how policy is made and implemented, and the types of acceptable policies.

Regionalism Intergovernmental collaboration at the regional level, recognized by Articles 52–54 of the U.N. Charter. These usually deal with economic, political, and security matters. Some believe these are stepping stones to universalism, but this has not been the case to date.

Regulatory Boards, Commissions, Agencies Quasi-legislative, judicial, and executive agencies with specific areas of responsibility such as the U.S. Federal Power Commission and the London Transport Board. These agencies sometimes set rules, enforce rules, and decide disputes. Their members are usually appointed for fixed terms.

Representation A process for making demands and translating them into policy. Representatives are people who act on behalf of other people in the decision-making process. In a democracy, these individuals are elected.

Restrictive Interest Groups Interest groups that speak principally for the narrow specific interests of their members. Examples are the National Rifle Association and the Real Estate Brokers Association.

Revealed Religion A religion based upon a special revelation of God in history, such as Christianity. This is in contrast with the revelation of God in nature, which is the essence of a religious belief called Deism. Many seventeenth and eighteenth century Deist philosophers, such as Thomas Hobbes and Jean-Jacques Rousseau, were critical of Christianity as a revealed religion.

Revisionists (Socialist) Characteristic of the socialist parties in Western Europe. Some democratic socialists look upon Marx as a great leader but believe many of his doctrines are in need of revision. Others, like the British Labor Party, have never been greatly influenced by Marx. All accept the parliamentary system and believe that Socialism can be attained by democratic means.

Revolutionary One-Party Systems Determined to make far-reaching changes in society after seizing power and to create a monolothic social order. Change, mobilization, and terror characterize the new system.

Reynolds* versus *Sims The 1964 U.S. Supreme Court decision ruling that state legislative districts of both houses must be substantially equal in population.

Role Involves standard or accepted expectations about how an individual or individuals should behave in specific situations or within particular institutional settings; for example, student, lobbyist, president, and bureaucrat.

Run-Off Ballot Used in France and many American primary elections when a majority is required to be elected or nominated. Because of multiple candidates no candidate receives a majority on the first ballot. A second or run-off ballot is required.

Science Usually raised when discussing how "scientific can political science be." Political science is not a physical or natural science that permits controlled experiments in a laboratory setting. It attempts to be scientific by its methods in terms of collecting, organizing, and examining data.

Secondary Associations   Formally organized groups created for specific purposes. Involve large numbers of people who do not regularly if ever act together daily on a face-to-face basis. Organized interest groups are secondary associations.

Security Council (of United Nations)   Composition and voting procedure emphasize big power (U.S.A., Soviet Union, China, France, and Great Britain) cooperation and control, acting as "world sheriff." The preceding five are permanent members and each has the power of veto. There also are 10 nonpermanent members elected biennially.

Secretary-General (of United Nations)   The chief administrative officer, elected by the General Assembly upon recommendation of the Security Council. Four persons have held this position, the most recent being Dr. Kurt Waldheim of Austria.

Separation of Powers   Usually associated with presidential government. The three branches of government (legislative, executive, judicial) have different powers, generally assigned by a constitution. Often one branch has some powers belonging to another; the result in practice is overlapping and not complete separation of powers.

Single-Cause Groups   Groups devoted uncompromisingly to supporting or opposing a single issue such as abortion, women's rights, tax reductions, nuclear power plants, etc.

Single-Member District   No matter what size an election district is, it elects only one individual at a time to a particular political office.

Smith Act   The 1940 act of the United States Congress that made teaching and advocacy of the overthrow of the government of the United States by force a criminal offense.

Social Contract   The theory that the state is the result of a contract voluntarily entered into by individuals. This theory postulates an original state of nature in which men originally lived. The most important philosophers identified with this concept are Thomas Hobbes, John Locke, and Jean-Jacques Rousseau. Except for Hobbes, this theory generally supports limited government.

Socialism   The doctrine that there should be common ownership of the means of production and exchange in the economic system. Socialists do not agree on the extent to which the economic system should be nationalized. Socialism is a response to the problems and abuses of the industrial revolution. Some socialists believe private property should be restricted; others believe it should be abolished. Although Socialism is frequently associated with the doctrines of Karl Marx, all socialists are not followers of Marx. Socialism is distinguished from Communism in that Socialists generally believe that the transition from Capitalism to Socialism can be attained by peaceful means.

Social Mobilization   Concept developed by Karl Deutsch. A set of quantifiably measurable social changes in society such as growth in urbanization, literacy, newspaper circulation, and industrialization, affecting politics and to which government must respond in terms of a wider range and increased outputs.

Socialization   Process by which individual and group attitudes are nurtured and shaped.

Solicitor   Office lawyers in Great Britain as distinguished from barristers. Solicitors handle a legal problem before the trial stage.

Solidarity Benefits   Psychological and nonmaterial rewards, such as affiliation and social interaction. Benefits interest group members receive from their organization and the principal reasons some individuals join.

Soviet Communism A variety of Communism initiated by Vladimir Lenin whose philosophy was based on a Marxism modified in light of developments in Russia. Unlike Marx, he believed the revolution could occur only through a vanguard of dedicated revolutionaries rather than the working class as a whole. Lenin also believed that an extended period of time was necessary after the revolution to attain the classless society. The power during this interim would be in the hands of the Communist party, which would rule in behalf of the proletariat.

Standing Committees Permanent legislative committees to which a bill is first referred after it is introduced. For example, there are 43 in the U.S. Congress and 6 in the British House of Commons.

Stare Decisis "Let the decision stand." A court follows previous decisions in similar cases unless it chooses to overrule the previous decision.

State of Nature A theoretical idyllic state, preceding political organization, with a small population; individuals are rational and there are few conflicts.

Statutory Law The interpretation courts give to statutes that determines the meaning of the statutes.

Stoicism The philosophy originating in Greece and Rome that emphasized the basic equality of all men regardless of wealth or social position. The individual was a citizen both of the secular state in which he was born and of the community of all men. Natural law was another important Stoic doctrine. See Natural Law.

Stratarchy Term to describe one type of democratic party organization opposite to the "iron law of oligarchy." There are numerous leaders and areas of influence. Power scattered; individuals higher in the organization often depend on support of those below them.

Strict Constructionist A U.S. Supreme Court Justice who interprets the powers of the court and the text of the Constitution narrowly so as to strike down as unconstitutional laws and interpretations of the Constitution not consistent with his judicial philosophy.

Suffrage The right to vote. In the democratic political systems suffrage was extended from a small percentage of property-owning adult males in the late eighteenth century to nearly all adults in the twentieth century. People given the vote are enfranchised.

Summit Meetings Meetings between the heads of several governments.

Support-Inputs Sometimes provided by foreign governments to maintain a regime in power and allowing for some influence on the supported government's policies.

Supports Given to a political system or regime by individuals even if they oppose a specific policy or leader. Includes such things as loyalty, patriotism, identity, and paying taxes.

Symbiosis Refers to the interaction and even interdependence of dissimilar parts, often with different objectives, in the social, economic, and political systems. There are, however, benefits to be achieved by all groups or components through associating together. An orientation that facilitates the evolution of political pluralism.

Symbolic Supports Attitudes or feelings of loyalty, patriotism, commitment to the political system. An extreme form is "my country right or wrong."

System Conflict Conflict over the basic nature of the political system and regime. Competition often is intense, uncompromising, and leads to political instability.

Tangible Supports Actions that show loyalty or identity with the political system such as voting as a citizen duty and paying taxes honestly.

Tariff   A tax on imports. Its objective is (1) to raise revenue; or (2) protect domestic agricultural or industrial producers by increasing the cost of the imported product. In the latter case, for example, some people argue that the United States ought to raise the tariff on imported Japanese cars because the American auto industry is in a slump.

Third Parties ˇ A political party that is formed when the two major parties fail to meet a need or demand. These parties are sometimes temporary and usually fail to get their candidate elected, but they get their interests recognized by the major parties.

Third World   Often used to refer to the developing world. First World consists of the democratic, industrialized countries. Second World the Communist Countries. Third World includes most of Africa, Asia, Latin America, and the Middle East.

Totalitarian   Political control by the elite permeates all of society. A single mass party, highly structured ideology and a terroristic secret police characterize such regimes. They usually try to spread their ideology and influence to other countries. Examples are Nazi Germany, Fascist Italy, Soviet Union, People's Republic of China, Cuba, and Vietnam.

Totalitarian Party   Committed to a dictatorial regime, controlled by one or a handful of leaders. A revolutionary organization to seize power and, if successful, control the political system, allowing no civil rights to the population.

Traditional Societies   Usually heavily agricultural, limited use of technology; change is gradual. Restricted participation in the decision-making process.

Transformation Stage   The most brutal stage of revolutionary one-party systems as the ol system is destroyed. Much loss of life occurs.

Transitional Political Systems   Systems in the Third World that are economically modernizing, emphasizing political integration and modifying the political process to allow more popular input.

Two-Party Systems   Such as in the United States and Great Britain. Third, fourth, etc. parties exist, but control of most political office alternates almost exclusively between the two principal parties.

Unicameral   A single-house legislature. One American state, Nebraska, has such a legislature. Several countries including Israel, Egypt, New Zealand, Finland, Panama, and Hungary also have one-house legislatures.

Unitary Government   All government power resides in the central government, which may through an ordinary legislative act delegate to local governments selected authority. All dictatorships in practice are unitary. However, unitary governments can be limited or constitutional governments such as France or Great Britain.

United Nations   Established in 1945. At the end of 1979 there were 151 members. Headquartered in New York City. Its objectives are to maintain international peace and security and to facilitate international cooperation in solving economic, social, and cultural problems.

Upper House   In a bicameral legislature usually the oldest, smaller, and more senior of the two Houses. The elected American Senate has slightly more power and prestige than the House of Representatives. In Britain, the hereditary and appointed House of Lords has little power today.

Vote of Confidence   A vote in a democratic parliamentary system of government. If the prime minister or premier loses the vote the government (prime minister and cabinet) must resign. A new government may be elected by the legislature or the defeated government may call for parliamentary elections in order that a new parliament will be able to form a working majority.

Warsaw Treaty Organization   Major Communist collective security organization designed to counter NATO. Established in 1955. Members are the Soviet Union and its East European allies.

Wesberry* versus *Sanders   The 1964 Supreme Court decision declaring that the U.S. Constitution requires one person, one vote.

Yates* versus *U.S. (1957)   Supreme Court decision that has made it more difficult to prosecute Communists. Urging people to act unlawfully is illegal, but only advocating that people believe in revolution or other aspects of Communist doctrine is not illegal.

Photo Credits

251:   Mary Anne Fackleman/The White House.
259:   Wide World Photos.
264:   Tass from Sovfoto.

Chapter 9
278:   Sylvia Johnson/Woodfin Camp.
280:   (top) Wide World Photos.
       (bottom) Eric Lessing/Magnum.
289:   Wide World Photos.
291:   Jim Moore/Gamma Liaison.
293:   Eve Arnold/Magnum.

Chapter 11
354:   UPI.

Chapter 12
399:   Alain Nogues/Sygma.
417:   Wide World Photos.

Chapter 13
448, 449 and 450:   Wide World Photos.

Chapter 14
475 and 476:   United Nations.

Index

NOTES

NOTES

NOTES

NOTES

NOTES

NOTES

NOTES